Interactive Web–Based Virtual Reality with Java 3D

Chi Chung Ko
National University of Singapore, Singapore

Chang Dong Cheng
National University of Singapore, Singapore

INFORMATION SCIENCE REFERENCE

Hershey · New York

Director of Editorial Content: Kristin Klinger
Managing Development Editor: Kristin Roth
Senior Managing Editor: Jennifer Neidig
Managing Editor: Jamie Snavely
Assistant Managing Editor: Carole Coulson
Copy Editor: Larissa Vinci
Typesetter: Amanda Appicello
Cover Design: Lisa Tosheff
Printed at: Yurchak Printing Inc.

Published in the United States of America by
          Information Science Reference (an imprint of IGI Global)
          701 E. Chocolate Avenue, Suite 200
          Hershey PA 17033
          Tel: 717-533-8845
          Fax: 717-533-8661
          E-mail: cust@igi-global.com
          Web site: http://www.igi-global.com/reference

and in the United Kingdom by
          Information Science Reference (an imprint of IGI Global)
          3 Henrietta Street
          Covent Garden
          London WC2E 8LU
          Tel: 44 20 7240 0856
          Fax: 44 20 7379 0609
          Web site: http://www.eurospanbookstore.com

Library of Congress Cataloging-in-Publication Data
Ko, Chi Chung.
  Interactive web-based virtual reality with Java 3D / by Chi Chung Ko and Chang Dong Cheng.
     p. cm.
  Includes bibliographical references and index.
  Summary: "This book provides both advanced and novice programmers with comprehensive, detailed coverage
of all of the important issues in Java 3D"--Provided by publisher.
  ISBN 978-1-59904-789-8 (hardcover) -- ISBN 978-1-59904-791-1 (ebook)
  1. Java3D. 2. Java (Computer program language) 3. Computer graphics. 4. Three-dimensional display systems.
5. Virtual reality. I. Cheng, Chang Dong. II. Title.
  QA76.73.J38K595 2008
  006.8--dc22
                                       200800910

British Cataloguing in Publication Data
A Cataloguing in Publication record for this book is available from the British Library.

All work contributed to this encyclopedia set is new, previously-unpublished material. The views expressed in
this encyclopedia set are those of the authors, but not necessarily of the publisher.

Table of Contents

Chapter IX

Chapter X

Chapter XI

Preface

With the emergence of the Java 3D API, the creation of high quality 3D animated graphics for Java applications and applets has become a possibility. Being a high-level API based on OpenGL and DirectX, Java 3D allows developers to produce object-oriented graphics applications that are platform-independent. Numerous applications in fields ranging from business, science, medical to education have been implemented based on this technology. One well known example is the Maestro project, which allows users to navigate the 3D world of Mars from a desktop computer based on inputs from eight 360-degree cameras onboard the rover.

In one of our research projects in this area, we have used Java 3D to develop a Web-based real time 3D oscilloscope experimentation system, which has been launched at National University of Singapore. This application enables users to carry out a physical electronic experiment that involves the use of an actual oscilloscope, a signal generator, and a circuit board remotely through the Internet. Specifically, the control of the various instruments are carried out in real time through the use of a Java 3D based interface on the client side, with the results of the experiment being also reflected or displayed appropriately on 3D instruments in the same interface.

In this application, Java 3D is used to create a virtual 3D world or room in which the 3D instruments reside. The mouse is used for both navigation in this world as well as for operating the instruments through, say, dragging a sliding control or a rotary control or clicking or switching appropriate buttons on the instruments. Associated commands that cause the real instruments in a remote physical laboratory to operate accordingly are then sent through the Internet in real-time. Experimental results corresponding to, say, a change in the real oscilloscope display, are then sent from the instrument control server back to the Java 3D client to result in a real-time change in the display of the virtual 3D oscilloscope in the virtual 3D world.

Apart from the room and instrument geometry, three important and difficult issues that have been tackled are navigating behavior, collision detection and picking behavior. Specifically, navigating behavior controls how the user is able to walk around in the virtual laboratory as well as the positions and angles of the view platform, as when the user attempts to get a better view. The use of appropriate collision detection ensures that the user is not able to traverse any solid objects such as walls, tables and instruments, while a customized picking behavior is necessary for the user to adjust the controls on the instruments precisely.

To satisfy these requirements and noting that the users will not be familiar with the use of special keys for 3D navigation, a more sophisticated and customized navigating system has been designed and developed. In this system, navigation can be done by using either the mouse or the keyboard. Specifically, the position and direction of the view platform or viewpoint can be changed by simply using the mouse to press two specially designed groups of control objects, a navigating speed slider, a translation, and a rotation icon.

To change the user's "walking" speed through the 3D virtual laboratory, the navigating speed slider can be adjusted. This will change the delays used in the main processing steps of the navigating function. An icon with six straight arrows allows the user to move in a straight translational manner. Pressing a ball in the center of the icon will reset the viewpoint to its initial position. The other icon with four curved arrows allows the user to rotate around the current position. The ball in the center will reset the viewpoint to a horizontal one.

With 3D scene-based navigation and manipulation implemented, the system is able to provide a more realistic 3D feel to users who are conducting real-time Web-based experimentations. In the course of designing and developing this application, a large number of Java 3D example and program codes has been written, and an API library for the creation of similar Web-based 3D experiments has been developed. Specifically, the library includes a series of code segments and classes for defining the geometry and appearance of control buttons, knobs, sliders, clips and scope displays as well as their behavior in a 3D world.

This has culminated in the writing of this book, which aims to provide programmers with a simple but yet complete, comprehensive, and detailed coverage of all the important topics in Java 3D.

In particular, this book includes a large number of programming examples for the reader to master this graphics API to develop sophisticated Java 3D graphic programs. Specifically, the use and significance of keywords, syntax, classes, methods, and features that make up the API are illustrated with 300 figures, 200 code fragments, and 100 examples throughout the 450 pages of the book to provide an easy-to-read and easy-to-use learning experience.

All of the important Java 3D topics, including geometry, appearance, navigation, picking, animation, interaction, texture, light, background, fog, shade, input device, sound, and advanced view will be covered. Both novice and advanced graphics programmers, including those who know Java but do not have any background in computer graphics, will find the book useful from the large number of working examples provided. In addition, each chapter is written in a relatively independent manner so that readers with specific interests can make use of the examples in certain chapters without the need to read through other chapters.

In total, the book consists of 13 chapters covering the various topics, and is organized in a step-by-step style. Discussions on basic 3D graphics, Java 3D overview, 3D geometry, appearance, texturing, animation, and interaction are discussed in the first six chapters. Subsequently, more advanced topics on navigating, picking, input device and are explored. The use of more complicated multiple views and audio are then discussed, culminating in the last chapter, which presents the Web-based 3D experiment application in detail. The following gives a brief synopsis on each of the chapters.

Chapter I provides an overview of interactive 3D graphics, OpenGL, virtual reality, VRML, Java 3D and mixed reality. The main purpose is to give an outline on the relationship between these related technologies and applications. This also serves to place Java 3D in the appropriate context from the general perspective of 3D graphics creation and presentation.

Although many programming languages are available for creating 3D graphical applications, only Java 3D, VRML and the subsequently developed X3D are suitable for Web-based virtual reality development. As a result, while other tools are also briefly introduced, this chapter will discuss, analyze and compare VRML and Java 3D in detail. Subsequent chapters in this book will focus on various aspects of Java 3D with an aim to provide a comprehensive experience in terms of understanding and programming using Java 3D technology.

From the discussions in this chapter, the differences between VRML and Java 3D will be better appreciated. It will be pointed out that, as one of the two important development tools for Web-based virtual reality, Java 3D has established itself as an important modeling and rendering languages for more specialized applications that involve, for example, database accesses, customized behaviors and home use mobile devices such as PDA, mobile phone, and pocket PC.

Chapter II is a relatively short chapter laying the ground work for the creation of a virtual world in Java 3D. This chapter introduces the programming paradigm or the scene graph approach. Specifically, after providing some basic knowledge on VirtualUniverse, SimpleUniverse, Locale, BranchGroup, and TransformGroup objects, which form the virtual world framework, this chapter outlines how one can build a virtual world through specifying a scene graph.

The scene graph in Java 3D is for the purpose of describing the objects in a virtual 3D world, and is a tree like structure consisting of a hierarchy of nodes containing information on objects or groups of objects on geometries, shapes, lights, sounds, interactions, and so on. Specifically, the root of the scene graph is a virtual universe that may have several local branches. Also, each locale may hold related objects that are next to one another at a certain location in the 3D world, and may be made up of many branch and transform groups.

Each branch group is a subgraph of the scene graph, and can be compiled for rendering efficiency. Also, by setting certain capabilities, branch groups can be attached or removed for interaction with the user during run time. In addition to the content branch, which describes the visual objects in the virtual world, the scene graph also needs at least a viewing branch for describing the how the user views the 3D world. The setting up of this branch can be carried out easily by invoking a simple universe. Alternatively, multiple views of the same virtual world can be obtained for applications involving multiple displays.

Chapter III focuses on creating shapes and 3D objects that can be rendered by Java 3D using both core and utility classes. Different approaches to object creation will be explored, helping programmers to construct complex shapes using simple building blocks.

In this chapter, several basic geometry classes that can be used to specify the geometry of visual objects in Java 3D will be introduced and discussed. Specifically, PointArray, LineArray, TriangleArray, and QuadArray are useful for building objects using a series of points, lines, triangles and quadrilaterals, while for structures where the series of lines or triangles are adjacent to each other in a certain manner, the use of LineStripArray, TriangleStripArray, and TriangleFanArray may be more convenient and lead to faster rendering.

The problem of requiring certain vertices to be repeated when these basic classes are used can be overcome through using their indexed versions, where the sequence of vertices can be supplied via some integer indexing arrays. Complex objects can also be created through appropriately combining objects built from different classes. Also, simple geometrical shapes such as boxes, spheres, cones or cylinders can be easily generated using some predefined utility classes in Java 3D.

In Chapter IV, the appearance of the created 3D objects is discussed, including some parameters that control how they will be presented to the user. Important appearance attributes are illustrated by using examples so that the effected changes can be better appreciated.

For most virtual reality or game applications, point, line and polygon are the basic primitives for constructing objects in the 3D world. The chapter therefore gives an in depth account of the various basic attribute settings, including rendering modes, visibilities, colors and material properties, that can be applied to these primitives.

Although extensive use of basic attributes such as color and material will be able to make an object realistic to the human user, the amount of programming codes needed will in general be very lengthy and time consuming to develop if the object has complicated geometry or appearance. As an example, to create an object with many color patterns on, say, a curve surface, many zones or strips may need to be individually defined using the appropriate color or material properties. Since this is time consuming, Java 3D allows the use of what is known as texturing and image mapping, which will be discussed in the next chapter.

Building on Chapter IV, Chapter V describes the technique of texture mapping to add realism to virtual scenes. The use of texture modes and attributes in Java 3D, which is relatively straightforward and effective for adding color and realistic details to the surface of a visual object, will be presented to give programmers a reasonable palette of texturing techniques with which to work on.

Specifically, texture objects are referenced by appearance objects, and have a variety of parameters that can be adapted to suit different needs through the Texture and TextureAttributes classes. The mapping of a texture image to a surface can be performed manually by using setTextureCoordinate to set texture coordinates. It can also be automatically carried out through the TexCoordGeneration class. The application of multiple textures to a surface can give a very realistic visual effect on the visual objects created in the virtual universe.

Chapter VI explores other issues that lead to better environmental realism. These including lighting, fog, and background that can be used to further enhance the appearance of the virtual world. In general, these environmental factors affect the appearance of the object through their interaction with its material attribute.

Specifically, the use of ambient, directional, point and spot lights will be presented. Topics involving material and normal settings, which determine how light will be reflected, will also be discussed. Some examples on the use of linear and exponential fog to smooth a scene and to prevent the sudden appearance of distant objects so as to enhance its emotional appearance will be given. Then, the use of simple color, image, and geometry based backgrounds will be illustrated.

Chapter VII discusses the use of interpolators and alpha classes for object animation in the virtual world. Simple animated movements such as rotation, translation and their combinations will be covered. More advanced animation techniques such as scaling, transparency, and morphing will also be discussed. In addition, The billboard and the level of detail (LOD) classes, which are useful for creating animation at a reduced rendering level, will be presented.

The various animation classes provided by Java3D are usually quite complete in terms of their functionality. Very often, just a few parameters will be sufficient to implement a variety of simple and basic animation in Web-base virtual reality applications. For more complex scenarios, these classes can be further defined with more specific codes to give rise to more complicated movements.

The movements of objects in a 3D world are very often the result of the user manipulating these objects or just navigation through them. As an example, the animation that allows a 3D clock hand to turn may need to be re-initiated if the user presses a certain reset button in the 3D world. The issue of interactions is therefore closely related to animation and is the main concern of the next chapter.

To detect and deal with interactions from the user, Chapter VIII delves into some basic issues on event detection and processing. These include capturing the key pressed, mouse movement, finding changes in the state of the virtual object and time lapsed. In Java 3D, the detection of these events or detection conditions are based on examination of the appropriate components of the behavior class of an object.

Specifically, to specify and implement an interaction, it is necessary to make use of some special behaviors and events that Java 3D provides or to refine or customize these interaction functions. In general, through the construction of custom wakeup conditions and criteria, the system will be able to provide changes to the virtual 3D scene and objects through some appropriate processStimulus methods when the relevant stimulus or trigger condition is received. Complicated behavior can be handled by creating specialized wakeup triggers that respond to combinations of wakeup conditions, by having behaviors that post events, by detecting object collisions as well as the entry and exit of objects and viewing platforms into certain spatial bounds.

After giving a basic foundation of event detection and processing, the next two chapters provide a more advanced coverage of the topic in two important interaction scenarios. These correspond to the picking of objects and use navigation in the 3D world.

Chapter IX discusses the use of the picking behavior class for the purpose of picking objects of interest. Using simple utility classes such as PickRotationBehavior, PickTranslateBehavior, and PickZoomBehavior is straightforward, although the picking behavior may not be flexible enough for most applications.

In general, the simple operation of picking an object in the real world is actually very complicated and involves many senses. To allow the user to pick objects in the virtual 3D world as realistically as possible, Java 3D has a variety of picking shapes, such as PickRay, PickConeRay PickCylinder and PickBounds, that can be used to customize the picking behavior. After discussing these in some detail in this chapter, an application example involving the use of the controls in a 3D instrument panel will be provided.

Chapter X is on another important interaction behavior, that for the user to navigate or move in the virtual world. At the beginning of this chapter, the basic navigation classes provided by Java 3D are introduced. Due to the fact that they are not very flexible, these classes cannot be used for navigating in most virtual reality applications.

As a result, there is a need to make use of Java 3D utility classes as well as more specialized user-defined behavior classes for designing customized navigation behavior in many virtual reality applications. This chapter will discuss how rotation and translation matrices can be used for calculating the position and orientation of the objects as the viewpoint changes. The use of navigation tools for moving and turning with the help of keyboard, mouse, joystick, and other external devices will also be presented. In addition, another important issue, that involves the collisions of objects and how these can be handled, will be discussed in this chapter.

In Chapter XI, some advanced topics needed for generating multiple views of the virtual universe in Java 3D will be discussed. Illustrated with examples on configuring the viewing window to the virtual world, one will be able to see the virtual world from different perspectives, resulting in customizing viewpoints. Real life applications such as portal view in immersive virtual reality environment and video wall configuration will be introduced.

In Chapter XII, how 3D sound sources and aural characteristics can be integrated into the virtual world built using Java 3D will be outlined. Java 3D supports three types of sound sources, BackgroundSound, PointSound, and ConeSound, which will become audible if the activation radius intersects with the scheduling bounds of the sound. Controls can also be made available to turn a sound source on or off, set its gain, release style, continuous playback style, looping, priority, and scheduling bounds. In addition, by creating a SoundScape object with appropriate AuralAttributes, a special acoustical environment can be simulated.

In the last chapter, we provide some detailed design and discussions on an application where Java 3D is used in a Web-based real time 3D oscilloscope experimentation system. Outlined earlier, this application enables users to carry out a physical electronic experiment that involves the use of an actual oscilloscope, a signal generator, and a circuit board remotely through the Internet.

We are particularly thankful to Prof. Ben M. Chen, Dr. Xiang Xu, and Dr Lu Shijian for their kind help and assistance. We are also thankful to Ye Jiunn Yee, Yupinto Ngadiman, Nguyen Trung Chinh, Henky Jatmiko Gunawan, Ang Wee Ngee, Au Heng Cheong, Teo Sing Miang, Lee Chi Shan, Tam Sai Cheong, Thian Boon Sim, Subramanian S/O Annamalai, Cheong Yew Nam, Ho Chang Sheng Herman, Wu Sin Wah, Ng Chea Siang, Lim Tiong Ming, and Thulasy Suppiah, for their help and contribution in the testing and debugging of the various source codes. Last, but certainly not least, we would like to acknowledge the National University of Singapore and the Singapore Advanced Research and Education Network for providing us with research funds that lead to this book.

January 2008
Ko Chi Chung
Cheng Chang Dong
Singapore

Chapter I
Virtual Reality and Java 3D

INTRODUCTION

Web-based virtual reality is fast becoming an important application and technological tools in the next generation of games and simulation as well as scientific research, visualization, and multi-user collaboration. While tools based on VRML (virtual reality modeling language) are frequently used for creating Web-based 3D applications, Java 3D has established itself as an important modeling and rendering languages for more specialized applications that involve, for example, database accesses, customized behaviors, and home use mobile devices such as the PDA, mobile phone, and pocket PC (Kameyama, Kato, Fujimoto, & Negishi, 2003).

Before discussing Java 3D is more detail, we will first give an overview of related topics on interactive 3D computer graphics, virtual reality, and Web-based virtual reality in this chapter. Specifically, a very brief introduction to VRML and OpenGL will be provided, including some comparisons of these tools with Java 3D. We will then embark on our journey on Java 3D by giving an overview of Java 3D through the use of a simple programming example.

INTERACTIVE 3D COMPUTER GRAPHICS

In general, the field of computer graphics includes the creation, collection, processing, and displaying of data using computer technology into a visual representation or form

(Rhyne, 1997). Very often, this is supplemented by the need for an interactive graphical user interface that captures user inputs through appropriate mouse, window, and widget functions. In terms of applications, computer graphics is an important subject in digital media technologies, scientific visualization, virtual reality, arts, and entertainment.

The basic theory for computer graphics can be found in the references by Pokorny (1994), Hearn and Baker (2006), and Foley, Dam, Feiner, and Hughes (2006). Very simply, in 3D computer graphic application, the components in a particular scene are often defined by using mathematical relationships or geometries. Specifically, these involve the use of graphical primitives that correspond to basic geometrical shapes for constructing graphical scenes. Each primitive may have many attributes including size and color.

To create 2D graphics, primitives such as line, circle, ellipse, arc, text, polygon, and spline are frequently used. For more complicated 3D applications, the primitives employed may include cylinder, sphere, cube, and cone. The main purpose of using these primitive-based representations is to speed up rendering in real-time. This is especially important in scenarios involving a large scale virtual world.

Since most display devices are 2D in nature, the projection or transformation of a 3D world on a 2D screen is an inherent process in most applications. This is not a trivial task, especially when there is a need to create immersive 3D effect by using lighting, volume, and shadowing techniques.

While the use of static 3D graphical primitives may satisfies the requirements in some cases, the ability for the user to interact with virtual or real objects in a 3D world are needed in a lot more applications. As examples, interactive 3D graphics can provide us with the capability to interact with movable objects or scenes, for exploring complex structures, and to better visualize time varying phenomena and architecture design. In general, with realistic interaction included in a 3D world, we arrive at what is commonly known as virtual reality.

To create 3D computer graphical applications, a variety of programming tools may be needed depending on the type of applications and hardware support available. A commonly

Figure 1. OpenGL rendering pipeline

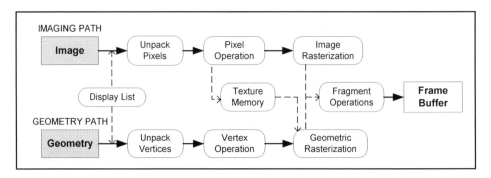

Figure 2. OpenGL in 3D graphics programming

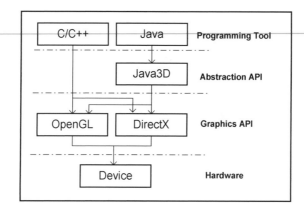

used programming tool, very often provided in the form of graphical libraries, is OpenGL (open graphics library). OpenGL is in turns based on GL (Graphics Library) from SGI. OpenGL has grown to be an industrial standard library for graphical application development, and consists of a set of procedures and functions that allow the programmer to specify objects and operations associated with producing high quality computer graphics. Figure 1 illustrates the rendering pipeline used in OpenGL.

An introduction to computer graphics and OpenGL programming, including some advanced topics such as Web3D, virtual reality, interconnection, and file formats, can be found in Chen (2003) and Chen (2006). A general introduction to OpenGL can also be obtained from the books written by Angle (2003) and Woo, Neider, and Davis (2006).

Another important tool that can be used for 3D graphics programming is DirectX, which is a set of graphical libraries developed by Microsoft. Obviously, DirectX is targeted for Microsoft Windows platform and is therefore not as platform-independent as OpenGL.

For the purpose of Web-based applications, which may involve different machines and platforms, OpenGL is a more suitable choice for program development. Figure 2 shows how OpenGL can be used for both native 3D graphics programming (with C/C++) as well as Web-based 3D programming (with Java3D). The latter is the main focus of this book and will be discussed in details subsequently.

VIRTUAL REALITY

Virtual reality has been defined by Hamit (1993) as "the presence of human in a computer generated space," or more specifically, "a highly interactive, computer-based, multimedia environment in which the user becomes a participant with the computer in a virtually real world."

Emphasizing the interaction and interface aspects, Stone in 1995 regarded virtual reality as an "interface between human and computerized applications based on real-time, three-dimensioned graphical worlds". Most VR systems therefore try as much as possible to provide users with the capability to interact with the system in the same way as their interaction with objects and events in the real world. Essentially, the basic objective is to provide a shared 3-D experience between people and computer with certain unique capabilities that allows the user to experience an artificially generated environment as if it is real.

To extend the impact of realistic visualization and experience, Isdale in 1995 defined virtual reality as "a way for humans to visualize, manipulate and interact with computers and extremely complex data". Such visualization is not limited to just graphics, but may also takes on a more general form of visual, auditory or other sensual outputs to the user.

According to these definitions, a virtual reality application has the following inherent important features.

- **Interactive:** Realistic interactions with virtual objects via data gloves and similar devices to support the manipulation, operation, and control of objects in a virtual world.
- **Real time:** Viewing, interactions, and other related tasks have to be executed with real-time response so that the resulting illusion of being fully immersed in an artificial world is as convincing as possible.
- **Immersive:** Head-referenced viewing can be taken as an example to provide a natural interface for navigation in a 3D space, and can give the user the ability to look-around, walk-around, and fly-through in the virtual environment. Sound, haptic devices, and other non-visual technologies can also be used to enhance the virtual experience significantly.

The creation of a realistic virtual 3D world is a long term goal in interactive computer graphics, requiring hardware and software systems that have yet to be constructed. Specifically, real-time rendering at the rate of at least 20fps very often requires significant computational power.

Since the rendering speed is a function of the number of polygons for the entire model in the application, this is a critical performance or complexity factor as a PC may only be able to render tens of thousands of polygons in real-time. In large scale applications involving complex models with up to a million polygons, powerful computer systems with special graphics hardware are often needed. This may be a major consideration in the deployment of virtual reality systems.

Unlike passive holographic or stereoscopic 3D video, virtual reality is inherently an interactive application. With the rapid advancement of computer hardware, the field of virtual reality, while initially focused on immersive viewing via expensive equipment, is rapidly expanding and includes a growing variety of systems for interacting with 3D computer models in real-time.

From an immersive graphical point of view, virtual reality can also be classified as follows.

- **Full-immersive 3D graphic:** Full immersive systems include full scale representation, stereoscopic viewing, and head-referenced navigation. The term virtual reality initially referred to these systems. Head-mounted display (HMD) is currently commercially available for providing users with a certain level of immersive virtual reality experience.
- **Semi-immersive 3D graphic:** Semi-immersive systems include large screen projections with or without stereo or table projection systems.
- **Non-immersive 3D graphic:** Non-immersive systems only have monitor-based viewing of 3D objects. This is the simplest way to display a virtual reality world through the use of appropriate projection. Most Web-based virtual reality systems are currently used on the use of non-immersive technology due to hardware, cost, and bandwidth constraints.

As applications of virtual reality, virtual world or virtual environment (VE) is often used to refer to the use of 3D graphics, 3D sound, and real-time interaction in an environmental simulation. Specifically, a VE is an environment, which is partially or totally based on user or computer generated sensory input, which may include information from the three most important senses of sight, hearing, and touch.

WEB-BASED VIRTUAL REALITY

The rapid development of the World Wide Web in recent decades has created an important variant of virtual reality applications, that of Web-based virtual reality. Applications in this domain are usually developed using the main programming languages of virtual reality modeling language (VRML) as well as the 3D API extension of the Java language. The former is a specification obtained from an extended subset of the SGI Open Inventor scene description language, which is a higher level programming tool for OpenGL.

Figure 3 presents the relationship between VRML and Java 3D. As shown, a 3D Web-based application will have programming codes in Java or Java3D in general. Some of these codes would invoke the Java3D API, which will in turn invoke lower level routines in libraries such as DirectX or OpenGL.

Regardless of the programming language used, a Web-based 3D application is typically carried out through a browser working under a client-server approach. The 3D plug-in that

Figure 3. Relationship of VRML and Java 3D

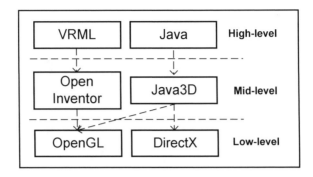

is associated with the 3D application must therefore be embedded into a 2D browser such as Netscape or Microsoft Internet Explorer.

Using a plug-in browser, the user can explore a virtual 3D world, zooming in and out, moving around and interacting with the virtual environment. With VRML, standard navigational tools like walk-trough or fly-over are provided by using the relevant plug-in. On the other hand, when a Java 3D plug-in is used, there is a need for the programmer to design and supply a more customized set of navigation tools to the user. In general, this requires more programming efforts, but will be able to provide a more flexible, realistic and professional interface to the user. As an example, it may allow the user to navigate through a 3D world model in an arbitrary way or along a predefined path by using, say, just the mouse.

Both VRML and Java 3D allow fairly complex 3D graphics to be transmitted across networks without the very high bandwidth capacity that would be necessary if the files were transmitted as standard graphic files. In general, the information transmitted may include platform-independent multimedia elements, such as texture images, video, and sounds.

VRML

Before discussing Java 3D in detail in this book, we will now give an outline of VRML in this section and discuss its relationship with Java 3D in subsequent sections.

VRML is a specification for producing 3D interactive worlds on the Web, and is the original and most popular form of Web3D. As a 3D scene description language and file format, VRML allows encoding and encapsulation of 3D content on the Internet. As given below, it has undergone a long history of evolving from versions 1.0 to X3D.

- **VRML 1.0:** This is the earliest version of VRML, and is evolved from SGI's Open Inventor scene description language. The key feature of this initial standard is a core set of object oriented constructs augmented by hypermedia links. VRML 1.0 allows for scene generation by Web browsers on Intel and Apple personal computers as well as UNIX workstations.

- **VRML 2.0:** This was released in August 96, and expands the specification to address real time animation on the Web. VRML 2.0 provides local and remote hooks, that is, an application programming interface or API, to graphical scene description. Dynamic scene changes are simulated by combinations of scripted actions, message passing, user commands, and behavior protocols such as Distributed Interaction Simulation (DIS) or Java.

- **VRML97:** VRML 2.0 was submitted to ISO (international standards organization) for publication in May 1997, and redefined as VRML97 by ISO. This became the industrial standard of non-proprietary file format for displaying scenes consist of three-dimensional objects on the Web.

- **X3D:** Currently, VRML (node structure) has evolved or mutated to X3D and much of it is incorporated into the MPEG-4 standard. X3D can support complex virtual reality applications. A wider range of interaction techniques and devices is now supported (Figueroa, Medina, Jimenez, Martýnez, & Albarracýn, 2005; Hudson, Couch, & Matsuba, 2003; Sommaruga & Catenazzi, 2007,). VRML browsers have also evolved, and new X3D browsers have been greatly expanded when compared with the earlier VRML 97 standards with extended media and texture/lighting capabilities. Technically, X3D is an integration of a new version of VRML using XML (extensible markup language). Its main disadvantage is that it is not well suited for constructing complex behaviors (Dachselt & Rukzio, 2003, Mesing & Hellmich, 2006).

3D models under VRML can be created directly and indirectly. Directly, we can use the descriptive language that VRML provides. The model is then defined in one or more VRML files, which are regular text files with a standardized syntax. The building blocks of a VRML model are called VRML nodes, and each node is specified using a standardized syntax and describes, for example, a three-dimensional shape, a light source, the path for an animation, the position of a sound source, and so on. The nodes are organized within what is called a scene graph, which is a hierarchical structure commonly used for building and managing complex three-dimensional content.

Very often, the virtual objects in VRML can be more easily created using other three-dimensional modeling software in an indirect manner. As an example, a CAD/CAM system may be used to create and export objects in the form of VRML nodes that can subsequently be inserted into a VRML file.

Although a VRML program may enable the user to control shapes and carry out some simple animation and interaction, it is often necessary for the programmer to write some short programs in Java or JavaScript for more advanced or sophisticated control. Under VRML, a script node that uses Javascript can be included to create customized behavior. This node can provide additional functionality and flexibility in the 3D application. However, these scripts are external to VRML and are therefore not compiled. As a result, complicated interactions that use sophisticated scripts may slow down the application. Another missing functionality in VRML is the capability to accessing databases and to carry out further parameterization.

JAVA 3D

Forming part of a Java API (application programmer interface), Java 3D is a set of standardized classes that have been extended under Java 2 for the creation of 3D graphics (Bouvier, 2006; Burrows & England, 2002; Java 3D API Specification, 2006; Selman, 2002; Walsh & Gehringer, 2002). Specifically, these are designed on top of lower level graphical API of OpenGL and DirectX, and can provide Java developers the ability to write Web-based applets as well as 3D interactive applications. It is a good representative example of a scene graph-based 3D toolkit, and has been used to implement a wide range of applications including computer aided design, Web advertising, motion picture special effects and computer games.

A variety of implementation examples using Java 3D are available. As examples, Java and Java3D are used in model visualization applications involving product components (Blanchebarbe & Diehl, 2001), proteins (Geroimenko & Geroimenko, 2000), and consciousness content (Can, Wan, Wang, & Su, 2003). Some examples for education and research purposes can be found in Zhang and Liang (2005), Tori, Jr, and Nakamura (2003), and Stritch and Best (2005). Other examples involving collaborative implementation are provided by Mendoza, Méndez, Ramos, Boyacá, and Pinzón (2006), Peralta and Silva (2006), Purnamadjaja, Iskandar, and Russell (2007), Wang, Wong, Shen, and Lang (2002), Wang (2003), Yu, Wu, & Wu (2005), and Xia, Song, and Zheng (2006).

One of the main advantages of Java 3D is that, being an API extension of Java, it is platform independent. Other advantages are:

- **High-level and object-oriented view of 3D graphics:** Java 3D accomplishes this by using a *scene graph*-based 3D graphics model. This approach can be important to programmers without much graphics or multimedia programming experience. Specifically, learning Java 3D is a rather straightforward and intuitive affair when compared with, say, OpenGL based on lower level and procedural 3D API.

- **Optimized speed wherever possible:** During runtime, rendering capability bits can be used to optimize the scene graph for the fastest possible renders. This allows Java 3D to be able to be used in, say, interactive graphics environments such as games, simulations, and low-latency situations, as well as in offline, high quality graphics applications.
- **A large and growing number of 3D loaders:** As an example, Java 3D VRML97 file loader and browser, together with their codes, are freely available.
- **Supports a number of exotic devices including wands, data gloves, and headsets:** The com.sun.j3d.utils.trackers package included with Sun's implementation provides classes for Fakespace, Logitech, and Polhemus devices.

On the other hand, the following lists downs some of the disadvantages of Java 3D.

- **Standard extension API:** Java 3D is a standard extension API to the Java2 platform. This dependence can sometimes be regarded as a risk that limits the portability of Java 3D code across platforms.
- **Availability constraints:** The only major vendor currently supporting Java 3D is Sun, through its implementation for Solaris and Win32. This is quite unlike OpenGL, which is available for a variety of Unix, Windows, and other systems. The issue of cross-platform portability is thus more severe for Java 3D.
- **Hiding of rendering pipeline details:** Since Java 3D is a high level API, it intentionally hides details of the rendering pipeline from the developer. This makes it unsuitable for applications where such details are important.
- **Heavyweight components:** Being heavyweight, Java 3D has a native non-Java peer that actually carries out the rendering. This may complicate GUI development if Java Swing and its all-Java, or lightweight, components are also used. While workarounds to these issues can be worked out, lightweight and heavyweight components in general do not mix well in the same container objects and windows.

While both Java 3D and VRML are commonly used for 3D graphics development, Java 3D is in general a more specialized tool for creating customized 3D graphical applications. Also, as illustrated by Liang, 2006, in a Java 3D logic design example that generates VRML-based files, it is possible to combine Java 3D and VRML and explore their advantages in the same application. The main differences between Java 3D and VRML are summarized below.

- **Program approach:** VRML adopts a content-centric approach, while Java 3D uses a program-centric approach in the building of 3D worlds.
- **Flexibility:** Java 3D is more flexible in terms of programming style and the functions available. Essentially, the larger number of functions available under Java 3D makes

it a better tool for developing more specialized and customized behavior and applications. This increased flexibility of course is at the expense of steeper learning curve. Specifically, Java 3D provides more extensive support for behaviors, interpolators, clipping and collision detection.

- **Application complexity:** VRML may be more suitable for simple graphics applications where the development time is at a premium. When the content or 3D world to be created is more complicated, Java 3D will be more suitable.
- **File format:** Being a text based modeling language for dynamic interpretation based on the source code directly, VRML has a file format that is more standardized. This is not the case for Java 3D, which has capability to support complied code using low level API for faster 3D graphics rendering.
- **Compatibility:** Java 3D is able to support VRML objects through the VRML97 loader. However, it is not possible for VRML to run Java 3D programs.
- **Dynamic variation of scene graph:** Since Java 3D nodes in the scene graph are instances of the corresponding classes, the scene graph that describe the virtual 3D world created under Java 3D can be dynamically changed. This is not possible for VRML.
- **Vendor support:** There are more vendors that support VRML.

It is worthwhile to note that some parts of Java 3D actually evolve from and is still dependent on OpenGL. At least in theory, OpenGL can be used for the creation of a 3D world completely. However, similar to writing assembly codes, it is not well suited for developing complicated 3D graphics applications due to programming, debugging, and maintenance efforts. This is a result of the older **procedural programming model** adopted in OpenGL.

MIXED REALITY

Mixed reality (MR), which involves the merging of real-world objects and computer generated graphics to provide the user with additional information and experience, is a more expansive form of virtual Reality and the continuum of merging between computer-generated content and the real world. Figure 4 shows the transition from real reality, mixed/augmented reality to virtual reality (Mark & Livingston, 2005; Wang, 2007).

Example applications include augmenting real objects with computer graphics for assisting archaeological excavation (Benko, Ishak, & Feiner, 2003), relaying stored experience (Correia, Alves, Sá, Santiago, & Romero, 2005), teleconference (Bekins et al., 2006), and virtual human interaction (Egges, Papagiannakis, & Magnenat-Thalmann, 2006). Some application of using MR for educational and training purposes can also be

Figure 4. From real reality to virtual reality

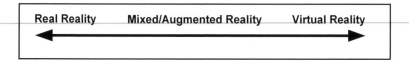

found in Cavazza, Charles, and Mead (2004), Hachimura, Kato, and Tamura (2004), and Radenkovic (2005).

In general, a typical MR application setup requires some sensors, HMDs, and tracking devices. For example, motion sensors are used by Bannach et al. (2006), wearable computers are used by Cheok et al. (2002), tracking devices are used by DiVerdi and Hollerer (2007). Some discussions on the use of head tracking sensors, firewire cameras and HMDs are provided by Qi (2004), Choy et al. (2005), and Nguyen et al. (2005).

Very often, these sensors are used for finding out the position and orientation of the user' head in the real-world before appropriate augmented graphical information can be shown to overlay to provide additional information on the user's display. As a result, MR systems have not yet evolved to a stage where Web-based applications can be integrated.

SUMMARY

Java 3D is an interactive object-orientated 3D graphics API for developing and presenting high level 3D content and sound in Java applications and applets. Designed for write-once, run-anywhere applications, Java 3D extends the entire set of Java APIs to give 3D Internet support for a wide range of platforms, multiple display environments and multiple input devices.

One advantage of Java 3D is that it allows the user to focus on creating the content of the application rather than on rendering optimization. The latter includes issues such as scene compilation, content culling, parallel and pipeline rendering.

Java 3D also has reasonably good graphic performance through the use of OpenGL/Direct3D and 3D graphic hardware acceleration. With portability and Internet support as main advantages, it can be used in a variety of platforms and operating systems with applications in scientific, medical, and information visualization (Hobona, 2006; Huang, 2004; Ko, 2002; Nielsen, 2006; Oellien, 2005; Speck, 1999; Zhuang, 2000). In particular, it is extensively used in simulation, computer-aided design (CAD), and geographical information systems (GIS) (Colon, 2006; Nikishkov, 2006; Oliveira, 2006; Ueda, 2006; Zhang et al., 2005).

In the following chapters, all the important topics on Java 3D will be discussed in detail. The discussion will start with the next chapter where a brief introduction on the use of Java 3D will be presented through a simple example program. In subsequent chapters, specific topics on the creation of geometries and appearance of 3D objects, the use of texturing and lighting techniques to create realistic effects, the ability for the user to interact with the virtual 3D world through animation, interaction and behavior, as well as the use of advanced methodologies such as multiple views and sound effects, will be discussed. Then, to illustrate how these various techniques can be used in a practical application, the final chapter will present an implementation of a Web-based 3D real-time laboratory experiment by using Java 3D.

REFERENCES

Angle, E. (2006). *Interactive computer graphics: A top-down approach with OpenGL.* Addison Wesley.

Bannach, D., Amft, O., Kunze, K. S., Heinz, E. A., Troster, G., & Lukowicz, P. (2007). Waving real hand gestures recorded by wearable motion sensors to a virtual car and driver in a mixed-reality parking game. *Proceedings of the IEEE Symposium on Computational Intelligence and Games* (pp. 32-39).

Bekins, D., Yost, S., Garrett, M., Deutsch, J., Htay, W. M., Xu, D., & Aliaga, D. (2006). Mixed reality tabletop (MRT): A low-cost teleconferencing framework for mixed-reality applications. *Proceedings of the IEEE Virtual Reality Conference* (pp. 34). Washington, DC: IEEE Computer Society.

Benko, H., Ishak, E. W., & Feiner, S. (2004). Collaborative mixed reality visualization of an archaeological excavation. *Proceedings of the 3rd IEEE and ACM International Symposium on Mixed and Augmented Reality* (pp. 132-140). Washington, DC: IEEE Computer Society.

Blanchebarbe, P., & Diehl, S. (2001). A framework for component based model acquisition and presentation using Java3D. *Proceedings of the 6th International Conference on 3D Web Technology* (pp. 117-125). New York: ACM.

Bouvier, D. J. (2006). Getting started with the Java 3D API, Sun Microsystems. Retrieved from http://java.sun.com/products/java-media/3D/collateral/j3d_tutorial_ch7.pdf

Burrows, A. L., & England, D. (2002). Java 3D, 3D graphical environments and behaviour. *Software—Practice and Experience, 32*(4), 359-376.

Can, T., Wan, Y., Wang, Y., & Su, J. (2003). FPV: Fast protein visualization using Java 3D. *Proceedings of the 2003 ACM Symposium on Applied Computing* (pp. 88-95). New York: ACM.

Cavazza, M., Charles, F., & Mead, S. J. (2004). Multimodal acting in mixed reality interactive storytelling. *IEEE MultiMedia, 11*(3), 30-39.

Chen, J. X. (2006). *Guide to graphics software tools.* Springer Verlag, latest version.

Chen, J. X., & Wegman, E. J. (2006). *Foundation of 3D graphics programming. Using JOGL and Java3D.* Springer Verlag.

Cheok, A. D., Fong, S. W., Yang, X., Wang, W., Lee, M. H., Billinghurst, M., & Hirokazu, K. (2002). Game-city: A ubiquitous large area multi-interface mixed reality game space for wearable computers. *Proceedings of the 6ᵗʰ International Symposium on Wearable Computers* (pp. 156-157).

Choy, C. S. T., Lu, K. C., Chow, W. M., Sit, K. M., Lay, K. H., & Ho, W. (2005). Mixed reality head-mounted display. *IEEE International Conference on Consumer Electronics* (pp. 427-428).

Correia, N., Alves, L., Sá, R., Santiago, J., & Romero, L. (2005). HyperMem: A system to store and replay experiences in mixed reality worlds. *Proceedings of the International Conference on Cyberworlds* (pp. 8).

Dachselt, R., & Rukzio, E. (2003). BEHAVIOR3D: An XML-based framework for 3D graphics behavior. *Proceeding of the 8ᵗʰ International Conference on 3D Web Technology* (pp. 101-112). New York: ACM.

DiVerdi, S., & Hollerer, T. (2007). GroundCam: A tracking modality for mobile mixed reality. *IEEE Virtual Reality Conference* (pp. 75-82).

Egges, A., Papagiannakis, G., & Magnenat-Thalmann, N. (2006). An interactive mixed reality framework for virtual humans. *Proceedings of the International Conference on Cyberworlds* (pp. 165-172). Washington, DC: IEEE Computer Society.

Figueroa, P., Medina, O., Jimenez, R., Martýnez, J., & Albarracýn, C. (2005). Extensions for interactivity and retargeting in X3D. *Proceedings of the 10ᵗʰ International Conference on 3D Web Technology* (pp. 103-110). New York: ACM.

Foley, J. D., Dam, A. V., Feiner, S. K., & Hughes, J. F. (2006). *Computer graphics: Principles and practice* (2ⁿᵈ ed.). Addison-Wesley.

Geroimenko, V., & Geroimenko, L. (2000). Visualising human consciousness content Using Java3D/X3D and psychological techniques. *Proceedings of the International Conference on Information Visualisation* (pp. 529). Washington, DC: IEEE Computer Society.

Hachimura, K., Kato, H., & Tamura, H. (2004). A prototype dance training support system with motion capture and mixed reality technologies. *Proceedings of the 13ᵗʰ IEEE International Workshop on Robot and Human Interactive Communication* (pp. 217-222).

Hamit, F. (1993). *Virtual reality and the exploration of cyberspace.* Carmel, IN: Sams Publishing.

Hearn, D., & Baker, M. P. (2006). *Computer graphics, C version* (2nd ed.). Prentice-Hall.

Hudson, A. D., Couch, J., & Matsuba, S. N. (2003). The Xj3D Browser: Community-Based 3D Software Development.

Isdale, J. (1995). *What is virtual reality?* Retrieved from http://www.cms.dmu.ac.uk/~cph/VR/whatisvr.html

Java3D Geometry. (2006). http://viz.aset.psu.edu/jack/java3d/geom.html.

Java 3D API Specification. (2006). http://java.sun.com/products/java-media/3D/forDevelopers/j3dguide/j3dTOC.doc.html

Java 3D Scene appearance. (2006). http://www.j3d.org/faq/appearance.html

Java 3D Explorer. (2006). http://web3dbooks.com/java3d/jumpstart/Java3DExplorer.html.

Kameyama, M., Kato, Y., Fujimoto, H., & Negishi, H. (2003). 3D graphics LSI core for mobile phone "Z3D." *Proceedings of the ACM SIGGRAPH/EUROGRAPHICS Conference on Graphics Hardware* (pp. 60-67). Aire-la-Ville, Switzerland: Eurographics Association.

Liang, J. S., & Pan, W. W. (2005). The research of Web-based 3D interactive technology for conceptual design system. *The 9th International Conference on Computer Supported Cooperative Work in Design Proceedings* (pp. 61-616).

MacEachren, A. M., Gahegan, M., Pike, W., Brewer, I., Cai, G., & Lengerich, E. (2004). Visualization viewpoints, geovisualization for knowledge construction and decision support. *IEEE Computer Graphics and Applications, 24*(1), 13-17.

Mesing, B., & Hellmich, C. (2006). Using aspect oriented methods to add behaviour to X3D documents. *Proceedings of the 11th International Conference on 3D Web Technology* (pp. 97-107). New York: ACM.

Mark, B. M., & Livingston, A. (2005). Moving mixed reality into the real world. *IEEE Computer Graphics and Applications, 25*(6), 22-23.

Mendoza, B. U., Méndez, L. M., Ramos, G. A., Boyacá, W. S., & Pinzón, A. (2006). Camera motion control from a Java 3D environment: Virtual studio application in decorative arts museum collections. *Proceedings of the IEEE Asia-Pacific Conference on Services Computing* (pp. 58-64). Washington, DC: IEEE Computer Society.

Nguyen, T. H. D., Qui, T. C. T., Xu, K., Cheok, A. D., Teo, S. L., Zhou, Z., Mallawaarachchi, A., Lee, S. P., Liu, W., Teo, H. S., Thang, L. N., Li, Y., & Kato, H. (2005). Real-time

3D human capture system for mixed-reality art and entertainment. *IEEE Transactions On Visualization and Computer Graphics, 11*(6), 706-721.

Peralta, L. M. R., & Silva, A. M. G. (2006). A model-based awareness approach for synchronous collaborative sessions on the Web. *Proceedings of the 4th Latin American Web Congress* (pp. 91-100). Washington, DC: IEEE Computer Society.

Pokorny, C. (1994). *Computer graphics: An object-oriented approach to the art and science.* Franklin, Beedle & Associates.

Purnamadjaja, A. H., Iskandar, J., & Russell, R. A. (2007). Pheromone communication simulation for mobile robots using Java 3D. The *6th IEEE/ACIS International Conference on Computer and Information Science* (pp. 261-266).

Qi, W. (2004). A prototype of video see-through mixed reality interactive system. *Proceedings of the 2nd International Symposium on 3D Data Processing, Visualization, and Transmission* (pp. 163-166). Washington, DC: IEEE Computer Society.

Radenkovic, M. (2005). Novel infrastructures for supporting mixed-reality experiences. *IEEE MultiMedia, 12*(2), 12-18.

Rhyne, T. M. (1997). Internetworked 3D computer graphics: Beyond the bottlenecks and roadblocks. *ACM SIGCOMM '97.*

Sharifi, M., Golpaygani, F. H., & Esmaeli, M. (2004). A new fractal-based approach for 3D visualization of mountains in VRML standard. *Proceedings of the 2nd International Conference on Computer Graphics and Interactive Techniques in Australasia and South East Asia* (pp. 100-105). New York: ACM.

Selman, D. (2002). *Java 3D Programming.* Manning Publications.

Sommaruga, L., & Catenazzi, N. (2007). Curriculum visualization in 3D. *Proceedings of the 12th International Conference on 3D Web Technology* (pp. 177-180). New York: ACM.

Stone, R. J. (1995). The reality of virtual reality. *World Class design to Manufacture, 2*(4), 11-17.

Stritch, T., & Best, J. (2005). A Java 3D visualization application for research use in astronomy. *Journal of Computing Sciences in Colleges, 21*(2), 49-58.

Stromer, J. N., Quon, G. T., Gordon, P. M. K., Turinsky, A. L., & Sensen, C. W. (2005). Jabiru: Harnessing Java 3D behaviors for device and display portability. *IEEE Computer Graphics and Applications, 25*(2), 70-80.

Tori, R., Jr, J. L. B., & Nakamura, R. (2006). Teaching introductory computer graphics Using Java 3D, games, and customized software: A Brazilian experience. *International Conference on Computer Graphics and Interactive Techniques* (pp. 12). New York: ACM.

Walsh, A. E., & Gehringer, D. (2002). *Java 3D API jump-start*. Prentice Hall.

Wang, X. (2007). Exploring an innovative collaborative design space through mixed reality boundaries. *Proceedings of the 11th International Conference on Computer Supported Cooperative Work in Design* (pp. 264-269). Melbourne, Australia

Wang, L., Wong, B., Shen, W., & Lang, S. (2002). A Java 3D-enabled cyber workspace. *Communications of the ACM: Vol. 45. Special Issue: Computer-supported cooperative work in design* (pp. 45-49). New York: ACM.

Woo, M., Neider, J., & Davis, T. (2006). *OpenGL programming guide.* Addison Wesley, latest version.

Xia, Y., Song, G., & Zheng, Y. (2006). Portal access to scientific computation and customized collaborative visualization on campus grid. *Proceedings of the IEEE Asia-Pacific Conference on Services Computing* (pp. 451-457). Washington, DC: IEEE Computer Society.

Yu, C., Wu, M., & Wu, H. (2005). Combining Java with VRML worlds for web-based collaborative virtual environment. *Proceedings of IEEE Networking, Sensing, and Control* (pp. 299-304).

Zhang, H., & Liang, Y. D. (2005). Undergraduate computer graphics using Java 3D. *Proceedings of the 43rd Annual Southeast Regional Conference: Vol. 1, Tutorials, workshops, and panels* (pp. 11-12). New York: ACM.

http://www2003.org/cdrom/papers/poster/p216/p216-kiss.html

http://www.icee.usm.edu/icee/Projects/P-Stadium_Training_(Justin_Nosser)/P-VR_Stadium_Training_Project_Page.htm

http://www.computer.org/portal/site/ieeecs/index.jsp

http://www.epic.noaa.gov/talks/nns/ams99/vrml/

http://vads.ahds.ac.uk/guides/vr_guide/vlib7.html

http://www.symbianone.com/content/view/2867/

http://java3d.j3d.org/faq/vrml.html

http://www.web3d.org/x3d/vrml/index.html

http://vrmlworks.crispen.org/faq/faq6.html

http://www.agocg.ac.uk/brief/vrml.htm

http://www.alchemists.com/vr-index.html

http://www.mcp.com/newriders/internet/vrml/ch3.html

http://www.sgi.com/Technology/openGL

http://vag.vrml.org

http://www.sdsc.edu/~nadeau/Talks/NASA_EOSDIS/java3d9.htm

Chapter II
Java 3D Overview

INTRODUCTION

In the last chapter, a brief introduction on the creation of 3D content through the use of Java 3D and other programming methodologies for virtual reality applications has been given.

Before giving details on the various Java 3D classes and functions in subsequent s, we will now discuss the basic Java 3D program structure in this . Specifically, JDK installation, programming and compiling tools, as well as the difference between Java 3D applet and application will be explained.

Originated from Sun Microsystems, the Java 3D API is made up of a few packages (Java platform API specification, 2006), which in turn contain the classes of some related components and elements. Specifically, the package javax.media.j3d (Package javax.media.j3d, 2006) contains the most basic classes, often referred to as core classes, which are needed to create a Java3D program.

Note, however, that a complete application will often use many other packages and classes as well. As an example, if there is a need to use vectors, points and matrices to draw the virtual universe, the package javax.vecmath (Package javax.media.j3d, 2006) has to be imported. Another important package is java.awt (AWT stands for Abstract Windowing Toolkit), which include classes to create a window to display the rendering. Associated with each class is a variety of methods to aid the programmer in creating the application.

Together, these classes and methods give the programmer the basic tools to construct a simple rotating cube system to a 3D virtual city.

An important concept in Java 3D programming is that the program and the programming objects created has a tree like structure. Thus, a Java3D program will create and instantiate Java 3D objects and places them in a virtual world through the use of a tree like scene graph. This will be explained in greater detail in subsequent sections

GETTING STARTED

To develop an application in Java3D, several tools for writing, compiling, running, and debugging Java3D programs are needed. Appendix A gives details on the various steps needed for downloading three major tools, the Java Development Kit (JDK), the JCreator Integrated Development Environment and the Java3D Application Programming Interface (API), for this purpose. Note that the steps described are for workstations that have not had any Java applications or programs installed in the system. For PCs with Java programming tools already installed, only step three will need to be carried out.

The JDK bundle comprises some programming tools and the Java Runtime Environment (JRE). The latter consists of the Java Virtual Machine and class libraries that will be used in a production environment. The programming tools include the following primary components:

- Javac, for converting a Java source code to a Java bytecode.
- Jar, for archiving related class libraries into a single JAR file.
- Javadoc, for generating documentation from source code comments.
- Jdb, the debugger.

A number of sample programs are also included in the JDK bundle.

The JCreator IDE serves to aid programmer in developing and running programs. It consists of a source code editor, a compiler, some build automation tools and a debugger. The JCreator IDE is for programming in Java (and Java3D) and will enable compiling, debugging and the running of Java programs using the appropriate menu options.

Perhaps most importantly, the Java3D API provides the tools needed for programming in Java3D and running 3D-programs. This API is basically an extension of the JDK bundle, and the downloaded files will simply be added to the appropriate .bin and .lib folders in the JRE that was created when the JDK bundle was installed onto the system.

Lastly, all these software are freely available from http://java.sun.com/.

A SIMPLE JAVA 3D PROGRAM FOR A RotatingCube

To illustrate the main principles and components needed for creating a Java3D application, Figure 1 shows a simple program for creating a rotating color cube.

Appendix B gives details of the various steps needed to compile and run the program. The steps involve first creating an empty workspace for writing the Java source code in the form of a project file, followed by compiling the code and running the program.

After performing the relevant steps to generate the executable file, a rotating cube as shown in Figure 2-2 will be displayed on the browser window. As can be seen, the cube has four colors and will be rotating continuously at the rate of 1 complete turn every four

Figure 1a. First part of RotatingCube

```
1. import javax.media.j3d.*;
2. import javax.vecmath.*;
3. import java.awt.*;
4. import java.awt.event.*;
5. import com.sun.j3d.utils.geometry.*;
6. import com.sun.j3d.utils.universe.*;
7.
8. public class RotatingCube extends Frame implements ActionListener
9. {        protected Button myButton=new Button("Exit");
10.        private SimpleUniverse U1 = null;
11.
12.        protected BranchGroup buildContentBranch(Node Geometry_Appearance)
13.        {
14.                BranchGroup BG_c=new BranchGroup();
15.                Transform3D S1=new Transform3D();
16.                S1.set(new AxisAngle4d(1.0,1.0,0.0,Math.PI/4.0));
17.            TransformGroup TG_c=new TransformGroup(S1);
18.                TG_c.setCapability
19.                    (TransformGroup.ALLOW_TRANSFORM_WRITE);
20.                BG_c.addChild(TG_c);
21.                TG_c.addChild(Geometry_Appearance);
22.                Transform3D yAxis = new Transform3D();
23.                Alpha rotationAlpha = new Alpha(-1,4000);
24.        RotationInterpolator B1 = new RotationInterpolator
25.            (rotationAlpha,TG_c,yAxis,0.0f,(float)Math.PI*2.0f);
26.                BoundingSphere bounds=new BoundingSphere
27.                    (new Point3d(0.0,0.0,0.0),100.0);
28.                B1.setSchedulingBounds(bounds);
29.                TG_c.addChild(B1);
30.                BG_c.compile();
31.                return BG_c;
32.        }//end
33.
```

Figure 1b. Second part of RotatingCube

```
34.     protected Node buildShape()
35.     {
36.       return new ColorCube(0.4);
37.     }
38.
39.     public void actionPerformed(ActionEvent e)
40.     {
41.             dispose();
42.             System.exit(0);
43.     }//end actionPerformed
44.
45.     public RotatingCube()
46.     {        GraphicsConfiguration
47.                     config=SimpleUniverse.getPreferredConfiguration();
48.             Canvas3D Canvas3D_1=new Canvas3D(config);
49.             BranchGroup scene=buildContentBranch(buildShape());
50.             U1=new SimpleUniverse(Canvas3D_1);
51.             U1.getViewingPlatform().setNominalViewingTransform();
52.             U1.addBranchGraph(scene);
53.             setTitle("RotatingCube");
54.             setSize(600,600);
55.             setLayout(new BorderLayout());
56.             add("Center",myCanvas3D);
57.             add("South",myButton);
58.             myButton.addActionListener(this);
59.             setVisible(true);
60.     }//end RotatingCube()
61.
62.     public static void main(String[] args)
63.     {
64.             RotatingCube rc=new RotatingCube();
65.     }
66. }//end RotatingCube class
```

seconds with respect to the vertical y axis. Note that there is an exit button that spans the entire window width at the bottom of the window and that the program can be stopped by pressing this button.

In the new few subsections, we will outline the fundamental underlying concepts and graphical model specified by the program code in Figure 1 and show how this leads to the 3D outputs of Figure 2. This will serve as an overview before these concepts and the associated applications are discussed in more details in subsequent chapters.

Figure 2. Rotating color cube from the program of Figure 1

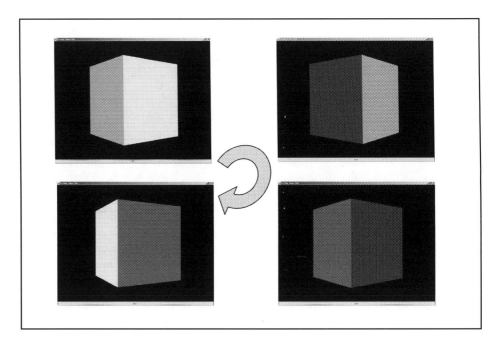

SCENE GRAPH BASICS

Under Java 3D, a 3D virtual world or scene is described in terms of a variety of objects arranged in a tree like graph called the scene graph. Some of the objects may give the geometry of visual objects in the virtual world, some on how the visual objects will behave when the user picks them up, some on the sounds that will be produced, and so on.

A Java 3D program builds the 3D world by creating these objects through instantiating the appropriate classes, setting their attributes, and linking them appropriately to form the scene graph. In subsequent chapters, we will describe and give examples on how different types of objects, including those on geometry, appearance, behaviors, sound, lights, transforms, viewpoint, location, and orientation, can be created and used.

Once the scene graph has been created, the description of the virtual universe is essentially complete. The rendering of the virtual universe into the physical world, which may consist of a simple monitor, multiple screen systems, head mounted or other displays, will be carried out by Java 3D.

For the purposes of illustration, Figure 2-3 shows a simple tree structure, with five nodes. Node A is the root, nodes B and C are its children, while nodes D and E have no

Figure 3. Simple tree structure

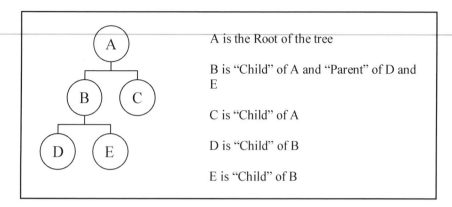

A is the Root of the tree

B is "Child" of A and "Parent" of D and E

C is "Child" of A

D is "Child" of B

E is "Child" of B

child and have node B as parent. In Java 3D scene graph terminology, both nodes A and B are group nodes as they have children nodes, while nodes C, D and E are leave nodes as they are at the end of the tree and have no child.

A simple graphics example would be that A corresponds to a viewing transformation, which describes how the children B and C under A would be viewed in terms of position and orientation. B and C may correspond to the geometry for a sphere and a cube in the virtual world. The children for B, D, and E, may be on a behavior for the sphere rendered under B to change in size depending on the user mouse clicks, as well as for giving an interesting sound whenever the sphere has been picked, respectively.

Depending on its nature, certain nodes or objects in the scene graph have capabilities that can be set to control read and write access to important information or data in the node. Without setting these node capabilities or permissions appropriately, it may not be possible to change these data once the node has become live or the associated code has been compiled. As an example, the relevant capabilities in the sound leave node must be set if it is desirable to change the aural characteristics of the sound during run time. However, increasing the number of capabilities will also reduce the ability for Java 3D to optimize the rendering process and increase computational requirements.

In the tree structure of Figure 3, the lines linking one node to another one corresponds basically to a parent child relationship (Liang, 2006). Apart from this, in a Java 3D scene graph, an object in a node can sometimes be referred to or linked in a reference manner to a NodeComponent object, which is often used to provide more information or attributes such as colors and appearance associated with the node. In this sense, the NodeComponent object can in fact be regarded as part of the node.

The advantage of having a tree structure is that only one path exists from the root of the tree to each of the leave nodes. Such paths are unique for distinct leave nodes and are called scene graph paths. Also, by tracing the scene graph path, it is possible to trace the actions and the bigger objects under which, say, a cube is created in a leave node.

SCENE GRAPH FOR THE RotatingCube

To illustrate the relationship of the scene graph structure and the corresponding Java 3D program, Figure 4 shows the scene graph tree structure for the RotatingCube program of Figure 1.

As can be seen from Figure 4, the scene graph for generating the rotating cube comprises of two major branches, the content branch and the view branch. The former gives details of the 3D objects to be set up in a 3D universe, while the other specifies how these objects will be viewed. Before discussing these in detail in the next few sections, we will first describe the root node of the graph briefly in this section.

Denoted by U1 in Figure 4, the root node of any scene graph in Java3D should be an instantiation of the VirtualUniverse class. The VirtualUniverse is the highest level container that will contain all scene graphs, and this includes a list of Locale objects. Most applications will require only one VirtualUniverse object even though it is possible for Java3D to support more. However, there may be several Locale nodes in each universe.

Figure 4. Scene graph diagram for RotatingCube example

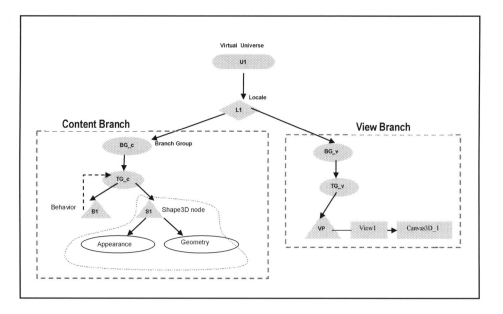

The Locale object, denoted by L1 in Figure 4, contains a set of branches, or BranchGroup subgraphs at a specified location in the VirtualUniverse. In terms of structure, the Locale is child node of the VirtualUniverse and the parent of BranchGroup objects. Each Locale node may be used for several visual, interaction, sound, and other objects that are next to a certain location in the universe. In the chapter on multiple views, we will see that each locale may also be used to provide a different view of the same universe.

Each Locale node may have many branches depending on applications. In the example in Figure 2-4, two BranchGroup nodes BG_v and BG_c, which serves as the root of the view and content subgraphs, are attached to the Locale node L1.

VIEW BRANCH FOR THE RotatingCube

The generic view branch shown in Figure 4 is primarily for defining the way the user sees the 3D objects in the virtual universe. In the RotatingCube example, the SimpleUniverse class is invoked to instantiate a view branch with default parameters. This is sufficient for many simple applications.

In more complicated applications, a more specific view branch may be needed for creating special views into the virtual 3D universe. An example for creating a customized view branch is given in Figure 5. This code segment can be used to replace line 10 as well as lines 47 and 48 in the RotatingCube code segment of Figure 1. With some other minor modifications, the same result, which is a rotating color cube, will be obtained.

Figure 5. A more specific view branch

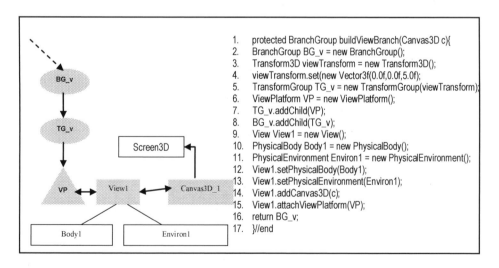

```
1.  protected BranchGroup buildViewBranch(Canvas3D c){
2.  BranchGroup BG_v = new BranchGroup();
3.  Transform3D viewTransform = new Transform3D();
4.  viewTransform.set(new Vector3f(0.0f,0.0f,5.0f);
5.  TransformGroup TG_v = new TransformGroup(viewTransform);
6.  ViewPlatform VP = new ViewPlatform();
7.  TG_v.addChild(VP);
8.  BG_v.addChild(TG_v);
9.  View View1 = new View();
10. PhysicalBody Body1 = new PhysicalBody();
11. PhysicalEnvironment Environ1 = new PhysicalEnvironment();
12. View1.setPhysicalBody(Body1);
13. View1.setPhysicalEnvironment(Environ1);
14. View1.addCanvas3D(c);
15. View1.attachViewPlatform(VP);
16. return BG_v;
17. }//end
```

CONTENT BRANCH FOR THE RotatingCube

The content branch, as its name suggests, is the container for the 3D objects, their attributes and behavior in a scene. From extracting the overall code fragment of Figure 1, Figure 6 shows the content branch in the RotatingCube example. In general, the 3D content of the scene will include the geometry, appearance and behavior attributes of the object and the scene.

Figure 6. Content branch and scene graph for the RotatingCube example

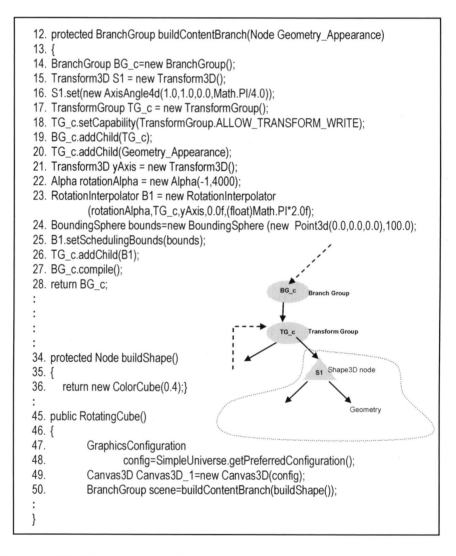

```
12. protected BranchGroup buildContentBranch(Node Geometry_Appearance)
13. {
14. BranchGroup BG_c=new BranchGroup();
15. Transform3D S1 = new Transform3D();
16. S1.set(new AxisAngle4d(1.0,1.0,0.0,Math.PI/4.0));
17. TransformGroup TG_c = new TransformGroup();
18. TG_c.setCapability(TransformGroup.ALLOW_TRANSFORM_WRITE);
19. BG_c.addChild(TG_c);
20. TG_c.addChild(Geometry_Appearance);
21. Transform3D yAxis = new Transform3D();
22. Alpha rotationAlpha = new Alpha(-1,4000);
23. RotationInterpolator B1 = new RotationInterpolator
            (rotationAlpha,TG_c,yAxis,0.0f,(float)Math.PI*2.0f);
24. BoundingSphere bounds=new BoundingSphere (new  Point3d(0.0,0.0,0.0),100.0);
25. B1.setSchedulingBounds(bounds);
26. TG_c.addChild(B1);
27. BG_c.compile();
28. return BG_c;
   :
   :
   :
   :

34. protected Node buildShape()
35. {
36.    return new ColorCube(0.4);}
   :
45. public RotatingCube()
46. {
47.          GraphicsConfiguration
48.              config=SimpleUniverse.getPreferredConfiguration();
49.          Canvas3D Canvas3D_1=new Canvas3D(config);
50.          BranchGroup scene=buildContentBranch(buildShape());
   :
}
```

For the RotatingCube example, the geometry and appearance of the cube are defined using the ColorCube class, while its behavior is that of rotation. The following subsections give a simple overview of the meaning and implications of the various lines of codes and the corresponding scene graph structure created.

In the RotatingCube example, the content branch is primarily built using the build-ContentBranch() function, shown starting from line 12 of Figure 6. The 3D content of this particular scene can be described in terms of the geometry, appearance and behavior of the multicolor cube to be realized.

The geometry and appearance of the multicolored 3D cube is specified under a Shape3D Node S1 in Figure 6. This node is created by the buildShape() function, which is a function outside the main content branch function. The buildShape() function returns a Node type shape and is given in lines 34 to 36 of Figure 6. After being invoked in line 50, the multicolor cube created is then passed as an argument to the buildContentBranch() function which proceeds to create the remaining attributes, including the rotation behavior B1 of the cube.

As given by lines 14 and 15, buildContentBranch() first creates new BranchGroup BG_c and TransformGroup TG_c nodes in Figure 6. The next subsection will give further information on these nodes, which are essential in the creation of the content branch.

From Figure 6, the behavior B1 node is connected to TG_c node by an arrow. This indicates that the behavior is time varying. Line 17 invokes the setCapability() function, which allows the real-time writing of transform information into an object. This is necessary for the cube to be rotated continuously. Lines 21 to 26 continue with the creation of the rotational attribute of the cube. Line 19 attaches TG_c to the newly created BG_c and lines 20 and 26 add the attributes of geometry and appearance, S1 and rotation B1 to TG_c. This completes the creation of the content branch, BG_c, for the RotatingCube scene graph.

BRANCH GROUP

In general, BranchGroup objects are for the purpose of organizing a scene graph. As previously described, the scene graph will have one viewing BranchGroup and another one for content in the most basic configuration.

A viewing or content BranchGroup can be linked as a child to another BranchGroup or node. The using and linking of BranchGroup objects or nodes are dependent on how objects in the virtual world are being organized and behaved as well as programming style.

A properly organized BranchGroup structure facilitates the addition and removal of visual objects in the virtual universe after the scene graph has become live. Specifically, by setting the appropriate capability and using the relevant detach method, a BranchGroup can be removed from its parent, thereby preventing all the underlying nodes from being rendered.

Each BranchGroup object also has a compile method for converting the subgraph under the object to an internal Java 3D format for faster rendering. As an example, several successive transformation matrices under the subgraph may be combined for rendering efficiency.

In the code segment of Figure 6 where a multicolor cube is created, line 14 first creates an empty BranchGroup node BG_c. Line 17 then creates a TransformGroup TG_c , which will be discussed in the next section, in Figure 6, and attaches it as a child node to BG_c. In line 27, the BranchGroup is compiled. A BranchGroup can be detached by invoking the detach() function.

In line 24, bounds are declared to specify a volume of space for a certain region of influence for appropriate objects and scene group nodes. This is essential for rendering and other purposes such as determining the influence of, for example, lightning and fog. In general, the volume specified may be within a box, a sphere or between sets of planes. In the RotatingCube example, an imaginary sphere within which the cube is to rotate is specified.

TRANSFORM GROUP

In addition to BranchGroup, TransformGroup is another commonly encountered object in a scene graph. Technically, a TransformGroup object serves as a container for Transform3D objects, through which translational, rotational and other transforms can be specified. All the child nodes under a certain TransformGroup node will be subject to the specified transforms so that the objects rendered will be appropriately translated, rotated and transformed.

In the RotatingCube example, a TransformGroup node TG_c, as depicted in Figure 6, is created for the behavior B1, Geometry and Appearance S1, of the multicolor cube object. Details on these nodes have been discussed earlier in Section 1.7.

SIMPLE UNIVERSE

As mentioned in previous section, the view branch defines how a viewer sees the virtual world. In the code fragment in Figure 5, specific parameters on the viewing position, orientation, screen size and so on are provided so that Java3D can render a certain desirable view of this 3D world on, for example, a 2D monitor.

A detailed discussion of various nodes and components under the view branch is given in the chapter on multiple views. However, in simpler applications where a single view is enough, it is not necessary to understand the full mechanism involved in the view branch.

Instead, by using a convenience utility class provided by Java3D, a simple universe comprising the structure within the boxed region in Figure 7 can be readily constructed

Figure 7. Code Segment for using the SimpleUniverse class

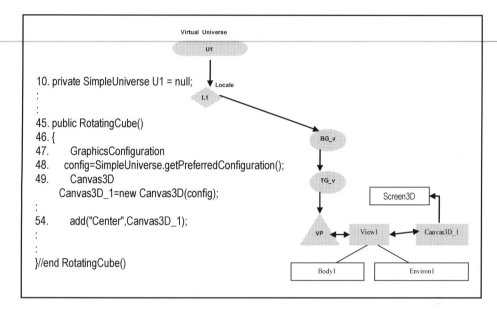

with default values used for the important parameters and nodes. The code segment for doing so is also provided in the figure.

Very briefly, line 10 in Figure 7 invokes the constructor to create a simple universe. In the java applet, all the variables in the method public RotatingCube(), starting from line 45, will then be initialized when the source code is compiled.

Lines 47 and 48 in Figure 7, invoke the SimpleUniverse.getPreferredConfiguration method for passing the Graphics Configuration to the Canvas3D constructor. The latter will construct a Canvas3D object, which corresponds to a 2D image plate in the 3D virtual world. Projecting the 3D objects onto this 2D image plate appropriately and painting this image plate onto the computer display will enable the user to view the virtual world. Line 54 adds the created Canvas3D canvas to the simple universe.

DIFFERENCE BETWEEN JAVA 3D APPLET AND APPLICATION

A standalone application of Java 3D and a Web-based Java 3D application in the form of an applet may share most of the classes. This implies that the codes written for the standalone application can easily be migrated to a Web-based applet application without much modification. However, there is a need to take into consideration of the following three issues in the event of a migration.

- In a standalone application, the entry function has a name of main as shown in Figure 1(b). However, in an applet, the entry function is its constructor. As an example, the constructor name is the same as the class name RotatingCube in Figure 1.
- The path of the files stored on the server has different representations. In a standalone application, a direct absolute or relative file path can be used. On the other hand, in an applet application, only URL-based path can be used. For example, the picture file picture1.gif, which is in the same directory as the java 3D code, can be loaded in Line 1 of Figure 1 in a standalone application. For an applet, the method given in D.6 of Appendix D has to be used instead.
- A standalone application can run under the Java runtime environment, while an applet must be embedded in a HTML file, and run under Internet Explorer or other browser.

In general, it is often easier to develop and test a standalone application first, before migrating to a Web-based applet for further debugging and evaluation.

SUMMARY

In Java 3D, the objects in a virtual 3D world are described in the form of a scene graph. This is a tree like structure consisting of a hierarchy of nodes containing information on objects or groups of objects on geometries, shapes, lights, sounds, interactions, and so on. Specifically, the root of the scene graph is a virtual universe that may have several locale branches. Also, each locale may hold related objects that are next to one another at a certain location in the 3D world, and may be made up of many branch and transform groups. Each branch group is a subgraph of the scene graph, and can be compiled for rendering efficiency. Also, by setting certain capabilities, branch groups can be attached or removed for interaction with the user during run time. In addition to the content branch, which describes the visual objects in the virtual world, the scene graph also needs at least a viewing branch for describing the how the user views the 3D world. The setting up of this branch can be carried out easily by invoking a simple universe. Alternatively, multiple views of the same virtual world can be obtained for applications involving multiple displays.

REFERENCES

Colon, E., Sahli, H., & Baudoin, Y. (2006). CoRoBa, a multi mobile robot control and simulation framework. *International Journal of Advanced Robotic Systems, 3*, 73-78.

Hobona, G., James P., & Fairbairn, D. (2006). Web-based visualization of 3D geospatial data using Java3D. *IEEE Computer Graphics and Applications, 26*, 28-33.

Huang, S., Baimouratov, R., & Nowinski, W. L. (2004). Building virtual anatomic models using Java3D. *Proceedings VRCAI—ACM SIGGRAPH International Conference on Virtual Reality Continuum and its Applications in Industry* (pp. 402-405).

Ko, C. C., Chen, B. M., Loke, C. M., Cheng, C. D., Xiang, X., Eapen, A. K., & Lim, T. S. (2002). Automation in creating Java 3D-based virtual Instruments. *Proceedings International Conference on Software Engineering Research and Practice.*

Java platform API specification. (2006). http://java.sun.com/j2se/1.4.2/docs/api/.

Liang, J. S. (2006). Conceptual design system in a Web-based virtual interactive environment for product development. *International Journal of Advanced Manufacturing Technology, 30*, 1010-1020.

Nielsen, J. F. (2006). A modular framework for development and interlaboratory sharing and validation of diffusion tensor tractography algorithms. *Journal of Digital Imaging, 19*, 112-117.

Nikishkov, G. P. (2006). Object oriented design of a finite element code in Java. *Computer Modeling in Engineering & Sciences, 11*, 81-90.

Oellien, F., Ihlenfeldt W., & Gasteiger, J. (2005). InfVis—Platform-independent visual data mining of multidimensional chemical data sets. *Journal of Chemical Information and Modeling, 45*, 1456-1467.

Oliveira, D., & AnaClaudia, M. T. G. (2006). Virtual reality framework for medical training: Implementation of a deformation class using Java. *Proceedings ACM International Conference on Virtual Reality Continuum and its Applications* (pp. 347-351).

Package javax.media.j3d. (2006). http://java.sun.com/products/java-media/3D/forDevelopers/J3D_1_2_API/j3dapi/.

Ueda, M. (2006). Making of the simplest interactive 3D digital globe as a tool for the world environmental problems. *WSEAS Transactions on Environment and Development, 2*, 973-979.

Zhang, L., Sheng, W., & Liu, X. (2005). 3D visualization of gene clusters and networks. *Proceedings SPIE* (pp. 316-326).

Chapter III
Geometry Objects

INTRODUCTION

To create 3D graphics, we have to build graphics or visual objects and position them appropriately in a virtual scene. In general, there are three possible approaches for doing this (Java 3D geometry, 2006).

One approach is to make use of geometry utility classes to create basic geometric shapes or primitives. The basic shapes are boxes, spheres, cones, and cylinders. Another approach is to employ commercial modeling tools, such as 3D studio max, and have the results loaded into Java 3D. Lastly, custom geometrical shapes or objects can also be created by defining their vertices.

While using utility classes or commercial modeling tools may be simpler and less time consuming, creating objects based on specifying vertices corresponds to the most general method. From a certain angle, the latter can in fact be regarded as the foundation from which the other approaches are based. The main thrust in this chapter will thus be on how objects can be built from their vertices, with some brief discussion on using utility classes presented toward the end of the chapter.

SHAPE3D

As specified in the constructor of Figure 1, the most basic method for creating and specifying the geometry and appearance of an object is through the Shape3D class. The geometry

Figure 1. Specifying geometry and appearance of Shape3D objects

```
Shape3D myShape = new Shape3D ();
// Constructs and initializes an object with default parameters of geometry and
// appearance as null. At the same time, centre is set to be at the origin (0,0,0).

Shape3D myShape1 = new Shape3D (myGeometry1);
// Constructs an object with geometry given by myGeometry1 and a null appearance.

Shape3D myShape2 = new Shape3D(myGeometry2, myAppearance2);
// Constructs and initialized an object with geometry given by Geometry2 and appearance given
// by myAppearance2.
```

component of this class hold the geometric data for the 3D object to be created, while the appearance component defines physical properties like color and line styles.

After its definition, a Shape3D class can be instantiated to create one or several Shape3D objects. These objects are usually added as child nodes to a BranchGroup, TransformGroup or any appropriate group node. The node components of the Shape3D object include objects under the Geometry and Appearance classes. The latter is optional, but will most likely be present.

Figure 2 shows the structure of a created Shape3D object and its components under a TransformGroup. The corresponding code segment is shown in Figure 3. Specifically, in

Figure 2. A Shape3D object and its components

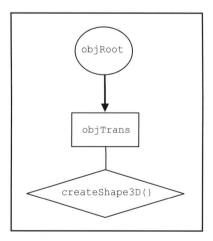

Figure 3. Code segment structure for setting up a scene with a single Shape3D node

```
1.    public class Testing extends Applet
2.    {
3.            . . .
4.
5.            public Testing()
6.            {
7.            }
8.
9.            public void init()
10.           { . . . }
11.
12.           public void destroy()
13.           { . . . }
14.
15.           public BranchGroup createSceneGraph()
16.           {
17.                   BranchGroup objRoot = new BranchGroup();
18.                   TransformGroup objTrans = new TransformGroup();
19.                   objRoot.addChild( objTrans );
20.                   objTrans.addChild( new createShape3D() );
21.                   objRoot.compile();
22.                   return objRoot;
23.           }
24.
25.           public static void main ( String[] args )
26.           { . . . }
27.
28.           public class createShape3D extends Shape3D
29.           {
30.                   public createShape3D()
31.                   {
32.                           this.setGeometry( createGeometry() );
33.                   }
34.
35.                   private Geometry createGeometry()
36.                   {
37.                           . . . return . . .;
38.                   }
39.           }
40.   }
```

line 17, objRoot is an instance of the branch group. Line 18 creates an object objTrans and add it as a child of objRoot in the scene graph. In line 20, the constructor for the create-Shape3D subclass is invoked and an instance of the Shape3D class is created and added to the TransformGroup. Using the setGeometry method, line 32 specifies the geometry for the created Shape3D object to that from a private createGeometry method. This private method specifies the geometrical shape of the visual object to be rendered. How this specification can be written will be discussed in subsequent sections.

GeometryArray CLASS

As discussed earlier in the first section, the shape of the visual object to be rendered is specified by a geometry object, which is a component under a Shape3D object. The creation of a geometry object can be done using the geometry class, which is an abstract superclass.

Under the geometry class (Java 3D API specification, 2006), a useful abstract subclass is the GeometryArray class and the class hierarchy is shown in Figure 4. Figure 5 illustrates the geometry subclasses.

Before any objects can be created, the number of vertices the object is going to have and their respective coordinates must first be planned out. One must remember to plan the coordinates in an anti-clockwise direction because this is the default for determining the front side of a polygon. Line, Quad, Triangle, and PointArrays have two general constructors. Figure 6 gives the format for specifying the vertices of Shape3D objects, where X stands for Point, Line, Quad, or Triangle.

The default coordinate system that is being used is the right hand system. Basically, when facing the screen, +X is to the right, +Y is up and +Z is towards the viewer as shown is Figure 7.

Figure 4. GeometryArray class hierarchy

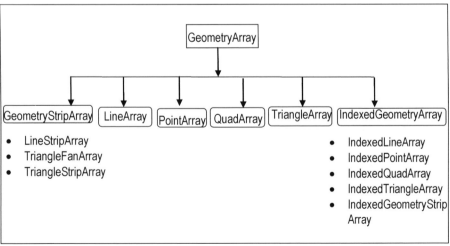

Figure 5. Geometry subclasses

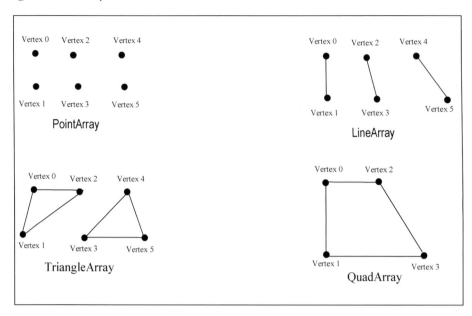

Figure 6. Specifying vertices of Shape3D objects

```
XArray myArray = new XArray(vertexCount, vertexFormat);
// Constructs and initializes an object with number of vertices given by vertexCount and
// type of components present in the vertex is given by vertexFormat.
// There are 4 types of flags that correspond to the mask in vertexFormat.  They are
// coordinates, normals, one of color_3 or color_4 (without or with //color information);
// and one of texture_coordinate_2, texture_coordinate_3 or //texture_coordinate_4 (2D, // // 3D or 4D).

XArray myArray = new XArray(vertexCount1, vertexFormat2,
texCoordSetCount, texCoordSetMap);
// Constructs and initializes an object with number of vertices given by vertexCount1 and
// type of components present in vertex is given by vertexFormat.  The number of texture // coordinate is given by the texCoordSetCount
and an array that maps texture coordinate // sets to texture units is given by texCoordSetMap.
```

Figure 7. Right hand coordinate system

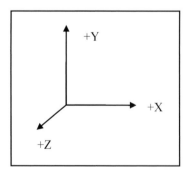

We will now discuss the last four most basic classes in the next few sections, noting that the first two classes, GeometryStripArray and IndexedGeometryArray, are again abstract classes which may also be useful and will be discussed in later sections.

PointArray

In the PointArray class, a series of vertices are drawn as individual points. Figure 8 shows the code segment and result for using PointArray to declare a set of points on a curve based on the equation $y = x^2$ and $z=0$. In line 13, the PointArray class is invoked and n vertices with coordinate masks are created. Note that since $z=0$, the 3D curve degenerates to become a 2D one. The variable r gives the x-axis range for the curve. This is set to be smaller than or equal to 2.0f as the maximum x-axis display width on the screen is 2.0f. With the

Figure 8. Code segment and result of PointArrayCurve.java

```
1.    public class Curve
2.    {
3.        private BranchGroup axisBG;
4.        public Curve()
5.        {           //this curve is draw based on this function y = square(x)
6.                axisBG = new BranchGroup();
7.            float r = 1.8f, x, y, dx;
8.
9.                int n = 100;        //n is number of points
10.               dx = r/n;           //dx is the x distance between 2 nearest point
11.
12.               //PointArray declaration of n vertices
13.               PointArray pA = new PointArray(n,
      GeometryArray.COORDINATES);
14.
15.               / / add the PointArray object to the BranchGraph
16.               axisBG.addChild(new Shape3D(pA));
17.       for (int i=0; i<n; i++)
18.         {
19.           x = -0.9f + dx*i;      //set the coordinate of x
20.           y = x*x;               //equivalent value of coordinate y
21.           pA.setCoordinate(i, new Point3f(x, y, 0.0f));
22.         }
23.        }
24.    public BranchGroup getBG()
25.        {
26.               return axisBG;
27.        }
28.    }
```

variable n corresponding to the number of points (vertices) for the curve, the variable dx = r/n gives the distance along the x-axis between 2 adjacent points.

LineArray

LineArray can be used to define an object based on drawing lines between pairs of points. This is illustrated in the code segment in Figure 9, which results in a star shaped figure.

Note that the vertices must be provided in the form of pairs as Java 3D will render a straight line, one pixel in thickness, between two vertices. Each of these vertices represents the endpoints of a line. Different line width and style can be achieved by using shape appearance attributes.

Figure 9. Code segment and result of LineArrayStar.java

```
1.    public class Star
2.    {
3.       private BranchGroup axisBG;
4.       public Star()
5.       {
6.       axisBG = new BranchGroup();
7.
8.       //define a LineArray of 10 vertices
9.       LineArray lineArr = new LineArray(10, LineArray.COORDINATES);
10.      axisBG.addChild(new Shape3D(lineArr));
11.
12.      float r = 0.6f, x, y;        //r is the distance from the origin to every vertex
13.      Point3f coor[] = new Point3f[5];
14.
15.      for (int i=0; i<=4; i++)
16.      {
17.       x = (float)Math.cos(Math.PI/180*(90+72*i))*r;
18.       y = (float)Math.sin(Math.PI/180*(90+72*i))*r;
19.       coor[i] = new Point3f(x, y, 0.0f);
20.      }
21.      for (int i=0; i<=4; i++)
22.      {
23.       lineArr.setCoordinate(i*2, coor[i]);
24.       lineArr.setCoordinate(i*2+1, coor[(i+2) % 5]);
25.      }
26.      }
27.      public BranchGroup getBG()
28.      {
29.              return axisBG;
30.      }
31.   }
```

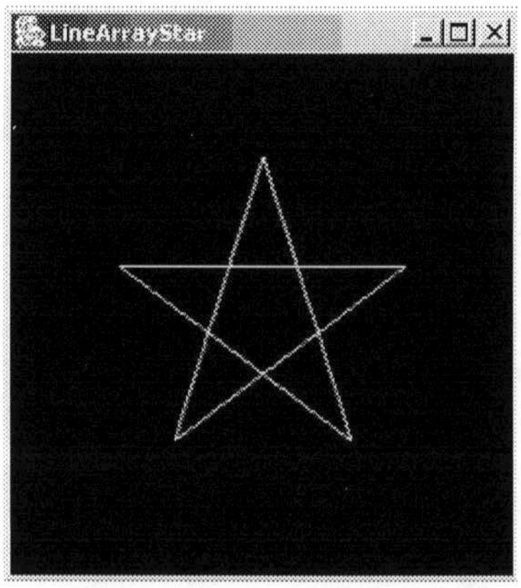

Since a star with 5 lines is to be created, the number of vertices is 10 and this is specified in line 9 when LineArray is invoked. The variable r gives the distance from the origin to every vertex. Note also that, with i <= 4, the index of coor[i+2] in line 24 may exceed its maximum bound. To ensure that this does not happen, a modulus or % operator is included in the code.

Note that the vertices must be provided in the form of pairs as Java 3D will render a straight line, one pixel in thickness, between two vertices.

QuadArray

Using QuadArray, 3D objects constructed by using quadrilaterals can be rendered by shape appearance attributes. Note: A quadrilateral must be planar and convex or results are undefined. In the case where vertexCount is less than 4 or is not a multiple of 4, an illegal argument exception will occur. Each quadrilateral will have a solid white by default, and will be drawn based on the coordinates of four vertices which defines the four sides of the quadrilateral.

Figures 10 to 13 show the code segment and result from using QuadArray in an example to build a house shaped object. Note that lines 86 to 90 set the appearance, which will be discussed in subsequent chapters, appropriately so that the outline of the object can be seen. Also, the house is built by specifying 12 vertices and then using appropriate combinations of these to construct several quadrilaterals that give the various faces of the object.

Figure 10. First code segment of House_Quad_Array.java

```
1.    import javax.media.j3d.*;
2.    import javax.vecmath.*;
3.
4.    public class House extends Shape3D
5.    {
6.        public House()
7.        {
8.            this.setGeometry(Draw_House());
9.            this.setAppearance(App());
10.       } //end of constructor
```

Figure 11. Second code segment of House_Quad_Array.java

```
11.     private Geometry Draw_House()
12.     {
13.     //constants for the front
14.     float fz = 0.5f;
15.     float tx = 0.25f;
16.     float ty = 0.6f;
17.     float mx = 0.5f;
18.     float my = 0.2f;
19.     float bz = -0.6f;
20.
21.     // coordinates for the six common vertices
22.             Vector3f topleft = new Vector3f(-tx,ty,fz);
23.             Vector3f midleft = new Vector3f(-mx,my,fz);
24.             Vector3f botleft = new Vector3f(-mx,-ty,fz);
25.
26.             Vector3f topright = new Vector3f(tx,ty,fz);
27.             Vector3f midright = new Vector3f(mx,my,fz);
28.             Vector3f botright = new Vector3f(mx,-ty,fz);
29.
30.             Vector3f btopleft = new Vector3f(-tx,ty,bz);
31.             Vector3f bmidleft = new Vector3f(-mx,my,bz);
32.             Vector3f bbotleft = new Vector3f(-mx,-ty,bz);
33.
34.             Vector3f btopright = new Vector3f(tx,ty,bz);
35.             Vector3f bmidright = new Vector3f(mx,my,bz);
36.             Vector3f bbotright = new Vector3f(mx,-ty,bz);
37.
38.     // define a Point3f array to store the coordinates of the vertices
39.     Point3f[] coords =
40.             {       //front trapezium
41.                     new Point3f(topleft), new Point3f (midleft),
42.                     new Point3f (midright), new Point3f (topright),
43.
44.                     //back trapezium
45.                     new Point3f(btopleft), new Point3f (bmidleft),
46.             new Point3f (bmidright), new Point3f (btopright),
47.
48.                     //bottom rectangle
49.                     new Point3f(botleft), new Point3f (botright),
50.
51.     new Point3f (bbotright), new Point3f (bbotleft),
52.
```

Specifically, lines 5 to 10 correspond to the constructor for the House class, which invokes two private methods, Draw_House() and App(). As the House class is an extension of the Shape3D class, the setGeometry() method in Shape3D is used with Draw_House()

Figure 12. Third code segment of House_Quad_Array.java

```
51.                          //front rectangle
52.                          new Point3f(midleft), new Point3f (botleft),
53.                          new Point3f (botright), new Point3f (midright),
54.
55.                          //left trapezium
56.                          new Point3f(btopleft), new Point3f (bmidleft),
57.                          new Point3f(midleft), new Point3f (topleft),
58.
59.                          //right trapezium
60.                          new Point3f (topright),new Point3f (midright),
61.                          new Point3f (bmidright),new Point3f (btopright),
62.
63.                          //back rectangle
64.                          new Point3f(bmidleft), new Point3f (bbotleft),
65.                          new Point3f (bbotright), new Point3f (bmidright)
66.              };
67.
68.        //define new QuadArray with the above vertices
69.        QuadArray House_struct = new QuadArray(coords.length, QuadArray.COORDINATES);
70.
71.        //coordinates will be filled starting from vertex 0
72.        House_struct.setCoordinates(0, coords);
73.
74.        return House_struct;
75.
76.    } // end of Draw_house method
77.
78.    private Appearance App()
79.    {
80.        Color3f lime = new Color3f(0.0f,2.0f,1.0f);
81.        Appearance look = new Appearance();
82.        ColoringAttributes ca = new ColoringAttributes(lime, ColoringAttributes.FASTEST);
83.        LineAttributes la = new LineAttributes(3, LineAttributes.PATTERN_SOLID, false);
84.        PolygonAttributes pa = new PolygonAttributes();
85.
86.        //to make no fill, only the frame
87.        pa.setPolygonMode(PolygonAttributes.POLYGON_LINE);
88.
89.        //to make both sides of the face appear
90.        pa.setCullFace(PolygonAttributes.CULL_NONE);
```

to define the geometry of the created House object. In the same way, the setAppearance() and App() methods are used to define the appearance of the object.

Lines 39 to 66 give the coordinates of 12 vertices for the object, based on which a Point3f array is created and initialized using relevant combinations of the coordinates of

Figure 13. Fourth code segment and result of House_Quad_Array.java

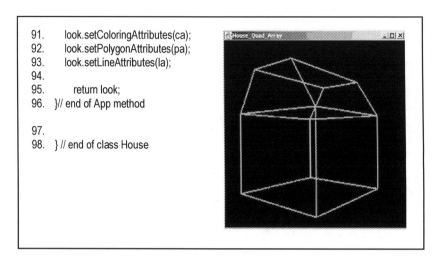

```
91.      look.setColoringAttributes(ca);
92.      look.setPolygonAttributes(pa);
93.      look.setLineAttributes(la);
94.
95.        return look;
96.    }// end of App method

97.
98.    } // end of class House
```

these vertices. A new QuadArray object, named House_Struct, is then instantiated in line 69, with a vertexFormat corresponding to coordinates.

The setCoordinates method of the GeometryArray class is used to set the coordinates for defining the various faces of House_Struct in line 72. The first argument of 0 dictates that the coordinates will be assigned starting from vertex 0. The second argument is simply the array which storing the coordinates.

TriangleArray

Instead of rendering objects based on four-sided quadrilaterals, three-sided triangles can also be used. Figures 14 to 16 give an example where an octahedron is constructed using 8 different triangles. Since each triangle requires 3 vertices, a total of 24 vertices would have to be specified to create the octahedron, even though many vertices are actually identical.

The global variable in line 3 specifies the number of vertices for each triangle, while lines 5 to 18 give the constructor for the Diamond class. In this example, every triangle is created using its own method, which includes the creation of a new TriangleArray object after specifying its coordinators using setCoordinate(). As mentioned, the rendering of, say, triangle 1 and 2 requires some common vertices to be specified twice.

Figure 14. First Code segment of DiamondTriangleArray.java

```
1.    public class Diamond extends Shape3D
2.    {
3.    int vertex = 3;
4.    //constructor
5.    public Diamond()
6.    {
7.
8.            this.setGeometry(Tri1Geometry());
9.            this.addGeometry(Tri2Geometry());
10.           this.addGeometry(Tri3Geometry());
11.           this.addGeometry(Tri4Geometry());
12.           this.addGeometry(Tri5Geometry());
13.           this.addGeometry(Tri6Geometry());
14.           this.addGeometry(Tri7Geometry());
15.           this.addGeometry(Tri8Geometry());
16.           this.setAppearance(DiamondAppearance());
17.
18.    }
19.    private Geometry Tri1Geometry()
20.    {
21.           //Triangle 1
22.           TriangleArray Tri1 = new TriangleArray (vertex, TriangleArray.COORDINATES );
23.           Tri1.setCoordinate(0, new Point3f(0.0f,0.8f,0.0f));
24.           Tri1.setCoordinate(1, new Point3f(0.0f,0.0f,0.5f));
25.           Tri1.setCoordinate(2, new Point3f(0.5f,0.0f,0.0f));
26.           return Tri1;
27.    }
28.
29.    private Geometry Tri2Geometry()
30.    {
31.           //Triangle 2
32.           TriangleArray Tri2 = new TriangleArray (vertex, TriangleArray.COORDINATES );
33.           Tri2.setCoordinate(0, new Point3f(0.0f,0.8f,0.0f));
34.           Tri2.setCoordinate(1, new Point3f(0.5f,0.0f,0.0f));
35.           Tri2.setCoordinate(2, new Point3f(0.0f,0.0f,-0.5f));
36.           return Tri2;
37.    }
38.
```

GeometryStripArray

From the previous sections, it is obvious that the use of the basic LineArray, QuadArray, TriangleArray, and PointArray classes to specify 3D objects is straightforward. However, it may also be rather cumbersome and tedious in terms of coding and rendering.

Figure 15. Second code segment of DiamondTriangleArray.java

```
39.     private Geometry Tri3Geometry()
40.     {
41.             //Triangle 3
42.             TriangleArray Tri3 = new TriangleArray (vertex, TriangleArray.COORDINATES);
43.             Tri3.setCoordinate(0, new Point3f(0.0f,0.8f,0.0f));
44.             Tri3.setCoordinate(1, new Point3f(0.0f,0.0f,-0.5f));
45.             Tri3.setCoordinate(2, new Point3f(-0.5f,0.0f,0.0f));
46.             return Tri3;
47.     }
48.
49.     private Geometry Tri4Geometry()
50.     {
51.             //Triangle 4
52.             TriangleArray Tri4 = new TriangleArray (vertex, TriangleArray.COORDINATES);
53.             Tri4.setCoordinate(0, new Point3f(0.0f,0.8f,0.0f));
54.             Tri4.setCoordinate(1, new Point3f(-0.5f,0.0f,0.0f));
55.             Tri4.setCoordinate(2, new Point3f(0.0f,0.0f,0.5f));
56.             return Tri4;
57.     }
58.     //Bottom
59.     private Geometry Tri5Geometry()
60.     {
61.             //Triangle 5
62.             TriangleArray Tri5 = new TriangleArray (vertex, TriangleArray.COORDINATES);
63.             Tri5.setCoordinate(0, new Point3f(0.0f,-0.8f,0.0f));
64.             Tri5.setCoordinate(1, new Point3f(0.5f,0.0f,0.0f));
65.             Tri5.setCoordinate(2, new Point3f(0.0f,0.0f,0.5f));
66.             return Tri5;
67.     }
68.
69.     private Geometry Tri6Geometry()
70.     {
71.             //Triangle 6
72.             TriangleArray Tri6 = new TriangleArray (vertex, TriangleArray.COORDINATES);
73.             Tri6.setCoordinate(0, new Point3f(0.0f,-0.8f,0.0f));
74.             Tri6.setCoordinate(1, new Point3f(0.0f,0.0f,-0.5f));
75.             Tri6.setCoordinate(2, new Point3f(0.5f,0.0f,0.0f));
76.             return Tri6;
77.     }
```

More complicated objects may instead be built more efficiently using GeometryStripArray, which is an abstract class and includes LineStripArray, TriangleStripArray and TriangleFanArray. Firgure 17 illustrates the basic shapes that can be constructed under these classes, while Figure 18 shows some typical application graphics that can be generated.

Figure 16. Third code segment of DiamondTriangleArray.java

```
78.    private Geometry Tri7Geometry()
79.    {
80.            //Triangle 7
81.            TriangleArray Tri7 = new TriangleArray (vertex, TriangleArray.COORDINATES);
82.            Tri7.setCoordinate(0, new Point3f(0.0f,-0.8f,0.0f));
83.            Tri7.setCoordinate(1, new Point3f(-0.5f,0.0f,0.0f));
84.            Tri7.setCoordinate(2, new Point3f(0.0f,0.0f,-0.5f));
85.            return Tri7;
86.    }
87.
88.    private Geometry Tri8Geometry()
89.    {
90.            //Triangle 8
91.            TriangleArray Tri8 = new TriangleArray (vertex, TriangleArray.COORDINATES);
92.            Tri8.setCoordinate(0, new Point3f(0.0f,-0.8f,0.0f));
93.            Tri8.setCoordinate(1, new Point3f(0.0f,0.0f,0.5f));
94.            Tri8.setCoordinate(2, new Point3f(-0.5f,0.0f,0.0f));
95.            return  Tri8;
96.    }
97. }
98.
```

Figure 17. Basic shapes from using LineStripArray (top left), TriangleStripArray (top right) and TriangleFanArray (bottom)

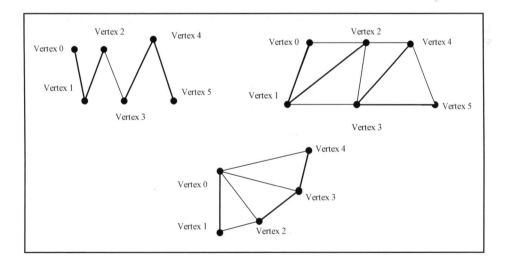

46 *Ko & Cheng*

Figure 18. Typical application graphics generated using LineStripArray, TriangleStripArray and TriangleFanArray

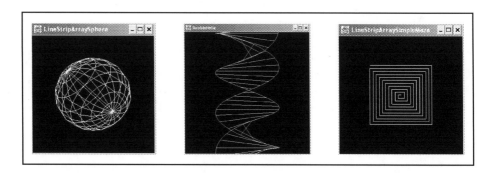

LineStripArray

We will now discuss the LineStripArray class in this section, before moving onto the other two more complicated classes in the next two sections. As illustrated in Figure 17, a LineStripArray object gives rise to a linked set of line segments drawn from an array of vertices. Figure 20 shows how a colored trapezium can be created by invoking LineStripArray.

Note that, before specifying the exact geometry of the trapezium, a Trapezium class is created by extending the Shape3D superclass in lines 6 and 7 in Figure 20.

The coordinators and color of vertices of the trapezium are then specified. Note also that while the trapezium has only four vertices, LineStripArray is supplied with five coordinates. This is because two points are needed to draw a line and so the starting point has to be included twice to form a closed trapezium.

Figure 21shows how the code segment in Figure 20 can be easily extended to create a 3D trapezoidal structure. In addition to the starting point, some physical vertices of the visual object will be visited more than once in building the structure using LineStripArray which draws lines between consecutive points. In this example, while the physical structure only has eight vertices, the number of vertices that need to be given to LineStripArray is 18.

Figure 19. Specifying the vertices and format of a LineStripArray object

```
LineStripArray line1= new LineStripArray (vertexCount, vertexFormat, stripVertexCounts)

// The number of vertices in a particular array is given by vertexCount and the format of // the pre-vertex data is given by VertexFormat.
```

Copyright © 2009, IGI Global, distributing in print or electronic forms without written permission of IGI Global is prohibited.

Figure 20. Code segment and result of Trapezium1.java

```
1.    public BranchGroup createSceneGraph(SimpleUniverse su)
2.    int vertex = 5;
3.    int StripCount[] = new int [1];
4.    StripCount[0] = vertex;
5.
6.    LineStripArray Trapezium =
7.      new LineStripArray(vertex, LineStripArray.COORDINATES|LineStripArray.COLOR_3,StripCount);
8.
9.    Trapezium.setCoordinate(0, new Point3f(0.75f, 0.75f, 0.0f));
10.   Trapezium.setCoordinate(1, new Point3f( 1.0f, -0.75f, 0.0f));
11.   Trapezium.setCoordinate(2, new Point3f( -1.0f,-0.75f, 0.0f));
12.   Trapezium.setCoordinate(3, new Point3f(-0.75f,0.75f, 0.0f));
13.   Trapezium.setCoordinate(4, new Point3f(0.75f,0.75f, 0.0f));
14.
15.   Trapezium.setColor(0, red);
16.   Trapezium.setColor(1, green);
17.   Trapezium.setColor(2, white);
18.   Trapezium.setColor(3, blue);
19.   Trapezium.setColor(4, red);
```

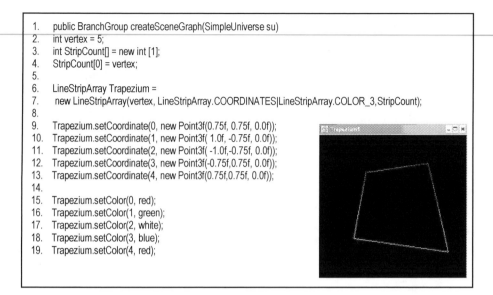

Figure 21. Code segment and result of Trapezium3D.java

```
1.    int vertex = 18;
2.    int StripCount[] = new int [1];
3.    StripCount[0] = vertex;
4.
5.    LineStripArray Trapezium =
new LineStripArray(vertex, LineStripArray.COORDINATES|LineStripArray.COLOR_3, StripCount);
6.
7.    Trapezium.setCoordinate(0, new Point3f(0.5f, 0.5f, 0.0f));
8.    Trapezium.setCoordinate(1, new Point3f( 0.75f, -0.5f, 0.0f));
9.    Trapezium.setCoordinate(2, new Point3f( -0.75f,-0.5f, 0.0f));
10.   Trapezium.setCoordinate(3, new Point3f(-0.5f,0.5f, 0.0f));
11.   Trapezium.setCoordinate(4, new Point3f(0.5f,0.5f, 0.0f));
12.   Trapezium.setCoordinate(5, new Point3f(0.5f,0.5f, -0.75f));
13.   Trapezium.setCoordinate(6, new Point3f(0.75f,-0.5f, -0.75f));
14.   Trapezium.setCoordinate(7, new Point3f(0.75f,-0.5f, 0.0f));
15.   Trapezium.setCoordinate(8, new Point3f(-0.75f,-0.5f, 0.0f));
16.   Trapezium.setCoordinate(9, new Point3f(-0.5f, 0.5f, 0.0f));
17.   Trapezium.setCoordinate(10, new Point3f( -0.5f, 0.5f, -0.75f));
18.   Trapezium.setCoordinate(11, new Point3f(-0.75f,-0.5f, -0.75f));
19.   Trapezium.setCoordinate(12, new Point3f( -0.75f,-0.5f, 0.0f));
20.   Trapezium.setCoordinate(13, new Point3f(-0.75f,-0.5f, -0.75f));
21.   Trapezium.setCoordinate(14, new Point3f(-0.5f, 0.5f, -0.75f));
22.   Trapezium.setCoordinate(15, new Point3f(0.5f,0.5f, -0.75f));
23.   Trapezium.setCoordinate(16, new Point3f(0.75f,-0.5f, -0.75f));
24.   Trapezium.setCoordinate(17, new Point3f(-0.75f,-0.5f, -0.75f));
25.
26.   for(int i= 0; i < vertex;i++)
27.   {
28.       Trapezium.setColor(i, green);
29.   }
```

Figure 22. Code segment and result of Tetrahedral1.java

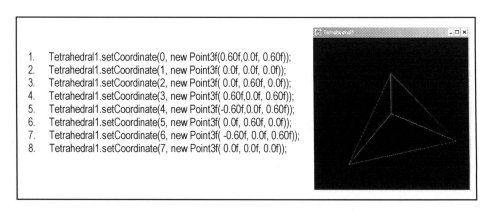

```
1.   Tetrahedral1.setCoordinate(0, new Point3f(0.60f,0.0f, 0.60f));
2.   Tetrahedral1.setCoordinate(1, new Point3f( 0.0f, 0.0f, 0.0f));
3.   Tetrahedral1.setCoordinate(2, new Point3f( 0.0f, 0.60f, 0.0f));
4.   Tetrahedral1.setCoordinate(3, new Point3f( 0.60f,0.0f, 0.60f));
5.   Tetrahedral1.setCoordinate(4, new Point3f(-0.60f,0.0f, 0.60f));
6.   Tetrahedral1.setCoordinate(5, new Point3f( 0.0f, 0.60f, 0.0f));
7.   Tetrahedral1.setCoordinate(6, new Point3f( -0.60f, 0.0f, 0.60f));
8.   Tetrahedral1.setCoordinate(7, new Point3f( 0.0f, 0.0f, 0.0f));
```

Figure 22 shows another example for creating a Tetrahedral. To render the structure most efficiently using LineStripArray, one side of the object has unavoidably had to be drawn twice. In practice, such overlaps should be avoided as much as possible to save rendering time.

Having discussed some simple examples to illustrate important concepts, we will now present two slightly more complicated applications discuss using LineStripArray. The first application is illustrated in Figure 23, where lines have been used to build a DNA type of structure with two helixes jointed at various positions.

Note that to cater for the possibility where the user changes the number of vertices dynamically, IndexedLineStripArray is not suitable for this application and LineStripArray is used instead. As can be seen from the code segment, the visual object can be built relatively easily by first writing down a suitable equation for the structure. One only needs to express the shape in its parametric form and set its corresponding coordinate.

Lastly, Figure 24 presents the code segment and result for creating a simple 3D maze structure using recursive programming techniques. Note that the variable m and dz give the separation between two layers and consecutive points. The construction of a maze with, say, six layers is obtained from a recursive call by using the same method to construct a maze with five layers, which in turn is obtained from a recursive call to build a maze with four layers, and so on.

TriangleStripArray

As illustrated in Figure 17, the use of TriangleStripArray will result in an object making up of a series of triangles formed from the vertices provided. Figure 25 gives a simple example where an hourglass shape is created based on five points or vertices.

Figure 23. Code segment and result of DoubleHelix.java

```
1.  int n = 360;        // number of vertices used
2.  double a = 0.5;     // radius of helix
3.  double i; int j;    // counting variables
4.
5.  int[] strip = new int[2 + n/2];
6.  strip[0] = n;                                   //for one of the helix
7.  strip[1] = n;                                   //for the other helix
8.  for ( int k=2; k<(2+n/2); k++ ) strip[k] = 2;   //for the lines connecting the two helix
9.
10. //there are n vertices on each helix, and n/2 lines connecting each
11. //helix, thus there are in total n+n+n vertices to be set.
12. LineStripArray lsa = new LineStripArray( (2*n + n ), GeometryArray.COORDINATES, strip );
13.
14. //for the first helix; i is in degrees. To do 720 degrees of revolution
15. for ( i=0,j=0; j<n; i=i+(720/n), j++ )
16.   lsa.setCoordinate( j, new Point3d((double)a*Math.cos(i*Math.PI/180),
17.       (double)(-1.25 + (i*Math.PI/180)/5.0 ), (double)a*Math.sin(i*Math.PI/180)));
18.
19. //for the second helix
20. for ( i=0, j=0; j<n; i=i+(720/n), j++ )
21.   lsa.setCoordinate( j+n, new Point3d( (double)-a*Math.cos(i*Math.PI/180),
22.       (double)(-1.25 + (i*Math.PI/180)/5.0 ), (double)-a*Math.sin(i*Math.PI/180) ) );
23.
24. //for the lines connecting the helix together
25. for ( i=0, j=0; j<n && i<720; i=i+(10*720/n) )
26. {
27.   lsa.setCoordinate( j+(2*n), new Point3d((double)a*Math.cos(i*Math.PI/180),
28.       (double)(-1.25 + (i*Math.PI/180)/5.0 ), (double)a*Math.sin(i*Math.PI/180) ) );
29.   j++;
30.   lsa.setCoordinate( j+(2*n), new Point3d((double)-a*Math.cos(i*Math.PI/180),
31.       (double)(-1.25 + (i*Math.PI/180)/5.0 ), (double)-a*Math.sin(i*Math.PI/180) ) );
32.   j++;
33. }
34.
```

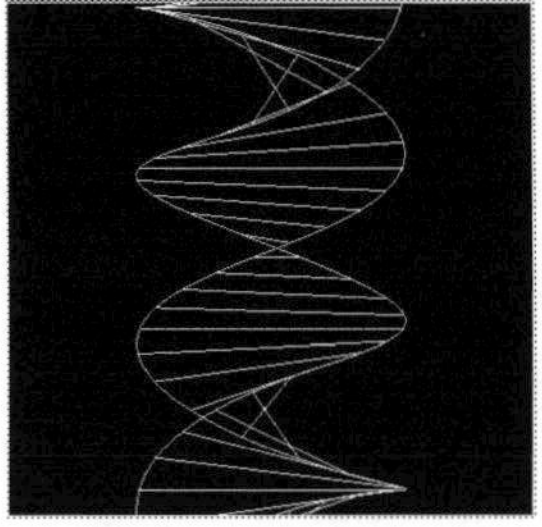

Figure 24. Code segment and result of LineStripArraySimpleMaze.java

```
1.    private BranchGroup axisBG;
2.    private int layer = 20;
3.    private float m = 0.05f;
4.    private float dz = 0.02f;
5.    private int[] counts = {layer*2+2};
6.
7.    public LineStripArray draw(int layer, float m, LineStripArray lineArr){
8.        if (layer==1) {
9.            lineArr.setCoordinate(0, new Point3f(0.0f, 0.0f, 0.0f));
10.           lineArr.setCoordinate(1, new Point3f(-m, 0.0f, dz));
11.           lineArr.setCoordinate(2, new Point3f(-m, -m, 2*dz));
12.           lineArr.setCoordinate(3, new Point3f(0.0f, -m, 3*dz));
13.       }
14.       else {
15.           lineArr = draw(layer-1, m, lineArr);
16.           int i=(layer-1)%2;
17.           float p1, p2, p3;
18.           p1 = (float)-Math.pow(-1,i)*m*(layer/2+(1-i));
19.           p2 = (float)Math.pow(-1,i)*m*(layer/2);
20.           p3 = dz*layer;
21.           lineArr.setCoordinate((layer-1)*2+1, new Point3f(p1, p2, p3));
22.           lineArr.setCoordinate((layer-1)*2+2, new Point3f(p1, p1, p3+dz));
23.           lineArr.setCoordinate((layer-1)*2+3, new Point3f(p2, p1, p3+2*dz));
24.       }
25.       return lineArr;
26.   }
27.
```

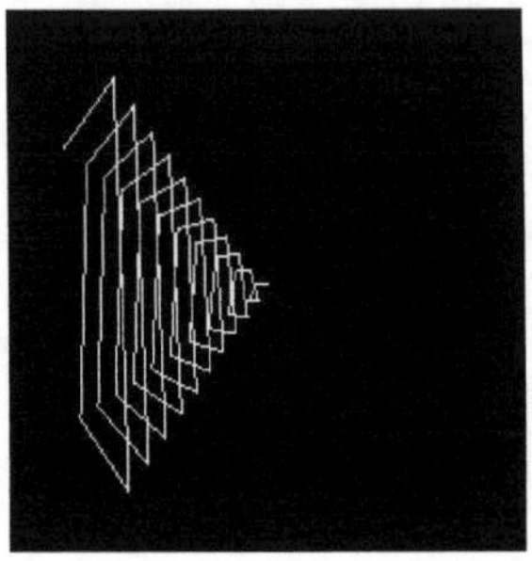

With five points and points 3 to 4 lying on a straight line, TriangleStripArray will give rise to two non-trivial triangles formed by points 1, 2, 3 and 3, 4, 5. However, the two triangles have a different sense in terms of the order of the coordinates, with the former being clockwise and the latter being anticlockwise in directions.

This difference in directions will result in the output as shown in Figure 25, where only one of the triangles will be visible at any instant. This is because the triangle with clockwise coordinates has a normal or face that points in the negative z direction, while the other with anticlockwise coordinates has a face in the opposite direction or points towards the positive z axis.

To overcome this difference in directions due to the ordering of the coordinators, the setNormal method can be used to set all the triangles to face the same direction. It is also possible to insert a dummy coordinate or vertice so that all the non-trivial triangles face the same direction. In this example, we can repeat point 3 and swap point 4 with point 5. Doing so will increase the number of vertices and rendering time slightly.

Figure 25. Code segment and result of Hourglass1.java

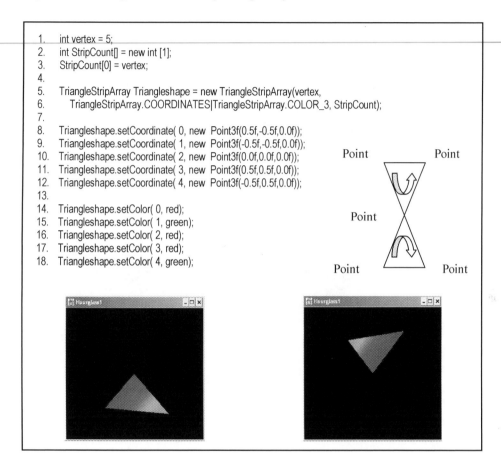

```
1.   int vertex = 5;
2.   int StripCount[] = new int [1];
3.   StripCount[0] = vertex;
4.
5.   TriangleStripArray Triangleshape = new TriangleStripArray(vertex,
6.       TriangleStripArray.COORDINATES|TriangleStripArray.COLOR_3, StripCount);
7.
8.   Triangleshape.setCoordinate( 0, new Point3f(0.5f,-0.5f,0.0f));
9.   Triangleshape.setCoordinate( 1, new Point3f(-0.5f,-0.5f,0.0f));
10.  Triangleshape.setCoordinate( 2, new Point3f(0.0f,0.0f,0.0f));
11.  Triangleshape.setCoordinate( 3, new Point3f(0.5f,0.5f,0.0f));
12.  Triangleshape.setCoordinate( 4, new Point3f(-0.5f,0.5f,0.0f));
13.
14.  Triangleshape.setColor( 0, red);
15.  Triangleshape.setColor( 1, green);
16.  Triangleshape.setColor( 2, red);
17.  Triangleshape.setColor( 3, red);
18.  Triangleshape.setColor( 4, green);
```

Yet another approach to resolve this is to set PolygonAttributes to the geometry created. This is illustrated in Figure 26 and will be discussed in detail in later chapters. Essentially, appearance class has been used to set appropriate polyAttributes. Note that the cull face has to be set to none to view the triangles under all rotation angles. Also, if POLYGON_LINE is used, the wire frame appearance shown will result.

The construction of structures that cannot be easily carried out by a single strip of triangles can sometimes be more conveniently done by using many strips. Figure 27 and 28 show an example where a diamond is constructed by having a few invocations of TriangleStripArray. Note that apart from the first strip, the other strips are added onto the existing geometry one after another. In programming, it may save time if it is possible to

Figure 26. Code segment and result of Hourglass1.java after setting PolygonAttributes

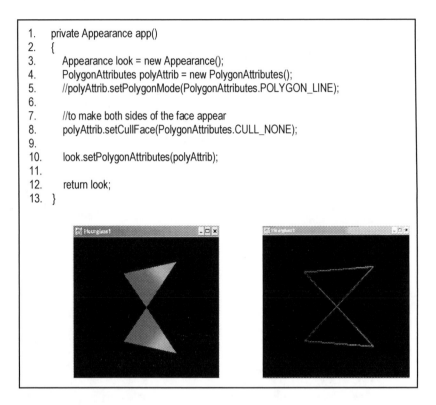

```
1.    private Appearance app()
2.    {
3.        Appearance look = new Appearance();
4.        PolygonAttributes polyAttrib = new PolygonAttributes();
5.        //polyAttrib.setPolygonMode(PolygonAttributes.POLYGON_LINE);
6.
7.        //to make both sides of the face appear
8.        polyAttrib.setCullFace(PolygonAttributes.CULL_NONE);
9.
10.       look.setPolygonAttributes(polyAttrib);
11.
12.       return look;
13.   }
```

define a few generic geometries and then have these appropriately added in an iterative or recursive manner.

TriangleFanArray

As shown in Figure 17, TriangleFanArray uses a set of vertices to produce a set of triangles fanning from a center. Specifically, triangles are drawn by using the current and previous vertices together with the first vertex.

The usage of the TriangleFanArray constructor is similar to that of LineStripArray and TriangleStripArray, and is illustrated in the simple example shown in Figure 29, where the combination of a number of fanning triangles of the same size gives rise to a circle eventually as the number of vertices is increased.

Obviously, TranigleFanArray is useful and efficient to construct objects that radiate from a central vertex. Two simple examples further illustrating this are given in Figures 30 and 31, where a two-pole speaker and a laser display are constructed.

Figure 27. First code segment for DiamondTriangleStripArray.java

```
1.    int vertex = 4;  int stripVertexCount [] = {vertex};
2.    public Diamond()
3.    {
4.      this.setGeometry(Strip1Geometry());          this.addGeometry(Strip2Geometry());
5.      this.addGeometry(Strip3Geometry());          this.addGeometry(Strip4Geometry());
6.      this.setAppearance(ColorAppearance());
7.    }
8.
9.    private Geometry Strip1Geometry() {          //Top TriangleStrip 1
10.    TriangleStripArray Triangle = new TriangleStripArray (vertex,
11.                     TriangleStripArray.COORDINATES , stripVertexCount);
12.    Triangle.setCoordinate(0, new Point3f(0.0f,0.0f,0.5f));
13.    Triangle.setCoordinate(1, new Point3f(0.0f,0.8f,0.0f));
14.    Triangle.setCoordinate(2, new Point3f(0.5f,0.0f,0.0f));
15.    Triangle.setCoordinate(3, new Point3f(0.0f,0.0f,-0.5f));
16.     return Triangle; }
17.
18.    private Geometry Strip2Geometry() {          //Top TriangleStrip 2
19.    TriangleStripArray Triangle2 = new TriangleStripArray (vertex,
20.                     TriangleStripArray.COORDINATES , stripVertexCount);
21.    Triangle2.setCoordinate(0, new Point3f(0.0f,0.0f,-0.5f));
22.    Triangle2.setCoordinate(1, new Point3f(-0.5f,0.0f,0.0f));
23.    Triangle2.setCoordinate(2, new Point3f(0.0f,0.8f,0.0f));
24.    Triangle2.setCoordinate(3, new Point3f(0.5f,0.0f,0.0f));
25.    return Triangle2; }
26.
27.    private Geometry Strip3Geometry() {          //Bottom TriangleStrip 3
28.    TriangleStripArray Triangle3 = new TriangleStripArray (vertex,
29.                     TriangleStripArray.COORDINATES , stripVertexCount);
30.    Triangle3.setCoordinate(0, new Point3f(0.0f,0.0f,0.5f));
31.    Triangle3.setCoordinate(3, new Point3f(0.5f,0.0f,0.0f));
32.    Triangle3.setCoordinate(2, new Point3f(0.0f,-0.8f,0.0f));
33.    Triangle3.setCoordinate(1, new Point3f(0.0f,0.0f,-0.5f));
34.    return Triangle3; }
```

Figure 28. Second code segment and result for DiamondTriangleStripArray.java

```
35.    private Geometry Strip4Geometry() {          //Bottom TriangleStrip 4
36.    TriangleStripArray Triangle4 = new TriangleStripArray (vertex,
37.                     TriangleStripArray.COORDINATES , stripVertexCount);
38.    Triangle4.setCoordinate(0, new Point3f(0.0f,0.0f,-0.5f));
39.    Triangle4.setCoordinate(1, new Point3f(-0.5f,0.0f,0.0f));
40.    Triangle4.setCoordinate(2, new Point3f(0.0f,-0.8f,0.0f));
41.    Triangle4.setCoordinate(3, new Point3f(0.0f,0.0f,0.5f));
42.    return Triangle4; }
```

Figure 29. Code segment and result of Circle1.java

```
1.   int vertex =100;                        //change accordingly
2.   int StripCount[] = new int [1];
3.   StripCount[0] = vertex;           //single strip is being used
4.
5.   TriangleFanArray Circle = new TriangleFanArray(vertex,
6.                    TriangleFanArray.COORDINATES|TriangleFanArray.COLOR_3, StripCount);
7.   objRoot.addChild(new Shape3D(Circle));
8.
9.   for (n =0, a=0; n < vertex;a = 2.0*Math.PI/(vertex) * ++n)
10.  {
11.     x = (float) (r * Math.cos(a));
12.     y = (float) (r * Math.sin(a));
13.     Circle.setCoordinate(n, new Point3f(x, y, 0.0f));
14.     Circle.setColor(n, red);
15.  }
16.
```

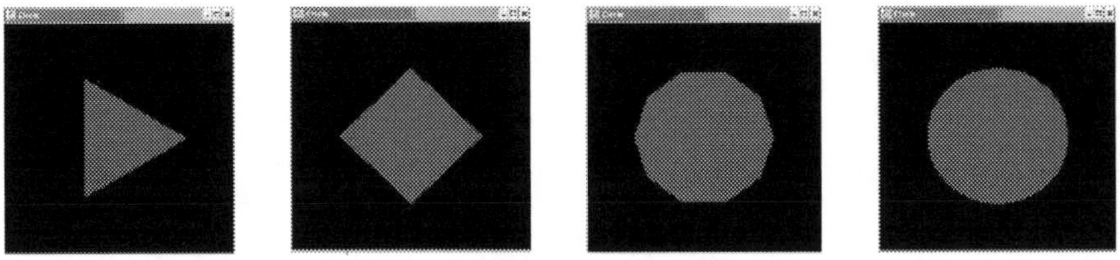

Figure 30. Code segment and result of Speaker1.java

```
1.    TriangleFanArray speaker = new TriangleFanArray(vertex,
2.                TriangleFanArray.COORDINATES|TriangleFanArray.COLOR_3, StripCount);
3.    speaker.setCoordinate(0, new Point3f(0.0f, 0.0f, 0.0f));
4.    speaker.setCoordinate(1, new Point3f(0.5f, 0.0f, 0.25f));
5.    speaker.setCoordinate(2, new Point3f(0.5f, 0.0f, -0.25f));
6.    speaker.setCoordinate(3, new Point3f(0.25f, 0.25f, -0.25f));
7.    speaker.setCoordinate(4, new Point3f(0.25f, 0.25f, 0.25f));
8.    speaker.setCoordinate(5, new Point3f(0.5f, 0.0f, 0.25f));
9.    speaker.setCoordinate(6, new Point3f(-0.5f, 0.0f, -0.25f));
10.   speaker.setCoordinate(7, new Point3f(-0.25f, 0.25f, -0.25f));
11.   speaker.setCoordinate(8, new Point3f(-0.25f, 0.25f, 0.25f));
12.   speaker.setCoordinate(9, new Point3f(-0.5f, 0.0f, 0.25f));
13.
14.   speaker.setColor(0, red);
15.   speaker.setColor(1, green);
16.   speaker.setColor(2, blue);
17.   speaker.setColor(3, white);
18.   speaker.setColor(4, red);
19.   speaker.setColor(5, blue);
20.   speaker.setColor(6, red);
21.   speaker.setColor(7, green);
22.   speaker.setColor(8, blue);
23.   speaker.setColor(9, white);
```

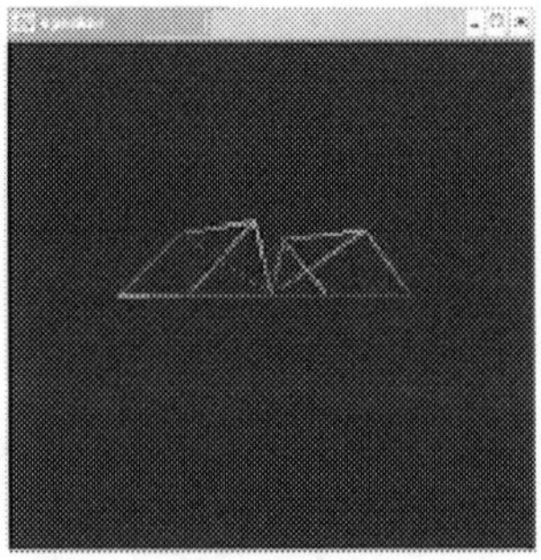

Figure 31. Code segment and result of Laser1.java

```
1.   TriangleFanArray laser = new TriangleFanArray(vertex,
2.              TriangleFanArray.COORDINATES|TriangleFanArray.COLOR_3, StripCount);
3.
4.   int vertex = 12;          // change this parameter
5.   int[] StripCount = {vertex};
6.
7.   for (n =0, a=0,z=100; n < vertex;a = 2*Math.PI/(vertex) * ++n)
8.   {
9.       x = (float) (r * Math.cos(a))/ z;
10.      y = (float) (r * Math.sin(a))/ z;
11.      z = (float) Math.sqrt (x*x + y*y);
12.      laser.setCoordinate(n, new Point3f(x, y, z));
13.      laser.setColor(n, red);
14.  }
```

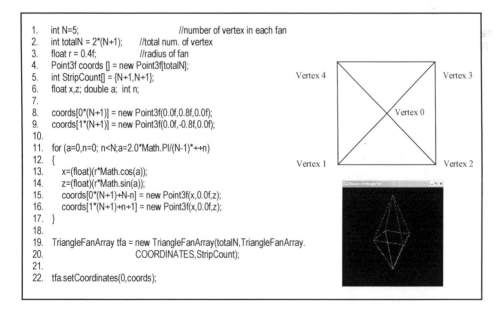

Figure 32. Code segment and result of DiamondTriangleFan.java

```
1.   int N=5;                              //number of vertex in each fan
2.   int totalN = 2*(N+1);      //total num. of vertex
3.   float r = 0.4f;           //radius of fan
4.   Point3f coords [] = new Point3f[totalN];
5.   int StripCount[] = {N+1,N+1};
6.   float x,z; double a;  int n;
7.
8.   coords[0*(N+1)] = new Point3f(0.0f,0.8f,0.0f);
9.   coords[1*(N+1)] = new Point3f(0.0f,-0.8f,0.0f);
10.
11.  for (a=0,n=0; n<N;a=2.0*Math.PI/(N-1)*++n)
12.  {
13.      x=(float)(r*Math.cos(a));
14.      z=(float)(r*Math.sin(a));
15.      coords[0*(N+1)+N-n] = new Point3f(x,0.0f,z);
16.      coords[1*(N+1)+n+1] = new Point3f(x,0.0f,z);
17.  }
18.
19.  TriangleFanArray tfa = new TriangleFanArray(totalN,TriangleFanArray.
20.              COORDINATES,StripCount);
21.
22.  tfa.setCoordinates(0,coords);
```

Lastly, the diamond implemented by using TriangleStripArray in Figure 28 can be easily implemented by using TriangleFanArray as well. This is shown in Figure 32, where the top and bottom parts of the object are implemented by using two strip arrays.

IndexedGeometryArray

In the same way as indirect addressing in computer systems, the IndexedGeometryArray class renders objects from accessing the vertices of the objects in an indirect manner. From this point of view, the various GeometryArray classes described in previous sections can be regarded as equivalent to the use of direct addressing.

Using IndexedGeometryArray class, information on the vertices must still be provided in arrays. However, these can be in any convenient order. Instead of accessing these directly to render the object in the prescribed manner, they can be accessed in any order through the use of additional integer arrays for indexing into the arrays of colors, normals, position, and texture coordinates. In a certain sense, the indexing arrays provide information on how vertices are connected in the rendering of the object.

The advantage of having indirect accessing capability is the possible reduction in the number of repeating vertices that will be needed under direct accessing as when GeometryArray class is used. However, the disadvantage is that time will have to be spent on this indirect accessing process and the rendering process may become slower. Specifically, using IndexedGeometryArray may save memory at the expense of speed.

The IndexedGeometryArray class includes the indexed versions of basically all the classes under the GeometryArray class discussed in earlier sections. In the same manner, our discussion of the IndexedGeometryArray class will start with the basic indexed classes first in the next few sections before moving on to discuss more complicated classes toward the end of the chapter.

IndexedPointArray

Figure 33 and 34 show the code segment and result on using IndexedPointArray to display a few points in space. The usage is similar to PointArray. In this simple example where there is no sharing of vertices, the vertex count is the number of points that will be displayed and the index count equals the vertex count. Specifically, a new integer array of indices is now declared to list down the sequence of vertices or points to be rendered.

IndexedLineArray

Figure 35 illustrates the use of IndexedLineArray to produce a trapezoidal object. Note that the code segment does not use any polygon attribute, the object is defined by its eight

Figure 33. First Code segment and result of Point.java

```
1.      public class Axis
2.      {
3.          private BranchGroup axisBG;
4.
5.          public Axis()
6.          {
7.                  axisBG = new BranchGroup();
8.                  IndexedPointArray array =
9.              new IndexedPointArray(11, PointArray.COORDINATES|PointArray.COLOR_3,11);
10.
11.                 Point3f []pts = new Point3f[11];
12.                 pts[0]  = new Point3f(0.5f, 0.5f, 0.5f);        pts[1]  = new Point3f(-0.5f, 0.5f, 0.5f);
13.                 pts[2]  = new Point3f(0.5f, 0.5f, -0.5f);       pts[3]  = new Point3f(-0.5f, 0.5f, -0.5f);
14.                 pts[4]  = new Point3f(0.5f, -0.5f, 0.5f);       pts[5]  = new Point3f(-0.5f, -0.5f, 0.5f);
15.                 pts[6]  = new Point3f(0.5f, -0.5f, -0.5f);      pts[7]  = new Point3f(-0.5f, -0.5f, -0.5f);
16.                 pts[8]  = new Point3f(0f, 0.5f, 0f);           pts[9]  = new Point3f(0f, -0.5f, 0f);
17.                 pts[10] = new Point3f(0f, 0f, 0f);
18.
19.                 int []indices = {0,1,2,3,4,5,6,7,8,9,10};
20.         array.setCoordinates(0,pts);
21.         array.setCoordinateIndices(0, indices);
```

Figure 34. Second code segment and result of Point.java

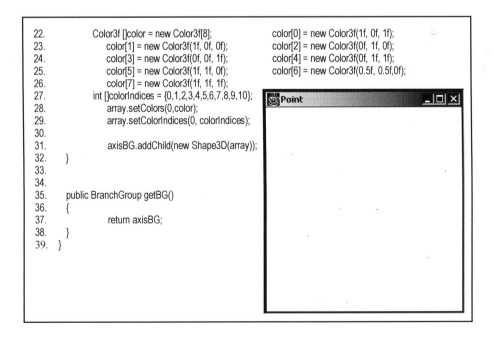

```
22.                 Color3f []color = new Color3f[8];          color[0] = new Color3f(1f, 0f, 1f);
23.                 color[1] = new Color3f(1f, 0f, 0f);        color[2] = new Color3f(0f, 1f, 0f);
24.                 color[3] = new Color3f(0f, 0f, 1f);        color[4] = new Color3f(0f, 1f, 1f);
25.                 color[5] = new Color3f(1f, 1f, 0f);        color[6] = new Color3f(0.5f, 0.5f,0f);
26.                 color[7] = new Color3f(1f, 1f, 1f);
27.                 int []colorIndices = {0,1,2,3,4,5,6,7,8,9,10};
28.                 array.setColors(0,color);
29.                 array.setColorIndices(0, colorIndices);
30.
31.                 axisBG.addChild(new Shape3D(array));
32.         }
33.
34.
35.         public BranchGroup getBG()
36.         {
37.                 return axisBG;
38.         }
39.     }
```

Figure 35. Code segment and result of LineTrapez.java

```
1.    public class Axis
2.    {
3.       private BranchGroup axisBG;
4.
5.       public Axis()
6.       {
7.                axisBG = new BranchGroup();
8.                IndexedLineArray array =
9.                     new IndexedLineArray(8,LineArray.COORDINATES|LineArray.COLOR_3,24);
10.
11.               Point3f []pts = new Point3f[8];
12.               pts[0] = new Point3f(0.5f, 0.75f, 0.5f);        pts[1] = new Point3f(-0.5f, 0.75f, 0.5f);
13.               pts[2] = new Point3f(0.5f, 0.75f, -0.5f);       pts[3] = new Point3f(-0.5f, 0.75f, -0.5f);
14.               pts[4] = new Point3f(0.75f, -0.25f, 0.75f);     pts[5] = new Point3f(-0.75f, -0.25f, 0.75f);
15.               pts[6] = new Point3f(0.75f, -0.25f, -0.75f);    pts[7] = new Point3f(-0.75f, -0.25f, -0.75f);
16.
17.               int []indices = {0,1,0,2,2,3,1,3,4,5,4,6,6,7,5,7,0,4,2,6,3,7,1,5};
18.               array.setCoordinates(0,pts);
19.               array.setCoordinateIndices(0, indices);
20.
21.               Color3f []color = new Color3f[8];
22.               color[0] = new Color3f(1f, 0f, 1f);            color[1] = new Color3f(1f, 0f, 0f);
23.               color[2] = new Color3f(0f, 1f, 0f);            color[3] = new Color3f(0f, 0f, 1f);
24.               color[4] = new Color3f(0f, 1f, 1f);            color[5] = new Color3f(0.5f, 0.5f, 0.5f);
25.               color[6] = new Color3f(0.5f, 0.5f,0f);         color[7] = new Color3f(1f, 1f, 1f);
26.
27.               int []colorIndices = {0,1,0,2,2,3,1,3,4,5,4,6,6,7,5,7,0,4,2,6,3,7,1,5};
28.               array.setColors(0,color);
29.               array.setColorIndices(0, colorIndices);
30.
31.               axisBG.addChild(new Shape3D(array));
32.       }
33.
34.       public BranchGroup getBG() return axisBG;
35.
36.
```

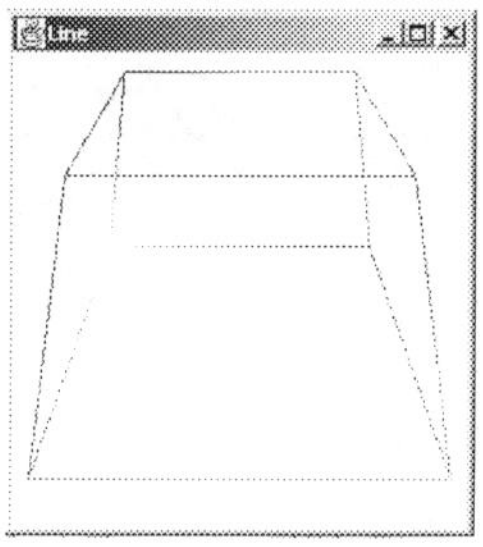

vertices, and joining two appropriate vertices will give a line forming one side of the object which has a total of 12 sides.

When the constructor of Axis is invoked, a BranchGroup object axisBG will be created in line 7. Lines 8 and 9 then create an IndexedLineArray object named array in the code segment. This object has a vertex count of eight and an index count of 24 to construct the visual trapezoidal object. The vertex format specified corresponds to the use of both co-ordinates for vertex positions and per vertex color. Since joining two appropriate vertices will produce a side and the visual object has 12 sides, a total of 24 indices for an index count of 24 are needed to render the object.

A Point3f array named pts with eight elements is created to store the eight coordinates of the vertices. This is followed by declaring an integer array named indices for storing the vertices in pairs, with each pair forming a line of the visual object. Next, the codes segment uses array.setCoordinates(0,pts) and array.setCoordinateIndices(0, indices) to set the coor-dinates associated with the vertices and the index array for accessing these coordinates.

The colors of the vertices, which influence the colors of the lines drawn in the manner as shown in the result in Figure 35, is set in the same way as that for the vertex coordinates. Specifically, a Color3f array is created with each element initiated to the colors needed. Note that this Color3f array need not have the same size as the Point3f array for the vertices. As an example, if only three colors are needed, the Color3f array will only be of size three and the colorIndices array declared subsequently will have values that are between 0 and 2.

Figure 36. First code segment of DemoSphere.java

```
1.    public class Axis
2.    {
3.        private BranchGroup axisBG;
4.
5.        public Axis()
6.        {
7.                axisBG = new BranchGroup();
8.                int n=200;  float z=0.5f;  Color3f color = new Color3f(0.2f, 0.3f, 0.2f);
9.                axisBG = drawSphere(n, z, color);
10.       }
11.
12.       public BranchGroup drawSphere(int n, float size, Color3f color)
13.       {
14.               BranchGroup axisBG = new BranchGroup();
15.               IndexedLineArray []array = new IndexedLineArray[n];
16.               for(int i=0; i<n; i++)
17.               {
18.                       float radius = (float)(Math.sin(Math.PI*i/n));
19.                       float dist = (float)(Math.cos(Math.PI*i/n));
20.                       array[i] = drawCircle(100,(float)(radius*size),0f,0f,(float)(dist*size), color);
21.                       axisBG.addChild(new Shape3D(array[i]));
22.               }
23.               return axisBG;
24.       }
```

Finally, after setting the IndexedLineArray object array up, it is constituted as a Shape3D node, which, in turn, is added as a child to the BranchGroup axisBG for the rendering of the trapezoidal object.

As another example, the code segment in Figures 36 and 37 illustrates the use of Indexed-LineArray to construct a sphere by using a series of circles. Specifically, the drawSphere method in the code segment will construct a sphere of radius given by the parameter size at the origin. It draws the sphere by iteratively invoking a drawCircle method, which builds a circle at (x, y, z) using n vertices with a radius given by the parameter size.

The drawing of the circle in the drawCircle method is carried out by drawing lines between adjacent equally spaced points along the circumference of the circle. The resulting shape will converge towards that for the desired circle if the number of points used is large

Figure 37. Second code segment and result of DemoSphere.java

```
1.    public IndexedLineArray drawCircle(int n, float size, double x, double y, double z, Color3f color)
2.    {
3.        IndexedLineArray lineArray =
4.          new IndexedLineArray(n+1,LineArray.COORDINATES|LineArray.COLOR_3,2*(n+1));
5.
6.        Point3f []linePts = new Point3f[n+1];
7.        for (int i=0; i<=n; i++)
8.        {
9.            float a = (float)(2*Math.PI/(n));
10.           linePts[i]= new
11.           Point3f((size*Math.cos(a*i)+x),(size*Math.sin(a*i)+y),(float)z);
12.       }
13.
14.       int []lineIndices = new int[2*n];
15.       for (int i=1, j=1; i<n+1; i++, j=j+2)
16.       {
17.           lineIndices[j-1]=i-1;
18.           lineIndices[j]=i;
19.       }
20.
21.       lineArray.setCoordinates(0,linePts);
22.       lineArray.setCoordinateIndices(0, lineIndices);
23.
24.       Color3f []lineColor = new Color3f[1];
25.       lineColor[0] = color;
26.       lineArray.setColors(0,lineColor);
27.   }
28.
29.   public BranchGroup getBG()
30.   {
31.       return axisBG;
32.   }
33. }
34.
```

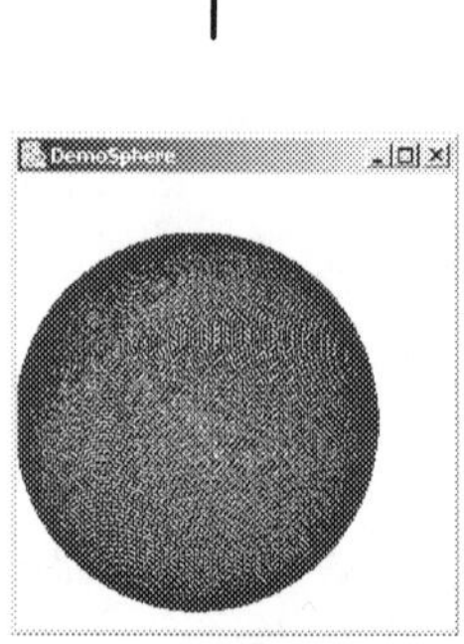

enough. Apart from the number of points used, the drawCircle method also has the radius, color and center of the circle as input parameters. Its makes use of an IndexedLineArray named linearray and created with n+1 vertices and 2(n+1) indices. Following the creation of IndexedLineArray, a Point3f array is created and filled to store vertex coordinates, before using another loop to fill up an appropriate indexing array on the lines to be drawn.

IndexedTriangleArray

Figure 38 gives an example on the use of IndexedTriangleArray to construct a solid tetrahedral. While the code is similar to that when IndexedLineArray is used, there are some important differences.

Figure 38. Code segment and result of Triangle.java

```
public class Axis
{
  private BranchGroup axisBG;

  public Axis()
  {
        axisBG = new BranchGroup();
        IndexedTriangleArray array = new
        IndexedTriangleArray(4, TriangleArray.COORDINATES|TriangleArray.COLOR_3, 12);

        Point3f []pts = new Point3f[4];
        pts[0] = new Point3f(0f, -0.5f, 0f);        pts[1] = new Point3f(1f, -0.5f, 0f);
        pts[2] = new Point3f(0f, 1f, 0f);           pts[3] = new Point3f(0f, -0.5f, 1f);
        int []indices = {0,3,2,0,2,1,0,1,3,2,3,1};
        array.setCoordinates(0,pts);
        array.setCoordinateIndices(0, indices);

        Color3f []color = new Color3f[4];
        color[0] = new Color3f(1f, 0f, 1f);
        color[1] = new Color3f(1f, 0f, 0f);
        color[2] = new Color3f(0f, 1f, 0f);
        color[3] = new Color3f(0f, 0f, 1f);
        int []colorIndices = {2,2,2,1,1,1,0,0,0,3,3,3};
        array.setColors(0,color);
        array.setColorIndices(0, colorIndices);

        axisBG.addChild(new Shape3D(array));
  }

  public BranchGroup getBG()
  {
        return axisBG;
  }
}
```

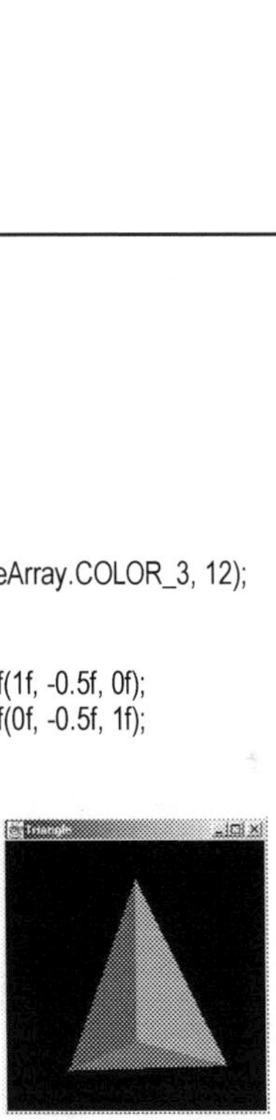

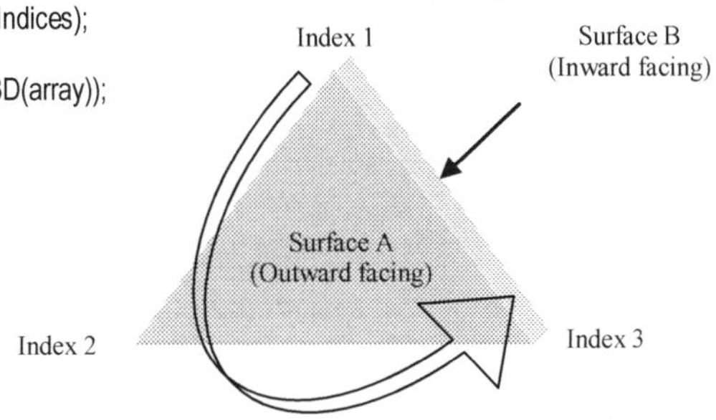

As can be seen, the tetrahedral has four vertices and is made up of four triangular faces. Since each face requires the drawing of a triangle with three vertices, three indices are needed for every face, and the total number of indices needed or the index count is 12.

After declaring this index count in the creation of the IndexedTriangleArray named array in the code segment, an integer array named indices is declared to store the indices to the vertex coordinates in groups of three, with each group defining a triangle. This is similar to when IndexedLineArray is used, where the indices are group in pairs for drawing a line between two vertices.

Figure 39. Code segment and result of DiamondIndexedTriangleArray.java

```
1.    public class DiamondIndexedTriangleArray extends Applet
2.    {
3.       public class Diamond extends Shape3D
4.       {
5.         public Diamond() //constructor
6.         {
7.           this.setGeometry(DiamondGeometry());
8.           this.setAppearance(DiamondAppearance());
9.         }
10.
11.        private Geometry DiamondGeometry()
12.        {
13.   IndexedTriangleArray Tri = new IndexedTriangleArray (6, GeometryArray.COORDINATES,24);
14.   Tri.setCoordinate( 0,new Point3f(0f, 0.8f, 0f)); Tri.setCoordinate(1,new Point3f(0.0f,0.0f,-0.5f));
15.   Tri.setCoordinate( 2,new Point3f(0.5f, 0f, 0f)); Tri.setCoordinate(3,new Point3f(-0.5f,0.0f,0.0f));
16.   Tri.setCoordinate( 4,new Point3f(0f, 0f, 0.5f)); Tri.setCoordinate(5, new Point3f(0f, -0.8f, 0.0f));
17.
18.        //Top Diamond
19.            Tri.setCoordinateIndex( 0, 0 );  Tri.setCoordinateIndex( 1, 4 );
20.            Tri.setCoordinateIndex( 2, 2 );  Tri.setCoordinateIndex( 3, 0 );
21.            Tri.setCoordinateIndex( 4, 2 );  Tri.setCoordinateIndex( 5, 1 );
22.            Tri.setCoordinateIndex( 6, 0 );  Tri.setCoordinateIndex( 7, 1 );
23.            Tri.setCoordinateIndex( 8, 3 );  Tri.setCoordinateIndex( 9, 0 );
24.            Tri.setCoordinateIndex( 10,3 );  Tri.setCoordinateIndex( 11,4 );
25.
26.            //Bottom Diamond
27.            Tri.setCoordinateIndex( 12,5 );  Tri.setCoordinateIndex( 13,4 );
28.            Tri.setCoordinateIndex( 14,2 );  Tri.setCoordinateIndex( 15,5 );
29.            Tri.setCoordinateIndex( 16,2 );  Tri.setCoordinateIndex( 17,1 );
30.            Tri.setCoordinateIndex( 18,5 );  Tri.setCoordinateIndex( 19,1 );
31.            Tri.setCoordinateIndex( 20,3 );  Tri.setCoordinateIndex( 21,5 );
32.            Tri.setCoordinateIndex( 22,3 );  Tri.setCoordinateIndex( 23,4 );
33.
34.            return Tri;
35.        }//end of GeometryDiamond method
36.   }//end of Diamond class
```

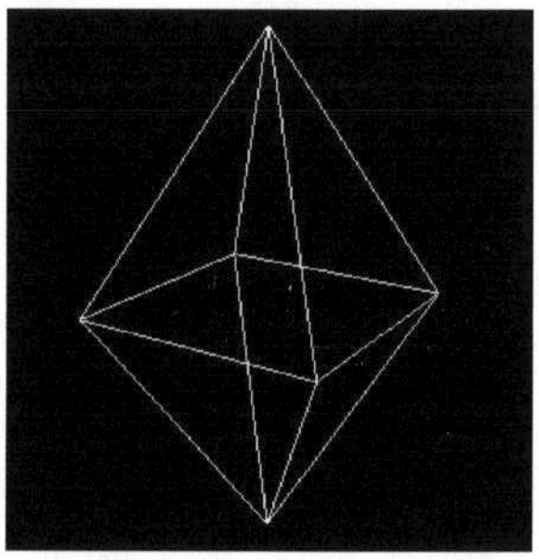

However, note that the ordering of the stored indices in the indexing array is associated with a certain sense of direction on whether the defined triangle will point towards one or the opposite direction. This corresponds to the use of the right hand rule and is also indicated in Figure 38. As an example, the indices 1, 2, 3 are associated with Surface A pointing outwards, while the indices 1, 3, 2 is associated with Surface A pointing inwards and forming an internal surface. For Surface A or its normal to be facing or pointing outward or forming an external surface, the indices have to be listed in an anti-clockwise manner as indicated.

After specifying the physical geometry, the color of the faces can be declared. This is done by creating a Color3f array for the colors and using an integer array to list down the color indices for the vertices in groups of three.

Figure 39 shows another example where IndexedTriangleArray is used to create a diamond shaped object. The code first specifies the coordinates of the six vertices of the object, and then creates and initiates an indexing array for building the eight faces of the diamond using eight triangles. Comparing with the program segment in Figures 14 to 16 for creating the same object using TriangleArray with 24 vertices, note that the use of IndexedTriangleArray only requires six vertices to be specified.

IndexedQuadArray

The usage of IndexedQuadArray is very similar to that of IndexedTriangleArray, apart from the fact that the basic shape is changed from a 3-sided triangle to a 4-sided quadrilateral. Figure 40 gives an example where a solid trapezoidal object is rendered.

Note that the number of vertices for the object is eight and the object has six faces, each formed from a quadrilateral. Thus, the index count used is 24 when the IndexedQuadArray array is first declared.

Since the basic shape is now a quadrilateral, the indexing array for specifying the physical geometry is provided in groups of four. Also, as for IndexedTriangleArray, each group of indices is associated with a certain sense of direction on the face created. This is illustrated in Figure 40 and is again associated with the use of the right hand rule. Thus, the use of 1, 3, 4, 2 in the indexing array corresponds to Surface A facing outward, while using 1, 2, 4, 3 will make it face inwards and will give rise to an internal surface.

IndexedStripArray

As with LineStripArray, the IndexedLineStripArray class is well suited to create complex objects making up of line segments. Figure 17 shows the basic shape for LineStripArray and its indirect access based indexing version, IndexedLineStripArray.

Figure 40. Code segment and result of Quad.java

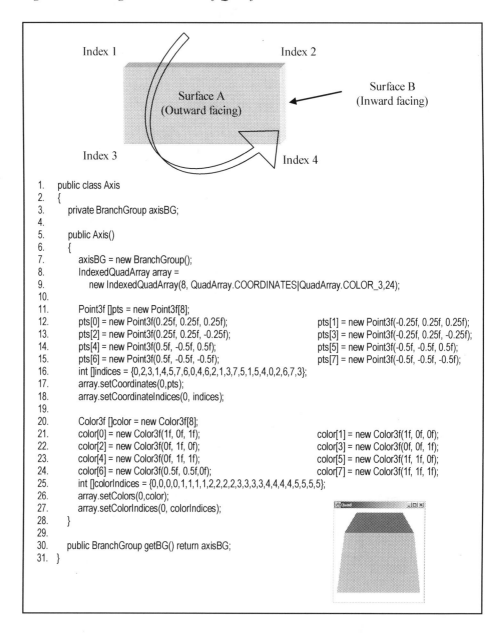

```
1.    public class Axis
2.    {
3.        private BranchGroup axisBG;
4.
5.        public Axis()
6.        {
7.            axisBG = new BranchGroup();
8.            IndexedQuadArray array =
9.                new IndexedQuadArray(8, QuadArray.COORDINATES|QuadArray.COLOR_3,24);
10.
11.           Point3f []pts = new Point3f[8];
12.           pts[0] = new Point3f(0.25f, 0.25f, 0.25f);          pts[1] = new Point3f(-0.25f, 0.25f, 0.25f);
13.           pts[2] = new Point3f(0.25f, 0.25f, -0.25f);         pts[3] = new Point3f(-0.25f, 0.25f, -0.25f);
14.           pts[4] = new Point3f(0.5f, -0.5f, 0.5f);            pts[5] = new Point3f(-0.5f, -0.5f, 0.5f);
15.           pts[6] = new Point3f(0.5f, -0.5f, -0.5f);           pts[7] = new Point3f(-0.5f, -0.5f, -0.5f);
16.           int []indices = {0,2,3,1,4,5,7,6,0,4,6,2,1,3,7,5,1,5,4,0,2,6,7,3};
17.           array.setCoordinates(0,pts);
18.           array.setCoordinateIndices(0, indices);
19.
20.           Color3f []color = new Color3f[8];
21.           color[0] = new Color3f(1f, 0f, 1f);                 color[1] = new Color3f(1f, 0f, 0f);
22.           color[2] = new Color3f(0f, 1f, 0f);                 color[3] = new Color3f(0f, 0f, 1f);
23.           color[4] = new Color3f(0f, 1f, 1f);                 color[5] = new Color3f(1f, 1f, 0f);
24.           color[6] = new Color3f(0.5f, 0.5f,0f);              color[7] = new Color3f(1f, 1f, 1f);
25.           int []colorIndices = {0,0,0,0,1,1,1,1,2,2,2,2,3,3,3,3,4,4,4,4,5,5,5,5};
26.           array.setColors(0,color);
27.           array.setColorIndices(0, colorIndices);
28.       }
29.
30.       public BranchGroup getBG() return axisBG;
31.   }
```

IndexedLineStripArray

The disadvantage of LineStripArray is, of course, that it is often necessary to repeat some vertices as when a complicated solid object is to be rendered. This disadvantage is overcome in IndexedLineStripArray by having an integer indexing array to point to the some unique coordinates on the object vertices that need to be used in the rendering process. However, as pointed out earlier, this may increase rendering time, and the issue is basically a memory vs. speed one.

Figure 41 shows the code segment and result of using IndexedLineStripArray to create a prism. The first three lines of the code segment create an integer array to be passed to IndexedLineStripArray. Basically, with two elements, there will be two strips. The first element has a value of six, indicating that the first strip will be made up of six vertices or five line segments. Similarly, the second element is assigned a value of two, specifying that the second strip will have two vertices or just one line segment.

Lines 6 and 7 creates an IndexedLineStripArray object through its constructor. The first argument passed to this constructor is the number of vertices the prism has, which is equal to four. The second parameter gives the vertex format. For this case, the indication is that it is the vertex coordinates and colors that will be supplied subsequently. The third argument is on the total number of indices used for rendering the object. In this scenario, eight is used as six indices are needed for the first strip and another two are required for the second strip. The fourth parameter is the name of the strip array set up earlier and described in the last paragraph.

Figure 41. Code segment and result of TertahedralMesh.java

```
1.   int[] strip = new int[2];
2.   strip[0] = 6;
3.   strip[1] = 2;
4.
5.   //creating a line array using indexed and strip method.  4 vertices and 8 index present.
6.   IndexedLineStripArray ilsa = new
7.   IndexedLineStripArray( 4, GeometryArray.COORDINATES|GeometryArray.COLOR_3, 8, strip );
8.
9.   Point3f[] pts = new Point3f[4];
10.  pts[0] = new Point3f( 0.0f, -0.5f, 0.0f );
11.  pts[1] = new Point3f( 0.75f, -0.5f, 0.0f );
12.  pts[2] = new Point3f( 0.0f, 0.75f, 0.0f );
13.  pts[3] = new Point3f( 0.0f, -0.5f, 0.75f );
14.
15.  int[] indices = { 0,1,2,3,0,2,1,3 };
16.  ilsa.setCoordinates( 0, pts );
17.  ilsa.setCoordinateIndices( 0, indices );
```

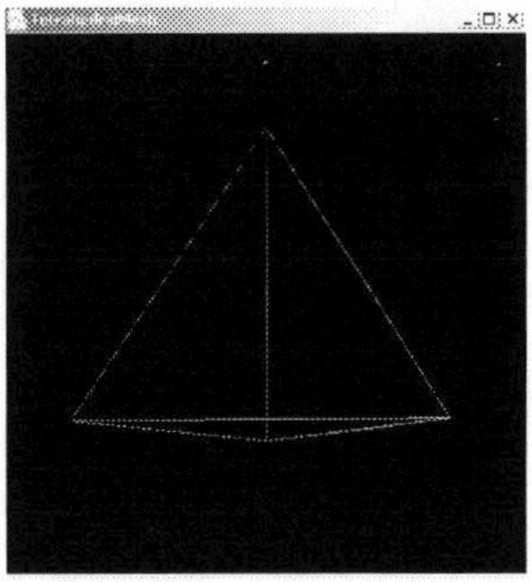

After creating the IndexedLineStripArray object, the vertex coordinators and indexing arrays are then defined and passed to the object for rendering in the remaining lines of the code segment.

Figure 42 gives another example of using IndexedLineStripArray to create a wedge shape object. The assignment of the indices for the various vertices is also shown together with the result of the program. Specifically, the object has six vertices and is drawn using four strips. The first strip draws the bottom of the object and this involves four vertices and five indices to draw four line segments. Two line segments each are drawn by the second

Figure 42. Code segment and result of IndexedLineArray.java

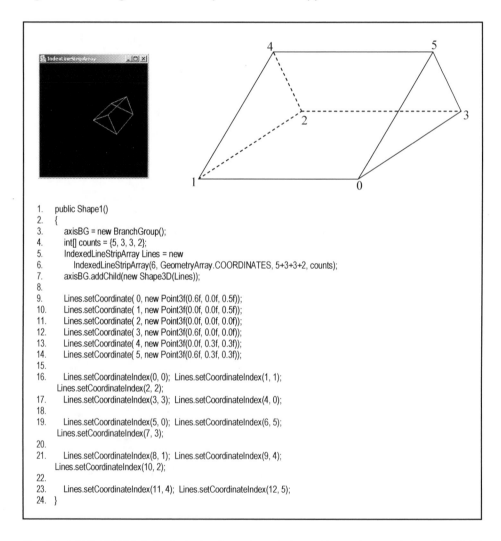

```
1.    public Shape1()
2.    {
3.        axisBG = new BranchGroup();
4.        int[] counts = {5, 3, 3, 2};
5.        IndexedLineStripArray Lines = new
6.            IndexedLineStripArray(6, GeometryArray.COORDINATES, 5+3+3+2, counts);
7.        axisBG.addChild(new Shape3D(Lines));
8.
9.        Lines.setCoordinate( 0, new Point3f(0.6f, 0.0f, 0.5f));
10.       Lines.setCoordinate( 1, new Point3f(0.0f, 0.0f, 0.5f));
11.       Lines.setCoordinate( 2, new Point3f(0.0f, 0.0f, 0.0f));
12.       Lines.setCoordinate( 3, new Point3f(0.6f, 0.0f, 0.0f));
13.       Lines.setCoordinate( 4, new Point3f(0.0f, 0.3f, 0.3f));
14.       Lines.setCoordinate( 5, new Point3f(0.6f, 0.3f, 0.3f));
15.
16.       Lines.setCoordinateIndex(0, 0);  Lines.setCoordinateIndex(1, 1);
          Lines.setCoordinateIndex(2, 2);
17.       Lines.setCoordinateIndex(3, 3);  Lines.setCoordinateIndex(4, 0);
18.
19.       Lines.setCoordinateIndex(5, 0);  Lines.setCoordinateIndex(6, 5);
          Lines.setCoordinateIndex(7, 3);
20.
21.       Lines.setCoordinateIndex(8, 1);  Lines.setCoordinateIndex(9, 4);
          Lines.setCoordinateIndex(10, 2);
22.
23.       Lines.setCoordinateIndex(11, 4);  Lines.setCoordinateIndex(12, 5);
24.   }
```

and third strips and these give rise to the left and right faces of the prism. Lastly, a final strip with a single line segment constructs the remaining top edge of the object.

IndexedTriangleStripArray

The relationship between IndexedTriangleStripArray and TriangleStripArray is the same as that between IndexedLineStripArray and LineStripArray. The basic shape that can be rendered under IndexedTriangleStripArray and TriangleStripArray is depicted in Figure 17. Essentially, both of these classes create a series of triangles based on a sequence of vertices with facing set automatically to align, regardless of the actual sequence of vertices, with that of the first triangle.

TirangleStripArray and its index version, IndexedTriangleStripArray, are very useful for building structures with complex polygons. Specifically, the indexing ability of the latter serves to save memory and time in programming at the expense of rendering speed.

Figure 43 illustrates a simple usage of IndexedTriangleStripArray to build a trapezoidal object with eight vertices. Note that each of the six faces of the object is a 4-sided quadrilateral and is build by using two triangles. A total of 14 indices giving rise to 12 triangles are used.

Figure 43. Code segment and result of Trapezium.java

```
1.   int[] strip = new int[1];  strip[0] = 14;
2.
3.   IndexedTriangleStripArray itsa = new IndexedTriangleStripArray
4.      ( 8,GeometryArray.COORDINATES|GeometryArray.COLOR_3, 14, strip );
5.
6.   Point3f[] pts = new Point3f[8];
7.   pts[0] = new Point3f( 0.5f, 0.5f, 0.0f );
8.   pts[1] = new Point3f( 0.0f, 0.5f, -0.5f );
9.   pts[2] = new Point3f( -0.5f, 0.5f, 0.0f );
10.  pts[3] = new Point3f( 0.0f, 0.5f, 0.5f );
11.  pts[4] = new Point3f( 0.75f, -0.25f, 0.0f );
12.  pts[5] = new Point3f( 0.0f, -0.25f, -0.75f );
13.  pts[6] = new Point3f( -0.75f, -0.25f, 0.0f );
14.  pts[7] = new Point3f( 0.0f, -0.25f, 0.75f );
15.
16.  int[] indices = { 0,1,3,2,6,1,5,0,4,3,7,6,4,5 };
17.  itsa.setCoordinates( 0, pts );
18.  itsa.setCoordinateIndices( 0, indices );
```

Figure 44. Code segment and result of DiamondIndexedTriangleStripArray.java

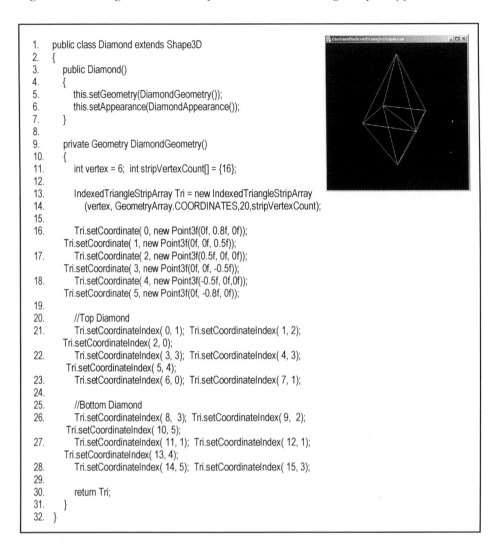

```
1.    public class Diamond extends Shape3D
2.    {
3.      public Diamond()
4.      {
5.        this.setGeometry(DiamondGeometry());
6.        this.setAppearance(DiamondAppearance());
7.      }
8.
9.      private Geometry DiamondGeometry()
10.     {
11.       int vertex = 6;  int stripVertexCount[] = {16};
12.
13.       IndexedTriangleStripArray Tri = new IndexedTriangleStripArray
14.         (vertex, GeometryArray.COORDINATES,20,stripVertexCount);
15.
16.       Tri.setCoordinate( 0, new Point3f(0f, 0.8f, 0f));
        Tri.setCoordinate( 1, new Point3f(0f, 0f, 0.5f));
17.       Tri.setCoordinate( 2, new Point3f(0.5f, 0f, 0f));
        Tri.setCoordinate( 3, new Point3f(0f, 0f, -0.5f));
18.       Tri.setCoordinate( 4, new Point3f(-0.5f, 0f,0f));
        Tri.setCoordinate( 5, new Point3f(0f, -0.8f, 0f));
19.
20.       //Top Diamond
21.       Tri.setCoordinateIndex( 0, 1);  Tri.setCoordinateIndex( 1, 2);
        Tri.setCoordinateIndex( 2, 0);
22.       Tri.setCoordinateIndex( 3, 3);  Tri.setCoordinateIndex( 4, 3);
        Tri.setCoordinateIndex( 5, 4);
23.       Tri.setCoordinateIndex( 6, 0);  Tri.setCoordinateIndex( 7, 1);
24.
25.       //Bottom Diamond
26.       Tri.setCoordinateIndex( 8, 3);  Tri.setCoordinateIndex( 9, 2);
        Tri.setCoordinateIndex( 10, 5);
27.       Tri.setCoordinateIndex( 11, 1);  Tri.setCoordinateIndex( 12, 1);
        Tri.setCoordinateIndex( 13, 4);
28.       Tri.setCoordinateIndex( 14, 5);  Tri.setCoordinateIndex( 15, 3);
29.
30.       return Tri;
31.     }
32.  }
```

Figure 44 presents another example where a diamond shaped object is constructed. Note that there are altogether six vertices and a single strip is used.

IndexedTriangleFanArray

IndexedTriangleFanArray is the indexed version of TriangleFanArray, which construct a series of triangles radiating or fanning from a central vertex as show in Figure 17. Figure

Figure 45. Code segment and result of Pyramid.java

```
1.   int[] strip = new int[2];  strip[0] = 6;  strip[1] = 4;
2.
3.   IndexedTriangleFanArray itfa = new IndexedTriangleFanArray
4.     ( 5, GeometryArray.COORDINATES|GeometryArray.COLOR_3, 10, strip );
5.
6.   Point3f[] pts = new Point3f[5];
7.   pts[0] = new Point3f( 0.0f, 0.75f, 0.0f );
8.   pts[1] = new Point3f( 0.75f, -0.25f, 0.0f );
9.   pts[2] = new Point3f( 0.0f, -0.25f, 0.75f );
10.  pts[3] = new Point3f( -0.75f, -0.25f, 0.0f );
11.  pts[4] = new Point3f( 0.0f, -0.25f, -0.75f );
12.
13.  int[] indices = { 0,2,1,4,3,2, 1,2,3,4 };
```

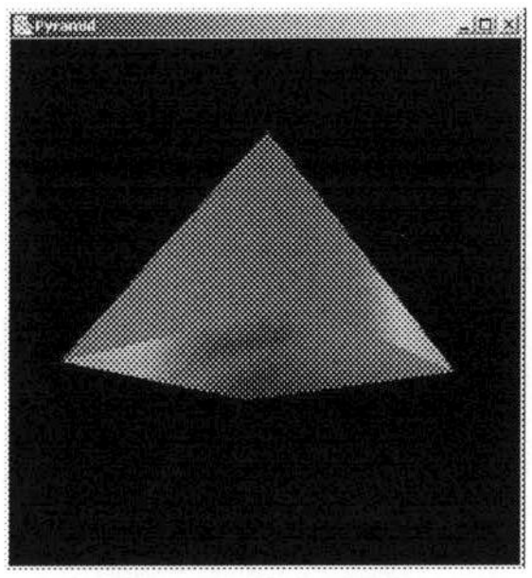

45 gives an example for constructing a pyramid using IndexedTriangleFanArray. Note that the object has five vertices and two fanning strips are used. The first strip involves five vertices and six indices to construct the four slanting triangular faces of the object, while the second strip uses two fanning triangles to construct the bottom square surface.

The next example, illustrated in Figure 46, constructs a diamond shaped object. Note that since two fanning strips, one for the top and one for the bottom part of the object, are used, the array VertexCount is now a two element array with both elements set to N, the number of vertices used in each fan.

CREATING AN OBJECT USING MULTIPLE GEOMETRY CLASSES

After discussing the various important geometry array classes individually, we will now show a slightly more complicated example where appropriate combinations of geometry classes are used to create a visual Shape3D object.

Figure 47 shows the constructor and result for the example, illustrating a scene where an artifact is housed inside a glass case. The artifact is created using IndexedTriangleFanArray and the glass case is built using IndexedQuadArray. Both belong to the geometry of a single Shape3D node.

Figure 46. Code segment and result of DiamondIndexedTriangleFanArray.java

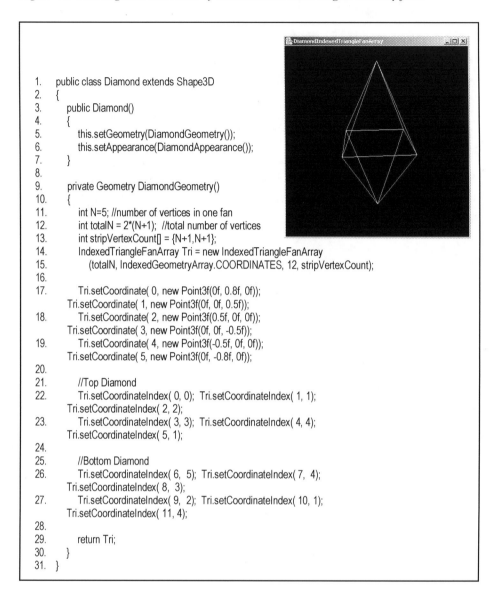

```
1.    public class Diamond extends Shape3D
2.    {
3.       public Diamond()
4.       {
5.          this.setGeometry(DiamondGeometry());
6.          this.setAppearance(DiamondAppearance());
7.       }
8.
9.       private Geometry DiamondGeometry()
10.      {
11.         int N=5; //number of vertices in one fan
12.         int totalN = 2*(N+1);  //total number of vertices
13.         int stripVertexCount[] = {N+1,N+1};
14.         IndexedTriangleFanArray Tri = new IndexedTriangleFanArray
15.            (totalN, IndexedGeometryArray.COORDINATES, 12, stripVertexCount);
16.
17.         Tri.setCoordinate( 0, new Point3f(0f, 0.8f, 0f));
           Tri.setCoordinate( 1, new Point3f(0f, 0f, 0.5f));
18.         Tri.setCoordinate( 2, new Point3f(0.5f, 0f, 0f));
           Tri.setCoordinate( 3, new Point3f(0f, 0f, -0.5f));
19.         Tri.setCoordinate( 4, new Point3f(-0.5f, 0f, 0f));
           Tri.setCoordinate( 5, new Point3f(0f, -0.8f, 0f));
20.
21.         //Top Diamond
22.         Tri.setCoordinateIndex( 0, 0);  Tri.setCoordinateIndex( 1, 1);
           Tri.setCoordinateIndex( 2, 2);
23.         Tri.setCoordinateIndex( 3, 3);  Tri.setCoordinateIndex( 4, 4);
           Tri.setCoordinateIndex( 5, 1);
24.
25.         //Bottom Diamond
26.         Tri.setCoordinateIndex( 6,  5);  Tri.setCoordinateIndex( 7,  4);
           Tri.setCoordinateIndex( 8,  3);
27.         Tri.setCoordinateIndex( 9,  2);  Tri.setCoordinateIndex( 10, 1);
           Tri.setCoordinateIndex( 11, 4);
28.
29.         return Tri;
30.      }
31.   }
```

Specifically, the constructor for the Exhibit class shown in Figure 47 is an extension of a Shape3D class. Line 3 invokes an Artefact() method which returns a geometry object for the creation of the artifact, with the setGeometry method placing the created geometry object as a geometry component at index 0. Similarly, the next line invokes a Glass_case()

Figure 47. Constructor and result of Museum_exhibit.java

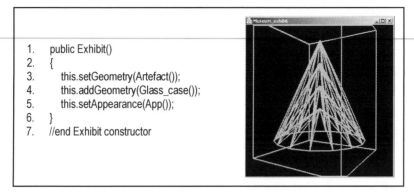

```
1.    public Exhibit()
2.    {
3.        this.setGeometry(Artefact());
4.        this.addGeometry(Glass_case());
5.        this.setAppearance(App());
6.    }
7.    //end Exhibit constructor
```

method to create a geometry object for the glass case and append this to the list of geometry components. Note that all appended objects should be equivalent in classes. That is, the list must consist of only Geometry or Raster or Text3D objects.

Figures 48 and 49 show the code segments for the Artefact() and Glass_case() methods. Created using IndexedTriangleFanArray, the artifact has 20 physical vertices and 72 accessing indices, and a few loops are used to set these to their appropriate values.

UTILITY CLASS

Rather than using basic and rather primitive geometry classes, the creation of some common objects can be easily achieved through geometry utility classes in Java 3D. These include the creation of boxes, spheres, cylinders, and cones. Figure 50 demonstrates how these can be done together with the results, including the use of lighting, which will be discussed in detail in later chapters, for illumination.

The creation of the first object, a sphere, is carried out in the block of codes starting from line five. Setting the translation of a Transform3D object, line six specifies the placement of a visual object at (0.5, 0.5, -0.5). Line 11 creates a sphere of radius 0.3 units using its constructor. Note that in addition to its radius, an optional appearance parameter on an appearance defined earlier is also passed. This is to avoid the creation of a default black sphere which will not be visible in a black background.

The next few blocks of codes for the building of a box, cone and cylinder are similar to that for the creation of the sphere. Lines 39 to 41, however, add lighting to the universe by attaching a created light object, which will be further discussed in subsequent chapters, to the initial TransformGroup.

Figure 48. Code segment for Artefact()

```
1.    private Geometry Artefact()
2.    {
3.        IndexedTriangleFanArray Indexedtfa;
4.        int N = 17;  int totalN = 4*(N+1); int stripCounts[] = {N+1,N+1,N+1,N+1};
5.        Point3f coords[] = new Point3f[totalN];
6.        float r = 0.6f;  int n,m;  double a;  float x, y;  int i,j;
7.
8.        Indexedtfa = new IndexedTriangleFanArray
9.                (20, IndexedTriangleFanArray.COORDINATES,totalN,stripCounts);
10.
11.       // set the central points for four triangle fan strips
12.       Indexedtfa.setCoordinate (16,new Point3f(0.0f, 0.0f, 0.8f));
13.       Indexedtfa.setCoordinate (17,new Point3f(0.0f, 0.0f, 0.5f));
14.       Indexedtfa.setCoordinate (18,new Point3f(0.0f, 0.0f, 0.2f));
15.       Indexedtfa.setCoordinate (19,new Point3f(0.0f, 0.0f, -0.1f));
16.
17.       //to avoid repeating the last vertice as vertice no 16 is the same as zero
18.       for(a = 0,n = 0,m=0; n < 17 && m < 16; a = 2.0*Math.PI/(N-1) * ++n,m++)
19.       {
20.               x = (float) (r * Math.cos(a));  y = (float) (r * Math.sin(a));
21.               Indexedtfa.setCoordinate (m,new Point3f(x,y,w));
22.       }
23.
24.       Indexedtfa.setCoordinateIndex( 0, 16);  Indexedtfa.setCoordinateIndex( 17, 0);
25.       for ( i=1; i<17; i++) Indexedtfa.setCoordinateIndex( i, i-1);
26.
27.       Indexedtfa.setCoordinateIndex( 18, 17);  Indexedtfa.setCoordinateIndex( 35, 0);
28.       for ( i=1, j=19; j<35; i++,j++) Indexedtfa.setCoordinateIndex( j, i-1);
29.
30.       Indexedtfa.setCoordinateIndex( 36, 18);  Indexedtfa.setCoordinateIndex( 53, 0);
31.       for ( i=1, j=37; j<53; i++,j++) Indexedtfa.setCoordinateIndex( j, i-1);
32.
33.       Indexedtfa.setCoordinateIndex( 54, 19); Indexedtfa.setCoordinateIndex( 71, 0);
34.       for ( i=1, j=55; j<71; i++,j++) Indexedtfa.setCoordinateIndex( j, i-1);
35.
36.       return Indexedtfa;
37.
38.   }//end of Artefact method
```

SUMMARY

We have introduced and discussed several basic geometry classes that can be used to specify the geometry of visual objects in Java 3D. PointArray, LineArray, TriangleArray,

Figure 49. Code segment for Glass_case()

```
1.    private Geometry Glass_case()
2.    {
3.        float c = 1.0f;  float d = -0.7f;  float e = 0.6f;
4.
5.        IndexedQuadArray qa = new IndexedQuadArray(8, QuadArray.COORDINATES, 16);
6.
7.        qa.setCoordinate(0,new Point3f(-e,e,c));      qa.setCoordinate(1,new Point3f(-e,-e,c));
8.        qa.setCoordinate(2,new Point3f(e,-e,c));      qa.setCoordinate(3,new Point3f(e,e,c));
9.        qa.setCoordinate(4,new Point3f(-e,e,d));      qa.setCoordinate(5,new Point3f(-e,-e,d));
10.       qa.setCoordinate(6,new Point3f(e,-e,d));      qa.setCoordinate(7,new Point3f(e,e,d));
11.
12.       //the front face and the back face using for loop
13.       for (int i=0; i<8;i++) qa.setCoordinateIndex(i,i);
14.       qa.setCoordinateIndex(8,5);        qa.setCoordinateIndex(9,6);
15.       qa.setCoordinateIndex(10,2);       qa.setCoordinateIndex(11,1);
16.       qa.setCoordinateIndex(12,4);       qa.setCoordinateIndex(13,0);
17.       qa.setCoordinateIndex(14,3);       qa.setCoordinateIndex(15,7);
18.
19.       return qa;
20.
21.    }//end of Glass_case method
```

and QuadArray are useful for building objects using a series of points, lines, triangles and quadrilaterals. For structures where the series of lines or triangles are adjacent to each other in a certain manner, the use of LineStripArray, TriangleStripArray, and TriangleFanArray may be more convenient and lead to faster rendering. The problem of requiring certain vertices to be repeated when these basic classes are used can be overcome through using their indexed versions, where the sequence of vertices can be supplied via some integer indexing arrays. Complex objects can be created through appropriately combining objects built from different classes. Also, simple geometrical shapes such as boxes, spheres, cones or cylinders can be easily generated using the predefined utility classes in Java 3D.

REFERENCES

Java 3D API specification. (2006). http://java.sun.com/products/java-media/3D/forDevelopers/j3dguide/j3dTOC.doc.html.

Java3D geometry. (2006). http://viz.aset.psu.edu/jack/java3d/geom.html.

Figure 50. Code segment and result for Util.java

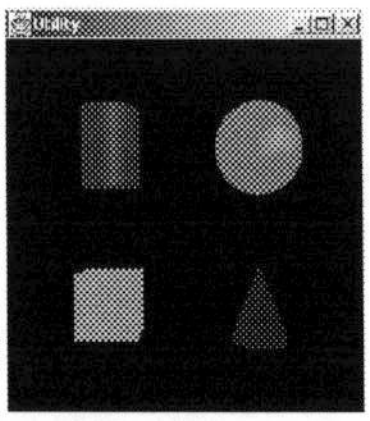

```
1.    public BranchGroup createSceneGraph()
2.    {
3.        BranchGroup objRoot = new BranchGroup();
4.
5.        Transform3D trans3d = new Transform3D();
6.        trans3d.setTranslation(new Vector3f(0.5f,0.5f,-0.5f));
7.        TransformGroup trans = new TransformGroup(trans3d);
8.        Material material = new Material(new Color3f(0.0f,0.0f,0.0f), new Color3f(0.5f,0.5f,0.0f),
9.                    new Color3f(0.0f,0.0f,0.0f), new Color3f(1.0f,1.0f,1.0f), 100f);
10.       Appearance appearance = new Appearance();  appearance.setMaterial(material);
11.       Sphere sphere = new Sphere(0.3f, appearance);
12.       objRoot.addChild(trans);  trans.addChild(sphere);
13.
14.       Material material1 = new Material(new Color3f(0.0f,0.0f,0.0f), new Color3f(0.2f,0.0f,0.9f),
15.                    new Color3f(0.0f,0.0f,0.0f), new Color3f(1.0f,1.0f,1.0f), 100f);
16.       Appearance appearance1 = new Appearance();  appearance1.setMaterial(material1);
17.       trans3d.setTranslation(new Vector3f(-0.5f,0.5f,-0.5f));
18.       TransformGroup trans1 = new TransformGroup(trans3d);
19.       Cylinder cylinder = new Cylinder(0.2f,0.5f, appearance1);
20.       objRoot.addChild(trans1); trans1.addChild(cylinder);
21.
22.       Material material2 = new Material(new Color3f(0.0f,0.0f,0.0f), new Color3f(0.0f,0.5f,0.9f),
23.                    new Color3f(0.0f,0.0f,0.0f), new Color3f(1.0f,1.0f,1.0f), 100f);
24.       Appearance appearance2 = new Appearance();  appearance2.setMaterial(material2);
25.       trans3d.setTranslation(new Vector3f(-0.5f,-0.5f,-0.5f));
26.       TransformGroup trans2 = new TransformGroup(trans3d);
27.       Box box = new Box(0.2f,0.2f,0.2f,appearance2);
28.       objRoot.addChild(trans2); trans2.addChild(box);
29.
30.       Material material3 = new Material(new Color3f(0.0f,0.0f,0.0f), new Color3f(0.4f,0.1f,0.3f),
31.                    new Color3f(0.0f,0.0f,0.0f), new Color3f(1.0f,1.0f,1.0f), 100f);
32.       Appearance appearance3 = new Appearance();  appearance3.setMaterial(material3);
33.       trans3d.setTranslation(new Vector3f(0.5f,-0.5f,-0.5f));
34.       TransformGroup trans3 = new TransformGroup(trans3d);
35.       Cone cone = new Cone(0.2f, 0.5f);
36.       cone.setAppearance(appearance3);
37.       objRoot.addChild(trans3);  trans3.addChild(cone);
38.
39.       DirectionalLight light = new DirectionalLight(new Color3f(1.0f,1.0f,0.0f), new Vector3f(-1f,0f,-
      1f));
40.       light.setInfluencingBounds(new BoundingSphere(new Point3d(), 1000d));
41.       trans.addChild(light);
42.
43.       return objRoot;
44.    }
```

Chapter IV
Appearance Objects

INTRODUCTION

In the last chapter, the creation of the skeletons or shapes of 3D objects has been discussed through the use of geometry objects in Java 3D. In order for these objects to be as realistic as possible to the user, it is often necessary for these objects to be covered with appropriate "skins" under good lighting conditions. In Java 3D, details on the skins can be specified by using color, texture, and material, which can be specified through the associated appearance objects.

In this chapter, all the important attributes, including the ways for rendering points, lines and polygons as well as color and material, for an appearance object will be discussed. The use of texturing will be covered in the next chapter.

As mentioned earlier, the creation of a virtual 3D object in a virtual world can be carried out using a Shape3D object in the associated scene graph. This object can reference a geometry object in Java 3D to create the skeleton of the virtual object. In addition, it can also reference an appearance object for specifying the skin of the virtual object.

On its own, an appearance object does not contain information on how the object will look like. However, it can reference other objects, such as "attribute objects," "texture-related objects," and "material objects," for getting appearance information to complement the object geometry.

Since the use of an appearance object to enhance the geometry in the creation of a virtual universe is a basic requirement in Java 3D, we will now discuss some important aspects of appearance object in this chapter.

The following steps are involved in the creation of an appearance object:

1. Create an appearance object.
2. Create the necessary attributes, materials object, and texture related objects.
3. Reference the objects in step 2 from the appearance object.
4. Reference the appearance object from the Shape3D object.

Figure 1 shows the how an appearance object is related to other relevant objects. As shown in Figure 1, an appearance object can refer to several different appearance attribute objects, which belong to basically the NodeComponent classes (Walsh & Gehringer, 2002). The important classes are

*   PointAttributes
*   LineAttributes
*   PolygonAttributes
*   ColoringAttributes
*   TransparencyAttributes
*   RenderingAttributes
*   Material
*   TextureAttributes
*   Texture
*   TexCoordGeneration

Figure 1. Relation of an appearance object with other objects and classes

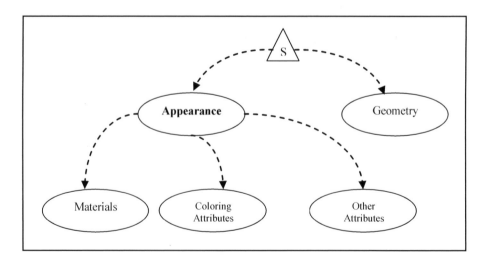

The first seven node components will be discussed in this chapter, while the remaining three classes are texture related and will be discussed in Chapter X.

Figure 2 shows the appearance constructor for creating an appearance object with all component object references initialized to null. Some important default values corresponding to null references are also listed in this figure.

To enable code sharing, it is possible for different Shape3D objects to reference the same appearance and NodeComponent Objects. An example is illustrated in Figure 3.

In addition to code sharing, using the same NodeComponents may also lead to an improvement in performance. For instance, if several appearance components share the same LineAttributes component and "antialiasing" is enabled, the Java3D rendering engine may decide to group the antialiased wire frame shapes together. This would minimize turning antialiasing on and off, and result in faster graphics rendering.

Figure 2. Appearance constructor and default values

Appearance appear = new Appearance ()

	Default values
Points and lines	Size and width of 1 pixel, no antialiasing
Intrinsic color	White
Transparency	Disabled
Depth buffer	Enabled, read and write accessible

Figure 3. Sharing appearance and NodeComponent objects

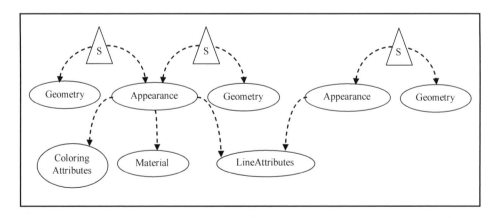

Figure 4. Images B and A rendered with and without antialising

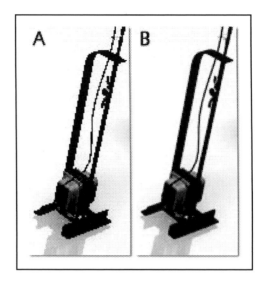

The issue of antialiasing is important in graphics display and can best be illustrated by comparing the two images shown in Figure 4.

Figure 5. Slanted line rendered with (bottom) and within (top) antialising

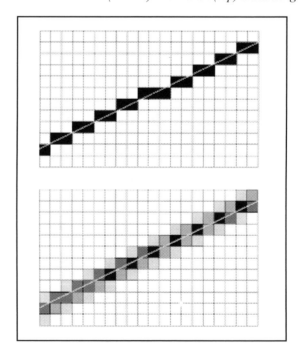

Obviously, Image B rendered with antialiasing appears smoother and looks better than Image A. This is because when a slanted line is drawn on a computer screen with limited resolution, it will actually be painted in a series of "steps" as shown in Figure 5. While this "aliasing" effect cannot be eliminated, the line will appear smoother if the graphic engine invokes an **antialiasing** process to paint adjacent pixels using some appropriate intermediate color or brightness.

PointAttributes

Beginning with PointAttributes, we will now start to discuss the important NodeComponent classes and illustrate how they can be used through some simple examples. Of course, for

Figure 6. Code segment PointAttributesExample1.java and result, illustrating PointAttributes

```
1.    // create a PointAttributes with point width = size
2.    public class aPoint extends Shape3D {
3.
4.    public aPoint(float xo, float yo, float zo, float size ) {
5.                  this.setGeometry(createPoint(xo, yo, zo));
6.                  this.setAppearance(createPointApp(size));
7.    }
8.
9.    private Geometry createPoint(float x, float y, float z) {
10.    // x, y, z are (x, y, z) coordinate of the point
11.    PointArray pt = new PointArray(1, GeometryArray.COORDINATES);
12.    pt.setCoordinate(0, new Point3f(x, y, z));
13.    return pt;
14. }
15.
16. private Appearance createPointApp(float size) {
17.    Appearance app = new Appearance();
18.            // and Point antialiasing = false
19.    PointAttributes pointAtt = new PointAttributes(size, false);
20.            app.setPointAttributes(pointAtt);
21.    return app;
22. }
23.
24. }
25.
26. public BranchGroup createSceneGraph() {
27.    BranchGroup objRoot = new BranchGroup();
28.    // add more point here with different coordinates and point width
29.    objRoot.addChild(new aPoint(0.3f, 0.4f, 0.0f, 4f));
30.    objRoot.addChild(new aPoint(0.4f, -0.3f, 0.0f, 8f));
31.    objRoot.addChild(new aPoint(-0.2f, 0.6f, 0.0f, 20f));
32.    objRoot.compile();
33.    return objRoot;
34. }
```

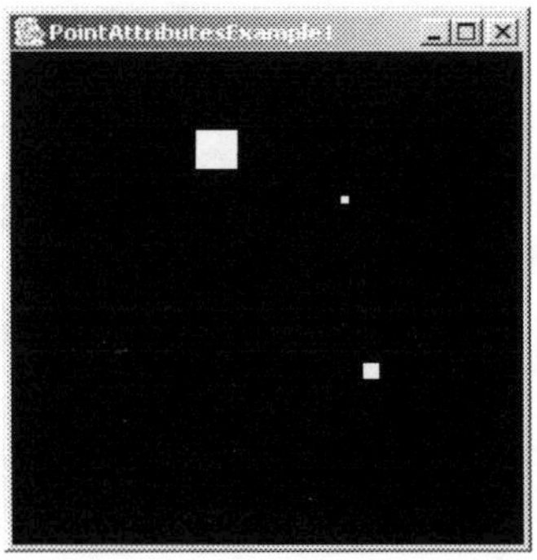

Figure 7. Additional code segment PointAttributesExample2.java and result

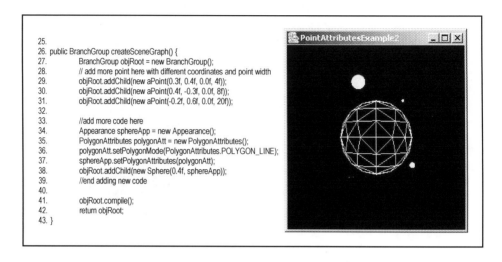

```
25.
26. public BranchGroup createSceneGraph() {
27.         BranchGroup objRoot = new BranchGroup();
28.         // add more point here with different coordinates and point width
29.         objRoot.addChild(new aPoint(0.3f, 0.4f, 0.0f, 4f));
30.         objRoot.addChild(new aPoint(0.4f, -0.3f, 0.0f, 8f));
31.         objRoot.addChild(new aPoint(-0.2f, 0.6f, 0.0f, 20f));
32.
33.         //add more code here
34.         Appearance sphereApp = new Appearance();
35.         PolygonAttributes polygonAtt = new PolygonAttributes();
36.         polygonAtt.setPolygonMode(PolygonAttributes.POLYGON_LINE);
37.         sphereApp.setPolygonAttributes(polygonAtt);
38.         objRoot.addChild(new Sphere(0.4f, sphereApp));
39.         //end adding new code
40.
41.         objRoot.compile();
42.         return objRoot;
43. }
```

Figure 8. First segment of LineAttributesExample1.java

```
1.     public class aLine extends Shape3D {
2.
3.     public aLine(float x1, float y1, float x2, float y2, float width, int pattern, boolean antialias) {
4.                 this.setGeometry(createLine(x1, y1, x2, y2));
5.                 this.setAppearance(createLineApp(width, pattern, antialias));
6.     }
7.
8.     private Geometry createLine(float x1, float y1, float x2, float y2) {
9.                 LineArray line = new LineArray(2, GeometryArray.COORDINATES);
10.     line.setCoordinate(0, new Point3f(x1, y1, 0.0f));
11.     line.setCoordinate(1, new Point3f(x2, y2, 0.0f));
12.     return line;
13. }
14.
15. private Appearance createLineApp(float width, int pattern, boolean antialias) {
16.                 Appearance app = new Appearance();
17.     // create a LineAttributes
18.     // and LineWidth = width, LinePattern = pattern, antialiasing = antialias
19.     LineAttributes lineAtt = new LineAttributes(width, pattern, antialias);
20.                 app.setLineAttributes(lineAtt);
21.     return app;
22. }
23.
24. }
```

any graphics system, Java 3D included, point and line attributes are the two most funda-mental attributes on which all visual objects are constructed.

In Java 3D, PointAttributes objects control how points in the virtual universe are ren-dered. The PointAttributes class has several methods to increase the size of a single point. However, note that a point will appear to be square in shape unless the setPointAntialias-ingEnable() method is set to true.

Figure 9. Second segment of LineAttributesExample1.java and result

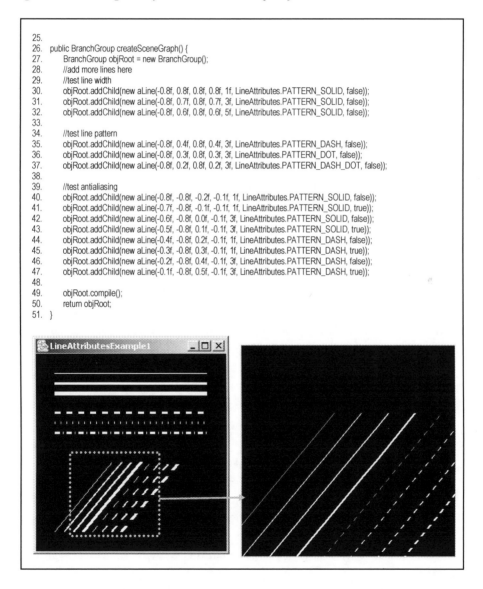

The code segment and result in Figure 6 illustrate how three points with different widths can be rendered at different locations. Note that in line 19, PointAttributes has set antialiasing to false to result in the output shown.

By adding a few more line of codes to those in Figure 6, Figure 7 shows how spherical or circular points can be rendered. Note that the additional code is to create a PolygonAttributes object (lines 10 and 11) in the same BranchGroup. Then, POLYGON_LINE is used and antialiasing is set to true to result in the output shown.

LineAttributes

LineAttributes objects change how line primitives are rendered by controlling the types (for example, solid or dashed) of the line patterns to be used, the width of the line, and whether antialiasing is enabled. Figures 8 and 9 show some sell-explanatory code segments and the corresponding results on some test lines rendered using LineWidth, LinePattern and Line Antialiasing properties.

PolygonAttributes

PolygonAttributes objects control how polygon primitives will be rendered. This includes how the polygon will be rasterized, and whether a special depth offset is set or culled. The default for filling polygons can also be easily changed using the setPolygonMode() method to show only the wire frame or vertices.

Furthermore, the PolygonAttribute class includes a method to reduce the number of polygons to be rendered through the use of setCullFace() method. This is illustrated in the code segment in Figure 10, where lines 15 to 23 set the appearance with the CULL_NONE attribute so that both the front and back of the object are rendered (Java 3D scene appearance, 2006). As illustrated in Figure 11, the result of this is that both the front and back of the letter E can be seen even after it has been rotated.

By changing CULL_NONE to CULL_FRONT in line 21 in the code segment of Figure 10, Java 3D will only render the polygons on the front of the letter E. Since the polygons at the back are not rendered, a black screen will result after rotation, as illustrated in Figure 12.

Similarly, by using CULL_BACK instead, only the polygons at the back will be rendered. As illustrated in Figure 13, it is the other side of the letter E that can be seen as it is rotated now.

Having discussed the issue of culling, we will now illustrate the use of POLYGON_ POINT to render just the vertices of the object. The code segment is shown in Figure 14, and is basically the same as that in Figure 10. However, an additional line of code (line 20) has been added to define the polygon mode. In this example, the PolygonMode is set using the setPolygonMode method to POLYGON_POINT to ensure that only the vertices are rendered. Specifically, line 17 creates a new Appearance object, line 18 creates a new PolygonAttributes object, line 20 sets the PolygonMode, and line 23 sets the PolygonAt-

Figure 10. Code segment PolygonAttributesExample1.java

```
1.      public class AppearanceCULL_NONE extends Applet
2.      {
3.       public class Letter_E extends Shape3D
4.        {
5.          int vertex = 4;
6.          //constructor
7.          public Letter_E()
8.          {
9.                  this.setGeometry(Quad1Geometry());
10.                 this.addGeometry(Quad2Geometry());
11.
12.                 this.addGeometry(Quad3Geometry());
13.                 this.addGeometry(Quad4Geometry());
14.                 this.setAppearance(Letter_E_Appearance());
15.          }
16.          private Appearance Letter_E_Appearance()
17.          {
18.                  Appearance look = new Appearance();
19.                  PolygonAttributes polyAttrib = new PolygonAttributes();
20.                  //to make both sides of the face appear
21.                  polyAttrib.setCullFace(PolygonAttributes.CULL_NONE);
22.                  look.setPolygonAttributes(polyAttrib);
23.                  return look;
24.          }
```

Figure 11. Results from PolygonAttributesExample1.java. Note that the CULL_NONE attribute results in both the front and back of the letter E to be seen even after it has been rotated

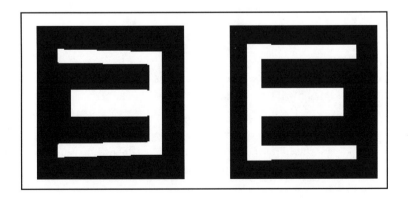

Figure 12. Results from PolygonAttributesExample1.java after changing CULL_NONE to CULL_FRONT. This renders only the front of the letter, resulting in a blank screen after rotation

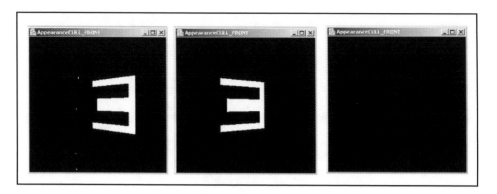

Figure 13. Results from PolygonAttributesExample1.java after changing CULL_NONE to CULL_BACK. This renders only the back of the letter, resulting in a blank screen after rotation

tributes for the new Appearance object. The result of the code is also given in Figure 14, showing clearly that only the vertices of the letter E can be seen.

Lastly, by using POLYGON_LINE instead of POLYGON_POINT in line 20, only the wire frame used to create the letter E will be rendered. Then, by using POLYGON_FILL instead, the polygons used for the letter E will be filled. These are illustrated in Figure 15. Note that the default mode is POLYGON_FILL.

Figure 14. Code segment and result of PolygonAttributesExample2.java

```
1.    public class AppearancePOLYGON_POINT extends Applet
2.    {
3.      public class Letter_E extends Shape3D
4.      {
5.        int vertex = 4;
6.        //constructor
7.        public Letter_E()
8.        {
9.              this.setGeometry(Quad1Geometry());
10.       this.addGeometry(Quad2Geometry());
11.       this.addGeometry(Quad3Geometry());
12.       this.addGeometry(Quad4Geometry());
13.       this.setAppearance(Letter_E_Appearance());
14.   }
15.   private Appearance Letter_E_Appearance()
16.   {
17.     Appearance look = new Appearance();
18.     PolygonAttributes polyAttrib = new PolygonAttributes();
19.     //use only the vertices to render the object
20.     polyAttrib.setPolygonMode(PolygonAttributes.POLYGON_POINT);
21.     //to make both sides of the face appear
22.     polyAttrib.setCullFace(PolygonAttributes.CULL_NONE);
23.     look.setPolygonAttributes(polyAttrib);
24.     return look;
25.   }
```

Figure 15. Results from PolygonAttributesExample2.java after changing POLYGON_POINT to POLYGON_LINE (left) and POLYGON_FILL (right)

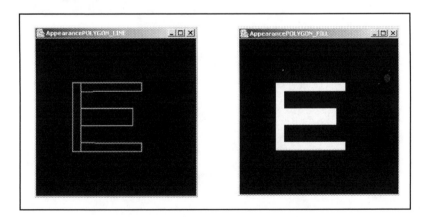

ColoringAttributes

ColoringAttributes controls how the various primitives will be colored. Colors can be specified in a variety of methods. As an example, colors may be defined at each vertex of a geometry object. In this case, as the geometry is created, the colors used in the geometry object will override the intrinsic color in ColoringAttributes. In addition, if lighting is used, the ColoringAttributes intrinsic color will be ignored completely and material color is used instead.

The code fragment in Figure 16 shows a simple example illustrating how the color of the object can be specified or changed. Line 21 creates a new ColoringAttributes object, and line 23 sets the new color. In this example, the use of Color3f(1.0f, 0.0f, 0.0f) corresponds to the use of red. Green and blue can similarly be specified by using (0.0f, 1.0f, 0.0f) and (0.0f, 0.0f, 1.0f), respectively.

Figure 16. Code segment and result of AppearanceCOLOR.java

```
1.    public class AppearanceCOLOR extends Applet
2.    {
3.        public class Letter_E extends Shape3D
4.        {
5.                int vertex = 4;
6.                //constructor
7.                public Letter_E()
8.                {
9.
10.                       this.setGeometry(Quad1Geometry());
11.                       this.addGeometry(Quad2Geometry());
12.                       this.addGeometry(Quad3Geometry());
13.                       this.addGeometry(Quad4Geometry());
14.                       this.setAppearance(Letter_E_Appearance());
15.
16.                }
17.
18.               private Appearance Letter_E_Appearance()
19.               {
20.                       Appearance look = new Appearance();
21.                       ColoringAttributes colorAttrib = new ColoringAttributes();
22.                       //set new color for the object
23.                       colorAttrib.setColor(new Color3f(1.0f,0.0f,0.0f));
24.                       PolygonAttributes polyAttrib = new PolygonAttributes();
25.                       //to make both sides of the face appear
26.                       polyAttrib.setCullFace(PolygonAttributes.CULL_NONE);
27.                       look.setColoringAttributes(colorAttrib);
28.                  look.setPolygonAttributes(polyAttrib);
29.                       return look;
30.               }
31.
```

TransparencyAttributes

TransparencyAttributes specifies transparency attributes, which are, in turn, depending on two parameters, the transparency mode, and the transparency value. Transparency mode (tmode) defines how transparency is applied to an appearance component object. The possibilities are listed below:

- **FASTEST:** Makes use of the fastest available method.
- **NICEST:** Uses the nicest available method.
- **SCREEN_DOOR:** Uses screen-door transparency. An on/off stipple pattern is used. The percentage of transparent pixels is approximately equal to the value specified by the transparency value.
- **BLENDED:** Uses alpha blended transparency. All the pixels are partially transparent at a percentage given by the transparency value.
- **NONE:** No transparency. The object is opaque.

Figure 17. Code segment and result of Sphere_exhibit.java

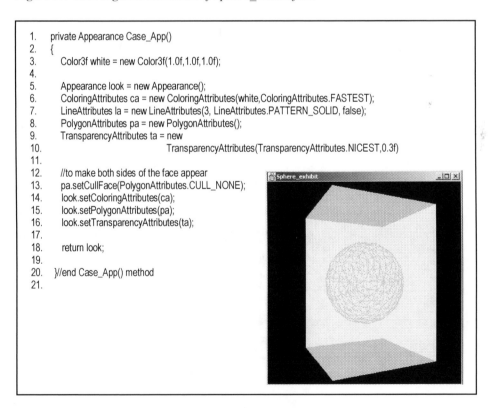

```
1.    private Appearance Case_App()
2.    {
3.        Color3f white = new Color3f(1.0f,1.0f,1.0f);
4.
5.        Appearance look = new Appearance();
6.        ColoringAttributes ca = new ColoringAttributes(white,ColoringAttributes.FASTEST);
7.        LineAttributes la = new LineAttributes(3, LineAttributes.PATTERN_SOLID, false);
8.        PolygonAttributes pa = new PolygonAttributes();
9.        TransparencyAttributes ta = new
10.                        TransparencyAttributes(TransparencyAttributes.NICEST,0.3f)
11.
12.        //to make both sides of the face appear
13.        pa.setCullFace(PolygonAttributes.CULL_NONE);
14.        look.setColoringAttributes(ca);
15.        look.setPolygonAttributes(pa);
16.        look.setTransparencyAttributes(ta);
17.
18.        return look;
19.
20.    }//end Case_App() method
21.
```

The transparency value (tval) specifies the object's opacity. 0.0f is for fully opaque and 1.0f for fully transparent. A better appreciation can be obtained from the code segment and result in Figure 17.

The results of using SCREEN_DOOR and BLENDED mode are given in Figure 18. As can be seen, the use of SCREEN_DOOR gives rise to a result that is rather unpleasant as 30% of the pixels are fully transparent and 70% of the pixels are fully opaque. Essentially, SCREEN_DOOR is faster than BLENDED at the expense of quality.

Figure 19 shows the results of having higher tval value so as to improve the transparency effect.

Figure 18. Results from Sphere_exhibit.java with tval equal to 0.3f and tmode given by SCREEN_DOOR (left) and BLENDED (right)

```
ıMovement(Node armingNode)
 WakeupOnCollisionMovement criterion.

ıMovement(Node armingNode, int speedHint)
 WakeupOnCollisionMovement criterion, where speedHint may be
 use geometric bounds as an approximation in computing collisions.
 Y - use geometry in computing collisions.

ıMovement(SceneGraphPath armingPath)
 WakeupOnCollisionMovement criterion.

ıMovement(SceneGraphPath armingPath, int speedHint)
 WakeupOnCollisionMovement criterion, where speedHint may be
 r USE_GEOMETRY.
```

Figure 19. Results from Sphere_exhibit.java with tval/ tmode given by 0.7f/NICEST (left), 0.85f/SCREEN_DOOR (middle), and 0.7f/BLENDED, CREEN_DOOR (right)

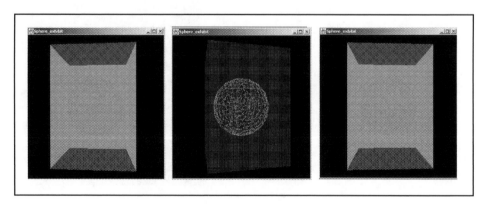

RenderingAttributes

RenderingAttributes controls how a graphical object will be rendered. It is best illustrated by using the code segment in Figures 20 and 21.

The code segment in lines 34 to 37 give rise to the instantiation of a new RenderingAttribute object, using which two different per-pixel rendering operations, the depth buffer test and the alpha test, can be controlled. As can be seen from the result in Figure 21 for this case when the rendering attributes are at their default values, the three rectangles are intercepted and partially blocked by the sphere.

The result of changing the first two rendering parameters, depthBufferEnable and depthBufferWriteEnable, in the rendering attribute constructor from true to false is shown in Figure 22. As can be seen, the parts of the rectangles that are behind and originally blocked have become visible and no longer blocked. This is because there is now no comparison

Figure 20. First segment of render.java

```
1.    public class rectangle extends Shape3D
2.    {
3.            public rectangle()
4.            {
5.                    this.setGeometry(CreateGeometry(0.0f, 0.8f));
6.                    this.addGeometry(CreateGeometry(0.2f, 1.0f));
7.                    this.addGeometry(CreateGeometry(-0.2f, 0.3f));
8.                    this.setAppearance(CreateApp());
9.            }
10.
11.           private Geometry CreateGeometry(float z, float alpha)
12.           {
13.                   QuadArray rect = new
14.           QuadArray(4,QuadArray.COORDINATES|QuadArray.COLOR_4);
15.                   rect.setCoordinate(0,new Point3f(-0.5f, 0.2f,z));
16.                   rect.setCoordinate(1,new Point3f(-0.5f, -0.2f,z));
17.                   rect.setCoordinate(2,new Point3f(0.5f, -0.2f,z));
18.                   rect.setCoordinate(3,new Point3f(0.5f, 0.2f,z));
19.
20.                   Color4f yellow = new Color4f(1.0f,1.0f,0.0f,alpha);
21.
22.                   rect.setColor(0,yellow);
23.                   rect.setColor(1,yellow);
24.                   rect.setColor(2,yellow);
25.                   rect.setColor(3,yellow);
26.                   return rect;
27.           }
28.
```

Figure 21. Second segment and result of render.java

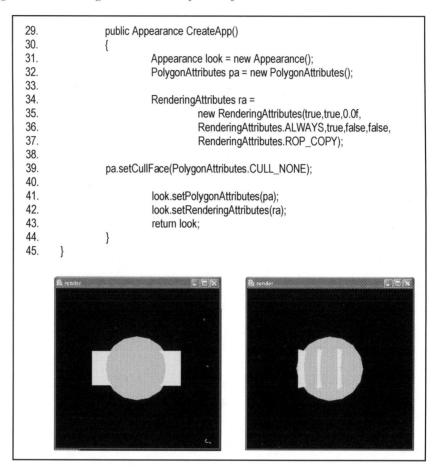

```
29.            public Appearance CreateApp()
30.            {
31.                    Appearance look = new Appearance();
32.                    PolygonAttributes pa = new PolygonAttributes();
33.
34.                    RenderingAttributes ra =
35.                            new RenderingAttributes(true,true,0.0f,
36.                            RenderingAttributes.ALWAYS,true,false,false,
37.                            RenderingAttributes.ROP_COPY);
38.
39.            pa.setCullFace(PolygonAttributes.CULL_NONE);
40.
41.                    look.setPolygonAttributes(pa);
42.                    look.setRenderingAttributes(ra);
43.                    return look;
44.            }
45.    }
```

Figure 22. Results from render.java, after changing the first two parameters in Rendering Attributes(true,true to RenderingAttributes(false,false

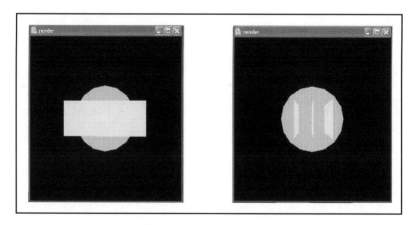

of depth or z-axis values between the geometries. As a result, all the objects have become visible and will be rendered, regardless of any occlusion and interception between them.

Next, alpha testing can be enabled by changing the third and fourth parameters in the rendering attribute constructor so that it becomes, for example, RenderingAttributes(true, true, ALPHA_TEST, RenderingAttributes.GREATER…). The results are given in Figure 23, which shows that some of the rectangles at different depth will not be rendered depending on the alpha test value, ALPHA_TEST, and the alpha value of the rectangle specified in line 20 of Figure 20.

Specifically, the alpha value serves as a multiplying factor when it is used with the TransparencyAttribute. If the transparency value in the TransparencyAttribute is 0.5f and the alpha value in color4f is 0.3f, the value of transparency will be 0.15f. In the above example when RenderingAttributes.GREATER is used as the fourth parameter in the rendering attribute constructor, the rendering of the object will be carried out only if the associated alpha values of the geometries are greater than the alpha test value set by the user.

Instead of using GREATER as in RenderingAttributes.GREATER, other possibilities and their associated actions are listed below.

- **ALWAYS:** Pixels are always drawn, irrespective of the alpha value. This is the default and, effectively, disables alpha testing.
- **NEVER:** Pixels are never drawn, irrespective of the alpha value.
- **EQUAL:** Pixels are drawn if the pixel alpha value is equal to the alpha test value.

Figure 23. Results from render.java, after changing the third and fourth parameters in RenderingAttributes(true,true,0.0f, RenderingAttributes.ALWAYS to RenderingAttributes(true,true,ALPHA_TEST,RenderingAttributes.GREATER. The value of ALPHA_TEST is 0.4f and 0.9f for the left and right diagram, respectively.

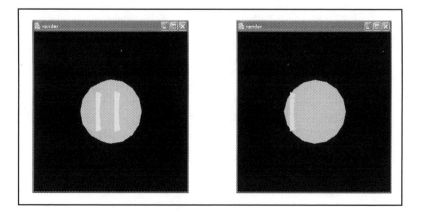

- **NOT_EQUAL:** Pixels are drawn if the pixel alpha value is not equal to the alpha test value.
- **LESS:** Pixels are drawn if the pixel alpha value is less than the alpha test value.
- **LESS_OR_EQUAL:** Pixels are drawn if the pixel alpha value is less than or equal to the alpha test value.
- **GREATER:** Pixels are drawn if the pixel alpha value is greater than the alpha test value.
- **GREATER_OR_EQUAL:** Pixels are drawn if the pixel alpha value is greater than or equal to the alpha test value.

Lastly, Figure 24 show the results when the other parameters in the rendering attribute constructor are changed. The fifth parameter controls visibility and, by changing it to false, the rectangles are not drawn as illustrated in the left diagram in the figure. Then, if the sixth ignoreVertexColors parameter is changed to true instead, the assigned yellow color of the rectangles will be ignored and the rectangles will now be rendered in white. The last two parameters in the rendering attribute constructor control raster operation and default values will be used most of the time.

Figure 24. Results from render.java, after changing the fifth and sixth parameters in Rendering Attributes(true,true,0.0f, RenderingAttributes.ALWAYS,true,false to RenderingAttributes(true,true,0.0f, RenderingAttributes.ALWAYS,false,false and RenderingAttributes(true,true,0.0f, RenderingAttributes.ALWAYS,true,true

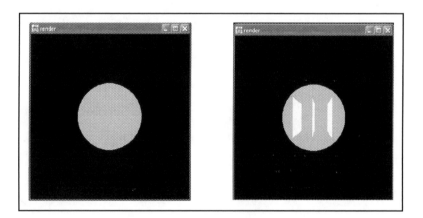

MATERIAL

Another way to add color and enhance visual effects to an object's appearance is to make use of material class. This, however, requires illumination from one or more light sources. Once these are specified, the appearance of the object can be determined.

A material object can have the following properties:

- **Ambient color:** The ambient RGB color reflected off the surface of the material. This gives the overall color of the object and is independent of the light source. The range of value for each primary color is 0.0f to 1.0f, with a default at (0.2f,0.2f,0.2f). Ambient color is visible only under ambient lighting.
- **Diffuse color:** The RGB color of the material when illuminated. Obviously, this color depends on the light source. Provided the object has no shininess, the surface of the material facing the light source will have this color. The range of value for each primary color is 0.0f to 1.0f, with a default diffuse color of (1.0f,1.0f,1.0f).
- **Specular color:** The RGB specular color of the material under highlights. The range of value for each primary color is 0.0f to 1.0f, with a default specular color of (1.0f,1.0f,1.0f).
- **Emissive color:** The RGB color of the light that the material emits, if any. The range of value for each primary color is 0.0f to 1.0f, with a emissive color of (0.0f,0.0f,0.0f) or black.
- **Shininess:** The material's shininess. The range is [1.0f, 128.0f], with 128.0f being not shiny and 1.0 being most shiny. The default value is 64.0f.
- Enabling or disabling of lighting.

Figure 25 shows an example using material class in the presence of two light sources, an ambient one and a directional one. Note that, with the ambient color set to green (0.0f,0.2f,0.0f), those parts of the object unaffected by the overhead directional light appear green in color. On the other hand, because the default diffuse and specular colors are white, the portion of the object illuminated by the overhead light appears white.

Figure 26 shows the result after each stage by changing the diffuse color to blue, the specular color to red, and then the emissive color to dirty green. Note that without the emissive color, the bottom part of the object still has an ambience color of green and looks the same as before. However, the color diffused from the overhead directional white light source now makes the top part of the object blue. Changing the specular color to red makes the highest part of the object that faces the directional light source directly red instead of white. The last change that overwrites the default emissive color of black (meaning that the object is not emitting any color) to dirty green results in quite a significant change to the appearance of the object. In general, setting strong emissive color will tend to override the colors from all the other sources.

Figure 25. Code segment and result of Material_Attribute.java

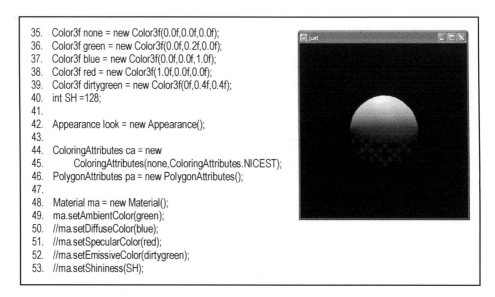

```
35.   Color3f none = new Color3f(0.0f,0.0f,0.0f);
36.   Color3f green = new Color3f(0.0f,0.2f,0.0f);
37.   Color3f blue = new Color3f(0.0f,0.0f,1.0f);
38.   Color3f red = new Color3f(1.0f,0.0f,0.0f);
39.   Color3f dirtygreen = new Color3f(0f,0.4f,0.4f);
40.   int SH =128;
41.
42.   Appearance look = new Appearance();
43.
44.   ColoringAttributes ca = new
45.       ColoringAttributes(none,ColoringAttributes.NICEST);
46.   PolygonAttributes pa = new PolygonAttributes();
47.
48.   Material ma = new Material();
49.   ma.setAmbientColor(green);
50.   //ma.setDiffuseColor(blue);
51.   //ma.setSpecularColor(red);
52.   //ma.setEmissiveColor(dirtygreen);
53.   //ma.setShininess(SH);
```

Figure 26. Results from Material_Attribute.java, after changing the diffuse color to blue (0.0f,0.0f, 1.0f), and then the specular color to red (1.0f,0.0f,0.0f), followed by the emissive color to dirty green (1.0f,0.4f,0.4f) resulting in the left, center and right hand displays, respectively.

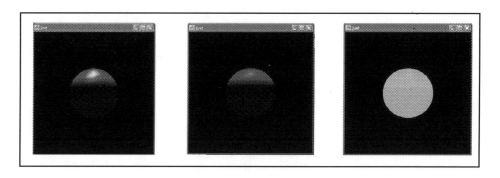

The shininess parameter is used to control the extent of the specular reflection. The higher the value, the smaller the extent of the reflection and the area being highlighted. Figure 27 shows the effect for different shininess of the same object with ambient and diffuse colors maintained at green and blue, and specular and emissive colors set to default.

Figure 27. Results from Material_Attribute.java, after changing the shininess parameter. The display on the left has a shininess of 128, while that on the right has a shininess of 10.

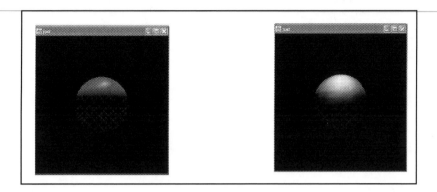

SUMMARY

Using an appearance object that references appropriate classes, the appearance of a geometry object can be further refined and enhanced (Java 3D explorer, 2006). Important classes are the attribute classes, material class and texture related classes.

The Sharing of appearance objects and the corresponding NodeComponent objects are possible and should be carried out for faster rendering. The NodeComponent objects discussed in this chapter are summarized in Figure 28.

Figure 28. Basic NodeComponent classes and their actions

PointAttributes	Point primitves
LineAttributes	Line primitives
PolygonAttributes	Polygon primitives
ColoringAttributes	Surface color
TransparencyAttirbutes	Geometry transparency
RenderingAttributes	Methods for rendering objects
Material	Surface color under illumination

REFERENCES

Java 3D explorer. (2006). http://web3dbooks.com/java3d/jumpstart/Java3DExplorer. html.

Java 3D scene appearance. (2006). http://www.j3d.org/faq/appearance.html

Walsh, A. E. & Gehringer, D. (2002). *Java 3D API Jump-Start*. Prentice Hall.

Chapter V
Textures

INTRODUCTION

Although extensive use of basic attributes such as color and material will be able to make an object realistic to the human user, it will be time consuming to develop the code for objects that have complicated geometries or appearances. As an example, to create an object with many color patterns on, say, a curve surface, many zones or strips may need to be individually defined using the appropriate color or material properties. To save programming effort, Java 3D allows the use of what is known as texturing and image mapping, which will be the concern of this chapter.

Specifically, there are four ways to apply colors to a visual object in Java 3D. The first one is to apply color by defining the color of each vertex in the associated geometry object introduced in Chapter III. Another two ways are to use the coloring attributes in an appearance object and use a material object explained in Chapter IV. Alternatively, as will be discussed in this chapter, we can also apply textures.

Texturing is a simple method of giving a geometrical object a realistic appearance. While a desert landscape can be created by simply setting the coloring attribute to golden brown, the result will be dull and unrealistic. However, by using a file with a digital photo for a real desert and applying this on top of the desert geometry, a realistic desert can be constructed in the virtual 3D world (Seamless textures pack, 2006).

With texturing, we have new means to add visual details without the need to have additional geometries. The image used for texturing is mapped on to the object at rendering time, and as for material and coloring attributes, the inclusion of texturing can be carried out through an appearance object (Meyer, 2006).

TEXTURE LOADING

The following four steps are involved for applying textures to a geometry:

- Prepare texture image.
- Load texture.
- Set texture through an appearance object.
- Specify texture coordinates.

The preparation of the best texture image is best performed using a good imaging editing software. However, it should be noted that the sides of the image must be integer powers of two such as 128 by 256, failing which may result in a runtime exception. Java 3D accepts a variety of picture formats, including gif and jpg.

The loading of the texture image can be done from files or through URLs. Lines 1 and 2 in Figure 1 give an example on how this can be performed. Basically, the first line loads the file, picture1.gif, to create an ImageComponent2D object, which can then be used by an appearance object. Note that image loading in Java 3D requires an image observer, which can be any of the AWT components and is specified in the second argument in line 1. The image observer is for the purpose of monitoring the image load process and can be queried on details concerning this process.

In addition to the previous method, the loading of images can also be performed by using the NewTextureLoader class, which is an extension of the TextureLoader class. This new class eliminates the need to specify an image observer component every time TextureLoader is instantiated. Rather, the image observer only needs to be specified once.

Figure 1. Loading texture

```
1.    TextureLoader loader = new Texture Loader("picture1.gif", this);
2.    ImageComponent2D image = loader.getImage();
3.
4.    Texture2D texture = new Texture2D();
5.    texture.setImage(0,image);
6.    Appearance appear = new Appearance();
7.    appear.setTexture(texture);
```

Having loaded the image, the created ImageComponent2D object must be added to the appropriate appearance bundle. The code segment from lines 4 to 7 in Figure 1 illustrates how this can be done.

TEXTURE COORDINATES

After loading the texture image and adding the created texture object to an appearance, we will now need to specify the texture coordinates that will be applied to each of all the vertices of the geometry object. This serves to define the 2D mapping that maps the 2D texture image to each face of the geometry object.

The texture coordinate is specified in the form of normalized (x, y) units, where (0, 0) is the bottom left corner and (1, 1) is the top right corner of the texture image. Using one of the several setTextureCoordinates methods, the code segment in Figure 2 illustrates how these coordinates can be specified and the result obtained in a simple example. The geometry is a 2D plane created using quad array, while the texture image consists of three compasses arranged in a row. The specification of the texture coordinates in the code segment is such that the entire texture image will be mapped to the entire 2D geometrical plane. It is therefore the most straightforward mapping with no rotation and distortion of the texture image.

To illustrate this mapping of the texture image to a surface more clearly, Figure 3 shows a more complicated example where a rectangular texture image is mapped to a triangular geometrical surface. The texture image consists of a red circle in blue background in a jpg file. As can be seen, the specification of the texture coordinates as shown lead to a non-linear mapping and the red circle becomes distorted.

Figure 2. Specifying texture coordinates without any distortion for a quad array plane

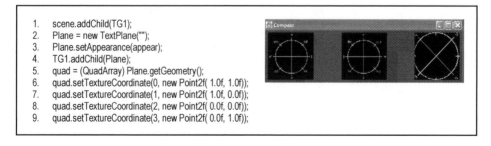

```
1.  scene.addChild(TG1);
2.  Plane = new TextPlane("");
3.  Plane.setAppearance(appear);
4.  TG1.addChild(Plane);
5.  quad = (QuadArray) Plane.getGeometry();
6.  quad.setTextureCoordinate(0, new Point2f( 1.0f, 1.0f));
7.  quad.setTextureCoordinate(1, new Point2f( 1.0f, 0.0f));
8.  quad.setTextureCoordinate(2, new Point2f( 0.0f, 0.0f));
9.  quad.setTextureCoordinate(3, new Point2f( 0.0f, 1.0f));
```

Figure 3. Specifying texture coordinates with distortion for a triangular geometry object

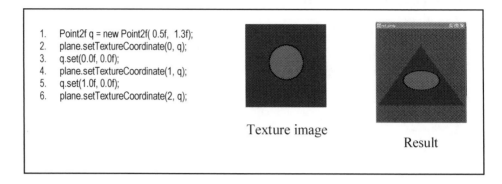

```
1.    Point2f q = new Point2f( 0.5f,  1.3f);
2.    plane.setTextureCoordinate(0, q);
3.    q.set(0.0f, 0.0f);
4.    plane.setTextureCoordinate(1, q);
5.    q.set(1.0f, 0.0f);
6.    plane.setTextureCoordinate(2, q);
```

Texture image

Result

TEXTURE PROPERTIES

The specification of the texture coordinates for the vertices of a 3D object corresponds to defining the mapping of the loaded 2D texture image to various 2D surfaces of the 3D object. This is one of the properties that can be changed in applying texture to an object. The other properties concern how the texture will blend in with the other attributes, say, the color, of the object.

In general, the application of texture can be specified through changing appropriate settings in the Texture and TextureAttributes classes. Figure 4 shows the relationship of these two classes to an appearance object.

Figure 4. Texture, TextureAttributes and Appearance classes

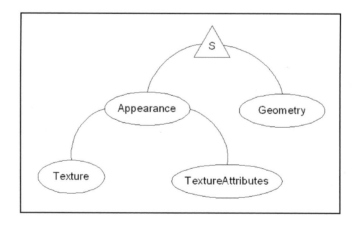

The Texture class can be used to define how texture will be rendered if the texture coordinates used have values which are not quite consistent or beyond the 0 to 1 normalized values for the entire texture image space. Specifically, the following possibilities are available:

- **Boundary mode:** WRAP or CLAMP. Boundary mode is on the rendering of texture when the texture coordinates are outside the image space. The default WRAP option specifies that the texture will be repeated to cover the entire surface. CLAMP uses the color at the edge of the image and stretches it across the remaining part of the uncovered surface. Specification of the boundary mode can be made for each of the horizontal and vertical dimensions of the image independently.
- **Filtering:** This is on how texture will be rendered when a displayed pixel is smaller or larger than a texel or the pixel for the texture image. A magnification filter can be specified for the former, while a minification filter can be defined for the latter.
- **Boundary color:** Allows a single color to be used outside the 0 to 1 range of the image space, that is, in the boundary region. This is applicable only if the boundary mode is CLAMP and the texture coordinates are beyond the 0 to 1 range.
- **Texture format:** Specifies the number of color bits and the color format for each texel and how these will affect the pixels on which they are rendered on. For example, using RGBA means that each texel will have 32-bit color value, and that the pixel color and alpha values will be modified by the corresponding texel.

TEXTURE ATTRIBUTES

Together with the Texture class, the TextureAttributes class provides the programmer with even greater control on the rendering of texture (Bouvier, 2006). In particular, as illustrated in Figure 5, it opens up the possibility for a texture to be shared by different geometries and yet for it to be customized based on having different texturing attributes.

Under texture attributes, it is possible to specify the texture mode, the blend color, the perspective correction, and the texture map transform to be used. In particular, the texture mode is on how the colors in the texture image will blend in with those from the object.

Figure 6 shows an example illustrating the effect of having different texture modes. In lines 4 to 5 of the code segment, the object is set to have a color of green. Also, line 2 specifies the texture mode and this is set to BLEND in the code segment. The texture image is a deck. This is the same as the third result, or when the texture mode is changed to REPLACE, the default mode signifying that the texture color will be used to replace the object color. Under this mode, the texture image will be used to provide the color and transparency for the final pixel, and all, except specular color with lighting enabled, will be ignored.

Figure 5. Using the same texture but having different texture attributes

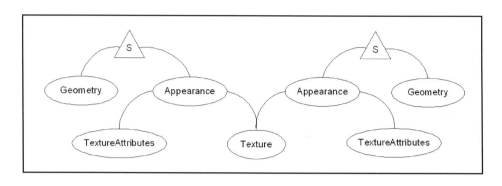

Under the BLEND mode, the color in the texture image can be seen to blend in with that of the geometry, with the former determining the amount of the non-texture color that will be added. The resulting transparency is the combination of the texture and material transparency. In addition, a blend color can also be supplied to result in a pixel color that is a combination of the texel and the blend color. By default, the blend color is black with an alpha value of 0.

When the texture mode is changed to MODULATE, the texture color is combined with the non-texture color in a modulating manner in the same way a signal modulates a carrier. The resulting transparency is also the sum of those due to the texture and material. Since the BLEND and MODULATE modes give rise to colors that depend on both the non-texture and the texture colors, they are useful for applying the same texture to different objects without having them giving the same look.

Lastly, in the DECAL mode, the texture color is applied as a decal on top of the non-texture color, and the transparency of the texture determines the amount of material color that will be applied, with the transparency of the pixel remaining unchanged. This mode requires a texture format of RGB or RGBA.

Since the mapping of textures to geometry takes place in image space, there may be a need to carry out perspective correction to have the rendered textured surface looks as realistically as possible in a 3D world. However, this will consume computational resources. Two options, FASTEST and NICEST, are thus provided for the programmer to choose in performing this correction.

Lastly, it is also possible to use a map transform for a texture to change, say the orientation of the texture image, before it is used for rendering. Figure 7 illustrates how this can be done to result in a 90-degree rotation of the rendered result when compared with those in Figure 6.

Figure 6. Texture modes

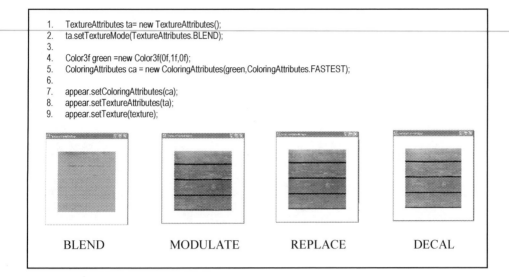

```
1.   TextureAttributes ta= new TextureAttributes();
2.   ta.setTextureMode(TextureAttributes.BLEND);
3.
4.   Color3f green =new Color3f(0f,1f,0f);
5.   ColoringAttributes ca = new ColoringAttributes(green,ColoringAttributes.FASTEST);
6.
7.   appear.setColoringAttributes(ca);
8.   appear.setTextureAttributes(ta);
9.   appear.setTexture(texture);
```

| BLEND | MODULATE | REPLACE | DECAL |

Figure 7. Texture map transform

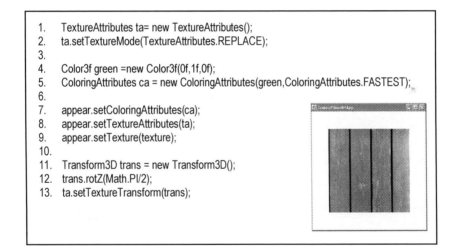

```
1.    TextureAttributes ta= new TextureAttributes();
2.    ta.setTextureMode(TextureAttributes.REPLACE);
3.
4.    Color3f green =new Color3f(0f,1f,0f);
5.    ColoringAttributes ca = new ColoringAttributes(green,ColoringAttributes.FASTEST);
6.
7.    appear.setColoringAttributes(ca);
8.    appear.setTextureAttributes(ta);
9.    appear.setTexture(texture);
10.
11.   Transform3D trans = new Transform3D();
12.   trans.rotZ(Math.PI/2);
13.   ta.setTextureTransform(trans);
```

TEXTURE COORDINATE GENERATION

As illustrated in previous sections, using texture to enhance the appearance of objects in a virtual 3D world is straightforward. The most cumbersome and time consuming operation is perhaps on specifying the texture coordinates as realistic objects usually have many vertices.

The generation of texture coordinates can be performed automatically for objects created from geometries in the utility class. An example is given in Figure 8, which shows that, by using the optional argument Primitive.GENERATE_TEXTURE_COORDS in the constructor in line 24, automatic generation of texture coordinates will be carried out.

Automatic generation of texture coordinates can also be carried out through the use of TexCoordGeneration for any graphical object. Figure 9 shows how this is done and the results obtained. The code segment is straightforward and the most crucial lines are from lines 9 to 11, where a TexCoordGeneration object is created for reference by the appearance bundle.

The first argument, TexCoordGeneration.OBJECT_LINEAR, in line 9 dictates the use of an object based linear projection technique in the generation process. Another linear projection method that can be selected is EYE_LINEAR, and the results for both methods are shown. Under OBJECT_LINEAR, the texture supplied will rotate with the object, whereas under the other mode, the texture will not rotate with the geometry and will appear more stationary.

For applications where the visual object is spherical in nature and the texture image is obtained from a fisheye lens, TexCoordGeneration offers yet another technique that may be useful. As illustrated in Figure 10, this can be selected by specifying SPHERE_MAP for sphere mapping. Clearly, under this mode, a visual effect that the object is reflecting its surrounding can be obtained.

Figure 8. Code segment and result for Myearth.java

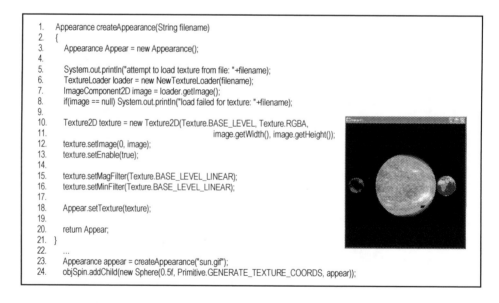

```
1.    Appearance createAppearance(String filename)
2.    {
3.        Appearance Appear = new Appearance();
4.
5.        System.out.println("attempt to load texture from file: "+filename);
6.        TextureLoader loader = new NewTextureLoader(filename);
7.        ImageComponent2D image = loader.getImage();
8.        if(image == null) System.out.println("load failed for texture: "+filename);
9.
10.       Texture2D texture = new Texture2D(Texture.BASE_LEVEL, Texture.RGBA,
11.                                    image.getWidth(), image.getHeight());
12.       texture.setImage(0, image);
13.       texture.setEnable(true);
14.
15.       texture.setMagFilter(Texture.BASE_LEVEL_LINEAR);
16.       texture.setMinFilter(Texture.BASE_LEVEL_LINEAR);
17.
18.       Appear.setTexture(texture);
19.
20.       return Appear;
21.   }
22.       ...
23.       Appearance appear = createAppearance("sun.gif");
24.       objSpin.addChild(new Sphere(0.5f, Primitive.GENERATE_TEXTURE_COORDS, appear));
```

Figure 9. Code segment and result for TexCoordGenApp.java

```
1.      Appearance createAppearance(){
2.
3.      Appearance Appear = new Appearance();
4.
5.      PolygonAttributes polyAttrib = new PolygonAttributes();
6.      polyAttrib.setCullFace(PolygonAttributes.CULL_NONE);
7.      Appear.setPolygonAttributes(polyAttrib);
8.
9.      TexCoordGeneration tcg = new TexCoordGeneration(TexCoordGeneration.OBJECT_LINEAR,
10.             TexCoordGeneration.TEXTURE_COORDINATE_2);
11.     Appear.setTexCoordGeneration(tcg);
12.
13.     String filename = "deck3.jpg";
14.     System.out.println("attempt to load texture from file: "+filename);
15.     TextureLoader loader = new TextureLoader(filename, this);
16.     ImageComponent2D image = loader.getImage();
17.     if(image == null) System.out.println("load failed for texture: "+filename);
18.
19.     Texture2D texture = new Texture2D(Texture.BASE_LEVEL, Texture.RGBA,
20.             image.getWidth(), image.getHeight());
21.     texture.setImage(0, image);
22.     texture.setEnable(true);
23.
24.     Appear.setTexture(texture);
25.
26.     return Appear; }
```

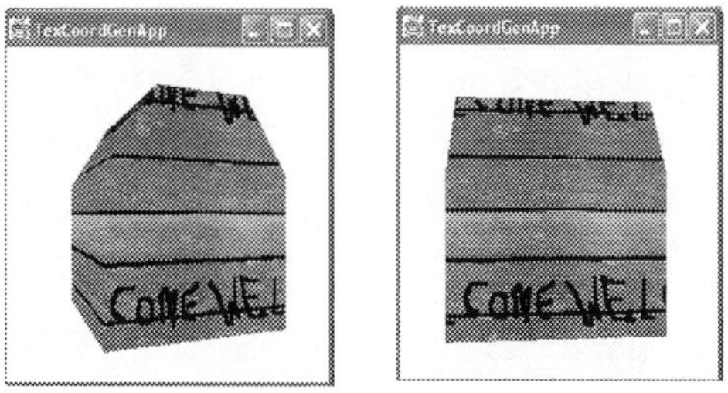

OBJECT_LINEAR   EYE_LINEAR

Figure 10. Code segment and result for SphereMap.java

```
1.   Appearance createAppearance()
2.   {
3.     TexCoordGeneration tcg = new TexCoordGeneration(TexCoordGeneration.SPHERE_MAP,
4.             TexCoordGeneration.TEXTURE_COORDINATE_3);
5.     Appear.setTexCoordGeneration(tcg);
6.
7.     String filename = "fisheye.jpg";
8.     System.out.println("attempt to load texture from file: "+filename);
9.     TextureLoader loader = new TextureLoader(filename, this);
10.  }
```

MULTILEVEL TEXTURING

The use of multiple levels of texture may lead to better rendering performance and give a more pleasant textured object in the 3D world as the distance between the object and the viewer is changed. Usually, this is done by loading a series of texture images at different resolutions and selecting the most appropriate one that match the size of the visual object on the screen. The latter will of course change depending on how far the viewer is from the object or as the user navigate through the virtual universe.

Using multilevel texturing is thus the same as using a DistanceLOD object. However, with the former, the visual object will be textured, whereas with the latter, the object may become untextured at certain distance.

Figure 11 shows an example of using multilevel texturing, activated with using the argument Texture.MULTI_LEVEL_MIPMAP for MIPmap in line 12. Under this mode, the series of texture images have sizes that decrease by a factor of 2 or areas that reduce by a factor of 4 for adjacent images, with the smallest size being 1x1.

In this example, the base level or level 0 of the image series is given by color256.gif, the minification filter is set to MULTI_LEVEL_POINT, and there are a total of 9 texture levels, each loaded individually. Note, also, that the example does not correspond to the normal usage of MIPmap, as each texture image actually corresponds to using a different color instead of having a realistic texture image at different resolution. However, as illustrated from the results obtained, this is for the purpose of illustrating how MIPmap works.

MultiTexture

With Multitexturing, different textures can be applied to a geometrical object, or more strictly to an appearance object, in a selective or combinational manner to create interesting visual effects (Engel, Hastreiter, Tomandl, Eberhardt, & Ertl, 2000). When we have only one texture, the appearance object will reference Texture, TextureAttributes and Texture-CoordGeneration directly. However, when there is more than one texture, the appearance object will reference these three texturing objects indirectly through a TextureUnitState object instead. This blending mechanism is illustrated in Figure 12.

From a programming point of view, all the TextureUnitStates can be grouped together to form a TextureUnitState array for passing to the appearance object. Note that the texture coordinates, which can be automatically generated as discussed in previous sections using TexCoordGeneration, for each texture may be different and must be explicitly specified.

Figures 13 and 14 give an example of using two textures, deck.jpg and lightmap.jpg, for a quadratic array object, in lines 9 and 10. The argument 1 in line 10 signifies that there will be only one set of texture coordinates, set 0. The next argument setmap is a 2-element

Figure 11. Code segment and result for MultiLevel.java

```
1.    Appearance createAppearance() {
2.        int imageWidth, imageHeight, imageLevel;  final int SMALLEST = 1;
3.        String filename = "color256.gif";  System.out.println("loading image: "+filename);
4.
5.        Appearance appear = new Appearance();
6.        System.out.println("loading image: "+filename);
7.        TextureLoader loader = new TextureLoader(filename, this);
8.        ImageComponent2D image = loader.getImage();
9.        if(image == null) System.out.println("load failed for texture: "+filename);
10.
11.       imageWidth = image.getWidth();  imageHeight = image.getHeight();
12.       Texture2D texture = new Texture2D(Texture.MULTI_LEVEL_MIPMAP, Texture.RGBA,
13.                  imageWidth, imageHeight);
14.
15.       imageLevel = 0;
16.       System.out.println("set image level: "+imageLevel+"  width: "+imageWidth+"  height:"+imageHeight);
17.       texture.setImage(imageLevel, image);
18.
19.       while (imageWidth > SMALLEST || imageHeight > SMALLEST) {
20.                  imageLevel++;
21.                  if (imageWidth > SMALLEST) imageWidth /= 2;
22.                  if (imageHeight > SMALLEST) imageHeight /= 2;
23.                  System.out.print("load image level: "+imageLevel+"  width: "+imageWidth
24.                             +"  height: "+imageHeight+" :: ");
25.                  filename = "color"+imageWidth+".gif";  System.out.print(filename + " ... ");
26.                  loader = new TextureLoader(filename, this);
27.                  image = loader.getImage();  System.out.println("set image");
28.                  texture.setImage(imageLevel, image); }
29.
30.       texture.setMagFilter(Texture.MULTI_LEVEL_POINT);
31.       texture.setMinFilter(Texture.MULTI_LEVEL_POINT);
32.
33.       appear.setTexture(texture);
34.       return appear; }
```

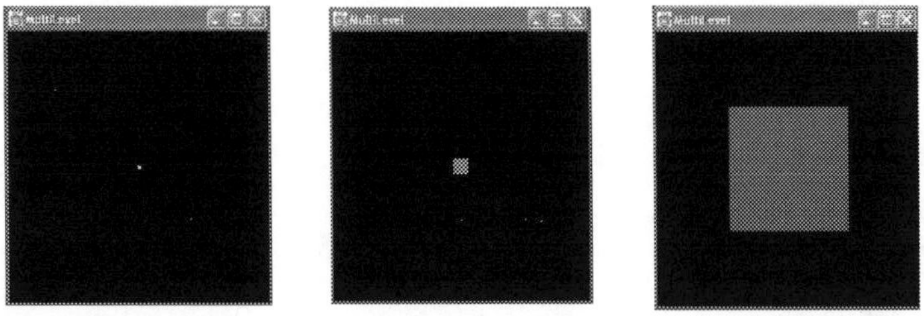

Very far   Far   Near

Figure 12. Multitexturing

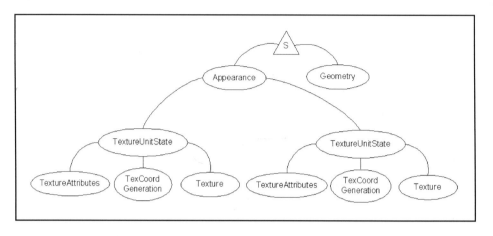

Figure 13. First code segment and result for Multitexture.java

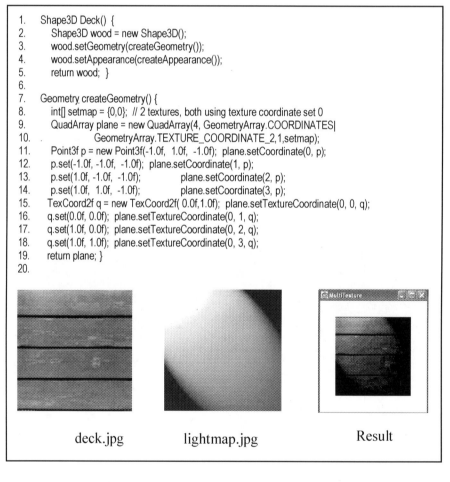

```
1.    Shape3D Deck() {
2.       Shape3D wood = new Shape3D();
3.       wood.setGeometry(createGeometry());
4.       wood.setAppearance(createAppearance());
5.       return wood;  }
6.
7.    Geometry createGeometry() {
8.       int[] setmap = {0,0};  // 2 textures, both using texture coordinate set 0
9.       QuadArray plane = new QuadArray(4, GeometryArray.COORDINATES|
10.                 GeometryArray.TEXTURE_COORDINATE_2,1,setmap);
11.      Point3f p = new Point3f(-1.0f,  1.0f,  -1.0f);  plane.setCoordinate(0, p);
12.      p.set(-1.0f, -1.0f,  -1.0f);  plane.setCoordinate(1, p);
13.      p.set(1.0f, -1.0f,  -1.0f);        plane.setCoordinate(2, p);
14.      p.set(1.0f,  1.0f, -1.0f);         plane.setCoordinate(3, p);
15.      TexCoord2f q = new TexCoord2f( 0.0f,1.0f);  plane.setTextureCoordinate(0, 0, q);
16.      q.set(0.0f, 0.0f);  plane.setTextureCoordinate(0, 1, q);
17.      q.set(1.0f, 0.0f);  plane.setTextureCoordinate(0, 2, q);
18.      q.set(1.0f, 1.0f);  plane.setTextureCoordinate(0, 3, q);
19.      return plane;  }
20.
```

deck.jpg   lightmap.jpg   Result

Figure 14. Second code segment for Multitexture.java

```
21.  Appearance createAppearance() {
22.      Appearance Appear = new Appearance();
23.
24.      TextureUnitState[] array = new TextureUnitState[2];
25.      TexCoordGeneration tcg = new TexCoordGeneration();
26.      tcg.setEnable(false);  // use the texture coordinates set above
27.
28.      String filename = "lightmap.jpg";  System.out.println("attempt to load texture from file: "+filename);
29.      TextureLoader loader = new TextureLoader(filename, this);
30.      ImageComponent2D image = loader.getImage();
31.      if(image == null) System.out.println("load failed for texture: "+filename);
32.      Texture2D texture = new Texture2D(Texture.BASE_LEVEL, Texture.RGBA,
33.              image.getWidth(), image.getHeight());
34.      texture.setImage(0, image);  texture.setEnable(true);
35.
36.      String filename2 = "deck.jpg";  System.out.println("attempt to load texture from file: "+filename2);
37.      TextureLoader loader2 = new TextureLoader(filename2, this);
38.      ImageComponent2D image2 = loader2.getImage();
39.      if(image2 == null) System.out.println("load failed for texture: "+filename2);
40.      Texture2D texture2 = new Texture2D(Texture.BASE_LEVEL, Texture.RGBA,
41.              image2.getWidth(), image2.getHeight());
42.      texture2.setImage(0, image2);  texture2.setEnable(true);
43.
44.      TextureAttributes ta = new TextureAttributes();  ta.setTextureMode(TextureAttributes.MODULATE);
45.
46.      TextureUnitState first = new TextureUnitState(texture,ta,tcg);
47.      first.setCapability(TextureUnitState.ALLOW_STATE_WRITE);  array[0]=first;
48.
49.      TextureUnitState second = new TextureUnitState(texture2,ta,tcg);
50.      second.setCapability(TextureUnitState.ALLOW_STATE_WRITE);  array[1]=second;
51.
52.      PolygonAttributes polyAttrib = new PolygonAttributes();
53.      polyAttrib.setCullFace(PolygonAttributes.CULL_NONE);
54.      Appear.setPolygonAttributes(polyAttrib);
55.
56.      Appear.setTextureUnitState(array);
57.      return Appear; }
```

integer array with both elements initialized to 0. This means that there will be 2 textures for the geometry, both using texture coordinate set 0. Basically, the elements of setmap are associated with corresponding elements in the TextureUnitState array instantiated in line 24.

Line 25 creates a new TexCoordGeneration object. The automatic generation of texture coordinates is however disabled in line 26. Instead, coordinates specified explicitly in lines 15 to 18 will be used. Another thing to note is the specification of MODULATE instead of the default REPLACE texture mode in line 44. Without this, the result will contain only one instead of the combined texture as shown.

TEXTURE IN APPLETS

There are some slight differences in using texture in applets and in applications. As illustrated in Figure 15, one difference is on how the location of the texture image can be specified. The first part of Figure 15 shows the usual loading procedure in applications, while the second part shows the corresponding one in applets.

Specifically, note the use of the method getCodeBase() in line 3 in the second code segment of Figure 15. Belonging to an applet class, this method will return the URL under which the current code can be found. The name of the texture file as well as other necessary path of the folder information from which the texture can be retrieved is appended to this URL. Essentially, in applets, the complete URL must be specified in order for the browser to locate the image file. On the other hand, loading image files in applications usually requires the name of the files to be specified because the default is that they reside in the same directory as the code segment.

While the loading of the image file in applets in Figure 15 is performed by finding out the URL of the current applet, we can of course also specify the URL directly if it is fixed and will not changed. Thus, we can also use, for example, go = new java.net.URL(http://vlab.ee.nus.edu.sg/vlab/earth.jpg).

Figure 15. Loading texture image in Java 3D and applets

```
1.  TextureLoader Loader = new Texture Loader("picture1.gif", this);
2.  ImageComponent2D image = loader.getImage();
3.  Texture2D texture = new Texture2D();
4.  texture.setImage(0,image);
5.  Appearance appear = new Appearance();
6.  appear.setTexture(texture);

1.  java.net.URL go =null;
2.  Texture texture =null;
3.  try { go= new java.net.URL(getCodeBase().toString()+"images/earth.jpg"); }
4.  catch (java.net.MalformedURLException ex) {
5.    System.out.println(ex.getMessage());
6.    System.exit(1); }
7.  texture = new TextureLoader(go, this).getTexture();
8.  Appearance appear = new Appearance();
9.  appear.setTexture(texture);
```

Apart from this difference, there are also other minor differences between programming for applets and applications. For example, the method init is used instead of the constructor in applets. Further information on this issue can be found from the Java Applet API documentation at http://java.sun.com/products/jdk/1.2/docs/api/java/applet/Applet.html and http://mercury.tvu.ac.uk/oop/oop_11.html. Figures 16 and 17 present an example code segment for an applet. Note the use of the method Load starting from line 29, and the fact that java.net.* has to be imported for using the URL class. Lastly, the code segment should be run as an index.html file in the context of a browser.

Figure 16. First code segment for Myearth_applet.java

```
1.    import java.applet.Applet;  import java.awt.BorderLayout;  import java.awt.Frame;
2.    import java.awt.event.*;  import java.awt.GraphicsConfiguration;
3.    import com.sun.j3d.utils.applet.MainFrame;  import com.sun.j3d.utils.universe.*;
4.    import com.sun.j3d.utils.image.TextureLoader;  import com.sun.j3d.utils.geometry.*;
5.    import javax.media.j3d.*;  import java.net.*;
6.
7.    public class Myearth_applet extends Applet {
8.        private java.net.URL go = null;
9.        private Texture texture = null;
10.       private SimpleUniverse simpleU= null;
11.
12.       public void init() { // initialize applet, equivalent to constructor in application
13.               setLayout(new BorderLayout());
14.               GraphicsConfiguration config = SimpleUniverse.getPreferredConfiguration();
15.               Canvas3D canvas3D = new Canvas3D(config);
16.               add("Center", canvas3D);  canvas3D.setStereoEnable(false);
17.               BranchGroup scene = createSceneGraph();
18.               simpleU = new SimpleUniverse(canvas3D);
19.               simpleU.getViewingPlatform().setNominalViewingTransform();
20.               simpleU.addBranchGraph(scene); }
21.
22.       public void destroy() { simpleU.removeAllLocales(); }
23.
24.       Appearance createAppearance() {
25.               Appearance Appear = new Appearance();
26.               Appear.setTexture(Load());
27.               return Appear; }
28.
29.       public Texture Load() {  // load texture
30.               try go= new java.net.URL(getCodeBase().toString()+"earth.jpg");
31.               catch (java.net.MalformedURLException ex) {
32.                       System.out.println(ex.getMessage());
33.                       System.exit(1); }
34.               texture = new TextureLoader(go, this).getTexture();
35.               return texture; }
36.
```

Figure 17. Second code segment for Myearth_applet.java

```
37.    public BranchGroup createSceneGraph() {
38.            BranchGroup contentRoot = new BranchGroup();
39.            TransformGroup objSpin = new TransformGroup();
40.            objSpin.setCapability(TransformGroup.ALLOW_TRANSFORM_WRITE);
41.            contentRoot.addChild(objSpin);
42.            Alpha rotationAlpha = new Alpha(-1, 16000);
43.            RotationInterpolator rotator = new RotationInterpolator(rotationAlpha, objSpin);
44.            BoundingSphere bounds = new BoundingSphere();
45.            rotator.setSchedulingBounds(bounds);
46.            objSpin.addChild(rotator);
47.            Appearance appear = createAppearance();  // create earth object
48.            objSpin.addChild(new Sphere(0.5f, Primitive.GENERATE_TEXTURE_COORDS, appear));
49.            contentRoot.compile();
50.            return contentRoot; }
51.
52.    public static void main(String[] args) { new MainFrame(new Myearth_applet(), 1024, 600); }
53.    }
```

SUMMARY

The use of texturing is relatively straightforward and effective for adding color and realistic details to the surface of a visual object. Texture objects are referenced by appearance objects, and have a variety of parameters that can be adapted to suit different needs through the Texture and TextureAttributes classes. The mapping of a texture image to a surface can be performed manually by using setTextureCoordinate to set texture coordinates. It can also be automatically carried out through the TexCoordGeneration class. The application of multiple textures to a surface can give a very realistic visual effect on the visual objects created in the virtual universe.

REFERENCES

Bouvier, D. J. (2006). Getting started with the Java 3D API, Sun Microsystems. Retrieved from http://java.sun.com/products/java-media/3D/collateral/j3d_tutorial_ch7.pdf

Engel, K., Hastreiter, P., Tomandl, B., Eberhardt, K., & Ertl, T. (2000). Combining local and remote visualization techniques for interactive volume rendering in medical applications. *Proceedings IEEE Conference on Visualization* (pp. 449-452).

Meyer, J. (2006). 3D volume modeling, feature identification and rendering of a human skull. *Proceedings IASTED International Conference on Modelling, Identification, and Control* (pp. 212-218).

Seamless textures pack. (2006). http://textures.forrest.cz/.

Chapter VI
Lighting, Fog, and Background

INTRODUCTION

How the properties of virtual 3D objects can be specified and defined has been discussed in earlier chapters. However, how a certain virtual object will appear to the user will in general depends also on human visual impression and perception, which depends to a large extent on the lighting used in illumination. As an example, watching a movie in a dark theatre and under direct sunlight will give rise to different feeling and immersion even though the scenes are the same.

Thus, in addition to defining the skeleton of a virtual object by using geometry objects in Java 3D in Chapter III, setting the appearance attributes in Chapter IV and applying texture in Chapter V to give a realistic skin to the virtual object, appropriate environmental concerns such as light, background and even fog are often necessary to make the virtual object appear as realistic to the user as possible. In this chapter, we will discuss topics related to the latter environmental issues.

The use of proper lighting is thus crucial to ensure that the 3D universe created is realistic in feeling and adds to strong emotional impressions in any application. For this purpose, Java 3D has a variety of light sources that can be selected and tailored to different scenarios.

Technically, light rays are not rendered. In fact, their effects will only become visible once they hit an object and reflect to the viewer. Of course, as with any object in the real world, the reflection depends on the material attributes of the objects.

In this chapter, we will discuss the use of different types of light source and their effects after describing the lighting properties or materials of visual objects. We will then outline the use of fogging techniques to turn a hard and straight computer image into a more realistic and smoother scene before discussing methods for immersing active visual objects in a background.

MATERIAL

The use of the material class has been discussed in Chapter III on appearance. Basically, four components, ambient, emissive, diffuse, specular and shininess, are involved in specifying a material.

Emissive corresponds to the color of the material that will be emitted, and is independent of other external light color and intensity. Ambient is associated with reflection from ambient light sources, specular and shininess are associated with highlight and strong reflections, while diffuse corresponds to normal reflection from diffused sources. Figure 1 gives a summary on how the various material components can be specified.

Note, however, that the material appearance of an object under various light sources will be properly seen only after setting the normal of the object properly. This is because the reflection of light is with respect to the normal direction, and changing the normal direction will affect the direction of the reflected lights.

Figure 2 illustrates the concepts of face normal and vertex normal, using a pyramid as an example. For the triangular face formed with vertices 1, 2, and 3 or points A, B, and C, the face normal will be the cross product of the vectors AC and AB. On the other hand, the vertex normal is the sum of all the normals of the faces that intercept to form the vertex.

The setting of the normal of faces can be carried out manually or automatically using com.sun.j3d.utils.geometry.GeometryInfo and com.sun.j3d.utils.geometry.NormalGenerator. This is illustrated in the examples in Figure 3.

Figure 1. Specifying material

```
Material material = new Material();
// create default material

Material material = new Material(Color3f ambient_colour, Color3f emissive_color,
        Color3f diffuse_color, Color3f specular_colour, float shinness);
// create material with specific lighting properties

Appearance appearance = new Appearance();
Appearance.setMaterial(material);
```

Figure 2. Face normal and vertex normal

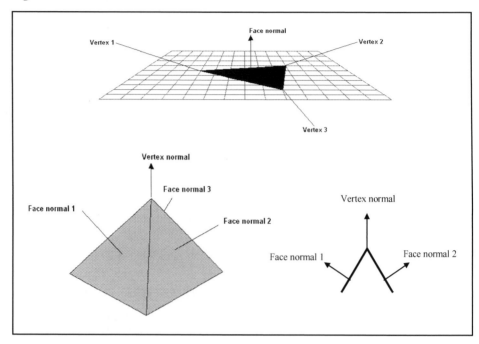

Figure 3. Setting the normal manually and automatically

```
1.    private Geometry plane() {
2.       TriangleFanArray tfa;
3.       int strip[] = {4};
4.       Point3f co[] = new Point3f[4];
5.       Color3f col[] = new Color3f[4];
6.       Vector3f v[] = new Vector3f[4];
7.       for (int i = 0; i<=3; i++) {
8.              col[i] = blue;
                v[i] = new Vector3f( 0f, 1f, 0f); } // all normal of z plane are the same
9.       co[0]=new Point3f(0f,0f,0f);
10.      co[1]=new Point3f(x,y,z);
11.      co[2]=new Point3f(x,y1,z);
12.      co[3]=new Point3f(x,y1,z1);
13.      tfa=new TriangleFanArray(4,TriangleFanArray.COORDINATES|TriangleFanArray.COLOR_3|
14.              TriangleFanArray. NORMALS,strip);
15.      tfa.setCoordinates(0,co);
16.      tfa.setColors(0,col);
17.      tfa.setNormals(0,v);
18.      return tfa; }

1.    private Geometry getnormal(Geometry g) {
2.       GeometryInfo gi = new GeometryInfo(g);
3.       NormalGenerator ng = new NormalGenerator();
4.       ng.generateNormals(gi);
5.       return gi.getGeometryArray(); }
```

Figure 4. Baising of normal

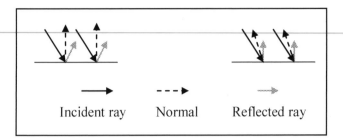

Incident ray   Normal   Reflected ray

To achieve special effects such as bumping, the normal can be set manually so that it becomes slanted as shown in Figure 4. As illustrated, the direction of the reflected ray will be changed correspondingly, leading to interesting visual effects.

AMBIENT LIGHT

Java 3D provides a variety of lights that can be controlled through parameters such as their influence boundaries, on and off states, and scopes (Lighting and textures, 2006). The on and off state of a light can be changed by using Lit.setEnable(boolean), while the scope of a light corresponds to the objects that will be affected by the light. By default, all objects in the scene will be affected. Figures 5 and 6 show an example code segment that can be used to illustrate the effects of having different types of light.

The purpose of ambient light is to fill the whole space with a light having uniform intensity from all directions. Its primary use is to provide background lighting for the whole environment. The presence of ambient light will enable every visual object to give at least a minimal amount of reflection.

In the example in Figure 6, an ambient light is created using AmbientLight(Color3f (0.5f, 0.5f, 0.5f)) which will give a weak white light. Changing the color of this light during run time is possible if the appropriate capabilities are set using lit.SetCapability(ALLOW_COLOR_READ) and lit.setCapability(ALLOW_COLOR_WRITE). Specifically, with these set, AmbientLight(Color3f (0f, 0f, 1f)) will give a blue ambient light.

The effect of having a weak white and a strong blue ambient light in the example of Figures 5 and 6 is compared in Figure 7. Obviously, the background planes take on the color of the ambient light, while the sphere has the same green color for both ambient lights. This is because the sphere is set to have a material with black ambient, black diffuse, white specular and green emissive colors. Thus, while there is no ambient reflection,

Figure 5. First code segment for J3d.java

```
1.    public BranchGroup createscenegraph() {
2.      // background object
3.      shape s = new shape();
4.      BranchGroup root = new BranchGroup();
5.      Transform3D rotation = new Transform3D();  Transform3D translation = new Transform3D();
6.      translation.set(new Vector3d( 0.0,-0.3, 0.0));  rotation.rotY(Math.PI/-4.0);  translation.mul(rotation);
7.      TransformGroup platform=new TransformGroup(translation);
8.      System.out.println("Enter the number of planes");
9.      BufferedReader in = new BufferedReader(new InputStreamReader(System.in));
10.     try { String userInput = in.readLine(); int res = Integer.parseInt(userInput); }
11.     catch (IOException ioe) { System.out.println("IO error trying to read input!"); System.exit(1); }
12.     platform.addChild(s.plane(5f,res));  root.addChild(platform);
13.
14.     // create a sphere
15.     Transform3D sphereposition= new Transform3D();
16.     TransformGroup sphere1 = new TransformGroup(sphereposition);
17.     TransformGroup sphere2 = new TransformGroup(sphereposition);
18.     Primitive shape = new Sphere(0.1f);
19.     Shape3D sphere = shape.getShape(1);
20.     Appearance appearance = new Appearance();
21.     Material material =new Material(s.black,s.green,s.black,s.white,100f);
22.     appearance.setMaterial(material);
23.     shape.setAppearance(appearance);
24.
```

the sphere does emit a green color and this emission dominates what is being seen at the position of the sphere.

DIRECTIONAL LIGHT

As its name suggests, directional light corresponds to light arriving from a certain direction in a uniform plane wave front (Lighting up the world, 2006). The intensity of the light is uniform, and it is usually used to simulate sky light or light from a distant source.

Line 35 in Figure 6 gives an example for creating a directional light. The first argument in the constructor DirectionalLight() corresponds to the color of the light, while the second argument specifies the direction of arrival of the rays. The capabilities, directionallght. setCapability(DirectionalLight.ALLOW_DIRECTION_WRITE) and directionallght. setCapability(DirectionalLight.ALLOW_DIRECTION_READ), must also be set if the

Figure 6. Second code segment for J3d.java

```
25.      System.out.println("1-Directional light");
26.      System.out.println("2-Point light");
27.      System.out.println("3-Spot light");
28.      System.out.println("other-Ambient light");
29.      in = new BufferedReader(new InputStreamReader(System.in));
30.      try { String userInput = in.readLine(); light=Integer.parseInt(userInput); }
31.    catch (IOException ioe) { System.out.println("IO error trying to read input!"); System.exit(1); }
32.
33.      // create light source at the origin
34.      lit = new AmbientLight(new Color3f( 0.5f, 0.5f, 0.5f));
35.      if (light==1){ lit = new DirectionalLight(new Color3f( 0.5f, 1.0f, 0.5f), new Vector3f( 0.2f,-0.5f,-1.0f));}
36.      if (light==2){ lit = new PointLight(new Color3f(1,1,1), new Point3f(0,0,0), new Point3f(1,1,0));}
37.      if (light==3){ lit = new SpotLight(new Color3f(1f,1f,1f), new Point3f(0.0f,0.0f,0.0f),
38.              new Point3f(1.0f,1.0f,0.0f), new Vector3f(0.0f,0.0f,1.0f), (float)(Math.PI/2.0f),0f);}
39.      lit.setInfluencingBounds(new BoundingSphere());
40.
41.      // make the light source move around the box
42.      Alpha alpha = new Alpha(-1,5000);
43.      Transform3D y = new Transform3D();
44.      float knots[] = {0.0f , 0.5f , 1.0f};
45.      Point3f pts[] = { new Point3f(-2f,0f, 2f), new Point3f( 2f,0f, 2f), new Point3f(-2f,0f, 2f)};
46.      PositionPathInterpolator posinterpolator = new PositionPathInterpolator(alpha,sphere1,y,knots,pts);
47.      RotationInterpolator rotinterpolator = new RotationInterpolator(alpha,sphere2);
48.      posinterpolator.setSchedulingBounds(new BoundingSphere());
49.      rotinterpolator.setSchedulingBounds(new BoundingSphere());
50.      sphere2.addChild(rotinterpolator);
51.      sphere1.addChild(posinterpolator);
52.      sphere2.addChild(shape);
53.      sphere2.addChild(lit);
54.      sphere1.addChild(sphere2);
55.      sphere1.setCapability(TransformGroup.ALLOW_TRANSFORM_WRITE);
56.      sphere2.setCapability(TransformGroup.ALLOW_TRANSFORM_WRITE);
57.      root.addChild(sphere1);
58.      return root;
59.  }
```

direction of the light is to be changed during run time. Also, care must be taken to ensure that the vertex and face normal of the objects being illuminated correctly has been properly set up, else biasing of the reflections may take place.

Figure 8 shows the result obtained from the code segment of Figures 5 and 6 when a directional light is selected. Comparing with the results in Figure 7 for ambient light, the directional characteristics of the light can be easily seen. Specifically, rather than the entire object, only the appropriate sides of the plane polygons have been lightened up.

Figure 7. Results from using weak white and strong blue ambient light

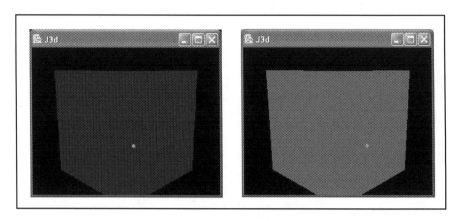

Figure 8. Result from using directional light

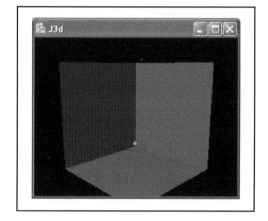

POINT LIGHT

Directional light gives rise to a uniform and planar light wave front from a certain direction and is useful for simulating the effects of distant sources. Point light, on the other hand, allows for the simulation of point light source placed anywhere in the scene. It is thus useful to produce the effects of light bulbs and candles that exist as nearby objects in the 3D world.

Figure 9. Point light and result

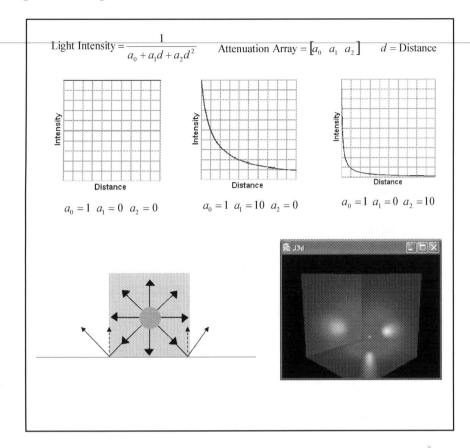

As illustrated in Figure 9, rays from a point source are emitted at all direction from the source. Line 36 in Figure 6 gives an example for creating a point light source by using the constructor PointLight(). The first argument in this constructor gives the light color emitted, the second gives the position of the source, while the last argument is a float array with three attenuation constants that will be used to calculate how the light will be attenuated as it propagates from the source.

Figure 9 also shows the equation for giving the light intensity as a function of distance as well as the results for three different sets of attenuation constants. The figure also shows the result obtained in the example of Figures 5 and 6. Again, note that reflections will be based on vertex and face normal, and the appropriate capabilities must be set if it is desirable to change certain parameters of a point light when running the program.

Figure 10. Spot light and results

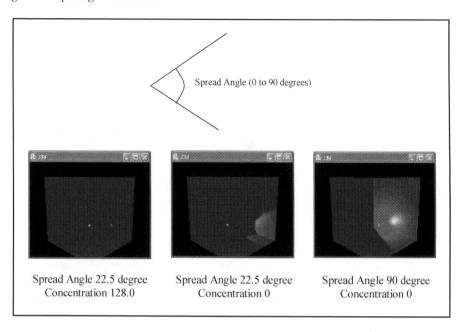

SPOT LIGHT OR CONE LIGHT

In a certain sense, spot light is a kind of point light. However, rather than emitting in all directions, the light will emitted towards a principal direction as illustrated in Figure 10. As for spot lights in the real world, using a spot or cone light enables certain objects to be highlighted.

Lines 37 and 38 in Figure 6 create an example spot light source by using SpotLight(). The first three arguments in this constructor are the same as those for point light, while the last three parameters give the direction of the light, its spread angle and its concentration. The range of the spread angle is from 0 to 0.5pi, while the concentration is from 0 to 128 for a focused and unfocused light, respectively. The effects of having different spread angle and concentration are illustrated in Figure 10.

LIGHT SCOPES

In Java 3D, the region of influence of a light source object can be controlled by setting appropriate Bounds or BoundingLeaf for the object. More exactly, this influence can be further limited by specifying a scope for the light object so that its influence is restricted to only a portion of the scene graph or to visual objects lying below an interesting group in the graph.

Figure 11 shows the code segment and result obtained from using this approach.

In this example, two crystals are illuminated by two spotlights and each spot light has a light scope given by lines 30 and 35 such that only the respective crystal will be illumi-

Figure 11. Code segment and result for LightAttenApp.java

```
1.     public LightAttenApp extends Applet {
2.         public BranchGroup createSceneGraph(){
3.         BranchGroup objRoot = new BranchGroup();
4.             TransformGroup objPath = new TransformGroup();
5.             objPath.setCapability(TransformGroup.ALLOW_TRANSFORM_WRITE);
6.             objRoot.addChild(objPath);
7.
8.             Transform3D trans1 = new Transform3D();  // move crystal to left
9.             trans1.setTranslation(new Vector3f(-0.3f, 0.0f, 0.0f));
10.            TransformGroup light1G = new TransformGroup(trans1);
11.            light1G.addChild(new Crystal());  objPath.addChild(light1G);
12.            Transform3D trans2 = new Transform3D();  // move crystal to right
13.            trans2.setTranslation(new Vector3f(0.3f, 0.0f, 0.0f));
14.            TransformGroup light2G = new TransformGroup(trans2);
15.            light2G.addChild(new Crystal());  objPath.addChild(light2G);
16.
17.            Alpha pathAlpha = new Alpha(-1, Alpha.INCREASING_ENABLE
18.                |Alpha.DECREASING_ENABLE, 0, 0, 2500, 0, 0, 2500, 0, 0);
19.            Transform3D pathAxis = new Transform3D();
20.            pathAxis.rotY(Math.PI/2.0f);
21.            PositionInterpolator path = new PositionInterpolator(pathAlpha, objPath, pathAxis, 0.8f, -0.8f);
22.            BoundingSphere bounds = new BoundingSphere(new Point3d(0.0,0.0,0.0), 100.0);
23.            path.setSchedulingBounds(bounds);  objPath.addChild(path);
24.            Vector3f lightDirectionA = new Vector3f(-1.0f, 0.0f, -1.0f);  lightDirectionA.normalize();
25.
26.            SpotLight lightS1 = new SpotLight();  // add spot light 1
27.            lightS1.setPosition(-0.3f, 0.0f, 1.2f);  lightS1.setAttenuation(0.0f, 0.0f, 3.0f);
28.            lightS1.setConcentration(100.0f);  lightS1.setSpreadAngle((float)Math.PI/5.0f);
29.            lightS1.setInfluencingBounds(new BoundingSphere(new Point3d(0.0,0.0,0.0), 5.0));
30.            lightS1.addScope(light1G);  objRoot.addChild(lightS1);
31.            SpotLight lightS2 = new SpotLight();  // add spot light 2
32.            lightS2.setPosition(0.3f, 0.0f, 1.2f);  lightS2.setAttenuation(0.0f, 3.0f, 0.0f);
33.            lightS2.setConcentration(100.0f);  lightS2.setSpreadAngle((float)Math.PI/5.0f);
34.            lightS2.setInfluencingBounds(new BoundingSphere(new Point3d(0.0,0.0,0.0), 5.0));
35.            lightS2.addScope(light2G);  objRoot.addChild(lightS2);
36.            DirectionalLight lightD = new DirectionalLight(new Color3f(0.5f, 0.5f, 0.5f), lightDirectionA);
37.            lightD.setInfluencingBounds(new BoundingSphere());  objRoot.addChild(lightD);
38.            AmbientLight lightA = new AmbientLight(new Color3f(1.0f, 1.0f, 1.0f));
39.            lightA.setInfluencingBounds(new BoundingSphere());  objRoot.addChild(lightA);
40.            objRoot.compile();  return objRoot;  }
```

nated. As can be seen from the result obtained, the effects of having different spread angles and concentration can be easily demonstrated by changing the appropriate parameters of the light sources.

FOG

Fog corresponds to the use of a fading effect for the purpose of enhancing realism and creating images, which are smoother and may lead to stronger emotional feelings (Brown & Petersen, 1999). This is achieved by blending the colors of visual objects with that of the fog depending on the distance of the objects from the view port. Objects, which are further away from the view port will take on a color that is closer to the fog color. With this fading in and out effects, distant objects will emerge into 3D world in a smoother manner, instead of appearing suddenly. In a certain way, the influence of atmospheric effects can be better simulated.

Figure 12. First code segment and for fogdemo.java

```
1.    public fogdemo(String title) {
2.      . . .
3.      if (getInput().equalsIgnoreCase("Y")){
4.        if (FogMode==1 || FogMode==2) {
5.          println ("Fog influencing distance"); fogdist=Double.parseDouble(getInput()); }
6.        if (FogMode==1){
7.          println("Fog Front Clip distance?"); print("?"); fogfront=Double.parseDouble(getInput());
8.          println("Fog Back Clip Distance?"); print("?"); fogback=Double.parseDouble(getInput());}
9.        if (FogMode==2){ println("Enter Fog Density"); print("?"); density=Float.parseFloat(getInput()); }
10.       println("Depth of objects to render"); print("?"); backClip=Double.parseDouble(getInput());
11.       println("The Detail of the scene"); print("?");buildings=Integer.parseInt(getInput()); }
12.     else { fogfront=0.1; fogback=400.0; fogdist=400.0; density=0.16f; backClip=400.0; }
13.     catch(Exception e) print("Error found"); println("Initializing......");
14.
15.     GraphicsConfiguration gc=SimpleUniverse.getPreferredConfiguration();
16.     Canvas3D canvas3d=new Canvas3D(gc);
17.     Rectangle rect=gc.getBounds();
18.     setSize(640,480);
19.     setLocation(rect.width/2+rect.x-320,rect.height/2+rect.y-240);
20.     SimpleUniverse simpleu=new SimpleUniverse(canvas3d);
21.     ViewPlatform vp=new ViewPlatform();
22.     TransformGroup tvg=new TransformGroup();
23.     tvg.setCapability(tvg.ALLOW_TRANSFORM_READ);
24.     tvg.setCapability(tvg.ALLOW_TRANSFORM_WRITE);
25.     tvg.addChild(vp);
26.
```

Figures 12 and 13 give the important code segment demonstrating how fog can be used in Java 3D. Specifically, after getting appropriate user inputs, a constructor for fog, which may be linear or exponential in nature, is invoked in either line 34 or 35 in Figure 13.

Linear fog uses a blending factor given by

$$f_{linear} = \frac{\text{backDistance} - \text{DistanceFromViewPort}}{\text{backDistance} - \text{frontDistance}},$$

where frontDistance is the distance at which objects will start to be obscured by the fog, and backDistance is the distance at which objects will become fully obscured. Linear fog has the advantage that it is easier to render, but the effect may however be not so natural.

Figure 13. Second code segment for fogdemo.java

```
27.    Alpha alp=new Alpha(-1,5000);  // create the animation path
28.    Transform3D zaxis=new Transform3D(); zaxis.rotZ(Math.PI/2f);
29.    float knot[]={0f,1f};  Point3f pos[]={new Point3f(0f,1.5f,0f),new Point3f(0f,1.5f,-400f)};
30.    PositionPathInterpolator ppi=new PositionPathInterpolator(alp,tvg,zaxis,knot,pos);
31.    tvg.addChild(ppi);  ppi.setSchedulingBounds(new BoundingSphere(new Point3d(),600.0));
32.
33.    Fog fogb=null;  //  create fog and its back clip distance
34.    if (FogMode==2) fogb=new ExponentialFog(0f,0f,1f,density);
35.    if (FogMode==1) fogb=new LinearFog(0f,0f,1f,fogfront,fogback);
36.    Clip clip=new Clip(backClip);
37.    clip.setApplicationBounds(new BoundingSphere(new Point3d(),backClip));
38.    tvg.addChild(clip);
39.    if (fogb!=null){
40.        fogb.setInfluencingBounds(new BoundingSphere(new Point3d(),fogdist));
41.        tvg.addChild(fogb); }
42.
43.    View view=simpleu.getViewer().getView();  // modify view branch
44.    view.setBackClipDistance(300.0f);  view.setFrontClipDistance(0.1);  view.attachViewPlatform(vp);
45.    BranchGroup brg=new BranchGroup();
46.    brg.addChild(tvg);
47.
48.    BranchGroup bgs=new BranchGroup();  // create the scene graph
49.    bgs.addChild(new shape());  bgs.addChild(building(buildings));
50.    DirectionalLight lit      =new DirectionalLight(new Color3f( 0.5f, 1.0f, 0.5f),new Vector3f( -2f,-2f,0f));
51.    lit.setInfluencingBounds(new BoundingSphere(new Point3d(),1000.0));
52.    bgs.addChild(lit);
53.    lit = new DirectionalLight(new Color3f( 0.5f, 0.5f, 1.0f),new Vector3f( 2f,-2f,0f));
54.    lit.setInfluencingBounds(new BoundingSphere(new Point3d(),1000.0));
55.    bgs.addChild(lit);
56.    Background bg=new Background(new Color3f(0f,0f,1f));
57.    bgs.addChild(bg);
58.    bg.setApplicationBounds(new BoundingSphere(new Point3d(),1500.0));
59.    bgs.compile(); }
```

In line 35 in Figure 13, a linear fog object is created with the first three parameters giving the RGB color of the fog to be used, and the last two parameters giving backDistance and frontDistance.

On the other hand, the blending factor for exponential fog depends only on a density factor and is given by

$$f_{exponential} = \frac{1}{e^{(density)(DistanceFromViewPort)}}$$

Exponential fog can often give rise to a more natural result at the expense of higher rendering time. The density factor controls the amount of exponential decrease in the use of fog as we move away from the camera. Setting the density factor to zero is equivalent to not using fog at all. The higher the density factor, the less visible it will be for distant objects. A density close to one will enable the viewer to see only nearby objects, with other objects in the scene covered by the fog used. In line 34 in Figure 13, an exponential fog object is constructed with the first three parameters giving the RGB color of the fog, and the last parameter giving the density factor.

Figure 14. Results from using fog

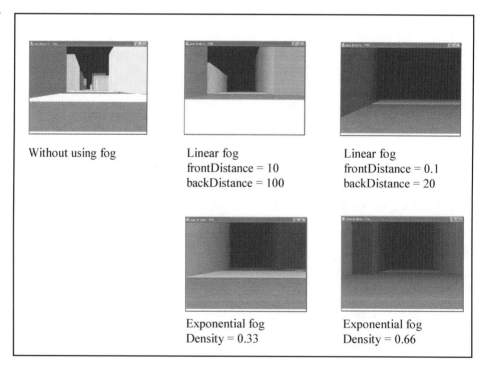

Figure 15. Using fog with influencing bound smaller than the distances to some objects

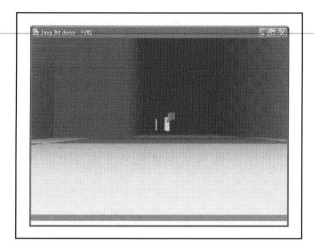

Based on the code segment of Figures 12 and 13, Figure 14 presents some results obtained using different fog settings. As can be seen, the original scene consists of a series of objects with sharp edges at different distances. The resolution is good, but the image has an artificial feeling. The use of fog reduces the resolution for distant objects, but gives rise to a smoother and more natural effect.

The influence of fog on the image rendered depends on the frontDistance and backDistance for the case of linear fog and on the density factor for the case of exponential fog. This is clearly illustrated in Figure 14.

Apart from these parameters, there are two other bounds or parameters that can determine whether objects will be influenced by the fog created. As set in lines 36 to 38 in Figure 13, the setting of a clipping bound by using Clip(clipDistance) will disable the rendering of all polygons lying beyond the clipping distance. By choosing a good clipping distance that matches the fog backDistance or effective distance that can possibly be seen by viewer, the task of rendering can be made more efficient, leading to a faster system.

In addition to the clipping bound, an influencing or activation bound for the fog can also be set. This is done in lines 39 to 41 in Figure 13 and, as illustrated in Figure 15, may produce interesting results. In this figure, the influencing bound of the fog is smaller than that needed to cover all the objects. As a result, some distant objects that fall outside the bound are rendered in the usual manner. Note that the default for the influencing bound for fog is 0 in Java 3D, corresponding to subjecting no object to the fog. Thus, in order for the effect of fog to be rendered, the influencing bound must be properly set.

BACKGROUND

In addition to using lighting and fog to enhance a virtual 3D world, the choice of a suitable background is also very important to enable interesting foreground 3D objects to stand out and be seen in the right context.

In Java 3D, a black background or window will be used if no background node is active, while generally, three types of non-trivial backgrounds may be used. Specifically, a simple constant color background, a more complicated background using a flat 2D image, or a more interesting background based on appropriate geometrical construction can be specified.

In the creation process, all these three types of background require a relevant color, image or geometry specification as well as a bounding volume that controls when and which background will be activated. Note that more than one background node may be added to the scene graph and the node, which is closest to the current one will be rendered.

Figure 16 shows the code segment and result for adding a simple constant color background node to the branch root. Note that regardless of how we navigate in the created 3D world, the background is static, dull, and has the same color.

Rather than using a simple constant color background, a slightly more complicated but more interesting background will be to use one based on an imported 2D image. Figure 17 shows how this can be done as well as the results obtained. Note that while the background is more interesting and impressive, it will not change even as we navigate around in the

Figure 16. Adding a constant color background and result

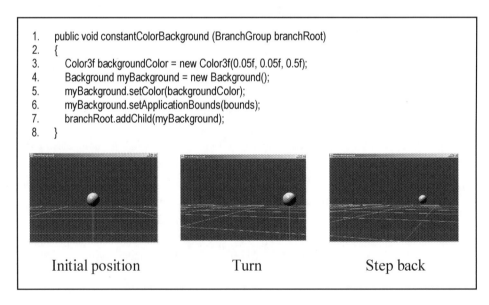

```
1.    public void constantColorBackground (BranchGroup branchRoot)
2.    {
3.       Color3f backgroundColor = new Color3f(0.05f, 0.05f, 0.5f);
4.       Background myBackground = new Background();
5.       myBackground.setColor(backgroundColor);
6.       myBackground.setApplicationBounds(bounds);
7.       branchRoot.addChild(myBackground);
8.    }
```

Initial position   Turn   Step back

Figure 17. A background based on a 2D image

```
1.    import com.sun.j3d.utils.image.*;
2.    public void flatImageBackground (BranchGroup branchRoot)
3.    {
4.        Background myBackground = new Background();
5.        myBackground.setImage(new TextureLoader("cloud.jpg", this).getImage());
6.        myBackground.setImageScaleMode(Background.SCALE_FIT_ALL);
7.                // SCALE_NONE, SCALE_FIT_MIN, SCALE_FIT_MAX, SCALE_FIT_ALL,
8.                // SCALE_REPEAT, SCALE_NONE_CENTER
9.        myBackground.setApplicationBounds(bounds);
10.       branchRoot.addChild(myBackground);
11.   }
```

| Initial position | Turn | Step back |

3D world. Also, the option SCALE_FIT_ALL has been selected so that the image will fill the entire window regardless of the display resolution of the monitor and the pixel size of the image. Other options as indicated in lines 7 and 8 are also possible. Specifically, SCALE_REPEAT will not scale the image to match the window size even though there is a mismatch in their resolutions. Instead, the image will be used in its original pixel resolution, but will be repeated in both horizontal and vertical directions to fill the entire window.

To have a more realistic background that befits a 3D environment, a relevant geometry model must be used for its construction (Creating a geometric background in Java3D, 2006). This way, as the user navigates around in the virtual 3D world, the background will change in an appropriate manner. A common geometry for creating a realistic 3D background would be that of a sphere with effectively infinite size, or size that enclose all the visual objects of interest.

Figure 18 shows an example code segment and the result obtained based on this approach. Specifically, to create a background based on spherical geometry, we need to create a background node myBackground and a branchgroup branchRoot, add the appropriate geometry to the branchgroup, use setGeometry to set the branchgroup into backgroup, set the application bound, and then add the background node to the branchroot. With this background, a better and more realistic visual effects can be obtained as the user navigates in the 3D world. In particular, while the background, at infinite distance effectively, will

Figure 18. A background based on a geometrical modeling

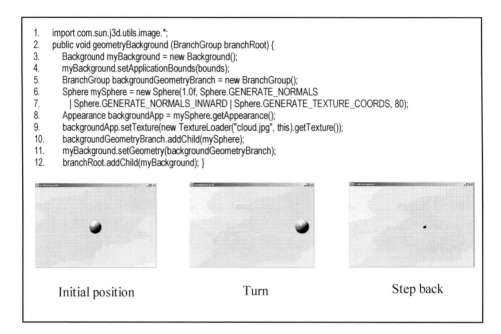

```
1.   import com.sun.j3d.utils.image.*;
2.   public void geometryBackground (BranchGroup branchRoot) {
3.       Background myBackground = new Background();
4.       myBackground.setApplicationBounds(bounds);
5.       BranchGroup backgroundGeometryBranch = new BranchGroup();
6.       Sphere mySphere = new Sphere(1.0f, Sphere.GENERATE_NORMALS
7.        | Sphere.GENERATE_NORMALS_INWARD | Sphere.GENERATE_TEXTURE_COORDS, 80);
8.       Appearance backgroundApp = mySphere.getAppearance();
9.       backgroundApp.setTexture(new TextureLoader("cloud.jpg", this).getTexture());
10.      backgroundGeometryBranch.addChild(mySphere);
11.      myBackground.setGeometry(backgroundGeometryBranch);
12.      branchRoot.addChild(myBackground); }
```

Initial position   Turn   Step back

not change if the user moves in a translational manner, it will change appropriately and realistically as the user turns.

SUMMARY

In this chapter, we have discussed some important advanced topics related to the use of lighting and other visual effects to create realistic 3D scenes with higher emotional appeal. The use of ambient, directional, point, and spot lights have been outlined. Using linear fog and exponential fog to smooth a scene and to prevent the sudden appearance of distant objects, we can enhance the emotional appearance of an artificial scene. Lastly, the use of simple color, image and geometry based backgrounds have also been illustrated.

REFERENCES

Brown, K., & Petersen, D. (1999). *Ready-to-Run Java 3D: With plug-and-play code*. Wiley & Sons.

Creating a geometric background in Java3D. (2006). http://www.java-tips.org/other-api-tips/java3d/creating-a-geometric-background-in-java3d.html.

Lighting and textures. (2006). http://www.crixler.de/meso2/ex0b.html.

Lighting up the world. (2006). http://www.java3d.org/lighting.html.

Chapter VII
Animation Objects

INTRODUCTION

We have discussed important Java 3D objects that are basically static in the last few chapters. Starting from this chapter, we will be looking at universe and objects that are dynamic in nature. Specifically, we will discuss issues on animation and interaction in this and the next chapter, respectively.

As well demonstrated by popular interactive computer games, animation, and interaction are crucial in making a Java 3D world more interesting. Technically, animation is associated with changes in graphical objects and images as time passes without any direct user action, while interaction corresponds to any such change in response to an action or input from the user (Tso, Tharp, Zhang, & Tai, 1999).

In any virtual reality or game application, animation and interaction are often crucial and critical. Through animation, the user is able to have a more realistic feel of the real 3D objects through looking at the object at different angles and perspectives. Through interaction with these objects, the user will become more integrated into the virtual 3D world in the same way as sensing our own reality in the real world.

Under Java 3D, the "behavior" class is used to define and control both animation and interaction. However, note that the behavior class is an abstract class and cannot be directly used (Stromer, Quon, Gordon, Turinsky, & Sensen, 2005). Instead, there are three classes that extend the behavior class and that are commonly used. They are the "interpolator," the "billboard," and the "level of detail (LOD)" class. Furthermore, we can create a new behavior class by extending the behavior class to fit any special need.

Briefly, in this chapter, we will discuss the important interpolator classes by using a number of illustrating examples, followed by some details discussions on the billboard and LOD classes.

BEHAVIOR AND ANIMATION

Java 3D implements animation through the use of behavior objects created under the behavior class. This is an abstract class that allows codes to be included so that the scene graph can be changed. Essentially, a behavior object in a scene graph serves to change the scene graph or some objects in the scene graph in response to some stimulus.

User actions such as pressing a key or moving the mouse correspond to stimulus associated with interaction and will be discussed in the next chapter. On the other hand, stimulus such as the passage of time, which requires no user action, is used in animation (Bund & Do, 2005; Burrows & England, 2002).

The Java 3D API provides a number of useful classes for animation, and it is in general not necessary for any new class to be created. In particular, the interpolator class can be used to create animation through the use of an interpolator and an "alpha" object, which will be discussed in the next section.

ALPHA OBJECT

Basically, an alpha object generates alpha values in the range of [0,1] when it is sampled over a period of time. The alpha values generated is for the primary use of an associated interpolator object, which will be discussed in the next section.

Depending on the parameters of the alpha object, the generated alpha value may change over time. Specifically, there are four phases in an alpha object waveform: increasing alpha, alpha at one, decreasing alpha, and alpha at zero. These four phases make up one cycle of the alpha waveform, and can be controlled by four sets of parameters of the alpha object. Also, the durations of the phases are given by an integer, which gives the duration in milliseconds.

An alpha object has the following important parameters.

- **loopCount:** The number of times that the alpha object will be run. The object will be run in an infinite loop manner if a value of –1 is given.
- **triggerTime:** The time in milliseconds after the system start time that the object will be first triggered. If the current time is equal to or more than the sum of the system start time and triggerTime, the object will be started as soon as possible.

- **phaseDelayDuration:** The time in milliseconds to wait after triggerTime before actually starting the object.
- **Mode:** May be set to INCREASING_ENABLE, DECREASING_ENABLE or the logical OR of the two values. INCREASING_ENABLE or DECREASING_ENABLE activates one of the two sets of corresponding parameters listed below.

The following parameters are associated with an alpha object in an increasing mode or when mode is set to INCREASING_ENABLE.

- **increasingAlphaDuration:** The length of time during which alpha goes from zero to one.
- **increasingAlphaRampDuration:** The length of time during which the object step size increases at the beginning of increasingAlphaDuration and, correspondingly, decreases at the end of increasingAlphaDuration. This parameter is clamped at a value equal to half of increasingAlphaDuration. When it is non-zero, constant positive acceleration at the beginning of the ramp and constant negative acceleration at the end of the ramp will result. If it is zero, the alpha value will have a constant velocity and zero acceleration, giving rise to a linearly increasing alpha ramp.
- **alphaAtOneDuration:** The length of time that alpha stays at one.

Similarly, the following parameters are associated with an alpha object in a decreasing mode or when mode is set to DECREASING_ENABLE.

- **decreasingAlphaDuration:** The length of time during which Alpha goes from one to zero.
- **decreasingAlphaRampDuration:** The length of time during which the object step size increases at the beginning of the decreasingAlphaDuration and, correspondingly, decreases at the end of the decreasingAlphaDuration. This parameter is clamped at a value equal to half of decreasingAlphaDuration. When it is non-zero, we have in effect constant positive acceleration at the beginning of the ramp and constant negative acceleration at the end of the ramp. If it is zero, the alpha value will have a constant velocity and zero acceleration, giving rise to a linearly decreasing alpha ramp.
- **alphaAtZeroDuration:** The length of time that alpha remains at zero.

INTERPOLATOR OBJECT

Interpolator is an abstract class that extends the behavior class to provide some common methods for use by associated interpolation subclasses. These include methods for initializing the behavior and for converting a time value into an alpha value.

Java 3D has provided, in the utility package, a number of interpolator classes, including ColorInterpolator, PositionInterpolator, RotationInterpolator, ScaleInterpolator, SwitchValueInterpolator, TransparencyInterpolator and PathInterpolator classes.

Technically, each interpolator is a custom behavior with a trigger for waking each frame along the time axis. Using the processStimulus method, an interpolator object will check the associated alpha object for the current alpha value, carry out some appropriate actions based on this value, and then reset its trigger to wake the next frame until the alpha is finished.

In general, an interpolator object has two values that serve to denote the end points of an interpolated action. For example, a RotationInterpolator object will have two angles that specify the entire span of the rotation. As new frame come along, the object will check the associated alpha value and make a suitable rotational adjustment to its target TransformGroup object. An alpha value of 0 will result in one of the ending angle being used, while an alpha value of 1 will lead to using the other extreme angle. On the other hand, if the alpha value is between 0 and 1, the interpolator will linearly interpolate between the two end point angles, and use the resulting interpolated angle to adjust the target object appropriately.

While most interpolator objects are for carrying out an implicit interpolation function, the SwitchValueInterpolator and PathInterpolator classes are for the purpose of branching or switching. As an example, SwitchValueInterpolator will choose one of the target nodes in a switch group based on the alpha value.

We will now give some illustrating examples on some of the important classes and discuss how they can be used in practice.

PositionInterpolator

The PositionInterpolator can be used to change the position of a visual object over time in a translational manner. An example on how this can be used is illustrated in the code segment and result in Figure 1.

In the code segment in Figure 1, a bounding sphere is defined in line 5. This specifies a "live" region, within which changes to the position of the visual object can be made. Then, an alpha object on how the position is changed is declared. Note that for smooth translation, both INCREASING_ENABLE and DECREASING_ENABLE are used.

Line 14 creates the PositionInterpolator object. The input parameters are the alpha object created earlier, the TransformGroup of the visual object, the axis of translation, and the initial and final positions. By default, the object will be translated along the x-axis. Thus, in order that the object moves along the y-axis, we need to rotate the axis of translation with respect to the z-axis. This is the purpose of declaring Transform3D in the code segment.

Figure 1. Code segment and result of DemoPositionInterpolator.java

```
1.    public BranchGroup createSceneGraph()
2.    {
3.       BranchGroup objRoot = createBranchScene();
4.
5.       BoundingSphere bound =  new BoundingSphere();
6.       Alpha alpha = new Alpha(-1, Alpha.INCREASING_ENABLE|Alpha.DECREASING_ENABLE, 0, 0,
      4000,2000,1000, 4000, 2000, 1000);
7.
8.       TransformGroup objPosition = new TransformGroup();
9.       objPosition.setCapability(TransformGroup.ALLOW_TRANSFORM_WRITE);
10.      objPosition.addChild(new Quad());
11.
12.      Transform3D axisPosition = new Transform3D();
13.      axisPosition.rotZ(Math.PI/2.0);
14.      PositionInterpolator positionInterpol = new PositionInterpolator(alpha,
      objPosition,axisPosition, 0f, 0.8f);
15.      positionInterpol.setSchedulingBounds(bound);
16.
17.      TransformGroup objTilt = new TransformGroup();
18.
19.      Transform3D tiltX = new Transform3D();
20.      Transform3D tiltY = new Transform3D();
21.      tiltX.rotX(Math.PI/5.0d);
22.      tiltY.rotY(Math.PI/5.0d);
23.      tiltX.mul(tiltY);
24.      objTilt.setTransform(tiltX);
25.
26.      objRoot.addChild(objTilt);
27.      objTilt.addChild(objPosition);
28.      objPosition.addChild(positionInterpol);
29.
30.      objRoot.compile();
31.
32.      return objRoot;
33.
34.   }
```

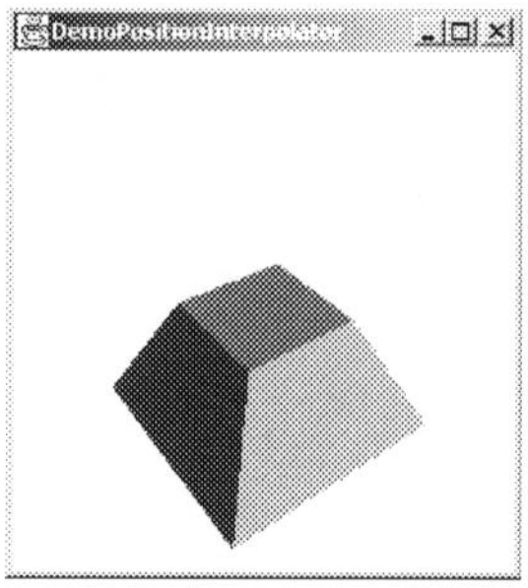

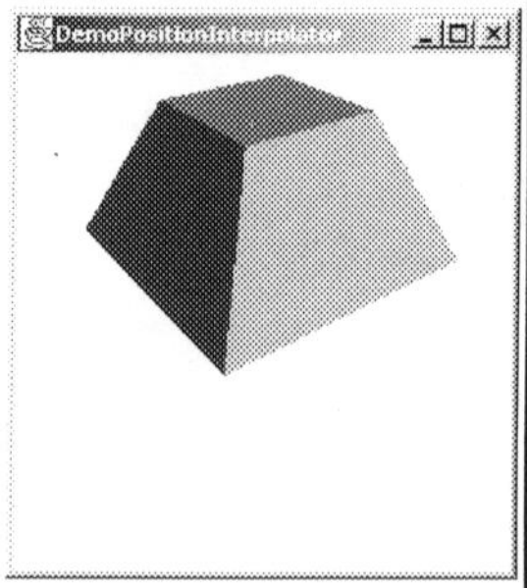

PositionPathInterpolator

The code segment and results in Figure 2 show how PositionPathInterpolator can be used together with the alpha values to change the translational position of the target Transfor-

Figure 2. Code segment and result of DemoPositionPathInterpolator.java

```
1.      public BranchGroup createSceneGraph()
2.      {
3.              BranchGroup objRoot = createBranchScene();
4.              Transform3D t3d = new Transform3D();
5.              t3d.rotY(Math.PI/4d);
6.              TransformGroup objRotate = new TransformGroup(t3d);
7.              TransformGroup objPositionPath = new TransformGroup();
8.              objRoot.addChild(objRotate);
9.              objRotate.addChild(objPositionPath);
10.             objPositionPath.addChild(new Axis().getBG());
11.             objPositionPath.setCapability(TransformGroup.ALLOW_TRANSFORM_WRITE);
12.             Point3f[] points = new Point3f[19];
13.             for (int i=0;i<18;i++) {
14.                     float x = (float) 0.5*(float)Math.sin((float)Math.PI*2*i/17);
15.                     float y = (float) 0.5*(float)Math.cos((float)Math.PI*2*i/17);
16.                     points[i] = new Point3f(x,y,0);
17.             }
18.             Points[18] = new Point3f(0f,0.5f,0f);
19.             float[] knots = new float[19];
20.             for (int i=1;i<18;i++) knots[i] = 1.0f*i/17f;
21.             knots[0] = 0f;
22.             knots[18] = 1.0f;
23.             Alpha posAlpha = new Alpha (-1, 5000);
24.             t3d.rotY(-Math.PI/4d);
25.             PositionPathInterpolator path =
26.                     new PositionPathInterpolator (posAlpha, objPositionPath, t3d, knots, points);
27.             BoundingSphere bounds = new BoundingSphere();
28.             path.setSchedulingBounds(bounds);
29.             objPositionPath.addChild(path);
30.             objRoot.compile();
31.             return objRoot;
32.     }
```

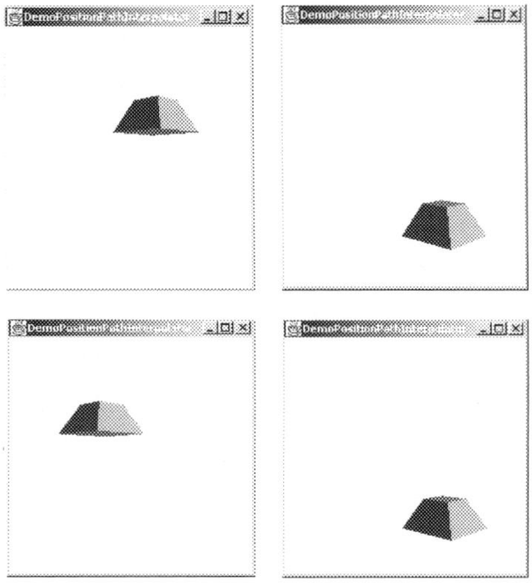

mGroup based on linear interpolating between a set of specified positions or knots. In particular, in this interpolator, the interpolated position is used to generate a translation transform of the local coordinate system. With the first and last knots associated with alpha values of 0.0f and 1.0f, respectively, an intermediate knot with index k will have an alpha value larger than those with indices less than k.

In Figure 2, a visual object is programmed to move in an anti-clockwise circular motion about the z-axis. Lines 13 to 17 specify a loop that gives rise to 18 points uniformly spaced on a circle of radius 0.5. PositionPathInterpolator is then invoked based on these points so that the visual object undergoes basically a circular motion.

Note that instead of defining points along a circular path and then using PositionPathInterpolator, rotation can also be achieved by using the RotationInterpolator class, which will be illustrated in the next section.

RotationInterpolator

This interpolator corresponds to a behavior class through which a visual object can be made to rotate (Palmer, 2001). The rotation is, by default, about the y-axis.

In the example of Figure 3, a trapezium is made to turn from an initial to a final angle by using RotationInterpolator. Line 5 specifies a bounding sphere for a live region to allow for the movement of the object. This is followed by declaring an alpha object on the characteristic of the motion. Both INCREASING_ENABLE and DECREASING_ENABLE are used so that the rotation is smooth.

Line 13 invokes the RotationInterpolator, with input arguments given by the defined alpha and the TransformGroup for the visual object. By default, this RotationInterpolator will rotate the object about the y-axis. In the event that rotation about another axis is needed, an appropriate Transform3D will have to be supplied for changing the rotation axis.

RotationPathInterpolator

The RotationInterpolator discussed in the last section makes use of a rotation matrix to effect rotation, which is limited to that about a main coordinate axis. For rotation about any direction, the class of RotationPathInterpolator can be used.

RotationPathInterpolator uses quaternions in the form q = [x y z w] to specify the rotation needed. Specifically, for rotation by an angle, 2b, about an axis given by (ax, ay, az), q will be given by

w = cos(b)
x = ax sin(b)

Figure 3. Code segment and result of DemoRotationInterpolator.java

```
1.    public BranchGroup createSceneGraph()
2.    {
3.        BranchGroup objRoot = createBranchScene();
4.
5.        BoundingSphere bound =  new BoundingSphere();
6.        Alpha alpha = new Alpha(-1, Alpha.INCREASING_ENABLE|Alpha.DECREASING_ENABLE, 0, 0,
7.                        4000, 2000,1000, 4000, 2000, 1000);
8.
9.        TransformGroup objRotate = new TransformGroup();
10.       objRotate.setCapability(TransformGroup.ALLOW_TRANSFORM_WRITE);
11.       objRotate.addChild(new Quad());
12.
13.       RotationInterpolator rotateInterpol = new RotationInterpolator(alpha, objRotate);
14.       rotateInterpol.setSchedulingBounds(bound);
15.
16.       TransformGroup objTilt = new TransformGroup();
17.       Transform3D tiltX = new Transform3D();
18.       tiltX.rotX(Math.PI/5.0d);
19.       objTilt.setTransform(tiltX);
20.
21.       objRoot.addChild(objTilt);
22.       objTilt.addChild(objRotate);
23.       objRotate.addChild(rotateInterpol);
24.
25.       objRoot.compile();
26.
27.       return objRoot;
28.   }
```

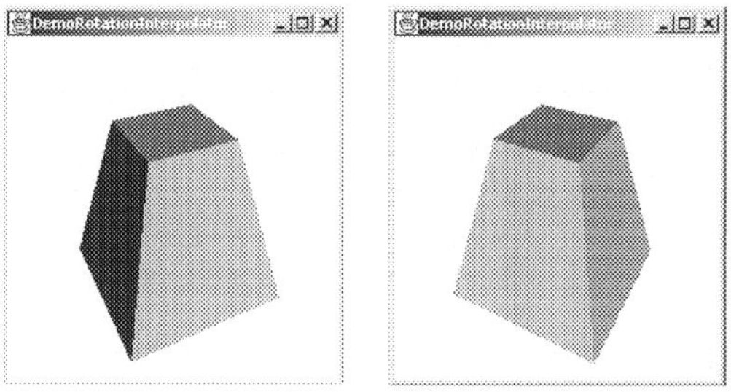

$$y = ay \sin(b)$$
$$z = az \sin(b)$$

As an example, to rotate by 180 degree about the y-axis, where ax = 0, ay = 1 and az = 0, the quaternion will be given by q = [0 1 0 0], and a declaration given by new Quat4f(0f,1f,0f,0f) will have to be invoked in Java3D. Note that the quaternion q = [0 0 0 1] corresponds to maintaining the original position with no rotation.

With the possibility to change the axis of rotation, RotationPathInterpolator allows for a complex sequence of rotations to be stringed together. This is illustrated in the example code segment and result of Figure 4. Note that the rotation depends on the local coordinate system as defined by the Transform3D object, and the size of the knots and quats arrays must be the same.

Figure 4. Code segment and result of RotPathInter.java

```
1.    public BranchGroup createSceneGraph()
2.    {
3.        BranchGroup objRoot = new BranchGroup();
4.
5.        TransformGroup objTrans = new TransformGroup();
6.        objTrans.setCapability( TransformGroup.ALLOW_TRANSFORM_WRITE );
7.        // this is essential for transformation in a live scene graph
8.        objRoot.addChild( objTrans );
9.
10.       Transform3D coordRot = new Transform3D();  //local coordinate system is set to default
11.
12.       float[] knots = { 0.0f, 0.25f, 0.5f, 0.75f, 1.0f };  //knot values to determine animation
13.
14.       Quat4f[] quats = new Quat4f[5];  // quaternions values needed to determine the rotation
15.       quats[0] = new Quat4f( 0.0f, -1.0f, 0.0f, 1.0f );
16.       quats[1] = new Quat4f( 0.0f, 1.0f, 0.0f, 1.0f );
17.       quats[2] = new Quat4f( 1.0f, 0.0f, 0.0f, 1.0f );
18.       quats[3] = new Quat4f( -1.0f, 0.0f, 0.0f, 1.0f );
19.       quats[4] = new Quat4f( 0.0f, -1.0f, 0.0f, 1.0f );
20.
21.       Alpha rotationAlpha = new Alpha( -1, 4000 );  //continuous loop of period 4000 miliseconds
22.       RotationPathInterpolator rotator =
23.       new RotationPathInterpolator( rotationAlpha, objTrans, coordRot, knots, quats );
24.
25.       BoundingSphere bounds = new BoundingSphere();
26.       rotator.setSchedulingBounds( bounds );
27.       objTrans.addChild ( rotator );
28.       // being a node leaf object, rotator have to be added to the appropriate group node.
29.
30.       objTrans.addChild( new createRotPathInter() );   //a RotPathInter shape node is added.
31.
32.       objRoot.compile();
33.
34.       return objRoot;
35.   }
```

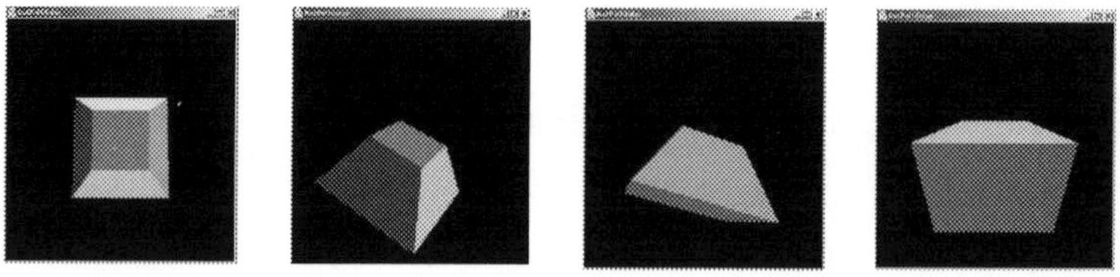

RotPosPathInterpolator

Combining the effects of both translation and rotation, the class RotPosPathInterpolator allows a visual object to undergo both translation and rotation along a specified path. Figure

5 shows an example code segment on this where an object of interest is made to translate and rotate along a set of knot/position and knot/orientation pairs. In this example, lines 15 to 20 define 5 translational positions for the object, while lines 9 to 14 specify 5 rotational movements.

Figure 5. Code segment and result of DemoRotPosPathInterpolator.java

```
1.      public BranchGroup createSceneGraph()
2.      {
3.          BranchGroup objRoot = createBranchScene();
4.          TransformGroup motion = new TransformGroup();
5.          motion.setCapability(TransformGroup.ALLOW_TRANSFORM_WRITE);
6.          objRoot.addChild(motion);
7.          motion.addChild(new Axis().getBG());
8.          Transform3D someAxis = new Transform3D();
9.          Quat4f[] quats = new Quat4f[5];
10.         quats[0] = new Quat4f(1.0f,0.0f,0.0f,1.0f);
11.         quats[1] = new Quat4f(1.0f,0.0f,1.0f,0.0f);
12.         quats[2] = new Quat4f(0.0f,1.0f,1.0f,0.0f);
13.         quats[3] = new Quat4f(0.0f,0.0f,0.0f,1.0f);
14.         quats[4] = quats[0];
15.         Point3f[] positions = new Point3f[5];
16.         positions[0] = new Point3f(-0.75f,  0.75f, -0.75f);
17.         positions[1] = new Point3f( 0.75f,  0.75f, -0.75f);
18.         positions[2] = new Point3f(-0.75f, -0.75f, -0.25f);
19.         positions[3] = new Point3f( 0.75f, -0.75f, -0.25f);
20.         positions[4] = positions[0];
21.         Alpha alpha = new Alpha(-1,10000);
22.         float[] knots = {0.0f, 0.25f, 0.5f, 0.75f, 1.0f};
23.         RotPosPathInterpolator rotpos =
24.         new RotPosPathInterpolator(alpha, motion, someAxis, knots, quats, positions);
25.         rotpos.setSchedulingBounds(new BoundingSphere());
26.         motion.addChild(rotpos);
27.         objRoot.compile();
28.         return objRoot;
29.     }
30.
```

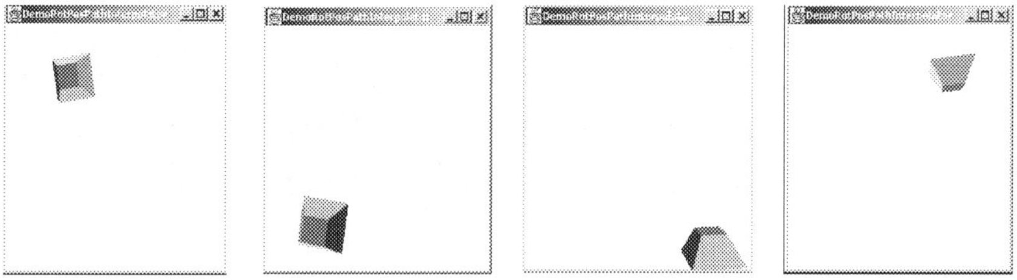

ScaleInterpolator

The ScaleInterpolator allows the apparent size of the object to be changed as time passes by generating appropriate scale transforms in the local coordinate system.

In the example code segment and result in Figure 6, a bounding sphere on a live region and an associated alpha object are first specified before invoking ScaleInterpolator to change the size of the trapezoidal object. The input parameter of 1.0f corresponds to the maximum scale or size, while 0.2f sets the minimum scale or size for the object. An appropriate Transform3D is then used to define the axis and the local coordinate system under which ScaleInterpolator operates.

Figure 6. Code segment and result of DemoScaleInterpolator.java

```
25.    System.out.println("1-Directional light");
26.    System.out.println("2-Point light");
27.    System.out.println("3-Spot light");
28.    System.out.println("other-Ambient light");
29.    in = new BufferedReader(new InputStreamReader(System.in));
30.    try { String userInput = in.readLine(); light=Integer.parseInt(userInput); }
31.    catch (IOException ioe) { System.out.println("IO error trying to read input!"); System.exit(1); }
32.
33.    // create light source at the origin
34.    lit = new AmbientLight(new Color3f( 0.5f, 0.5f, 0.5f));
35.    if (light==1){ lit = new DirectionalLight(new Color3f( 0.5f, 1.0f, 0.5f), new Vector3f( 0.2f,-0.5f,-1.0
36.    if (light==2){ lit = new PointLight(new Color3f(1,1,1), new Point3f(0,0,0), new Point3f(1,1,0));}
37.    if (light==3){ lit = new SpotLight(new Color3f(1f,1f,1f), new Point3f(0.0f,0.0f,0.0f),
38.            new Point3f(1.0f,1.0f,0.0f), new Vector3f(0.0f,0.0f,1.0f), (float)(Math.PI/2.0f),0f);}
39.    lit.setInfluencingBounds(new BoundingSphere());
40.
41.    // make the light source move around the box
42.    Alpha alpha = new Alpha(-1,5000);
43.    Transform3D y = new Transform3D();
44.    float knots[] = {0.0f , 0.5f , 1.0f};
45.    Point3f pts[] = { new Point3f(-2f,0f, 2f), new Point3f( 2f,0f, 2f), new Point3f(-2f,0f, 2f)};
46.    PositionPathInterpolator posinterpolator = new PositionPathInterpolator(alpha,sphere1,y,knots,
47.    RotationInterpolator rotinterpolator = new RotationInterpolator(alpha,sphere2);
48.    posinterpolator.setSchedulingBounds(new BoundingSphere());
49.    rotinterpolator.setSchedulingBounds(new BoundingSphere());
50.    sphere2.addChild(rotinterpolator);
51.    sphere1.addChild(posinterpolator);
52.    sphere2.addChild(shape);
53.    sphere2.addChild(lit);
54.    sphere1.addChild(sphere2);
55.    sphere1.setCapability(TransformGroup.ALLOW_TRANSFORM_WRITE);
56.    sphere2.setCapability(TransformGroup.ALLOW_TRANSFORM_WRITE);
57.    root.addChild(sphere1);
58.    return root;
59. }
```

RotPosScalePathInterpolator

Similar to RotPosPathInterpolator, which combines translation and rotation, RotPos-ScalePathInterpolator allows an object to be rotated, translated, and scaled. As illustrated

Figure 7. Code segment and result of RotPosScalePathInter.java

```
1.    public BranchGroup createSceneGraph()
2.    {
3.       BranchGroup objRoot = new BranchGroup();
4.       TransformGroup objTrans = new TransformGroup();
5.       objTrans.setCapability( TransformGroup.ALLOW_TRANSFORM_WRITE );
6.       objRoot.addChild( objTrans );
7.       Alpha rotationAlpha = new Alpha( -1, 4000 );
8.       Transform3D axisRot = new Transform3D();
9.       float[] knots = { 0.0f, 0.25f, 0.5f, 0.75f, 1.0f };
10.      Quat4f[] quats = new Quat4f[5]; //quaternions for rotation
11.      quats[0] = new Quat4f( 0.0f, -1.0f, 0.0f, 1.0f );
12.      quats[1] = new Quat4f( 0.0f, 1.0f, 0.0f, 1.0f );
13.      quats[2] = new Quat4f( 1.0f, 0.0f, 0.0f, 1.0f );
14.      quats[3] = new Quat4f( -1.0f, 0.0f, 0.0f, 1.0f );
15.      quats[4] = new Quat4f( 0.0f, -1.0f, 0.0f, 1.0f );
16.      Point3f[] postns = new Point3f[5];   //coordinates of waypoints for translation
17.      postns[0] = new Point3f( 0.0f, 0.0f, 0.0f );
18.      postns[1] = new Point3f( 0.5f, 0.0f, 0.0f );
19.      postns[2] = new Point3f( 0.0f, 0.5f, 0.0f );
20.      postns[3] = new Point3f( -0.5f, 0.0f, 0.0f );
21.      postns[4] = new Point3f( 0.0f, 0.0f, 0.0f );
22.      float[] scales = { 1.0f, 0.5f, 0.1f, 0.5f, 1.0f };  // scaling factor for each position
23.      RotPosScalePathInterpolator rotator =
24.        new RotPosScalePathInterpolator( rotationAlpha, objTrans, axisRot, knots, quats, postns, scales );
25.      BoundingSphere bounds = new BoundingSphere();
26.      rotator.setSchedulingBounds( bounds );
27.      objTrans.addChild( rotator );
28.      objTrans.addChild( new createRotPosScalePathInter() );
29.      objRoot.compile();
30.      return objRoot;
31.   }
32.
```

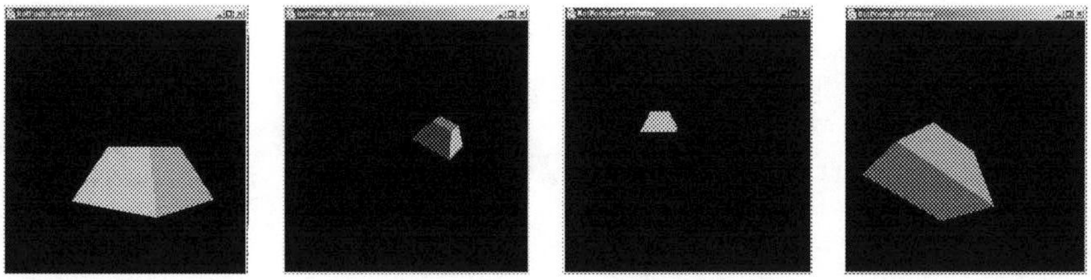

in the example of Figure 7, three arrays specifying rotation, translation, and scaling have to be supplied at each position, in addition to the knots array.

SwitchValueInterpolator

This class of interpolator allows the child of the target switch node to be selected. Specifically, if the target switch node has n children, the child index selected using SwitchValueInterpolator can range from 0 to n-1.

In the illustrating example of Figure 8, the target switch node has 2 children. Specifically, line 6 defines the target switch node, and line 7 sets its capability to ALLOW_SWITCH_WRITE, enabling the selected child to be modified. Lines 10 and 11 add the children for this node, with the first child index being associated with a trapezoidal object, and the second child index being that for a prism.

Figure 8. Code segment and result of RotPosScalePathInter.java

```
1.   public BranchGroup createSceneGraph()
2.   {
3.   BranchGroup objRoot = createBranchScene();
4.   BoundingSphere bound =  new BoundingSphere();
5.   Alpha alpha = new Alpha(-1, Alpha.INCREASING_ENABLE|Alpha.DECREASING_ENABLE, 0, 0, 0,
       0, 4000,  0, 0, 4000);
6.   Switch objSwitch = new Switch();
7.   objSwitch.setCapability(Switch.ALLOW_SWITCH_WRITE);
8.   SwitchValueInterpolator switchInterpol = new SwitchValueInterpolator (alpha, objSwitch);
9.   switchInterpol.setSchedulingBounds(bound);
10.  objSwitch.addChild(new Quad());
11.  objSwitch.addChild(new Triangle());
12.  TransformGroup objTilt = new TransformGroup();
13.  Transform3D tiltX = new Transform3D();
14.  Transform3D tiltY = new Transform3D();
15.  tiltX.rotX(Math.PI/5.0d);
16.  tiltY.rotY(Math.PI/5.0d);
17.  tiltX.mul(tiltY);
18.  objTilt.setTransform(tiltX);
19.  objRoot.addChild(objTilt);
20.  objTilt.addChild(objSwitch);
21.  objTilt.addChild(switchInterpol);
22.  switchInterpol.setLastChildIndex(1);
23.  objRoot.compile();
24.  return objRoot;
25.  }
```

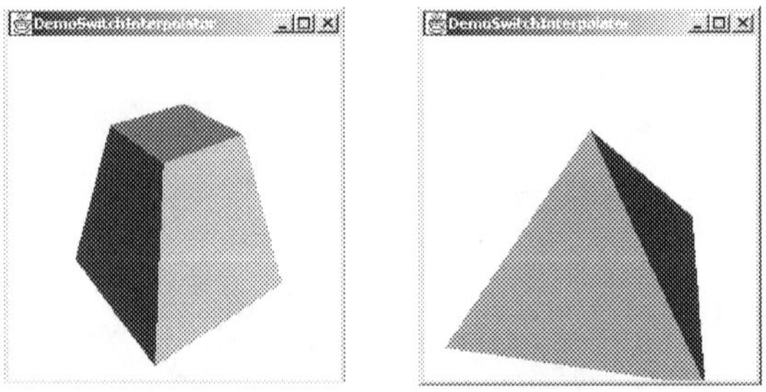

The alpha object for this simulation has alphaAtOneDuration and alphaAtZeroDuration equal to 4000. With these values, the visual object observed will be a trapezoidal one for 4 seconds before changing to a prism. SwitchValueInterpolator is invoked in line 8, with its input arguments being the alpha object and the target switch node.

TransparencyInterpolator

The TransparencyInterpolator class can be used to change the transparency of an visual object by altering its transparency attributes.

In the example of Figure 9, a visual trapezoidal object is declared in line 8. Line 10 creates an appearance object, and the appearance of the visual object is passed to this appearance

Figure 9. Code segment and result of DemoTransparencyInterpolator.java

```
1.    public BranchGroup createSceneGraph()
2.    {
3.    BranchGroup objRoot = createBranchScene();
4.    BoundingSphere bound = new BoundingSphere();
5.    Alpha alpha = new Alpha(-1, Alpha.INCREASING_ENABLE|Alpha.DECREASING_ENABLE, 0, 0,
         4000, 2000, 1000, 4000, 2000, 1000);
6.    TransformGroup objTransparency = new TransformGroup();
7.    objTransparency.setCapability(TransformGroup.ALLOW_TRANSFORM_WRITE);
8.    Shape3D quadTransparentObj = new Quad();
9.    objTransparency.addChild(quadTransparentObj);
10.   Appearance quadTransparentObjAppear = quadTransparentObj.getAppearance();
11.   TransparencyAttributes transparencyAttr = new TransparencyAttributes();
12.   transparencyAttr.setCapability(TransparencyAttributes.ALLOW_VALUE_WRITE);
13.   transparencyAttr.setTransparencyMode(TransparencyAttributes.BLENDED);
14.   quadTransparentObjAppear.setTransparencyAttributes(transparencyAttr);
15.   TransparencyInterpolator transparencyInterpol = new TransparencyInterpolator(alpha,
         transparencyAttr, 0f, 1f);
16.   transparencyInterpol.setSchedulingBounds(bound);
17.   TransformGroup objTilt = new TransformGroup();
18.   Transform3D tiltX = new Transform3D();
19.   Transform3D tiltY = new Transform3D();
20.   tiltX.rotX(Math.PI/5.0d);
21.   tiltY.rotY(Math.PI/5.0d);
22.   tiltX.mul(tiltY);
23.   objTilt.setTransform(tiltX);
24.   objRoot.addChild(objTilt);
25.   objTilt.addChild(objTransparency);
26.   objTransparency.addChild(transparencyInterpol);
27.   objRoot.compile();
28.   return objRoot;
29.   }
```

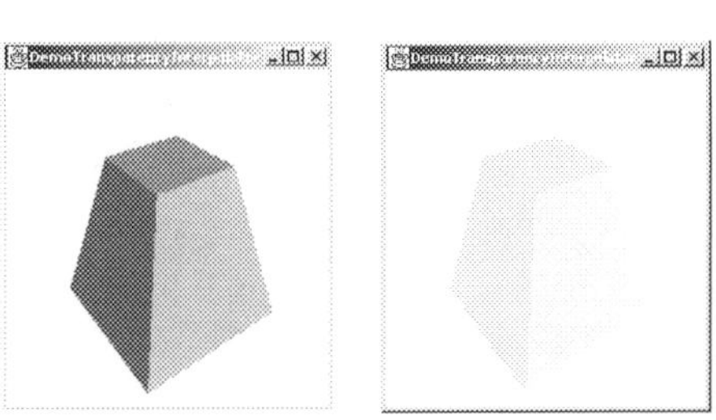

object. Lines 10 to 12 declare a TransparencyAttributes object and set its characteristic to ALLOW_VALUE_WRITE and BLENDED. With these declarations, the appearance of the visual object can be set using the TransparencyAttributes object.

Line 15 invokes the TransparencyInterpolator, which takes in an associated alpha object, the TransparencyAttributes object, and the maximum and minimum transparency values as arguments. A transparency value of 1.0f corresponds to a situation when the visual object is fully opaque, while a transparency value of 0.0f gives rise to a fully transparent object. In this example, the object is made to change from a fully opaque object to one that is more transparent with a transparency value of 0.2.

ColorInterpolator

Through ColorInterpolator class, the diffuse color of the associated material objects may be altered. Note that this behavior class and the material object may have more than one target visual objects. Also, if Lighting is not set, the effect of ColorInterpolator will not be visible.

In the example in Figure 10, a material object is created at line 7 to define the appearance of a visual object under illumination. The use of ALLOW_COMPONENT_WRITE sets this object to allow for the possibility to change individual component field information.

ColorInterpolator is invoked in line 9. After specifying the alpha and material object used, the initial and the final color are stated in the subsequent lines. SchedulingBounds is also specified so that the change in color can be seen. Also, as the presence of lighting is needed, directional light is declared in line 27. The visual object is declared as a Shape3D object starting from line 13, and its appearance node is modified using the material object declared earlier.

BILLBOARD

In its default mode, the Billboard class supports rotation about the y-axis only, and allows the user to view the declared 3D objects in a 2D view as the viewing angle rotates. An example is presented in Figures 11 to 15.

In the code segments in Figures 11 and 12, four visual 3D objects are declared. Of these, the road markers and tree shape objects are individually created and translated into the scene graph by adding transform groups.

The inclusion of the relevant billboard objects into the scene graph is then carried out in the loops in Figure 14. Specifically, the following steps are followed.

Figure 10. Code segment and result of DemoColorInterpolator.java

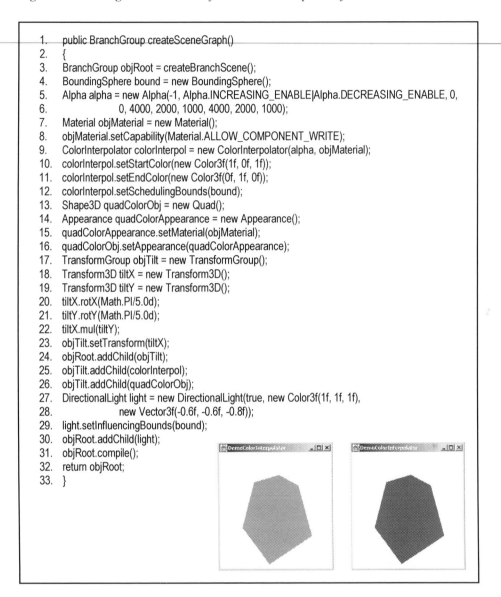

```
1.    public BranchGroup createSceneGraph()
2.    {
3.    BranchGroup objRoot = createBranchScene();
4.    BoundingSphere bound = new BoundingSphere();
5.    Alpha alpha = new Alpha(-1, Alpha.INCREASING_ENABLE|Alpha.DECREASING_ENABLE, 0,
6.              0, 4000, 2000, 1000, 4000, 2000, 1000);
7.    Material objMaterial = new Material();
8.    objMaterial.setCapability(Material.ALLOW_COMPONENT_WRITE);
9.    ColorInterpolator colorInterpol = new ColorInterpolator(alpha, objMaterial);
10.   colorInterpol.setStartColor(new Color3f(1f, 0f, 1f));
11.   colorInterpol.setEndColor(new Color3f(0f, 1f, 0f));
12.   colorInterpol.setSchedulingBounds(bound);
13.   Shape3D quadColorObj = new Quad();
14.   Appearance quadColorAppearance = new Appearance();
15.   quadColorAppearance.setMaterial(objMaterial);
16.   quadColorObj.setAppearance(quadColorAppearance);
17.   TransformGroup objTilt = new TransformGroup();
18.   Transform3D tiltX = new Transform3D();
19.   Transform3D tiltY = new Transform3D();
20.   tiltX.rotX(Math.PI/5.0d);
21.   tiltY.rotY(Math.PI/5.0d);
22.   tiltX.mul(tiltY);
23.   objTilt.setTransform(tiltX);
24.   objRoot.addChild(objTilt);
25.   objTilt.addChild(colorInterpol);
26.   objTilt.addChild(quadColorObj);
27.   DirectionalLight light = new DirectionalLight(true, new Color3f(1f, 1f, 1f),
28.              new Vector3f(-0.6f, -0.6f, -0.8f));
29.   light.setInfluencingBounds(bound);
30.   objRoot.addChild(light);
31.   objRoot.compile();
32.   return objRoot;
33.   }
```

- The object locations are set by inserting appropriate values into a Vector3f array.
- A transform group is created and the translation of the Vector3f point is set.
- The Billboard constructor is created and the scheduling bound is specified.
- A transform group is added as a child to the object root.

Figure 11. First code segment of BillboardDemo.java

```
1.    import java.applet.Applet;
2.    import java.awt.Frame;
3.    import com.sun.j3d.utils.applet.MainFrame;
4.    import com.sun.j3d.utils.universe.*;
5.    import javax.media.j3d.*;
6.    import javax.vecmath.*;
7.    import com.sun.j3d.utils.behaviors.keyboard.*;
8.    import com.sun.j3d.utils.geometry.Sphere;
9.
10.   public class BillboardDemo extends Applet
11.   {
12.     Shape3D createGrass()
13.     {
14.       Color3f brown = new Color3f(0.7f, 0.5f, 0.6f);
15.       int vertex = 4;
16.       int StripCount[] = {vertex};
17.       TriangleStripArray Grass = new TriangleStripArray(vertex,
18.       TriangleStripArray.COORDINATES|TriangleStripArray.COLOR_3, StripCount);
19.        Grass.setCoordinate(0, new Point3f(-50.0f,0.0f, -50.0f));
20.       Grass.setCoordinate(1, new Point3f(-10.0f, 0.0f,-50.0f));
21.       Grass.setCoordinate(2, new Point3f(-10.0f, 0.0f,50.0f));
22.       Grass.setCoordinate(3, new Point3f( -50.0f, 0.0f,50.0f));
23.       for(int i = 0; i < 4; i++) Grass.setColor( i, brown);
24.       return new Shape3D(Grass);
25.     }
26.
27.     Shape3D createGrass1()
28.     {
29.       Color3f brown = new Color3f(0.7f, 0.5f, 0.6f);
30.       int vertex = 4;
31.       int StripCount[] = {vertex};
32.       TriangleStripArray Grass1 = new TriangleStripArray(vertex,
33.       TriangleStripArray.COORDINATES|TriangleStripArray.COLOR_3,
34.       StripCount);
35.        Grass1.setCoordinate(0, new Point3f(50.0f,0.0f, -50.0f));
36.        Grass1.setCoordinate(1, new Point3f(10.0f, 0.0f,-50.0f));
37.       Grass1.setCoordinate(2, new Point3f(10.0f, 0.0f,50.0f));
38.       Grass1.setCoordinate(3, new Point3f(50.0f, 0.0f,50.0f));
39.       for(int i = 0; i < 4; i++)  Grass1.setColor( i, brown);
40.       return new Shape3D(Grass1);
41.     }
42.
```

Figure 12. Second code segment of BillboardDemo.java

```
44.   Shape3D createRunway()
45.   {
46.       Color3f black = new Color3f(0.0f, 0.0f, 0.0f);
47.       int vertex = 4;
48.       int StripCount[] = {vertex};
49.       TriangleStripArray Runway1 = new TriangleStripArray(vertex,
50.       TriangleStripArray.COORDINATES|TriangleStripArray.COLOR_3,
51.       StripCount);
52.       Runway1.setCoordinate(0, new Point3f(-10.0f,0.0f, -50.0f));
53.       Runway1.setCoordinate(1, new Point3f(-10.0f, 0.0f,50.0f));
54.       Runway1.setCoordinate(2, new Point3f(10.0f, 0.0f,-50.0f));
55.       Runway1.setCoordinate(3, new Point3f(10.0f, 0.0f,50.0f));
56.       for(int i = 0; i < 4; i++) Runway1.setColor( i, black);
57.       return new Shape3D(Runway1);
58.   }
59.
60.   Shape3D createTree()
61.   {
62.       int vertex = 14;
63.       int StripCount[] = {vertex};
64.       LineStripArray tree = new LineStripArray(vertex,
65.       LineStripArray.COORDINATES|LineStripArray.COLOR_3, StripCount);
66.       tree.setCoordinate(0, new Point3f(-0.5f,0.0f, 0.0f));
67.       tree.setCoordinate(1, new Point3f(-0.25f, 0.2f,0.0f));
68.       tree.setCoordinate(2, new Point3f(-0.5f, 0.2f,0.0f));
69.       tree.setCoordinate(3, new Point3f(-0.25f, 0.4f,0.0f));
70.       tree.setCoordinate(4, new Point3f(-0.5f,0.4f, 0.0f));
71.       tree.setCoordinate(5, new Point3f(0.0f,0.6f, 0.0f));
72.       tree.setCoordinate(6, new Point3f(0.5f,0.4f, 0.0f));
73.       tree.setCoordinate(7, new Point3f(0.25f,0.4f, 0.0f));
74.       tree.setCoordinate(8, new Point3f(0.5f,0.2f, 0.0f));
75.       tree.setCoordinate(9, new Point3f(0.25f,0.2f, 0.0f));
76.       tree.setCoordinate(10, new Point3f(0.5f,0.0f, 0.0f));
77.       tree.setCoordinate(11, new Point3f(0.25f,-0.2f, 0.0f));
78.       tree.setCoordinate(12, new Point3f(-0.25f,-0.2f, 0.0f));
79.       tree.setCoordinate(13, new Point3f(-0.5f,0.0f, 0.0f));
80.       Color3f green = new Color3f(0.0f, 1.0f, 0.5f);
81.       Color3f brown = new Color3f(0.7f, 0.5f, 0.5f);
82.       for(int i = 0; i <11; i++) tree.setColor( i, green);
83.       for (int j=11; j<14;j++)  tree.setColor(j,brown);
84.       return new Shape3D(tree);
85.   }
86.
```

Figure 13. Third code segment of BillboardDemo.java

```
87.   public BranchGroup createSceneGraph(SimpleUniverse su)
88.   {
89.     TransformGroup viewplatformTrans = null;
90.     BranchGroup objRoot = new BranchGroup();
91.     ColoringAttributes ca = new ColoringAttributes();
92.     ca.setColor(1.0f,0.0f,0.0f);
93.     Appearance app = new Appearance();
94.     app.setColoringAttributes(ca);
95.     Vector3f translate = new Vector3f();
96.     Transform3D t3D= new Transform3D();
97.     TransformGroup translateGroup = null;
98.     TransformGroup TGroup = null;
99.     Billboard billboard = null;
100.    BoundingSphere bSphere = new BoundingSphere();
101.    objRoot.addChild(createGrass());
102.    objRoot.addChild(createGrass1());
103.    objRoot.addChild(createRunway());
104.    Vector3f location[] = new Vector3f [9];
105.    location[0] = new Vector3f(10f, 0.2f,-40.0f);
106.    location[1] = new Vector3f(-10.0f, 0.2f,-30.0f);
107.    location[2] = new Vector3f(10f, 0.2f,-20.0f);
108.    location[3] = new Vector3f(-10.0f, 0.2f,-10.0f);
109.    location[4] = new Vector3f(10f, 0.2f,0.0f);
110.    location[5] = new Vector3f(-10.0f, 0.2f,10.0f);
111.    location[6] = new Vector3f(10f, 0.2f,20.0f);
112.    location[7] = new Vector3f(-10.0f, 0.2f,30.0f);
113.    location[8] = new Vector3f(10f, 0.2f,40.0f);
114.    Vector3f location1[] = new Vector3f [9];
115.    location1[0] = new Vector3f(0.0f, 0.0f,-40.0f);
116.    location1[1] = new Vector3f(0.0f, 0.0f,-30.0f);
117.    location1[2] = new Vector3f(0.0f, 0.0f,-20.0f);
118.    location1[3] = new Vector3f(0.0f, 0.0f,-10.0f);
119.    location1[4] = new Vector3f(0.0f, 0.0f,0.0f);
120.    location1[5] = new Vector3f(0.0f, 0.0f,10.0f);
121.    location1[6] = new Vector3f(0.0f, 0.0f,20.0f);
122.    location1[7] = new Vector3f(0.0f, 0.0f,30.0f);
123.    location1[8] = new Vector3f(0.0f, 0.0f,40.0f);
```

- The Billboard constructor is added as a child to the object root.
- The billboard object or the object shape is added as a child to the transform group created earlier.

Figure 14. Fourth code segment of BillboardDemo.java

```
124. for (int i = 0; i < location1.length; i++)
125. {
126.     translate.set(location1[i]);
127.     t3D.setTranslation(translate);
128.     translateGroup = new TransformGroup(t3D);
129.     TGroup = new TransformGroup();
130.     TGroup.setCapability(TransformGroup.ALLOW_TRANSFORM_WRITE);
131.     billboard = new Billboard(TGroup);
132.     billboard.setSchedulingBounds(bSphere);
133.     objRoot.addChild(translateGroup);
134.     objRoot.addChild(billboard);
135.     translateGroup.addChild(TGroup);
136.     TGroup.addChild(new Sphere(0.1f,app));
137. }
138. for (int i = 0; i < location.length; i++)
139. {
140.     translate.set(location[i]);
141.     t3D.setTranslation(translate);
142.     translateGroup = new TransformGroup(t3D);
143.     TGroup = new TransformGroup();
144.     TGroup.setCapability(TransformGroup.ALLOW_TRANSFORM_WRITE);
145.     billboard = new Billboard(TGroup);
146.     billboard.setSchedulingBounds(bSphere);
147.     objRoot.addChild(translateGroup);
148.     objRoot.addChild(billboard);
149.     translateGroup.addChild(TGroup);
150.     TGroup.addChild(createTree());
151. }
152. viewplatformTrans = su.getViewingPlatform().getViewPlatformTransform();
153. translate.set( 0.0f, 0.3f, 0.0f);
154. t3D.setTranslation(translate);
155. viewplatformTrans.setTransform(t3D);
156. KeyNavigatorBehavior keyNavBeh = new KeyNavigatorBehavior(viewplatformTrans);
157. keyNavBeh.setSchedulingBounds(new BoundingSphere(new Point3d(),1000.0));
158. objRoot.addChild(keyNavBeh);
159. Background background = new Background();
160. background.setColor(0.3f, 0.3f, 1.0f);               // set background colour
161. background.setApplicationBounds(new BoundingSphere());
162. objRoot.addChild(background);
163. objRoot.compile();
164. return objRoot;
165. } // end of CreateSceneGraph method of Billboard
166.
```

Figure 15. Fifth code segment and result of BillboardDemo.java

```
167. public BillboardDemo()
168. {
169.   setLayout(new BorderLayout());
170.   Canvas3D canvas3D = new Canvas3D(null);
171.   add("Center", canvas3D);
172.   SimpleUniverse simpleU = new SimpleUniverse(canvas3D);
173.   BranchGroup scene = createSceneGraph(simpleU);
174.   simpleU.addBranchGraph(scene);
175.
176. } // end of BillboardDemo (constructor)
177.
178.
179.   public static void main(String[] args)
180.   {
181.     System.out.print("A demonstration of the Billboard Behavior \n");
182.     System.out.println("It uses KeyNavigatorBehavior to explore the scene.");
183.     System.out.println("At all times the 2D objects found in the scene will face  the user.\n");
184.     Frame frame = new MainFrame(new BillboardDemo(), 256, 256);
185.   } // end of main (method of BillboardDemo)
186. }
187.
```

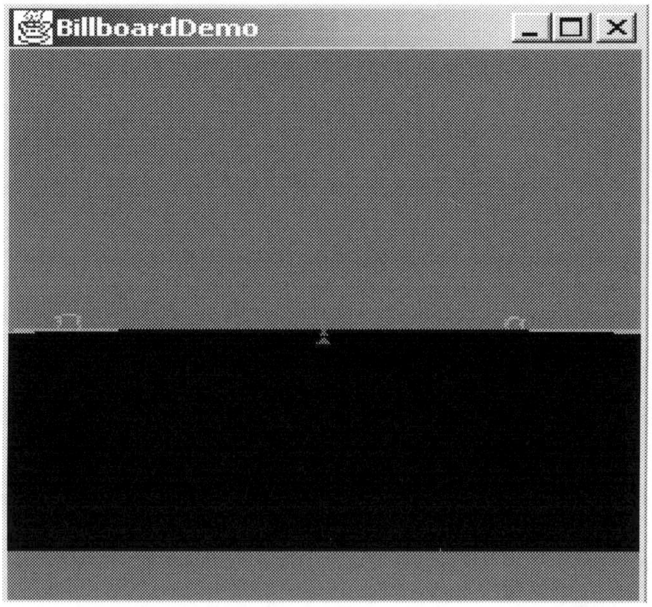

LEVEL OF DETAIL (LOD)

This makes use of the DistanceLOD class to manage variation in the display as the distance between the user and visual objects is changed. Specifically, if the distance is increased, the

Figure 16. First code segment of LOD.java

```
1.    import java.applet.Applet;
2.    import java.awt.BorderLayout;
3.    import java.awt.Frame;
4.    import com.sun.j3d.utils.applet.MainFrame;
5.    import com.sun.j3d.utils.geometry.*;
6.    import com.sun.j3d.utils.universe.*;
7.    import javax.media.j3d.*;
8.    import javax.vecmath.*;
9.    public class LOD extends Applet
10.   {
11.     public BranchGroup createSceneGraph()
12.     {
13.       BranchGroup objRoot = new BranchGroup();
14.       BoundingSphere bounds = new BoundingSphere();
15.       TransformGroup objMove = new TransformGroup();
16.       objMove.setCapability(TransformGroup.ALLOW_TRANSFORM_WRITE);
17.       Alpha alpha = new Alpha (-1, Alpha.INCREASING_ENABLE + Alpha.DECREASING_ENABLE,
18.               0, 0, 5000, 1000, 1000, 5000, 1000, 1000);
19.       AxisAngle4f axisTrans = new AxisAngle4f(0.0f,1.0f,0.0f,(float)Math.PI/-2.0f); // translation axis
20.       Transform3D T3D= new Transform3D();
21.       T3D.set(axisTrans);
22.
23.       // create position interpolator
24.       PositionInterpolator positionInt = new PositionInterpolator (alpha, objMove, T3D, -2.5f, -25.0f);
25.       positionInt.setSchedulingBounds(bounds);
26.
27.       // create DistanceLOD target object
28.       Switch SwitchTarget = new Switch();
29.       SwitchTarget.setCapability(Switch.ALLOW_SWITCH_WRITE);
30.
31.       ColoringAttributes caA = new ColoringAttributes();
32.       caA.setColor(1.0f,0.0f,0.0f);
33.       Appearance appA = new Appearance();
34.       appA.setColoringAttributes(caA);
35.       ColoringAttributes caB = new ColoringAttributes();
36.       caB.setColor(0.0f,0.0f,1.0f);
37.       Appearance appB = new Appearance();
38.       appB.setColoringAttributes(caB);
39.       SwitchTarget.addChild(new Cylinder(0.9f,0.9f,appA));
40.       SwitchTarget.addChild(new Cylinder(0.75f,0.75f,appB));
41.       SwitchTarget.addChild(new Cylinder(0.5f,0.5f,appA));
42.       SwitchTarget.addChild(new Cylinder(0.25f,0.25f,appB));
```

amount of details that need to be rendered for the object can be reduced. This will reduce rendering time and complexity (Hu & Di, & Li, 2005).

In the example program in Figures 16 to 18, we have four switch objects. The object in the middle will change its color between blue and red as it moves towards and away from the user, respectively. Each of the switch objects must have its distances between the previous and the next switch objects specified.

In this scenario, a cone object from the utility class is used along with appropriate color attributes. Furthermore, the appearance attributes must be defined. Since PositionInterpo-

Figure 17. Second code segment of LOD.java

```
43.      float[] distances = { 5.0f, 10.0f, 15.0f};
44.      DistanceLOD distanceLOD = new DistanceLOD(distances, new Point3f());
45.      distanceLOD.addSwitch(SwitchTarget);
46.      distanceLOD.setSchedulingBounds(bounds);
47.
48.      if((SwitchTarget.numChildren()-1) != distanceLOD.numDistances())
49.      {
50.          System.out.println("Error in creating LOD ");
51.      }
52.
53.      objRoot.addChild(objMove);
54.      objRoot.addChild(positionInt);
55.      objMove.addChild(distanceLOD);
56.      objMove.addChild(SwitchTarget);
57.
58.      // show the object at a nearer distance
59.      Transform3D sCylinder = new Transform3D();
60.      sCylinder.set(new Vector3f(0.7f, 0.0f, 0.0f));
61.      TransformGroup smallCylinder = new TransformGroup(sCylinder);
62.      objRoot.addChild(smallCylinder);
63.      smallCylinder.addChild(new Cylinder(0.25f,0.25f,appB));
64.
65.      // show the object at a further distance
66.      sCylinder.set(new Vector3f(-10.0f, 0.0f, -30.0f));
67.      TransformGroup smallCylinder1 = new TransformGroup(sCylinder);
68.      objRoot.addChild(smallCylinder1);
69.      smallCylinder1.addChild(new Cylinder(0.9f,0.9f,appA));
70.
71.      // a white background is better for printing images in tutorial
72.      Background background = new Background();
73.      background.setColor(1.0f, 1.0f, 1.0f);
74.      background.setApplicationBounds(new BoundingSphere());
75.      objRoot.addChild(background);
76.      objRoot.compile();
77.      return objRoot;
78.  }
```

Figure 18. Third code segment and result of LOD.java

```
79.   public LOD()
80.   {
81.        setLayout(new BorderLayout());
82.        Canvas3D canvas3D = new Canvas3D(null);
83.        add("Center", canvas3D);
84.        BranchGroup scene = createSceneGraph();
85.        SimpleUniverse simpleU = new SimpleUniverse(canvas3D);
86.        simpleU.getViewingPlatform().setNominalViewingTransform();
87.        simpleU.addBranchGraph(scene);
88.   }
89.
90.   public static void main(String[] args)
91.   {
92.        Frame frame = new MainFrame(new LOD(), 256, 256);
93.   }    // end of method LOD
94.
95.   } // end of class LOD
```

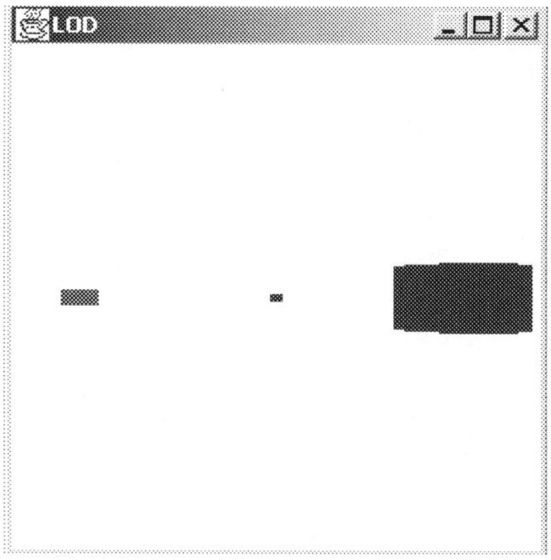

lator is used to move the object back and forth in this example, the alpha of the object, the axis of translation and the start and end positions must also be declared.

MORPH

If it is desired to produce animation that cannot be created by pre-determined behavior such as those under interpolators, billboard or LOD, the Morph class can be used. The effect will be similar to that of flipping pages of slightly different still pictures to create an illusion of moving objects or images.

Under the morph class, these pages of still make up an array of GeometryArray objects, as illustrated in line 15 to line 19 in Figure 19. Each element of the array is associated with a GeometryArray object for the morph class to combine and smooth for the purpose of animation.

In addition the morph class, the animation sequence must also be defined. This is done by declaring a separate class on the behavior of the morph object as illustrated in Figure 20.

To declare a behavior class, the initialize() and processStimulus() classes must be specified. Also, for MorphBehaviour, it is necessary to define an array of weights. These serve

Figure 19. Morph class

```
1.    public BranchGroup createSceneGraph()
2.    {
3.        BranchGroup objRoot = new BranchGroup();
4.        TransformGroup objTrans = new TransformGroup();
5.        objTrans.setCapability( TransformGroup.ALLOW_TRANSFORM_WRITE );
6.        objRoot.addChild( objTrans );
7.
8.        Alpha alphas = new Alpha( -1, 5000 );
9.        RotationInterpolator rotator =
10.               new RotationInterpolator( alphas, objTrans );
11.       BoundingSphere bounds = new BoundingSphere();
12.       rotator.setSchedulingBounds( bounds );
13.       objTrans.addChild( rotator );
14.
15.       GeometryArray[] geoarry = new GeometryArray[4];
16.       geoarry[0] = createGeometry1();
17.       geoarry[1] = createGeometry2();
18.       geoarry[2] = createGeometry3();
19.       geoarry[3] = createGeometry4();
20.
21.       Morph objMorph = new Morph( geoarry );
22.       objMorph.setCapability( Morph.ALLOW_WEIGHTS_WRITE );
23.
24.       MorphBehaviour behave = new MorphBehaviour( objMorph, alphas );
25.       behave.setSchedulingBounds( bounds );
26.
27.       objTrans.addChild( objMorph );
28.       objRoot.addChild( behave );
29.       objRoot.compile();
30.
31.       return objRoot;
32.    }
```

to determine the extent the corresponding GeometryArray objects will contribute to the rendered shape at any specified time. The index of the array weights should thus be the same as the index of the GeometryArray array. Also, the weights must all add up to unity.

Figure 20. Morph behavior and result

```
1.    public class MorphBehaviour extends Behavior
2.    {
3.      private Morph objMorph;
4.      private Alpha alpha;
5.      private double[] weights = new double [4];
6.      private WakeupCondition trigger = new WakeupOnElapsedFrames(0);
7.
8.      MorphBehaviour(Morph objMorph, Alpha alpha)
9.      {
10.       this.objMorph = objMorph;
11.       this.alpha = alpha;
12.     }
13.
14.     public void initialize()  this.wakeupOn(trigger);
15.
16.     public void processStimulus(Enumeration criteria)
17.     {
18.       weights[0] = 0;      //initialize all weights to 0
19.       weights[1] = 0;
20.       weights[2] = 0;
21.       weights[3] = 0;
22.       float alphaValue = 4f*alpha.value(); // multiply by 4f to spread the alpha duration equally
23.                                            // between the 4 trapezium states
24.       int alphaIndex = (int)alphaValue;
25.
26.       //morphing between the current state and next state
27.       if (alphaIndex>3) // upper limits to prevent alphaIndex from going above 3
28.       weights[3] = 1.0;
29.       else if (alphaIndex<=0) // lower limits to prevent alphaIndex from going below 0
30.       {
31.         weights[0] = (double)(alphaValue - (double)alphaIndex);
32.         weights[3] = 1.0 - weights[alphaIndex];
33.       }
34.        else
35.       {
36.         weights[alphaIndex] = (double)(alphaValue - (double)alphaIndex);
37.         weights[alphaIndex-1] = 1.0 - weights[alphaIndex];
38.       }
39.
40.     objMorph.setWeights(weights);
41.     this.wakeupOn(trigger);
42.     }
43.  }
```

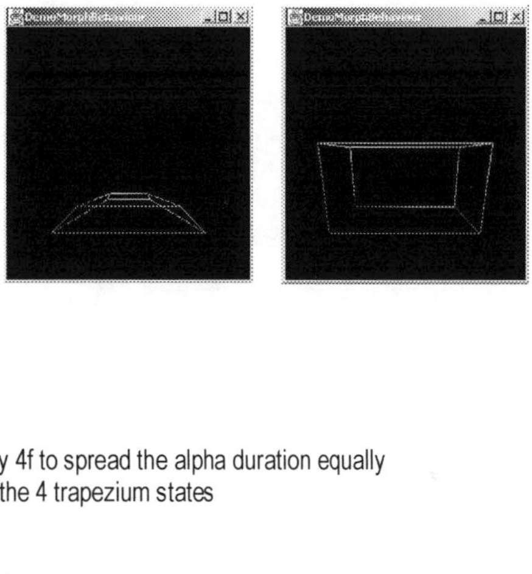

As can be seen from Figure 20, the weights have indices determined from the alpha values. Specifically, with alphaIndex giving the next GeometryArray object to be formed, the visual object will be made up of two GeometryArray objects, indexed by alphaIndex and alphaIndex-1. Their contributions to the rendered shape will be determined by the values of the elements of weights array with the same index. Note that the weight for alphaIndex change from 0 to 0 that for alphaIndex-1 changes from 1 to 0. This way, the rendered shape will morph from one geometry to another.

SUMMARY

This chapter has introduced the Alpha class and how it is used in animations together with the important interpolator classes. In particular, the Billboard and the Level of Detail (LOD) classes are useful for creating animation with reduced rendering. Lastly, the Morph class has been presented with an example on a key frame animation.

REFERENCES

Burrows, A. L., & England, D. (2002). Java 3D, 3D graphical environments and behaviour. *Software - Practice and Experience*, *32*(4), 359-376.

Bund, S., & Do, E. Y. (2005). Fetch light: Interactive navigable 3D visualization of direct sunlight. *Automation in Construction*, *14*, 181-188.

Hu, C., Di, L., & Li, G. (2005). 3D visualization of city residence district based on Java3D. *Proceedings SPIE*, 6043.

Palmer, I. (2001). *Essential Java3D fast: Developing 3D graphics applications in Java*. Springer-Verlag.

Stromer, J. N., Quon, G. T., Gordon, P. M. K., Turinsky, A. L., & Sensen, C. W. (2005). Jabiru: Harnessing Java 3D behaviors for device and display portability. *IEEE Computer Graphics and Applications*, *25*, 70-80.

Tso, K. S., Tharp, G. K., Zhang, W., & Tai, A. T. (1999). A multi-agent operator interface for Unmanned Aerial Vehicles. *Proceedings 18th Digital Avionics Systems Conference*, 6.A.4.1-6.A.4.8.

Chapter VIII
Interaction

INTRODUCTION

In Chapter VII, we discussed how animation can be applied in Java 3D to increase the visual impact of a virtual 3D world and illustrate the dynamic of the various 3D objects to the user (Tate, Moreland, & Bourne, 2001). In this chapter, we will continue this process to make the virtual 3D universe even more interesting and appealing by adding the ability for the user to interact with the 3D objects being rendered.

In Java 3D, both animation and interaction can be accomplished through the use of the behavior class. Having discussed how this class helps to carry out animation in the last chapter, we will now concentrate on the mechanism of using behavior class to achieve interaction.

Technically, the behavior class is an abstract class with mechanisms for the scene graph to be changed. Being an extension of the leaf class, it can also be a part of a normal scene. In particular, it may be a leaf node in the scene graph and can be placed in the same way as geometry is placed.

For instance, in an application where it is necessary to render and control a rotating cube, the rotation behavior for the animation and interaction can be placed under the same transform group as the geometry object for rendering the cube. The main objective of adding a behavior object in a scene graph is of course to change the scene graph in response to a stimulus in the form of, say, pressing a key, moving a mouse, colliding objects, or a combination of these and other events. The change in the virtual 3D world may consist of translating or rotating objects, removing some objects, changing the attributes of others, or any other desirable outcomes in the specific application.

BEHAVIOR CLASS

In Java 3D, all behavior must be based on extending the behavior base class. Specifically, to create an animation or interaction behavior, this base class must first be appropriately extended before it is added to the appropriate position in the scene graph for changing the associated visual objects.

The object that a behavior will act upon is called the object of change. It is through this object that the behavior will be able to change the virtual world. Specifically, the following shows the general code development procedure for creating a custom behavior class.

1. Create the relevant constructors with references to the object of change. Any behavior created will need a reference to an object of change so that the system will know the 3D objects that will be affected by the behavior.
2. Specify the initial wakeup criteria using the initialization() method. The system will invoke this method when the scene graph containing the behavior class becomes live. It sets the initial conditions or triggers under which the behavior should be executed.
3. Decode the trigger condition using the processStimulus() method, and act upon this appropriately. In other words, we need to determine the condition or event, be it a key stroke, mouse click, mouse movement, or other relevant events, being activated and then carry out appropriate processing.

The processStimulus() method will be invoked during runtime by the system when the appropriate trigger conditions have occurred. Initially, the trigger conditions set in the initialization() method will be used. Subsequently, the trigger conditions may be changed in the processStimulus() method itself after it has been invoked.

Note that the calling of processStimulus() depends on the stimulus and many events may be encoded as a single trigger condition. For example, since different mouse actions such as clicking or moving are taken as a single WakeupOnAWTEvent, processStimulus() must carry out some appropriate decoding to find out the specific user input, say, right click or left click. After this, relevant changes to the object of change can be made, resulting in changes in the objects in the virtual 3D world.

With valid stimulus, the invocation of processStimulus() will be invoked by the system between the rendering of adjacent frames. Since the rendering of complicated 3D objects may be compute and system intensive, careful consideration must be taken to ensure that the processing will not result in a substantial reduction of the frame rate or animation speed.

The code fragment in Figure 1 gives an example where a custom behavior class is created for moving a cube upwards when a mouse button is clicked. The example includes the three basic steps outlined in the previous code development procedure.

Firstly, a constructor is created with a reference to a TransformGroup object of change. This is done from lines 16 to 20. Secondly, from lines 22 to 26, the initialization() method is used to specify the initial trigger wakeup condition which, for this case, is an AWTEvent

Figure 1. Code segment for SimpleMouseBehavior.java

```
1.    import java.awt.event.*;
2.    import java.util.Enumeration;
3.
4.    public class SimpleMouseBehavior extends Applet
5.    {
6.        private WakeupCriterion events[] = new WakeupCriterion[1];
7.        private WakeupOr allEvents;
8.
9.        public class SimpleMouseMovement extends Behavior
10.       {
11.               private TransformGroup targetTG;
12.               private Transform3D trans = new Transform3D();
13.               private double TransX = 0.0;
14.               private double TransY = 0.0;
15.
16.               //create SimpleBehavior
17.               SimpleMouseMovement (TransformGroup targetTG)
18.               {
19.                       this.targetTG = targetTG;
20.               }
21.
22.               //initialize the behavior; set initial wakeup condition; called when behavior becomes live
23.               public void initialize()
24.               {
25.                       this.wakeupOn(new WakeupOnAWTEvent(MouseEvent.MOUSE_PRESSED));
26.               }
27.
28.               public void processStimulus(Enumeration criteria)
29.               {
30.                       //decode event ; do what is necessary
31.                       TransY+=0.05;
32.                       trans.set(new Vector3f((float)TransX,(float)TransY,0.0f));
33.                       targetTG.setTransform(trans);
34.                       this.wakeupOn(new WakeupOnAWTEvent(MouseEvent.MOUSE_PRESSED));
35.               }
36.       }
37.  }
```

for a mouse click. Lastly, the processStimulus() method is supplied for defining the action to be taken when the event or condition is triggered. In this simple example with only one triggering condition, no decoding is needed and the processStimulus() method simply increases the value of the TransY variable to move the cube up by a certain amount vertically

Figure 2. Adding SimpleMouseBehavior.java

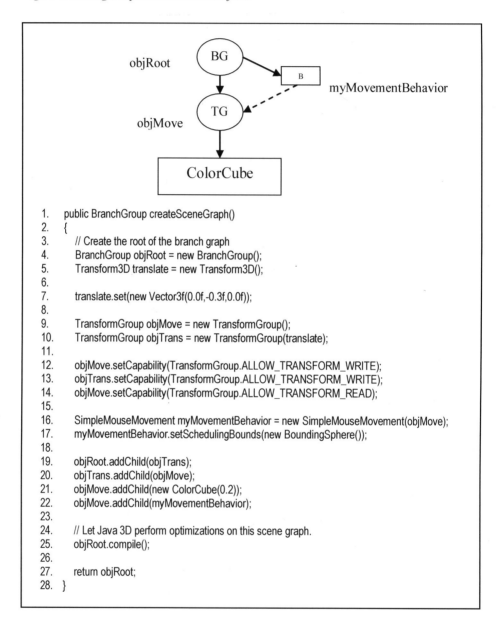

```
1.    public BranchGroup createSceneGraph()
2.    {
3.        // Create the root of the branch graph
4.        BranchGroup objRoot = new BranchGroup();
5.        Transform3D translate = new Transform3D();
6.
7.        translate.set(new Vector3f(0.0f,-0.3f,0.0f));
8.
9.        TransformGroup objMove = new TransformGroup();
10.       TransformGroup objTrans = new TransformGroup(translate);
11.
12.       objMove.setCapability(TransformGroup.ALLOW_TRANSFORM_WRITE);
13.       objTrans.setCapability(TransformGroup.ALLOW_TRANSFORM_WRITE);
14.       objMove.setCapability(TransformGroup.ALLOW_TRANSFORM_READ);
15.
16.       SimpleMouseMovement myMovementBehavior = new SimpleMouseMovement(objMove);
17.       myMovementBehavior.setSchedulingBounds(new BoundingSphere());
18.
19.       objRoot.addChild(objTrans);
20.       objTrans.addChild(objMove);
21.       objMove.addChild(new ColorCube(0.2));
22.       objMove.addChild(myMovementBehavior);
23.
24.       // Let Java 3D perform optimizations on this scene graph.
25.       objRoot.compile();
26.
27.       return objRoot;
28.    }
```

in the direction of the positive y axis. After this movement, the trigger is reset in line 34. Thus, subsequent mouse clicks will move the cube up by the same amount every time.

Note that the code segment in Figure 1 includes two import statements for the behavior class. Specifically, java.awt.event.* is for mouse interaction, while java.util.Enumeration is for the purpose of decoding the wake up conditions.

Having created a desirable behavior for moving an object in Figure 1, Figure 2 shows how this can be incorporated into the main code segment for the creation of the Java 3D virtual world. The created scene graph is also shown. As depicted, before adding the appropriate behavior, a TransformGroup, which is at a level above the cube to be rotated, is first created which will serve as the target of the behavior subsequently.

Next, an instance of the behavior class is added to the scene graph. Note that if the scene graph is not live, the behavior will not be initialized. Lastly, scheduling bounds are provided for the behavior. This behavior will only be active for the receiving of stimulus when its scheduling bounds intersect the activation volume of a ViewPlatform. We will discuss this in more detail in the next section.

BOUNDING REGION

setSchedulingBounds from javax.media.j3d.Behavior is a method that allows the bounding region of a behavior to be specified. If this region intersects with the region of the ViewPlatform as illustrated in Figure 3, this behavior will be able to receive user and event stimulus and will be able to render changes in the virtual 3D world.

Conceptually, as illustrated, the view region is a region that can be seen by the user and corresponds to the user view, while the behavior region is a region where something interesting may be going on. However, the user can only see what is happening in his or her view and if this happens not to contain the region where interesting behavior is going on, the user will still not be able to see the latter.

Technically, the ViewingPlatform is a property of the universe in Java3D, with a default region centered at the origin and an activation radius of 62. On the other hand, the bounding region for a behavior can be specified under the BoundingSphere class, and has a default center at the origin and a radius of one. Thus, the default bounding sphere will intersect the normal ViewingTransform, and the behavior will be visible. However, if the latter is changed to those values given in Figure 4 (which show the normal declaration formats of ViewingPlatform and bounding sphere), there will be no interaction and the behavior will not be visible.

Figure 3. Illustration of bounding region and ViewPlatform

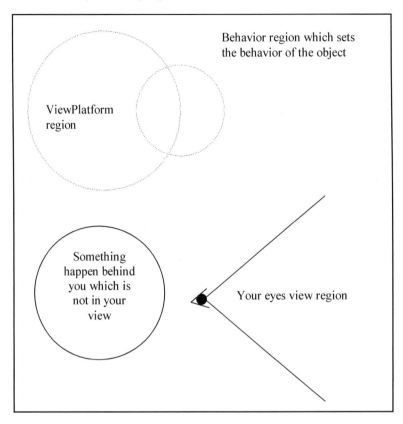

Figure 4. ViewPlatform and bounding sphere declaration

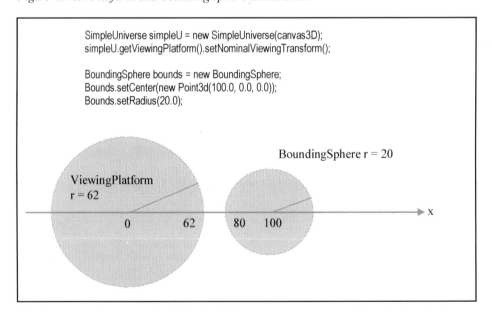

WAKEUP CONDITION AND CRITERION

As discussed in the last section, a behavior is active and will be able to receive a triggering stimulus if its scheduling bound is able to intersect with the activation volume of the ViewPlatform. When this happens, the occurrence of one or more of the defined wakeup stimuli will cause the system to invoke the relevant parts of the processStimulus() method, resulting in changes in the Java 3D world.

A variety of stimuli can be defined to correspond to the detection of associated user actions or system events. Technically, this is done through specifying the wakeup stimuli in terms of appropriate descendants of the WakeupCondition class.

WakeupCondition is an abstract class that provides the foundation of all the wakeup classes in Java 3D. Under this abstract class, there are five important extended classes. The first four allow multiple wakeup conditions to be composed in a single wakeup condition, while the last one corresponds to WakeupCriterion, which is an abstract method for 14 specific wakeup criterion classes.

As summarized in Figure 5, two important methods are provided for the WakeupCondition class. The first one, allElemnts, returns an enumeration list of all the wakeup criteria for a WakeupCondition object. The other, triggeredElements, provides information on the specific wakeup criterion that has resulted in the triggering of the behavior. Obviously, this method will be most useful in decoding the event that has led to the running of a processStimulus method of a behavior.

On the other hand, WakeupCriterion is an abstract class for 14 specific wakeup criterion classes. Under this abstract class, only one method, hasTriggered, is provided. Figure 6 gives a summary for this as well as the specific wakeup events under WakeupCriterion. Note that since the functionality of the hasTriggered method can be captured under the triggeredElements method of WakeupCondition, the former method is often not used in program development.

Figure 5. WakeupCondition and methods

```
WakeupCondition()
// Constructor for creating a WakeupCondition object.

Enumeration allElements()
// Method that returns an enumeration of all WakeupCriterion objects.

Enumeration triggeredElements()
// Method that returns an enumeration of all triggered WakeupCriterion objects
```

Figure 6. WakeupCriterion and method

WakeupCriterion()
// Constructor for creating a WakeupCriterion object.

boolean hasTriggered()
// method returning a true if the specified criterion has given rise to the wakeup trigger.

Wakeup criterion	Triggering event
WakeupOnActivation	An object's scheduling region starts to intersect with the ViewPlatform's activation volume
WakeupOnDeactivation	An object's scheduling region no longer intersects with the ViewPlatform's activation volume
WakeupOnAWTEvent	A specific AWT event occurs
WakeupOnBehaviorPost	A behavior object posts a specific event
WakeupOnCollisionEntry	A specified object collides with other objects
WakeupOnCollisionExit	A specified object no longer collides with other objects
WakeupOnCollisionMovement	A specified object moves while colliding with other objects
WakeupOnElapsedFrames	The elapsing of a specified number of frames
WakeupOnElapsedTime	The elapsing of a specific number of milliseconds
WakeupOnSensorEntry	A sensor has started to intersect a specified boundary
WakeupOnSensorExit	The sensor no longer intersects the specified boundary
WakeupOnTransformChange	The transform in a specified TransformGroup has changed
WakeupOnViewPlatformEntry	The ViewPlatform's activation volume intersects with the specified boundary
WakeupOnViewPlatformExit	The ViewPlatform's activation volume no longer intersects the specified boundary

A simple example illustrating the use of wakeup criterions is presented in Figure 7. In this example, two wakeup criteria, WakeupOnActivation and WakeupOnDeactivation, are used.

At the beginning, the bound region has a radius of 50 and the initial wakeup trigger condition is set to correspond to that for WakeupOnActivation or when the ViewingPlatform intersects the scheduling regions. Since the two regions do overlap at this time as illustrated, the system will generate a trigger and control will be passed to the processStimulus method to deal with this trigger.

In this simple example, the processStimulus method changes the scheduling region by reducing its bound radius. As can be seen, the new scheduling region will not be intersecting

Figure 7. Code segment for WakeupOnActivationAndDeactivation.java

```
1.    public class SimpleBehavior extends Behavior
2.    {
3.      private TransformGroup targetTG;
4.      private WakeupCriterion Activation = new WakeupOnActivation();
5.      private WakeupCriterion DeActivation = new WakeupOnDeactivation();
6.      private BoundingSphere bound = new BoundingSphere(new Point3d(100.0, 0.0, 0.0), 50.0);
7.
8.      SimpleBehavior(TransformGroup TG)
9.      {
10.           this.targetTG = TG;
11.           this.setSchedulingBounds(bound); // set SchedulingBounds - center (100, 0, 0), radius 50
12.     }
```

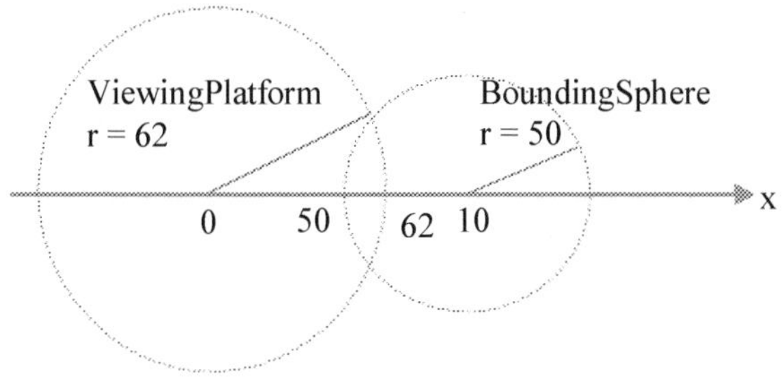

```
13.     public void initialize()
14.     {
15.           this.wakeupOn(Activation); //set initial wakeup criterion as Activation
16.     }
17.
18.     public void processStimulus(Enumeration criteria)
19.     {
20.           bound.setRadius(20.0); // change the radius to 20.0
21.           this.setSchedulingBounds(bound);  // reset the SchedulingBounds
```

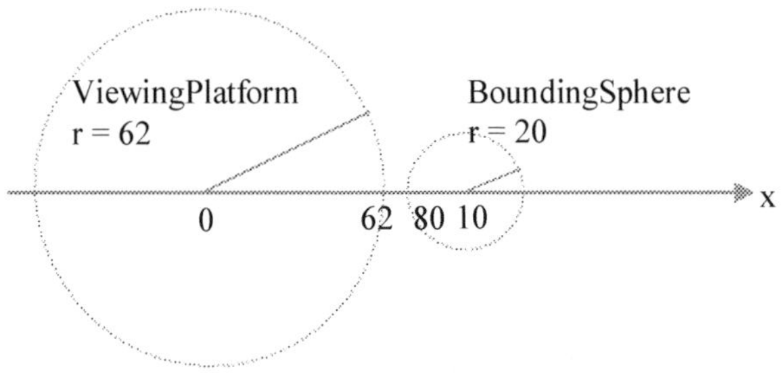

```
22.           if (DeActivation.hasTriggered()) // check for DeActivation
23.                 System.out.println("Deactivation = True");
24.           else
25.                 System.out.println("Deactivation = False");
26.           this.wakeupOn(DeActivation); // set the new wakeup criterion to DeActivation
27.     }
28. }
```

the ViewingPlatform region after the change and will result in a WakeupOnDeactivation trigger after the current invocation of the processStimulus method has been completed.

The completion of the current invocation of processStimulus requires the checking of the logical triggering status of the DeActivation criterion and then printing this out as a system message. Since the running of the current processStimulus method is due to a WakeupOnActivation trigger, the output is of course false in nature. After printing this message, a new wakeup trigger condition, which is based on WakeupOnDeactivation, is set.

After finishing the current processStimulus method and with the scheduling region changed to be non-overlapping with the ViewingPlatform, a new trigger for WakeupOnDeactivation will be generated. The same processStimulus method will be invoked by the system to deal with this trigger, and it is easy to see that the status message printed out will now be true.

It is worthwhile to note that the setting of a new wakeup trigger condition, which is based on WakeupOnDeactivation, is crucial. Without this, the processStimulus method will not be invoked to deal with the WakeupOnDeactivation wakeup criterion. Also, as illustrated in the code segment and the straightforward task involved in this simple example, it is easy to make mistakes and difficult to debug programs involving complicated behavior. In general, careful planning in the setting up of appropriate wakeup trigger conditions is essential to ensure that objects in the Java 3D world behave in accordance with expectation.

KEYBOARD AND MOUSE EVENTS

The most common events that need to be dealt with in any Java 3D program are perhaps those corresponding to changes in mouse and keyboard status, which result in WakeupOnAWTEvent (Geroimenko & Geroimenko, 2000). The usage of the latter and the common associated AWT events are presented in Figure 8.

The code segment in Figure 9 shows how key strokes can be captured and processed through WakeupOnAWTEvent. Lines 4 to 6 define the keys that will give rise to a trigger for the behavior. Lines 21 to 27 correspond to the initialization method, which sets up the initial trigger condition. Lines 29 to 43 give the processStimulus method, which will be invoked by the system when the specified events have happened. Note that in this example, the processStimulus method will simply decode the key that have been pressed, and then pass this to a keyPressed method for relevant processing.

Figures 10 and 11 present an example for the processing of mouse events instead of key strokes. The code is similar to that in Figure 9 for key strokes. Note that the method MouseEvent is called after decoding the type of mouse movement or mouse button pressed (Vormoor, 2001). Also, the method is supplied with an integer argument that identifies the movement or button.

Figure 8. WakeupOnAWTEvent and usage

```
WakeupOnAWTEvent(int AWTId)
// Constructor for a new WakeupOnAWTEvent object.
// AWTId is the AWT ids that we would like to intercept.  Common values are:
// KeyEvent.KEY_TYPED, KeyEvent.KEY_PRESSED, KeyEvent.KEY_RELEASED
// MouseEvent.MOUSE_CLICKED, MouseEvent.MOUSE_PRESSED,
// MouseEvent.MOUSE_RELEASED, MouseEvent.MOUSE_MOVED,
// MouseEvent.MOUSE_DRAGGED

WakeupOnAWTEvent(long eventMask)
// Constructor for a new WakeupOnAWTEvent object using EVENT_MASK values in
// logical or format.  Common values are:
// KEY_EVENT_MASK, MOUSE_EVENT_MASK
// MOUSE_MOTION_EVENT_MASK

AWTEvent[] getAWTEvent()
// Method for retrieving the array of consecutive AWT event triggering the wakeup.
```

POSTED EVENTS

Other than user and external events such as the pressing of keys or buttons or mouse movement, it is also possible for a behavior to post an event to the system. This is the same as
having an external stimulus and will result in a wakeup trigger, perhaps resulting in the
execution of the appropriate prosessStimulus method and leading to a change in the 3D
world being rendered.

The mechanism for achieving this is through the setting of the WakeupOnBehaviorPost
condition together with an integer postId for identification purposes. Figure 12 shows the
usage of this mechanism as well as some accompanying methods for setting and identify-
ing the behavior and postId causing the wakeup.

The ability for posting events is very useful for developing codes involving the movement
of different objects or complicated behavior. It allows for different behaviors to coordinate
with one another after the virtual world has gone through some identifiable important
changes. For instance, in a simple application involving the opening and closing of a door,
it may be easier to develop two different individual behaviors for the two different actions,
and have one behavior posting a message to wakeup the other behavior if a door closing
operation is to follow a door closing one.

The code segment in Figures 13 to 15 illustrate the use of WakeupOnBehaviorPost for
shifting an object to the right if a key is pressed, to the left when the next key is pressed,

Figure 9. Code segment for KeyBoardBehavior.java

```
1.    public class KeyBoardBehaviour extends Applet
2.    {
3.        private static final int
4.          UP = KeyEvent.VK_UP, DOWN = KeyEvent.VK_DOWN, LEFT = KeyEvent.VK_LEFT,
5.          RIGHT = KeyEvent.VK_RIGHT, MOVEUP = KeyEvent.VK_W, MOVEDWN  = KeyEvent.VK_S,
6.          MOVERGT = KeyEvent.VK_D, MOVELEFT = KeyEvent.VK_A;
7.
8.        private WakeupCriterion events[] = new WakeupCriterion[1];
9.        private WakeupOr allEvents;
10.
11.       public class SimpleBehavior extends Behavior
12.       {
13.               private TransformGroup targetTG;
14.               private Transform3D tempRotation = new Transform3D();
15.               private Transform3D rotation = new Transform3D();
16.               private Transform3D trans = new Transform3D();
17.               private double anglex = 0.0, angley = 0.0, TransX = 0.0, TransY = 0.0;
18.
19.               SimpleBehavior(TransformGroup targetTG) this.targetTG = targetTG;
20.
21.               public void initialize()
22.               {
23.                       events[0]=new WakeupOnAWTEvent(KeyEvent.KEY_PRESSED);
24.                       this.wakeupOn(new WakeupOnAWTEvent(KeyEvent.KEY_PRESSED));
25.                       allEvents=new WakeupOr(events);
26.                       wakeupOn(allEvents);
27.               }
28.
29.               public void processStimulus(Enumeration criteria)
30.               {
31.                       WakeupCriterion wakeup;  AWTEvent[] event ;
32.                       while(criteria.hasMoreElements())
33.                       {
34.                               wakeup = (WakeupCriterion) criteria.nextElement();
35.                               if(wakeup instanceof WakeupOnAWTEvent)
36.                               {
37.                                       event = ((WakeupOnAWTEvent)wakeup).getAWTEvent()
38.                                       keyPressed((KeyEvent)event[0]);
39.
40.                               }
41.                       }
42.                       this.wakeupOn(allEvents);
43.               }
44.       } //end of class SimpleBehavior
```

and so on. Lines 12 to 56 build the MoveRight behavior class to shift the object right, and this is initialized by a WakeupOnAWTEvent. When a key is pressed, its processStimulus method is invoked and the object is shifted right using WakeupOnElaspedFrame. Once

Figure 10. First code segment of MouseBehaviorUserDefine.java

```
1.      public class MouseBehaviourUserDefine extends Applet
2.      {
3.        private static final int UP = 1;
4.        private static final int DOWN = 2;
5.        private static final int LEFT = 3;
6.        private static final int RIGHT = 4;
7.
8.        private WakeupCriterion events[] = new WakeupCriterion[4];
9.        private WakeupOr allEvents;
10.
11.       public class MouseMovement extends Behavior
12.       {
13.         private TransformGroup targetTG;
14.         private Transform3D trans = new Transform3D();
15.         private double TransX = 0.0;
16.         private double TransY = 0.0;
17.
18.         MouseMovement (TransformGroup targetTG) this.targetTG = targetTG;
19.
20.         public void initialize()
21.         {
22.           //set initial wakeup condition
23.           events[0]=new WakeupOnAWTEvent(MouseEvent.MOUSE_DRAGGED);
24.           events[1]=new WakeupOnAWTEvent(MouseEvent.MOUSE_PRESSED);
25.           events[2]=new WakeupOnAWTEvent(MouseEvent.MOUSE_RELEASED);
26.           events[3]=new WakeupOnAWTEvent(MouseEvent.MOUSE_MOVED);
27.
28.           allEvents=new WakeupOr(events);
29.           wakeupOn(allEvents);
30.         }
31.
```

this shift right operation has finished, an appropriate postID will be posted to wake up a partner MoveLeft class in line 51.

The MoveLeft class is presented from lines 57 onwards. As shown in line 81, it is initialized by WakeupOnBehaviorPost instead of WakeupOnAWTEvent. Line 86 checks if the postId for the wakeup is proper. If it is, lines 88 to 90 will be executed, setting the next WakeupCriterion to be AWTEvent or the pressing of a key. When the next key stroke is detected, the object will thus shift left, and once this operation has been accomplished, the next WakeupCriterion will be set to WakeupOnBehaviorPost and a new postID will be posted to its partner MoveRight.

Ko & Cheng

Figure 11. Second code segment of MouseBehaviorUserDefine.java

```
32.       public void processStimulus(Enumeration criteria)
33.       {
34.         WakeupCriterion wakeup;
35.         AWTEvent[] event;
36.         int eventID;
37.         while(criteria.hasMoreElements())
38.         {
39.           wakeup = (WakeupCriterion) criteria.nextElement();
40.           if(wakeup instanceof WakeupOnAWTEvent)
41.           {
42.             event = ((WakeupOnAWTEvent)wakeup).getAWTEvent();
43.             for(int i=0;i<event.length;i++)
44.             {
45.               eventID = event[i].getID();
46.               if((eventID==MouseEvent.MOUSE_PRESSED)&&
47.                     !((MouseEvent)event[i]).isAltDown()&& !((MouseEvent)event[i]).isMetaDown())
48.               {
49.                     MouseEvent(3);  //Left Mouse Button
50.
51.               }
52.               if((eventID==MouseEvent.MOUSE_PRESSED)&&
53.                     !((MouseEvent)event[i]).isAltDown()&& ((MouseEvent)event[i]).isMetaDown())
54.               {
55.                     MouseEvent(4);  //Right Mouse Button
56.               }
57.               if((eventID==MouseEvent.MOUSE_PRESSED)&&
58.                     ((MouseEvent)event[i]).isAltDown()&&!((MouseEvent)event[i]).isMetaDown())
59.               {
60.                     MouseEvent(1);  //Center Mouse Button
61.               }
62.               if((eventID==MouseEvent.MOUSE_DRAGGED)&&
63.                     !((MouseEvent)event[i]).isAltDown()&& !((MouseEvent)event[i]).isMetaDown())
64.               {
65.                     MouseEvent(2);  //Combination of click and drag of the mouse
66.               }
67.             }
68.           }
69.         }
70.         this.wakeupOn(allEvents);
71.       }
72.     }
73.   }
```

Figure 12. WakeupOnBehaviorPost event and usage

```
WakeupOnBehaviorPost (Behavior behavior, int postId)
// Constructor for a new WakeupOnBehaviorPost criterion.

Behavior getBehavior()
// Method for returning the behavior for an object

int getPostId()
// Retrieves the postId

Behavior getTriggeringBehavior()
// Returns the behavior that triggered the wakeup.

int getTriggeringPostId()
// Returns the postId that caused the behavior to wakeup.
```

Figure 13. First code segment of PostBehavior.java

```
1.    public class PostBehaviour extends Applet
2.    {
3.        public class MoveRight extends Behavior
4.        {
5.                private TransformGroup  targetTG;
6.                private Transform3D trans = new Transform3D();
7.                private WakeupCriterion pairPostCondition;
8.                private WakeupCriterion wakeupNextFrame;
9.                private WakeupCriterion AWTEventCondition;
10.               private double transX;
11.
12.               MoveRight(TransformGroup targetTG)
13.               {
14.                       this.targetTG = targetTG;
15.                       AWTEventCondition = new WakeupOnAWTEvent(KeyEvent.KEY_PRESSED);
16.                       wakeupNextFrame = new WakeupOnElapsedFrames(0);
17.               }
18.
19.               public void setBehaviorObjectPartner(Behavior behaviorObject)
20.               {
21.                       pairPostCondition = new WakeupOnBehaviorPost(behaviorObject, 2);
22.               }
23.
24.               public void initialize()
25.               {
26.                       this.wakeupOn(AWTEventCondition);
27.                       transX = 0.0;
28.               }
29.
```

Figure 14. Second code segment of PostBehavior.java

```
30.            public void processStimulus(Enumeration criteria)
31.            {
32.                    if (criteria.nextElement().equals(pairPostCondition))
33.                    {
34.                            System.out.println("ready to shift");
35.                            this.wakeupOn(AWTEventCondition);
36.                            transX = 0.0f;
37.                    }
38.                    else
39.                    {
40.                            if (transX < 0.7)
41.                            {
42.                                    transX += 0.1;
43.                                    trans.set(new Vector3f((float)transX,0.0f,0.0f));
44.                                    targetTG.setTransform(trans);
45.                                    this.wakeupOn(wakeupNextFrame);
46.                            }
47.                            else
48.                            {
49.                                    System.out.println("block shifted right");
50.                                    this.wakeupOn(pairPostCondition);
51.                                    postId(1);
52.                            }
53.                    }
54.            }
55.    }
56.
57.    public class MoveLeft extends Behavior
58.    {
59.            private TransformGroup  targetTG;
60.            private WakeupCriterion pairPostCondition;
61.            private Transform3D trans = new Transform3D();
62.            private WakeupCriterion wakeupNextFrame;
63.            private WakeupCriterion AWTEventCondition;
64.            private double transX;
65.
66.            MoveLeft(TransformGroup targetTG)
67.            {
68.                    this.targetTG = targetTG;
69.                    AWTEventCondition = new WakeupOnAWTEvent(KeyEvent.KEY_PRESSED);
70.                    wakeupNextFrame = new WakeupOnElapsedFrames(0);
71.            }
72.
```

Figure 15. Third code segment of PostBehavior.java

```
73.              public void setBehaviorObjectPartner(Behavior behaviorObject)
74.              {
75.                      pairPostCondition = new WakeupOnBehaviorPost(behaviorObject, 1);
76.              }
77.
78.              public void initialize()
79.              {
80.                      this.wakeupOn(pairPostCondition);
81.                      transX = 0.7f;
82.              }
83.
84.              public void processStimulus(Enumeration criteria)
85.              {
86.                      if (criteria.nextElement().equals(pairPostCondition))
87.                      {
88.                              System.out.println("ready to shift");
89.                              this.wakeupOn(AWTEventCondition);
90.                              transX = 0.7f;
91.                      }
92.                      else
93.                      {
94.                              if (transX > 0.0)
95.                              {
96.                                      transX -= 0.1;
97.                                      trans.set(new Vector3f((float)transX,0.0f,0.0f));
98.                                      targetTG.setTransform(trans);
99.                                      this.wakeupOn(wakeupNextFrame);
100.                             }
101.                             else
102.                             {
103.                                     System.out.println("block shifted left");
104.                                     this.wakeupOn(pairPostCondition);
105.                                     postId(2);
106.                             }
107.                     }
108.             }
109.
110.     }
111.
112. }
```

COLLISION EVENTS

Sudden changes to how objects should be rendered in a 3D world will most likely be necessary when two objects collide with each other. The detection of collisions and how they can be handled are therefore important issues in Java 3D.

However, since these issues are complicated, we will not discuss the topic in detail in this chapter. Instead, for the sake of completeness, a summary of the important classes and methods that can be used for handling collisions are presented in Figures 16, 17, and 18. Specifically, the setting of wakeup events for detecting when a specific object has collided with other objects, when it no longer collide with any other objects, and when it moves while in collision are summarized in the respective figures. A detailed example on the use of these wakeup events will be presented later.

ELAPSED TIME AND FRAME EVENTS

For handling situations where objects are evolving or changing as a function of time and in animation, the use of classes that provide wakeup triggers after a certain number of frames or milliseconds have passed may be very useful.

Figure 19 gives a summary of the usage of the WakeupOnElapsedFrames and WakeupOnElapsedTime classes for such applications. Note that the wakeup criterion may be passive or non-passive. If the latter is selected, the rendering of the various objects will proceed to be carried out continuously. Also, the execution of behaviors and rendering will not be synchronized in general, except for the case when a frame count of 0 is specified. In this situation, the relevant behavior will be invoked every frame, and changes to the objects being rendered will take effect in the same rendering frame.

A simple example on the use of WakeupOnElapsedFrames is given in Figure 20. The wakeup criteria for the program correspond to that of pressing the mouse or when 100 frames have passed. When triggers for these events are received and the processStimulus method is invoked, a relevant system message will be printed.

Figure 21 gives the code segment and result from using WakeupOnElapsedTime to render a clock that ticks at the same rate as the system clock. The methods for the drawing of the clock frame and its three hands are not shown. Essentially, two arrays are used to store vertices that can be used to draw the clock and its hands corresponding to specified time using appropriate methods. Note, however, that for the position for the hands to be varied, the Shape3D capability has to be changed to ALLOW_GEOMETRY_WRITE.

As specified in the initial wake up criterion, the clock is started by the pressing of a key. When this happens, the processStimulus method retrieves the system time, invokes the relevant methods to render the clock hands according to the system time, which is in 24-hour format, and then sets the new wake up criterion to that for a time lapsed of 1000

Figure 16. WakeupOnCollisonEntry event and usage

```
WakeupOnCollisionEntry(Bounds armingBounds)
// Constructs a new WakeupOnCollisionEntry criterion.

WakeupOnCollisionEntry(Node armingNode, int speedHint)
// Constructs a new WakeupOnCollisionEntry criterion, where speedHint may be
// USE_BOUNDS - use geometric bounds as an approximation in computing collisions.
// USE_GEOMETRY - use geometry in computing collisions.

WakeupOnCollisionEntry(SceneGraphPath armingPath)
// Constructs a new WakeupOnCollisionEntry criterion with USE_BOUNDS.

WakeupOnCollisionEntry(SceneGraphPath armingPath, int speedHint)
// Constructs a new WakeupOnCollisionEntry criterion, where speedHint may be
// USE_BOUNDS or USE_GEOMETRY.
```

Figure 17. WakeupOnCollisonExit event and usage

```
WakeupOnCollisionExit(Bounds armingBounds)
// Constructs a new WakeupOnCollisionExit criterion.

WakeupOnCollisionExit(Node armingNode)
// Constructs a new WakeupOnCollisionExit criterion.

WakeupOnCollisionExit(Node armingNode, int speedHint)
// Constructs a new WakeupOnCollisionExit criterion, where speedHint may be
// USE_BOUNDS - use geometric bounds as an approximation in computing collisions.
// USE_GEOMETRY - use geometry in computing collisions.

WakeupOnCollisionExit(SceneGraphPath armingPath)
// Constructs a new WakeupOnCollisionExit criterion.

WakeupOnCollisionExit(SceneGraphPath armingPath, int speedHint)
// Constructs a new WakeupOnCollisionExit criterion, where speedHint may be
// USE_BOUNDS or USE_GEOMETRY.

Bounds getArmingBounds()
// Returns the bound an object used in specifying collision condition.

SceneGraphPath getArmingPath()
// Returns the path used in specifying collision condition.

Bounds getTriggeringBounds()
// Returns the bound of an object that caused a collision

SceneGraphPath getTriggeringPath()
// Returns the path describing the object that caused a collision.
```

Figure 18. WakeupOnCollisonMovement event and usage

```
WakeupOnCollisionMovement(Bounds armingBounds)
// Constructs a new WakeupOnCollisionMovement criterion.

WakeupOnCollisionMovement(Node armingNode)
// Constructs a new WakeupOnCollisionMovement criterion.

WakeupOnCollisionMovement(Node armingNode, int speedHint)
// Constructs a new WakeupOnCollisionMovement criterion, where speedHint may be
// USE_BOUNDS - use geometric bounds as an approximation in computing collisions.
// USE_GEOMETRY - use geometry in computing collisions.

WakeupOnCollisionMovement(SceneGraphPath armingPath)
// Constructs a new WakeupOnCollisionMovement criterion.

WakeupOnCollisionMovement(SceneGraphPath armingPath, int speedHint)
// Constructs a new WakeupOnCollisionMovement criterion, where speedHint may be
// USE_BOUNDS or USE_GEOMETRY.

Bounds getArmingBounds()
// Returns the bound an object used in specifying the collision condition.

SceneGraphPath getArmingPath()
// Returns the path used in specifying the collision condition.

Bounds getTriggeringBounds()
// Returns the bound of the object that caused the collision.

SceneGraphPath getTriggeringPath()
// Returns the path describing the object that caused the collision.
```

Figure 19. WakeupOnElapsedFrames and WakeupOnElapsedTime events and usage

```
WakeupOnElapsedFrames(int frameCount)
// Constructs a non-passive WakeupOnElapsedFrames criterion.

WakeupOnElapsedFrames(int frameCount, boolean passive)
// Constructs a new WakeupOnElapsedFrames criterion.

getElapsedFrameCount()
// Retrieve the elapsed frame count used when constructing a certain criterion.

WakeupOnElapsedTime(long miliseconds)
// Constructs a new WakeupOnElapsedTime criterion.

getElapsedFrameTime()
// Retrieve the WakeupCriterion's elapsed time used when constructing a certain criterion.
```

Figure 20. Code segment for SimpleElapsedFrames.java

```
1.    public class SimpleElapsedFrames extends Applet
2.    {
3.      private WakeupCriterion events[] = new WakeupCriterion[2];
4.      private WakeupOr allEvents;
5.
6.      public class SimpleFrames extends Behavior
7.      {
8.              private TransformGroup targetTG;
9.
10.             SimpleFrames (TransformGroup targetTG)
11.             {
12.                     this.targetTG = targetTG;
13.             }
14.
15.             public void initialize()
16.             {
17.                     events[0]=new WakeupOnAWTEvent(MouseEvent.MOUSE_PRESSED);
18.                     events[1]=new WakeupOnElapsedFrames(100);
19.                     allEvents=new WakeupOr(events);
20.                     wakeupOn(allEvents);
21.             }
22.
23.             public void processStimulus(Enumeration criteria)
24.             {
25.                     WakeupCriterion wakeup;
26.                     while(criteria.hasMoreElements())
27.                     {
28.                             wakeup = (WakeupCriterion) criteria.nextElement();
29.                             if(wakeup instanceof WakeupOnAWTEvent)
30.                                     System.out.println("MOUSE_CLICK");
31.                             else
32.                                     System.out.println("100 FRAMES HAVE ELAPSED");
33.                     }
34.                     this.wakeupOn(allEvents);
35.             }
36.    }
```

milliseconds or 1 second. The passing of 1 second will lead to a triggering of the same processStimulus method to update the clock hands, giving the visual effect of a ticking clock.

Figure 21. Code segment and result of WakeupOnElapsedTimeClock.java

```
1.   aHand SecHand, MinHand, HourHand;
2.   Point3f coor[] = new Point3f[120];  // contains coordinates to draw the clock
3.   Point3f coorHand[][] = new Point3f[3][60]; // 3 subarray contains coordinates to draw the 3 hands
4.
5.   public class SimpleBehavior extends Behavior
6.   {
7.       private TransformGroup targetTG;
8.       SimpleBehavior(TransformGroup TG) this.targetTG = TG;
9.
10.      public void initialize() this.wakeupOn(new WakeupOnAWTEvent(KeyEvent.KEY_PRESSED));
11.
12.      public void processStimulus(Enumeration criteria)
13.      {
14.              Date timenow = new Date();  // get current time
15.              int sec, min, hour;
16.              sec = timenow.getSeconds();
17.              min = timenow.getMinutes();
18.              hour = timenow.getHours()%12;
19.              SecHand.setPos(sec, 0);  //reset three hands
20.              MinHand.setPos(min, 1);
21.              HourHand.setPos(hour*5+min/12, 2);
22.
23.              this.wakeupOn(new WakeupOnElapsedTime(1000)); // set the WakeupCriterion for 1 sec
24.      }
25.  }
```

EVENTS DUE TO CHANGES IN POSITIONS AND TRANSFORMS

Changes in the positions and the transform of objects in the 3D universe can be detected through the use of the WakeupOnTransformChange criterion, which will give rise to a trigger event for a behavior when the TransformGroup attached to it is changed. From a certain point of view, it provides another way for the implementation of WakeupOnPost-

Figure 22. WakeupOnPostBehavo event and usage

```
WakeupOnTransformChange(TransformGroup node)
// Constructs a new WakeupOnTransformChange Criterion.

TransformGroup getTransformGroup()
// Return the TransformGroup node used in creating a certain WakeupCriterion.
```

Figure 23. First code segment of TransformChange.java

```
1.   MoveBehavior(TransformGroup targetTG)
2.   {
3.      keyboardevent=new WakeupOnAWTEvent(KeyEvent.KEY_PRESSED);
4.      this.targetTG = targetTG;
5.   }
6.
7.   public void initialize() this.wakeupOn(keyboardevent);
8.
9.   public void keyPressed(KeyEvent e)
10.  {
11.     int key = e.getKeyCode();  direction = key;
12.     switch(key)
13.     {
14.             case up:    transY+=0.01;
15.                                 translate.set(new Vector3f((float)transX, float)transY,0.0f));
16.                                 targetTG.setTransform(translate); direct="forward"; break;
17.             case down:      transY-=0.01;
18.                                 translate.set(new Vector3f((float)transX, (float)transY, 0.0f));
19.                                 targetTG.setTransform(translate); direct="back"; break;
20.             case right: transX+=0.01;
21.                                 translate.set(new Vector3f((float)transX,(float)transY,0.0f));
22.                                 targetTG.setTransform(translate); direct="right"; break;
23.             case left:   transX-=0.01;
24.                                 translate.set(new Vector3f((float)transX,(float)transY,0.0f));
25.                                 targetTG.setTransform(translate); direct="left"; break;
26.             default:
27.     }
28.
29.  public void processStimulus(Enumeration criteria)
30.  {
31.     WakeupCriterion wakeup;
32.     AWTEvent[] event;
33.     while(criteria.hasMoreElements())
34.     {
35.             wakeup = (WakeupCriterion) criteria.nextElement();
36.             event = ((WakeupOnAWTEvent)wakeup).getAWTEvent();
37.             keyPressed((KeyEvent)event[0]);
38.     }
39.     this.wakeupOn(keyboardevent);
40.  }
41.
```

Behavior criterion in making sure that different behaviors are applied appropriately to a visual object.

Figure 22 shows how this criterion can be set and the supported method. Figures 23 and 24 present a simple example on its use. Specifically, Figure 23 shows the important code segment for detecting some key strokes and changing the transform for a translational movement of some objects, while Figure 24 gives the code for printing out appropriate movement messages when the transform has been changed.

Line 7 in the code segment of Figure 23 initializes a behavior for the movement of the objects. As indicated, the behavior will be woken up when a key is pressed. The associated processStimulus method then carries out some key decoding and then changes the transform

Figure 24. Second code segment and result of TransformChange.java

```
1.    public ChangeBehavior(TransformGroup targetTG)
2.    {
3.        ourTG=targetTG;
4.        event= new WakeupOnTransformChange(ourTG);
5.    }
6.
7.    public void initialize()
8.    {
9.        System.out.println("Started!");
10.       this.wakeupOn(event);
11.   }
12.
13.   public void processStimulus(java.util.Enumeration criteria)
14.   {
15.       WakeupCriterion wakeup;
16.       while (criteria.hasMoreElements())
17.       {
18.               wakeup = (WakeupCriterion) criteria.nextElement();
19.               if (wakeup instanceof WakeupOnTransformChange)
20.               {
21.
22.                       System.out.println("You're moving "+direct);
23.               }
24.               this.wakeupOn(event);
25.       }
26.   }
```

```
C:\yupinto\programs\JCreator LENGE2001.exe                    _ □ ×
DEMONSTRATION ON USING WakeupOnTransformChange criterion

Started!
You're moving forward
You're moving back
You're moving left
You're moving right
```

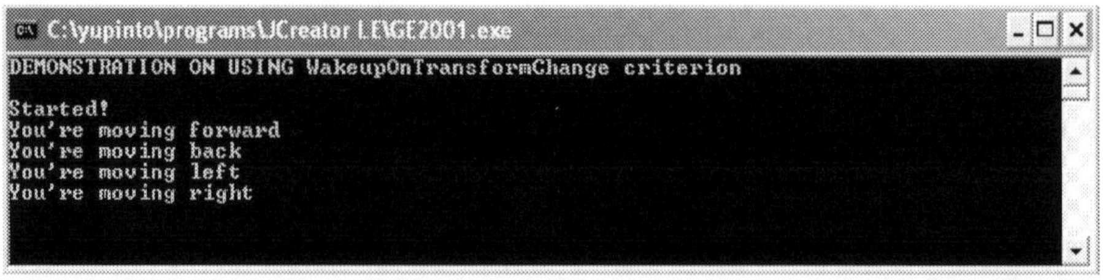

accordingly, leading to an appropriate translational movement of the associated objects. A string variable is also changed to correspond to the type of movement.

In Figure 24, another behavior is set up to detect the change in the movement by enabling it to be triggered whenever the transform group targetTG leading to the movement is changed. The processStimulus method of this behavior does nothing but just print out a relevant message based on the modified string, which gives information on the movement type.

It is worthwhile noting that, for obvious reasons of good programming practice, the system will not allow the detection of a transform change in the same behavior for the transform.

PLATFORM ENTRY AND EXIT EVENTS

Using the WakeupOnViewPlatformEntry and WakeupOnViewPlatformExit criteria, one can detect if the viewing platform is entering or leaving a certain volume. This will be useful to decide if there is a need to carry out processing that may be specific to a particular volume.

Note that there is a minor but significant difference between these two criteria on the platform with WakeupOnActivation and WakeuponDeactivation. Specifically, for the latter two criteria, which deal with objects and the platform in the virtual world, intersection of the activation volume with the scheduling regions of the relevant objects will result in the event triggering. On the other hand, WakeupOnViewPlatformEntry and its companion do not require any object in the virtual universe. Instead, a certain bound needs to be passed when the wakeup criterion is set up. Once this bound overlaps with the viewing platform, appropriate triggers will be generated.

The usage of WakeupOnViewPlatformEntry and WakeupOnViewPlatformExit is given in Figure 25, whereas Figure 26 gives a simple example where two sets of bounds are set

Figure 25. WakeupOnViewPlatformEntry and WakeupOnViewPlatformExit

```
WakeupOnViewPlatformEntry(Bounds region)
// Constructs a new WakeupOnEntry criterion.

WakeupOnViewPlatformExit(Bounds region)
// Constructs a new WakeupOnExit criterion.

Bounds getBounds()
// Return the bound specified.
```

Figure 26. Code segment for Zoo.java

```
1.    public class ViewBehavior extends Behavior
2.    {
3.        private TransformGroup targetTG; private Transform3D rotation = new Transform3D();
4.        private double angle = 0.0; private float angley, anglex;
5.        private BoundingSphere bounds = new BoundingSphere(new Point3d(0f,0f,10f), 1.0);
6.        private BoundingSphere bounds2 = new BoundingSphere(new Point3d(0f,0f,1f), 1.0);
7.        private WakeupCriterion eventsCondition[] = new WakeupCriterion[4];
8.        private WakeupOr allEvents;
9.
10.       ViewBehavior(TransformGroup targetTG) this.targetTG = targetTG;
11.
12.       public void initialize()
13.       {
14.               eventsCondition[0] = new WakeupOnViewPlatformEntry(bounds);
15.               eventsCondition[1] = new WakeupOnViewPlatformExit(bounds);
16.               eventsCondition[2] = new WakeupOnViewPlatformEntry(bounds2);
17.               eventsCondition[3] = new WakeupOnViewPlatformExit(bounds2);
18.               allEvents = new WakeupOr(eventsCondition);  wakeupOn(allEvents);
19.       }
20.
21.       public void processStimulus(Enumeration criteria)
22.       {
23.               WakeupCriterion wakeup;
24.               while (criteria.hasMoreElements())
25.               {
26.                       wakeup = (WakeupCriterion) criteria.nextElement();
27.                       if (wakeup instanceof WakeupOnViewPlatformEntry)
28.                       {
29.                               if(((WakeupOnViewPlatformEntry)wakeup)==eventsCondition[0])
30.                                   System.out.println("WELCOME TO THE ZOO!");
31.                               if(((WakeupOnViewPlatformEntry)wakeup)==eventsCondition[2])
32.                                   System.out.println("TIGERS ARE AN ENDANGERED SPECIES");
33.                       }
34.                       if (wakeup instanceof WakeupOnViewPlatformExit)
35.                       {
36.                               if(((WakeupOnViewPlatformExit)wakeup)==eventsCondition[1])
37.                                   System.out.println("DON'T FORGET TO LOOK AT THE TIGERS!");
38.                               if(((WakeupOnViewPlatformExit)wakeup)==eventsCondition[3])
39.                                   System.out.println("ROAR!");
40.                       }
41.               }
42.               this.wakeupOn(allEvents);
43.       }
44.   }
```

for the platform. Whenever the ViewPlatform enter the first bound, a trigger event will be generated and the message "WELCOME TO THE ZOO!" will be printed. On leaving this bound, the message "DON'T FORGET TO LOOK AT THE TIGERS" will be printed.

Figure 27. WakeupOnSensorEntry and WakeupOnSensorExit

```
WakeupOnSensorEntry(Bounds region)
// Constructs a new WakeupOnEntry criterion for a sensor.

WakeupOnSensorExit(Bounds region)
// Constructs a new WakeupOnExit criterion for a sensor.

Bounds getBounds()
// Return the bound from a relevant object.
```

Similarly, when the platform enters the second set of bound, the user will see a message "TIGERS ARE AN ENDANGERED SPECIES." On exit, the message "ROAR!" will be shown.

SENSOR ENTRY AND EXIT EVENTS

Similar to detecting the entry and exit of the viewing platform into and out of certain spatial regions, it is also possible to detect whether specific sensors have crossed certain boundaries in entry or exit. The relevant constructors and methods are listed in Figure 27.

COMBINING DIFFERENT WAKEUP CRITERIA

The detection of complicated behavior with excitations from various user and object inputs may sometimes be better handled by combining several relevant wakeup criteria to form a single WakeupCondition. This can be done by using the constructors of Figure 28, the first

Figure 28. Forming a single wakeup condition by logically combining wakeup criteria

```
WakeupOr(WakeupCriterion[] conditions)

WakeupAnd(WakeupCriterion[] conditions)

WakeupAndOfOrs(WakeupOr[] conditions)

WakeupOrsOfAnds(WakeupAnd[] conditions)
```

Figure 29. Code segment for MouseBehaviorUserDefine.java

```
1.    public void initialize()
2.    {
3.        //set initial wakeup condition
4.        events[0]=new WakeupOnAWTEvent(MouseEvent.MOUSE_DRAGGED);
5.        events[1]=new WakeupOnAWTEvent(MouseEvent.MOUSE_PRESSED);
6.        events[2]=new WakeupOnAWTEvent(MouseEvent.MOUSE_RELEASED);
7.        events[3]=new WakeupOnAWTEvent(MouseEvent.MOUSE_MOVED);
8.        allEvents=new WakeupOr(events);
9.        wakeupOn(allEvents);
10.   }
```

two of which create a WakeupCondition from several WakeupCriterion through a logical And and Or operation. Similarly, the last two constructors allow for the composition of the first two classes into more complex WakeupCondition objects.

The code fragment in Figure 29 illustrates the use of WakeupOr to construct a behavior trigger for capturing any of the event mouse conditions stated.

SUMMARY

In this chapter, we have discussed how behavior class can be used to detect user inputs and changes in the graphical objects for the purpose of allowing the user to interact with a Java 3D created virtual world (Wang, Wong, Shen, & Lang, 2001). Specifically, through the construction of custom wakeup conditions and criteria, the system will be able to provide changes to the virtual 3D scene and objects through some appropriate processStimulus methods when the relevant stimulus or trigger condition is received. Complicated behavior can be handled by creating specialized wakeup triggers that respond to combinations of wakeup conditions, by having behaviors that post events, by detecting object collisions as well as the entry and exit of objects and viewing platforms into certain spatial bounds.

REFERENCES

Geroimenko, V., & Geroimenko, L. (2000). Visualizing human consciousness content using Java 3D/X3D and psychological techniques. *Proceedings IEEE Conference on Information Visualization* (pp. 529-532).

Tate, J. G., Moreland, J. L., & Bourne, P. E. (2001). Design and implementation of a collaborative molecular graphics environment. *Journal of Molecular Graphics & Modeling, 19*, 280-287.

Vormoor, O. (2001). Quick and easy interactive molecular dynamics using Java 3D. *Computing in Science & Engineering. 3*(5), 98-104.

Wang, L., Wong, B., Shen, W., & Lang, S. (2001). A Web-based collaborative workspace using Java 3D. *Proceedings 6th International Conference on Computer Supported Cooperative Work in Design* (pp. 77-82).

Chapter IX
Picking

INTRODUCTION

The last two chapters have discussed how animation and interaction can be created in Java 3D to increase visual impact, to show object dynamics and hidden views, and to allow the user to interact with the objects in a virtual 3D universe (Emoto et al., 2001, Shyamsundar & Gadh, 2001). Our discussion has been carried in a general tone through the use of the behavior class to capture all types of events to cater to all possibilities.

However, it is common that interaction with 3D objects in many applications involves the user to pick up relevant objects and change its positions, angles, and even texture and

Figure 1. Illustration of picking behavior when the user picks and moves the cube

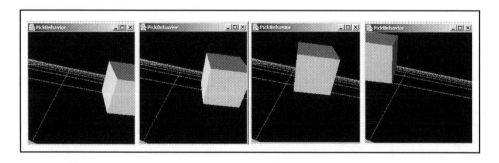

shapes for a variety of purposes. As a simple example of picking behavior, Figure 1 shows snapshots in an application where the user uses the mouse to pick up a cube and moves it to a new position through a mouse dragging operation.

In this chapter, we will discuss how the picking behavior class in Java 3D can be made use of to create interesting customized dynamical picking interaction with any specific visual object. We will start in the next section with the use of some standard picking behavior classes, before embarking on to discuss how custom picking classes can be constructed to suit specific applications.

PickRotateBehavior, PickTranslateBehavior, AND PickZoomBehavior

The standard PickRotateBehavior, PickTranslateBehavior, and PickZoomBehavior classes in Java 3D include capabilities that allow the user to interactively pick and then rotate, translate, and zoom visual objects in a 3D scene (Nakano, Sato, Matsuo, & Ishimasa, 2000).

Figures 2 to 4 give the code segment and result snapshots in a simple example illustrating the use of these three classes in a picking behavior involving a sphere and a color cube. The interaction includes translation, rotation, and zooming.

In this example, the objects are immersed in a landscape matrix so that it will be easier to visualize how the objects are being moved or changed as they are picked by using the mouse. Specifically, dragging a visual object while pressing the left mouse button will make the picked object rotate, doing so with the right button pressed will translate the object, and dragging the object with the middle button pressed will make the object zoom in or out.

Note that the picking behavior is unique for individual objects in the same scene. Also, Enable_Pick_Reporting is set for the appropriate transform groups.

PICKING CLASSES IN GENERAL

The picking classes described in the last section are relatively easy to use and can provide some standard interaction between visual objects and the user. However, the interaction may be too rigid to cater to every scenario. Examples are knobs that only allow the user to turn and buttons that can only be pressed as they are pushed in the 3D world.

To satisfy requirements such as those mentioned in the examples, there are very often needs to create customized picking behaviors for certain specific objects in applications. We will now discuss techniques and methods that can be used for constructing customized picking classes for this purpose.

Before discussing details and giving illustrating examples in the following sections, we would first like to highlight a few general categories of picking classes and describe how

Figure 2. First code segment for PickBehaviour.java

```
1.    import java.applet.Applet;
2.    import java.awt.BorderLayout;
3.    import java.awt.Frame;
4.    import com.sun.j3d.utils.applet.MainFrame;
5.    import com.sun.j3d.utils.geometry.*;
6.    import com.sun.j3d.utils.universe.*;
7.    import com.sun.j3d.utils.picking.behaviors.*;
8.    import javax.media.j3d.*;
9.    import javax.vecmath.*;
10.   import java.awt.event.*;
11.   import java.util.Enumeration;
12.   import com.sun.j3d.utils.behaviors.keyboard.*;
13.
14.   public class pickApp extends Applet
15.   {
16.     Shape3D Landscape()
17.     {
18.             LineArray landGeom = new LineArray(44, GeometryArray.COORDINATES |
19.                     GeometryArray.COLOR_3);
20.             float l = -100.0f;
21.             for(int c = 0; c < 44; c+=4)
22.             {
23.                     landGeom.setCoordinate( c+0, new Point3f( -100.0f, 0.0f,  l ));
24.                     landGeom.setCoordinate( c+1, new Point3f(  100.0f, 0.0f,  l ));
25.                     landGeom.setCoordinate( c+2, new Point3f(  l  , 0.0f, -100.0f ));
26.                     landGeom.setCoordinate( c+3, new Point3f(  l  , 0.0f,  100.0f ));
27.                     l += 10.0f;
28.             }
29.
30.     Color3f c = new Color3f(0.1f, 0.8f, 0.1f);
31.     for(int i = 0; i < 44; i++) landGeom.setColor( i, c);
32.
33.     return new Shape3D(landGeom);
34.     }
35.
```

they are related to one another. This is described below and shows the processing and flow involved in a typical picking operation:

- **PickTool:** This is the base class in picking, and defines the tool that will be used in the process. The associated method will return a PickResult object for each object picked.
- **PickCanvas:** This is a subclass of PickTool for the purpose of simplifying picking based on mouse events from a canvas, and allows for picking using positional locations on a canvas through the generation of appropriate pick shape.

Figure 3. Second code segment for PickBehaviour.java

```
36.     public BranchGroup createSceneGraph(Canvas3D canvas)
37.     {
38.             BranchGroup objRoot = new BranchGroup();
39.
40.             TransformGroup objTranslate = null;  Transform3D transform = new Transform3D();
41.             BoundingSphere bounds = new BoundingSphere(new Point3d( ), 1000.0 );
42.
43.             ColoringAttributes caA = new ColoringAttributes();  caA.setColor(0.9f,0.5f,0.4f);
44.             Appearance appA = new Appearance();      appA.setColoringAttributes(caA);
45.
46.             objTranslate = new TransformGroup (transform);
47.             objTranslate.setCapability(TransformGroup.ALLOW_TRANSFORM_WRITE);
48.             objTranslate.setCapability(TransformGroup.ALLOW_TRANSFORM_READ);
49.             objTranslate.setCapability(TransformGroup.ENABLE_PICK_REPORTING);
50.
51.             objRoot.addChild(objTranslate);
52.             objTranslate.addChild(Landscape());
53.             objTranslate.addChild(new Sphere(0.4f, appA));
54.
55.             transform.setTranslation(new Vector3f( 1.0f, 0.0f, -0.5f));
56.             objTranslate = new TransformGroup(transform);
57.             objTranslate.setCapability(TransformGroup.ALLOW_TRANSFORM_WRITE);
58.             objTranslate.setCapability(TransformGroup.ALLOW_TRANSFORM_READ);
59.             objTranslate.setCapability(TransformGroup.ENABLE_PICK_REPORTING);
60.
61.             objRoot.addChild(objTranslate);
62.             objTranslate.addChild(new ColorCube(0.4));
63.
64.             PickTranslateBehavior pickTranslate
65.                     = new PickTranslateBehavior(objRoot, canvas, bounds);
66.             objRoot.addChild(pickTranslate);
67.             PickZoomBehavior pickZoom = new PickZoomBehavior (objRoot, canvas, bounds);
68.             objRoot.addChild(pickZoom);
69.
70.             PickRotateBehavior pickRotate = new PickRotateBehavior(objRoot, canvas, bounds);
71.             objRoot.addChild(pickRotate);
72.
73.             objRoot.compile();
74.
75.             return objRoot;
76.     }
77.
```

- **PickResult:** This stores information on the picked object when picking occurs. By setting appropriate capability bits in the scene graph Node, detailed information on the pick and intersection of the PickShape with the picked Node can be obtained.

Figure 4. Third code segment and result snapshoots for PickBehaviour.java

```
78.     public pickApp()
79.     {
80.             setLayout(new BorderLayout());
81.             Canvas3D canvas3D = new Canvas3D(null);
82.             add("Center", canvas3D);
83.             SimpleUniverse simpleU = new SimpleUniverse(canvas3D);
84.             BranchGroup scene = createSceneGraph(canvas3D);
85.             simpleU.getViewingPlatform().setNominalViewingTransform();
86.             simpleU.addBranchGraph(scene);
87.
88.     }
89.
90.     public static void main(String[] args)
91.     {
92.             Frame frame = new MainFrame(new pickApp(), 256, 256);
93.     }
94.
95.  }// end of class pickApp
```

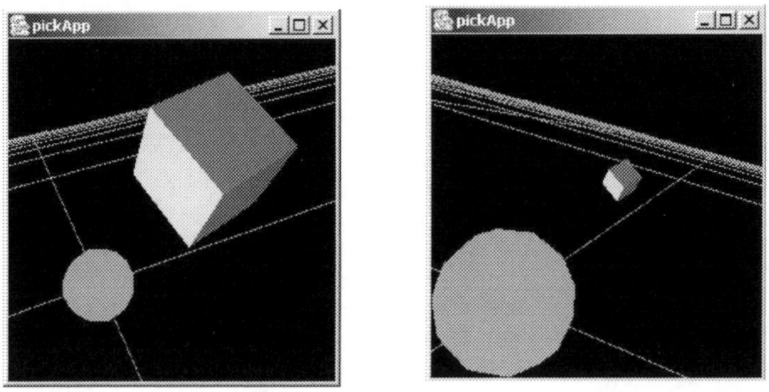

PickTool.setCapabilties(Node, int) can be used to ensure that the relevant capabilities are set. A CapabilityNotSet exception will be generated if attempts are made to obtain data without having the right capabilities set.
•   **PickIntersection:** This is a part of PickResult and holds information on an intersection of a PickShape with a Node, including intersected geometry, intersected primitive, intersection point, and closest vertex.

CUSTOMIZING PICKING BEHAVIOR CLASS

Since picking, despite its importance, is still a behavior class, methods, and techniques for dealing with picking follow the same methodology as those discussed in previous chapters on behavior objects.

Specifically, code development for a customized picking behavior requires the specification of a constructor, an initialization method, wakeup criteria and conditions, and an appropriate processStimulus method for carrying out appropriate processing once certain specified events have happened.

For picking, the constructor usually has arguments that inform the system of the canvas3D and branchgroup of interest. Essentially, the constructor will give rise to an object to carry out the task of implementing picking behavior using the canvas on the branchgroup specified. In addition, the capability of the PickTool to be used can be defined.

Figure 5 shows a simple example picking constructor based on the use of PickCanvas in Java 3D. Using PickCanvas is simple and appropriate for implementing picking behavior based on the mouse. Under this, the picking shape is set by default to either PickRay with a tolerance value of zero or PickConeRay with a non-zero tolerance value.

Following the constructor, an appropriate initialize function or method has to be provided to create the initial data under the picking behavior as well as to specify the

Figure 5. A simple picking behavior constructor based on using PickCanvas

```
1.    public PickingBehavior(Canvas3D canvas3D, BranchGroup branchGroup)
2.    {
3.        pickCanvas = new PickCanvas(canvas3D, branchGroup);
4.        pickCanvas.setTolerance(0.0f);
5.        pickCanvas.setMode(PickCanvas.GEOMETRY_INTERSECT_INFO);
6.        pickCanvas.setMode(PickCanvas.GEOMETRY);
7.        pickCanvas.setMode(PickTool.GEOMETRY);
8.    }
```

Figure 6. A few line of code in processStimulus for dealing with mouse location inputs

```
1.    int x_m = ((MouseEvent)event[i]).getX();
2.    int y_m = ((MouseEvent)event[i]).getY();
3.    pickCanvas.setShapeLocation(x_m, y_m);
```

keyboard, mouse or other wakeup events that will trigger the behavior. The various types of wakeup events have been extensively described in the last chapter on interaction and behavior in general.

Lastly, it is necessary to provide an appropriate processStimulus method that will be invoked by the system when wakeup stimuli for the specified events or some logical combinations of these have been received. Figure 6 shows a few line of codes in a processStimulus method for getting mouse locations.

PICKTOOL

In many applications, the use of simple PickRay or PickConeRay is not satisfactory and the specification of a more customized PickTool with a desired picking shape is needed

Figure 7. Constructor for PickTool and transforming 2D mouse to 3D virtual positions

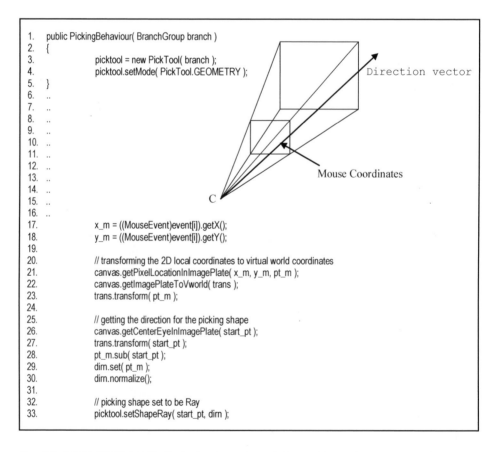

```
1.    public PickingBehaviour( BranchGroup branch )
2.    {
3.              picktool = new PickTool( branch );
4.              picktool.setMode( PickTool.GEOMETRY );
5.    }
6.    ..
7.    ..
8.    ..
9.    ..
10.   ..
11.   ..
12.   ..
13.   ..
14.   ..
15.   ..
16.   ..
17.             x_m = ((MouseEvent)event[i]).getX();
18.             y_m = ((MouseEvent)event[i]).getY();
19.
20.             // transforming the 2D local coordinates to virtual world coordinates
21.             canvas.getPixelLocationInImagePlate( x_m, y_m, pt_m );
22.             canvas.getImagePlateToVworld( trans );
23.             trans.transform( pt_m );
24.
25.             // getting the direction for the picking shape
26.             canvas.getCenterEyeInImagePlate( start_pt );
27.             trans.transform( start_pt );
28.             pt_m.sub( start_pt );
29.             dirn.set( pt_m );
30.             dirn.normalize();
31.
32.             // picking shape set to be Ray
33.             picktool.setShapeRay( start_pt, dirn );
```

(Barrilleaux, 2001). Figure 7 shows the constructor that can be used as well as the code segment in an accompanying processStimulus method for converting 2D mouse positions to 3D coordinates in the virtual 3D world.

The transformation of the 2D mouse position to a 3D location in the virtual world is an important process in picking. This is because what is shown on the computer display is really a degenerated 2D view of the underlying 3D world. The former is often referred to as the viewing plane, and the mouse position is always registered with respect to this plane.

The visual objects rendered in a Java 3D scene are nevertheless 3D in nature and the user is actually picking 3D objects. A transformation of the 2D mouse position to a 3D coordinates in the virtual universe will therefore need to be done in many applications, as illustrated in lines 17 to 23 in the code segment in Figure 7.

Other useful information that may be needed in picking the correct 3D objects are the direction of the picking shape and the virtual world coordinates of the starting point, as denoted by C in the perspective projection in Figure 7. The former is obtained from lines 26 and 27, while the latter is obtained from subtracting the mouse pick point from the starting point coordinates. Lastly, line 30 normalizes the direction vector found.

POINT AND RAY PICKING SHAPE

Rather than using the default PickShape object for picking, it is often necessary to create customized PickShape objects for the purpose of picking in various scenarios. As an example, in a 3D room environment, it will be more appropriate have a PickShape object to pick only objects that are nearby instead of something far away.

Technically, the class of PickShape objects is used together with PickTool in defining a picking operation. Starting from this section, we will proceed to discuss the various types of PickShape objects that can be employed.

PickRay is the most basic picking shape, and will pick objects in the same way as a penetrating ray of radiation. Essentially, the picking ray extends into the scene infinitely in a specific direction and any object intersected by this ray will be picked.

The code segment and result snapshots in Figure 8 illustrate how PickRay can be used to pick an object and change its color and at the same time print out a relevant message. The program segment first obtains and then transforms the local mouse and eye positions from the viewing plane to 3D world coordinates. The normalized ray direction that projects indefinitely into the scene is then calculated, the closest intersected objects is retrieved, and its properties is modified to give rise to a change in color. Note that in order for the program to run properly, the appropriate picking capabilities must be set.

Apart from PickRay, another basic PickShape is PickPoint. As its name implies, using PickPoint corresponds to using a single point for picking. This, of course, may not be very user-friendly, as it will be difficult to pick objects at exact 3D locations with a mouse that

Figure 8. Code segment and result for PickRayBehaviour.java

```
1.    case MouseEvent.MOUSE_CLICKED:
2.        int x = ((MouseEvent)event[i]).getX();  int y = ((MouseEvent)event[i]).getY();
3.        Point3d point3d = new Point3d();  canvas.getPixelLocationInImagePlate(x,y,point3d);
4.        Point3d center = new Point3d();  canvas.getCenterEyeInImagePlate(center);
5.        Transform3D transform3D = new Transform3D();  canvas.getImagePlateToVworld(transform3D);
6.        transform3D.transform(point3d);  transform3D.transform(center);
7.
8.        Vector3d mouseVec;  mouseVec = new Vector3d();  mouseVec.sub(point3d, center);
9.        mouseVec.normalize();
10.
11.       picktool.setShapeRay(point3d, mouseVec);
12.
13.       if ( picktool.pickClosest() != null )
14.       {
15.           System.out.println( "Object picked " + picktool.getPickShape() );
16.           System.out.println("Direction vector =" + mouseVec);
17.           pickresult = picktool.pickClosest();
18.
19.           PickIntersection pickint = pickresult.getClosestIntersection(center);
20.           shape3d = (Shape3D) pickresult.getNode(PickResult.SHAPE3D);
21.           IndexedGeometryArray quadarray = (IndexedGeometryArray) shape3d.getGeometry();
22.
23.           quadarray.getColor( 0, temp);
24.           if ( temp.equals( red ) ) quadarray.setColor(0,blue);         else quadarray.setColor(0,red);
25.       }
26.       else
27.           System.out.println( "Target not aacquired !!" );
28.   break;
```

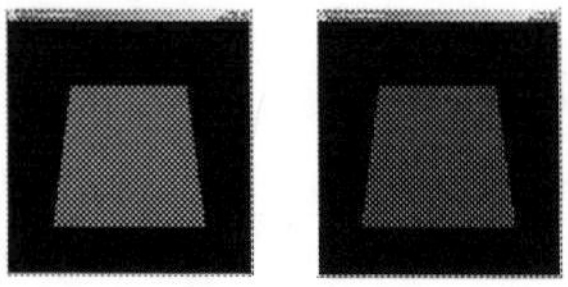

have inherent system inaccuracies. Nevertheless, PickPoint can be used in BranchGroup and Locale pick testing as well as for picking package classes.

RAY SEGMENT PICKING SHAPE

As discussed, the use of PickRay will pick all objects that intersect a ray of infinite extent. Obviously, in a scene with many objects, this may give to problems in determining the exact object that the user is trying to pick. PickSegment attends to overcome this to a certain degree by using only a ray with appropriate starting and ending points

We will now illustrate how PickSegment can be used to change the transparency values of a few rows of trapezoidal objects and will discuss the important program segments in greater details. Specifically, we will discuss the overall structure, variable declaration, constructor, initialize(), and processStimulus() methods one after another.

Firstly, Figure 9 shows the overall code segment structure of the picking behavior class to be developed for this application. As can be seen, there is a constructor, an initialize() method, a processStimulus() method, a findEyeAndEndPos() method for determining the two end points of PickSegment, a changeAppearance() method to change the appearance of the picked object, and a printInfo() method to give relevant message information on the picking process.

Figure 10 shows the second code segment, listing all the important variables that will be used. Lines 1 and 2 declare suitable wakeup criteria variables that will be used. Specifically, line 2 declares a WakeupOr variable, while line 1 gives rise to a WakeupCriterion variable array. The array has only one element, because the only event of interest corresponds to a mouse click in this example.

Lines 4 and 5 declare BranchGroup and Canvas3D variables that will correspond to the branchGroup and canvas3D of the scene for the picking behavior. Lines 7 to 9 declare Shape3D, Appearance and TransparencyAttributes variables for the purpose of changing the appearance of the picked visual objects. In lines 11 to 14, relevant variables for the picking class are declared. The variables from lines 16 to 20 are for use in the findEyeAndEndPos() method to determine the starting and ending point of the pick segment. Lastly, x and y in lines 22 to 23 serve as stores for the mouse position on the image plate and will also be used in determining the two end points of the pick segment.

Figure 9. First code segment for PickSegmentBehavior.java

```
1.    public class SimplePickingSegmentBehavior extends Behavior
2.    {
3.          public SimplePickingSegmentBehavior(Canvas3D canvas3D, BranchGroup branchGroup)
4.          {     // constructor of SimplePickingSegmentBehavior class   }
5.
6.          public void initialize()
7.          {     // initialize method   }
8.
9.          public void processStimulus(Enumeration criteria)
10.         {     // actions to be taken this behavior class is triggered   }
11.
12.         private void findEyeAndEndPos()
13.         {     // set the start and end position of PickSegment   }
14.
15.         private void changeAppearance()
16.         {     // used by processStimulus to change transparency attributes of picked object   }
17.
18.         private void printInfo(int eventID)
19.         {     // print out relevant information messages       }
20.   }
```

198 *Ko & Cheng*

Figure 10. Second code segment for PickSegmentBehavior.java

```
1.     private WakeupCriterion []allEvents = new WakeupCriterion[1];
2.     private WakeupOr allEventsCriterion;
3.
4.     private BranchGroup branchGroup;
5.     private Canvas3D canvas3D;
6.
7.     private Shape3D geo3D = new Shape3D();
8.     private Appearance appear;
9.     private TransparencyAttributes transAttr;
10.
11.    private PickCanvas pickCanvas;
12.    private PickResult pickResult;
13.    private PickTool pickTool;
14.    private PickIntersection pickIntersect;
15.
16.    private Point3d eyepos = new Point3d();
17.    private Point3d mousepos = new Point3d();
18.    private Point3d endpos = new Point3d();
19.    private Vector3d dirn = new Vector3d();
20.    private Transform3D trans = new Transform3D();
21.
22.    private int x;
23.    private int y;
```

Figure 11. Third code segment for PickSegmentBehavior.java

```
1.  public      SimplePickingSegmentBehavior(Canvas3D canvas3D, BranchGroup branchGroup)
2.  {
3.       this.branchGroup = branchGroup;
4.       this.canvas3D = canvas3D;
5.       geo3D.setCapability(Shape3D.ALLOW_APPEARANCE_READ);
6.       geo3D.setCapability(Shape3D.ALLOW_APPEARANCE_WRITE);
7.
8.       pickTool = new PickTool(branchGroup);
9.       pickTool.setMode(PickTool.GEOMETRY_INTERSECT_INFO);
10.      pickTool.setMode(PickTool.GEOMETRY);
11. }
12.
13. public void initialize()
14. {
15.      allEvents[0] = new WakeupOnAWTEvent(MouseEvent.MOUSE_CLICKED);
16.      allEventsCriterion = new WakeupOr(allEvents);
17.      wakeupOn(allEventsCriterion);
18. }
```

With the important variables declared, the first part of Figure 11 shows the code segment for the constructor of the pick behavior class in our application. Lines 3 and 4 set the branchGroup and canvas3D of our behavior object to that of the external one invoking it. Lines 8 to 10 set or turn on the necessary capabilities of the pickTool. Specifically, picking will start from the branchGroup and with PickTool.GEOMETRY specified, picking will be carried out based on the geometries of objects rather than their bounds. Similarly, lines 5 and 6 set the capability of Shape3D to allow for the reading and writing of the appearance of visual object. Note that the setting of this capability must be performed in the constructor or during initializing. It cannot be carried out in processStimulus() when the object is already live. This is because capabilities cannot be set or modify for a live node.

Figure 12. Fourth code segment for PickSegmentBehavior.java

```
1.    public void processStimulus(Enumeration criteria)
2.    {
3.         WakeupCriterion wakeup;  AWTEvent []event;  int eventID;
4.
5.         while(criteria.hasMoreElements())
6.         {
7.              wakeup = (WakeupCriterion)criteria.nextElement();
8.              if(wakeup instanceof WakeupOnAWTEvent)
9.              {
10.                 event = ((WakeupOnAWTEvent)wakeup).getAWTEvent();
11.                 for(int i=0; i<event.length; i++)
12.                 {
13.                      eventID = event[i].getID();
14.                      if(eventID == MouseEvent.MOUSE_CLICKED)
15.                      {
16.                           x = ((MouseEvent)event[i]).getX();
17.                           y = ((MouseEvent)event[i]).getY();
18.                           findEyeAndEndPos();
19.                           pickTool.setShapeSegment(eyepos, endpos);
20.                           pickResult = pickTool.pickClosest();
21.                           if (pickResult!=null)
22.                           {
23.                                pickIntersect = pickResult.getClosestIntersection(eyepos);
24.                                geo3D = (Shape3D) pickResult.getNode(PickResult.SHAPE3D);
25.                                changeAppearance();
26.                           }
27.                           printInfo(eventID);
28.                      }
29.                 }
30.              }
31.              this.wakeupOn(allEventsCriterion);
32.         }
33.    }
```

The second part in the code segment of Figure 11 shows the initialize method for the initial wakeup of our behavior. Specifically, as only mouse click event is of interest, the array allEvents[] only has 1 element corresponding to a MOUSE_CLICKED event.

Figure 12 shows the code segment for the processStimulus method that will carry out the necessary processing when the behavior is triggered. The method starts with checking whether a mouse click event has indeed result in the trigger. If this is the case, the code segment within the first if statement will be executed. The execution includes the use of PickSegment with appropriate starting and ending points to define a ray segment and to pick visual objects. In particular, the findEyeAndEndPos() method is used to determine the start and end point of the pick segment, after which pickTool is set to PickSegment. With the newly selected pickTool, the system will carry out picking to find the nearest object in the picked region and have the result stored in pickResult. A null pickResult means that the operation has resulted in nothing. Otherwise, a visual object has been picked and its appearance will be changed. Note that PickIntersect will give the Shape3D obtained from the picking operation.

Snapshots of the result from the code segments in Figures 9 to 12 are shown in Figure 13. A 3 by 3 array of trapeziums are placed at different distance from the viewing platform. The appearance attribute of a particular trapezium can be changed by clicking at the trapezium with a mouse, and the trapezium will change from translucent to opaque or the other way round.

Note that it is not necessary to be within a trapezium for it to be selected. Clicking outside the trapezium may also select the object as the picking behavior is set to pick by object geometries rather than bounds. The left and middle diagrams in Figure 13 illustrate the changes that occurred when the relevant trapeziums are selected using mouse clicks. The right diagram, however, show that the third row of visual objects cannot be selected.

Figure 13. Result from PickSegmentBehavior.java

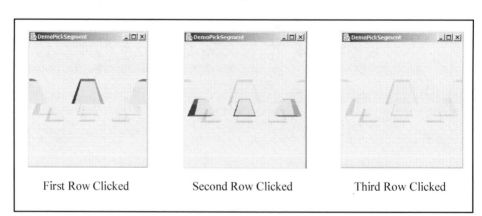

| First Row Clicked | Second Row Clicked | Third Row Clicked |

This is because the pickTool used is a PickSegment of length 4 extending from the eye position into the virtual universe, and this will not intersect the objects in the third row, which are at a distance of more than four from the eye position.

CONE PICKING SHAPE

PickConeRay and PickConeSegment belong to the abstract base class of PickCone. The main difference between the picking shapes under PickCone and PickRay, which have been discussed in previous sections, is that the former is conic in shape while the latter is a ray or a line with theoretically zero width or thickness. Obviously, picking visual objects using a conic type of shape will be advantageous if the object has a cross section or size that is too small to be picked or intersected by a line.

To illustrate the use of PickConeRay, which has a picking shape that corresponds to a cone with infinite length, we will now outline an example consisting of 3 spheres, a bigger sphere at the origin, and two smaller ones at other locations. Point light sources are also placed at the same positions as the two smaller spheres so that they are emitting light effectively. By using the mouse, the two smaller spheres can be picked. Clicking the left mouse button will turn the light sources on and off, while clicking using the right button will change its color. The resulting visual effect is illustrated in Figure 14.

In this application, it should be clear that using PickRay may not give satisfactory results as the smaller spheres are too small to be easily picked. Instead, using PickCone will be more appropriate as it will be easier for the spheres, despite their small size, to be intersected by a conic picking shape.

Another point to note is that the application actually requires the development of a program that modifies other objects as the user clicked on another one. This is sometimes necessary if the object to be modified in the live scene graph is transparent or cannot be

Figure 14. Result from PickConeRayBehavior.java

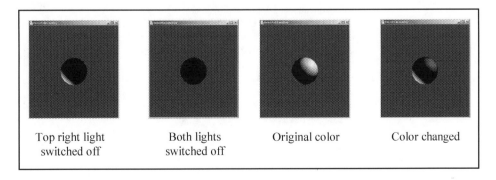

| Top right light switched off | Both lights switched off | Original color | Color changed |

seen, as picking will not work for these objects. For instance, the back face of a solid object, a fully transparent window or a light source cannot be picked. In such applications, another object that can be picked will have to be created to control the unpickable target object indirectly.

Since the program will need to change the attributes of objects in a live scene graph, the appropriate capabilities must be set. For this application, ENABLE_PICK_REPORTING must be set for the relevant transform group so that it is possible for the scene graph to be

Figure 15. First code segment for PickConeRayBehavior.java

```
1.    public BranchGroup createSceneGraph()
2.    {
3.        BranchGroup objRoot = new BranchGroup();
4.        TransformGroup objTrans1 = new TransformGroup();
5.        TransformGroup objTrans2 = new TransformGroup();
6.        objRoot.addChild (objTrans1 );
7.        objRoot.addChild (objTrans2 );
8.
9.        // setting the appropriate capabilities
10.       objTrans1.setCapability ( Group.ALLOW_CHILDREN_READ );
11.       objTrans1.setCapability ( TransformGroup.ENABLE_PICK_REPORTING );
12.       objTrans2.setCapability ( Group.ALLOW_CHILDREN_READ );
13.       objTrans2.setCapability ( TransformGroup.ENABLE_PICK_REPORTING );
14.
15.       Background backgd = new Background( 0.0f, 0.0f, 1.0f );
16.       BoundingSphere bounds = new BoundingSphere();
17.       backgd.setApplicationBounds( bounds );
18.       objRoot.addChild( backgd );
19.
20.       // creating a small sphere to be picked in the scene.
21.       Sphere small_sphere1 = new Sphere( 0.005f, createAppearance1() );
22.       objTrans1.addChild( small_sphere1 );
23.       PointLight pointlight1 = new PointLight();
24.       Color3f light_colour = new Color3f( 1.0f, 0.0f, 0.0f );
25.       pointlight1.setColor( light_colour );
26.       pointlight1.setInfluencingBounds( bounds );
27.       pointlight1.setCapability ( Light.ALLOW_STATE_WRITE );
28.       pointlight1.setCapability ( Light.ALLOW_STATE_READ );
29.       pointlight1.setCapability ( Light.ALLOW_COLOR_READ );
30.       pointlight1.setCapability ( Light.ALLOW_COLOR_WRITE );
31.       objTrans1.addChild( pointlight1 );
32.       Transform3D translate = new Transform3D();
33.       translate.set( new Vector3f( 0.5f, 0.5f, 0.5f ) );
34.       objTrans1.setTransform( translate );
35.
```

used in tracing our way to the desired node from the picked node. Also, as the light sources will be modified, all the relevant capabilities must be set to prevent getting Capability Not Set exceptions. With these points in mind, Figure 15 and 16 shows the code segments for creating the scene in this application.

To incorporate the picking behavior for this scene in the manner described, Figure 17 shows the structure of the customized picking behavior class needed. Again, as in the example in the last section, the code structure includes declaration for a set of variables, a constructor, an initialize and a processStimulus method.

Note that in the code segment for the constructor in Figure 17, the mode of picking is set to be bounds rather than geometry based as has been done in earlier examples. This will save time needed for intersection checking in the picking process, and will be satisfactory in this application where the only picking operation is just to turn something on and off through the smaller spheres. Since only mouse click will be used, the initialize method sets up an initial wakeup criterion to correspond to MOUSE_CLICKED only.

Figure 16. Second code segment for PickConeRayBehavior.java

```
36.     Sphere small_sphere2 = new Sphere( 0.005f, createAppearance1() );
37.     objTrans2.addChild( small_sphere2 );
38.     PointLight pointlight2 = new PointLight();
39.     light_colour.set( 1.0f, 1.0f, 1.0f );
40.     pointlight2.setColor( light_colour );
41.     pointlight2.setInfluencingBounds( bounds );
42.     pointlight2.setCapability ( Light.ALLOW_STATE_WRITE );
43.     pointlight2.setCapability ( Light.ALLOW_STATE_READ );
44.     pointlight2.setCapability ( Light.ALLOW_COLOR_READ );
45.     pointlight2.setCapability ( Light.ALLOW_COLOR_WRITE );
46.     objTrans2.addChild( pointlight2 );
47.     translate.set( new Vector3f( -0.5f, -0.5f, 0.0f ) );
48.     objTrans2.setTransform( translate );
49.
50.     // creating a big sphere at the origin. Note that this sphere is not pickable
51.     Sphere big_sphere = new Sphere( 0.3f, createAppearance2() );
52.     big_sphere.setPickable( false ); //setting the sphere to be unpickable
53.     objRoot.addChild( big_sphere );
54.     PickingBehaviour behave = new PickingBehaviour( objRoot );
55.     behave.setSchedulingBounds( bounds );
56.     objRoot.addChild( behave );
57.     objRoot.compile();
58.     return objRoot;
59. }
```

Figure 17. Third code segment for PickConeRayBehavior.java

```
1.     public class PickingBehaviour extends Behavior
2.     {
3.         private WakeupCriterion[] allEvents;
4.         private PickTool picktool;
5.         private PickResult result;
6.         private Point3d pt_m = new Point3d();
7.         private Transform3D trans = new Transform3D();
8.         private Point3d start_pt = new Point3d();
9.         private Vector3d dirn = new Vector3d( );
10.        private int x_m;
11.        private int y_m;
12.        private TransformGroup picked_tg = new TransformGroup();
13.        int mouse_button;
14.        private PointLight lighting = new PointLight();
15.        private Color3f light_colour = new Color3f();
16.        private Color3f red = new Color3f( 1.0f, 0.0f, 0.0f );
17.        private Color3f white = new Color3f( 1.0f, 1.0f, 1.0f );
18.
19.        public PickingBehaviour( BranchGroup branch ) // constructor for behavior class
20.        {
21.            picktool = new PickTool( branch );
22.            picktool.setMode( PickTool.BOUNDS );
23.        }
24.
25.        public void initialize()  // initialize method
26.        {
27.            allEvents = new WakeupCriterion[1];
28.            allEvents[0] = new WakeupOnAWTEvent( MouseEvent.MOUSE_CLICKED );
29.            wakeupOn ( new WakeupOr( allEvents ) );
30.        }
31.
32.        public void processStimulus(Enumeration criteria)
33.        {    // actions to be taken by this behavior class when triggered   }
34.    }
```

Figures 18 and 19 show the important code segment in the processStimulus method which will be invoked for carrying out the necessary processing when a mouse click event has occurred. Essentially, the method checks that a mouse click event has indeed happened before finding the local mouse position on the 2D image plane, transforming this to 3D world coordinators, and calculating the principal 3D pick shape direction.   .

A cone ray is then selected as the picking shape to detect the sphere that the user is trying to pick or select. As mentioned, the use of cone ray is crucial in this application

Figure 18. Fourth code segment for PickConeRayBehavior.java

```
1.    if( wakeup instanceof WakeupOnAWTEvent )
2.    {
3.          event = ((WakeupOnAWTEvent) wakeup).getAWTEvent();
4.          for( int i=0; i<event.length; i++ )
5.          {
6.                eventId = event[i].getID();
7.                ( eventId )
8.                {
9.                case MouseEvent.MOUSE_CLICKED:
10.
11.                     // get mouse position on 2D viewing plane
12.                     x_m = ((MouseEvent)event[i]).getX();
13.                     y_m = ((MouseEvent)event[i]).getY();
14.
15.                     // transform 2D local to virtual world coordinates
16.                     canvas.getPixelLocationInImagePlate( x_m, y_m, pt_m );
17.                     canvas.getImagePlateToVworld( trans );
18.                     trans.transform( pt_m );
19.
20.                     // get pick shape direction
21.                     canvas.getCenterEyeInImagePlate( start_pt );
22.                     trans.transform( start_pt );
23.                     pt_m.sub( start_pt );
24.                     dirn.set( pt_m );
25.                     dirn.normalize();
26.
27.                     // set pick shape to ConeRay
28.                     picktool.setShapeConeRay( start_pt, dirn, 2*Math.PI/180 );
29.
```

as the smaller spheres that can be picked have very small sizes. If a simple ray with zero thickness is used, the chance of intersecting the smaller spheres will be small and it will be difficult for the user to pick the visual objects.

After specifying the pick shape, the nearest object that intersects with this shape is retrieved. With ENABLE_PICK_REPORTING capability for transform group set, the transform group of the picked object can also be retrieved. This in turns enables the light node, the second child added to the transform group, to be retrieved using the getChild(int x) method with x being equal to 1 (0 for the first child and 1 for the second child). The light node can subsequently be changed to result in the visual effects in the live scene as illustrated in Figure 14.

Figure 19. Fifth code segment for PickConeRayBehavior.java

```
30.              // get intersected object and process
31.              result = picktool.pickClosest();
32.              if( result != null )
33.              {
34.                      picked_tg = (TransformGroup)result.getNode( PickResult.TRANSFORM_GROUP);
35.                      lighting = (PointLight ) picked_tg.getChild( 1 );
36.                      mouse_button = ((MouseEvent)event[i]).getButton();
37.                      switch ( mouse_button )
38.                      {
39.                      case MouseEvent.BUTTON1:  // left mouse button clicked
40.                          if ( lighting.getEnable ( ) == false ) lighting.setEnable ( true );
41.                          else lighting.setEnable ( false );  break;
42.                      case MouseEvent.BUTTON2:  // other mouse button clicked
43.                      case MouseEvent.BUTTON3:
44.                          if ( lighting.getEnable ( ) == true )
45.                          {
46.                                  lighting.getColor( light_colour );
47.                                  if ( light_colour.equals( red ) ) lighting.setColor( white );
48.                                  else lighting.setColor( red );
49.                          };  break;
50.                      }
51.              }
52.              break;
53.      ...
```

With relationship similar to that between PickRaySegment and PickRay, PickConeRay-Segment is also a variation of PickConeRay with an additional control on the length of the cone ray that can be specified. Specifically, PickConeRay has rays within a conic volume that is infinite in length, whereas the length of the cone in PickConeRaySegment can be specified and finite. The usage of PickConeRaySegment is similar to that of PickConeRay, although it may be more useful in applications for picking objects of different depths.

CYLINDER PICKING SHAPE

The use of conic picking shape is most appropriate for applications where a 3D prospective view is involved when rendering the virtual world. However, in scenarios where the view or projection used is primarily or approximately parallel in nature, it may be more useful to choose a picking shape that is cylindrical in nature for picking or interacting with objects. The abstract base picking class for this purpose is PickCylinder with subclasses PickCylinderRay and PickCylinderSegment. Both PickCylinderRay and PickCylinderSegment give rise to a pick shape that is cylindrical in nature with a certain circular cross section. However, the former is infinite in its length, whereas the latter has a length that is finite and can be specified.

Figures 20 and 21 illustrate the use of PickCylinderRay to pick a trapezoidal object and transforming it to become a square. Figure 20 shows the important variables, the construc-

Figure 20. First code segment and result for PickCylinderRayBehavior.java

```
1.    public class SimpleBehavior extends Behavior
2.    {
3.         private WakeupCriterion[] allEvents;
4.         private PickCanvas pickCanvas;
5.         private Point3d p_3d;
6.         private PickResult pickres;
7.         private Shape3D shape3d;
8.         private BranchGroup branch;
9.
10.        public SimpleBehavior ( Canvas3D canvas, BranchGroup branchgroup )  // constructor
11.        {
12.             pickCanvas = new PickCanvas( canvas, branchgroup );
13.             pickCanvas.setTolerance( 0.0f );
14.             pickCanvas.setMode( PickCanvas.GEOMETRY );
15.             pickCanvas.setMode( PickTool.GEOMETRY );
16.             pickCanvas.setMode( PickCanvas.GEOMETRY_INTERSECT_INFO );
17.             branch = branchgroup;
18.        }
19.
20.        public void initialize()
21.        {
22.             allEvents = new WakeupCriterion[2];
23.             allEvents[0] = new WakeupOnAWTEvent( MouseEvent.MOUSE_DRAGGED );
24.             allEvents[1] = new WakeupOnAWTEvent( MouseEvent.MOUSE_PRESSED );
25.             wakeupOn ( new WakeupOr( allEvents ) );
26.        }
27.        public void processStimulus(Enumeration criteria)
28.        {     // actions to take when triggered   }
29.    }
```

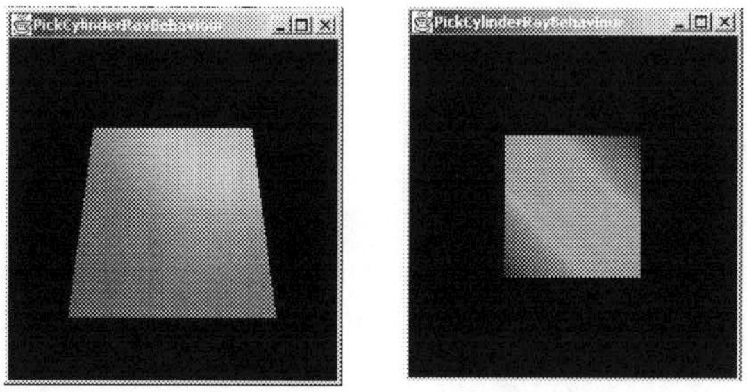

Trapezoidal object becomes a square through pressing or dragging the mouse

Figure 21. Second code segment for PickCylinderRayBehavior.java

```
42.  public void processStimulus(Enumeration criteria)
43.  {
44.      WakeupCriterion wakeup;  AWTEvent[] event;  int eventId;
45.      while ( criteria.hasMoreElements() )
46.      {
47.          wakeup = (WakeupCriterion) criteria.nextElement();
48.          if ( wakeup instanceof WakeupOnAWTEvent )
49.          {
50.              event = ((WakeupOnAWTEvent) wakeup).getAWTEvent();
51.              for ( int i=0; i<event.length; i++ )
52.              {
53.                  eventId = event[i].getID();
54.                  switch ( eventId )
55.                  {
56.                  case MouseEvent.MOUSE_PRESSED:
57.                  case MouseEvent.MOUSE_DRAGGED:
58.                      int x_m = ((MouseEvent)event[i]).getX();
59.                      int y_m = ((MouseEvent)event[i]).getY();
60.                      Point3d start_pt = new Point3d();
61.                      Transform3D trans = new Transform3D();
62.                      canvas.getPixelLocationInImagePlate( x_m, y_m, start_pt );
63.                      canvas.getImagePlateToVworld( trans );
64.                      trans.transform( start_pt );
65.                      pickCanvas.setShapeCylinderRay( start_pt, new Vector3d( 0,0,-1),0.1);
66.                      if ( pickCanvas.pickClosest() != null )
67.                      {
68.                          pickres = pickCanvas.pickClosest();
69.                          PickIntersection pickint = pickres.getClosestIntersection(p_3d);
70.                          shape3d = (Shape3D) pickres.getNode(PickResult.SHAPE3D);
71.                          shape3d.addGeometry(new Square().getGeometry());
72.                          shape3d.removeGeometry(0);
73.                      }
74.                      break;
75.                  default: ;
76.                  }
77.              }
78.          }
79.          this.wakeupOn( new WakeupOr( allEvents ) );
80.      }
81.  }
```

tor and the initialize method for a customized picking behavior class for this application, whereas Figure 21 shows the important code segment in the processStimulus method. Note that the transformation of the visual object can be done through pressing or dragging the mouse, while clicking the mouse will have no effect. Also, a CylinderRay pick shape that propagates towards the negative z-axis infinitely is selected for picking the object.

PICKING OBJECTS WITHIN A SPECIFIED BOUND FROM A CERTAIN POSITION

Instead of picking objects using a standard pick shape and finding intersection of the shape with visual objects, it may sometimes be more convenient to pick objects within some specified bounds from a certain position. The position and the bound can of course be updated dynamically depending on changes in the viewpoint of the user or as the user navigates within the 3D virtual world using, say, the mouse. The underlying class for implementation in this approach is PickBound, where only the shape and the position of the bound are important.

The next few figures illustrate a simple example using PickBound in an application where the colors of some spherical objects as shown in Figure 22 can be changed by using the mouse. Figure 23 shows the code segment for the creation of the six spherical objects at different locations. Note that spheres 3 and 6 are green in color and are closer to the screen while the others are positioned in two different clusters.

Clicking the mouse near the two cluster groups will create an appropriate picking bound at a 3D coordinate associated with the current mouse position and will result in the picking of all the spheres enveloped by the specified bound. Subsequently, the coloring attributes of the picked spheres will be changed, resulting in a change in the visual color of the objects. Note, however, that since the program is such that the green spheres are quite far away from the bound, they will not be picked.

Figure 22. Result from PickBoundsBehavior.java

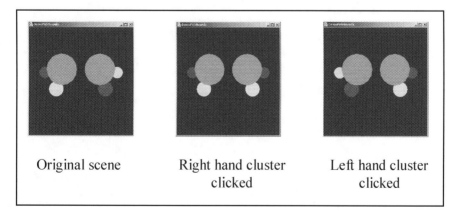

| Original scene | Right hand cluster clicked | Left hand cluster clicked |

Figure 23. First code segment for PickBoundsBehavior.java

```
1.   Sphere sphere1 = new Sphere( 0.1f, createAppearance1() );
2.   sphere1.setCapability( Primitive.ENABLE_APPEARANCE_MODIFY );
3.   sphere1.getShape().setCapability( Shape3D.ALLOW_APPEARANCE_READ );
4.   sphere1.getShape().setCapability( Shape3D.ALLOW_APPEARANCE_WRITE );
5.   objTrans1.addChild( sphere1 );  Transform3D translate = new Transform3D();
6.   translate.set( new Vector3f( 0.65f, 0.15f, 0.15f ) );  objTrans1.setTransform( translate );
7.
8.   Sphere sphere2 = new Sphere( 0.15f, createAppearance2() );
9.   sphere2.setCapability( Primitive.ENABLE_APPEARANCE_MODIFY );
10.  sphere2.getShape().setCapability( Shape3D.ALLOW_APPEARANCE_READ );
11.  sphere2.getShape().setCapability( Shape3D.ALLOW_APPEARANCE_WRITE );
12.  objTrans2.addChild( sphere2 );  translate.set( new Vector3f( 0.5f, -0.15f, -0.15f ) );
13.  objTrans2.setTransform( translate );
14.
15.  Sphere sphere3 = new Sphere( 0.2f, createAppearance3() );
16.  sphere3.setCapability( Primitive.ENABLE_APPEARANCE_MODIFY );
17.  sphere3.getShape().setCapability( Shape3D.ALLOW_APPEARANCE_READ );
18.  sphere3.getShape().setCapability( Shape3D.ALLOW_APPEARANCE_WRITE );
19.  objTrans3.addChild( sphere3 );  translate.set( new Vector3f( 0.25f, 0.15f, 0.75f ) );
20.  objTrans3.setTransform( translate );
21.
22.  Sphere sphere4 = new Sphere( 0.1f, createAppearance2() );
23.  sphere4.setCapability( Primitive.ENABLE_APPEARANCE_MODIFY );
24.  sphere4.getShape().setCapability( Shape3D.ALLOW_APPEARANCE_READ );
25.  sphere4.getShape().setCapability( Shape3D.ALLOW_APPEARANCE_WRITE );
26.  objTrans4.addChild( sphere4 );  translate.set( new Vector3f( -0.65f, 0.15f, 0.15f ) );
27.  objTrans4.setTransform( translate );
28.
29.  Sphere sphere5 = new Sphere( 0.15f, createAppearance1() );
30.  sphere5.setCapability( Primitive.ENABLE_APPEARANCE_MODIFY );
31.  sphere5.getShape().setCapability( Shape3D.ALLOW_APPEARANCE_READ );
32.  sphere5.getShape().setCapability( Shape3D.ALLOW_APPEARANCE_WRITE );
33.  objTrans5.addChild( sphere5 );  translate.set( new Vector3f( -0.5f, -0.15f, -0.15f ) );
34.  objTrans5.setTransform( translate );
35.
36.  Sphere sphere6 = new Sphere( 0.2f, createAppearance3() );
37.  sphere6.setCapability( Primitive.ENABLE_APPEARANCE_MODIFY );
38.  sphere6.getShape().setCapability( Shape3D.ALLOW_APPEARANCE_READ );
39.  sphere6.getShape().setCapability( Shape3D.ALLOW_APPEARANCE_WRITE );
40.  objTrans6.addChild( sphere6 );  translate.set( new Vector3f( -0.25f, 0.15f, 0.75f ) );
41.  objTrans6.setTransform( translate );
```

Figure 24 shows the important code segment for implementing the behavior described. Upon the occurrence of a mouse click event, the mouse position will be transformed to

Figure 24. Second code segment for PickBoundsBehavior.java

```
1.    case MouseEvent.MOUSE_CLICKED:
2.
3.    // getting the mouse position on the 2D viewing plane
4.    x_m = ((MouseEvent)event[i]).getX();  y_m = ((MouseEvent)event[i]).getY();
5.
6.    // transforming the 2D local coordinates to virtual world coordinates
7.    canvas.getPixelLocationInImagePlate( x_m, y_m, pt_m );
8.    canvas.getImagePlateToVworld( trans );
9.    trans.transform( pt_m );
10.
11.   // getting the direction for the picking shape
12.   canvas.getCenterEyeInImagePlate( start_pt );
13.   trans.transform( start_pt );
14.   pt_m.sub( start_pt );
15.   dirn.set( pt_m );
16.   dirn.normalize();
17.   dirn.scale( 2.5 );
18.   end_pt.add( start_pt, dirn );
19.
20.   BoundingSphere bounding = new BoundingSphere ( end_pt, 0.5 );
21.   picktool.setShapeBounds( bounding, start_pt );
22.
23.   result = picktool.pickAllSorted();
24.
25.   if( result != null )
26.   {
27.       Primitive[] picked_node = new Primitive[result.length];
28.       for ( int j=0; j < result.length && result[j] != null; j++ )
29.       {
30.           picked_node[j] = (Primitive)result[j].getNode( PickResult.PRIMITIVE );
31.           current_attr = picked_node[j].getAppearance().getColoringAttributes();
32.           current_attr.getColor( current_clr );
33.           if ( current_clr.equals( yellow ) ) current_attr.setColor( red );
34.           else current_attr.setColor( yellow );
35.       }
36.   }
37.
38.   break;
```

obtain the corresponding 3D coordinate in the same way as other examples in previous sections, and a spherical bound with a certain radius is specified to pick up objects within the sphere. The color attributes of the objects picked are then changed.

PICKING IN A VIRTUAL INSTRUMENT PANEL

We will now outline a more complete and interesting application to implement the front panel of an instrument in a 3D virtual laboratory using the various picking techniques discussed (Xiang, 2001). The entire system involves the rendering of a Java 3D based laboratory in a room with an oscilloscope and one signal generator for carrying out a real-time real-life experiment. The virtual instruments that the user can operate on remotely in a client Internet site actually correspond to equivalent real instruments in a physical laboratory.

After navigating to the instrument of interest in the virtual 3D world, the user can use mouse drag, press and click to adjust the various types of controls such as pushbuttons, sliders and knobs on the instrument. Any change in the instrument control panel will be transmitted to the server, which will send commands to change the actual settings on the real instrument in the laboratory. The resulting changes in waveforms and other measurements will also be sent back to the client to provide update in the Java 3D virtual world on the client side.

In this application, many objects corresponding to a variety of control knobs, sliders and pushbuttons may be picked and different controls will have different behavioral requirements. Illustrated to some degrees in Figure 25 in the control panel for the signal generator, a knob can only be turned, a pushbutton must be pushed in a certain direction, and a slider can only be dragged in a specific direction.

Figure 25. Signal generator control panel

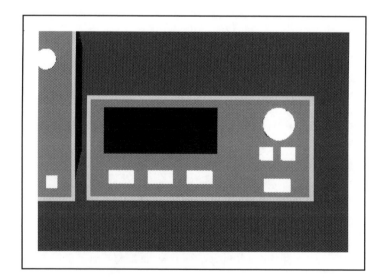

Obviously, utility classes such as PickRotationBehavior, PickTranslateBehavior and PickZoomBehavior, which have been discussed in the beginning of this chapter, have rather restricted performance and will not have enough flexibility in this application. Instead, we need to develop a more dedicated and sophisticated picking behavior class to support the development of different types of 3D instrument controls in the virtual laboratory.

Figure 26 shows the important code segment for implementing the picking behavior, where the control being picked and the action to be taken is obtained from the type of mouse events as well as the identity number of the picked objects or controls. The following gives a more detailed description on the subtleties in the implementation.

Figure 26. First code segment for Oscilloscope.java

```
1.    public void processStimulus (Enumeration criteria) {
2.        ...
3.        if (eventId == MouseEvent.MOUSE_MOVED) {
4.            Point3d []ptw = pi.getPrimitiveCoordinatesVW();
5.            Point3d []pt = pi.getPrimitiveCoordinates();
6.            if (pt.length() == 3) if (pt[0].z>0&&pt[1].z>0&&pt[2].z>0) {
7.                Point3f RPt = new Point3f(ptw[0]);
8.                obj = whichObject(RPt.x, RPt.y, RPt.z); }
9.            else {
10.               if (pt[0].z>=0&&pt[1].z>=0&&pt[2].z>=0&&pt[3].z>=0)
11.               if (pt[0].x>=0&&pt[1].x>=0&&pt[2].x>=0&&pt[3].x>=0) {
12.                   Point3f RPt = new Point3f((ptw[2].x+ptw[3].x)/2.0f, (ptw[2].y+ptw[3].y)/2.0f, ptw[0].z);
13.                   obj = whichObject(RPt.x, RPt.y, RPt.z); }
14.               else {
15.                   Point3f RPt =new Point3f((ptw[0].x+ptw[2].x)/2.0f, (ptw[0].y+ptw[2].y)/2.0f, ptw[0].z);
16.                   obj = whichObject(RPt.x, RPt.y, RPt.z); }}
17.       if (eventId == MouseEvent.MOUSE_PRESSED) {
18.           if (obj==id) ... // activate or deactivate a button;  ... }
19.       if (eventId == MouseEvent.MOUSE_RELEASED) {
20.           if (obj==id) ... // deactivate a button or send out a network command;  ...}
21.       if (eventId == MouseEvent.MOUSE_DRAGGED) {
22.           if (obj==id) ... // rotate a knob, or drag a slider or connector;  ...}
23.       ...
24.   public int whichObject(float x, float y, float z) {
25.       if (isObject(posi[i], x, y, z)) return id;
26.       else return 0;
27.   }
28.
29.   public boolean isObject(Point3f object, float x, float y, float z) {
30.       float d;
31.       d = (object.x-x)*(object.x-x)+(object.y-y)*(object.y-y)+ (object.z-z)*(object.z-z);
32.       if (d < DIFFERENCE) return true;
33.       else return false;
34.   }
```

- Instrument buttons, sliders, and connectors have geometries constructed using QuadArray, while knobs are built using TriangleStripArray.
- In the standard Java 3D API, an object in a 3D virtual scene cannot be identified directly using mouse events. To create a picking function that can be used for the various types of control, we assign to each control a unique identity number based on its position.
- For the instrument to behave as realistically as possible, controls on the instrument panel should not be adjustable unless the mouse is on their front face. Thus, when the side of a button is pressed, it should not be activated or deactivated. This is different from the basic picking behavior from Java 3D, where picking from other faces may also be possible. To obtain the intended behavior, the origin of the local coordinate system for a 3D button, slider, and knob is taken to be the geometric center of the front face of the control, while that for a 2D connector is the center of its left edge.
- To obtain the identity number of a control, the coordinates of all the controls, which may have changed depending on how the user has used the instruments, have to be

Figure 27. Second code segment for Oscilloscope.java

```
1.    public boolean isObject(Point3f object, float x, float y)
2.    {
3.        float d;
4.        d = (object.x-x)*(object.x-x)+(object.y-y)*(object.y-y);
5.        System.out.println(d);
6.        if (d < 0.00001f) return true;
7.        else return false;
8.    }
9.
10.   public int whichObject(float x, float y)
11.   {
12.       if (isObject(osci_knobposi[0], x, y)) return 1101;
13.       …
14.       if (isObject(osci_knobposi[9], x, y)) return 1110;
15.       if (isObject(osci_buttonposi[0], x, y)) return 1201;
16.       if (isObject(osci_slideposi[0], x, y)) return 1301;
17.       …
18.       if (isObject(osci_slideposi[4], x, y)) return 1305;
19.       if (isObject(sg_knobposi[0], x-0.47f, y+0.075f)) return 2101;
20.       if (isObject(sg_buttonposi[0], x-0.47f, y+0.075f)) return 2201;
21.       …
22.       if (isObject(sg_buttonposi[5], x-0.47f, y+0.075f)) return 2206;
23.       return 0;
24.   }
```

retrieved. This is done in lines 4 and 5, where the arrays pt and ptw give the local and global coordinates. Subsequently, Lines 6 and 10 check for the mouse being on the front face, and the global coordinates of the controls are calculated in lines 7, 12 and 15.

- To identify or find out the identity number of the control being picked, the global coordinates of the controls have to be compared with the values in the original setup. The latter can be obtained from the former using a series of linear geometric transformation based on the hierarchy structure that defines the virtual laboratory in terms of instruments and controls.

In the code fragment in Figure 26, the functions whichObject and isObject are for the purpose of finding the identity of the control picked from comparing global coordinates. These two functions are given in Figure 27. Specifically, in the whichObject method, an appropriate integer that identifies a specific control in the scene is returned if any of the if statements is correct. The values of x and y correspond to the global coordinates of the center of the picked object, which is placed along the z axis.

SUMMARY

This chapter has discussed the use of picking behavior class for the purpose of picking objects of interest. Using simple utility classes such as PickRotationBehavior, PickTranslateBehavior, and PickZoomBehavior is straightforward, although the picking behavior may not be flexible enough for most applications. The use of a variety of picking shapes, such as PickRay, PickConeRay, PickCylinder, and PickBounds, to customize the picking behavior is then discussed, followed by an example involving the controls in 3D instrument panels.

REFERENCES

Barrilleaux, J. (2001). *3D user interfaces with Java 3D*. Manning Publications.

Emoto, M., Narlo, J., Kaneko, O., Komori, A., Iima, M., Yamaguchi, S., & Sudo, S. (2001). 3D real-time monitoring system for LHD plasma heating experiment. *Fusion Engineering and Design*, *56*, 1017-1021.

Nakano, H., Sato, Y., Matsuo, S., & Ishimasa, T. (2000). Development of 3D Visualization system for the study of physical properties of quasicrystals. *Materials Science and Engineering*, 542-547.

Shyamsundar, N., & Gadh, R. (2001). Internet-based collaborative product design with assembly features and virtual design spaces. *Computer-Aided Design, 33*, 637-651.

Xiang, X., Cheng, C. D., Ko, C. C., Chen, B. M., & Lu, S. J. (2001). API for virtual laboratory instrument using Java 3D. *Proceedings 3rd International Conference on Control Theory and Applications.*

Chapter X
Navigation, Input Devices, and Collision

INTRODUCTION

One of the most useful and important advantages of 3D graphics rendering and applications is that there is the possibility for the user to navigate through the 3D virtual world in a seamless fashion. Complicated visual objects can be better appreciated from different angles and manipulation of these objects can be carried out in the most natural manner.

To support this important function of navigation, the user will often need to use a variety of input devices such as the keyboard, mouse, and joystick in a fashion that befits a 3D scenario. Also, collision handling is important as it will be unnatural if the user can, say, walk through solid walls in the virtual world.

The functionality of navigation therefore has a close relationship with input devices and collision detection, all of which can be handled in Java 3D through a variety of straightforward but not so flexible utility classes as well as more complicated but at the same time more flexible user defined methods.

The main requirement of navigation is of course to handle or refresh changes in the rendered 3D view as the user moves around in the virtual universe (Wang, 2006). As illustrated in Figure 1, this will require a modification of the platform transform as the user changes his or her position in the universe. Essentially, as will be illustrated in the next section, we will first need to retrieve the ViewPlatformTransform object from the SimpleUniverse object.

Figure 1. Basic view branch graph showing view platform transform

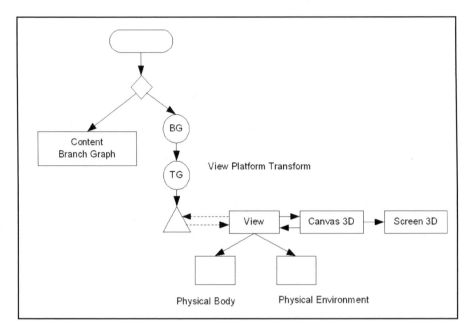

KEYBOARD NAVIGATION USING KeyBoardBehavior

The keyboard is perhaps still the simplest and the most comprehensive hardware available for navigation in a 3D virtual world. To use this hardware in Java 3D, two approaches can be adopted. The most straightforward but rather rigid approach is to make use of the existing KeyNavigatorBehavior utility class, which is summarized in Figure 2. On the other hand, for more flexible behavior and performance, more programming effort can be spent to define the behavior for each individual key to suit a specific application. The former approach will be dealt with in this section, while the latter will be discussed in the next section.

Essentially, the use of the KeyNavigatorBehaviour utility class requires the following steps to be carried out:

- Create a KeyNavigatorBehavior object for the transform group of interest.
- Add the KeyNavigatorBehavior object to the scene graph.
- Define appropriate bounds for the KeyNavigatorBehavior object.

Figure 3 shows the code segment for a simple example in the use of the KeyNavigator-Behavior class for navigation. Note that the navigation functionalities of the various keys are provided in Figure 2.

Figure 2. Using KeyNavigatorBehavior

```
KeyNavigatorBehavior(TransformGroup targetTG)
// constructs a new key navigator behavior node that operates on the specified transform group.

initialize()
// Override behavior's initialize method to setup wakeup criteria.

processStimulus(java.util.Enumeration criteria)
// Override behavior's stimulus method to handle stimulus event.
```

Key	Movement
←	Rotate left
→	Rotate Right
↑	Move forward
↓	Move backward
PgUp	Rotate up
PgDn	Rotate down
+	Restore back clip distance (and return to the origin)
-	Reduce back clip distance
=	Return to center of universe

As can be seen from Figure 3, the TransformGroup for the ViewPlatform needs to be retrieved before it can be appropriately changed as the user moves. Thus, we pass the relevant SimpleUniverse object to the createSceneGraph () method in the code segment, and use it to retrieve the TransformGroup containing the ViewPlatform in line 10. Line 12 creates a new KeyNavigatorBehavior object and line 13 defines bounds for that object.

It should be emphasized that the main advantage of using KeyNavigatorBehavior is that one can use some well-known pre-defined keystrokes for navigation. However, the main disadvantage is that it may not be flexible enough for specific applications. In particular, the rate of movement or the speed at which the user moves through the virtual world cannot be changed.

USER DEFINED KEYBOARD NAVIGATION

The requirement of user friendliness often dictates the use of custom defined key functions in 3D navigation. This will involve detecting the relevant keys and making changes to some transforms to give the effect of moving forward or backward, sidestepping left or right, up or down, as well as turning left and right.

Figure 3. Code segment for KeyBoardUtil.java

```
1.    public class KeyBoardUtil extends Applet
2.    {
3.        SimpleUniverse universe = null;
4.
5.        public BranchGroup createSceneGraph(SimpleUniverse universe, Canvas3D c)
6.        {
7.                BranchGroup objRoot = new BranchGroup();  // create root of branch graph
8.
9.                TransformGroup viewTrans = new TransformGroup();
10.               viewTrans = universe.getViewingPlatform().getViewPlatformTransform();
11.
12.               KeyNavigatorBehavior keyNav = new KeyNavigatorBehavior(viewTrans);
13.               keyNav.setSchedulingBounds(new BoundingSphere());
14.               objRoot.addChild(keyNav);
15.
16.               objRoot.addChild(new ColorCube(0.1f));
17.               objRoot.addChild(createFloor());
18.
19.               objRoot.compile();  /// Java 3D to perform optimization on this scene graph
20.
21.               return objRoot;
22.       }
23.
24.       public void init()
25.       {
26.               setLayout(new BorderLayout());
27.               GraphicsConfiguration config = SimpleUniverse.getPreferredConfiguration();
28.
29.               Canvas3D canvas3D = new Canvas3D(config);
30.               add("Center", canvas3D);
31.               universe = new SimpleUniverse(canvas3D);
32.
33.               BranchGroup scene = createSceneGraph(universe,canvas3D);
34.               TransformGroup joy = new TransformGroup();
35.
36.               // Move ViewPlatform back a bit so the objects can be viewed.
37.               universe.getViewingPlatform().setNominalViewingTransform();
38.               universe.addBranchGraph(scene);
39.       }
```

Essentially, two types of movement, translation, and rotation are involved. Mathematically, we will need to incorporate two types of transformation matrix in the program code. For rotation, which includes turning left or right, or pitching up or down, the transformation can be described by

$$\mathbf{M}^{(i+1)} = (\mathbf{M}^{(i)T})^{-1} \begin{bmatrix} \cos\alpha & 0 & \sin\alpha \\ 0 & 1 & 0 \\ -\sin\alpha & 0 & \cos\alpha \end{bmatrix}$$

and

$$\mathbf{M}^{(i+1)} = (\mathbf{M}^{(i)T})^{-1} \begin{bmatrix} 1 & 0 & 0 \\ 0 & \cos\beta & -\sin\beta \\ 0 & \sin\beta & \cos\beta \end{bmatrix},$$

where α and β are the increases in angles for turning left and pitching up, and $\mathbf{M}^{(i)}$ is the directional cosine matrix in the ith rotation.

In the example code segment shown from Figures 4 to 7, the previous equation is used in lines 12 to 35 to form and return a transformation matrix for the purpose of rotation about one of the two possible axes x and y. In lines 36 to 46, the rotation operation is carried out in a function whose first argument corresponds to the target transform group that needs to be worked on. For this navigation example, the target transform group is of course the one for the ViewPlatform. The second argument of the function is the angle to be used in the rotation, and this may be equal to either α or β depending on the value of the third argument. The latter is an integer mode argument with 1 denoting left rotation and 2 denoting up pitching.

In the same manner, the mathematical formula for translation is given by

$$\begin{cases} x_{i+1} = x_i + \Delta \sin\alpha \\ z_{i+1} = z_i + \Delta \cos\alpha, \end{cases}$$

$$\begin{cases} x_{i+1} = x_i + \Delta \sin\left(\alpha + \dfrac{\pi}{2}\right) \\ z_{i+1} = z_i + \Delta \cos\left(\alpha + \dfrac{\pi}{2}\right) \end{cases}$$

and

$$y_{i+1} = y_i + \Delta$$

for implementing forward, left and up movements, respectively. Note that x_i, y_i and z_i are the x, y and z coordinates of the viewpoint, and Δ is the movement increment. Lines 48 to 55 of Figure 5 give the code for the function for translation.

222   *Ko & Cheng*

Figure 4. First code segment for KeyBoardNavigation.java

```
1.    public void initialize()
2.    {
3.        events[0]=new WakeupOnAWTEvent(KeyEvent.KEY_PRESSED); // set initial wakeup condition
4.        this.wakeupOn(new WakeupOnAWTEvent(KeyEvent.KEY_PRESSED));
5.        allEvents=new WakeupOr(events);
6.        wakeupOn(allEvents);
7.        comMat.m00 = 1.0f;  comMat.m01 = 0.0f;  comMat.m02 = 0.0f;
8.        comMat.m10 = 0.0f;  comMat.m11 = 1.0f;  comMat.m12 = 0.0f;
9.        comMat.m20 = 0.0f;  comMat.m21 = 0.0f;  comMat.m22 = 1.0f;
10.   }
11.
12.   private Matrix3f coMatrix(int mode, float angle)
13.   {
14.       Matrix3f tempMat = new Matrix3f();
15.       switch (mode)
16.       {
17.       case 1:
18.         tempMat.m00 = Math.cos(angle);  tempMat.m01 = 0.0f;  tempMat.m02 = Math.sin(angle);
19.         tempMat.m10 = 0.0f;  tempMat.m11 = 1.0f;  tempMat.m12 = 0.0f;
20.         tempMat.m20 = -Math.sin(angle);  tempMat.m21 = 0.0f;  tempMat.m22 = Math.cos(angle);
21.         break;
22.       case 2:
23.         tempMat.m00 = 1.0f;  tempMat.m01 = 0.0f;  tempMat.m02 = 0.0f;
24.         tempMat.m10 = 0.0f;  tempMat.m11 = Math.cos(angle);  tempMat.m12 = Math.sin(angle);
25.         tempMat.m20 = 0.0f;  tempMat.m21 = -Math.sin(angle);  tempMat.m22 = Math.cos(angle);
26.         break;
27.       case 3:
28.         tempMat.m00 = Math.cos(angle);  tempMat.m01 = -Math.sin(angle);  tempMat.m02 = 0.0f;
29.         tempMat.m10 = Math.sin(angle);  tempMat.m11 = Math.cos(angle);  tempMat.m12 = 0.0f;
30.         tempMat.m20 = 0.0f;  tempMat.m21 = 0.0f;  tempMat.m22 = 1.0f;
31.         break;
32.       default:
33.       }
34.       return tempMat;
35.   }
```

The keys to be used for this user-defined keyboard based navigation example are defined in lines 58 and 59 in Figure 6. Lines 85 to 88 use the setRotation3D function described to give rise a rotational movement of the ViewPlatform, while lines 89 to 94 use the seTranslation3D function to give a translation movement.

The initialize method from lines 74 to 80 sets the keyboard event conditions that will wakeup this navigational behavior. Specifically, WakeupOnAWTEvent will enable the behavior to receive any keyboard event stimulus. Lastly, the processStimulus function will

Figure 5. Second code segment for KeyBoardNavigation.java

```
36.  private Transform3D setRotation3D(TransformGroup Trans, float angle, Matrix3f rotMat, int mode)
37.  {  // to set the position after rotation
38.      Transform3D rt3d = new Transform3D();
39.      Trans.getTransform(rt3d);
40.      rotMat.transpose();
41.      rotMat.invert();
42.      rotMat.mul(rotMat, coMatrix(mode, angle));
43.      rt3d.setRotation(rotMat);
44.      Trans.setTransform(rt3d);
45.      return rt3d;
46.  }
47.
48.  private Transform3D setPosition3D(TransformGroup Trans, Point3f point)
49.  {  // to set the position after movement
50.      Transform3D t3d = new Transform3D();
51.      Trans.getTransform(t3d);
52.      t3d.setTranslation(new Vector3d(point));
53.      Trans.setTransform(t3d);
54.      return t3d;
55.  }
```

carry out any necessary processing when the behavior has been awoken. In the current example, the identity of the key pressed is passed as information to the keypressed function, which will decide if a predefined key has been pressed, and then subsequently modify the orientation and position of the ViewPlatform accordingly.

NAVIGATION USING MOUSE UTILITY CLASS

In addition to the keyboard, the mouse and other appropriate input devices can also be used for navigation. Using the mouse is convenient and requires less training than using the keyboard, especially in the presence of mouse dragging and clicking based 3D navigational tools on the screen.

In Java 3D, a number of straightforward utility behaviors that allow the mouse to be used for interaction and navigation are available. These are summarized in Figure 8 and include classes for translating, zooming, and rotating objects based on mouse movements.

In general, these behavior classes can be used to manipulate visual objects in the manner specified. In particular, they can be used for 3D navigation in the virtual universe. Note that the three classes have very similar structures, and have constructors, which

Figure 6. Third code segment for KeyBoardNavigation.java

```
56.   public class KeyBoardNavigation extends Applet
57.   {
58.     private static final int      UP = KeyEvent.VK_UP, DOWN = KeyEvent.VK_DOWN,
59.                                    LEFT = KeyEvent.VK_LEFT, RIGHT = KeyEvent.VK_RIGHT;
60.     private static final float  PAI= 3.14159f, ANGLEPAI = 2.0f*PAI/360.0f,
61.                                    SPAN = 0.02f,  ANGLESTEP = 0.01f;
62.     private float x, y, z, turningAngle = 0.0f;  int direction = 1;
63.     private Matrix4d matrix = new Matrix4d();  private Matrix3f comMat = new Matrix3f();
64.     private WakeupCriterion events[] = new WakeupCriterion[1]; private WakeupOr allEvents;
65.     SimpleUniverse universe = null;
66.
67.     public class KeyBoardBehavior extends Behavior
68.     {
69.        private TransformGroup targetTG;
70.        Point3f viewposi = new Point3f(0.0f,0.0f,2.5f);
71.
72.        KeyBoardBehavior(TransformGroup targetTG) { this.targetTG = targetTG; }
73.
74.        public void initialize() {
75.           events[0]=new WakeupOnAWTEvent(KeyEvent.KEY_PRESSED);
76.           this.wakeupOn(new WakeupOnAWTEvent(KeyEvent.KEY_PRESSED));
77.           allEvents=new WakeupOr(events);  wakeupOn(allEvents);
78.           comMat.m00 = 1.0f;  comMat.m01 = 0.0f;  comMat.m02 = 0.0f;
79.           comMat.m10 = 0.0f;  comMat.m11 = 1.0f;  comMat.m12 = 0.0f;
80.           comMat.m20 = 0.0f;  comMat.m21 = 0.0f;  comMat.m22 = 1.0f;  }
81.
82.        public void keyPressed(KeyEvent e){
83.           int key=e.getKeyCode();
84.           switch(key) {
85.           case RIGHT: turningAngle -= ANGLESTEP;
86.                       setRotation3D(targetTG, -ANGLESTEP, comMat, 1);  break;
87.           case LEFT:  turningAngle += ANGLESTEP;
88.                       setRotation3D(targetTG, ANGLESTEP, comMat, 1);  break;
89.           case UP:  viewposi.x = viewposi.x-3.0f*SPAN*(float)Math.sin(turningAngle);
90.                       viewposi.z = viewposi.z-3.0f*SPAN*(float)Math.cos(turningAngle);
91.                       setPosition3D(targetTG, viewposi);  break;
92.           case DOWN: viewposi.x = viewposi.x+1.0f*SPAN*(float)Math.sin(turningAngle);
93.                       viewposi.z = viewposi.z+1.0f*SPAN*(float)Math.cos(turningAngle);
94.                       setPosition3D(targetTG, viewposi);  break;
95.           default: }
96.        }
```

may take in an argument of MouseBehavior.INVERT_INPUTS. The latter specifies that the mouse response will be in a direction opposite to that normally used for manipulation objects, and will be appropriate for changing the TransformGroup for the ViewPlatform in 3D navigation.

Figure 7. Fourth code segment for KeyBoardNavigation.java

```
97.    public void processStimulus(Enumeration criteria)
98.    {
99.      WakeupCriterion wakeup;  AWTEvent[] event ;
100.     while(criteria.hasMoreElements())
101.     {
102.        wakeup = (WakeupCriterion) criteria.nextElement();
103.        if(wakeup instanceof WakeupOnAWTEvent)
104.        {
105.           event = ((WakeupOnAWTEvent)wakeup).getAWTEvent();
106.           keyPressed((KeyEvent)event[0]);
107.        }
108.     }
109.     this.wakeupOn(allEvents);
110.   }
111.
112. } // end of class KeyBoardBehavior
```

Figure 8. Mouse interaction utility class

```
MouseRotate()
// constructor for a default mouse rotate behavior.

MouseRotate(int flags)
// create a rotate behavior with flags.  Flags may be MouseBehavior.INVERT_INPUT or
// MouseBehavior.MANUAL_WAKEUP for inverting input or manual wakeup, respectively.

MouseRotate(TransformGroup transformGroup)
// create a rotate behavior given the transform group.

MouseTranslate()
MouseTranslate(int flags)
MouseTranslate(TransformGroup transformGroup)
// equivalent constructors for translation instead of rotation

MouseZoom()
MouseZoom(int flags)
MouseZoom(TransformGroup transformGroup)
// equivalent constructors for zooming instead of rotation
```

MouseBehavior Class	Response to Mouse Action	Mouse Action
MouseRotate	Rotate object	Left-button held with mouse movement
MouseTranslate	Translate object in a plane parallel to image plate	Right-button held with mouse movement
MouseZoom	Translate the object in a plane orthogonal to the image plate	Middle-button held with mouse movement

Similar to other utility classes, using the mouse behavior classes is quite straightforward and requires the following steps:

- Create an appropriate MouseBehavior object.
- Set the target transform group.
- Define bounds for the MouseBehavior object.
- Add the MouseBehavior object to the scene graph.

The code segment listed in Figure 9 exemplifies instances where the three mouse behavior classes are used for navigational. Note that MouseBehavior.INVERT_INPUTS is selected and the target transform group is the ViewPlatform transform.

Figure 9. Code segment for MouseInteractionUtil.java

```
1.    public class MouseInteractionUtil extends Applet
2.    {
3.        SimpleUniverse universe = null;
4.
5.        public BranchGroup createSceneGraph(SimpleUniverse universe, Canvas3D c)
6.        {
7.            BranchGroup objRoot = new BranchGroup(); // create root of the branch graph
8.
9.            TransformGroup viewTrans = new TransformGroup();
10.           viewTrans = universe.getViewingPlatform().getViewPlatformTransform();
11.
12.           MouseRotate Rotate = new MouseRotate(MouseBehavior.INVERT_INPUT); // rotate
13.           Rotate.setTransformGroup(viewTrans);
14.           Rotate.setSchedulingBounds(new BoundingSphere());
15.           objRoot.addChild(Rotate);
16.
17.           MouseTranslate Translate = new MouseTranslate(MouseBehavior.INVERT_INPUT); // translate
18.           Translate.setTransformGroup(viewTrans);
19.           Translate.setSchedulingBounds(new BoundingSphere());
20.           objRoot.addChild(Translate);
21.
22.           MouseZoom Zoom = new MouseZoom(MouseBehavior.INVERT_INPUT); // zoom
23.           Zoom.setTransformGroup(viewTrans);
24.           Zoom.setSchedulingBounds(new BoundingSphere());
25.           objRoot.addChild(Zoom);
26.
27.           objRoot.addChild(new ColorCube(0.1f));
28.           objRoot.addChild(createFloor());
29.
30.           objRoot.compile(); // Java optimization
31.           return objRoot;
32.       }
```

USER-DEFINED MOUSE NAVIGATION

The reason for implementing a user-defined mouse navigation tool and behavior is the same as that in user-defined keyboard navigation. Specifically, while it takes more programming

Figure 10. First code segment for MouseNavigation.java

```
1.    public class MouseNavigation extends Applet
2.    {
3.        private static final int UP = 1, DOWN = 2, LEFT = 3, RIGHT = 4;
4.        private float  x, y, z, turningAngle = 0.0f;  int direction = 1;
5.        private Matrix4d matrix = new Matrix4d();  private Matrix3f comMat = new Matrix3f();
6.        private static final float PAI = 3.14159f, ANGLEPAI = 2.0f*PAI/360.0f, SPAN = 0.02f,
7.            ANGLESTEP = 0.01f;
8.        private WakeupCriterion events[] = new WakeupCriterion[4];  private WakeupOr allEvents;
9.        SimpleUniverse universe = null;
10.
11.       public class MouseMovement extends Behavior
12.       {
13.           private TransformGroup targetTG;
14.           Point3f viewposi = new Point3f(0.0f,0.0f,2.5f);
15.
16.           MouseMovement (TransformGroup targetTG) {
17.               this.targetTG = targetTG; } // create behavior
18.
19.           public void initialize() {
20.               events[0]=new WakeupOnAWTEvent(MouseEvent.MOUSE_DRAGGED);
21.               events[1]=new WakeupOnAWTEvent(MouseEvent.MOUSE_PRESSED);
22.               events[2]=new WakeupOnAWTEvent(MouseEvent.MOUSE_RELEASED);
23.               events[3]=new WakeupOnAWTEvent(MouseEvent.MOUSE_MOVED);
24.               allEvents=new WakeupOr(events);  wakeupOn(allEvents);
25.               comMat.m00 = 1.0f;  comMat.m01 = 0.0f;  comMat.m02 = 0.0f;
26.               comMat.m10 = 0.0f;  comMat.m11 = 1.0f;  comMat.m12 = 0.0f;
27.               comMat.m20 = 0.0f;  comMat.m21 = 0.0f;  comMat.m22 = 1.0f;  }
28.
29.           public void MouseEvent(int direction) {
30.               switch(direction) {
31.                   case UP:       viewposi.x = viewposi.x-3.0f*SPAN*(float)Math.sin(turningAngle);
32.                                  viewposi.z = viewposi.z-3.0f*SPAN*(float)Math.cos(turningAngle);
33.                                  setPosition3D(targetTG, viewposi);  break;
34.                   case DOWN:     viewposi.x = viewposi.x+1.0f*SPAN*(float)Math.sin(turningAngle);
35.                                  viewposi.z = viewposi.z+1.0f*SPAN*(float)Math.cos(turningAngle);
36.                                  setPosition3D(targetTG, viewposi);  break;
37.                   case LEFT:     turningAngle += ANGLESTEP;
38.                                  setRotation3D(targetTG, ANGLESTEP, comMat, 1);  break;
39.                   case RIGHT:    turningAngle -= ANGLESTEP;
40.                                  setRotation3D(targetTG, -ANGLESTEP, comMat, 1);  break;
41.                   default: }}
42.
```

effort, the resulting behavior can be tailored to the specific application in mind, leading to a more user friendliness system (Ball & Mirmehdi, 1999).

The steps involved in defining specific mouse navigation behavior are similar to those for the keyboard discussed in the previous section. However, instead of keyboard events, we will now need to detect and process mouse events.

An example on having user-defined mouse navigation is provided in the code segment in Figures 10 and 11. As with other behavior classes, the customized MouseMovement navigation class includes a constructor, an initialize method to specify the initial wakeup events, a processStimulus method to detect the exact event and carry out processing when any of the mouse events has occurred, as well as a support MouseEvent method for carrying out the necessary transform.

Specifically, the processStimulus method in Figure 11 decodes the specific user interaction with the mouse and then invokes the MouseEvent method with the decoded interaction to carry out the necessary transform. Obviously, it is easy to modify the processStimulus and MouseEvent methods to include capabilities to change the rate of movement and other advanced features.

Figure 11. Secondcode segment for MouseNavigation.java

```
43.      public void processStimulus(Enumeration criteria)
44.      {
45.        WakeupCriterion wakeup;  AWTEvent[] event;  int eventID;
46.        while(criteria.hasMoreElements())
47.        {
48.          wakeup = (WakeupCriterion) criteria.nextElement();
49.          if(wakeup instanceof WakeupOnAWTEvent)
50.          {
51.            event = ((WakeupOnAWTEvent)wakeup).getAWTEvent();
52.            for(int i=0;i<event.length;i++)
53.            {
54.              eventID = event[i].getID();
55.              if((eventID==MouseEvent.MOUSE_PRESSED)&& !((MouseEvent)event[i]).isAltDown()
56.                && !((MouseEvent)event[i]).isMetaDown()) MouseEvent(3);  // left button
57.              if((eventID==MouseEvent.MOUSE_PRESSED)&& !((MouseEvent)event[i]).isAltDown()
58.                && ((MouseEvent)event[i]).isMetaDown()) MouseEvent(4);  // right button
59.              if((eventID==MouseEvent.MOUSE_PRESSED)&& ((MouseEvent)event[i]).isAltDown()
60.                && !((MouseEvent)event[i]).isMetaDown()) MouseEvent(1);  // center button
61.              if((eventID==MouseEvent.MOUSE_DRAGGED)&& !((MouseEvent)event[i]).isAltDown()
62.                && !((MouseEvent)event[i]).isMetaDown()) MouseEvent(2); // click and drag
63.            }
64.          }
65.        }
66.        this.wakeupOn(allEvents);
67.      }
```

INPUT DEVICE

Since the mouse and keyboard are basically 2D devices with a third dimension in terms of button clicking and key pressing, it is sometimes more convenient to carry out 3D navigation and object manipulation using more sophisticated devices such as a joystick, head tracker, motion capture suit, and space ball.

For this purpose, Java 3D provides an InputDevice interface for adding a device into an application. The runtime environment will support the device in the same manner as for a mouse. In Java 3D, any source that provides information with six degrees of freedom can be taken as an input device (Sowizral & Deering, 1999). The input devices may also have an unlimited number of buttons. As an example, a 6-button joystick will be a valid input device.

When the mouse and keyboard are used to capture user interactions, standard AWT event mechanisms are available and we have discussed how these events can be captured and processed for object manipulation and navigation in the 3D world. However, the capturing of events and getting information from other devices for processing in Java 3D require both the InputDevice interface and a Sensor class. The former encompasses the entire object interface, while the latter corresponds to one element of input from the device.

Figure 12. Specifying joystick device driver

```
40.   public class Joystick
41.   {
42.       public static final int BUTTON1 = 0x0001, BUTTON2 = 0x0002, BUTTON3 = 0x0004,
43.           BUTTON4 = 0x0008;
44.       static { System.loadLibrary("joystick"); }
45.       private int joyID = 0;
46.       public native int getNumDevs(),getButtons(int id);
47.       public native float getXPos(int id), getYPos(int id), getZPos(int id);
48.
49.       public Joystick(int id) { joyID = id; }
50.
51.       public float getXPos() { return getXPos(joyID); }
52.
53.       public float getYPos() { return getYPos(joyID); }
54.
55.       public float getZPos() { return getZPos(joyID); }
56.
57.       public int getButtons() { return getButtons(joyID); }
58.
59.       public String toString() { return "Joystick"; }
60.   }
```

In this section, the joystick will be used as an example input device. Note that, in general, a custom device driver that suits the specific joystick used will be required in any implementation. Specifically, the required native functions from the device driver must be obtained and specified in a *.java file.

In the example in this section, we will take the device driver as joystick.dll. In addition, as shown in the code segment in Figure 12, there are five native methods that are provided by the device driver. However, before discussing how these are used in our example implementation, it is worthwhile to take note of the following three generic ways for getting information from the device or device driver:

- **Blocking:** This signifies that the device driver is a blocking one and that Java 3D should be scheduled to read from the driver regularly. Technically, a blocking driver is one that can cause the thread (pollAndProcessInput in Java 3D) accessing the driver to be blocked while data is being transferred.
- **Non Blocking:** This signifies that the device driver is a non blocking one and that Java 3D should be scheduled to read from the driver regularly. Technically, a non blocking driver is one that will not cause the thread accessing the driver to be blocked while data is being retrieved. When there is no data available, pollAndProcessInput will return without any updating of the relevant sensor read value.
- **Demand Driven:** This is in a certain way non-blocking also and will give the current sensor value on demand whenever pollAndProcessInput is called through one of the getRead methods for the sensors of the device. The implication is that there is no need for scheduled regular reads.

Figures 13 and 14 show the code segment in an example for using the joystick as an input device. A demand driven device driver is assumed. Essentially, we need to perform the following operations:

- Construct the appropriate class and any necessary supporting methods.
- Read from the device and perform preprocessing.
- Use the input values to change the runtime environment.

Specifically, the setting up of the JoystickInputDevice class starts with creating instances from the Joystick, Sensor, and SensorRead classes in lines 3 to 5 in Figure 13. After declaring the other important variables and objects, the class constructor is declared with input arguments given by the transform groups that need to be modified. In this navigation example, the main interest is the transform group that contains the ViewPlatform and any other attached objects.

Next, an initialize method that will be invoked by the system upon initialization is supplied in lines 22 to 28 so that the joystick can be properly initialized. In this example, the transformation matrix is set up and checks for any device driver link error are performed.

Figure 13. First code segment for JoystickInputDevice.java

```
1.    public class JoystickInputDevice implements InputDevice
2.    {
3.        private Joystick joy[] = new Joystick[1];
4.        private Sensor joySensor[] = new Sensor[1];
5.        private SensorRead joySensorRead = new SensorRead();
6.        private Matrix4d matrix = new Matrix4d();  private Matrix3f comMat = new Matrix3f();
7.        private float   x, y, z, turningAngle = 0.0f;  int direction = 1;
8.        private static final float PAI = 3.14159f, ANGLEPAI = 2.0f*PAI/360.0f; SPAN = 0.02f,
9.            ANGLESTEP = 0.01f;
10.       TransformGroup tran, bodyTrans;
11.       Collision fcollision;
12.       Point3f viewposi;
13.
14.       public JoystickInputDevice(TransformGroup tran, Shape3D body3d,
15.           TransformGroup bodyTrans, Point3f viewposi) {
16.           this.tran = tran;
17.           this.bodyTrans = bodyTrans;
18.           this.viewposi = viewposi;
19.           System.out.println(viewposi);
20.           fcollision = new Collision(tran, body3d, bodyTrans); }
21.
22.       public boolean initialize() {
23.           try { joy[0] = new Joystick(0); } catch (SecurityException se) {} catch (UnsatisfiedLinkError ule) {}
24.           joySensor[0] = new Sensor(this);  // make a sensor object out of the input device
25.           comMat.m00 = 1.0f;  comMat.m01 = 0.0f;  comMat.m02 = 0.0f;
26.           comMat.m10 = 0.0f;  comMat.m11 = 1.0f;  comMat.m12 = 0.0f;
27.           comMat.m20 = 0.0f;  comMat.m21 = 0.0f;  comMat.m22 = 1.0f;
28.           return true; }
29.
30.       public void close() {}
31.
32.       public int getProcessingMode() {    return DEMAND_DRIVEN; }
33.
34.       public int getSensorCount() { return 1; }
35.
36.       public Sensor getSensor(int id) {    return joySensor[id]; }
37.
38.       public void setProcessingMode(int mode) {}
39.
```

Finally, a ProcessInput function is supplied to process the input from the joystick when the pollAndProcessInput method in line 76 is invoked. Lines 41 and 42 obtain information on the x and y coordinates, which will be 0 if no button is pressed, and the pressed button of the joystick. These are used for the purpose of navigation in the virtual world. The movement, be it rotational or translational, is determined by the button and the coordinates which of

Figure 14. Second code segment for JoystickInputDevice.java

```
40.   public void ProcessInput(Joystick joy, Sensor joySensor) {
41.      int buttons = joy.getButtons(); joySensorRead.setTime(System.currentTimeMillis());
42.      x = joy.getXPos(); z = joy.getYPos();  // determine button press on the directional keypad
43.      if (Math.abs(x) < 0.3f)  x = 0.0f;  if (Math.abs(z) < 0.3f) z = 0.0f;
44.      if (z<0 && x==0) { direction = 1; System.out.println(direction + " Forward");
45.         viewposi.x = viewposi.x-1.0f*SPAN*(float)Math.sin(turningAngle);
46.         viewposi.z = viewposi.z-1.0f*SPAN*(float)Math.cos(turningAngle);
47.         setPosition3D(tran, viewposi); setPosition3D(bodyTrans, viewposi); }
48.      if(z>0 && x==0) { direction = 2; System.out.println(direction+ " Backward");
49.         viewposi.x = viewposi.x+1.0f*SPAN*(float)Math.sin(turningAngle);
50.         viewposi.z = viewposi.z+1.0f*SPAN*(float)Math.cos(turningAngle);
51.         setPosition3D(tran, viewposi); setPosition3D(bodyTrans, viewposi); }
52.      if(x<0 && z==0) { direction = 3; System.out.println(direction + " Rotate right");
53.         turningAngle += ANGLESTEP; setRotation3D(tran, ANGLESTEP, comMat, 1);
54.         setRotation3D(bodyTrans, ANGLESTEP, comMat, 1);
55.         setRotation3D(bodyTrans, -ANGLESTEP, comMat, 1); }
56.      if(x>0 && z==0) { direction = 4; System.out.println(direction + " Rotate left");
57.         turningAngle -= ANGLESTEP; setRotation3D(tran, -ANGLESTEP, comMat, 1);
58.         setRotation3D(bodyTrans, -ANGLESTEP, comMat, 1);
59.         setRotation3D(bodyTrans, ANGLESTEP, comMat, 1); }
60.      if ( ((buttons & Joystick.BUTTON1) != 0)) { direction = 5; System.out.println(direction + " Elevate");
61.         viewposi.y = viewposi.y+SPAN/2.0f; setPosition3D(tran, viewposi);
62.         setPosition3D(bodyTrans, viewposi); return; }
63.      if ( ((buttons & Joystick.BUTTON2) != 0)) { direction = 6;          System.out.println(direction + " Land");
64.         viewposi.y = viewposi.y-SPAN/2.0f; setPosition3D(tran, viewposi);
65.         setPosition3D(bodyTrans, viewposi); return; }
66.      if ( ((buttons & Joystick.BUTTON3) != 0)) { direction = 7; System.out.println(direction + " Shift R");
67.         viewposi.x = viewposi.x+SPAN*(float)Math.sin(turningAngle+Math.PI/2.0);
68.         viewposi.z = viewposi.z+SPAN*(float)Math.cos(turningAngle+Math.PI/2.0);
69.         setPosition3D(tran, viewposi); setPosition3D(bodyTrans, viewposi); return; }
70.      if ( ((buttons & Joystick.BUTTON4) != 0)) { direction = 8;          System.out.println(direction + " Shift left");
71.         viewposi.x = viewposi.x-SPAN*(float)Math.sin(turningAngle+Math.PI/2.0);
72.         viewposi.z = viewposi.z-SPAN*(float)Math.cos(turningAngle+Math.PI/2.0);
73.         setPosition3D(tran, viewposi); setPosition3D(bodyTrans, viewposi); return; }
74.      joySensor.setNextSensorRead( joySensorRead ); }
75.
76.   public void pollAndProcessInput() { ProcessInput(joy[0], joySensor[0]); }
77.
78.   public void processStreamInput() {}
```

course is associated with the joystick position. Subsequently, the appropriate transformation can be calculated and invoked to change the view from the ViewPlatform.

SENSORS

From a programming point of view, sensors serve to obtain and translate inputs from external devices such as a joystick into digital data that can be used within the scene graph in the virtual world. While it is possible that a single device may have many sensors, a sensor can provide information corresponding to six degrees of freedom and some buttons, and is usually associated with a single device.

A typical joystick with forwards/backwards and left/right movements has two degrees of freedom and at least two buttons. The inputs these provide are thus well within what can be provided for by a single sensor.

In java 3D, the creation of an input device will require the construction of all the associated sensors that will be needed. This is usually done during initialization and is carried out in line 25 in the example in Figure 13, where reference to the specific input device is provided.

Retrieving data and information from a sensor can be carried out through the use of SensorRead, which can provide information such as a timestamp, a transform, and optional button values. Note, however, that the short time gap between two consecutive SensorRead invocations may give different values depending on how much and how fast the input device has changed.

Figure 15 shows the skeleton code segment for a customized behavior class for getting data from the sensor and calling the Sensor.getRead method to update the new position of the view platform in the virtual world.

After specifying and creating the input device interface and the associated sensor class, new input device can be added into the environment. As can be seen in the example in Figure 16, the addInputDevice method is used. This passes an existing instance of the created InputDevice and registers it with the system at runtime. Then, with an instance of

Figure 15. First Code segment for SensorBehavior.java

```
1.    public class SensorBehavior extends Behavior
2.    {
3.        private WakeupOnElapsedFrames conditions = new WakeupOnElapsedFrames(0);
4.        private TransformGroup transformGroup;
5.        private Sensor sensor;
6.        private Transform3D transform = new Transform3D();
7.
8.        public SensorBehavior(Sensor sensor ) { this.sensor = sensor; }
9.
10.       public void initialize() { wakeupOn(conditions); }
11.
12.       public void processStimulus(Enumeration criteria) {
13.           sensor.getRead(transform);
14.           wakeupOn(conditions); }
15.   }
```

Figure 16. Second code segment and result for SensorBehavior.java

```
1.   public BranchGroup createSceneGraph(SimpleUniverse universe, Canvas3D c)
2.   {
3.       TransformGroup viewTrans = new TransformGroup();
4.       viewTrans = universe.getViewingPlatform().getViewPlatformTransform();
5.       setPosition(viewTrans, initviewpoint);
6.       setPosition(holdBody, initviewpoint);
7.       holdBody.addChild(body);
8.       setPosition(body, new Point3f(0.0f, -0.2f, -1.5f));
9.
10.      joyDevice = new JoystickInputDevice(viewTrans, body.getShape(), holdBody, initviewpoint);
11.      joyDevice.initialize();
12.      universe.getViewer().getPhysicalEnvironment().addInputDevice(joyDevice);
13.
14.      Sensor joystick = joyDevice.getSensor(0);
15.      SensorBehavior s = new SensorBehavior(joystick);
16.      s.setSchedulingBounds(new BoundingSphere(new Point3d(0.0,0.0,0.0), Float.MAX_VALUE));
17.      root.addChild(s);
18.      ...
```

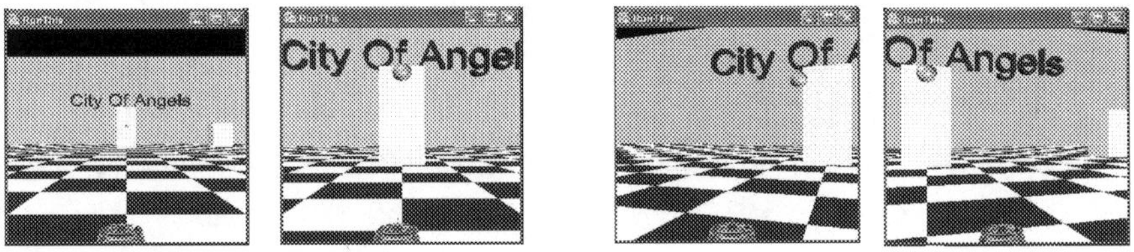

Translational movement   Rotational movement

the sensor class assigned to the created joyDevice in line 14, the joystick will become fully functional and will allow the user to navigate in the 3D world as shown.

COLLISIONS

In addition to a change of view, another important issue in 3D navigation is collision of the viewer with other visual objects (Bishop, Hembruch, & Trudeau, 1999). Obviously, this has to be properly taken care of if the 3D world built is to be as realistic as possible.

As discussed in earlier chapters, object collisions can be detected through setting up the proper wakeup criteria. Specifically, WakeupOnCollisionEntry, WakeupOnCollisionMovement and WakeupOnCollisionExit can be used. The first criterion will generate a trigger when an object first collides with another, the second one will be triggered while the two objects are still in collision and there is relative movement, and the third will give a stimulus when collisions no longer exist.

Figure 17. First code segment for collision detection

```
1.    public class Collision extends Behavior
2.    {
3.        private TransformGroup collisiontran, collisionbodyTrans;
4.        private Shape3D target;
5.        private WakeupCriterion events[] = new WakeupCriterion[3];  private WakeupOr allEvents;
6.        private BoundingSphere bounds     = new BoundingSphere(new
7.        Point3d(0.0,0.0,0.0), 0.1);
8.
9.        public Collision(TransformGroup collisiontran, Shape3D target, TransformGroup collisionbodyTrans)
10.       {
11.           this.collisiontran = collisiontran;
12.           this.collisionbodyTrans = collisionbodyTrans;
13.           this.target  = target;
14.       }
15.
16.       public void initialize()
17.       {
18.           events[0]=new WakeupOnCollisionEntry(collisionbodyTrans);
19.           events[1]=new WakeupOnCollisionExit(collisionbodyTrans);
20.           events[2]=new WakeupOnCollisionMovement(collisionbodyTrans);
21.           allEvents=new WakeupOr(events);
22.           wakeupOn(allEvents);
23.       }
24.
```

Based on the triggers generated from the above collision criteria, appropriate methods must be provided to, say, prevent objects from passing through one another or for the viewer to walk through solid walls in the 3D universe (The Colliding Grabbers, 2006).

Figures 17 and 18 give the code segment for handling collisions in a navigation example. As with other behavior classes, the customized collision behavior class contains an initialize and a processStimulus method. The former sets the collision detection criteria of interest, while the latter detects the collision type and takes the necessary actions. Specifically, in lines 60 and 61, the method CollisionEvent is invoked to prevent a collision whenever WakeupOnCollisionEntry is detected.

CollisionEvent prevents collision through re-position the relevant colliding object appropriately. Note that the new position of the object after collision is crucial as it must be fully out of the collision zone. Lines 27 to 54 illustrates this.

Figure 18. Second code segment for handling collisions

```
25.     public void CollisionEvent() {
26.        System.out.println("collision"+ " " + direction);
27.        if (direction == 1) { System.out.println("Moving back");
28.           viewposi.x = viewposi.x+3.0f*SPAN*(float)Math.sin(turningAngle);
29.           viewposi.z = viewposi.z+3.0f*SPAN*(float)Math.cos(turningAngle);
30.           setPosition3D(collisiontran, viewposi);  setPosition3D(collisionbodyTrans, viewposi); }
31.        if (direction == 2 ) { System.out.println("Moving forward");
32.           viewposi.x = viewposi.x-3.0f*SPAN*(float)Math.sin(turningAngle);
33.           viewposi.z = viewposi.z-3.0f*SPAN*(float)Math.cos(turningAngle);
34.           setPosition3D(collisiontran, viewposi);  setPosition3D(collisionbodyTrans, viewposi); }
35.        if (direction == 3) { System.out.println("Moving right");
36.           viewposi.x = viewposi.x+3.0f*SPAN*(float)Math.sin(turningAngle+Math.PI/2.0);
37.           viewposi.z = viewposi.z+3.0f*SPAN*(float)Math.cos(turningAngle+Math.PI/2.0);
38.           setPosition3D(collisiontran, viewposi);  setPosition3D(collisionbodyTrans, viewposi); }
39.        if (direction == 4) { System.out.println("Moving left");
40.           viewposi.x = viewposi.x-3.0f*SPAN*(float)Math.sin(turningAngle+Math.PI/2.0);
41.           viewposi.z = viewposi.z-3.0f*SPAN*(float)Math.cos(turningAngle+Math.PI/2.0);
42.           setPosition3D(collisiontran, viewposi);  setPosition3D(collisionbodyTrans, viewposi); }
43.        if (direction == 5) { System.out.println("Moving down");  viewposi.y = viewposi.y-0.02f-SPAN;
44.           setPosition3D(collisiontran, viewposi);  setPosition3D(collisionbodyTrans, viewposi); }
45.        if (direction == 6) { System.out.println("Moving up");  viewposi.y = viewposi.y+0.02f+SPAN;
46.           setPosition3D(collisiontran, viewposi);  setPosition3D(collisionbodyTrans, viewposi); }
47.        if (direction == 7) { System.out.println("Moving left");
48.           viewposi.x = viewposi.x-3.0f*SPAN*(float)Math.sin(turningAngle+Math.PI/2.0);
49.           viewposi.z = viewposi.z-3.0f*SPAN*(float)Math.cos(turningAngle+Math.PI/2.0);
50.           setPosition3D(collisiontran, viewposi);  setPosition3D(collisionbodyTrans, viewposi); }
51.        if (direction == 8) { System.out.println("Moving right");
52.           viewposi.x = viewposi.x+3.0f*SPAN*(float)Math.sin(turningAngle+Math.PI/2.0);
53.           viewposi.z = viewposi.z+3.0f*SPAN*(float)Math.cos(turningAngle+Math.PI/2.0);
54.           setPosition3D(collisiontran, viewposi);  setPosition3D(collisionbodyTrans, viewposi); } }
55.
56.     public void processStimulus(Enumeration criteria) {
57.        WakeupCriterion wakeup;  AWTEvent[] event;
58.        while(criteria.hasMoreElements()) {
59.           wakeup = (WakeupCriterion) criteria.nextElement();
60.           if(wakeup instanceof WakeupOnCollisionEntry) { System.out.println("Collision Entry");
61.              CollisionEvent(); }
62.           if(wakeup instanceof WakeupOnCollisionExit) System.out.println("Collision Exit");
63.           if(wakeup instanceof WakeupOnCollisionMovement) System.out.println("Collision Movement"); }
64.        this.wakeupOn(allEvents); }
65.
66.  }
```

SUMMARY

This chapter has discussed how navigation in the 3D virtual world can be handled through the use of the keyboard, mouse and external device. The use of Java 3D utility classes as well as user-defined behavior classes has been highlighted. Lastly, the handling of collisions, which is important for realistic navigation, has also been discussed.

REFERENCES

Ball, D., & Mirmehdi, M. (1999). A prototype hotel browsing system using Java 3D. *Proceedings IEEE International Conference on Information Visualization* (pp. 464-469).

Bishop, W., Hembruch, M., & Trudeau, C. (1999). Simulating colliding particles in Java using Parsimony. *Proceedings IEEE Canadian Conference on Electrical and Computer Engineering* (pp. 255-260).

Sowizral, H. A., & Deering, M. F. (1999). The Java 3D API and virtual reality. *IEEE Computer Graphics and Applications*, *19*(3), 12-15.

The Colliding Grabbers. (2006). http://fivedots.coe.psu.ac.th/~ad/jg/chN4/index.html.

Wang, L. (2006). J3D-based monitoring and control for e-ShopFloor. *International Journal of Manufacturing Technology and Management*, *8*, 126-140.

Chapter XI
Multiple Views

INTRODUCTION

Our discussions in previous chapters have centered on the creation and interaction of visual objects in a virtual 3D world. The objects and scenes constructed, however, will ultimately have to be shown on appropriate display devices such as a single PC monitor, a stereoscopic head mount display (HMD), or a multi screen project system (Salisbury, Farr, & Moore, 1999).

Also, it is quite often that we may need to show different views of the created universe at the same time for certain applications. Even for the case of a single PC monitor, showing different views of the same objects in different windows will be instructive and informative, and may be essential in some cases.

While we have been using a single simple view in earlier chapters, Java 3D has inherent capabilities to give multiple views of the created 3D world for supporting, say, the use of head tracking HMD systems for user to carry out 3D navigation (Yabuki, Machinaka, & Li, 2006). In this chapter, we will discuss how multiple views can be readily generated after outlining the view model and the various components that make up the simple universe view used previously.

Figure 1. View model

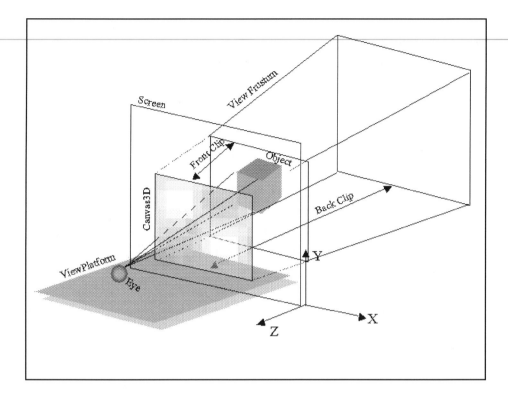

VIEW MODEL

Figure 1 shows the view model used in Java 3D. As can be seen, the ViewPlatform is essential a magic carpet on which the eye of the user is located. By default, it is positioned at the origin and looks into the negative z-axis. Technically, the eye forms part of a View object, which also consists of a PhysicalBody and PhysicalEnvironment objects. The latter two give the actual physical characteristics of the user such as the eye and ear positions.

As shown, the eye sees a single view of the 3D world with bounds defined by the view frustum. Visual objects within this volume will be rendered onto a canvas or a Canvas3D object. Basically a 2D window to the 3D virtual world, it is the Canvas3D object that will be rendered for display on the appropriate 2D system display device.

SINGLE VIEW

The single eye view of the 3D world as depicted in Figure 1 corresponds to what has been used in previous chapters through the SimpleUniverse utility class. The availability of this utility allows one to develop a 3D application that uses a single view rapidly and easily without the need to understand the mechanism of viewing fully.

However, to develop multiple view applications, be it based on multiple view platforms, canvas, or other means, an appreciation of how the view model is implemented is needed. In this section, we will outline the structure of the SimpleUniverse class and show how it can be implemented using core API functions. This will form the foundation for making changes to result in multiple views.

Figure 2 shows the scene graph structure of a typical Java 3D program. The SimpleUniverse object, created from using the relevant utility class to provide a minimal Virtual Universe, corresponds to the group of objects within the dashed line. To implement the SimpleUniverse object using core API functions, we need to create all the necessary components in the same manner as shown. Specifically, the following steps should be carried out:

Figure 2. Simple Universe scene graph

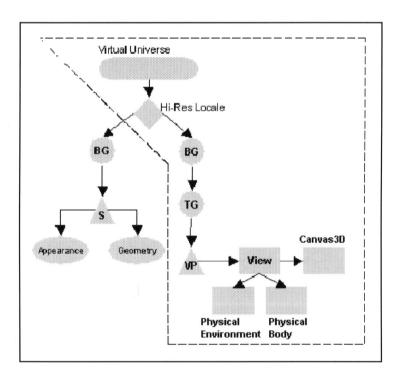

- Create a VirtualUniverse object.
- Create a relevant Locale object and attach this to the VirtualUniverse.
- Construct content branches.
- Compile branch graphs and attach to Locale.
- Construct view branch and attach to Locale.
- Create a Canvas3D object.
- Create a TransformGroup TG.
- Create a ViewPlatform object VP and attach to the TransformGroup TG.
- Create a View object and attach to the ViewPlatform.
- Create a Canvas3D object and attach to the View.
- Create a PhysicalBody object and attach to the View.

Figure 3. Code segment for setting up simple universe

```
1.    public SimpleUniverseApp () {
2.        virtualUniverse = new VirtualUniverse();      Locale locale = new Locale(virtualUniverse);
3.        VirtualWorld vWorld = new VirtualWorld();  BranchGroup scene = vWorld.createVirtualWorld();
4.        scene.compile();  locale.addBranchGraph(scene);
5.        BranchGroup view = createViewGraph();  enableInteraction(view);  view.compile();
6.        locale.addBranchGraph(view); }
7.
8.    public BranchGroup createViewGraph() {
9.        Canvas3D canvas3D = new Canvas3D();  String caption = "Example 1";
10.       TransformGroup viewPlatform;  viewManager = new ViewManager(this, 1, 1);
11.       BranchGroup viewRoot = new BranchGroup();
12.       TransformGroup transformGroup = new TransformGroup();
13.       viewRoot.addChild(transformGroup);
14.       GraphicsConfiguration config = viewManager.getPreferredGraphicsConfiguration();
15.       canvas3D = new Canvas3D(config);  viewManager.add(canvas3D, caption);
16.       viewPlatform = createViewPlatform(canvas3D, 0);
17.       transformGroup.addChild(viewPlatform);
18.       return viewRoot;  }
19.
20.    public TransformGroup createViewPlatform(Canvas3D canvas3D, int mode) {
21.       Transform3D transform3D = vpTransform3D(mode);
22.       ViewPlatform viewPlatform = new ViewPlatform();
23.       TransformGroup objTransform = new TransformGroup(transform3D);
24.       objTransform.addChild(viewPlatform);
25.       View view = new View();
26.       view.attachViewPlatform(viewPlatform);
27.       view.addCanvas3D(canvas3D);
28.       view.setPhysicalBody(new PhysicalBody());
29.       view.setPhysicalEnvironment(new PhysicalEnvironment());
30.       return objTransform; }
```

- Create a PhysicalEnvironment object and attach to the View.
- Attach the TransformGroup to view branch.

Note that the creation and use of a TransformGroup for attaching the ViewPlatform is to ensure that the viewing angle or position can be changed by using the appropriate transformation. The code segment in Figure 3 gives an example showing how the structure of a SimpleUniverse object can be set up.

Figure 4. Code structure for multiple views

```
1.    public class ViewModelApp extends JApplet implements ActionListener
2.    {
3.       public void main(String[] args)
4.       {          // main method to run the application, specify screen size
5.       }
6.
7.       public ViewModel()
8.       {          // constructor, calls createViewGraph() and createVirtualWorld() from VirtualWorld.java
9.       }
10.
11.      public void destroy()
12.      {          // destructor
13.      }
14.
15.      public BranchGraph createViewGraph()
16.      {          // uses ViewManager.java to format and insert captions; calls createViewPlatform()
17.      }
18.
19.      public TransformGroup createViewPlatform(Canvas3D canvas3D, int mode)
20.      {          // most of the settings on the view model made here; calls vpTransform3D
21.      }
22.
23.      public Transform3D vpTransform3D(int mode)
24.      {          // specify the orientation and position of the View Platform
25.      }
26.
27.      public void enableInteraction(BranchGroup viewRoot)
28.      {          // functionality for keyboard and mouse navigation in the virtual world
29.      }
30.
31.      public void createPanel(int mode)
32.      {          // adds control such as buttons and check boxes for interaction
33.      }
34.
35.      public void actionPerformed(ActionEvent e)
36.      {          // specify the changes to be made when a control element is clicked
37.      }
38.   }
```

MULTIPLE VIEWS

Before studying how multiple views can be created and the various issues involved, Figure 4 shows the code structure that will be used in our ensuring discussion. The methods createViewGraph, createViewPlatform, and vpTransform3D are especially important as these are where different views can be created and changed. Also, viewManager as used in subsequent code segments corresponds to an instance of a custom utility class View-Manager, which is given in Appendix C. Basically, this formats the Canvas3D objects on the window to the same size, adds appropriate captions, facilitates the addition of controls such as buttons, drop down, and check boxes to the window, and have these laid out in a grid manner.

As an illustrating example, Figure 5 shows the scene graph for getting a front, side, and overhead view of the visual objects in 3D world. To obtain these three views at the same time, the scene graph will now consist of three transform groups and three sets of view platforms under two levels of transforms.

The first transform group TG, a child of the branch group BG, is for the purpose of navigation, while the second level of transforms allows the user to see different views from different orientation and position at the current location. Obviously, getting multiple

Figure 5. Multiple view scene graph

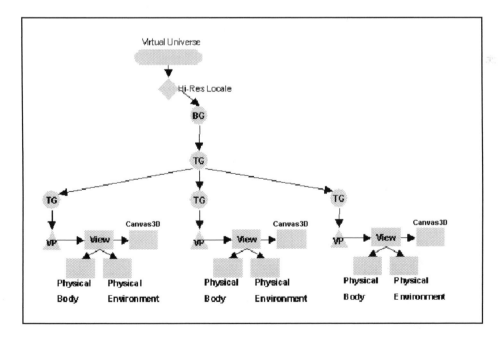

Figure 6. Code segment and result for MultiViewApp.java

```
1.    public BranchGroup createViewGraph() {
2.       final int numberOfViews = 4;
3.       Canvas3D canvas3D[] = new Canvas3D[numberOfViews];
4.       String caption[] = {"Front View", "Side View", "Plan View", "Zoom Out View"};
5.       TransformGroup viewPlatform;
6.       viewManager = new ViewManager(this, 2, 2);
7.       BranchGroup viewRoot = new BranchGroup();
8.       TransformGroup transformGroup = new TransformGroup();
9.       viewRoot.addChild(transformGroup);
10.      GraphicsConfiguration config = viewManager.getPreferredGraphicsConfiguration();
11.      for (int i = 0; i < numberOfViews; i++) {
12.         canvas3D[i] = new Canvas3D(config);
13.         viewManager.add(canvas3D[i], caption[i]);
14.         viewPlatform = createViewPlatform(canvas3D[i], i);
15.         transformGroup.addChild(viewPlatform); }
16.      return viewRoot; }
17.
18.   public TransformGroup createViewPlatform(Canvas3D canvas3D, int mode) {
19.      Transform3D transform3D = vpTransform3D(mode);
20.      ViewPlatform viewPlatform = new ViewPlatform();
21.      TransformGroup objTransform = new TransformGroup(transform3D);
22.      objTransform.addChild(viewPlatform);
23.      View view = new View();
24.      view.attachViewPlatform(viewPlatform);
25.      view.addCanvas3D(canvas3D);
26.      view.setPhysicalBody(new PhysicalBody());
27.      view.setPhysicalEnvironment(new PhysicalEnvironment());
28.      return objTransform; }
29.
30.   public Transform3D vpTransform3D(int mode) {
31.      Transform3D transform3D = new Transform3D();
32.      switch (mode) {
33.         case FRONT_VIEW:  break;
34.         case SIDE_VIEW:        transform3D.rotY(Math.PI / 2.0d);  break;
35.         case PLAN_VIEW:        transform3D.rotX(-1 * Math.PI / 2.0d);  break;
36.         case ZOOM_OUT:         transform3D.setTranslation(new Vector3f(0.0f, 0.0f, 3.0f));  break; }
37.      return transform3D; }
```

views can be readily done by using appropriate transforms and associating these with the relevant view platforms.

Following this approach, Figure 6 shows the code segment and result for getting four views by using a loop to create a number of transform groups, view platforms, and canvas. The transform for each platform is then initiated depending on a specific view needed by using the method vpTransform3D.

VIEW ATTACH POLICY AND ACTIVATION RADIUS

Having described the basic principles of generating multiple views in Java 3D, we will now proceed to discuss in more details the options and settings that are available in the customization of the various components in the process.

As depicted in Figures 1 and 2, the most important component in view generation is the view platform. Usually under a suitable TransformGroup for navigation and other similar purposes, a ViewPlatform defines a view point on the virtual world. It controls the location and orientation of the user, and also serves as a node in the scene graph for attaching a View object. As illustrated in Figure 5, a virtual universe may have many view platforms. However, each ViewPlatform can only have one View object.

Every ViewPlatform object has a view attach policy and an activation radius. The latter defines a spherical region surrounding the center of the ViewPlatform. As discussed in previous chapters, if this activation region intersects with the bounding and scheduling regions for behaviors, fogs and similar objects, stimulus for the associated behaviors and rendering of the fogs will be activated.

Figure 7. View attach policy and activation radius

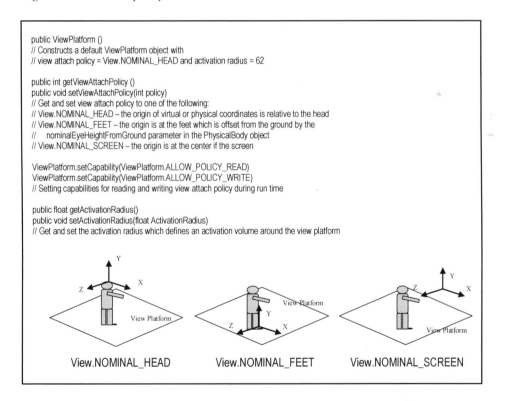

```
public ViewPlatform ()
// Constructs a default ViewPlatform object with
// view attach policy = View.NOMINAL_HEAD and activation radius = 62

public int getViewAttachPolicy ()
public void setViewAttachPolicy(int policy)
// Get and set view attach policy to one of the following:
// View.NOMINAL_HEAD – the origin of virtual or physical coordinates is relative to the head
// View.NOMINAL_FEET – the origin is at the feet which is offset from the ground by the
//    nominalEyeHeightFromGround parameter in the PhysicalBody object
// View.NOMINAL_SCREEN – the origin is at the center if the screen

ViewPlatform.setCapability(ViewPlatform.ALLOW_POLICY_READ)
ViewPlatform.setCapability(ViewPlatform.ALLOW_POLICY_WRITE)
// Setting capabilities for reading and writing view attach policy during run time

public float getActivationRadius()
public void setActivationRadius(float ActivationRadius)
// Get and set the activation radius which defines an activation volume around the view platform
```

View.NOMINAL_HEAD   View.NOMINAL_FEET   View.NOMINAL_SCREEN

For the situation when the View, which will be discussed in the next section, is set to have a default screen scale policy of SCALE_SCREEN_SIZE, the actual activation radius is given by multiplying 0.5 to the physical monitor screen size and the activation radius. For instance, for a default screen size of 0.35 meters and a default activation radius value of 62, the actual activation radius would be 10.85 meters.

Figure 7 summarizes the characteristics of the ViewPlatform objectm, including some illustrations on the meaning of the view attach policy and some of the important methods. As can be seen, the view attach policy defines basically the origin of the coordinate system used.

PROJECTION POLICY

As illustrated in Figures 1 and 2, each ViewPlatform has a View object, which basically controls what a virtual person standing on the platform will see as the various 3D visual objects are rendered on a canvas through the Canvas3D object. Note that a number of Canvas3D objects can in fact be attached to a View object, which can reference a PhysicalBody and a PhysicalEnvironment object.

By invoking the constructor

Public View ()

a View object will be created with the following default parameters:

View policy = View.SCREEN_VIEW
Projection policy = View.PERSPECTIVE_PROJECTION
Screen Scale = View.SCALE_SCREEN_SIZE
Window resize policy = View.PHYSICAL_WORLD
Window movement policy = View.PHYSICAL_WORLD
Window Eyepoint policy = View.RELATIVE_TO_FIELD_OF_VIEW
Front clip policy = View.PHYSICAL_EYE
Back clip policy = View.PHYSICAL_EYE
Visibility policy = View.VISIBILITY_DRAW_VISIBLE
Coexistence centering flag = true
Compatibility mode = false
Left projection = identity
Right projection = identity
Physical body = null
Physical environment = null
Screen scale = 1.0

Field of view = π/4
Front clip distance = 0.1
Back clip distance = 10.0
View platform = null
Minimum frame duration = 0

Some of the important parameters will be discussed in this section using illustrative examples.

Figure 8. Projection policy

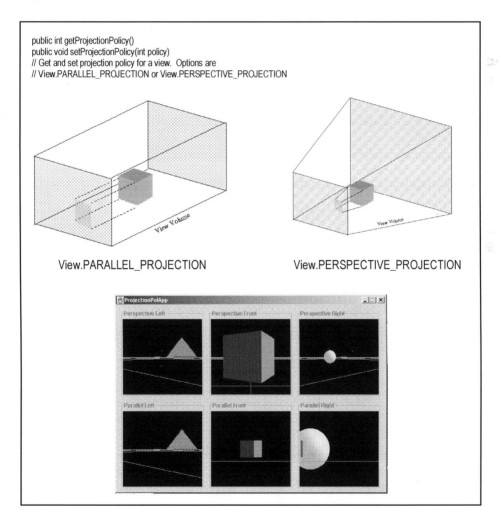

Firstly, one of the important controls that can be selected in View is the projection policy, which may be parallel or perspective in nature. Under parallel projection, the view volume is cubic in shape and objects rendered will not change in size even as the viewing distance has changed. The rendering is based on projecting parallel rays from the objects on to the canvas. On the other hand, in perspective projection, the view volume or frustum has a pyramid shape with apex cut off. Perspective projection is of course the same as that used in the human visual system, with nearer objects appearing bigger in size. Figure 8 illustrates how the projection policy can be set and the results obtained.

CLIP DISTANCE

As shown in Figure 1, the front and back clip distances define the starting and ending planes for the volume of space in which objects will be rendered. Before specifying these distances as illustrated in Figure 9, the unit and point of reference of their measurements can be set through methods on the clip polices. Specifically, the measurement may be in physical or virtual units relative to the eye or screen position.

WINDOW EYEPOINT POLICY AND FIELD OF VIEW

Apart from the clipping distances, which determine the front and back planes of the view volume, another set of parameters that defines the view volume is the window eyepoint

Figure 9. Clip policy and distance

```
public int getFrontClipPolicy
public void setFrontClipPolicy(int policy)
public int getBackClipPolicy
public void setBackClipPolicy(int policy)
// Get and set the front and back clipping policies.  Options are
// View.PHYSICAL_EYE – measurement relative to the eye position in meter
// View.PHYSICAL_SCREEN – measurement relative to screen in meter
// View.VIRTUAL_EYE – measurement relative to the eye in virtual distance
// View.VIRTUAL_SCREEN – measurement relative to the screen in virtual distance

public double getFrontClipDistance
public void setFrontClipDistance(double distance)
public double getBackClipDistance
public void setBackClipDistance(double distance)
// Get and set front and back clip distances.  The defaults are 0.1 and 10.0, respectively.
```

Figure 10. Window eyepoint policy and field of view

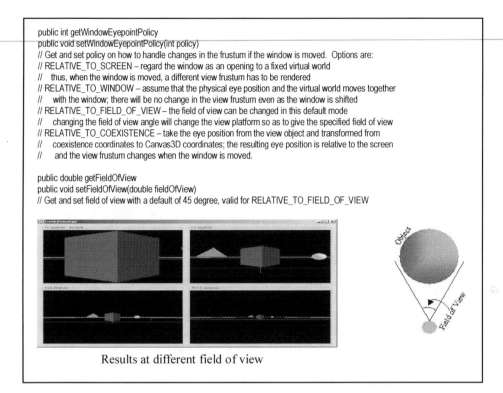

```
public int getWindowEyepointPolicy
public void setWindowEyepointPolicy(int policy)
// Get and set policy on how to handle changes in the frustum if the window is moved.  Options are:
// RELATIVE_TO_SCREEN – regard the window as an opening to a fixed virtual world
//    thus, when the window is moved, a different view frustum has to be rendered
// RELATIVE_TO_WINDOW – assume that the physical eye position and the virtual world moves together
//    with the window; there will be no change in the view frustum even as the window is shifted
// RELATIVE_TO_FIELD_OF_VIEW – the field of view can be changed in this default mode
//    changing the field of view angle will change the view platform so as to give the specified field of view
// RELATIVE_TO_COEXISTENCE – take the eye position from the view object and transformed from
//    coexistence coordinates to Canvas3D coordinates; the resulting eye position is relative to the screen
//    and the view frustum changes when the window is moved.

public double getFieldOfView
public void setFieldOfView(double fieldOfView)
// Get and set field of view with a default of 45 degree, valid for RELATIVE_TO_FIELD_OF_VIEW
```

Results at different field of view

policy and the field of view. Figure 10 summarizes the possible options which are valid and selectable in a non-head tracked environment.

Note that both the eyepoint policy and field of view are given by the horizontal field of view and apex angle in the pyramid in the perspective projection in Figure 8. Under the third option, which is the default, a horizontal field of view angle can be specified. The eye position is then calculated to give the specific field of view needed. The maximum field of view is π, which corresponds to the ability to see the entire horizon.

CONVENTIONAL CAMERA-BASED VIEW

Java 3D provides methods for generating the transform groups needed to obtain views by using essentially a camera on the virtual world. These are summarized in Figure 11, and serve to provide compatibility and links to 3D graphic programs developed using the traditional camera based viewing model (Sowizral, Rushforth, & Deering, 2000). Note,

Figure 11. Methods for camera based viewing model

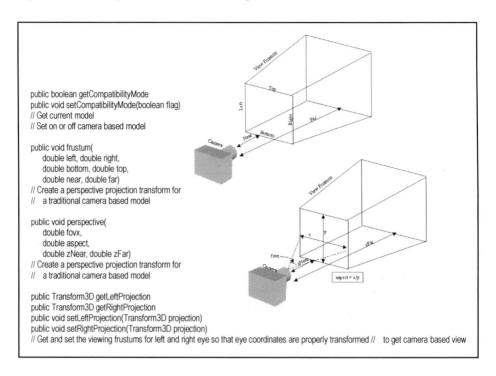

however, that using these will not be compatible with developing advanced applications using, say, head mounted displays.

Figure 12 shows the important code segment and results obtained in a simple example illustrating the use of the methods for this compatibility mode provided by Java 3D. The code segment takes relevant inputs from the user, calculates the relevant transformation needed and then render the view.

The actionPerformed method corresponds to the last one in the overall code structure of Figure 4, and is meant for processing the inputs from the user whenever a mouse click is received over the window. The updateView method is a generic function for detecting user inputs on the sets of buttons and returning value that has been changed. For instance, for the parameter topVal, updateView detects topInc and topDec, and updates topLabel accordingly. topVal is then passed as a parameter to the frustum method.

Figure 12. Code segment and result for ViewProjectionApp.java

```
1.    public void actionPerformed(ActionEvent e) {
2.        Object target = e.getSource();  // sync step sizes for both panels
3.        if (target == stepSizeSel) stepSizeSel2.setSelectedIndex(stepSizeSel.getSelectedIndex());
4.        else if (target == stepSizeSel2) stepSizeSel.setSelectedIndex(stepSizeSel2.getSelectedIndex());
5.
6.        double topVal = updateView(topInc, topDec, topLabel, target);  // get inputs for frustum projection
7.        double botVal = updateView(botInc, botDec, botLabel, target);
8.        double lefVal = updateView(lefInc, lefDec, lefLabel, target);
9.        double rigVal = updateView(rigInc, rigDec, rigLabel, target);
10.       double neaVal = updateView(neaInc, neaDec, neaLabel, target);
11.       double farVal = updateView(farInc, farDec, farLabel, target);
12.       Transform3D viewFrustum = new Transform3D();  // update view frustum
13.       viewFrustum.frustum(lefVal, rigVal, botVal, topVal, neaVal, farVal);
14.       view[0].setLeftProjection(viewFrustum);
15.
16.       double fovVal = updateView(fovInc, fovDec, fovLabel, target);  // get inputs for perspective proj.
17.       double aspVal = updateView(aspInc, aspDec, aspLabel, target);
18.       double zneVal = updateView(zneInc, zneDec, zneLabel, target);
19.       double zfaVal = updateView(zfaInc, zfaDec, zfaLabel, target);
20.       Transform3D viewPerspective = new Transform3D();  // update view perspective
21.       viewPerspective.perspective(Math.toRadians(fovVal), aspVal, zneVal, zfaVal);
22.       view[1].setLeftProjection(viewPerspective);  }
23.
24.   private double updateView(JButton incButton, JButton decButton, JLabel value, Object target) {
25.       double tarVal = Double.parseDouble(value.getText());
26.       if (target == incButton)   tarVal += ((Double) stepSizeSel.getSelectedItem()).doubleValue();
27.       if (target == decButton) tarVal -= ((Double) stepSizeSel.getSelectedItem()).doubleValue();
28.       DecimalFormat df = new DecimalFormat("#0.00");  value.setText(df.format(tarVal));
29.       return Double.parseDouble(value.getText());  }
```

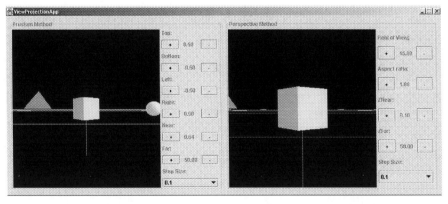

Figure 13. Visibility, screen scale, window movement and minimum frame cycle time

```
public int getVisibilityPolicy()
public void setVisibilityPolicy(int policy)
// Get and set the visibility policy for current view.  Options are:
//   View.VISIBILITY_DRAW_VISIBLE – only draw visible objects (default)
//   View.VISIBILITY_DRAW_INVISIBLE – only draw invisible objects
//   View.VISIBILITY_DRAW_ALL – draw all objects

public int getScreenScalePolicy()
public void setScreenScalePolicy(int policy)
// Get and set screen scale policy for current view.  Options are:
//   view.SCALE_SCREEN_SIZE – scale equals half of physical screen width (default)
//   view.SCALE_EXPLICIT – scale equals user-provided screenScale parameter.

public int getWindowMovementPolicy()
Public void setWindowMovementPolicy(int policy)
// Get and set window movement policy.  Options are:
//   view.VIRTUAL_WORLD – window is an opening to virtual world; image will change when window shifts
//   view.PHYSICAL_WORLD – image in window remain unchanged when window shifts (default)

public long getMinimiumFrameCycleTime()
public void setMinimiumFrameCycleTime(long minimiumTime)
// Get and set the minimum time, in milliseconds, for refreshing one frame for current view.  The default is 0
```

VISIBILITY, SCREEN SCALE, WINDOW MOVEMENT, AND FRAME CYCLE TIME

Other important policies that can be specified under View are the minimum frame cycle time, visibility, screen scale and window movement. The various options available and their significance are indicated in Figure 13.

Canvas3D

As shown in Figures 1 and 2, the object Canvas3D is basically a 2D canvas on which 3D objects in the virtual universe will be painted or rendered on. Thus, there must be at least one Canvas3D object attached to a View object. Figure 14 gives the constructor for a Canvas3D object and shows how it can be attached to a View object. The various default values are also shown.

Note that Canvas3D should not be initialized with a null argument. Instead, its GraphicsConfiguration argument should be properly set up. This can be done manually or by

Figure 14. Setting up Canvas3D objects

```
public Canvas3D (GraphicsConfiguration graphicsConfiguration)
public Canvas3D (GraphicsConfiguration graphicsConfiguration, boolean offScreen)
// construct a Canvas3D object with the following default parameters:
//    left manual eye in image plate = (0.142, 0.135, 0.4572)
//    right manual eye in image plate = (0.208, 0.135, 0.4572)
//    stereo enable = true
//    double buffer enable = true
//    monoscopic view policy = View.CYCLOPEAN_EYE_VIEW
//    off-screen mode = false
//    off-screen buffer = null
//    off-screen location = (0,0)

View view = new View();
GraphicsConfiguration config = viewManager.getPreferredGraphicsConfiguration();
Canvas3D canvas3D1 = new Canvas3D(config);
Canvas3D canvas3D2 = new Canvas3D(config);
View.addCanvas3D(canvas3D1);
View.addCanvas3D(canvas3D2);
```

simply using the getPreferredgraphicsConfiguration method in ViewManager. Also, an off-screen Canvas3D object cannot be used for normal rendering and it must not be added into any Container object for displaying on screen.

There are three monoscopic policies that can be selected for the rendering of a monoscopic view. They correspond to producing a view based on the left, right and a fictional center eye. The use of the center eye is the default. Figure 15 illustrates the important code segment for selecting these policies and the results that are rendered.

Note that the code segment adds three Canvas3D objects to a View object through the use of an array for the rendering of three different views, each based on a different monoscopic view policy.

Through a Canvas3D object, the positions of the eyes can be changed manually at run time. Figures 16 to 18 give the code segment and results in an interactive example where the user can alter the eye positions by clicking some relevant buttons and observe the results.

In the createViewGraph method, lines 5 to 7 are for the purpose of creating buttons, while line 13 invokes the createPanel method of Figure 17 to create the panels for two views. Lines 14 and 15 set the left and right Canvas3D objects to show the views of the left and right eyes, respectively. Then, a ZOOM_OUT view is specified instead of the standard FRONT_VIEW in line 39.

Figure 15. Code segment and result for MonoscopicPolicyApp.java

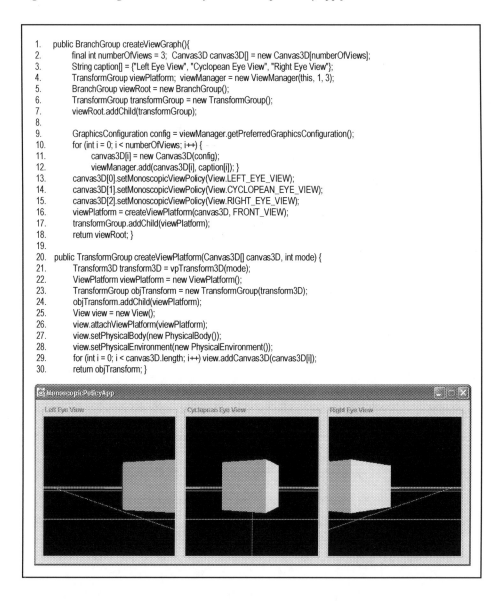

In the createViewPlatform method, line 26 dictates the use of a View.RELATIVE_ TO_SCREEN policy. This is essential in order for manual eye adjustment to work. In the createPanel method of Figure 17, the switch statement in line 47 retrieves either the left or right eye coordinates depending on the panel index. The coordinates are then placed in

Figure 16. First code segment for ManualEyeApp.java

```
1.    public BranchGroup createViewGraph() {
2.       final int numberOfViews = 2;  canvas3D = new Canvas3D[numberOfViews];
3.       String caption[] = {"Left Eye View", "Right Eye View"};
4.       TransformGroup viewPlatform; viewManager = new ViewManager(this, 1, 2);
5.       label = new ArrayList();  minus = new ArrayList();
6.       value = new ArrayList();  plus = new ArrayList();
7.       jPanels = new ArrayList();  eye = new Point3d();
8.       BranchGroup viewRoot = new BranchGroup();
9.       TransformGroup transformGroup = new TransformGroup();
10.      viewRoot.addChild(transformGroup);
11.      GraphicsConfiguration config = viewManager.getPreferredGraphicsConfiguration();
12.      for (int i = 0; i < numberOfViews; i++) { canvas3D[i] = new Canvas3D(config);
13.         jPanels.add(viewManager.add(canvas3D[i], caption[i]));  createPanel(i); }
14.      canvas3D[0].setMonoscopicViewPolicy(View.LEFT_EYE_VIEW);
15.      canvas3D[1].setMonoscopicViewPolicy(View.RIGHT_EYE_VIEW);
16.      viewPlatform = createViewPlatform(canvas3D, ZOOM_OUT);
17.      transformGroup.addChild(viewPlatform);
18.      return viewRoot; }
19.
20.   public TransformGroup createViewPlatform(Canvas3D[] canvas3D, int mode) {
21.      Transform3D transform3D = vpTransform3D(mode);
22.      ViewPlatform viewPlatform = new ViewPlatform();
23.      TransformGroup objTransform = new TransformGroup(transform3D);
24.      objTransform.addChild(viewPlatform);
25.      View view = new View();
26.      view.setWindowEyepointPolicy(View.RELATIVE_TO_SCREEN);
27.      view.attachViewPlatform(viewPlatform);
28.      view.setPhysicalBody(new PhysicalBody());
29.      view.setPhysicalEnvironment(new PhysicalEnvironment());
30.      for (int i = 0; i < canvas3D.length; i++) view.addCanvas3D(canvas3D[i]);
31.      return objTransform; }
32.
33.   public Transform3D vpTransform3D(int mode) {
34.      Transform3D transform3D = new Transform3D();
35.      switch (mode) {
36.         case FRONT_VIEW: transform3D.setTranslation(new Vector3f(0.0f, 0.0f, 1.5f)); break;
37.         case SIDE_VIEW: transform3D.rotY(Math.PI / 2.0d);
38.            transform3D.setTranslation(new Vector3f(1.5f, 0.0f, 0.0f));  break;
39.         case PLAN_VIEW: transform3D.rotX(-1 * Math.PI / 2.0d);
40.            transform3D.setTranslation(new Vector3f(0.0f, 1.5f, 0.0f)); break;
41.         case ZOOM_OUT: transform3D.setTranslation(new Vector3f(0.0f, 0.0f, 20.0f)); break; }
42.      return transform3D; }
```

the various JLabels variables. Similarly, in Figure 18, lines 71 to 74 retrieves the appropriate eye position so that this can be subsequently updated in the Canvas3D object to give a refreshed view based on the button pressed.

Figure 17. Second code segment for ManualEyeApp.java

```
43.   public void createPanel(int index) {
44.       JLabel currentLabel; JButton currentMinus; JLabel currentValue; JButton currentPlus;
45.       viewManager.createControlPanel();
46.       String[] labelString = {"X", "Y", "Z"};
47.       switch (index)   {
48.          case 0: canvas3D[index].getLeftManualEyeInImagePlate(eye); break;
49.          case 1: canvas3D[index].getRightManualEyeInImagePlate(eye); break; }
50.       for (int i = 0; i < 3; i++) {
51.          currentLabel = new JLabel(labelString[i]);
52.          currentMinus = new JButton("-"); currentPlus = new JButton("+");
53.          switch (i) {
54.             case 0: currentValue = new JLabel(String.valueOf(eye.x)); break;
55.             case 1: currentValue = new JLabel(String.valueOf(eye.y)); break;
56.             case 2: currentValue = new JLabel(String.valueOf(eye.z)); break;
57.             default: currentValue = new JLabel(""); }
58.          currentValue.setHorizontalAlignment(JLabel.RIGHT);
59.          currentMinus.addActionListener (this); currentPlus.addActionListener (this);
60.          label.add(currentLabel);
61.          minus.add(currentMinus);  value.add(currentValue); plus.add(currentPlus);
62.          viewManager.addControl(currentLabel, 1, 3);  viewManager.addControl(currentMinus);
63.          viewManager.addControl(currentValue);  viewManager.addControl(currentPlus); } }
```

As can be seen from the screen shot in Figure 18, the left and right eyes show slightly more of the left and right sides of the virtual world, respectively. Figure 19 shows some results when the x, y, and z coordinates of the eyes are changed.

The values reflected on the panel show the default position for the left and right eyes respectively. This is with respect to the image plate coordinate, with the positive x axis pointing to the right, positive y axis pointing to up, and the positive z axis pointing out of the image plate.

The left eye view and the right eye view significantly differ from the ones in MonoscopicPolicyApp, this is because of the different View policies being used. MonoscopicPolicyApp uses the default View policy, that is View.RELATIVE_TO_FIELD_OF_VIEW, while ManualEyeApp uses the View.RELATIVE_TO_SCREEN policy. It is also because of this policy that the portion of the virtual world that is rendered changes as the window is moved around the screen.

Since the left eye view is independent of the right eye view, it is possible to observe the changes on one view and expect the other view to respond in the same manner. Setting the x position of the left eye to 0.202, essentially moving the eye to the right, results in more of the left portion of the virtual world being rendered. Similarly, moving the left eye to the left to x position 0.52 results in more of the right portion of the virtual world being rendered.

Figure 18. Third code segment and results for ManualEyeApp.java

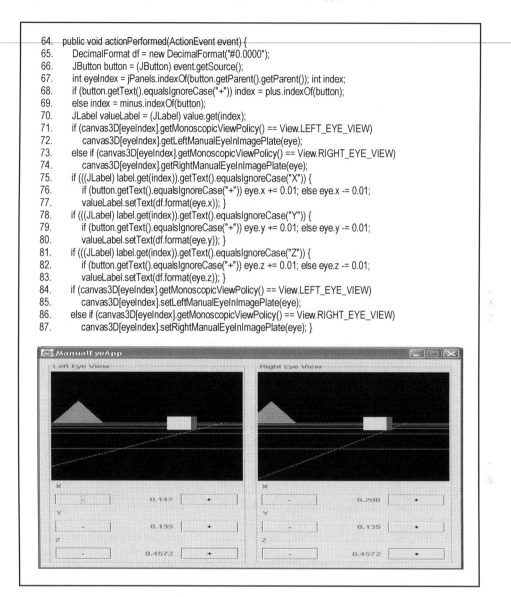

```
64.   public void actionPerformed(ActionEvent event) {
65.      DecimalFormat df = new DecimalFormat("#0.0000");
66.      JButton button = (JButton) event.getSource();
67.      int eyeIndex = jPanels.indexOf(button.getParent().getParent()); int index;
68.      if (button.getText().equalsIgnoreCase("+")) index = plus.indexOf(button);
69.      else index = minus.indexOf(button);
70.      JLabel valueLabel = (JLabel) value.get(index);
71.      if (canvas3D[eyeIndex].getMonoscopicViewPolicy() == View.LEFT_EYE_VIEW)
72.         canvas3D[eyeIndex].getLeftManualEyeInImagePlate(eye);
73.      else if (canvas3D[eyeIndex].getMonoscopicViewPolicy() == View.RIGHT_EYE_VIEW)
74.         canvas3D[eyeIndex].getRightManualEyeInImagePlate(eye);
75.      if (((JLabel) label.get(index)).getText().equalsIgnoreCase("X")) {
76.         if (button.getText().equalsIgnoreCase("+")) eye.x += 0.01; else eye.x -= 0.01;
77.         valueLabel.setText(df.format(eye.x)); }
78.      if (((JLabel) label.get(index)).getText().equalsIgnoreCase("Y")) {
79.         if (button.getText().equalsIgnoreCase("+")) eye.y += 0.01; else eye.y -= 0.01;
80.         valueLabel.setText(df.format(eye.y)); }
81.      if (((JLabel) label.get(index)).getText().equalsIgnoreCase("Z")) {
82.         if (button.getText().equalsIgnoreCase("+")) eye.z += 0.01; else eye.z -= 0.01;
83.         valueLabel.setText(df.format(eye.z)); }
84.      if (canvas3D[eyeIndex].getMonoscopicViewPolicy() == View.LEFT_EYE_VIEW)
85.         canvas3D[eyeIndex].setLeftManualEyeInImagePlate(eye);
86.      else if (canvas3D[eyeIndex].getMonoscopicViewPolicy() == View.RIGHT_EYE_VIEW)
87.         canvas3D[eyeIndex].setRightManualEyeInImagePlate(eye); }
```

A similar effect is observed when the y position is modified, except that the effect will be observed vertically instead of horizontally. Likewise, changing the z position has the effect of moving forward and backward.

Figure 19. Views from changing eye positions

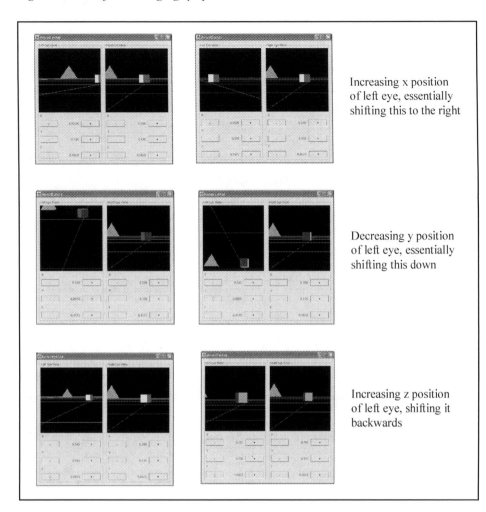

Increasing x position of left eye, essentially shifting this to the right

Decreasing y position of left eye, essentially shifting this down

Increasing z position of left eye, shifting it backwards

PhysicalBody AND PhysicalEnvironment

The objects that we have discussed so far in the construction of views exist mainly in the virtual world. For applications such as those that use head mounted displays to provide the user with the experience of, say walking through a virtual city, there is a need to match virtual world to the physical world. Specifically, the important dimensions and sizes of the two world must match so that objects rendered based on the virtual universe appear in the right size to the user.

Two objects that can be referenced by a View object for such purposes are the Physical-Body and PhysicalEnvironment objects. The former gives the physical characteristics of the user and includes parameters such as the physical locations of the eyes and ears. These are measured in meters with a head coordinate system that has an origin that is half way between the left and right eye. A right hand coordinate system is used with the positive x-axis pointing to the right, the y-axis pointing up and the z-axis pointing backwards. Figure 20 summarizes the important attributes of the PhysicalBody object and the important associated methods.

As its name implies, the PhysicalEnvironment object deals with the physical environment of the user, including the physical dimensions of the devices available to help the user in seeing and interacting with the virtual world. Figure 21 gives a summary of this object and the important methods for setting parameters for devices such as audio and tracking sensor hardware.

Figure 20. PhysicalBody object and methods

```
public PhysicalBody ()
// Construct a PhysicalBody object with the following default parameters:
//    Left eye position = (-0.033, 0.0, 0.0)
//    Right eye position = (0.033, 0.0, 0.0)
//    Left ear position = (-0.080, -0.030, 0.095)
//    Right ear position = (0.080, -0.030, 0.095)
//    nominalEyeHeightFromGround = 1.68
//    nominalEyeOffsetFromNominalScreen = 0.4572

public Point3d getLeftEyePosition ()
public Point3d getRightEyePosition ()
public void setLeftEyePosition(Point3d position)
public void setRightEyePosition(Point3d position)
// Get and set center of rotation of left and right eyes of user in head coordinates

public Point3d getLeftEarPosition ()
public Point3d getRightEarPosition ()
public void setLeftEarPosition(Point3d position)
public void setRightEarPosition(Point3d position)
// Get and set position of the left and right ears of user in head coordinates

public double getNominalEyeHeightFromGround ()
public void setNominalEyeHeightFromGround(double height)
// Get and set user nominal eye height from ground to the center eye or origin of head coordinates

public double getNominalEyeOffsetFromNominalScreen ()
public void setNominalEyeOffsetFromNominalScreen(double offset)
// Get and set distance between center eye and center of display screen
```

Figure 21. PhysicalEnvironment object and methods

```
public PhysicalEnvironment ()
// Construct a PhysicalEnvironment object with the following default parameters:
//    Sensor count = 3
//    Sensors = null
//    headIndex = 0
//    rightHandIndex = 1
//    leftHandIndex = 2
//    dominantHandIndex = 1
//    nonDominantHandIndex = 2
//    trackingAvailable = false
//    audioDevice = null
//    inputDeviceList = empty
//    coexistenceToTrackerBase = identity
//    coexistenceCenterInPworldPolicy = View.NOMINAL_SCREEN

public boolean getTrackingAvaible ()
// Get status indicating if tracking mode is available

public AudioDevice getAudioDevice ()
public void setAudioDevice(AudioDevice device)
// Get and set the device through which audio rendering can be performed

public void addInputDevice(InputDevice device)
public InputDevice removeInputDevice (InputDevice device)
// Add and remove input device to and from the list of input device

public Sensor getSensor (int index)
public void setSensor(int index, Sensor sensor)
// Get and set sensor corresponding to an allocated index in the sensor list

public int getCoexistenceCenterInPworldPolicy ()
public void setCoexistenceCenterInPworldPolicy (int policy)
// get and set physical coexistence policy.  This is on how the eye point will be placed.
//    Options are View.NOMINAL_HEAD, View.NOMINAL_FEET, and View.NOMINAL_SCREEN

public double getNominalEyeOffsetFromNominalScreen ()
public void setNominalEyeOffsetFromNominalScreen(double offset)
// Get and set distance between center eye and center of display screen
```

EXAMPLE APPLICATIONS

We will now outline two examples on the creation of a portal and video wall viewing system to illustrate how multiple views can be used in typical applications.

Figure 22 shows the view branch of the scene graph, the important code segment, the result and the display configuration in creating a portal view of a virtual world using three monitor panels with a tilting angle of 45 degrees.

As shown, each panel of the system has its ViewPlatform and View objects. The TransformGroups of these panels come under a parent TransformGroup associated with

Figure 22. Portal view system

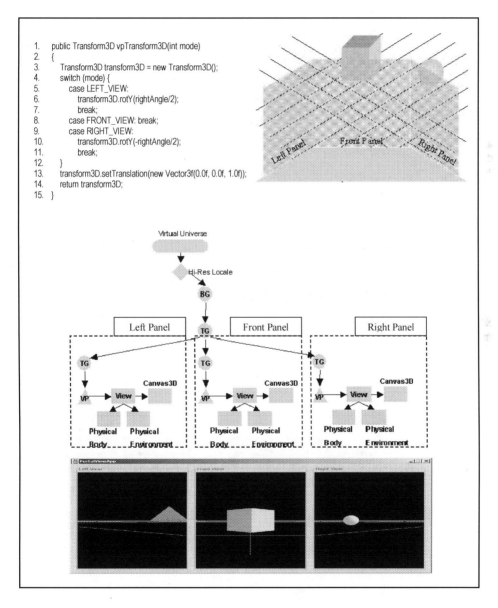

an attached keyboard and mouse navigation behaviour node. With each panel having its own TransformGroup and ViewPlatform, a different Transform3D can be used to provide each panel with the desired view to the virtual universe.

Figure 23. Video wall viewing system

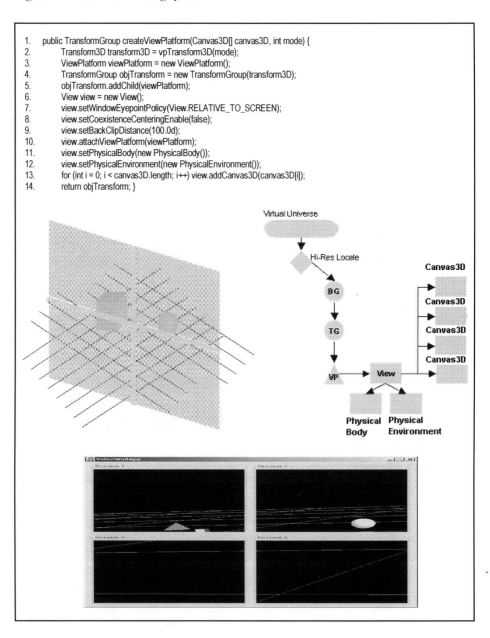

```
1.    public TransformGroup createViewPlatform(Canvas3D[] canvas3D, int mode) {
2.        Transform3D transform3D = vpTransform3D(mode);
3.        ViewPlatform viewPlatform = new ViewPlatform();
4.        TransformGroup objTransform = new TransformGroup(transform3D);
5.        objTransform.addChild(viewPlatform);
6.        View view = new View();
7.        view.setWindowEyepointPolicy(View.RELATIVE_TO_SCREEN);
8.        view.setCoexistenceCenteringEnable(false);
9.        view.setBackClipDistance(100.0d);
10.       view.attachViewPlatform(viewPlatform);
11.       view.setPhysicalBody(new PhysicalBody());
12.       view.setPhysicalEnvironment(new PhysicalEnvironment());
13.       for (int i = 0; i < canvas3D.length; i++) view.addCanvas3D(canvas3D[i]);
14.       return objTransform; }
```

The next example is illustrated in Figure 23, which is on a video wall viewing system. The system renders the virtual world using four monitors arranged in a tile manner. Unlike the previous example, the Java 3D program in this example uses a different approach to generate views for the different monitors.

Instead of several TransformGroups, each with its own ViewPlatform, View, and Canvas3D objects, a single View object is used this time with several Canvas3D objects attached. Each canvas captures an adjacent view of the virtual world. Note that the examples are developed based on using ViewManager.java and VirtualWorld.java. The former is a custom utility class in Appendix C for formatting canvas layout, inserting caption and control buttons, while the latter is for specifying the scene graph content.

SUMMARY

This chapter has discussed some advanced topics needed for generating multiple views of the virtual universe. The Java 3D view model has been outlined together with the important components making up the view branch of the scene graph. By having multiple ViewPlatform and Canvas3D objects, it is relatively straightforward to create applications with multiple views to enhance the experience of observing and interacting in a virtual 3D world.

REFERENCES

Salisbury, C. F., Farr, S. D., & Moore, J. A. (1999). Web-based simulation visualization using Java 3D. *Proceedings Winter Simulation Conference* (Vol. 2, pp. 1425-1429).

Sowizral, H., Rushforth, K., & Deering, M. (2000). *The Java 3D API Specification*. Addison-Wesley.

Yabuki, N., Machinaka, H., & Li, Z. (2006). A cooperative engineering environment using virtual reality with sensory user interfaces for steel bridge erection. *Proceedings International Conference Cooperative Design, Visualization, and Engineering* (pp. 83-90).

Chapter XII
Audio

INTRODUCTION

Of all the human perceptions, two of the most important ones are perhaps vision and sound, for which we have developed highly specialized sensors over millions of years of evolution. The creation of a realistic virtual world therefore calls for the development of realistic 3D virtual objects and sceneries supplemented by associated sounds and audio signals.

The development of 3D visual objects is of course the main domain of Java 3D. However, as in watching a movie, it is also essential to have realistic sound and audio in some applications. In this chapter, we will discuss how sound and audio can be added and supported by Java 3D.

The Java 3D API provides some functionalities to add and control sound in a 3D spatialized manner. It also allows the rendering of aural characteristics for the modeling of real world, synthetic or special acoustical effects (Warren, 2006).

From a programming point of view, the inclusion of sound is similar to the addition of light. Both are the results of adding nodes to the scene graph for the virtual world. The addition of a sound node can be accomplished by the abstract Sound class, under which there are three subclasses on BackgroundSound, PointSound, and ConeSound (Osawa, Asai, Takase, & Saito, 2001).

Multiple sound sources, each with a reference sound file and associated methods for control and activation, can be included in the scene graph. The relevant sound will become audible whenever the scheduling bound associated with the sound node intersects the activation volume of the listener.

By creating an AuralAttributes object and attaching it to a SoundScape leaf node for a certain sound in the scene graph, we can also specify the use of certain acoustical effects in the rendering of the sound. This is done through using the various methods to change important acoustic parameters in the AuralAttributes object.

BackgroundSound

This is a subclass of the Sound class for audio and sound that are unattenuated and nonspatialized. That is, similar to ambient lighting, the sound generated will not have a specific position or direction and will be independent of where the user is in the virtual 3D world. However, unlike a background scenery, more than one BackgroundSound node can be enabled and played at the same time.

Figure 1. Code segment for SoundBackgroundPanel.java

```
1.    BackgroundSound back_sound = new BackgroundSound();
2.
3.    public void addSound ()
4.    {
5.       MediaContainer sample1 = new MediaContainer("file:sound files/sample1.wav");
6.       sample1.setCacheEnable(true);
7.
8.       back_sound.setCapability(ConeSound.ALLOW_SOUND_DATA_READ);
9.       back_sound.setCapability(ConeSound.ALLOW_SOUND_DATA_WRITE);
10.      back_sound.setCapability(ConeSound.ALLOW_ENABLE_READ);
11.      back_sound.setCapability(ConeSound.ALLOW_ENABLE_WRITE);
12.      back_sound.setCapability(ConeSound.ALLOW_LOOP_READ);
13.      back_sound.setCapability(ConeSound.ALLOW_LOOP_WRITE);
14.      back_sound.setCapability(ConeSound.ALLOW_RELEASE_READ);
15.      back_sound.setCapability(ConeSound.ALLOW_RELEASE_WRITE);
16.      back_sound.setCapability(ConeSound.ALLOW_CONT_PLAY_READ);
17.      back_sound.setCapability(ConeSound.ALLOW_CONT_PLAY_WRITE);

18.      back_sound.setSoundData(sample1);
19.      back_sound.setInitialGain(2.0f);
20.      back_sound.setLoop(0);
21.      back_sound.setReleaseEnable(false);
22.      back_sound.setContinuousEnable(false);
23.      back_sound.setEnable(false);
24.      back_sound.setSchedulingBounds(bounds);
25.      back_sound.setPriority(1.0f);
26.   }
```

Figure 1 shows the code segment in an example for adding a background sound in our virtual 3D world. In line 5, the sound file is opened and loaded by a MediaContainer from the current directory. Alternatively, a path can be specified or the sound data can come from the Internet through a URL such as http://vlab.ee.nus.edu.sg/vlab/sound.wav.

Lines 8 to 17 declare some reading and writing capabilities to the sound node created in Line 1. With these capabilities set, it is now possible to change the sound data and alter the enable, loop, release and continuous play functionality of the node through some of the methods in lines 18 to 25.

Specifically, line 18 uses the setSoundData method to change the sound source to correspond to that loaded earlier. Line 19 sets the initial amplitude gain for playing the sound, line 20 uses the setLoop method to specify number of times that sound will be repeated. In the current case, the argument is 0 and the sound will be played once. An argument of −1 will repeat the sound indefinitely.

Line 21 sets the setReleaseEnable flag to false. This flag is only valid when the sound is played once. Setting this flag to true will force the sound to be played until it finishes even in the presence of a stop request.

Similarly, line 22 set the setContinuousEnable flag to false. Setting this to true gives rise to the effect that the sound will be played continuously in a silent mode even if the node is no longer active as when it is outside the scheduling bound. A false setting will play the sound from the beginning when the audio object reenters the scheduling bound.

Changing the setEnable flag in line 23 is similar to pressing the play or stop button in an audio system. A true will play the sound, while a false will stop it. Essentially, it is straightforward to set up and use sound in Java 3D. We just need to create an audio object, load the sound track to a MediaContainer, link the MediaContainer to the audio object, enable the latter, and set the scheduling bound.

PointSound

With BackgroundSound being similar to ambient light, PointSound, another subclass of Sound, is similar to point light. Essentially, as illustrated in Figure 2, a point sound source has a spatial location and generates sound that radiates uniformly in all directions from that location. However, the amplitude of the sound will decrease as it travels further and further away from the source.

To realize this attenuation characteristic, an array of points giving the system gains at different distances from the source can be specified. This will enable Java 3D to interpolate the gain at other distance in a linear manner. In the example code segment in Figure 2 for the creation of a point sound source, line 3 specifies that the gain on the amplitude will still be 1 at a short distance of 1 from the source, but will decrease to 0.5 at a distance of 5. At a further distance of 10, the gain becomes 0 or that the sound will become silent.

Figure 2. Point sound source and code segment for SoundPointPanel.java

```
1.    PointSound point_sound = new PointSound();
2.
3.    Point2f[] Attenuation_Strong = { new Point2f(1,1), new Point2f(5,0.5), new Point2f(10,0) };
4.    Point2f[] Attenuation_Average = { new Point2f(5,1), new Point2f(15,0.5), new Point2f(30,0) };
5.    Point2f[] Attenuation_Weak = { new Point2f(20,1), new Point2f(40,0.5), new Point2f(60,0) };
6.
7.    public void addSound ()
8.    {
9.        MediaContainer sample1 = new MediaContainer("file:sound files/sample1.wav");
10.       sample1.setCacheEnable(true);
11.
12.       point_sound.setCapability(ConeSound.ALLOW_SOUND_DATA_READ);
13.       point_sound.setCapability(ConeSound.ALLOW_SOUND_DATA_WRITE);
14.       point_sound.setCapability(ConeSound.ALLOW_ENABLE_READ);
15.       point_sound.setCapability(ConeSound.ALLOW_ENABLE_WRITE);
16.       point_sound.setCapability(ConeSound.ALLOW_LOOP_READ);
17.       point_sound.setCapability(ConeSound.ALLOW_LOOP_WRITE);
18.       point_sound.setCapability(ConeSound.ALLOW_RELEASE_READ);
19.       point_sound.setCapability(ConeSound.ALLOW_RELEASE_WRITE);
20.       point_sound.setCapability(ConeSound.ALLOW_CONT_PLAY_READ);
21.       point_sound.setCapability(ConeSound.ALLOW_CONT_PLAY_WRITE);
22.       point_sound.setCapability(ConeSound.ALLOW_DISTANCE_GAIN_READ);
23.       point_sound.setCapability(ConeSound.ALLOW_DISTANCE_GAIN_WRITE);
24.
25.       point_sound.setSoundData(sample1);
26.       point_sound.setInitialGain(2.0f);
27.       point_sound.setLoop(0);
28.       point_sound.setReleaseEnable(false);
29.       point_sound.setContinuousEnable(false);
30.       point_sound.setEnable(false);
31.       point_sound.setSchedulingBounds(bounds);
32.       point_sound.setPriority(1.0f);
33.       point_sound.setPosition(0.0f, 0.0f, 0.0f);
34.       point_sound.setDistanceGain( Attenuation_Weak);
35.   }
```

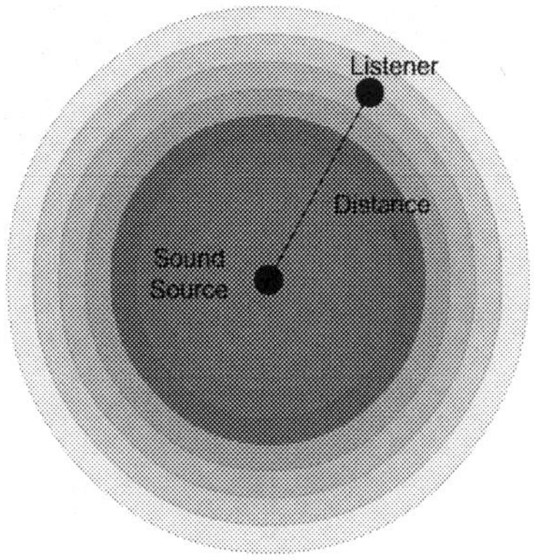

The setting of the various capabilities and the functionality flags in Figure 2 are similar to those in Figure 1 for the background sound. However, the sound source position and distance gain relationship can now be set as in lines 33 and 34, respectively.

CONESOUND

ConeSound creates a sound source that has characteristics similar to using a spot or cone light source that points at a certain direction. Basically, similar to a point sound, a cone sound source is located at a certain position, and gives out acoustic sounds that radiates from this position. Of course, the sound becomes weaker of get attenuated the further it travels.

Figure 3. Cone sound source and code segment for SoundConePanel.java

```
1.    ConeSound cone_sound = new ConeSound();
2.    Point2f[] myFrontAtten = { new Point2f(100,1), new Point2f(350,0.5), new Point2f(600,0) };
3.    Point2f[] myBackAtten = { new Point2f(50,1), new Point2f(100,0.5), new Point2f(200,0) };
4.    Point3f[] smallAngular = { new Point3f(0,1,20000),
5.        new Point3f( (float)Math.PI/20, 0.5f, 5000.0f ), new Point3f( (float)Math.PI/10, 0.0f, 2000.0f ) };
6.    Point3f[] averageAngular = { new Point3f( 0,1,20000),
7.        new Point3f( (float)Math.PI/8, 0.5f, 5000.0f ), new Point3f( (float)Math.PI/4, 0.0f, 2000.0f ) };
8.    Point3f[] largeAngular = { new Point3f(0,1,20000),
9.        new Point3f( (float)Math.PI/4, 0.5f, 5000.0f ), new Point3f( (float)Math.PI/2, 0.0f, 2000.0f ) };
10.
11.   public void addSound ()
12.   {
13.       MediaContainer sample1 = new MediaContainer("file:sound files/sample1.wav");
14.       sample1.setCacheEnable(true);
15.
16.       cone_sound.setCapability(ConeSound.ALLOW_SOUND_DATA_READ);
17.       cone_sound.setCapability(ConeSound.ALLOW_SOUND_DATA_WRITE);
18.       cone_sound.setCapability(ConeSound.ALLOW_ENABLE_READ);
19.       cone_sound.setCapability(ConeSound.ALLOW_ENABLE_WRITE);
20.       cone_sound.setCapability(ConeSound.ALLOW_LOOP_READ);
21.       cone_sound.setCapability(ConeSound.ALLOW_LOOP_WRITE);
22.       cone_sound.setCapability(ConeSound.ALLOW_RELEASE_READ);
23.       cone_sound.setCapability(ConeSound.ALLOW_RELEASE_WRITE);
24.       cone_sound.setCapability(ConeSound.ALLOW_CONT_PLAY_READ);
25.       cone_sound.setCapability(ConeSound.ALLOW_CONT_PLAY_WRITE);
26.       cone_sound.setCapability(ConeSound.ALLOW_ANGULAR_ATTENUATION_READ);
27.       cone_sound.setCapability(ConeSound.ALLOW_ANGULAR_ATTENUATION_WRITE);
28.
29.       cone_sound.setSoundData(sample1);
30.       cone_sound.setInitialGain(2.0f);
31.       cone_sound.setLoop(0);
32.       cone_sound.setReleaseEnable(false);
33.       cone_sound.setContinuousEnable(false);
34.       cone_sound.setEnable(false);
35.       cone_sound.setSchedulingBounds(bounds);
36.       cone_sound.setPriority(1.0f);
37.       cone_sound.setPosition(0.0f, 0.0f, -12.5f);
38.       cone_sound.setDirection( new Vector3f( 0.0f, 0.0f, 1.0f ) );
39.       cone_sound.setDistanceGain( myFrontAtten, myBackAtten );
40.       cone_sound.setAngularAttenuation( smallAngular );
41.   }
```

However, while a point sound source will radiates uniformly in all directions, a cone sound is directional and radiates more strongly at a certain direction, in the same way that a spot light has more light output shining at an object of interest.

Technically, the amplitude of the sound from a cone sound depends on both the distance from the source as well as the angle the user has with the sound source in the virtual world. Figure 3 gives an example for creating a cone sound. The codes are similar to those in Figure 2, except for some additional controls that can be specified regarding how the sound will be attenuated at different directions.

Specifically, the principal direction of the sound is given in line 38. On attenuation or gain as a function of distance, two front and back distance gain attenuations are provided in lines 2, 3 and 39. A single distance gain attenuation is also possible, corresponding to using the same profile for both distance attenuation for front and back propagation.

Lines 4, 5, and 40 specify the variation of gain as a function of direction, giving the coning profile for the sound. The specification of this is in the form of an array of triples. The first of the triple gives the angle separation from the main direction, the second one gives the gain factor, and the last one is a filter cut off frequency used for implementing a low pass filter to remove the higher frequency components of the sound.

AURAL ENVIRONMENT

In addition to placing multiple sound sources through the Sound leaf node in a virtual world, it is also possible in Java 3D to implement specific acoustical characteristics so as to simulate some special aural effects and add realism to the environment (View Model, 2006). We will outline in this section two examples on how this can be done by using the appropriate classes and methods.

The code segment for the first example is given in Figures 4 to 6, in the form of codes for three files, MultiViewApp.java, PointSoundScape.java, and ViewManager.java. The main method is MultiViewApp.java and is shown in Figure 4. A modified version of a similar problem from the chapter on multiple views, this allows the user to navigate in the virtual world.

Essentially, MultiViewApp creates a PointSoundScape object and invokes methods from the PointSoundScape class. The most important line in this example is line 10, which add an avatar to the virtual world, and lines 20 and 21, which initialize the sound in Java 3D.

An explicit method for initializing the sound is implemented as a customized view branch has been used. The same effect can be accomplished by using the getViewer(). createAudioDevice() method implicitly from the SimpleUniverse utility class. Note that Sound and Soundscape will become active when the ActivationVolume of the ViewPlatform overlaps their scheduling or activation bounds.

Figure 4. Code segment and screen capture for MultiViewApp.java

```
1.      public TransformGroup createViewPlatform(Canvas3D canvas3D, int mode)
2.      {
3.        Transform3D transform3D = vpTransform3D(mode);
4.        ViewPlatform viewPlatform = new ViewPlatform();
5.        viewPlatform.setActivationRadius(10.0f);
6.        TransformGroup objTransform = new TransformGroup(transform3D);
7.        objTransform.addChild(viewPlatform);
8.
9.        // call method in PointSoundScape; add a colored cube and a footsteps PointSound as avatar
10.       if (mode == 0) myWorld.addAvatar(objTransform);
11.
12.       View view = new View();
13.       view.attachViewPlatform(viewPlatform);
14.       view.addCanvas3D(canvas3D);
15.       view.setPhysicalBody(new PhysicalBody());
16.       PhysicalEnvironment physicalEnvironment = new PhysicalEnvironment();
17.       view.setPhysicalEnvironment(physicalEnvironment);
18.
19.       if(mode == 0) { // Initializes sound
20.          JavaSoundMixer javaSoundMixer = new JavaSoundMixer(physicalEnvironment);
21.          javaSoundMixer.initialize(); }
22.
23.       return objTransform;
24.    }
```

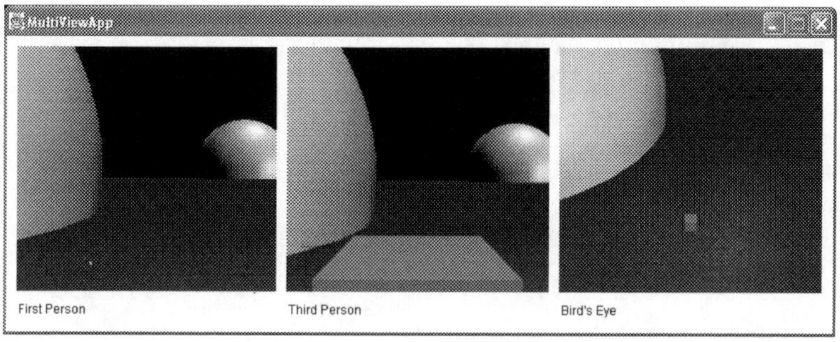

Figure 5 shows the code segment for PointSoundScape.java, where two methods, addSound and addAvatar, are provided to add stationary PointSound sources and a Soundscape are added to the scene graph. Specifically, addAvatar adds a PointSound to simulate footsteps at the current position, while addSound adds two other PointSound sources.

Lines 6 and 7 of addSound specify the sound files to be used for these two PointSound sources, line 5 sets the position of one source, while lines 10 and 11 provide the attenuation characteristics of both sources through a series of distance gain pairs in an array.

Three different SoundScape objects are then created, each having different AuralAt-tributes. As defined in line 20, the first Soundscape increases the frequency of the sound 20 times. However, as given by lines 22 and 23, the second Soundscape has no effect on

Figure 5. Code segment for PointSoundScape.java

```
1.    private void addSound() {
2.        BoundingSphere sBounds1 = new BoundingSphere(new Point3d(), 40.0);
3.        BoundingSphere sBounds2 = new BoundingSphere(new Point3d(-20.0f, 0.0f, 60.0f), 40.0);
4.        PointSound sound1 = new PointSound();
5.        PointSound sound2 = new PointSound();  sound2.setPosition(-20.0f, 0.0f, 60.0f);
6.        MediaContainer data1 = new MediaContainer("file:sound files/howdeep.wav");
7.        MediaContainer data2 = new MediaContainer("file:sound files/ifihadu.wav");
8.        sound1.setSoundData(data1);  sound1.setInitialGain(1.0f);
9.        sound2.setSoundData(data2);  sound2.setInitialGain(1.0f);
10.       Point2f distanceGain[] = { new Point2f(0,2), new Point2f(10,1.5), new Point2f( 20,1),
11.            new Point2f(30,0.5), new Point2f(50,0) };
12.       sound1.setDistanceGain(distanceGain);        sound2.setDistanceGain(distanceGain);
13.       sound1.setLoop(Sound.INFINITE_LOOPS);  sound2.setLoop(Sound.INFINITE_LOOPS);
14.       sound1.setEnable(true);  sound2.setEnable(true);
15.       sound1.setSchedulingBounds(sBounds1); sound2.setSchedulingBounds(sBounds2);
16.       BoundingSphere sScapeBounds1 = new BoundingSphere(new Point3d(), 1.0);
17.       BoundingSphere sScapeBounds2 = new BoundingSphere(new Point3d(), 1000.0);
18.       BoundingSphere sScapeBounds3 = new BoundingSphere(new Point3d(-20.0f, 0.0f, 60.0f), 1.0);
19.       AuralAttributes aAttributes1 = new AuralAttributes();
20.       aAttributes1.setFrequencyScaleFactor(20.0f); // increases frequency of the sound rendered
21.       Soundscape sScape1 = new Soundscape(sScapeBounds1, aAttributes1);
22.       AuralAttributes aAttributes2 = new AuralAttributes();
23.       Soundscape sScape2 = new Soundscape(sScapeBounds2, aAttributes2); // default AuralAttribute
24.       AuralAttributes aAttributes3 = new AuralAttributes();
25.       aAttributes3.setReverbDelay(600); // model a large cavern
26.       aAttributes3.setReflectionCoefficient(1);  aAttributes3.setReverbOrder(20);
27.       Soundscape sScape3 = new Soundscape(sScapeBounds3, aAttributes3);
28.       this.addChild(sScape2);  this.addChild(sScape1);  this.addChild(sScape3);
29.       this.addChild(sound1);  this.addChild(sound2); }
30.
31.   public static void addAvatar(TransformGroup objTransform) {
32.       objTransform.addChild(new ColorCube(0.25f));  PointSound sound = new PointSound();
33.       MediaContainer data = new MediaContainer("file:sound files/footsteps.wav");
34.       sound.setSoundData(data);  sound.setInitialGain(0.0f);
35.       sound.setCapability(Sound.ALLOW_INITIAL_GAIN_WRITE);
36.       sound.setLoop(Sound.INFINITE_LOOPS);  sound.setEnable(true);
37.       sound.setSchedulingBounds(new BoundingSphere());  objTransform.addChild(sound);
38.       KeySoundBehavior keySoundBehavior = new KeySoundBehavior(sound);
39.       keySoundBehavior.setSchedulingBounds(new BoundingSphere(new Point3d(),1000.0));
40.       objTransform.addChild(keySoundBehavior);
41.       PointLight lightPW = new PointLight(new Color3f(1,1,1), new Point3f(0,0,0), new Point3f(1,1,0));
42.       lightPW.setInfluencingBounds(new BoundingSphere(new Point3d(), 5.0));
43.       objTransform.addChild(lightPW); }
```

the sound rendered, and has application bounds that covers all other areas not under the bounds of the other two Soundscapes.

Lines 25 and 26 creates a third Soundscape that simulates being in a large cavern. This is done by have a large ReverbDelay, a unit ReflectionCoefficient and a large ReverbOrder. The large ReverbDelay increases the lengths of echoes, a unit ReflectionCoefficient removes the absorption of reflected sounds, and a large ReverbOrder increases the lifespan of echoes by allowing a higher number of multiple reflections.

The use of various PointSounds and Soundscapes with different ApplicationBounds enables us to create a 3D virtual world with sounds where the user can move around, see objects from different perspectives, and experience the resulting positional and reverberation effects.

In the addAvatar method in Figure 5, a PointSound is added to simulate footsteps. This is done by using a custom behavior class KeySoundBehavior, the code segment for which is given in Figure 6. In particular, through lines 9 to 10, the pressing of a navigation key will set the gain of the PointSound to 1 and make it audible, while the releasing of the key will set the gain to 0 and make it inaudible. With the PointSound set to loop infinitely in line 36 in Figure 5, an effect similar to that of footsteps is obtained.

Some screen captures for the example described are shown in Figure 4. Note that the sphere gives the ApplicationBounds of the SoundScape, and when this intersects with the ActivationVolume of the ViewPlatform, the AuralAttributes specified will be applied to the sound being rendered.

Figures 7 and 8 show the code segment and screen capture in another example where the aural or acoustical characteristics can be changed during run time. This is done by extending the TestApplet class and using JComponent based controls. Note that in order for the aural parameters to be varied in real-time after the objects have become live, the appropriate capabilities have to be set.

Figure 6. Code segment for KeySoundBehavior.java

```
1.    public void processStimulus( Enumeration criteria ) {
2.        WakeupCriterion wakeup;
3.        AWTEvent[] event;
4.        while( criteria.hasMoreElements() ) {
5.            wakeup = (WakeupCriterion) criteria.nextElement();
6.            if( !(wakeup instanceof WakeupOnAWTEvent) ) continue;
7.            event = ((WakeupOnAWTEvent)wakeup).getAWTEvent();
8.            for( int i = 0; i < event.length; i++ ) {
9.                if( event[i].getID() == KeyEvent.KEY_PRESSED) pSound.setInitialGain(1.0f);
10.               else if(event[i].getID() == KeyEvent.KEY_RELEASED) pSound.setInitialGain(0.0f); } }
11.       wakeupOn( keyCriterion );}
```

Figure 7. First code segment for SoundTest.java

```
24.  aAttributes.setCapability(AuralAttributes.ALLOW_ATTRIBUTE_GAIN_WRITE);
25.  aAttributes.setCapability(AuralAttributes.ALLOW_FREQUENCY_SCALE_FACTOR_WRITE);
26.  aAttributes.setCapability(AuralAttributes.ALLOW_REFLECTION_COEFFICIENT_WRITE);
27.  aAttributes.setCapability(AuralAttributes.ALLOW_REVERB_DELAY_WRITE);
28.  aAttributes.setCapability(AuralAttributes.ALLOW_REVERB_ORDER_WRITE);
29.  aAttributes.setCapability(AuralAttributes.ALLOW_ROLLOFF_WRITE);
30.  aAttributes.setCapability(AuralAttributes.ALLOW_VELOCITY_SCALE_FACTOR_WRITE);
31.  aAttributes.setDistanceFilter(distanceFilter);
32.  sound.setCapability(Sound.ALLOW_ENABLE_WRITE);
33.  sound.setCapability(Sound.ALLOW_ENABLE_READ);
34.  sound.setCapability(PointSound.ALLOW_DISTANCE_GAIN_WRITE);
35.  sound.setSchedulingBounds(sBounds);
36.  sound.setSoundData(data);
37.  sound.setInitialGain(2.0f);
38.  sound.setLoop(Sound.INFINITE_LOOPS);
39.  sScape.setCapability(Soundscape.ALLOW_ATTRIBUTES_WRITE);
40.  sScape.setCapability(Soundscape.ALLOW_APPLICATION_BOUNDS_WRITE);
41.  sScape.setAuralAttributes(aAttributes);
42.  sScape.setApplicationBounds(sScapeBounds);
43.
44.  protected void decode(ParamSlider paramSlider, int idx) {
45.      float value = paramSlider.getValue();
46.      try switch(idx) {
47.          case 0: aAttributes.setAttributeGain(value); break;
48.          case 1: aAttributes.setFrequencyScaleFactor(value); break;
49.          case 2: aAttributes.setReflectionCoefficient(value); break;
50.          case 3: aAttributes.setReverbDelay(value); break;
51.          case 4: aAttributes.setReverbOrder((int)value); break;
52.          case 5: aAttributes.setRolloff(value); System.out.println(value); break;
53.          case 6: aAttributes.setVelocityScaleFactor(value); break;
54.          case 7: v3f.set(0.0f, 0.0f, -value); t3d.setTranslation(v3f); tg.setTransform(t3d); break;
55.          default: };
56.      catch (NumberFormatException e){}
57.      sScape.setApplicationBounds(sScapeBounds);
58.  }
```

SUMMARY

In this chapter, we have outlined how 3D sound sources and aural characteristics can be integrated into the virtual world built using Java 3D. Three types of sources, Background-Sound, PointSound and ConeSound, are supported, and this become audible if the activation radius intersects with the scheduling bounds of the sound. Controls are also available to

Figure 8. Second code segment and result for SoundTest.java

```
1.    // Selection of distanceFilter models
2.    JRadioButton fModel1 = new JRadioButton("No filter");
3.    JRadioButton fModel2 = new JRadioButton("Model 1");
4.    JRadioButton fModel3 = new JRadioButton("Model 2");
5.
6.    fModel1.addActionListener(new ActionListener() {
7.       public void actionPerformed(ActionEvent e) {
8.          aAttributes.setDistanceFilter(distanceFilter1);
9.          tg.setTransform(t3d);
10.         if(!sound.getEnable()) { sound.setEnable(true); sound.setDistanceGain(distanceGain); }}};
11.
12.   fModel2.addActionListener(new ActionListener() {
13.      public void actionPerformed(ActionEvent e) {
14.         aAttributes.setDistanceFilter(distanceFilter2);
15.         tg.setTransform(t3d);
16.         if(!sound.getEnable()) { sound.setEnable(true); sound.setDistanceGain(distanceGain); }}};
17.
18.   fModel3.addActionListener(new ActionListener() {
19.      public void actionPerformed(ActionEvent e) {
20.         aAttributes.setDistanceFilter(distanceFilter3);
21.         tg.setTransform(t3d);
22.         if(!sound.getEnable()) { sound.setEnable(true); sound.setDistanceGain(distanceGain); }}};
```

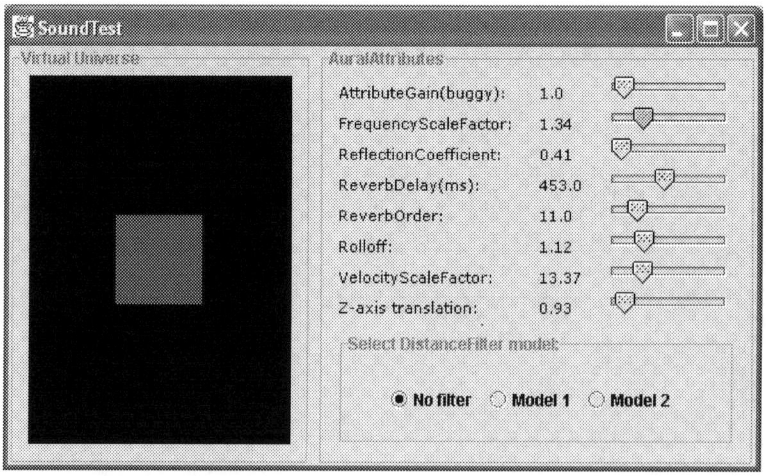

turn a sound source on or off, set its gain, release style, continuous playback style, looping, priority, and scheduling bounds. In addition, by creating a SoundScape object with appropriate AuralAttributes, an special acoustical environment can be simulated.

REFERENCES

Osawa, N., Asai, K., Takase, N., & Saito, F. (2001). An immersive system for editing and playing music on network-connected computers. *Proceedings 5ᵗʰ International Conference on Information Visualization* (pp. 630-635).

View Model. (2006). http://download.java.net/media/java3d/javadoc/1.4.0-latest/javax/media/j3d/doc-files/ViewModel.html

Warren, D. (2006). *Renderering MIDI in Java3D*. Retrieved from http://www.mail-archive.com/java3d-interest@sun.com/msg02749.html

Chapter XIII
A Web–Based 3D Real Time Oscilloscope Experiment

INTRODUCTION

In this final chapter, we will describe the use of Java 3D as a visualization technology in the development of a Web-based 3D real time oscilloscope experiment.

Developed and launched under a research project at the National University of Singapore, this application enables students to carry out a physical electronic experiment that involves the use of an actual oscilloscope, a signal generator and a circuit board remotely through the Internet (Ko 2000, and 2001). Specifically, this system addresses 3D visualization schemes on the client side (Bund, 2005, Hobona, 2006, Liang, 2006, Ueda, 2006, Wang, 2006), as well as Web-based real time control and 3D-based monitoring between the client and server (Nielsen, 2006; Qin, Harrison, West, & Wright, 2004).

The control of the various instruments are carried out in real time through the use of a Java 3D based interface on the client side, with the results of the experiment being also reflected or displayed appropriately on 3D instruments in the same interface.

Basically, Java 3D is used to create a virtual 3D world or room in which the 3D instruments reside. The mouse is used for both navigation in this world as well as to operate the instruments through, say, dragging a sliding control or a rotary control or clicking or switching appropriate buttons on the instruments. Associated commands that cause the real instruments in a remote physical laboratory to operate accordingly are then sent through the Internet in real-time. Experimental results corresponding to, say, a change in the real oscilloscope display, are then sent from the instrument control server back to the

Java 3D client to result in a real-time change in the display of the virtual 3D oscilloscope in the virtual 3D world.

Figures 1 and 2 show some screen capture of the application. Specifically, Figure 1 shows the initial scene of the virtual laboratory room for carrying out the experiment. Note that the experiment and apparatus are inside the room and the user has to make use of the navigational controls at the bottom of the screen to "walk" toward the room and open the door after typing an user access password. The bottom rightmost control allows the user to make turns in four possible directions, while a similarly shaped adjacent control on the left allows the user to move linearly. These controls are custom designed for the application and can be activated by using just the mouse, even though keyboard activation is also possible. While this adds an additional level of complexity to the interface and makes it more difficult to develop the program, it is felt to be essential for the users who are primarily students with no experience in using a 3D-based software.

The main advantage of using Java 3D is of course the ability to create a virtual 3D world with realistic instruments and objects that occupy 3D space and linked to real instruments in a real physical laboratory. This will enhance the experience of the user or student in operating the various instruments, even though the actual physical apparatus may be very far away and the usual laboratory opening hour may well have past. Also, from a safety point of view, the user will sustain no injury even if the instruments are incorrectly oper-

Figure 1 Virtual room in the real-time oscilloscope experiment

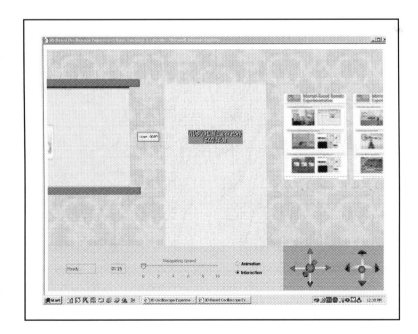

ated. Another advantage is that the experiment can be accessed and run using a Java and Java 3D runtime installed Web browser with a vrml97 plug-in.

Figure 2 show two typical screen capture after the user has entered the virtual room and walked to the laboratory bench. Note that since most practical instruments consist of a large

Figure 2. Virtual instruments in the real-time oscilloscope experiment

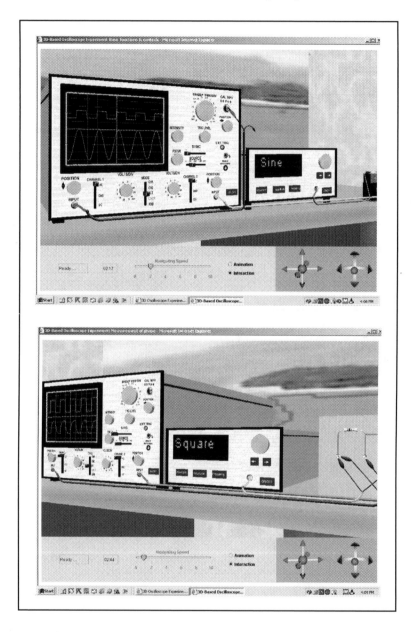

number of knobs, buttons, sliders, and connectors, creation of a realistic 3D instrument and experiment is an inherently complicated task. Thus, to do this as efficiently as possible, we have developed a large API library for creating various controls and components needed in the instruments and virtual laboratory.

Apart from the room and instrument geometry, three important and difficult issues to bear in mind in such an application are navigating behavior, collision detection and picking behavior. Specifically, navigating behavior controls how the user is able to walk around in the virtual laboratory as well as the positions and angles of the view platform, as when the user attempts to get a better view. The use of appropriate collision detection ensures that the user is not able to traverse any solid objects such as walls, tables, and instruments, while a customized picking behavior is necessary for the user to adjust the controls on the instruments precisely.

Note that besides the use of Java 3D to create the 3D virtual scene, the complete application also requires other software components for the control of actual physical instruments. Also, there is a need to stream real-time experimental data from the actual equipments in the remote laboratory to the client.

SYSTEM REFERENCE MODEL AND WORKING PRINCIPLE

Before giving details of the Java 3D code in the application, we will first briefly discuss the framework for the creation of the Web-based 3D real time experimentation. As shown in Figure 3, this framework makes use of Java 3D to produce an applet to combine with Java for 3D visualization and the realization of a network connection on the client side.

Note that, usually, 3D visualization consists of both geometry and behavior objects. The former will include picked, moved, animated and static objects, while the latter consists of navigating, collision detection, picking, and animating behaviors.

SCENE GRAPH AND MAIN APPLET

As discussed in earlier chapters, the programming model in Java 3D is based on the use of scene graph, which provides a simple and flexible mechanism for representing and rendering scenes. Basically, the scene graph gives a complete description of the entire scene, and is makes up of Java 3D objects, called nodes, arranged in a tree structure. The scene graph of the 3D experiment is given in Figure 4.

In Figure 4, TG denotes a TransformGroup object, BG denotes a BranchGroup object, S denotes a Shape3D object, and B denotes a Behavior object. There is one higher level BG object for hosting all the visual objects, which include an oscilloscope, a signal generator,

Figure 3. Framework for creating Web-based real time experimentation

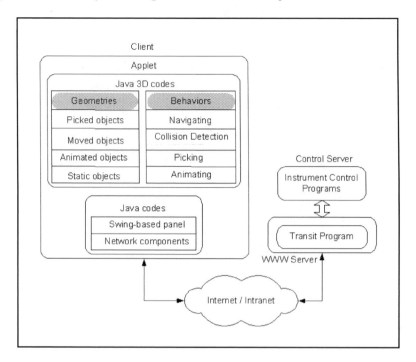

Figure 4. Scene graph of experiment

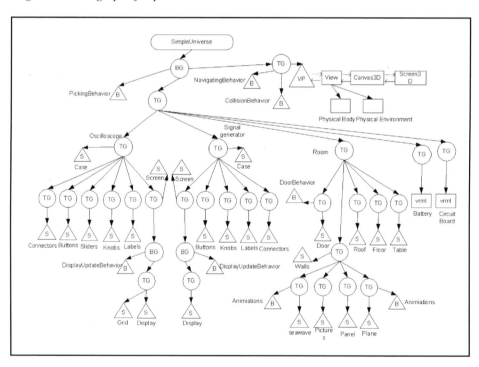

a room, and two VRML models in the laboratory. This higher level BG object also has an attached picking behavior.

For the purpose of refreshing the displays of the oscilloscope and the signal generator, the scene graph has two other lower level BG objects for attaching or detaching the two respective display objects. The updating can then be done by using two associated DisplayUpdatingBehavior objects.

The scene graph also includes a view branch for managing the viewing platform or user viewpoint. Appropriate navigating and collision detection behavior is attached to a TG of this branch.

The code for the important high level functions for implementing the Applet for the 3D client Interface of the experiment is quite lengthy and is given in Appendices D and E. Appendix D is the main Applet for the client interface. Certain statements in this appendix invokes the code in Appendix E, which basically creates the scene graph for the application. Note that the code are for the realization of a 3D world where the user can enter a virtual laboratory by moving to press a button and walking through a door as shown in Figure 1. After entering the laboratory, the user will see a 3D room with floor, ceiling, a few walls, two windows with a view where aircrafts land and one door. To carry out the experiment, the user can walk to a bench where an oscilloscope, a signal generator, a circuit board, and a battery are placed.

As given in Appendix D, Section D.9 gives the entry to the main applet for the client interface. This invokes the initialization function in Section D.3, which then loads the VRML-based circuit board and the 3D scene. The handles to the navigation controls are then obtained and the view mode is set up. After this, the pictures for texturing various instruments and the 3D room are loaded.

The initialization function then invokes scene3d = new Scene3D in Section D.3 to create a Java scene graph for the entire experiment. This Scene3D class is defined in Appendix E and corresponds to the structure of Figure 4.

Specifically, Appendix E first uses the code in Section E.8 to create the appropriate lighting environment by using spot, directional and ambient light sources. This section then creates a Branch Group branchRoot, which corresponds to BG in Figure 4. All of the light sources are added to this node as child nodes. Section E.7 is then invoked to obtain a handle to BG so that the remaining parts of the scene graph can be constructed according to the structure in Figure 4.

As an example, the Transform Group objTrans in the code segment corresponds to the first TG node that lies just below the node BG in the scene graph, while the Transform Group vpTrans corresponds to the TG in the View Platform branch of the scene graph. According to the scene graph in Figure 4, the TG node corresponding to objTrans in the code segment should have five child nodes. The one corresponding to the oscilloscope TG is named osciTrans in the code segment. Similarly, the next one corresponding to the signal generator TG is named sgTrans in the code segment.

Note that those picking behavior that are associated with important 3D objects such as the door, oscilloscope and signal generator controls are added to the BG node or objRoot in the code segment. On the other hand, navigation and collision detection behavior are associated with the view platform, and are invoked through the view platform TG node or vpTrans in the code segment.

CONTROL BUTTONS, SLIDERS, KNOBS, AND OTHER OBJECTS

To realize 3D instruments in the 3D world, a number of 3D visual objects for controlling the apparatus have to be made use of. While the number of such lower level component objects may be larger, they can often be classified as belonging to a few classes including buttons, knobs, sliders, screens, and frames.

Although each object has its own appearance attributes, it is more convenient to define and construct these in a standardized manner. Specifically, the following methodologies are adopted.

1.   Each of these objects is created by specifying the vertex coordinates of the polygon surfaces that make it up. To achieve better rendering performance, subclasses of GeometryStripArray are used as far as possible so as to reuse as many vertices as possible.
2.   To reduce the complexity of the model, coaxial cables, circuit board, battery, and static clips are created using VRML format, and are loaded into the 3D virtual scene using the vrml97 loader.
3.   Some visual objects such as those shown in Figure 5 are realized through the use of appropriate textures on appropriate surfaces such as an instrument panel.

Figure 5. Texture for realizing the front surface of a button test point, a test point, and a clip

As an example, Appendix F gives the code segment for the knob class, which can be invoked to create a knob of arbitrary size, position, and orientation relative to an attached instrument face. Specifically, a knob is defined by five parameters: its radius, length, number of segments, mark color and face texture. The knob class belongs to Transform-Group node in the scene graph, with geometry-based on the use of TriangleFanArray. The color of the knob is set by using TexCoordGeneration. The position and orientation of the knob on the face of the instrument panel can be changed using the methods setRotationX, setRotationY, setRotationZ, setPosition. In order that the knob can be turned, PickTool is set to an appropriate capability.

CUSTOM BEHAVIOR

After defining and creating the numerous geometry objects for the 3D experiment, it is necessary to specify how the user can interact with these objects for the purpose of carrying out the experiment. As an example, the position of a control button may need to be changed after being pressed by the user.

The proper functioning of the instruments and their responses depend on many behavior objects. The important ones are described below and the corresponding code segments are given in Appendices G and H.

1. **Navigating behavior:** Since only one viewpoint is provided in the 3D laboratory, a SimpleUniverse object is used. This will reduce the time and effort needed to create the view branch graph significantly. Through the use of the NavigatingBehavior class provided in Appendix G, the user will be able to explore the virtual laboratory as if walking around in a real laboratory while carrying out the experiment.
2. **Collision detection:** This is based on using a cylinder of height 1.7m and diameter 0.3m in width to model a human body.
3. **Picking behavior:** The PickingBehavior object given in Appendix H enables the user to turn a knob, press a button, and drag a slider or a connector. As can be seen, the code segment for realizing the various picking behavior is quite lengthy, illustrating the fact that interaction is very often more difficult and time consuming to develop.
4. **Door operating behavior:** This is for the opening and closing of the door to the virtual laboratory. It is implemented through the use of both interaction and animation techniques.
5. **Outdoor behavior:** An outdoor scene with an island, some sea waves, and flying planes is included to give a more dynamic feel of being in a real laboratory. This scene can be viewed through the two windows in the 3D world and is implemented using standard scale and position interpolators.

Since behavior is crucial and more difficult to realize, the next few sections will provide some more details on the overall design and implementation of the important behaviors for the application.

NAVIGATION BEHAVIOR

This is crucial for allowing the user to move or walk around in the virtual world and is a very important aspect in the design of any 3D system. In the original Java 3D API, some basic navigating functions are provided. This is through the use of the class KeyNavigator-Behavior and is based on keystrokes. The drawback is that it is not a natural interface, as many keys are involved and it is not possible to change the movement step size. For most users who are not familiar with the many keys involved, it will be much easier if only the mouse is needed for navigation by clicking or pressing some movement icons.

With this consideration, a more sophisticated navigating system has been designed and developed. In this system, navigation can be done by using either the mouse or the keyboard. Specifically, the position and direction of the view platform or viewpoint can be changed by simply using the mouse to press the appropriate icons of Figure 6.

As shown in Figure 6, navigation using the designed interface can be done by using three control objects: a navigating speed slider, a translation, and a rotation icon. To change the user's "walking" speed through the 3D virtual laboratory, the navigating speed slider can be adjusted. This will change the delays used in the main processing steps of the navigating function. The icon with six straight arrows allows the user to move in a straight translational manner. Pressing the ball in the center will reset the viewpoint to its initial position. The other icon with four curved arrows allows the user to rotate around the current position. The ball in the center will reset the viewpoint to a horizontal one.

As given in Appendix G, navigation and collision detection are implemented in the following manner.

1. **Navigation with mouse:** When a mouse click is detected on the navigation icons, the system will activate the MousePressed function in Section G.17. This will find out the selected navigation direction and pass this information to a variable buttonvalue. The main processStimulus function in Section F.14 is then invoked to calculate the position and orientation parameters for the movement.
2. **Navigation with keys:** When an appropriate navigation key is pressed, the system will invoke the main processStimulus function in Section G.14. The processKeyEvent function in Section G.13 will be invoked to calculate the position and orientation parameters for the movement.
3. **Movement:** Once the position and orientation parameters for the movement have been obtained, the code in Section G.11 or 9 is then invoked to implement the translation

Figure 6. Navigating icons

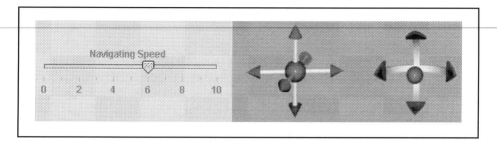

or orientation necessary for the view platform and human body. Note that this may involve the detection of collision detection events. For the application, movements in four directions, forward, backward, shift left or right may generate collision events. When one of these has occurred, anti-collision will be activated. This may result in a movement, which is opposite to the one specified by the user. Further discussion on the implementation of collision detection in the Java 3D application is given in the next section.

COLLISION DETECTION BEHAVIOR

To achieve realistic navigation in a 3D environment, the use of collision detection is essential to guarantee that the viewing platform or user does not traverse any solid object. The Java 3D API provides only two event conditions, WakeupOnCollisionEntry and WakeupOnCollisionExit, for detecting collisions. There is no provision on follow-up actions when these events occur.

As given in Appendix G, a custom collision detection conditions has been designed and developed to provide better support for post-collision processing in the 3D virtual laboratory application. Specifically, a cylinder with appropriate height and radius is used to represent a human body, and this is used to detect collision with objects in the 3D virtual scene. Once the cylinder collides with geometric objects such as virtual instruments, doors or walls, a collision event is generated for post-collision processing so that the user will be prevented from making any further offending movement.

Figure 7 shows the flow chart for post-collision processing. Note that since collision occurs only when the movement is forward, backward, left or right, the processing is only restricted to these four kinds of movements. Also, to make the effect of collision as obvious to the user as possible, a significantly larger incremental movement in a direction opposite to the current movement is used when there is a collision.

Figure 7. Post-collision processing

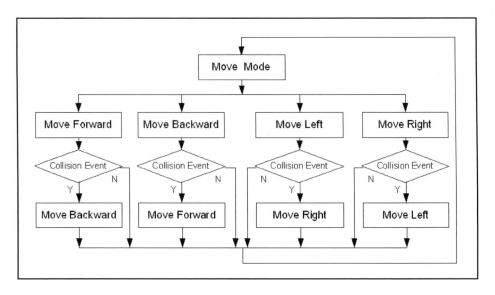

PICKING BEHAVIOR

This behavior class is the most complicated as a variety of control component objects such as buttons, knobs, sliders and connectors for the equipment and experiment can be picked in different ways as shown in Figure 8. In addition, the picking of a control object may result in changes on some curve, text, and screen displays on the virtual instruments.

With these considerations, the 3D laboratory application depends on many custom designed picking functions for appropriately adjusting the various controls in the virtual laboratory. The standard utility classes for picking in the Java 3D API, including Pick-RotationBehavior, PickTranslateBehavior, and PickZoomBehavior, provide only limited capabilities for picking an object. Many controls, which may require different actions to be taken, are not differentiated in the standard Java 3D utility class. Also, it is not possible to implement different functions for different controls of the same type. For example, the vertical position and horizontal position knobs are both knobs, but require different functions to be implemented when they are turned.

As given in Appendix H, the picking classed used are combined with mouse events so that when the focus of the mouse is on the front face of a pickable object, the identity number of the object can be retrieved through the event associated with the mouse movement, and the necessary actions or processing can then be performed.

Figure 8. Example picking controls on instruments

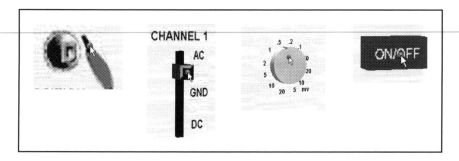

Some examples of the type of controls for the instruments in the application are shown in Figure 8. In general, the behavior for interacting with these controls in the laboratory are implemented in the following manner.

1. **Main processStimulus function:** This is given in Section H.32 and will be invoked by the system whenever a mouse move event is detected. The closest object that intersects with the picking ray is captured.
2. **Object identification:** The type and ID of the object being picked is then identified. Specifically, button and knob objects can be differentiated based on the fact that a knob is created by using TriangleFanArray while a button is created by using QuadArray. The identity number of the object can be obtained by using the WhichObject function in Section H.17.
3. **Manipulation:** The turning of a knob is based on pressing the left button of the mouse and dragging the mouse to turn the knob. As the mouse is dragged, the knob should turn accordingly. The total angle of the mouse dragging operation relative to the initial position when the mouse left button is first pressed corresponds to the angle that the knob should be turned. In implementation, the first pressing of the left button of the mouse will be detected and a knob turning operation will be taken to have started. Then, the change in mouse movement will be detected periodically while the mouse left button is held down. When this change exceeds the smallest angle for turning the knob after an normalization operation to convert from screen position to knob angle, the knob will be turned by invoking the appropriate function. Also, the new knob position will be stored so that any further dragging of the mouse will be regarded as relative to this position. The moving of sliders and the pressing of buttons are simpler operations and are implemented in the same way.
4. **Visualization:** To make it as user friendly as possible, a red dot will be displayed when the mouse is over a control that has received focus. As shown in Figure 8, the

operation of turning a knob a slider, pressing a button, adjusting a slider and making a connection to a terminal can be done through simply dragging the mouse to move the relevant control when the control is in focus.

SUMMARY

The main functions and features of the experiment and laboratory can be summarized as follows.

1.   A 3D virtual laboratory controlling actual instruments and displaying real signals is implemented through a dynamic virtual scene in Java 3D. The laboratory has an oscilloscope, a signal generator, a battery, a circuit, a few cables, and some other visual objects.
2.   A navigation tool for walking around the virtual laboratory has been custom designed. Shown in Figure 6, the tool allows the user to move around the virtual laboratory and view instruments from different positions and directions in a very user friendly manner through the mouse.
3.   A collision detection mechanism is implemented. This guarantees that the viewing platform will not traverse any solid objects such as walls, doors, windows, tables, and virtual instruments.
4.   Through the appropriate picking function, the user can adjust individual controls on the virtual instruments and connect circuits in the same way as he or she operates an actual instrument in the real laboratory.
5.   The adjusted controls are converted into the relevant commands and sent to the instrument control server for implementation by real instruments in the actual physical laboratory. The result of the experiment is sent back by the server to the client to be displayed in the 3D virtual laboratory in real time.
6.   A lively outdoor scene with an island and a flying plane through the window of the virtual laboratory gives a good and realistic feeling of being in a real laboratory.

REFERENCES

Bund, S., & Do, E. Y. (2005). SPOT! fetch light: interactive Interactive navigable 3D visualization of direct sunlight. *Automation in Construction, 14*, 181-188.

Hobona, K., James, P., & Fairbairn, D. (2006). Web-based visualization of 3D geospatial data using Java3D. *IEEE Computer Graphics and Applications, 26*, 28-33.

Ko, C. C., Chen, B. M., Chen, J., Zhuang, Y., & Tan, K. C. (2001). Development of a Web-based laboratory for control experiments on a coupled tank apparatus. *IEEE Transactions on Education, 44*(1), 76-86.

Ko, C. C., Chen, B. M., Chen, S. H., Ramakrishnan, V., Chen, R., Hu, S. Y., & Zhuang, Y. (2000). A large scale Web-based virtual oscilloscope laboratory experiment. *IEE Engineering Science and Education Journal, 9*(2), 69-76.

Ko, C. C., Chen, B. M., Hu, S. Y., Ramakrishnan V., Cheng C. D., Zhuang, Y., & Chen, J. (2001). A Web-based virtual laboratory on a frequency modulation experiment. *IEEE Transactions on Systems, Man, and Cybernetics, Part C: Applications and Reviews, 31*(3), 295-303.

Liang, J. S. (2006). Conceptual design system in a Web-based virtual interactive environment for product development. *International Journal of Advanced Manufacturing Technology, 30,* 1010-1020.

Nielsen, J. F. (2006). A modular framework for development and interlaboratory sharing and validation of diffusion tensor tractography algorithms, *Journal of Digital Imaging, 19,* 112-117.

Oellien, F., Ihlenfeldt, W., & Gasteiger, J. (2005). InfVis—Platform-independent visual data mining of multidimensional chemical data sets. *Journal of Chemical Information and Modeling, 45,* 1456-1467.

Qin, S. F., Harrison, R., West, A. A., & Wright, D. K. (2004). Development of a novel 3D simulation modeling system for distributed manufacturing. *Computers in Industry, 54,* 69-81.

Ueda, M. (2006). Making of the simplest interactive 3D digital globe as a tool for the world environmental problems, *WSEAS Transactions on Environment and Development, 2,* 973-979.

Wang, L. (2006). J3D-based monitoring and control for e-ShopFloor. *International Journal of Manufacturing Technology and Management, 8,* 126-140.

Appendix A
Downloading Software

STEP 1: JDK BUNDLE

1. Visit "http://java.sun.com/j2se/1.4/download.html."
2. Click "Download J2SE SDK" and then "Accept License Agreement."
3. Click the "j2sdk-1_4_2_12-windows-i586-p.exe" link. Save the file in an appropriate directory, for instance the C:\ drive.
4. Once the download of the file is complete, double-click the "setup" icon.
5. Follow the setup instructions and install the software.

STEP 2: JCREATOR

1. Visit "http://www.jcreator.com."
2. Click the "DOWNLOAD AND TRY OUT JCREATOR" tab. On the next screen, click "the DOWNLOAD" button for JCreator LE v2.50.
3. In the dialog box that pops up, click the "Save to Disk" button and then click "OK" to save the file in the C:\ drive.
4. Once the download is complete, unzip JCrea250.zip.
5. After unzipping, close all applications and proceed to install the program by double-clicking the "setup" icon in the JCrea250 folder.
6. After the installation is complete, launch JCreator from the icon that has been created and placed on the desktop.

Figure 1. Setting the Classpath (Step 7)

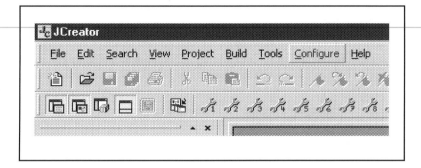

7. Next, to ensure that JCreator points to the JDK folder, click "Configure/Options/Editor" under "Configure" as illustrated in Figure 1.
8. Click JDK Profiles. As shown in Figure 2 in the JDK Profiles window that results, the default classpath of the selected JDK profile slot must contain appropriate information on the classpath. If this is not the case, click "JDK version 1.3" or "JDK version 1.4" profile at the top of the window.

Figure 2. Setting the Classpath (Step 8)

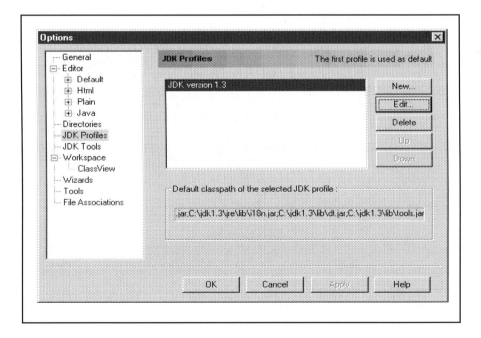

Figure 3. Setting the Classpath (Step 9)

Figure 4. Setting the Classpath (Step 10)

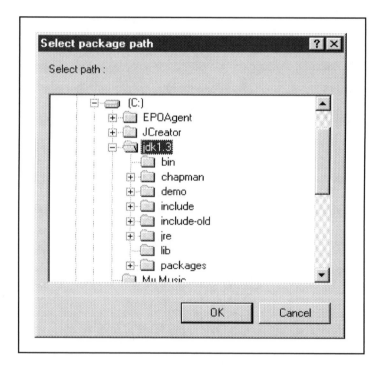

Figure 5. Setting the Classpath (Step 11)

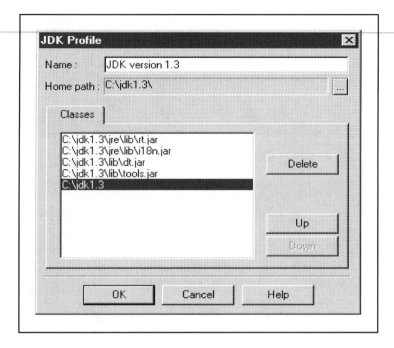

9. Click "Edit," and in the Classes window of Figure 3, click "Add."
10. Choose "Add Path." Select the folder containing the JDK documentation as illustrated in Figure 4 and then click "OK."
11. The selected JDK directory will now appear at the bottom of the list in the Classes window as depicted in Figure 5. Click "OK" to accept and, finally, "OK" in the original window.
12. The "Build" option from the menu in Figure A-1 can be used to compile and run a program. One may wish to explore this and other functions using some sample Java programs to ensure that the installation of the JDK bundle has been successfully carried out.

STEP 3: JAVA 3D API

1. Visit "http://java.sun.com/products/java-media/3D/downloads/."
2. Click the "1.4.0_01 API Download" tab. In the next screen, click the "DOWNLOAD" button under Download Java 3D API 1.4.0_01.

Figure 6. Installing Java3D API

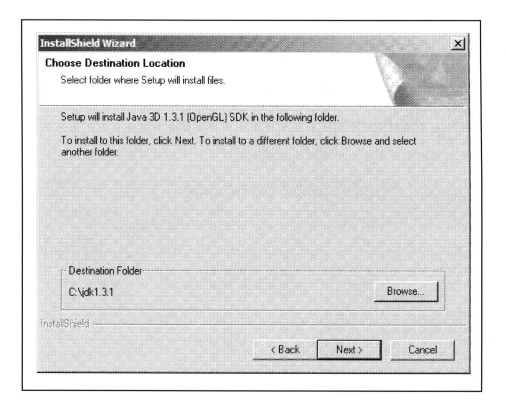

3. Click "Accept License Agreement" and then the "java3d-1_4_0_01-windows-i586. exe" link under Windows Platform - Java 3D API 1.4.0_01. Save in the C:\ drive.
4. Once the download is complete, run the setup process by double-clicking the "java3d-1_4_0_01-windows-i586" icon.
5. As illustrated in Figure A-6, install the Java3D API into the JDK or JRE folder. This step will automatically install all the j3d extensions into the respective JDK lib and bin folders.

Appendix B
Running the Rotating Cube Program

The following gives a step-by-step procedure for running the rotating cube example program presented in Chapter I.

STEP 1: LAUNCH JCREATOR

By doubling clicking the "JCreator" icon on the desktop, the JCreator IDE application can be launched. Figure 1 shows the main window of the application when no project has been created.

STEP 2: CREATE WORKSPACE AND PROJECT

To create a workspace for the editing, compiling and running of Java3D programs, select "File→New" on the menu of the main window. This is illustrated in Figure 2.

Subsequently, a dialog box as shown in Figure 3 will pop up. Click the "Projects" tab and select the "Empty Project" option. Enter an appropriate name for the project in the Project name textbox. In Figure 3, the project is named "FirstJava3D." Ensure that the "Create new workspace" option is checked and that the location at which the project will be saved is appropriate. Click "OK" when finished.

Figure 1. JCreator IDE application window

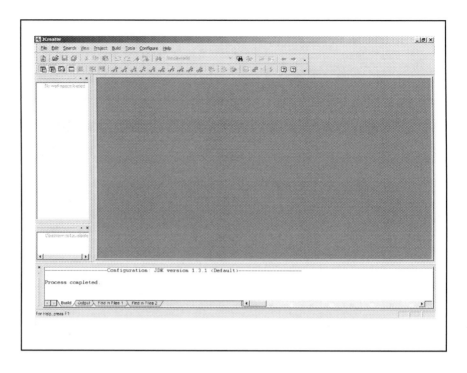

Figure 2. Create workspace

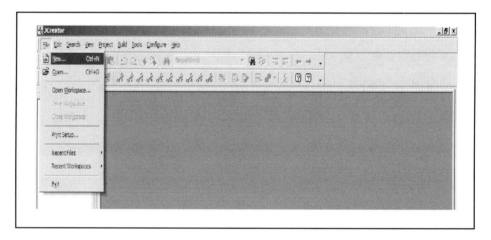

Figure 3. Create project

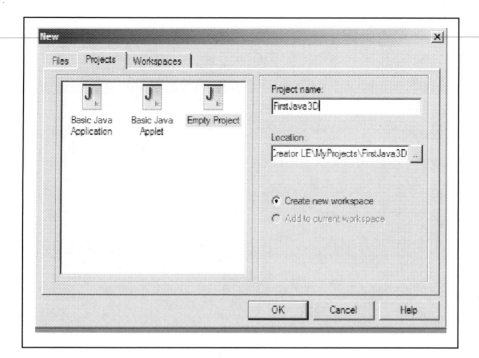

STEP 3: ADD JAVA FILES

After creating an empty workspace and project, we can proceed to add Java files to the project. Select "File→New" or use the keyboard shortcut "Ctrl+N." A dialog box, as shown in Figure 4 will appear. Under the "Files" tab, select the "Java File" option. Enter an appropriate "Filename" and "Location." Also ensure that that "Add to Project" box is checked before clicking "OK."

After carrying out the previous steps, the main window would now be as shown in Figure 5. By double-clicking "FirstJava3D," all the files created in the project workspace can be viewed. This includes of course the recently created "RotatingCube" Java file.

STEP 4: COPY AND EDIT CODES AND COMPILING

The program code on the Rotating Cube program in Chapter I can now be copied and pasted. After this and any appropriate editing has been completed, click the "Compile Project" button as highlighted in Figure 6.

Figure 4. Add files

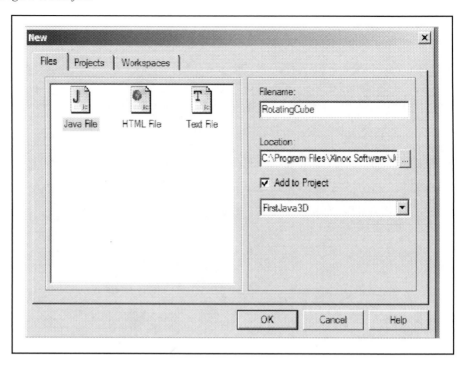

Figure 5. Main window after adding files

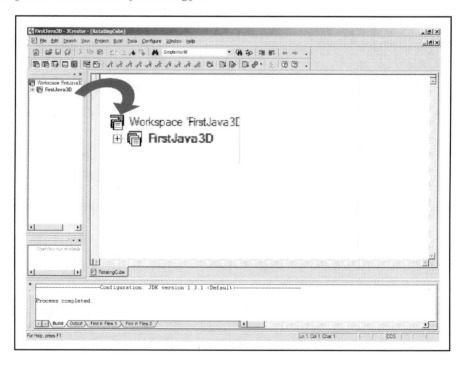

Figure 6. Compile program

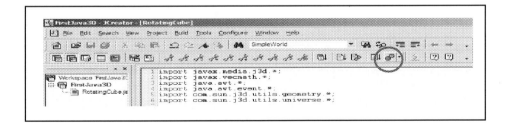

Figure 7. Compilation message

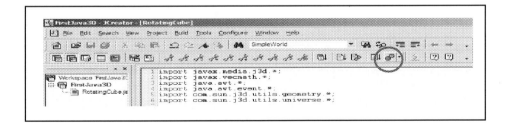

When any project has been successfully compiled, an appropriate message as shown in Figure 7 will appear at the bottom of the window. In particular, the Rotating Cube program in Chapter I should compile without any error.

STEP 5: BUILD AND EXECUTE PROGRAM

With a successful compilation, the program can be built and executed. This can be done by clicking the "Execute Project" icon as shown in Figure 8.

Figure 8. Build and execute program

Finally, as the program is executed, a rotating cube as shown in Figure 9 will appear.

Figure 9. Running program

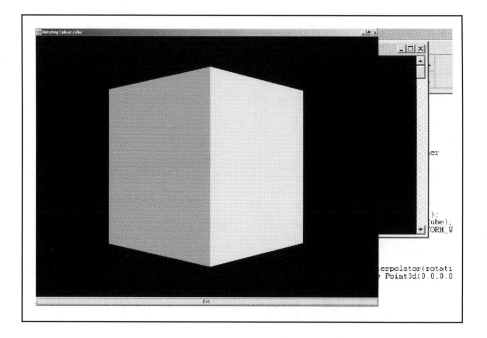

Appendix C
ViewManager

SWING COMPONENTS

Even though the focus of this book is on Java 3D, it is not possible to ignore the use of Swing components completely. This is because, ultimately, a Java 3D virtual world has to be displayed onto the screen using these. However, through using the ViewManager, a custom utility class, this distraction, or burden can be significantly relieved, resulting in codes that are more easily understandably.

ViewManager places each of the Canvas3D inside a JPanel with the title of the Canvas3D put at the border of that panel. If a Graphical User Interface (GUI) is required, ViewManager can be invoked to add a sub-JPpanel into the panel that holds the Canvas3D. The layout within each of the Canvas3D panels can be performed using BorderLayout, while the whole applet can be organized using GridBagLayout.

ViewManager

Figure 1 shows how ViewManager can be instantiated as well as an example.

If, in the example in Figure 1, the number of Canvas3D objects to be displayed is not equal to totalRows multiplied by totalColumns, ViewManager will use the value of totalColumns and wrap the Canvas3D objects accordingly. That is, if View Manager is requested to handle objects in a 1-row by 3-column fashion but there are four Canvas3D objects, the

Figure 1. ViewManager constructor and example

```
ViewManager (JApplet jApplet, int totalRows, int totalColumns);
//   jApplet - the JApplet that ViewManager should manage
//   totalRows - number of rows of Canvas3D objects to be displayed in jApplet
//   totalColumns - number of columns of Canvas3D objects to be displayed in jApplet

ViewManager viewManager = new ViewManager(this, 2, 2);
//   Current applet to display 4 Canvas3D objects in a 2 by 2 configuration
```

first three objects will be positioned in one row whereas the fourth one will in the second row below the first Canvas3D object.

ADDING Canvas3D

Figure 2 summarizes the usage and format of methods for adding Canvas3D objects.

Note that the methods shown can be broadly divided into three different groups. The first group adds Canvas3D objects without specifying locations, relying instead on ViewManager

Figure 2. Methods for adding Canvas3D objects

```
viewManager.add (Canvas3D canvas3D, String title);
viewManager.add (Canvas3D canvas3D, String title, JPanel jPanel);
viewManager.add (Canvas3D canvas3D, String title, JPanel jPanel, String location);
viewManager.add (Canvas3D canvas3D, String title, int index);
viewManager.add (Canvas3D canvas3D, String title, JPanel jPanel, int index);
viewManager.add (Canvas3D canvas3D, String title, JPanel jPanel, String location, int index);
viewManager.add (Canvas3D canvas3D, String title, int row, int column);
viewManager.add (Canvas3D canvas3D, String title, JPanel jPanel, int row, int column);
viewManager.add (Canvas3D canvas3D, String title, JPanel jPanel, String location, int row, int
     column);
// canvas3D - Canvas3D to be added into the applet
// title - title to identify the Canvas3D
// jPanel - additional panel for holding, say, the Panel1 controls, to be added into the Panel1
// location – may be ViewManager.TOP_CONTROL, ViewManager.RIGHT_CONTROL,
//     ViewManager.BOTTOM_CONTROL or ViewManager.LEFT_CONTROL for specifying
//     the position for adding jPanel with respect to the Canvas3D
// row      - specify the row for adding the Canvas3D
// column - specify the column for adding the Canvas3D
// index    - specify the index of the Canvas3D to be added
```

to place the objects automatically. The second group is based on the index of the Canvas3D object to being added. Using this, we can control the sequence of the Canvas3D objects to be added into the applet. The last group allows complete control on where Canvas3D should be added, through the row and column of the position of the Canvas3D in the applet.

In the methods for each group, the first one allows one to add just the Canvas3D and its title. The second one has the additional ability to add a JPanel into the panel that holds the Canvas3D, with a default position that is below the Canvas3D. With the third method in each group, we can even specify the position of the JPanel with respect to the Canvas3D.

Most applications will however use just the first method, as ViewManager can also be used to create the control panel. Nevertheless, the other two methods can also be invoked to construct a JPanel manually if the needs arise. Note that all of the methods will return the JPanel that holds the Canvas3D. This gives the handle for any further modifications to be made.

As a usage example, if viewManager is an instantiated object of ViewManager, and there is a need to add a Canvas3D canvas3D with the title "test," we can use the method

    viewManager.add(canvas3D, "test");

This can be repeated to add other Canvas3D objects into the applet. ViewManager will automatically position the Canvas3D, starting from the top left corner of the applet.

ADDING CONTROL PANEL

As previously mentioned, ViewManager allows for the addition of a control panel for each Canvas3D. However, instead of performing this through the constructor, the SetControlPanel method illustrated in Figure 3 can also be used for this purpose.

Note that since ViewManager will only help in positioning, the control panel must be fully programmed before it is added to the Canvas3D.

Figure 3. setControlPanel method of ViewManager

```
void viewManager.setControlPanel(JPanel jPanel);
void viewManager.setControlPanel(JPanel jPanel, String location);
// jPanel - panel to be added to the most recently added Canvas3D
// location – may be ViewManager.TOP_CONTROL, ViewManager.RIGHT_CONTROL,
//    ViewManager.BOTTOM_CONTROL or ViewManager.LEFT_CONTROL for
//    specifying the position for adding jPanel with respect to the Canvas3D
```

Yet another way is add a control panel is to use ViewManager to create an empty panel first and then add the controls later. The method that can be used for this purpose is illustrated in Figure 4.

Invoking createControlPanel() without any parameter will create a control panel at defaults given by location = ViewManager.BOTTOM_CONTROL, row = 1, and column = 3. Although this default is only for 3 controls in a single row, more controls can in fact be added through the usual wrapping process.

Note however that the setControlPanel and createControlPanel methods are applicable only to the last Canvas3D added. Also, each Canvas3D can only have one control panel. Thus, invoking one of these methods will overwrite any control panel that has been set or created earlier.

Figure 4. createControlPanel method of ViewManager

```
JPanel viewManager.createControlPanel();
JPanel viewManager.createControlPanel(int row, int column);
JPanel viewManager.createControlPanel(String location, int row, int column);
//   location – May be ViewManager.TOP_CONTROL, ViewManager.RIGHT_CONTROL,
//      ViewManager.BOTTOM_CONTROL or ViewManager.LEFT_CONTROL
//      specifying the position for the jPanel to be added with respect to the Canvas3D
//   row - total number of rows of controls to be added
//   column - total number of columns of the controls to be added
```

Figure 5. Using ViewManager correctly

```
1.        viewManager.add(canvas3D1, "canvas3D1");
2.        viewManager.createControlPanel();
3.        viewManager.add(canvas3D2, "canvas3D2");
4.        viewManager.createControlPanel():
```

Figure 6. Using ViewManager incorrectly

```
1.        viewManager.add(canvas3D1, "canvas3D1");
2.        viewManager.add(canvas3D2, "canvas3D2");
3.        viewManager.createControlPanel();
4.        viewManager.createControlPanel():
```

As an example, Figure 5 shows how two Canvas3D, canvas3D1 and canvas3D2 with a control panel each, can be added to viewManager, an instantiated object of ViewManager.

If the code sequence is in the wrong order as illustrated in Figure 6, an error will result. Specifically, this code segment will add canvas3D1 without any control panel, while canvas3D2 will have only one control panel. This is despite the two attempts to create two control panels, with the second one overwriting the first one.

ADDING CONTROLS

Since ViewManager only helps us to position the controls for a Canvas3D object, the creation of these controls and their ActionListener have to be carried out manually. Note that, in this process, we need to invoke the createControlPanel method first. Specifically, the addControl methods illustrated in Figure 7 can only be used in conjunction with the appropriate createControlPanel method. The setControlPanel method cannot be used for the addition of controls.

Figure 7. addControl method summary

```
JComponent viewManager.addControl(JComponent jComponent);
JComponent viewManager.addControl(JComponent jComponent, int height, int width);
JComponent viewManager.addControl(JComponent jComponent, int index);
JComponent viewManager.addControl(JComponent jComponent, int index, int height, int width);
JComponent viewManager.addControl(JComponent jComponent, int row, int column, int height,
//                                  int width);
//  jComponent – an object from JComponent or any of its subclasses to be added
//  index - index of the jComponent with respect to other jComponent objects
//  row - row for adding jComponent, with respect to other jComponent objects
//  column - column for adding jComponent, with respect to other jComponent objects
//  height - number of rows jComponent would stretch across
//  width - number of columns jComponent would stretch across
```

Figure 8. Using addControl

```
1.      viewManager.addControl (title, 1, 3);
2.      viewManager.addControl (minus);
3.      viewmanager.addControl (value);
4.      viewManager.addControl (plus);
```

JComponent has many subclasses and two or more commonly used ones are JLabel and JButtons, the usage of which are given in the Java API.

As an example, suppose viewManager is an instantiated object of ViewManager, a Canvas3D object has been added, and an createControlPanel method has been invoked. Then, the code segment in Figure 8 will add a JLabel title that stretches over three columns, a JButton minus, a JLabel value, and a JButton plus. Specifically, ViewManager will position the JLabel title in the first row and have it stretch over three columns, and place the other controls in the second row, in the order of minus, value, and plus.

GETTING OPTIMUM WIDTH AND HEIGHT

The optimum width and height of the applet, or the width and height without stretching, can be obtained by using the methods in Figure 9.

These methods are particularly useful when it is used together with the MainFrame utility class that allows applets to be run as applications. An example code segment is provided in Figure 10. The lines are from the main method of ViewModelApp, which uses the MainFrame utility class to enable it to be run as an application. Here, ViewManager is called using viewModel.viewManager because only the ViewManager object that has been used to manage the application layout is able to return the correct width and height. A new instance of ViewManager created in the main method will not be able to return the correct width and height.

Figure 9. Methods for getting applet size

```
int viewManager.getOptimumFrameWidth();
int viewManager.getOptimumFrameHeight();
```

Figure 10. ViewManager and Mainframe

```
1.     ViewModelApp viewModel = new ViewModelApp();
2.     Frame frame = new MainFrame( viewModel,
3.             viewModel.viewManager.getOptimumFrameWidth(),
4.             viewModel.viewManager.getOptimumFrameHeight() );
```

FRAME CENTERING

This method shown in Figure 11 places the frame in the centre of the screen, and can be used in conjunction with the MainFrame utility class. The line, which uses ViewManager to place the frame in the centre of the screen, is taken from the main method in View-ModelApp. The object frame is an instance of MainFrame that holds the viewModel, an instance of ViewModel.

GETTING CONFIGURATION FOR Canvas3D

Figure 12 illustrates the method that can be used to return the GraphicsConfiguration that can be used for Canvas3D. Note that a warning will be given if Canvas3D is instantiated using null for its GraphicsConfiguration.

Figure 11. palceInScreenCenter method

```
viewModel.viewManager.placeInScreenCenter(frame);
```

Figure 12. GraphicsConfiguration

```
1.      GraphicsConfiguration config = viewManager.getPreferredGraphicsConfiguration();
2.      Canvas3D canvas3D = new Canvas3D(config);
```

Appendix D
Main Applet for Web–Based 3D Experiment

D.1 IMPORTING LIBRARIES

```
import java.awt.BorderLayout;
import java.applet.Applet;
import java.awt.event.*;
import com.sun.j3d.utils.applet.MainFrame;
import com.sun.j3d.utils.universe.*;
import javax.media.j3d.*;
import com.sun.j3d.utils.image.TextureLoader;
import java.net.*;
import javax.swing.*;
import java.awt.*;
```

D.2 MAIN APPLET FOR CREATING ALL OBJECTS IN LABORATORY

```
public class Oscilloscope extends Applet implements ActionListener
{
    // ---------------------------Osci
    private java.net.URL Ch1 = null;
    private java.net.URL Ch2 = null;
    private java.net.URL Vposi = null;
    private java.net.URL Mode = null;
    private java.net.URL Volts = null;
```

```
private java.net.URL Source = null;
private java.net.URL Sync = null;
private java.net.URL Ac = null;
private java.net.URL Add = null;
private java.net.URL Hposi = null;
private java.net.URL Vdiv = null;
private java.net.URL Trig = null;
private java.net.URL Tdiv = null;
private java.net.URL Focus = null;
private java.net.URL Intensity = null;
private java.net.URL Blank = null;
private java.net.URL Cal = null;
private java.net.URL Input = null;
private java.net.URL Output = null;
private java.net.URL Line = null;
private java.net.URL Gnd = null;
private java.net.URL Branch = null;
// ----------------------------Sg
private java.net.URL Case = null;
private java.net.URL Backside = null;
private java.net.URL Leftside = null;
private java.net.URL Rightside = null;
private java.net.URL Calconnector = null;
private java.net.URL Power = null;
private java.net.URL Left = null;
private java.net.URL Right = null;
private java.net.URL Wave = null;
private java.net.URL Amp = null;
private java.net.URL Freq = null;
private java.net.URL switcher = null;
private java.net.URL Dot = null;
private java.net.URL Battery = null;

// ----------------------------Pass
private java.net.URL brick = null;
private java.net.URL floor = null;
private java.net.URL ceiling = null;
private java.net.URL Door = null;
private java.net.URL Desk = null;
private java.net.URL Desk1 = null;
private java.net.URL Outside01 = null;
private java.net.URL Outside02 = null;
private java.net.URL Airbus01 = null;
private java.net.URL Picture01 = null;
private java.net.URL Picture02 = null;
private java.net.URL Picture03 = null;
private java.net.URL Picture04 = null;
private java.net.URL Vlabposter01 = null;
private java.net.URL Vlabposter02 = null;
private java.net.URL Vlabname = null;
private java.net.URL D0 = null;
private java.net.URL D1 = null;
```

```
private java.net.URL D2 = null;
private java.net.URL D3 = null;
private java.net.URL D4 = null;
private java.net.URL D5 = null;
private java.net.URL D6 = null;
private java.net.URL D7 = null;
private java.net.URL D8 = null;
private java.net.URL D9 = null;
private java.net.URL C = null;
private java.net.URL OK = null;
private java.net.URL Yellowplug = null;
private java.net.URL Redplug = null;
private java.net.URL Blueplug = null;
private java.net.URL Greenplug = null;
private java.net.URL image = null;
private java.net.URL image1 = null;
private URL helpfile = null;
private java.net.URL cir_board = null;


// -----------------------------------------------------
private View view = null;
private SimpleUniverse u = null;
private Scene3D scene3d = null;
private static final int VIRTUAL_EYE = 2;
private OPanel panel;
```

D.3 INITIALIZATION FUNCTION FOR MAIN APPLET

```
public void init()
{
  setLayout(new BorderLayout());
  Canvas3D c = new Canvas3D(SimpleUniverse.getPreferredConfiguration());
  add("Center", c);

  timerField timer = new timerField(4);
  String path = getCodeBase().toString();

  LoadPanel();
  panel = new OPanel(image, image1, timer); //Loading the panel of the 2D part
  add("South", panel);
  panel.Forward.addActionListener(this);

    LoadCir_Board();
    scene3d = new Scene3D(cir_board);              //Loading the the 3D part

    scene3d.setPanel(panel);//Loading the the 3D part
    LoadTextured();
    u = new SimpleUniverse(c);
    BranchGroup scene = scene3d.createSceneGraph(u, c);
    u.addBranchGraph(scene);
```

```
        view = u.getViewer().getView();
        view.setFrontClipPolicy(VIRTUAL_EYE);
        view.setFrontClipDistance(0.05);
        view.setWindowResizePolicy(1);
        view.setWindowMovementPolicy(1); //Modifying the view parameters
    }
```

D.4 DESTROYING FUNCTION FOR MAIN APPLET

```
    public void destroy()
    {
        if (scene3d!=null)
            scene3d.closeAll();
        u.removeAllLocales();

    }
```

D.5 LOADING VRML BASED CIRCUIT BOARD OBJECT FOR MAIN APPLET

```
    public void LoadCir_Board()
    {
        try {
            cir_board =  new java.net.URL(getCodeBase().toString()+"models/Battary.WRL");
        } catch (java.net.MalformedURLException ex) {
            System.out.println(ex.getMessage());
            System.exit(1);
        }

    }
```

D.6 LOADING PICTURES FOR 3D WALLS AND ENVIRONMENT FOR MAIN APPLET

```
    public void LoadPanel()
    {
        try {
            image = new java.net.URL(getCodeBase().toString()+"images/rectangle.jpg");
        } catch (java.net.MalformedURLException ex) {
            System.out.println(ex.getMessage());
            System.exit(1);
        }
        try {
            image1 =  new java.net.URL(getCodeBase().toString()+"images/rotate.jpg");
        } catch (java.net.MalformedURLException ex) {
```

```
                System.out.println(ex.getMessage());
                System.exit(1);
        }
}
```

D.7 DEFINIG USUAL FUNCTION FOR KEYBOARD AND MOUSE INPUTS FOR MAIN APPLET

```
public void actionPerformed(ActionEvent event)
{
        /*
        if (event.getSource()==panel.Forward)
        {
                try{
                        helpfile = new URL(getCodeBase().toString() + "vrosciexp1.html");
                } catch(java.net.MalformedURLException ex) {
                        System.out.println(ex.getMessage());
                        System.exit(1);
                }
                getAppletContext().showDocument(helpfile,"help");
        }
        */
}
```

D.8 LOADING PICTURES FOR DEFINING TEXTURE ON INSTRUMENTS FOR MAIN APPLET

```
public void LoadTextured()
{
        // -----------------------------------------------------------Osci
        try {
                Ch1 = new java.net.URL(getCodeBase().toString() + "images/Ch1.gif");
        } catch (java.net.MalformedURLException ex) {
                System.out.println(ex.getMessage());
                System.exit(1);
        }
        scene3d.Ch1 = new TextureLoader(Ch1, this).getTexture();
        try {
                Ch2 = new java.net.URL(getCodeBase().toString() + "images/Ch2.gif");
        } catch (java.net.MalformedURLException ex) {
                System.out.println(ex.getMessage());
                System.exit(1);
        }
        scene3d.Ch2 = new TextureLoader(Ch2, this).getTexture();
        try {
                Vposi = new java.net.URL(getCodeBase().toString() + "images/Vposi.gif");
```

```
        } catch (java.net.MalformedURLException ex) {
            System.out.println(ex.getMessage());
            System.exit(1);
        }
    scene3d.Vposi = new TextureLoader(Vposi, this).getTexture();
    try {
            Mode = new java.net.URL(getCodeBase().toString() + "images/Mode.gif");
        } catch (java.net.MalformedURLException ex) {
            System.out.println(ex.getMessage());
            System.exit(1);
        }
    scene3d.Mode = new TextureLoader(Mode, this).getTexture();
    try {
            Volts = new java.net.URL(getCodeBase().toString() + "images/Volts.gif");
        } catch (java.net.MalformedURLException ex) {
            System.out.println(ex.getMessage());
            System.exit(1);
        }
    scene3d.Volts = new TextureLoader(Volts, this).getTexture();
    try {
            Source = new java.net.URL(getCodeBase().toString() + "images/Source.gif");
        } catch (java.net.MalformedURLException ex) {
            System.out.println(ex.getMessage());
            System.exit(1);
        }
    scene3d.Source = new TextureLoader(Source, this).getTexture();
    try {
            Sync = new java.net.URL(getCodeBase().toString() + "images/Sync.gif");
        } catch (java.net.MalformedURLException ex) {
            System.out.println(ex.getMessage());
            System.exit(1);
        }
    scene3d.Sync = new TextureLoader(Sync, this).getTexture();
    try {
            Ac = new java.net.URL(getCodeBase().toString() + "images/Ac.gif");
        } catch (java.net.MalformedURLException ex) {
            System.out.println(ex.getMessage());
            System.exit(1);
        }
    scene3d.Ac = new TextureLoader(Ac, this).getTexture();
    try {
            Add = new java.net.URL(getCodeBase().toString() + "images/Add.gif");
        } catch (java.net.MalformedURLException ex) {
            System.out.println(ex.getMessage());
            System.exit(1);
        }
    scene3d.Add = new TextureLoader(Add, this).getTexture();
    try {
            Hposi = new java.net.URL(getCodeBase().toString() + "images/Hposi.gif");
        } catch (java.net.MalformedURLException ex) {
            System.out.println(ex.getMessage());
            System.exit(1);
```

```
        }
        scene3d.Hposi = new TextureLoader(Hposi, this).getTexture();
        try {
                Vdiv = new java.net.URL(getCodeBase().toString() + "images/Vdiv.gif");
        } catch (java.net.MalformedURLException ex) {
                System.out.println(ex.getMessage());
                System.exit(1);
        }
        scene3d.Vdiv = new TextureLoader(Vdiv, this).getTexture();
        try {
                Trig = new java.net.URL(getCodeBase().toString() + "images/Trig.gif");
        } catch (java.net.MalformedURLException ex) {
                System.out.println(ex.getMessage());
                System.exit(1);
        }
        scene3d.Trig = new TextureLoader(Trig, this).getTexture();
        try {
                Tdiv = new java.net.URL(getCodeBase().toString() + "images/Tdiv.gif");
        } catch (java.net.MalformedURLException ex) {
                System.out.println(ex.getMessage());
                System.exit(1);
        }
        scene3d.Tdiv = new TextureLoader(Tdiv, this).getTexture();
        try {
                Focus = new java.net.URL(getCodeBase().toString() + "images/Focus.gif");
        } catch (java.net.MalformedURLException ex) {
                System.out.println(ex.getMessage());
                System.exit(1);
        }
        scene3d.Focus = new TextureLoader(Focus, this).getTexture();
        try {
                Intensity = new java.net.URL(getCodeBase().toString() + "images/Intensity.gif");
        } catch (java.net.MalformedURLException ex) {
                System.out.println(ex.getMessage());
                System.exit(1);
        }
        scene3d.Intensity = new TextureLoader(Intensity, this).getTexture();
        try {
                Blank = new java.net.URL(getCodeBase().toString() + "images/Blank.gif");
        } catch (java.net.MalformedURLException ex) {
                System.out.println(ex.getMessage());
                System.exit(1);
        }
        scene3d.Blank = new TextureLoader(Blank, this).getTexture();
        try {
                Cal = new java.net.URL(getCodeBase().toString() + "images/Cal.gif");
        } catch (java.net.MalformedURLException ex) {
                System.out.println(ex.getMessage());
                System.exit(1);
        }
        scene3d.Cal = new TextureLoader(Cal, this).getTexture();
        try {
```

```
            Input = new java.net.URL(getCodeBase().toString() + "images/Input.gif");
        } catch (java.net.MalformedURLException ex) {
            System.out.println(ex.getMessage());
            System.exit(1);
        }
        scene3d.Input = new TextureLoader(Input, this).getTexture();
        try {
            Output = new java.net.URL(getCodeBase().toString() + "images/Output01.gif");
        } catch (java.net.MalformedURLException ex) {
            System.out.println(ex.getMessage());
            System.exit(1);
        }
        scene3d.Output = new TextureLoader(Output, this).getTexture();
        try {
            Gnd = new java.net.URL(getCodeBase().toString() + "images/Gnd.gif");
        } catch (java.net.MalformedURLException ex) {
            System.out.println(ex.getMessage());
            System.exit(1);
        }
        scene3d.Gnd = new TextureLoader(Gnd, this).getTexture();
        // -------------------------------------------------------Sg
        try {
            Case = new java.net.URL(getCodeBase().toString() + "images/Case.jpg");
        } catch (java.net.MalformedURLException ex) {
            System.out.println(ex.getMessage());
            System.exit(1);
        }
        scene3d.Case = new TextureLoader(Case, this).getTexture();
        try {
            Backside = new java.net.URL(getCodeBase().toString() + "images/Backside.gif");
        } catch (java.net.MalformedURLException ex) {
            System.out.println(ex.getMessage());
            System.exit(1);
        }
        scene3d.Backside = new TextureLoader(Backside, this).getTexture();
        try {
            Rightside = new java.net.URL(getCodeBase().toString() + "images/Rightside.gif");
        } catch (java.net.MalformedURLException ex) {
            System.out.println(ex.getMessage());
            System.exit(1);
        }
        scene3d.Rightside = new TextureLoader(Rightside, this).getTexture();
        try {
            Leftside = new java.net.URL(getCodeBase().toString() + "images/Leftside.gif");
        } catch (java.net.MalformedURLException ex) {
            System.out.println(ex.getMessage());
            System.exit(1);
        }
        scene3d.Leftside = new TextureLoader(Leftside, this).getTexture();
        try {
        Calconnector = new java.net.URL(getCodeBase().toString() + "images/connector.gif");
        } catch (java.net.MalformedURLException ex) {
```

```
                    System.out.println(ex.getMessage());
                    System.exit(1);
            }
            scene3d.Calconnector = new TextureLoader(Calconnector, this).getTexture();
            try {
                    Power = new java.net.URL(getCodeBase().toString() + "images/Power.gif");
            } catch (java.net.MalformedURLException ex) {
                    System.out.println(ex.getMessage());
                    System.exit(1);
            }
            scene3d.Power = new TextureLoader(Power, this).getTexture();
            try {
                    Left = new java.net.URL(getCodeBase().toString() + "images/Left.gif");
            } catch (java.net.MalformedURLException ex) {
                    System.out.println(ex.getMessage());
                    System.exit(1);
            }
            scene3d.Left = new TextureLoader(Left, this).getTexture();
            try {
                    Right = new java.net.URL(getCodeBase().toString() + "images/Right.gif");
            } catch (java.net.MalformedURLException ex) {
                    System.out.println(ex.getMessage());
                    System.exit(1);
            }
            scene3d.Right = new TextureLoader(Right, this).getTexture();
            try {
                    Wave = new java.net.URL(getCodeBase().toString() + "images/Wave.gif");
            } catch (java.net.MalformedURLException ex) {
                    System.out.println(ex.getMessage());
                    System.exit(1);
            }
            scene3d.Wave = new TextureLoader(Wave, this).getTexture();
            try {
                    Amp = new java.net.URL(getCodeBase().toString() + "images/Amp.gif");
            } catch (java.net.MalformedURLException ex) {
                    System.out.println(ex.getMessage());
                    System.exit(1);
            }
            scene3d.Amp = new TextureLoader(Amp, this).getTexture();
            try {
                    Freq = new java.net.URL(getCodeBase().toString() + "images/Freq.gif");
            } catch (java.net.MalformedURLException ex) {
                    System.out.println(ex.getMessage());
                    System.exit(1);
            }
            scene3d.Freq = new TextureLoader(Freq, this).getTexture();
            try {
                    switcher = new java.net.URL(getCodeBase().toString() + "images/switcher.gif");
            } catch (java.net.MalformedURLException ex) {
                    System.out.println(ex.getMessage());
                    System.exit(1);
            }
```

```
scene3d.switcher = new TextureLoader(switcher, this).getTexture();
try {
      Dot = new java.net.URL(getCodeBase().toString() + "images/Plug02.gif");
} catch (java.net.MalformedURLException ex) {
      System.out.println(ex.getMessage());
      System.exit(1);
}
scene3d.Dot = new TextureLoader(Dot, this).getTexture();
try {
      Redplug = new java.net.URL(getCodeBase().toString() + "images/redplug.gif");
} catch (java.net.MalformedURLException ex) {
      System.out.println(ex.getMessage());
      System.exit(1);
}
scene3d.Redplug = new TextureLoader(Redplug, this).getTexture();
try {
Greenplug = new java.net.URL(getCodeBase().toString() + "images/greenplug.gif");
} catch (java.net.MalformedURLException ex) {
      System.out.println(ex.getMessage());
      System.exit(1);
}
scene3d.Greenplug = new TextureLoader(Greenplug, this).getTexture();
try {
      Blueplug = new java.net.URL(getCodeBase().toString() + "images/blueplug.gif");
} catch (java.net.MalformedURLException ex) {
      System.out.println(ex.getMessage());
      System.exit(1);
}
scene3d.Blueplug = new TextureLoader(Blueplug, this).getTexture();
try {
Yellowplug = new java.net.URL(getCodeBase().toString() + "images/yellowplug.gif");
} catch (java.net.MalformedURLException ex) {
      System.out.println(ex.getMessage());
      System.exit(1);
}
scene3d.Yellowplug = new TextureLoader(Yellowplug, this).getTexture();
// ------------------------------------------------------------Pass
try {
      brick = new java.net.URL(getCodeBase().toString() + "images/Wall.jpg");
} catch (java.net.MalformedURLException ex) {
      System.out.println(ex.getMessage());
      System.exit(1);
}
scene3d.brick = new TextureLoader(brick, this).getTexture();
try {
      floor = new java.net.URL(getCodeBase().toString() + "images/Floor.jpg");
} catch (java.net.MalformedURLException ex) {
      System.out.println(ex.getMessage());
      System.exit(1);
}
scene3d.texfloor = new TextureLoader(floor, this).getTexture();
try {
```

```
            ceiling = new java.net.URL(getCodeBase().toString() + "images/Ceiling.jpg");
    } catch (java.net.MalformedURLException ex) {
            System.out.println(ex.getMessage());
            System.exit(1);
    }
    scene3d.ceiling = new TextureLoader(ceiling, this).getTexture();
    try {
            Door = new java.net.URL(getCodeBase().toString() + "images/Door.gif");
    } catch (java.net.MalformedURLException ex) {
            System.out.println(ex.getMessage());
            System.exit(1);
    }
    scene3d.Door = new TextureLoader(Door, this).getTexture();
    try {
            Desk = new java.net.URL(getCodeBase().toString() + "images/Desk.jpg");
    } catch (java.net.MalformedURLException ex) {
            System.out.println(ex.getMessage());
            System.exit(1);
    }
    scene3d.Desk = new TextureLoader(Desk, this).getTexture();
    try {
            Desk1 = new java.net.URL(getCodeBase().toString() + "images/Desk1.jpg");
    } catch (java.net.MalformedURLException ex) {
            System.out.println(ex.getMessage());
            System.exit(1);
    }
    scene3d.Desk1 = new TextureLoader(Desk1, this).getTexture();
    try {
            Outside01 = new java.net.URL(getCodeBase().toString() + "images/Outside.jpg");
    } catch (java.net.MalformedURLException ex) {
            System.out.println(ex.getMessage());
            System.exit(1);
    }
    scene3d.Outside01 = new TextureLoader(Outside01, this).getTexture();
    try {
     Outside02 = new java.net.URL(getCodeBase().toString() + "images/Outside02.gif");
    } catch (java.net.MalformedURLException ex) {
            System.out.println(ex.getMessage());
            System.exit(1);
    }
    scene3d.Outside02 = new TextureLoader(Outside02, this).getTexture();
    try {
            Airbus01 = new java.net.URL(getCodeBase().toString() + "images/Airbus01.gif");
    } catch (java.net.MalformedURLException ex) {
            System.out.println(ex.getMessage());
            System.exit(1);
    }
    scene3d.Airbus01 = new TextureLoader(Airbus01, this).getTexture();
    try {
            Picture01 = new java.net.URL(getCodeBase().toString() + "images/Picture01.jpg");
    } catch (java.net.MalformedURLException ex) {
            System.out.println(ex.getMessage());
```

```
            System.exit(1);
      }
      scene3d.Picture01 = new TextureLoader(Picture01, this).getTexture();
      try {
            Picture02 = new java.net.URL(getCodeBase().toString() + "images/Picture02.jpg");
      } catch (java.net.MalformedURLException ex) {
            System.out.println(ex.getMessage());
            System.exit(1);
      }
      scene3d.Picture02 = new TextureLoader(Picture02, this).getTexture();
      try {
            Picture03 = new java.net.URL(getCodeBase().toString() + "images/Picture03.jpg");
      } catch (java.net.MalformedURLException ex) {
            System.out.println(ex.getMessage());
            System.exit(1);
      }
      scene3d.Picture03 = new TextureLoader(Picture03, this).getTexture();
      try {
            Picture04 = new java.net.URL(getCodeBase().toString() + "images/Picture04.jpg");
      } catch (java.net.MalformedURLException ex) {
            System.out.println(ex.getMessage());
            System.exit(1);
      }
      scene3d.Picture04 = new TextureLoader(Picture04, this).getTexture();
      try {
      Vlabposter01 = new java.net.URL(getCodeBase().toString() + "images/Vlabposter01.jpg");
      } catch (java.net.MalformedURLException ex) {
            System.out.println(ex.getMessage());
            System.exit(1);
      }
      scene3d.Vlabposter01 = new TextureLoader(Vlabposter01, this).getTexture();
      try {
      Vlabposter02 = new java.net.URL(getCodeBase().toString() + "images/Vlabposter02.jpg");
      } catch (java.net.MalformedURLException ex) {
            System.out.println(ex.getMessage());
            System.exit(1);
      }
      scene3d.Vlabposter02 = new TextureLoader(Vlabposter02, this).getTexture();
      try {
       Vlabname = new java.net.URL(getCodeBase().toString() + "images/Vlabname.gif");
      } catch (java.net.MalformedURLException ex) {
            System.out.println(ex.getMessage());
            System.exit(1);
      }
      scene3d.Vlabname = new TextureLoader(Vlabname, this).getTexture();
      try {
            C = new java.net.URL(getCodeBase().toString() + "images/c.gif");
      } catch (java.net.MalformedURLException ex) {
            System.out.println(ex.getMessage());
            System.exit(1);
      }
      scene3d.C = new TextureLoader(C, this).getTexture();
```

```
        try {
                OK = new java.net.URL(getCodeBase().toString() + "images/ok.gif");
        } catch (java.net.MalformedURLException ex) {
                System.out.println(ex.getMessage());
                System.exit(1);
        }
        scene3d.OK = new TextureLoader(OK, this).getTexture();

}
```

D.9 DEFINING COUNTDOWN TIMER OBJECT FOR GIVING REMAINING TIME FOR MAIN APPLET

```
class timerField extends JTextField implements Runnable
{
        private boolean running = false;
        private Thread timerThread;

        public timerField(int col)
        {
                setColumns(col);
                setEditable(false);
                //setBackground(Color.white);
                //setBounds(1, 1, 20, 20);
                running = true;
                timerThread = new Thread(this);
                timerThread.start();
        }

        public void run()
        {
                int min, sec;
                String minute, second;
                long startTime, currentTime;

                startTime = System.currentTimeMillis();
                while (running)
                {
                        currentTime = System.currentTimeMillis();
                        min = Math.round((currentTime - startTime) / 60000L);
                        sec = Math.round((currentTime - startTime - min * 60000L) / 1000);
                        minute = Integer.toString(min);
                        second = Integer.toString(sec);
                        if (minute.length() < 2) {
                                minute = "0" + minute;
                        }
                        if (second.length() < 2) {
                                second = "0" + second;
                        }
                        setText(""+minute+":"+second);
```

```
            if (min==29&&sec==59)
            {
                if (scene3d!=null)
                    scene3d.closeAll();
                running = false;
            }
            try {
                timerThread.sleep(1000);
            } catch (Exception ie) {
                System.out.println("Interrupted Exception!");
            }
        }
    }
}
```

D.10 ENTRY FOR MAIN APPLET

```
// The following allows it to be run as an application as well as an applet
public static void main(String[] args)
    {
    new MainFrame(new Oscilloscope(), 1024, 600);
    }
}
```

Appendix E
Scene Graph Implementation for Web–Based 3D Experiment

E.1 IMPORTING LIBRARIES

```
import java.awt.*;
import javax.media.j3d.*;
import javax.vecmath.*;
import com.sun.j3d.utils.universe.*;
import com.sun.j3d.utils.picking.PickTool;
import com.sun.j3d.loaders.vrml97.VrmlLoader;
import com.sun.j3d.loaders.ParsingErrorException;
import com.sun.j3d.loaders.IncorrectFormatException;
import com.sun.j3d.loaders.Scene;
import java.io.*;
```

E.2 DEFINING CLASS

```
public class Scene3D
{
    // Create a bounds for the behavior methods
    private BoundingSphere bounds = new BoundingSphere(new Point3d(0.0,0.0,0.0), 100.0);

    private static final float PAI = 3.14159f;
    private static final float ANGLEPAI = 2.0f*PAI/360.0f;;
```

```
private static final float TRACKWIDTH = 0.06f;

private OPanel panel;
private Appearance appimage = null;
private PickingBehavior pickingbehavior=null;

    // ----------------------Osci
    Texture texture = null;
    Texture Ch1 = null;
    Texture Ch2 = null;
    Texture Vposi = null;
    Texture Mode = null;
    Texture Volts = null;
    Texture Source = null;
    Texture Sync = null;
    Texture Ac = null;
    Texture Add = null;
    Texture Hposi = null;
    Texture Vdiv = null;
    Texture Trig = null;
    Texture Tdiv = null;
    Texture Focus = null;
    Texture Intensity = null;
    Texture Blank = null;
    Texture Cal = null;
    Texture Input = null;
    Texture Output = null;
    Texture Line = null;
    Texture Gnd = null;
    Texture Branch = null;
    // ----------------------Sg
    Texture Case = null;
    Texture Backside = null;
    Texture Leftside = null;
    Texture Rightside = null;
    Texture Calconnector = null;
    Texture Power = null;
    Texture Left = null;
    Texture Right = null;
    Texture Wave = null;
    Texture Amp = null;
    Texture Freq = null;
    Texture switcher = null;
Texture Dot = null;
    Texture Battery = null;
    // ----------------------Pass
Texture brick = null;
Texture texfloor = null;
Texture ceiling = null;
Texture Sky = null;
Texture Door = null;
Texture Desk = null;
```

```
Texture Desk1 = null;
Texture Outside01 = null;
    Texture Outside02 = null;
    Texture Airbus01 = null;
Texture Clock = null;
Texture Shelf = null;
Texture Picture01 = null;
Texture Picture02 = null;
Texture Picture03 = null;
Texture Picture04 = null;
Texture Vlabposter01 = null;
Texture Vlabposter02 = null;
Texture Vlabname = null;
Texture D0 = null;
Texture D1 = null;
Texture D2 = null;
Texture D3 = null;
Texture D4 = null;
Texture D5 = null;
Texture D6 = null;
Texture D7 = null;
Texture D8 = null;
Texture D9 = null;
Texture C = null;
Texture OK = null;
Texture Empty = null;
Texture Yellowplug = null;
Texture Redplug = null;
Texture Blueplug = null;
Texture Greenplug = null;

java.net.URL cir_board = null;
```

E.3 DEFINING CONSTRUCTOR

```
public Scene3D(java.net.URL cirboard)
{
   this.cir_board = cirboard;
}
```

E.4 OBTAINING HANDLES TO GUI CONTROL

```
public void setPanel(OPanel panel)
{
   this.panel = panel;
}
```

E.5 OBTAINING HANDLES TO APPEARANCE

```
public void setAppearance(Appearance appimage)
{
    this.appimage = appimage;
}
```

E.6 CLEARING PICKING BEHAVIOR OBJECT AFTER SYSTEM EXIT

```
public void closeAll()
{
        if (pickingbehavior!=null)
        pickingbehavior.closeAll();
}
```

E.7 MAIN SCENE GRAPH CREATION FUNCTION

```
public BranchGroup createSceneGraph(SimpleUniverse su, Canvas3D c)
    {
        // Initializing the parameters used below
        int j;

        Point3f initviewpoint = new Point3f(0.75f, 1.60f, 8.0f);
        Point3f outsideposi = new Point3f(0.75f, 1.75f, -7.0f);
        Point3f doorposi = new Point3f(1.5f, 0.0f, 2.0f);
        Point3f aircraftposi = new Point3f(0.0f, 0.6f, 0.01f);

        Color3f objColor = null;
        Color3f black = new Color3f(0.0f, 0.0f, 0.0f);
        Color3f white = new Color3f(1.0f, 1.0f, 1.0f);

        Appearance text_look = new Appearance();
        Appearance knob_look = new Appearance();
        Appearance track_look = new Appearance();
        Appearance panel_look = new Appearance();
        Appearance dis_look = new Appearance();

        objColor = new Color3f(0.65f, 0.65f, 0.65f);
        knob_look.setMaterial(new Material(objColor, black, objColor, white, 100.0f));

        objColor = new Color3f(0.15f, 0.15f, 0.15f);
        panel_look.setMaterial(new Material(objColor, black, objColor, white, 100.0f));

        objColor = new Color3f(0.0f, 0.0f, 0.0f);
        track_look.setMaterial(new Material(objColor, black, objColor, white, 100.0f));
```

```
objColor = new Color3f(0.05f, 0.05f, 0.05f);
dis_look.setMaterial(new Material(objColor, black, objColor, white, 100.0f));

Transform3D yAxis1 = new Transform3D();
Transform3D yAxis2 = new Transform3D();
Transform3D yAxis3 = new Transform3D();
///////////////////////////////////// for the oscilloscope
final float enlarge = 2.2f;
float osci_length = 0.45f*enlarge;
float osci_width  = 0.24f*enlarge;
float osci_height = 0.14f*enlarge;
Point3f osciposi = new Point3f(-0.2f, 1.16f, -4.48f);

Knob3D osci_knob[] = new Knob3D[10];
Point3f osci_knobposi[] = new Point3f[10];
float osci_knobangle[] = new float[10];

osci_knobposi[0] = new Point3f(-0.40f*osci_width,-0.31f*osci_height,
    0.5f*osci_length+0.0025f*enlarge);
osci_knobposi[1] = new Point3f(-0.15f*osci_width,-0.35f*osci_height,
    0.5f*osci_length+0.0025f*enlarge);
osci_knobposi[2] = new Point3f( 0.10f*osci_width,-0.35f*osci_height,
    0.5f*osci_length+0.0025f*enlarge);
osci_knobposi[3] = new Point3f( 0.35f*osci_width,-0.31f*osci_height,
    0.5f*osci_length+0.0025f*enlarge);
osci_knobposi[4] = new Point3f( 0.12f*osci_width,-0.10f*osci_height,
    0.5f*osci_length+0.0025f*enlarge);
osci_knobposi[5] = new Point3f( 0.12f*osci_width, 0.10f*osci_height,
    0.5f*osci_length+0.0025f*enlarge);
osci_knobposi[6] = new Point3f( 0.12f*osci_width, 0.30f*osci_height,
    0.5f*osci_length+0.0025f*enlarge);
osci_knobposi[7] = new Point3f( 0.28f*osci_width, 0.33f*osci_height,
    0.5f*osci_length+0.0025f*enlarge);
osci_knobposi[8] = new Point3f( 0.28f*osci_width, 0.10f*osci_height,
    0.5f*osci_length+0.0025f*enlarge);
osci_knobposi[9] = new Point3f( 0.42f*osci_width, 0.20f*osci_height,
    0.5f*osci_length+0.0025f*enlarge);

osci_knobangle[0] =  60.0f*ANGLEPAI;
osci_knobangle[1] = 105.0f*ANGLEPAI;
osci_knobangle[2] = 105.0f*ANGLEPAI;
osci_knobangle[3] = 120.0f*ANGLEPAI;
osci_knobangle[4] = 120.0f*ANGLEPAI;
osci_knobangle[5] = 150.0f*ANGLEPAI;
osci_knobangle[6] = 180.0f*ANGLEPAI;
osci_knobangle[7] =  45.0f*ANGLEPAI;
osci_knobangle[8] =  90.0f*ANGLEPAI;
osci_knobangle[9] =  90.0f*ANGLEPAI;

Shape3D osci_button[] = new Button3D[2];
Point3f osci_buttonposi[] = new Point3f[2];
```

```
osci_buttonposi[0] = new Point3f(0.44f*osci_width+0.007f, -0.41f*osci_height,
    0.5f*osci_length+0.01f);


Slide3D osci_slide[] = new Slide3D[5];
Point3f osci_slideposi[] = new Point3f[5];

osci_slideposi[0] = new Point3f(-0.30f*osci_width,
-0.385f*osci_height+TRACKWIDTH/2.0f, 0.5f*osci_length+0.01f);
osci_slideposi[1] = new Point3f(-0.05f*osci_width,
-0.385f*osci_height+TRACKWIDTH/2.0f, 0.5f*osci_length+0.01f);
osci_slideposi[2] = new Point3f( 0.20f*osci_width,
-0.385f*osci_height+TRACKWIDTH/2.0f, 0.5f*osci_length+0.01f);
osci_slideposi[3] = new Point3f( 0.23f*osci_width-TRACKWIDTH/2.0f, -0.05f*osci_height,
0.5f*osci_length+0.01f);
osci_slideposi[4] = new Point3f( 0.23f*osci_width-TRACKWIDTH/4.0f, -0.15f*osci_height,
0.5f*osci_length+0.01f);

Point3f osci_connposi[] = new Point3f[3];
float osci_connangle[] = new float[3];

osci_connposi[0] = new Point3f( 0.485f*osci_width,       0.255f*osci_height,
    0.5f*osci_length+0.002f);
osci_connposi[1] = new Point3f(-0.350f*osci_width+0.0055f, -0.520f*osci_height+0.006f,
    0.5f*osci_length+0.000f);
osci_connposi[2] = new Point3f( 0.350f*osci_width+0.031f, -0.520f*osci_height+0.0057f,
    0.5f*osci_length+0.000f);
osci_connangle[0] = 105.0f*ANGLEPAI;
osci_connangle[1] = 125.0f*ANGLEPAI;
osci_connangle[2] = 123.0f*ANGLEPAI;

Track3D osci_track[] = new Track3D[5];
Point3f osci_trackposi[] = new Point3f[5];

osci_trackposi[0] = new Point3f(-0.30f*osci_width, -0.385f*osci_height,
    0.5f*osci_length+0.0025f);
osci_trackposi[1] = new Point3f(-0.05f*osci_width, -0.385f*osci_height,
    0.5f*osci_length+0.0025f);
osci_trackposi[2] = new Point3f( 0.20f*osci_width, -0.385f*osci_height,
    0.5f*osci_length+0.0025f);
osci_trackposi[3] = new Point3f( 0.23f*osci_width, -0.05f*osci_height,
    0.5f*osci_length+0.0025f);
osci_trackposi[4] = new Point3f( 0.23f*osci_width, -0.15f*osci_height,
    0.5f*osci_length+0.0025f);

Panel3D osci_panel[] = new Panel3D[4];
Point3f osci_panelposi[] = new Point3f[4];
osci_panelposi[0] = new Point3f(0.0f, -0.5f*osci_height-0.003f-0.01f, 0.5f*osci_length);
osci_panelposi[1] = new Point3f(0.0f,  0.5f*osci_height+0.003f+0.01f, 0.5f*osci_length);
osci_panelposi[2] = new Point3f( 0.5f*osci_width+0.003f, 0.0f, 0.5f*osci_length);
osci_panelposi[3] = new Point3f(-0.5f*osci_width-0.003f, 0.0f, 0.5f*osci_length);

Panel3D osci_bottom[] = new Panel3D[4];
```

```
Point3f osci_bottomposi[] = new Point3f[4];
osci_bottomposi[0] = new Point3f(-0.46f*osci_width, -0.5f*osci_height-0.014f,
     0.46f*osci_length);
osci_bottomposi[1] = new Point3f( 0.46f*osci_width, -0.5f*osci_height-0.014f,
     0.46f*osci_length);
osci_bottomposi[2] = new Point3f(-0.46f*osci_width, -0.5f*osci_height-0.014f,-
     0.46f*osci_length);
osci_bottomposi[3] = new Point3f( 0.46f*osci_width, -0.5f*osci_height-0.014f,
     -0.46f*osci_length);

Label2D osci_label[] = new Label2D[30];

//////////////////////////////////// for the signal generator
float sg_length = 0.6f;
float sg_width = 0.35f;
float sg_height = 0.15f;
Point3f sgposi = new Point3f(0.27f, 1.08f, -4.28f);

Knob3D sg_knob[] = new Knob3D[2];
Point3f sg_knobposi[] = new Point3f[2];
float sg_knobangle[] = new float[2];

sg_knobposi[0] = new Point3f(0.35f*sg_width, 0.25f*sg_height, 0.5f*sg_length+0.01f);
sg_knobangle[0] =  60.0f*ANGLEPAI;

Shape3D sg_button[] = new Button3D[6];
Point3f sg_buttonposi[] = new Point3f[6];

sg_buttonposi[0] = new Point3f( 0.40f*sg_width, -0.38f*sg_height, 0.5f*sg_length+0.005f);
sg_buttonposi[1] = new Point3f( 0.30f*sg_width, -0.05f*sg_height, 0.5f*sg_length+0.005f);
sg_buttonposi[2] = new Point3f( 0.40f*sg_width, -0.05f*sg_height, 0.5f*sg_length+0.005f);
sg_buttonposi[3] = new Point3f(-0.36f*sg_width, -0.30f*sg_height, 0.5f*sg_length+0.005f);
sg_buttonposi[4] = new Point3f(-0.18f*sg_width, -0.30f*sg_height, 0.5f*sg_length+0.005f);
sg_buttonposi[5] = new Point3f( 0.00f*sg_width, -0.30f*sg_height, 0.5f*sg_length+0.005f);

Point3f sg_connposi[] = new Point3f[2];
float sg_connangle[] = new float[2];

sg_connposi[0] = new Point3f( 0.180f*sg_width,        -0.480f*sg_height,
     0.5f*sg_length+0.000f);
sg_connposi[1] = new Point3f( 0.220f*sg_width-0.003f,  -0.480f*sg_height-0.008f,
     0.5f*sg_length+0.000f);
sg_connangle[0] = 160.0f*ANGLEPAI;
sg_connangle[1] =  88.0f*ANGLEPAI;

Panel3D sg_panel[] = new Panel3D[4];
Point3f sg_panelposi[] = new Point3f[4];

sg_panelposi[0] = new Point3f(0.0f, -0.5f*sg_height-0.003f, 0.5f*sg_length);
sg_panelposi[1] = new Point3f(0.0f,  0.5f*sg_height+0.003f, 0.5f*sg_length);
sg_panelposi[2] = new Point3f( 0.5f*sg_width+0.003f, 0.0f, 0.5f*sg_length);
sg_panelposi[3] = new Point3f(-0.5f*sg_width-0.003f, 0.0f, 0.5f*sg_length);
```

```
Panel3D sg_bottom[] = new Panel3D[4];
Point3f sg_bottomposi[] = new Point3f[4];
sg_bottomposi[0] = new Point3f(-0.46f*sg_width, -0.5f*sg_height-0.014f, 0.46f*sg_length);
sg_bottomposi[1] = new Point3f( 0.46f*sg_width, -0.5f*sg_height-0.014f, 0.46f*sg_length);
sg_bottomposi[2] = new Point3f(-0.46f*sg_width, -0.5f*sg_height-0.014f,-0.46f*sg_length);
sg_bottomposi[3] = new Point3f( 0.46f*sg_width, -0.5f*sg_height-0.014f,-0.46f*sg_length);

Label2D sg_label[] = new Label2D[5];

///////////////////////////////////////// for the circuit board
Point3f cc_connposi[] = new Point3f[2];
float cc_connangle[] = new float[2];

cc_connposi[0] = new Point3f(1.0f*sg_width+0.026f, -0.135f*sg_height-0.06f,
        0.5f*sg_length+0.004f);
cc_connposi[1] = new Point3f(1.17f*sg_width+0.0128f, -0.13f*sg_height-0.06f,
        0.5f*sg_length-0.005f);
cc_connangle[0] = 90.0f*ANGLEPAI;
cc_connangle[1] = 95.0f*ANGLEPAI;

///////////////////////////////////////// for the virtual house
float pass_length = 0.05f;
float pass_width = 0.3f;
float pass_height = 0.12f;
Point3f passposi = new Point3f(-0.22f, 1.75f, 0.12f);
Point3f frontleftwallposi = new Point3f(0.0f, 0.0f, 2.0f);

Shape3D pass_button[] = new Button3D[12];
Point3f pass_buttonposi[] = new Point3f[12];

pass_buttonposi[1 ] = new Point3f(-0.25f*pass_width,  0.10f*pass_height,
        0.5f*pass_length+0.005f);
pass_buttonposi[2 ] = new Point3f( 0.00f*pass_width,  0.10f*pass_height,
        0.5f*pass_length+0.005f);
pass_buttonposi[3 ] = new Point3f( 0.25f*pass_width,  0.10f*pass_height,
        0.5f*pass_length+0.005f);
pass_buttonposi[4 ] = new Point3f(-0.25f*pass_width, -0.05f*pass_height,
        0.5f*pass_length+0.005f);
pass_buttonposi[5 ] = new Point3f( 0.00f*pass_width, -0.05f*pass_height,
        0.5f*pass_length+0.005f);
pass_buttonposi[6 ] = new Point3f( 0.25f*pass_width, -0.05f*pass_height,
        0.5f*pass_length+0.005f);
pass_buttonposi[7 ] = new Point3f(-0.25f*pass_width, -0.20f*pass_height,
        0.5f*pass_length+0.005f);
pass_buttonposi[8 ] = new Point3f( 0.00f*pass_width, -0.20f*pass_height,
        0.5f*pass_length+0.005f);
pass_buttonposi[9 ] = new Point3f( 0.25f*pass_width, -0.20f*pass_height,
        0.5f*pass_length+0.005f);
pass_buttonposi[10] = new Point3f(-0.25f*pass_width, -0.0f*pass_height,
        0.5f*pass_length+0.005f);
pass_buttonposi[0 ] = new Point3f( 0.00f*pass_width, -0.35f*pass_height,
        0.5f*pass_length+0.005f);
```

```
        pass_buttonposi[11] = new Point3f( 0.25f*pass_width, -0.0f*pass_height,
              0.5f*pass_length+0.005f);

        Panel3D pass_panel[] = new Panel3D[4];
        Point3f pass_panelposi[] = new Point3f[4];

        pass_panelposi[0] = new Point3f(0.0f,           -0.5f*pass_height-0.003f, 0.5f*pass_length);
        pass_panelposi[1] = new Point3f(0.0f,            0.5f*pass_height+0.003f, 0.5f*pass_length);
        pass_panelposi[2] = new Point3f( 0.5f*pass_width+0.003f,  0.0f,           0.5f*pass_length);
        pass_panelposi[3] = new Point3f(-0.5f*pass_width-0.003f,  0.0f,           0.5f*pass_length);

        //////////////////////////////////////////// Create the root of the branch graph
        BranchGroup objRoot = createBranchEnvironment();

        TransformGroup objTrans = new TransformGroup();
        objTrans.setCapability(TransformGroup.ALLOW_TRANSFORM_WRITE);
        objTrans.setCapability(TransformGroup.ALLOW_TRANSFORM_READ);
        objRoot.addChild(objTrans);

        BoundingSphere bounds =
          new BoundingSphere(new Point3d(0.0,0.0,0.0), 100.0);

        // Create the transform group node for navigation behavior ----
        TransformGroup vpTrans = new TransformGroup();
        vpTrans = su.getViewingPlatform().getViewPlatformTransform();
        setPosition(vpTrans, initviewpoint);

        Body3D body = new Body3D(0.3f, 0.6f);
        setPosition(body, new Point3f(initviewpoint.x, initviewpoint.y, initviewpoint.z));
        objTrans.addChild(body);

// Create an oscilloscope --------------------------------------------------------//
TransformGroup osciTrans = new Case3D(osci_length, osci_width, osci_height+0.02f, Case,
                Backside, Leftside, Rightside, Case, Case);
osciTrans.setCapability(TransformGroup.ALLOW_TRANSFORM_WRITE);
osciTrans.setCapability(TransformGroup.ALLOW_TRANSFORM_READ);
osciTrans.setCapability(TransformGroup.ALLOW_PICKABLE_READ);
osciTrans.setCapability(TransformGroup.ALLOW_PICKABLE_WRITE);
osciTrans.setCapability(TransformGroup.ENABLE_PICK_REPORTING);
setPosition(osciTrans, osciposi);
objTrans.addChild(osciTrans);

osci_label[0] = new Label2D(0.044f, 0.011f, Ch1);
  osci_label[0].setPosition(new Point3f(-0.30f*osci_width, -0.35f*osci_height+0.03f,
      0.5f*osci_length+0.002f));
  osciTrans.addChild(osci_label[0]);

  osci_label[1] = new Label2D(0.044f, 0.011f, Ch2);
  osci_label[1].setPosition(new Point3f(0.20f*osci_width, -0.35f*osci_height+0.03f,
      0.5f*osci_length+0.002f));
  osciTrans.addChild(osci_label[1]);
```

```
osci_label[2] = new Label2D(0.044f, 0.033f, Vposi);
osci_label[2].setPosition(new Point3f(-0.40f*osci_width-0.008f,-0.31f*osci_height+0.011f,
      0.5f*osci_length+0.002f));
osciTrans.addChild(osci_label[2]);


osci_label[3] = new Label2D(0.044f, 0.033f, Vposi);
osci_label[3].setPosition(new Point3f(0.35f*osci_width-0.008f,-0.31f*osci_height+0.011f,
      0.5f*osci_length+0.002f));
osciTrans.addChild(osci_label[3]);

osci_label[4] = new Label2D(0.0246f, 0.011f, Mode);
osc_label[4].setPosition(new Point3f(-0.05f*osci_width, -0.35f*osci_height+0.03f,
      0.5f*osci_length+0.002f));
osciTrans.addChild(osci_label[4]);

osci_label[5] = new Label2D(0.044f, 0.011f, Volts);
osci_label[5].setPosition(new Point3f(-0.15f*osci_width, -0.35f*osci_height+0.04f,
      0.5f*osci_length+0.002f));
osciTrans.addChild(osci_label[5]);

osci_label[6] = new Label2D(0.044f, 0.011f, Volts);
osci_label[6].setPosition(new Point3f(0.10f*osci_width, -0.35f*osci_height+0.04f,
      0.5f*osci_length+0.002f));
osciTrans.addChild(osci_label[6]);

osci_label[7] = new Label2D(0.066f, 0.0176f, Source);
osci_label[7].setPosition(new Point3f(0.23f*osci_width, -0.15f*osci_height+0.015f,
      0.5f*osci_length+0.002f));
osciTrans.addChild(osci_label[7]);

osci_label[8] = new Label2D(0.066f, 0.0176f, Sync);
osci_label[8].setPosition(new Point3f(0.23f*osci_width, -0.05f*osci_height+0.015f,
      0.5f*osci_length+0.002f));
osciTrans.addChild(osci_label[8]);

osci_label[9] = new Label2D(0.015f, 0.06f, Ac);
osci_label[9].setPosition(new Point3f(-0.30f*osci_width+0.015f, -0.35f*osci_height-0.008f,
      0.5f*osci_length+0.002f));
osciTrans.addChild(osci_label[9]);


osci_label[10] = new Label2D(0.015f, 0.06f, Ac);
osci_label[10].setPosition(new Point3f(0.20f*osci_width+0.015f, -0.35f*osci_height-0.008f,
      0.5f*osci_length+0.002f));
osciTrans.addChild(osci_label[10]);

osci_label[11] = new Label2D(0.022f, 0.07f, Add);
osci_label[11].setPosition(new Point3f(-0.05f*osci_width+0.018f, -0.35f*osci_height-0.01f,
      0.5f*osci_length+0.002f));
osciTrans.addChild(osci_label[11]);

osci_label[12] = new Label2D(0.04f, 0.02f, Hposi);
osci_label[12].setPosition(new Point3f(0.42f*osci_width-0.005f, 0.20f*osci_height+0.02f,
```

```
        0.5f*osci_length+0.002f));
    osciTrans.addChild(osci_label[12]);

    osci_label[13] = new Label2D(0.055f, 0.055f, Vdiv);
    osci_label[13].setPosition(new Point3f(-0.15f*osci_width+0.0015f, -0.35f*osci_height-0.0015f,
        0.5f*osci_length+0.002f));
    osciTrans.addChild(osci_label[13]);

    osci_label[14] = new Label2D(0.055f, 0.055f, Vdiv);
    osci_label[14].setPosition(new Point3f(0.10f*osci_width+0.0015f, -0.35f*osci_height-0.0015f,
        0.5f*osci_length+0.002f));
    osciTrans.addChild(osci_label[14]);

    osci_label[15] = new Label2D(0.044f, 0.011f, Trig);
    osci_label[15].setPosition(new Point3f(0.28f*osci_width, 0.10f*osci_height+0.024f,
        0.5f*osci_length+0.002f));
    osciTrans.addChild(osci_label[15]);

    osci_label[16] = new Label2D(0.0836f, 0.088f, Tdiv);
    osci_label[16].setPosition(new Point3f(0.28f*osci_width, 0.33f*osci_height+0.005f,
        0.5f*osci_length+0.002f));
    osciTrans.addChild(osci_label[16]);

    osci_label[17] = new Label2D(0.0264f, 0.011f, Focus);
    osci_label[17].setPosition(new Point3f(0.12f*osci_width,-0.10f*osci_height+0.022f,
        0.5f*osci_length+0.002f));
    osciTrans.addChild(osci_label[17]);

    osci_label[18] = new Label2D(0.044f, 0.011f, Intensity);
    osci_label[18].setPosition(new Point3f(0.12f*osci_width,0.10f*osci_height+0.022f,
        0.5f*osci_length+0.002f));
    osciTrans.addChild(osci_label[18]);

    osci_label[19] = new Label2D(0.055f, 0.088f, Blank);
    osci_label[19].setPosition(new Point3f(0.4f*osci_width,-0.01f*osci_height-0.02f,
        0.5f*osci_length+0.002f));
    osciTrans.addChild(osci_label[19]);

    osci_label[20] = new Label2D(0.0484f, 0.055f, Cal);
    osci_label[20].setPosition(new Point3f(0.42f*osci_width,0.4f*osci_height,
        0.5f*osci_length+0.002f));
    osciTrans.addChild(osci_label[20]);

    osci_label[21] = new Label2D(0.0286f, 0.0308f, Input);
    osci_label[21].setPosition(new Point3f(-0.40f*osci_width, -0.43f*osci_height,
        0.5f*osci_length+0.002f));
    osciTrans.addChild(osci_label[21]);

    osci_label[22] = new Label2D(0.0286f, 0.0308f, Input);
    osci_label[22].setPosition(new Point3f(0.35f*osci_width, -0.43f*osci_height,
        0.5f*osci_length+0.002f));
    osciTrans.addChild(osci_label[22]);

    Connector2D osci_calconn1 = new Connector2D(0.0484f, 0.011f, Calconnector);
```

```
osci_calconn1.setPosition(osci_connposi[0]);
    osci_calconn1.setRotationZ(osci_connangle[0]);
osciTrans.addChild(osci_calconn1);

Connector2D osci_calconn2 = new Connector2D(0.043f, 0.017f, Redplug);
osci_calconn2.setPosition(osci_connposi[1]);
osci_calconn2.setRotationZ(osci_connangle[1]);
osciTrans.addChild(osci_calconn2);

Connector2D osci_calconn3 = new Connector2D(0.043f, 0.017f, Yellowplug);
osci_calconn3.setPosition(osci_connposi[2]);
osci_calconn3.setRotationZ(osci_connangle[2]);
osciTrans.addChild(osci_calconn3);

// Create the panel
for (j=0;j<4;j++)
{
switch (j)
{
case 0:
    osci_panel[0] = new Panel3D(0.01f, osci_width+0.012f, 0.006f, panel_look);
    break;

case 1:
    osci_panel[1] = new Panel3D(0.01f, osci_width+0.012f, 0.006f, panel_look);
    break;

case 2:
    osci_panel[2] = new Panel3D(0.01f, 0.006f, osci_height+0.003f+0.02f, panel_look);
    break;

case 3:
    osci_panel[3] = new Panel3D(0.01f, 0.006f, osci_height+0.003f+0.02f, panel_look);
    break;

default:
}
TransformGroup oscipanel_Trans = new TransformGroup();
setPosition(oscipanel_Trans, osci_panelposi[j]);
oscipanel_Trans.addChild(osci_panel[j]);
osciTrans.addChild(oscipanel_Trans);
}

    for (j=0;j<4;j++)
    {
        switch (j)
        {
        case 0:
            osci_bottom[0] = new Panel3D(0.028f, 0.028f, 0.028f, panel_look);
            break;

        case 1:
```

```
                        osci_bottom[1] = new Panel3D(0.028f, 0.028f, 0.028f, panel_look);
                        break;

                case 2:
                        osci_bottom[2] = new Panel3D(0.028f, 0.028f, 0.028f, panel_look);
                        break;

                case 3:
                        osci_bottom[3] = new Panel3D(0.028f, 0.028f, 0.028f, panel_look);
                        break;

                default:
                }
                TransformGroup oscibottom_Trans = new TransformGroup();
                setPosition(oscibottom_Trans, osci_bottomposi[j]);
                oscibottom_Trans.addChild(osci_bottom[j]);
                osciTrans.addChild(oscibottom_Trans);
        }

        for (j=0;j<10;j++)
        {
// Create the knob.
                switch (j)
                {
                case 0:
        osci_knob[0] = new Knob3D(0.0075f*enlarge, 0.005f*enlarge, 20, knob_look, Desk);
                        break;
                case 1:
                        osci_knob[1] = new Knob3D(0.0075f*enlarge, 0.005f*enlarge, 20, knob_look, Desk);
                        break;
                case 2:
                        osci_knob[2] = new Knob3D(0.0075f*enlarge, 0.005f*enlarge, 20, knob_look, Desk);
                        break;
                case 3:
                        osci_knob[3] = new Knob3D(0.0075f*enlarge, 0.005f*enlarge, 20, knob_look, Desk);
                        break;
                case 4:
                        osci_knob[4] = new Knob3D(0.0075f*enlarge, 0.005f*enlarge, 20, knob_look, Desk);
                        break;
                case 5:
                        osci_knob[5] = new Knob3D(0.0075f*enlarge, 0.005f*enlarge, 20, knob_look, Desk);
                        break;
                case 6:
                        osci_knob[6] = new Knob3D(0.0075f*enlarge, 0.005f*enlarge, 20, knob_look, Desk);
                        break;
                case 7:
                        osci_knob[7] = new Knob3D(0.0130f*enlarge, 0.005f*enlarge, 20, knob_look, Desk);
                        break;
                case 8:
                        osci_knob[8] = new Knob3D(0.0075f*enlarge, 0.005f*enlarge, 20, knob_look, Desk);
                        break;
                case 9:
```

```
                    osci_knob[9] = new Knob3D(0.0075f*enlarge, 0.005f*enlarge, 20, knob_look, Desk);
                    break;
              default:
              }
              if (j!=6)
              {
osci_knob[j].setPosition(osci_knobposi[j]);
              osci_knob[j].setRotationZ(osci_knobangle[j]);
              osciTrans.addChild(osci_knob[j]);
              }
}

      for (j=0;j<5;j++)
      {
              // Create the sliders.
              switch (j)
              {
              case 0:
                    osci_slide[j] = new Slide3D(0.01f*enlarge, 0.01f, 0.01f, switcher);
                    break;
              case 1:
                    osci_slide[j] = new Slide3D(0.01f*enlarge, 0.01f, 0.01f, switcher);
                    break;
              case 2:
                    osci_slide[j] = new Slide3D(0.01f*enlarge, 0.01f, 0.01f, switcher);
                    break;
              case 3:
                    osci_slide[j] = new Slide3D(0.01f*enlarge, 0.01f, 0.01f, switcher);
                    break;
              case 4:
                    osci_slide[j] = new Slide3D(0.01f*enlarge, 0.01f, 0.01f, switcher);
                    break;
              default:
              }
              osci_slide[j].setCapability(Shape3D.ALLOW_APPEARANCE_READ);
              osci_slide[j].setCapability(Shape3D.ALLOW_APPEARANCE_WRITE);
              PickTool.setCapabilities(osci_slide[j], PickTool.INTERSECT_FULL);
              TransformGroup oscislideTrans = new TransformGroup();
              oscislideTrans.setCapability(TransformGroup.ALLOW_TRANSFORM_WRITE);
              oscislideTrans.setCapability(TransformGroup.ALLOW_TRANSFORM_READ);
              oscislideTrans.setCapability(TransformGroup.ALLOW_PICKABLE_READ);
              oscislideTrans.setCapability(TransformGroup.ALLOW_PICKABLE_WRITE);
              oscislideTrans.setCapability(TransformGroup.ENABLE_PICK_REPORTING);
              setPosition(oscislideTrans, osci_slideposi[j]);
              oscislideTrans.addChild(osci_slide[j]);
              osciTrans.addChild(oscislideTrans);
      }

      for (j=0;j<5;j++)
      {
              // Create the tracks.
              switch (j)
```

```
                    {
                    case 0:
                        osci_track[0] = new Track3D(0.005f, 0.005f, TRACKWIDTH, track_look);
                        break;
                    case 1:
                        osci_track[1] = new Track3D(0.005f, 0.005f, TRACKWIDTH, track_look);
                        break;
                    case 2:
                        osci_track[2] = new Track3D(0.005f, 0.005f, TRACKWIDTH, track_look);
                        break;
                    case 3:
                        osci_track[3] = new Track3D(0.005f, TRACKWIDTH, 0.005f, track_look);
                        break;
                    case 4:
                        osci_track[4] = new Track3D(0.005f, TRACKWIDTH, 0.005f, track_look);
                        break;
                    default:
                    }
                    TransformGroup oscitrackTrans = new TransformGroup();
                    setPosition(oscitrackTrans, osci_trackposi[j]);
                    oscitrackTrans.addChild(osci_track[j]);
                    osciTrans.addChild(oscitrackTrans);
            }

// Create the buttons.
osci_button[0] = new Button3D(0.01f*enlarge, 0.016f*enlarge, 0.008f*enlarge, Power);
PickTool.setCapabilities(osci_button[0], PickTool.INTERSECT_FULL);

TransformGroup oscibuttonTrans = new TransformGroup();
        oscibuttonTrans.setCapability(TransformGroup.ALLOW_TRANSFORM_WRITE);
        oscibuttonTrans.setCapability(TransformGroup.ALLOW_TRANSFORM_READ);
oscibuttonTrans.setCapability(TransformGroup.ALLOW_PICKABLE_READ);
oscibuttonTrans.setCapability(TransformGroup.ALLOW_PICKABLE_WRITE);
oscibuttonTrans.setCapability(TransformGroup.ENABLE_PICK_REPORTING);
setPosition(oscibuttonTrans, osci_buttonposi[0]);
oscibuttonTrans.addChild(osci_button[0]);
osciTrans.addChild(oscibuttonTrans);

        // here add the real time video
        Shape3D osci_screen = new Screen3D(0.01f, 0.125f*enlarge, 0.09f*enlarge, dis_look);
        osci_screen.setCapability(Shape3D.ALLOW_APPEARANCE_READ);
        osci_screen.setCapability(Shape3D.ALLOW_APPEARANCE_WRITE);
        osci_screen.setCapability(Shape3D.ALLOW_APPEARANCE_OVERRIDE_READ);
        osci_screen.setCapability(Shape3D.ALLOW_APPEARANCE_OVERRIDE_WRITE);
        osci_screen.setPickable(false);

        TransformGroup osciscreenTrans = new TransformGroup();
        osciscreenTrans.setCapability(Group.ALLOW_CHILDREN_WRITE);
        osciscreenTrans.setCapability(Group.ALLOW_CHILDREN_EXTEND);
        setPosition(osciscreenTrans, new Point3f(-0.20f*osci_width, 0.14f*osci_height,
            0.5f*osci_length+0.01f));
        osciscreenTrans.addChild(osci_screen);
```

```
osciTrans.addChild(osciscreenTrans);

Shape3D osci_screen1 = new Screen3D(0.015f, 0.125f*enlarge, 0.018f, dis_look);
osci_screen1.setPickable(false);

TransformGroup osciscreenTrans1 = new TransformGroup();
setPosition(osciscreenTrans1, new Point3f(0.0f, -0.045f*enlarge+0.0035f, 0.0025f));
osciscreenTrans1.addChild(osci_screen1);
osciscreenTrans.addChild(osciscreenTrans1);

Shape3D osci_screen2 = new Screen3D(0.015f, 0.125f*enlarge, 0.018f, dis_look);
osci_screen2.setPickable(false);

TransformGroup osciscreenTrans2 = new TransformGroup();
setPosition(osciscreenTrans2, new Point3f(0.0f, 0.045f*enlarge-0.0035f, 0.0025f));
osciscreenTrans2.addChild(osci_screen2);
osciscreenTrans.addChild(osciscreenTrans2);

Shape3D osci_screen3 = new Screen3D(0.015f, 0.008f, 0.09f*enlarge, dis_look);
osci_screen3.setPickable(false);

TransformGroup osciscreenTrans3 = new TransformGroup();
setPosition(osciscreenTrans3, new Point3f(-0.0625f*enlarge+0.004f, 0.0f, 0.0025f));
osciscreenTrans3.addChild(osci_screen3);
osciscreenTrans.addChild(osciscreenTrans3);

Shape3D osci_screen4 = new Screen3D(0.015f, 0.008f, 0.09f*enlarge, dis_look);
osci_screen4.setPickable(false);

TransformGroup osciscreenTrans4 = new TransformGroup();
setPosition(osciscreenTrans4, new Point3f(0.0625f*enlarge-0.004f, 0.0f, 0.0025f));
osciscreenTrans4.addChild(osci_screen4);
osciscreenTrans.addChild(osciscreenTrans4);

    // Create a signal generator -------------------------------------------------------------//
    TransformGroup sgTrans = new Case3D(sg_length, sg_width, sg_height, Case,
                Backside, Leftside, Rightside, Case, Case);
    sgTrans.setCapability(TransformGroup.ALLOW_TRANSFORM_WRITE);
    sgTrans.setCapability(TransformGroup.ALLOW_TRANSFORM_READ);
    sgTrans.setCapability(TransformGroup.ALLOW_PICKABLE_READ);
    sgTrans.setCapability(TransformGroup.ALLOW_PICKABLE_WRITE);
    sgTrans.setCapability(TransformGroup.ENABLE_PICK_REPORTING);
    setPosition(sgTrans, sgposi);
    objTrans.addChild(sgTrans);

    sg_label[0] = new Label2D(0.028f, 0.031f, Output);
    sg_label[0].setPosition(new Point3f(0.26f*sg_width, -0.36f*sg_height+0.01f,
        0.5f*sg_length+0.002f));
    sgTrans.addChild(sg_label[0]);

    sg_label[1] = new Label2D(0.018f, 0.020f, Gnd);
    sg_label[1].setPosition(new Point3f(0.15f*sg_width, -0.40f*sg_height+0.01f,
```

```
                0.5f*sg_length+0.002f));

Connector2D sg_calconn1 = new Connector2D(0.035f, 0.008f, Calconnector);
sg_calconn1.setPosition(sg_connposi[0]);
sg_calconn1.setRotationZ(sg_connangle[0]);

Connector2D sg_calconn2 = new Connector2D(0.043f, 0.017f, Greenplug);
sg_calconn2.setPosition(sg_connposi[1]);
sg_calconn2.setRotationZ(sg_connangle[1]);
sgTrans.addChild(sg_calconn2);

    // Create the panel for the signal generator
    for (j=0;j<4;j++)
    {
        switch (j)
        {
        case 0:
            sg_panel[0] = new Panel3D(0.01f, sg_width+0.012f, 0.006f, panel_look);
            break;

        case 1:
            sg_panel[1] = new Panel3D(0.01f, sg_width+0.012f, 0.006f, panel_look);
            break;

        case 2:
            sg_panel[2] = new Panel3D(0.01f, 0.006f, sg_height+0.003f, panel_look);
            break;

        case 3:
            sg_panel[3] = new Panel3D(0.01f, 0.006f, sg_height+0.003f, panel_look);
            break;

        default:
        }
        TransformGroup sgpanel_Trans = new TransformGroup();
        setPosition(sgpanel_Trans, sg_panelposi[j]);
        sgpanel_Trans.addChild(sg_panel[j]);
        sgTrans.addChild(sgpanel_Trans);
    }

    for (j=0;j<4;j++)
    {
        switch (j)
        {
        case 0:
            sg_bottom[0] = new Panel3D(0.016f, 0.016f, 0.028f, panel_look);
            break;

        case 1:
            sg_bottom[1] = new Panel3D(0.016f, 0.016f, 0.028f, panel_look);
            break;
```

```
            case 2:
                sg_bottom[2] = new Panel3D(0.016f, 0.016f, 0.028f, panel_look);
                break;

            case 3:
                sg_bottom[3] = new Panel3D(0.016f, 0.016f, 0.028f, panel_look);
                break;

            default:
            }
            TransformGroup sgbottom_Trans = new TransformGroup();
            setPosition(sgbottom_Trans, sg_bottomposi[j]);
            sgbottom_Trans.addChild(sg_bottom[j]);
            sgTrans.addChild(sgbottom_Trans);
    }

    // Create the knob.
    sg_knob[0] = new Knob3D(0.025f, 0.008f, 20, knob_look, Desk);
    sgTrans.addChild(sg_knob[0]);
    sg_knob[0].setPosition(sg_knobposi[0]);
    sg_knob[0].setRotationZ(sg_knobangle[0]);

    for (j=0; j<6; j++)
    {
        switch (j)
        {
        case 0:
            sg_button[0] = new Button3D(0.01f, 0.04f, 0.02f, Power);
            break;
        case 1:
            sg_button[1] = new Button3D(0.01f, 0.02f, 0.02f, Left);
            break;
        case 2:
            sg_button[2] = new Button3D(0.01f, 0.02f, 0.02f, Right);
            break;
        case 3:
            sg_button[3] = new Button3D(0.01f, 0.04f, 0.02f, Wave);
            break;
        case 4:
            sg_button[4] = new Button3D(0.01f, 0.04f, 0.02f, Amp);
            break;
        case 5:
            sg_button[5] = new Button3D(0.01f, 0.04f, 0.02f, Freq);
            break;
        default:
        }

        sg_button[j].setCapability(Shape3D.ALLOW_APPEARANCE_READ);
        sg_button[j].setCapability(Shape3D.ALLOW_APPEARANCE_WRITE);
        PickTool.setCapabilities(sg_button[j], PickTool.INTERSECT_FULL);

        TransformGroup sgbuttonTrans = new TransformGroup();
```

```
        sgbuttonTrans.setCapability(TransformGroup.ALLOW_TRANSFORM_WRITE);
        sgbuttonTrans.setCapability(TransformGroup.ALLOW_TRANSFORM_READ);
        sgbuttonTrans.setCapability(TransformGroup.ALLOW_PICKABLE_READ);
        sgbuttonTrans.setCapability(TransformGroup.ALLOW_PICKABLE_WRITE);
        sgbuttonTrans.setCapability(TransformGroup.ENABLE_PICK_REPORTING);
        setPosition(sgbuttonTrans, sg_buttonposi[j]);
        sgbuttonTrans.addChild(sg_button[j]);
        sgTrans.addChild(sgbuttonTrans);
}

Shape3D sg_screen = new Screen3D(0.005f, 0.18f, 0.07f, dis_look);
TransformGroup sgscreenTrans = new TransformGroup();

sgscreenTrans.setCapability(Group.ALLOW_CHILDREN_WRITE);
sgscreenTrans.setCapability(Group.ALLOW_CHILDREN_EXTEND);
setPosition(sgscreenTrans, new Point3f(-0.18f*sg_width, 0.18f*sg_height,
        0.5f*sg_length+0.005f));
sgscreenTrans.addChild(sg_screen);
sgTrans.addChild(sgscreenTrans);

// Create a circuit board -----------------------------------------------------//
Transform3D t3d = new Transform3D();

TransformGroup ccTrans = new TransformGroup();
TransformGroup objScale = new TransformGroup();
t3d.setScale(0.1);
t3d.setTranslation(new Vector3d(0.67, 1.17, -4.04));
objScale.setTransform(t3d);

objRoot.addChild(ccTrans);

ccTrans.addChild(objScale);
VrmlLoader f = new VrmlLoader();
Scene s = null;
try {
        s = f.load(cir_board);
}
catch (FileNotFoundException e) {
        System.err.println(e);
        System.exit(1);
}
catch (ParsingErrorException e) {
        System.err.println(e);
        System.exit(1);
}
catch (IncorrectFormatException e) {
        System.err.println(e);
        System.exit(1);
}

s.getSceneGroup().setPickable(false);
objScale.addChild(s.getSceneGroup());
```

```
Connector2D cc_calconn1 = new Connector2D(0.0484f, 0.011f, Calconnector);
cc_calconn1.setPosition(cc_connposi[0]);
cc_calconn1.setRotationZ(cc_connangle[0]);

Connector2D cc_calconn2 = new Connector2D(0.0484f, 0.011f, Calconnector);
cc_calconn2.setPosition(cc_connposi[1]);
cc_calconn2.setRotationZ(cc_connangle[1]);

// Create a room with password permission -------------------------------------------------//
Windows3D frontleftwall = new Windows3D(0.16f, 15.0f, 3.5f, 0.5f, 1.0f, 3.0f, 1.5f, 2, brick);
frontleftwall.setPosition(frontleftwallposi);
objTrans.addChild(frontleftwall);

Glass3D window = new Glass3D(0.0f, 3.0f, 1.5f);
window.setPosition(new Point3f(-2.0f, 1.75f, 0.0f));
window.setTransP(0.5f);
frontleftwall.addChild(window);

Wall3D frontrightwall = new Wall3D(0.16f, 13.5f, 3.5f, 2, brick);
frontrightwall.setPosition(new Point3f(15.0f, 0.0f, 2.0f));
objTrans.addChild(frontrightwall);

Wall3D fronttopwall = new Wall3D(0.16f, 1.5f, 1.0f, 2, brick);
fronttopwall.setPosition(new Point3f(1.5f, 2.5f, 2.0f));
objTrans.addChild(fronttopwall);

Door3D door = new Door3D(0.04f, 1.5f, 2.5f, false, Door);
door.setRotation(0.0f*ANGLEPAI);
door.setPosition(doorposi);
objTrans.addChild(door);

TexturePlate vlabname = new TexturePlate(0.02f, 0.8f, 0.2f, Vlabname);
setPosition(vlabname, new Point3f(-0.75f, 1.75f, 0.03f));
vlabname.setPickable(false);
door.addChild(vlabname);

Wall3D rightwall = new Wall3D(0.0f, 8.0f, 3.5f, 1, brick);
rightwall.setPosition(new Point3f(4.0f, 0.0f, 2.0f));
rightwall.setRotation(-90.0f*ANGLEPAI);
objTrans.addChild(rightwall);

Wall3D leftwall = new Wall3D(0.0f, 8.0f, 3.5f, 1, brick);
leftwall.setPosition(new Point3f(-4.0f, 0.0f, -6.0f));
leftwall.setRotation(90.0f*ANGLEPAI);
objTrans.addChild(leftwall);

Windows3D rearwall = new Windows3D(0.16f, 10.0f, 3.5f, 3.0f, 1.0f, 4.0f, 1.5f, 1, brick);
rearwall.setPosition(new Point3f(5.0f, 0.0f, -6.0f));
objTrans.addChild(rearwall);

TexturePlate outside = new TexturePlate(0.0f, 10.0f, 2.0f, Outside01);
outside.setCapability(TransformGroup.ALLOW_TRANSFORM_WRITE);
```

342 *Ko & Cheng*

```
outside.setCapability(TransformGroup.ALLOW_TRANSFORM_READ);
setPosition(outside, outsideposi);
objTrans.addChild(outside);

TexturePlate outside02 = new TexturePlate(0.0f, 10.0f, 2.0f, Outside02);
outside02.setCapability(TransformGroup.ALLOW_TRANSFORM_WRITE);
outside02.setCapability(TransformGroup.ALLOW_TRANSFORM_READ);
setPosition(outside02, new Point3f(0.0f, 0.0f, 0.01f));
outside.addChild(outside02);

Alpha outAlpha = new Alpha(-1, Alpha.INCREASING_ENABLE
      |Alpha.DECREASING_ENABLE, 0, 0, 1000, 400, 500, 1000, 400, 500);

Quat4f outquats[] = new Quat4f[2];
float outknots[] = {0.0f, 1.0f};
Point3f outposi[] = new Point3f[2];

outquats[0] = new Quat4f(0.0f, 0.0f, 0.0f, 1.0f);
outquats[1] = new Quat4f(0.0f, 0.0f, 0.0f, 1.0f);
outposi[0] = new Point3f(-0.03f, 0.01f, 0.01f);
outposi[1] = new Point3f( 0.01f,-0.01f, 0.01f);
RotPosPathInterpolator outshift = new RotPosPathInterpolator(outAlpha, outside02, yAxis1,
      outknots, outquats, outposi);

outshift.setSchedulingBounds(bounds);
objTrans.addChild(outshift);

TransformGroup air = new TransformGroup();
air.setCapability(TransformGroup.ALLOW_TRANSFORM_WRITE);
air.setCapability(TransformGroup.ALLOW_TRANSFORM_READ);
setPosition(air, new Point3f( 6.5f,-0.2f, 0.01f));
outside.addChild(air);

TexturePlate aircraft = new TexturePlate(0.0f, 1.5f, 0.4f, Airbus01);
aircraft.setCapability(TransformGroup.ALLOW_TRANSFORM_WRITE);
aircraft.setCapability(TransformGroup.ALLOW_TRANSFORM_READ);
setPosition(aircraft, new Point3f(0.0f, 0.0f, 0.0f));
air.addChild(aircraft);

Alpha comAlpha = new Alpha(-1, Alpha.INCREASING_ENABLE, 0, 0, 15000, 10000, 0,
      0, 0, 0);
ScaleInterpolator scale = new ScaleInterpolator(comAlpha, aircraft, yAxis2, 1.0f, 0.0f);
scale.setSchedulingBounds(bounds);
objTrans.addChild(scale);

Quat4f quats[] = new Quat4f[2];
float knots[] = {0.0f, 1.0f};
Point3f airposi[] = new Point3f[2];

quats[0] = new Quat4f(0.0f, 0.0f, 0.0f, 1.0f);
quats[1] = new Quat4f(0.0f, 0.0f, 0.0f, 1.0f);
airposi[0] = new Point3f( 6.5f,-0.2f, 0.01f);
```

Copyright © 2009, IGI Global, distributing in print or electronic forms without written permission of IGI Global is prohibited.

```
airposi[1] = new Point3f(-3.5f, 0.6f, 0.01f);
RotPosPathInterpolator shift = new RotPosPathInterpolator(comAlpha,
    air, yAxis3, knots, quats, airposi);
```

```
shift.setSchedulingBounds(bounds);
objTrans.addChild(shift);
```

```
Floor floor = new Floor(10.0f, 8.0f);
floor.setPosition(new Point3f(0.0f, 0.0f, -2.0f));
floor.setAutoTexture(texfloor);
objTrans.addChild(floor);
```

```
Floor cliff = new Floor(10.0f, 8.0f);
cliff.setPosition(new Point3f(0.0f, 3.5f, -2.0f));
cliff.setRotationX(180.0f*ANGLEPAI);
cliff.setAutoTexture(ceiling);
objTrans.addChild(cliff);
```

```
Wall3D limitleftwall = new Wall3D(0.0f, 10.0f, 3.5f, 1, null);
limitleftwall.setPosition(new Point3f(-7.0f, 0.0f, 2.0f));
limitleftwall.setRotation(90.0f*ANGLEPAI);
limitleftwall.setLimit(1.0f);
objTrans.addChild(limitleftwall);
```

```
Wall3D limitrightwall = new Wall3D(0.0f, 10.0f, 3.5f, 1, null);
limitrightwall.setPosition(new Point3f(7.0f, 0.0f, 12.0f));
limitrightwall.setRotation(-90.0f*ANGLEPAI);
limitrightwall.setLimit(1.0f);
objTrans.addChild(limitrightwall);
```

```
Wall3D limitrearwall = new Wall3D(0.0f, 14.0f, 3.5f, 1, null);
limitrearwall.setPosition(new Point3f(-7.0f, 0.0f, 12.0f));
limitrearwall.setRotation(180.0f*ANGLEPAI);
limitrearwall.setLimit(1.0f);
objTrans.addChild(limitrearwall);
```

```
TexturePlate picture01 = new TexturePlate(0.02f, 0.75f, 1.0f, Picture01);
setPosition(picture01, new Point3f(-2.5f, 1.75f, 0.01f));
leftwall.addChild(picture01);
```

```
TexturePlate picture03 = new TexturePlate(0.02f, 1.0f, 0.75f, Picture03);
setPosition(picture03, new Point3f(-5.5f, 1.75f, 0.01f));
leftwall.addChild(picture03);
```

```
TexturePlate picture02 = new TexturePlate(0.02f, 0.75f, 1.0f, Picture02);
setPosition(picture02, new Point3f(-5.5f, 1.75f, 0.01f));
rightwall.addChild(picture02);
```

```
TexturePlate picture04 = new TexturePlate(0.02f, 1.0f, 0.75f, Picture04);
setPosition(picture04, new Point3f(-2.5f, 1.75f, 0.01f));
rightwall.addChild(picture04);
```

```
TexturePlate vlabposter01 = new TexturePlate(0.02f, 0.9f, 1.2f, Vlabposter01);
setPosition(vlabposter01, new Point3f(-12.8f, 1.75f, 0.09f));
frontrightwall.addChild(vlabposter01);

TexturePlate vlabposter02 = new TexturePlate(0.02f, 0.9f, 1.2f, Vlabposter02);
setPosition(vlabposter02, new Point3f(-11.8f, 1.75f, 0.09f));
frontrightwall.addChild(vlabposter02);

Table3D table = new Table3D(1.2f, 2.0f, 0.95f, Desk, Desk1);
setPosition(table, new Point3f(0.0f, 0.475f, -4.5f));
objTrans.addChild(table);

TransformGroup battery = new Case3D(0.1f, 0.1f, 0.18f, Battery,
            Battery, Battery, Battery, Desk, Desk);
battery.setCapability(TransformGroup.ALLOW_TRANSFORM_WRITE);
battery.setCapability(TransformGroup.ALLOW_TRANSFORM_READ);
setRotationZ(battery, ANGLEPAI*90.0f);
setPosition(battery, new Point3f(0.65f, 1.06f, -4.05f));

// Create a card reader ------------------------------------------------------------//
TransformGroup passTrans = new Case3D(pass_length, pass_width, pass_height, Empty,
            Empty, Empty, Empty, Empty, Empty);
passTrans.setCapability(TransformGroup.ALLOW_TRANSFORM_WRITE);
passTrans.setCapability(TransformGroup.ALLOW_TRANSFORM_READ);
passTrans.setCapability(TransformGroup.ALLOW_PICKABLE_READ);
passTrans.setCapability(TransformGroup.ALLOW_PICKABLE_WRITE);
passTrans.setCapability(TransformGroup.ENABLE_PICK_REPORTING);
setPosition(passTrans, passposi);
frontleftwall.addChild(passTrans);

for (j=0;j<4;j++)
{
    switch (j)
    {
    case 0:
        pass_panel[0] = new Panel3D(0.01f, pass_width+0.012f, 0.006f, panel_look);
        break;

    case 1:
        pass_panel[1] = new Panel3D(0.01f, pass_width+0.012f, 0.006f, panel_look);
        break;

    case 2:
        pass_panel[2] = new Panel3D(0.01f, 0.006f, pass_height+0.003f, panel_look);
        break;

    case 3:
        pass_panel[3] = new Panel3D(0.01f, 0.006f, pass_height+0.003f, panel_look);
        break;

    default:
    }
```

```
            TransformGroup passpanel_Trans = new TransformGroup();
            setPosition(passpanel_Trans, pass_panelposi[j]);
            passpanel_Trans.addChild(pass_panel[j]);
            passTrans.addChild(passpanel_Trans);
    }

    for (j=0; j<12; j++)
    {
        switch (j)
        {
        case 0:
            pass_button[0] = new Button3D(0.01f, 0.05f, 0.05f, D0);
            break;
        case 1:
            pass_button[1] = new Button3D(0.01f, 0.05f, 0.05f, D1);
            break;
        case 2:
            pass_button[2] = new Button3D(0.01f, 0.05f, 0.05f, D2);
            break;
        case 3:
            pass_button[3] = new Button3D(0.01f, 0.05f, 0.05f, D3);
            break;
        case 4:
            pass_button[4] = new Button3D(0.01f, 0.05f, 0.05f, D4);
            break;
        case 5:
            pass_button[5] = new Button3D(0.01f, 0.05f, 0.05f, D5);
            break;
        case 6:
            pass_button[6] = new Button3D(0.01f, 0.05f, 0.05f, D6);
            break;
        case 7:
            pass_button[7] = new Button3D(0.01f, 0.05f, 0.05f, D7);
            break;
        case 8:
            pass_button[8] = new Button3D(0.01f, 0.05f, 0.05f, D8);
            break;
        case 9:
            pass_button[9] = new Button3D(0.01f, 0.05f, 0.05f, D9);
            break;
        case 10:
            pass_button[10] = new Button3D(0.01f, 0.13f, 0.065f, C);
            break;
        case 11:
            pass_button[11] = new Button3D(0.01f, 0.13f, 0.065f, OK);
            break;
        default:
        }

        if (j==10||j==11)
        {
            pass_button[j].setCapability(Shape3D.ALLOW_APPEARANCE_READ);
```

```
            pass_button[j].setCapability(Shape3D.ALLOW_APPEARANCE_WRITE);
            PickTool.setCapabilities(pass_button[j], PickTool.INTERSECT_FULL);

            TransformGroup passbuttonTrans = new TransformGroup();
            passbuttonTrans.setCapability(TransformGroup.ALLOW_TRANSFORM_WRITE);
            passbuttonTrans.setCapability(TransformGroup.ALLOW_TRANSFORM_READ);
            passbuttonTrans.setCapability(TransformGroup.ALLOW_PICKABLE_READ);
            passbuttonTrans.setCapability(TransformGroup.ALLOW_PICKABLE_WRITE);
            passbuttonTrans.setCapability(TransformGroup.ENABLE_PICK_REPORTING);
            setPosition(passbuttonTrans, pass_buttonposi[j]);
            passbuttonTrans.addChild(pass_button[j]);
            passTrans.addChild(passbuttonTrans);
        }
    }

Shape3D pass_screen = new Screen3D(0.005f, 0.25f, 0.07f, dis_look);
TransformGroup passscreenTrans = new TransformGroup();

passscreenTrans.setCapability(Group.ALLOW_CHILDREN_WRITE);
passscreenTrans.setCapability(Group.ALLOW_CHILDREN_EXTEND);
setPosition(passscreenTrans, new Point3f(0.0f*pass_width, 0.30f*pass_height,
    0.5f*pass_length+0.005f));
passscreenTrans.addChild(pass_screen);

// Creating the navigating and picking behavior --------------------------------------//
NavigatorBehavior naviObject = new NavigatorBehavior(vpTrans, body, body.getShape());

naviObject.initPosition(initviewpoint);
naviObject.setOutside(outside, outsideposi);
naviObject.setObject(panel.FrameDelay);

panel.FrameDelay.addChangeListener(naviObject);
panel.Animation.addActionListener(naviObject);
panel.Interaction.addActionListener(naviObject);
panel.addMouseListener(naviObject);

naviObject.setSchedulingBounds(bounds);
objRoot.addChild(naviObject);

pickingbehavior = new PickingBehavior (c, objRoot);

pickingbehavior.setDisplay(osciscreenTrans, sgscreenTrans, passscreenTrans);
pickingbehavior.setAppearance(appimage, dis_look, osci_screen);
pickingbehavior.setOsciPositions(osciposi, osci_knobposi, osci_buttonposi, osci_slideposi);
pickingbehavior.setSgPositions(sgposi, sg_knobposi, sg_buttonposi);
pickingbehavior.setPassPositions(passposi, pass_buttonposi, frontleftwallposi);
pickingbehavior.setAngles(osci_knobangle, sg_knobangle);
pickingbehavior.setConnStatus(osci_connposi, sg_connposi, cc_connposi, osci_connangle,
    sg_connangle, cc_connangle);
pickingbehavior.setDoor(door);
pickingbehavior.setPanel(panel);
pickingbehavior.setSchedulingBounds(bounds);
```

```
        objRoot.addChild (pickingbehavior);

        objRoot.compile();
        return objRoot;

    }
```

E.8 SETTING UP OF LIGHT SOURCES

```
BranchGroup createBranchEnvironment()
  {
  // Create the root of the branch graph
    BranchGroup branchRoot = new BranchGroup();

  // Set up the background
  Color3f bgColor = new Color3f(0.05f, 0.05f, 0.5f);
  Background bgNode = new Background(bgColor);
  bgNode.setApplicationBounds(bounds);
  branchRoot.addChild(bgNode);

  // Set up the ambient light
  Color3f ambientColor = new Color3f(0.55f, 0.55f, 0.55f);
  AmbientLight ambientLightNode = new AmbientLight(ambientColor);
  ambientLightNode.setInfluencingBounds(bounds);
  branchRoot.addChild(ambientLightNode);

  // Set up the directional lights
  Color3f lightColor = new Color3f(0.65f, 0.65f, 0.65f);
  Vector3f light1Direction  = new Vector3f(0.0f, -1.0f, -1.0f);
    Vector3f light2Direction  = new Vector3f(0.0f, -1.0f,  1.0f);

  DirectionalLight light1
    = new DirectionalLight(lightColor, light1Direction);
  light1.setInfluencingBounds(bounds);
  branchRoot.addChild(light1);

  DirectionalLight light2
    = new DirectionalLight(lightColor, light2Direction);
  light2.setInfluencingBounds(bounds);

  boolean lighton = true;
  Color3f spotlightColor = new Color3f(0.8f, 0.8f, 0.75f);

  Point3f attenuation = new Point3f(1.0f,0.0f,0.0f);
  Vector3f lightDirection  = new Vector3f(0.0f, -1.0f, 0.0f);
  float spreadangle = 90.0f*ANGLEPAI;
  float concentration = 0.0f;
  SpotLight spotlight;
  Point3f position = new Point3f(0.0f, 4.0f, -3.0f);
```

```
      spotlight = new SpotLight(lighton, spotlightColor, position, attenuation,
                  lightDirection, spreadangle, concentration);
      spotlight.setInfluencingBounds(bounds);
      branchRoot.addChild(spotlight);

      return branchRoot;
  }
```

E.9 ROTATING A TRANSFORM GROUP BY A SPECIFIC ANGLE RELATIVE TO Z-AXIS

```
  private void setRotationZ(TransformGroup Trans, float angle)
  {
      Matrix3d rotMat = new Matrix3d();
      Transform3D rt3d = new Transform3D();

      Trans.getTransform(rt3d);
      rt3d.getRotationScale(rotMat);
      rotMat.m00 = Math.cos(angle);
      rotMat.m11 = rotMat.m00;
      rotMat.m10 = Math.sin(angle);
      rotMat.m01 = -rotMat.m10;
      rt3d.setRotation(rotMat);
      Trans.setTransform(rt3d);
  }
```

E.10 MOVING A TRANSFORM GROUP TO SPECIFIC POINT

```
  private void setPosition(TransformGroup Trans, Point3f point)
  {
      Transform3D t3d = new Transform3D();

      Trans.getTransform(t3d);
      t3d.setTranslation(new Vector3d(point));
      Trans.setTransform(t3d);
  }
```

E.11 SCALING A TRNASFORM GROUP WITH SPECIFIC VALUE

```
  private void setScality(TransformGroup Trans, float scalevalue)
  {
      Transform3D t3d = new Transform3D();
```

```
        Trans.getTransform(t3d);
        t3d.setScale(scalevalue);
        Trans.setTransform(t3d);
    }
}
```

Appendix F
Knob Class for Web–Based 3D Experiment

F.1 IMPORTING LIBRARIES

```
import java.lang.Math.*;
import javax.media.j3d.*;
import javax.vecmath.*;

import com.sun.j3d.utils.picking.PickTool;
```

F.2 DEFINING CLASS FOR CONTROL KNOB

```
public class Knob3D extends TransformGroup
{
    public Knob3D(float radius, float length, int segmentCount, Appearance look, Texture texture)
    {
        // The direction of the ray from the knob's center
        float xDirection, yDirection;
        float xKnob, yKnob;
        Appearance frontfacelook = new Appearance();

        // The z coordinates for the knob's faces
        float frontZ = 0.5f * length;
        float rearZ = -0.5f * length;

        int knobFaceVertexCount;                    // #(vertices) per knob face
        int knobFaceTotalVertexCount;               // total #(vertices) in all teeth
```

```
int knobFaceStripCount[] = new int[1]; // per knob vertex count
int knobVertexCount;                                    // #(vertices) for knob
int knobStripCount[] = new int[1];       // #(vertices) in strip/strip
```

```
// Front facing normals for the knob's faces
Vector3f frontNormal = new Vector3f(0.0f, 0.0f, 1.0f);
Vector3f outNormal = new Vector3f(1.0f, 0.0f, 0.0f);

// Temporary variables for storing coordinates and vectors
Point3f coordinate = new Point3f(0.0f, 0.0f, 0.0f);
Shape3D newShape;

// The angle subtended by a single segment
double segmentAngle = 2.0 * Math.PI/segmentCount;
double tempAngle;

this.setCapability(TransformGroup.ALLOW_TRANSFORM_WRITE);

// Construct the knob's front and rear face
knobFaceVertexCount = segmentCount + 2;
knobFaceStripCount[0] = knobFaceVertexCount;

TriangleFanArray frontKnobFace = new TriangleFanArray(knobFaceVertexCount,
GeometryArray.COORDINATES | GeometryArray.NORMALS, knobFaceStripCount);

coordinate.set(0.0f, 0.0f, frontZ);
frontKnobFace.setCoordinate(0, coordinate);
frontKnobFace.setNormal(0, frontNormal);

for(int index = 1; index < segmentCount+2; index++)
{
    tempAngle = segmentAngle * (double)index;
    coordinate.set(radius * (float)Math.cos(tempAngle), radius * (float)Math.sin(tempAngle), frontZ);
    frontKnobFace.setCoordinate(index, coordinate);
    frontKnobFace.setNormal(index, frontNormal);
}

TexCoordGeneration tcg = new TexCoordGeneration(TexCoordGeneration.OBJECT_LINEAR,
                TexCoordGeneration.TEXTURE_COORDINATE_2);
frontfacelook.setTexCoordGeneration(tcg);
frontfacelook.setTexture(texture);
newShape = new Shape3D(frontKnobFace, frontfacelook);
PickTool.setCapabilities(newShape, PickTool.INTERSECT_FULL);
this.addChild(newShape);

// Construct knob's outer skin (the cylinder body)
knobVertexCount = 2 * segmentCount + 2;
knobStripCount[0] = knobVertexCount;

TriangleStripArray outerknobFace = new TriangleStripArray(knobVertexCount,
            GeometryArray.COORDINATES|GeometryArray.NORMALS, knobStripCount);
outNormal.set(1.0f, 0.0f, 0.0f);
```

```
coordinate.set(radius, 0.0f, frontZ);
outerknobFace.setCoordinate(0, coordinate);
outerknobFace.setNormal(0, outNormal);

coordinate.set(radius, 0.0f, rearZ);
outerknobFace.setCoordinate(1, coordinate);
outerknobFace.setNormal(1, outNormal);

for(int count = 0; count < segmentCount; count++)
{
    int index = 2 + count * 2;
    tempAngle = segmentAngle * (double)(count + 1);
    xDirection = (float)Math.cos(tempAngle);
    yDirection = (float)Math.sin(tempAngle);
    xKnob = radius * xDirection;
    yKnob = radius * yDirection;
    outNormal.set(xDirection, yDirection, 0.0f);

        coordinate.set(xKnob, yKnob, frontZ);
        outerknobFace.setCoordinate(index, coordinate);
        outerknobFace.setNormal(index, outNormal);

        coordinate.set(xKnob, yKnob, rearZ);
        outerknobFace.setCoordinate(index + 1, coordinate);
        outerknobFace.setNormal(index + 1, outNormal);
        }
    newShape = new Shape3D(outerknobFace, look);
    PickTool.setCapabilities(newShape, PickTool.INTERSECT_FULL);
    this.addChild(newShape);

    Appearance dotlook = new Appearance();
    Color3f black = new Color3f(0.0f, 0.0f, 0.0f);
    Color3f white = new Color3f(1.0f, 1.0f, 1.0f);
    Color3f objColor = new Color3f(1.0f, 0.0f, 0.0f);
    dotlook.setMaterial(new Material(objColor, black, objColor, white, 100.0f));

    Point3f[] verts =
    {
        // front face
        new Point3f(1.0f*radius, -0.06f*radius,  0.52f*length),
        new Point3f(1.0f*radius,  0.06f*radius,  0.52f*length),
        new Point3f(0.92f*radius,  0.06f*radius,  0.52f*length),
        new Point3f(0.92f*radius, -0.06f*radius,  0.52f*length),
        // right face
        new Point3f(1.0f*radius, -0.06f*radius, -0.52f*length),
        new Point3f(1.0f*radius,  0.06f*radius, -0.52f*length),
        new Point3f(1.0f*radius,  0.06f*radius,  0.52f*length),
        new Point3f(1.0f*radius, -0.06f*radius,  0.52f*length),
        // top face
        new Point3f(1.0f*radius,  0.06f*radius,  0.52f*length),
        new Point3f(1.0f*radius,  0.06f*radius, -0.52f*length),
        new Point3f(0.92f*radius,  0.06f*radius, -0.52f*length),
```

```
                new Point3f(0.92f*radius,  0.06f*radius,  0.52f*length),
                // bottom face
                new Point3f(0.92f*radius, -0.06f*radius,  0.52f*length),
                new Point3f(0.92f*radius, -0.06f*radius, -0.52f*length),
                new Point3f(1.0f*radius, -0.06f*radius, -0.52f*length),
                new Point3f(1.0f*radius, -0.06f*radius,  0.52f*length),
        };

        Vector3f[] normals =
        {
                new Vector3f( 0.0f,  0.0f,  1.0f),        // front face
                new Vector3f( 1.0f,  0.0f,  0.0f),        // right face
                new Vector3f( 0.0f,  1.0f,  0.0f),        // top face
                new Vector3f( 0.0f, -1.0f,  0.0f),        // bottom face
        };

        int i;
        QuadArray mark = new QuadArray(20, QuadArray.COORDINATES|QuadArray.NORMALS
                |QuadArray.TEXTURE_COORDINATE_2);

        for (i = 0; i < 16; i++)
        {
                mark.setCoordinate(i, verts[i]);
        }
        for (i = 0; i < 16; i++)
        {
            mark.setNormal(i, normals[i/4]);
        }
        mark.setCapability(Geometry.ALLOW_INTERSECT);

        newShape = new Shape3D(mark, dotlook);
        PickTool.setCapabilities(newShape, PickTool.INTERSECT_FULL);
        this.addChild(newShape);

    this.setCapability(TransformGroup.ALLOW_TRANSFORM_WRITE);
    this.setCapability(TransformGroup.ALLOW_TRANSFORM_READ);
    this.setCapability(TransformGroup.ALLOW_PICKABLE_READ);
    this.setCapability(TransformGroup.ALLOW_PICKABLE_WRITE);
    this.setCapability(TransformGroup.ENABLE_PICK_REPORTING);
  }
```

F.3 FUNCTION FOR CHANGING ORIENTATION OF KNOB

```
public void setRotationX(float angle)
{
    Matrix3d rotMat = new Matrix3d();
    Transform3D rt3d = new Transform3D();

    this.getTransform(rt3d);
    rt3d.getRotationScale(rotMat);
```

```
      rotMat.m11 = Math.cos(angle);
      rotMat.m22 = rotMat.m11;
      rotMat.m12 = Math.sin(angle);
      rotMat.m21 = -rotMat.m12;
      rt3d.setRotation(rotMat);
      this.setTransform(rt3d);
   }

   public void setRotationY(float angle)
   {
      Matrix3d rotMat = new Matrix3d();
      Transform3D rt3d = new Transform3D();

      this.getTransform(rt3d);
      rt3d.getRotationScale(rotMat);
      rotMat.m00 = Math.cos(angle);
      rotMat.m22 = rotMat.m00;
      rotMat.m02 = Math.sin(angle);
      rotMat.m20 = -rotMat.m02;
      rt3d.setRotation(rotMat);
      this.setTransform(rt3d);
   }

   public void setRotationZ(float angle)
   {
      Matrix3d rotMat = new Matrix3d();
      Transform3D rt3d = new Transform3D();

      this.getTransform(rt3d);
      rt3d.getRotationScale(rotMat);
      rotMat.m00 = Math.cos(angle);
      rotMat.m11 = rotMat.m00;
      rotMat.m10 = Math.sin(angle);
      rotMat.m01 = -rotMat.m10;
      rt3d.setRotation(rotMat);
      this.setTransform(rt3d);
   }
```

F.4 FUNCTION FOR CHANGING POSITION OF KNOB

```
   public void setPosition(Point3f point)
   {
      Transform3D t3d = new Transform3D();

      this.getTransform(t3d);
      t3d.setTranslation(new Vector3d(point));
      this.setTransform(t3d);
      this.setTransform(t3d);
   }
}
```

Appendix G
Navigation and Collision Detection for Web–Based 3D Experiment

G.1 IMPORTING LIBRARIES

```
import javax.media.j3d.*;
import javax.vecmath.*;
import java.awt.event.*;
import java.awt.AWTEvent;
import java.util.Enumeration;
import javax.swing.event.*;
import javax.swing.*;
```

G.2 DEFINING CLASS FOR NAVIGATION AND COLLISION DETECTION

```
public class NavigatorBehavior extends Behavior implements MouseListener,
        MouseMotionListener, ActionListener, ItemListener, ChangeListener
{
    private TransformGroup viewTrans;
    private TransformGroup bodyTrans;
    private TransformGroup outsideTrans;
    private Matrix3f comMat = new Matrix3f();

    private Shape3D bodyshape;
    private int direction;
    private WakeupCriterion eventsCondition[] = new WakeupCriterion[3];
```

```
private WakeupOr allEvents;

private String buttonvalue = new String();
private boolean poststop = false;
private float turningAngle = 0.0f;
private float pitchAngle = 0.0f;
private Point3f viewposi = new Point3f();
private Point3f firstviewposi = new Point3f();
private Point3f outsideposi = new Point3f();
private boolean ticked = false;
private int delay = 20;
private JSlider FrameDelay;

private Animation animator; //for animating thread;
private boolean animating = false;
private BoundingSphere bounds = new BoundingSphere(new Point3d(0.0,0.0,0.0), 0.1);
private static final float PAI = 3.14159f;
private static final float ANGLEPAI = 2.0f*PAI/360.0f;
private static final float SPAN = 0.02f;
private static final float ANGLESTEP = 0.01f;
private static final float Outsidescale = 0.4f;
private static final int VIEWMOTION = 5001;
private static final int DOOROPEN = 401;
private static final int DOORCLOSE = 402;
private static final int ANIMATION = 501;
private static final int INTERACTION = 502;

private static final int Forward = KeyEvent.VK_UP;
private static final int Backward = KeyEvent.VK_DOWN;
private static final int LEFT = KeyEvent.VK_LEFT;
private static final int RIGHT = KeyEvent.VK_RIGHT;
private static final int SHIFTRIGHT = KeyEvent.VK_R;
private static final int SHIFTLEFT = KeyEvent.VK_L;
private static final int Up = KeyEvent.VK_U;
private static final int Down = KeyEvent.VK_D;
```

G.3 CONSTRUCTOR OF NAVIGATION AND COLLISION DETECTION FUNCTION

```
NavigatorBehavior(TransformGroup viewTrans, TransformGroup bodyTrans, Shape3D bodyshape)
{
   this.bodyshape = bodyshape;
   this.viewTrans = viewTrans;
   this.bodyTrans = bodyTrans;
}
```

G.4 VIEW PLATFORM POSITION INITIALIZATION

```
public void initPosition(Point3f initposi)
{
    this.viewposi = new Point3f(initposi);
    firstviewposi = new Point3f(initposi);
    init();
}
```

G.5 SETTING REFERENCE FOR OUTSIDE SCENE

```
public void setOutside(TransformGroup outsideTrans, Point3f outsideposi)
{
    this.outsideTrans = outsideTrans;
    this.outsideposi = new Point3f(outsideposi);
}
```

G.6 SETTING REFERENCE FOR SPEED CONTROL SLIDER FOR NAVIGATION

```
public void setObject(JSlider FrameDelay)
{
    this.FrameDelay = FrameDelay;
}
```

G.7 PARAMETER INITIALIZATION

```
private void init()
{
    comMat.m00 = 1.0f;
    comMat.m01 = 0.0f;
    comMat.m02 = 0.0f;
    comMat.m10 = 0.0f;
    comMat.m11 = 1.0f;
    comMat.m12 = 0.0f;
    comMat.m20 = 0.0f;
    comMat.m21 = 0.0f;
    comMat.m22 = 1.0f;
}
```

G.8 FUNCTION FOR CALCULATION OF ROTATION MATRIX FROM ROTATION ANGLE

```
private Matrix3f coMatrix(int mode, float angle)
{
  Matrix3f tempMat = new Matrix3f();
  switch (mode)
  {
  case 1:
    tempMat.m00 = (float)(Math.cos(angle));
    tempMat.m01 = 0.0f;
   tempMat.m02 = (float)(Math.sin(angle));
   tempMat.m10 = 0.0f;
   tempMat.m11 = 1.0f;
   tempMat.m12 = 0.0f;
   tempMat.m20 = (float)(-Math.sin(angle));
   tempMat.m21 = 0.0f;
   tempMat.m22 = (float)(Math.cos(angle));
   break;
  case 2:
   tempMat.m00 = 1.0f;
   tempMat.m01 = 0.0f;
   tempMat.m02 = 0.0f;
   tempMat.m10 = 0.0f;
   tempMat.m11 = (float)(Math.cos(angle));
   tempMat.m12 = (float)(Math.sin(angle));
   tempMat.m20 = 0.0f;
   tempMat.m21 = (float)(-Math.sin(angle));
   tempMat.m22 = (float)(Math.cos(angle));
   break;
  case 3:
   tempMat.m00 = (float)(Math.cos(angle));
   tempMat.m01 = (float)(-Math.sin(angle));
   tempMat.m02 = 0.0f;
   tempMat.m10 = (float)(Math.sin(angle));
   tempMat.m11 = (float)(Math.cos(angle));
   tempMat.m12 = 0.0f;
   tempMat.m20 = 0.0f;
   tempMat.m21 = 0.0f;
   tempMat.m22 = 1.0f;
   break;
  default:
  }
  return tempMat;
}
```

G.9 FUNCTION FOR IMPLEMENTATION OF ROTATION FOR VIEW PLATFORM

```
private void setRotation(TransformGroup Trans, float angle, Matrix3f rotMat, int mode)
{
    Transform3D rt3d = new Transform3D();
    Trans.getTransform(rt3d);
    rotMat.transpose();
    rotMat.invert();
    rotMat.mul(rotMat, coMatrix(mode, angle));
    rt3d.setRotation(rotMat);
    Trans.setTransform(rt3d);
}
```

G.10 FUNCTION FOR IMPLEMENTATION OF TRANSLATION FOR VIEW PLATFORM

```
private Point3f setTranslation(Matrix3f rotMat, Point3f posi)
{
    Point3f tempposi = new Point3f();
    tempposi.x = rotMat.m00*posi.x + rotMat.m01*posi.y + rotMat.m02*(posi.z+0.01f);
    tempposi.y = rotMat.m10*posi.x + rotMat.m11*posi.y + rotMat.m12*(posi.z+0.01f);
    tempposi.z = rotMat.m20*posi.x + rotMat.m21*posi.y + rotMat.m22*(posi.z+0.01f);
    return tempposi;
}
```

G.11 FUNCTION FOR IMPLEMENTATION OF TRANSLATION AND ROTATION FOR TRANSFORM GROUP

```
private void setPosition(TransformGroup Trans, Point3f point)
{
    Transform3D t3d = new Transform3D();

    Trans.getTransform(t3d);
    t3d.setTranslation(new Vector3d(point));
    Trans.setTransform(t3d);
}
```

G.12 EVENT INITIALIZATION FUNCTION

```
public void initialize()
{
    eventsCondition[0] = new WakeupOnAWTEvent(KeyEvent.KEY_PRESSED);
    eventsCondition[1] = new WakeupOnCollisionEntry(bodyshape);
    eventsCondition[2] = new WakeupOnBehaviorPost(null, VIEWMOTION);

    allEvents = new WakeupOr(eventsCondition);
    wakeupOn(allEvents);
```

}

G.13 KEY EVENTS RESPONSE FUNCTION FOR KEYBOARD NAVIGATION

```
private void processKeyEvent(KeyEvent e)
{
  int key = e.getKeyCode();
  direction = key;
  switch(key)
  {
  case Forward:
    direction = Forward;
      viewposi.x = viewposi.x-2.0f*SPAN*(float)Math.sin(turningAngle);
      viewposi.z = viewposi.z-2.0f*SPAN*(float)Math.cos(turningAngle);
    setPosition(bodyTrans, viewposi);
    setPosition(viewTrans, viewposi);
    if (outsideTrans!=null)
      setPosition(outsideTrans, new Point3f(Outsidescale*viewposi.x, outsideposi.y, outsideposi.z));
    break;
  case Backward:
    direction = Backward;
      viewposi.x = viewposi.x+2.0f*SPAN*(float)Math.sin(turningAngle);
      viewposi.z = viewposi.z+2.0f*SPAN*(float)Math.cos(turningAngle);
    setPosition(bodyTrans, viewposi);
    setPosition(viewTrans, viewposi);
    if (outsideTrans!=null)
      setPosition(outsideTrans, new Point3f(Outsidescale*viewposi.x, outsideposi.y, outsideposi.z));
    break;
  case LEFT:
      if (pitchAngle!=0)
      {
       setRotation(viewTrans, -pitchAngle, comMat, 2);
       pitchAngle = 0.0f;
      }
      setRotation(viewTrans, ANGLESTEP, comMat, 1);
      turningAngle += ANGLESTEP;
    break;
  case RIGHT:
      if (pitchAngle!=0)
      {
          setRotation(viewTrans, -pitchAngle, comMat, 2);
          pitchAngle = 0.0f;
      }
      setRotation(viewTrans, -ANGLESTEP, comMat, 1);
      turningAngle -= ANGLESTEP;
      break;
  case Up:
      if (viewposi.y<1.7f)
```

```
        {
              viewposi.y = viewposi.y+SPAN/2.0f;
              setPosition(viewTrans, viewposi);
              setPosition(bodyTrans, viewposi);
        }
        break;
   case Down:
        if (viewposi.y>1.0f)
        {
              viewposi.y = viewposi.y-SPAN/2.0f;
              setPosition(viewTrans, viewposi);
              setPosition(bodyTrans, viewposi);
        }
        break;
   case SHIFTLEFT:
      direction = SHIFTLEFT;
      viewposi.x = viewposi.x-SPAN*(float)Math.sin(turningAngle+Math.PI/2.0);
      viewposi.z = viewposi.z-SPAN*(float)Math.cos(turningAngle+Math.PI/2.0);
      setPosition(bodyTrans, viewposi);
      setPosition(viewTrans, viewposi);
      if (outsideTrans!=null)
          setPosition(outsideTrans, new Point3f(Outsidescale*viewposi.x, outsideposi.y, outsideposi.z));
      break;
   case SHIFTRIGHT:
      direction = SHIFTRIGHT;
      viewposi.x = viewposi.x+SPAN*(float)Math.sin(turningAngle+Math.PI/2.0);
      viewposi.z = viewposi.z+SPAN*(float)Math.cos(turningAngle+Math.PI/2.0);
      setPosition(bodyTrans, viewposi);
      setPosition(viewTrans, viewposi);
      if (outsideTrans!=null)
          setPosition(outsideTrans, new Point3f(Outsidescale*viewposi.x, outsideposi.y, outsideposi.z));
      break;
   default:
   }
}
```

G.14 MAIN EVENTS RESPONSE FUNCTION FOR NAVIGATING AND COLLISION DETECTION

```
public void processStimulus(Enumeration criteria)
{
   WakeupCriterion wakeup;
   AWTEvent[] event;
   int eventId;

   if (!animating)
   {
   while (criteria.hasMoreElements())
   {
```

```
wakeup = (WakeupCriterion) criteria.nextElement();
if (wakeup instanceof WakeupOnAWTEvent)
{
      event = ((WakeupOnAWTEvent)wakeup).getAWTEvent();
      for (int i=0; i<event.length; i++)
      {
            processKeyEvent((KeyEvent) event[i]);
      }
}
if (wakeup instanceof WakeupOnBehaviorPost)
{
      try {
            Thread.sleep(delay);
      } catch (Exception ie) {
            System.out.println("Interrupted Exception!");
      }
      if (buttonvalue.indexOf("Forward") != -1)
      {
            direction = Forward;
            viewposi.x = viewposi.x-2.0f*SPAN*(float)Math.sin(turningAngle);
            viewposi.z = viewposi.z-2.0f*SPAN*(float)Math.cos(turningAngle);
            setPosition(bodyTrans, viewposi);
            setPosition(viewTrans, viewposi);
            if (outsideTrans!=null)
setPosition(outsideTrans, new Point3f(Outsidescale*viewposi.x, outsideposi.y, outsideposi.z));
      }
      else if (buttonvalue.indexOf("Backward") != -1)
      {
            direction = Backward;
            viewposi.x = viewposi.x+2.0f*SPAN*(float)Math.sin(turningAngle);
            viewposi.z = viewposi.z+2.0f*SPAN*(float)Math.cos(turningAngle);
            setPosition(bodyTrans, viewposi);
            setPosition(viewTrans, viewposi);
            if (outsideTrans!=null)
setPosition(outsideTrans, new Point3f(Outsidescale*viewposi.x, outsideposi.y, outsideposi.z));
}
      else if (buttonvalue.indexOf("Turnleft") != -1)
      {
            if (pitchAngle!=0)
            {
            setRotation(viewTrans, -pitchAngle, comMat, 2);
            pitchAngle = 0.0f;
            }
            setRotation(viewTrans, ANGLESTEP, comMat, 1);
            turningAngle += ANGLESTEP;
            }
            else if (buttonvalue.indexOf("Turnright") != -1)
            {
            if (pitchAngle!=0)
            {
                  setRotation(viewTrans, -pitchAngle, comMat, 2);
                  pitchAngle = 0.0f;
```

```
            }
            setRotation(viewTrans, -ANGLESTEP, comMat, 1);
            turningAngle -= ANGLESTEP;
            }
            else if (buttonvalue.indexOf("Pitchup") != -1)
            {
            if (pitchAngle>-10.0f*ANGLEPAI)
            {
                setRotation(viewTrans, -ANGLESTEP, comMat, 2);
                pitchAngle -= ANGLESTEP;
                }
            }
            else if (buttonvalue.indexOf("Pitchdown") != -1)
            {
                if (pitchAngle<10.0f*ANGLEPAI)
                {
                setRotation(viewTrans, ANGLESTEP, comMat, 2);
                pitchAngle += ANGLESTEP;
                }
            }
            else if (buttonvalue.indexOf("Yawleft") != -1)
            {
            }
            else if (buttonvalue.indexOf("Yawright") != -1)
            {
            }
            else if (buttonvalue.indexOf("Horizontal") != -1)
            {
                if (pitchAngle!=0)
                {
                    setRotation(viewTrans, -pitchAngle, comMat, 2);
                    pitchAngle = 0.0f;
                }
            }
            else if (buttonvalue.indexOf("Original") != -1)
            {
                viewposi = new Point3f(firstviewposi);
                if (pitchAngle!=0)
                {
                    setRotation(viewTrans, -pitchAngle, comMat, 2);
                    pitchAngle = 0.0f;
                }
                if (turningAngle!=0)
                {
                    setRotation(viewTrans, -turningAngle, comMat, 1);
                    turningAngle = 0.0f;
                }
                setPosition(bodyTrans, viewposi);
                setPosition(viewTrans, viewposi);
                if (outsideTrans!=null)
    setPosition(outsideTrans, new Point3f(Outsidescale*viewposi.x, outsideposi.y, outsideposi.z));
            }
```

```
        else if (buttonvalue.indexOf("Up") != -1)
        {
            if (viewposi.y<1.7f)
            {
                viewposi.y = viewposi.y+SPAN/2.0f;
                setPosition(viewTrans, viewposi);
                setPosition(bodyTrans, viewposi);
            }
        }
        else if (buttonvalue.indexOf("Down") != -1)
        {
            if (viewposi.y>1.0f)
            {
                viewposi.y = viewposi.y-SPAN/2.0f;
                setPosition(viewTrans, viewposi);
                setPosition(bodyTrans, viewposi);
            }
        }
        else if (buttonvalue.indexOf("Shiftleft") != -1)
        {
            direction = SHIFTLEFT;
viewposi.x = viewposi.x-SPAN*(float)Math.sin(turningAngle+Math.PI/2.0);
    viewposi.z = viewposi.z-SPAN*(float)Math.cos(turningAngle+Math.PI/2.0);
            setPosition(bodyTrans, viewposi);
            setPosition(viewTrans, viewposi);
            if (outsideTrans!=null)
setPosition(outsideTrans, new Point3f(Outsidescale*viewposi.x, outsideposi.y, outsideposi.z));
        }
        else if (buttonvalue.indexOf("Shiftright") != -1)
        {
            direction = SHIFTRIGHT;
                viewposi.x = viewposi.x+SPAN*(float)Math.sin(turningAngle+Math.PI/2.0);
                viewposi.z = viewposi.z+SPAN*(float)Math.cos(turningAngle+Math.PI/2.0);
            setPosition(bodyTrans, viewposi);
            setPosition(viewTrans, viewposi);
            if (outsideTrans!=null)
setPosition(outsideTrans, new Point3f(Outsidescale*viewposi.x, outsideposi.y, outsideposi.z));
        }
        if (poststop) postId(VIEWMOTION);
        }
        if (wakeup instanceof WakeupOnCollisionEntry)
        {
        // The imprememtation of the collision function, go back two step when
        // the collision occurs in order to obtain the next collision ability
        switch (direction)
        {
        case Forward:
            viewposi.x = viewposi.x+4.0f*SPAN*(float)Math.sin(turningAngle);
            viewposi.z = viewposi.z+4.0f*SPAN*(float)Math.cos(turningAngle);
            setPosition(bodyTrans, viewposi);
            setPosition(viewTrans, viewposi);
            if (outsideTrans!=null)
```

```
setPosition(outsideTrans, new Point3f(Outsidescale*viewposi.x, outsideposi.y, outsideposi.z));
        break;
    case Backward:
    viewposi.x = viewposi.x-4.0f*SPAN*(float)Math.sin(turningAngle);
    viewposi.z = viewposi.z-4.0f*SPAN*(float)Math.cos(turningAngle);
    setPosition(bodyTrans, viewposi);
    setPosition(viewTrans, viewposi);
    if (outsideTrans!=null)
setPosition(outsideTrans, new Point3f(Outsidescale*viewposi.x, outsideposi.y, outsideposi.z));
        break;
    case SHIFTLEFT:
    viewposi.x = viewposi.x+2.0f*SPAN*(float)Math.sin(turningAngle+Math.PI/2.0);
    viewposi.z = viewposi.z+2.0f*SPAN*(float)Math.cos(turningAngle+Math.PI/2.0);
    setPosition(bodyTrans, viewposi);
    setPosition(viewTrans, viewposi);
    if (outsideTrans!=null)
setPosition(outsideTrans, new Point3f(Outsidescale*viewposi.x, outsideposi.y, outsideposi.z));
        break;
    case SHIFTRIGHT:
    viewposi.x = viewposi.x-2.0f*SPAN*(float)Math.sin(turningAngle+Math.PI/2.0);
    viewposi.z = viewposi.z-2.0f*SPAN*(float)Math.cos(turningAngle+Math.PI/2.0);
    setPosition(bodyTrans, viewposi);
    setPosition(viewTrans, viewposi);
    if (outsideTrans!=null)
    setPosition(outsideTrans, new Point3f(Outsidescale*viewposi.x, outsideposi.y, outsideposi.z));
        break;
    default:
        }
    }
    }
    }
    this.wakeupOn(allEvents);
    }
```

G.15 EVENTS FUNCTION FOR NAVIGATION CONTROL PANEL

```
public void actionPerformed(ActionEvent e)
{
    String radiobutton = e.getActionCommand();

if (radiobutton.indexOf("Animation")!=-1)
{
    animating = true;
    viewposi = new Point3f(firstviewposi);
    if (pitchAngle!=0)
    {
    setRotation(viewTrans, -pitchAngle, comMat, 2);
        pitchAngle = 0.0f;
```

```
                }
                if (turningAngle!=0)
                {
                setRotation(viewTrans, -turningAngle, comMat, 1);
                    turningAngle = 0.0f;
                }
                setPosition(bodyTrans, viewposi);
                setPosition(viewTrans, viewposi);
                if (outsideTrans!=null)
                setPosition(outsideTrans, new Point3f(Outsidescale*viewposi.x, outsideposi.y,
                        outsideposi.z));
                postId(DOOROPEN);
                if (animator == null)
                {
                    animator = new Animation();
                    animator.running = true;
                }
                else if (!animator.running)
                {
                    animator.running = true;
                }
            }
        else if (radiobutton.indexOf("Interaction")!=-1)
        {
            animating = false;
            viewposi = new Point3f(firstviewposi);
            if (pitchAngle!=0)
            {
                setRotation(viewTrans, -pitchAngle, comMat, 2);
                pitchAngle = 0.0f;
            }
            if (turningAngle!=0)
            {
                setRotation(viewTrans, -turningAngle, comMat, 1);
                turningAngle = 0.0f;
            }
            setPosition(bodyTrans, viewposi);
            setPosition(viewTrans, viewposi);
            if (outsideTrans!=null)
            setPosition(outsideTrans, new Point3f(Outsidescale*viewposi.x, outsideposi.y, outsideposi.z));
            postId(DOORCLOSE);
            if (animator != null)
            {
                if (animator.AnimationThread.isAlive())
                {
                    animator.running = false;          //quit the measuring loop
                }
            }
            animator = null;
        }
    }
}
```

G.16 MOUSE RELEASE EVENTS FUNCTION

```
public void mouseReleased(MouseEvent e)
{
        poststop = false;
}
```

G.17 FUNCTION FOR MOUSE PRESSED EVENTS FOR IDENTIFYING ICONS ON NAVIGATING PANEL

```
public void mousePressed(MouseEvent e)
{
     buttonvalue = null;
     int positionX = e.getX();
     int positionY = e.getY();
     if(positionX>722 && positionX<734 && positionY>58 && positionY<71)
     {
       buttonvalue = "Shiftleft";
     }
     else if(positionX>826 && positionX<839 && positionY>55 && positionY<69)
     {
       buttonvalue = "Shiftright";
     }
     else if(positionX>772 && positionX<788 && positionY>7 && positionY<21)
     {
       buttonvalue = "Up";
     }
     else if(positionX>772 && positionX<788 && positionY>102 && positionY<114)
     {
       buttonvalue = "Down";
     }
     else if(positionX>785 && positionX<798 && positionY>40 && positionY<52)
     {
       buttonvalue = "Forward";
     }
     else if(positionX>758 && positionX<771 && positionY>74 && positionY<86)
     {
       buttonvalue = "Backward";
     }
     else if(positionX>767 && positionX<791 && positionY>52 && positionY<64)
     {
          buttonvalue = "Original";
     }
     else if(positionX>883 && positionX<896 && positionY>53 && positionY<73)
     {
       buttonvalue = "Turnleft";
     }
     else if(positionX>974 && positionX<985 && positionY>52 && positionY<75)
     {
```

Copyright © 2009, IGI Global, distributing in print or electronic forms without written permission of IGI Global is prohibited.

```
      buttonvalue = "Turnright";
    }
    else if(positionX>922 && positionX<944 && positionY>14 && positionY<22)
    {
      buttonvalue = "Pitchup";
    }
    else if(positionX>922 && positionX<942 && positionY>100 && positionY<113)
    {
      buttonvalue = "Pitchdown";
    }
    else if(positionX>925 && positionX<942 && positionY>57 && positionY<77)
    {
            buttonvalue = "Horizontal";
    }
    if (buttonvalue != null)
    {
      poststop = true;
      postId(VIEWMOTION);
    }
}
```

G.18 FUNCTION FOR MOUSE EXIT EVENT

```
public void mouseExited(MouseEvent e)
{
}
```

G.19 FUNCTION FOR MOUSE ENTRY EVENT

```
public void mouseEntered(MouseEvent e)
{
}
```

G.20 FUNCTION FOR MOUSE CLICK EVENT

```
public void mouseClicked(MouseEvent e)
{
}
```

G.21 FUNCTION FOR MOUSE MOVE EVENT

```
public void mouseMoved(MouseEvent e)
{
}
```

G.22 FUNCTION FOR MOUSE DRAG EVENT

```
public void mouseDragged(MouseEvent e)
{
}
```

G.23 FUNCTION FOR DRAGGING OF SPEED CONTROL SLIDER PANEL

```
public void stateChanged(ChangeEvent e)
{
    if (e.getSource().toString().indexOf("majorTickSpacing=2")!=-1)
    {
        delay = (10-FrameDelay.getValue())*15;
    }
}
```

G.24 FUNCTION FOR CLICKING MODE BUTTONS ON NAVIGATION PANEL

```
public void itemStateChanged(ItemEvent e)
{
    if (e.getSource().toString().indexOf("Keyboard")!=-1)
    {
        if (e.getStateChange() == ItemEvent.DESELECTED)
        {
            ticked = false;
        }
        else ticked = true;
    }
}
```

G.25 ANIMATION THREAD CLASS FOR CONTINUOUS MOVEMENT WHILE NAVIGATING ICONS IS HELD OR ANIMATION MODE BUTTON IS CLICKED

```
class Animation implements Runnable
{
    boolean running = false;
    Thread AnimationThread;

    public Animation()
    {
        AnimationThread = new Thread(this);
        AnimationThread.start();    //call function run() to begin to measure
    }

    public void run()
    {
        try {
            AnimationThread.sleep(1000);
        } catch (Exception ie) {
            System.out.println("Interrupted Exception!");
        }

        while (running)
        {
        if (viewposi.z>-2.0f)
        {
            viewposi.z = viewposi.z - 2.0f*SPAN;
                setPosition(bodyTrans, viewposi);
                setPosition(viewTrans, viewposi);
                if (outsideTrans!=null)
                setPosition(outsideTrans, new Point3f(Outsidescale*viewposi.x, outsideposi.y,
                    outsideposi.z));
        }
        else
        {
            viewposi.z=-2.0f;
            setRotation(viewTrans, ANGLESTEP, comMat, 1);
            turningAngle += ANGLESTEP;
        }
        try {
            AnimationThread.sleep(80);
        } catch (Exception ie) {
            System.out.println("Interrupted Exception!");
        }
        }
        AnimationThread.interrupt();          //stop measuring
    }
}
}    // end of class NavigatorBehavior
```

Appendix H
Picking for Web–Based 3D Experiment

H.1 IMPORTING LIBRARIES

```
import java.net.*;
import java.io.*;
import java.awt.*;
import java.awt.event.*;
import java.util.*;
import javax.media.j3d.*;
import javax.vecmath.*;
import com.sun.j3d.utils.picking.*;
import com.sun.j3d.utils.geometry.*;
```

H.2 DEFINING CLASS FOR PICKING BEHAVIOR

```
public class PickingBehavior extends Behavior
{
      private PickCanvas pickCanvas;
      private PickResult pickResult;
      private TransformGroup trans = new TransformGroup();
      private Point3f CurrentPt = new Point3f();
      private float currentangle;
      private float lastangle;
      private int obj = 0;
      private boolean animating = false;
      private boolean initosci = false;
      private long deltatime;
```

```
private long stime;
private int ch1length, ch2length;
private int counter = 10;
private WakeupCriterion[] allEvents;
private WakeupCriterion[] mouseandpostidEvents;
private WakeupOr alleventsCriterion;
private WakeupOr mouseandpostidCriterion;
private TransformGroup sphTrans = new TransformGroup();
private Point3f sphposi = new Point3f(0.0f, 0.0f, 14.0f);
private BoundingSphere bounds = new BoundingSphere(new Point3d(0.0,0.0,0.0), 100.0);
OPanel panel;

//---------------------------------------- for the oscilloscope
private Point3f osciposi = new Point3f();
private Point3f osci_knobposi[] = new Point3f[10];
private Point3f osci_slideposi[] = new Point3f[5];
private Point3f osci_buttonposi[] = new Point3f[2];
private Point3f osci_connposi[] = new Point3f[3];
private TransformGroup osciknobTrans[] = new TransformGroup[10];
private TransformGroup oscibuttonTrans[] = new TransformGroup[2];
private TransformGroup oscislideTrans[] = new TransformGroup[5];
private TransformGroup osciconnTrans[] = new TransformGroup[3];
private Shape3D osci_screen;
private Appearance appimage;
private Appearance appblack;
private boolean oscibuttonaction[] = new boolean[2];
private boolean osciconn[] = new boolean[3];
private float osci_knobangle[] = new float[10];
private float osci_connangle[] = new float[3];
private final float osciknob1_circleposi[] = new float[11];
private final float osciknob2_circleposi[] = new float[11];
private final float osciknob3_circleposi[] = new float[11];
private final float osciknob4_circleposi[] = new float[11];
private final float osciknob8_circleposi[] = new float[16];
private final float osciknob9_circleposi[] = new float[11];
private final float osciknob10_circleposi[] = new float[11];
private final float osciconn1_circleposi[] = new float[2];
private final float osciconn2_circleposi[] = new float[2];
private final float osciconn3_circleposi[] = new float[2];
private float oscislider1_posi[] = new float[3];
private float oscislider2_posi[] = new float[3];
private float oscislider3_posi[] = new float[3];
private float oscislider4_posi[] = new float[2];
private float oscislider5_posi[] = new float[2];
private UDP_OSCI_1 udp_osciservice=null;
private TCP_OSCI tcp_osciservice=null;
private Group osciCurvebranchParent;
private BranchGroup osciCurvebranch;
private float coordinate_Y1[] = new float[200];
private float coordinate_Y2[] = new float[200];
private Scope3D_1 ch1curve3D, ch21curve3D;
private Scope3D ch22curve3D;
```

```
        private Grid3D grid;
        private Box3D box_11, box_12, box_21, box_22;
        private Triangle3D tri;
        private UTriangle3D utri;
        private TransformGroup Transbox_11, Transbox_12, Transbox_21, Transbox_22;
        private TransformGroup Transtri, Transutri;
        private Coord3D_1 coord_1;
        private Coord3D_2 coord_2;
        private long starttime;
        private boolean ch1on = true;
        private boolean ch2on = false;
        private boolean triggerch1 = true;
        private boolean triggerch2 = false;
        private int positionch1 = 6;
        private int positionch2 = 4;
        private int counterch1 = 0;
        private int counterch2 = 0;
        private float heightch1 = 0.0f;
        private float heightch2 = 0.0f;
        private int hposition = 0;
        private int triggerposition = 5;
        private int triggerch1coun = 100;
        private int triggerch2coun = 100;
        private float sweeptime = 0.0005f;
        private float cycle=0.5f; //sgfrq*sweeptime

        //--------------------------------------- for the signal generator
        private Point3f sgposi = new Point3f();
        private Point3f sg_knobposi[] = new Point3f[2];
        private Point3f sg_buttonposi[] = new Point3f[6];
        private Point3f sg_connposi[] = new Point3f[2];
        private TransformGroup sgknobTrans[] = new TransformGroup[1];
        private TransformGroup sgbuttonTrans[] = new TransformGroup[6];
        private TransformGroup sgconnTrans[] = new TransformGroup[2];
        private boolean sgbuttonaction[] = new boolean[6];
        private boolean sgconn[] = new boolean[2];
        private float sg_knobangle[] = new float[2];
        private float sg_connangle[] = new float[2];
        private final float sgknob1_circleposi[] = new float[7];
        private final float sgconn1_circleposi[] = new float[2];
        private final float sgconn2_circleposi[] = new float[2];
        private TCP_OSCI tcp_sgservice=null;
        private Group sgCurvebranchParent;
        private BranchGroup sgCurvebranch;
        private int sgvalue = 1000;
        private int sgamp = 1000;
        private int sgfrq = 1000;
        private int sgdigit = 4;
        private int sglast_digit = 4;
        private int sgcurrent_digit = 4;
        private boolean sgsquare =true;
        private String sgdisplayvalue;
```

```java
private String sgunit = new String("Hz");
private Text2D sgtext;

//--------------------------------------- for the circuit board
private TransformGroup ccconnTrans[] = new TransformGroup[2];
private Point3f cc_connposi[] = new Point3f[2];
private float cc_connangle[] = new float[2];
private boolean ccconn[] = new boolean[2];
private final float ccconn1_circleposi[] = new float[2];
private final float ccconn2_circleposi[] = new float[2];

//------------------------------ for the room with the password permission
private Point3f passposi = new Point3f();
private Point3f frontleftwallposi = new Point3f();
private Point3f passbuttonposi[] = new Point3f[12];
private TransformGroup passbuttonTrans[] = new TransformGroup[12];
private boolean passbuttonaction[] = new boolean[6];
private TransformGroup doorTrans = new TransformGroup();
private Alpha doorAlpha = new Alpha(1, Alpha.INCREASING_ENABLE, 0, 0, 1500, 0, 0, 0, 0);
private RotPosPathInterpolator doorcontrol;
private Quat4f quats[] = new Quat4f[2];
private float knots[] = {0.0f, 1.0f};
private Point3f doorposi[] = new Point3f[2];
private long startTime = System.currentTimeMillis();
private boolean dooropen = false;
private Group passCurvebranchParent;
private BranchGroup passCurvebranch;

private String passdisplayvalue = new String("");
private String passstorevalue = new String("");
private Text2D passtext;
private int passdigit = 0;

//------------------------------ for the constants
private static final int OSCION = 101;
private static final int OSCIOFF = 102;
private static final int SGON = 201;
private static final int SGOFF = 202;
private static final int SGINC = 203;
private static final int SGDEC = 204;
private static final int PASSON = 301;
private static final int DOOROPEN = 401;
private static final int DOORCLOSE = 402;
private static final int ANIMATION = 501;
private static final int INTERACTION = 502;
private static final int DISCONN = 601;
private static final float DIFFERENCE = 0.00001f;
private static final float PAI = 3.14159f;
private static final float ANGLEPAI = 2.0f*PAI/360.0f;;
private static final float KNOBFACE = 0.003f;
private static final float BUTTONFACE = 0.004f;
```

```
private static final float TRACKWIDTH = 0.06f;
private static final int STEPDELAY = 100;
private static final int COUNCH1 = 15;
private static final int COUNCH2 = 15;
private static final int COUNTER = 10;
```

H.3 CONSTRUCTOR FOR PICKING BEHAVIOR

```
public PickingBehavior(Canvas3D canvas3D, BranchGroup branchGroup)
{
    pickCanvas = new PickCanvas(canvas3D, branchGroup);
    pickCanvas.setTolerance(0.0f);
    pickCanvas.setMode(PickCanvas.GEOMETRY_INTERSECT_INFO);
    pickCanvas.setMode(PickCanvas.GEOMETRY);
    pickCanvas.setMode(PickTool.GEOMETRY);

        // Create an Appearance.
        Appearance redlook = new Appearance();
        Color3f objColor = new Color3f(1.0f, 0.0f, 0.0f);
        Color3f black = new Color3f(0.0f, 0.0f, 0.0f);
        Color3f white = new Color3f(1.0f, 1.0f, 1.0f);
        redlook.setMaterial(new Material(objColor, black, objColor, white, 50.0f));
        redlook.setCapability(Appearance.ALLOW_MATERIAL_WRITE);
        Sphere sph = new Sphere(0.002f, redlook);
        sph.setPickable (false);
        sphTrans.setCapability (TransformGroup.ALLOW_TRANSFORM_READ);
        sphTrans.setCapability (TransformGroup.ALLOW_TRANSFORM_WRITE);
        sphTrans.addChild(sph);
        branchGroup.addChild(sphTrans);
}
```

H.4 OBTAINING HANDLES TO DISPLAYS OF OSCILLOSCOPE, SIGNAL GENERATOR AND DOOR PANEL

```
public void setDisplay(Group oscidisparent, Group sgdisparent, Group passdisparent)
{
    this.osciCurvebranchParent = oscidisparent;
    this.sgCurvebranchParent = sgdisparent;
    this.passCurvebranchParent = passdisparent;
}
```

H.5 OBTAINING HANDLE TO NAVIGATION PANEL

```
public void setPanel(OPanel panel)
{
```

```
        this.panel = panel;
    }
```

H.6 OBTAINING HANDLES FOR SHOWING REAL-TIME VIDEO ON OSCILLOSCOPE DISPLAY

```
public void setAppearance(Appearance appimage, Appearance appblack, Shape3D osci_screen)
{
    this.appimage = appimage;
    this.appblack = appblack;
    this.osci_screen = osci_screen;
}
```

H.7 OBTAINING INITIAL POSITIONS OF CONTROLS ON OSCILLOSCOPE

```
public void setOsciPositions(Point3f osciposi, Point3f osci_knobposi[], Point3f osci_buttonposi[],
    Point3f osci_slideposi[])
{
    this.osciposi = osciposi;
    this.osci_knobposi = osci_knobposi;
    this.osci_slideposi = osci_slideposi;
    this.osci_buttonposi = osci_buttonposi;
}
```

H.8 OBTAINING INITIAL POSITIONS OF CONTROLS ON SIGNAL GENERATOR

```
public void setSgPositions(Point3f sgposi, Point3f sg_knobposi[], Point3f sg_buttonposi[])
{
    this.sgposi = sgposi;
    this.sg_knobposi = sg_knobposi;
    this.sg_buttonposi = sg_buttonposi;
}
```

H.9 OBTAINING INITIAL POSITIONS OF CONTROLS ON DOOR CONTROL

```
public void setPassPositions(Point3f passposi, Point3f passbuttonposi[], Point3f frontleftwallposi)
{
    this.passposi = passposi;
    this.passbuttonposi = passbuttonposi;
```

```
        this.frontleftwallposi = frontleftwallposi;
    }
```

H.10 OBTAINING INITIAL KNOB ORIENTATION ANGLES ON OSCILLOSCOPE AND SIGNAL GNERATOR

```
    public void setAngles(float osci_knobangle[], float sg_knobangle[])
    {
        this.osci_knobangle = osci_knobangle;
        this.sg_knobangle = sg_knobangle;
    }
```

H.11 OBTAINING INITIAL CONNECTING STATUS OF CLIPS

```
    public void setConnStatus(Point3f osci_connposi[], Point3f sg_connposi[], Point3f cc_connposi[],
        float osci_connangle[], float sg_connangle[], float cc_connangle[])
    {
        this.osci_connposi = osci_connposi;
        this.osci_connangle = osci_connangle;
        this.sg_connposi = sg_connposi;
        this.sg_connangle = sg_connangle;
        this.cc_connposi = cc_connposi;
        this.cc_connangle = cc_connangle;
        initparamters();
    }
```

H.12 OBTAINING DOOR OPENING OR CLOSING STATUS

```
    public void setDoor(TransformGroup doorTrans)
    {
      Transform3D yis = new Transform3D();

        this.doorTrans = doorTrans;
        quats[0] = new Quat4f(0.0f, 0.0f, 0.0f, 1.0f);
        quats[1] = new Quat4f(0.0f, 0.0f, 0.0f, 1.0f);
        doorposi[0] = new Point3f(1.5f, 0.0f, 2.0f);
        doorposi[1] = new Point3f(1.5f, 0.0f, 2.0f);
        doorcontrol = new RotPosPathInterpolator(doorAlpha, this.doorTrans, yis, knots, quats,
            doorposi);
        quats[1] = new Quat4f(0.0f, 1.0f, 0.0f, 1.0f);
        doorcontrol.setSchedulingBounds(bounds);
        this.doorTrans.addChild(doorcontrol);
    }
```

H.13 CLOSE FUNCTION FOR DISCONNECTING TCP/IP LINKS

```
public void closeAll()
{
    if (tcp_osciservice!=null)
    {
        tcp_osciservice.stop();
        tcp_osciservice=null;
    }
    stime = System.currentTimeMillis();
    do
    {
        deltatime = System.currentTimeMillis() - stime;
    } while (deltatime<STEPDELAY);
    if (tcp_sgservice!=null)
    {
        tcp_sgservice.stop();
        tcp_sgservice=null;
    }
    if (udp_osciservice!=null)
    {
        udp_osciservice.shownoCurve();

        stime = System.currentTimeMillis();
        do
        {
            deltatime = System.currentTimeMillis() - stime;
        } while (deltatime<3000);
        udp_osciservice.stop();
        udp_osciservice=null;
    }
}
```

H.14 INITIALIZING ORIENTATONS AND POSITIONS OF ALL CONTROLS

```
private void initparamters()
{
    osciknob1_circleposi[0]  = 240.0f*ANGLEPAI;
    osciknob1_circleposi[1]  = 210.0f*ANGLEPAI;
    osciknob1_circleposi[2]  = 180.0f*ANGLEPAI;
    osciknob1_circleposi[3]  = 150.0f*ANGLEPAI;
    osciknob1_circleposi[4]  = 120.0f*ANGLEPAI;
    osciknob1_circleposi[5]  =  90.0f*ANGLEPAI;
    osciknob1_circleposi[6]  =  60.0f*ANGLEPAI;
    osciknob1_circleposi[7]  =  30.0f*ANGLEPAI;
    osciknob1_circleposi[8]  =   0.0f*ANGLEPAI;
    osciknob1_circleposi[9]  = 330.0f*ANGLEPAI;
    osciknob1_circleposi[10] = 300.0f*ANGLEPAI;
```

```
osciknob2_circleposi[0]  = 225.0f*ANGLEPAI;
osciknob2_circleposi[1]  = 195.0f*ANGLEPAI;
osciknob2_circleposi[2]  = 165.0f*ANGLEPAI;
osciknob2_circleposi[3]  = 135.0f*ANGLEPAI;
osciknob2_circleposi[4]  = 105.0f*ANGLEPAI;
osciknob2_circleposi[5]  =  75.0f*ANGLEPAI;
osciknob2_circleposi[6]  =  45.0f*ANGLEPAI;
osciknob2_circleposi[7]  =  15.0f*ANGLEPAI;
osciknob2_circleposi[8]  = 345.0f*ANGLEPAI;
osciknob2_circleposi[9]  = 315.0f*ANGLEPAI;
osciknob2_circleposi[10] = 285.0f*ANGLEPAI;
osciknob3_circleposi[0]  = 225.0f*ANGLEPAI;
osciknob3_circleposi[1]  = 195.0f*ANGLEPAI;
osciknob3_circleposi[2]  = 165.0f*ANGLEPAI;
osciknob3_circleposi[3]  = 135.0f*ANGLEPAI;
osciknob3_circleposi[4]  = 105.0f*ANGLEPAI;
osciknob3_circleposi[5]  =  75.0f*ANGLEPAI;
osciknob3_circleposi[6]  =  45.0f*ANGLEPAI;
osciknob3_circleposi[7]  =  15.0f*ANGLEPAI;
osciknob3_circleposi[8]  = 345.0f*ANGLEPAI;
osciknob3_circleposi[9]  = 315.0f*ANGLEPAI;
osciknob3_circleposi[10] = 285.0f*ANGLEPAI;
osciknob4_circleposi[0]  = 240.0f*ANGLEPAI;
osciknob4_circleposi[1]  = 210.0f*ANGLEPAI;
osciknob4_circleposi[2]  = 180.0f*ANGLEPAI;
osciknob4_circleposi[3]  = 150.0f*ANGLEPAI;
osciknob4_circleposi[4]  = 120.0f*ANGLEPAI;
osciknob4_circleposi[5]  =  90.0f*ANGLEPAI;
osciknob4_circleposi[6]  =  60.0f*ANGLEPAI;
osciknob4_circleposi[7]  =  30.0f*ANGLEPAI;
osciknob4_circleposi[8]  =   0.0f*ANGLEPAI;
osciknob4_circleposi[9]  = 330.0f*ANGLEPAI;
osciknob4_circleposi[10] = 300.0f*ANGLEPAI;
osciknob8_circleposi[0]  = 225.0f*ANGLEPAI;
osciknob8_circleposi[1]  = 205.0f*ANGLEPAI;
osciknob8_circleposi[2]  = 185.0f*ANGLEPAI;
osciknob8_circleposi[3]  = 165.0f*ANGLEPAI;
osciknob8_circleposi[4]  = 145.0f*ANGLEPAI;
osciknob8_circleposi[5]  = 125.0f*ANGLEPAI;
osciknob8_circleposi[6]  = 105.0f*ANGLEPAI;
osciknob8_circleposi[7]  =  85.0f*ANGLEPAI;
osciknob8_circleposi[8]  =  65.0f*ANGLEPAI;
osciknob8_circleposi[9]  =  45.0f*ANGLEPAI;
osciknob8_circleposi[10] =  25.0f*ANGLEPAI;
osciknob8_circleposi[11] =   5.0f*ANGLEPAI;
osciknob8_circleposi[12] = 345.0f*ANGLEPAI;
osciknob8_circleposi[13] = 325.0f*ANGLEPAI;
osciknob8_circleposi[14] = 305.0f*ANGLEPAI;
osciknob8_circleposi[15] = 285.0f*ANGLEPAI;
osciknob9_circleposi[0]  = 240.0f*ANGLEPAI;
osciknob9_circleposi[1]  = 210.0f*ANGLEPAI;
osciknob9_circleposi[2]  = 180.0f*ANGLEPAI;
```

```
osciknob9_circleposi[3]  = 150.0f*ANGLEPAI;
osciknob9_circleposi[4]  = 120.0f*ANGLEPAI;
osciknob9_circleposi[5]  =  90.0f*ANGLEPAI;
osciknob9_circleposi[6]  =  60.0f*ANGLEPAI;
osciknob9_circleposi[7]  =  30.0f*ANGLEPAI;
osciknob9_circleposi[8]  =   0.0f*ANGLEPAI;
osciknob9_circleposi[9]  = 330.0f*ANGLEPAI;
osciknob9_circleposi[10] = 300.0f*ANGLEPAI;
osciknob10_circleposi[0] = 240.0f*ANGLEPAI;
osciknob10_circleposi[1] = 210.0f*ANGLEPAI;
osciknob10_circleposi[2] = 180.0f*ANGLEPAI;
osciknob10_circleposi[3] = 150.0f*ANGLEPAI;
osciknob10_circleposi[4] = 120.0f*ANGLEPAI;
osciknob10_circleposi[5] =  90.0f*ANGLEPAI;
osciknob10_circleposi[6] =  60.0f*ANGLEPAI;
osciknob10_circleposi[7] =  30.0f*ANGLEPAI;
osciknob10_circleposi[8] =   0.0f*ANGLEPAI;
osciknob10_circleposi[9] = 330.0f*ANGLEPAI;
osciknob10_circleposi[10] = 300.0f*ANGLEPAI;
oscislider1_posi[0] = osci_slideposi[0].y;
oscislider1_posi[1] = osci_slideposi[0].y-TRACKWIDTH/2.0f;
oscislider1_posi[2] = osci_slideposi[0].y-TRACKWIDTH;
oscislider2_posi[0] = osci_slideposi[1].y;
oscislider2_posi[1] = osci_slideposi[1].y-TRACKWIDTH/4.0f;
oscislider2_posi[2] = osci_slideposi[1].y-TRACKWIDTH/2.0f;
oscislider3_posi[0] = osci_slideposi[2].y;
oscislider3_posi[1] = osci_slideposi[2].y-TRACKWIDTH/2.0f;
oscislider3_posi[2] = osci_slideposi[2].y-TRACKWIDTH;
oscislider4_posi[0] = osci_slideposi[3].x+TRACKWIDTH/3.0f;
oscislider4_posi[1] = osci_slideposi[3].x;
oscislider5_posi[0] = osci_slideposi[4].x+TRACKWIDTH/4.0f;
oscislider5_posi[1] = osci_slideposi[4].x;
osciconn1_circleposi[0] = 130.0f*ANGLEPAI;
osciconn1_circleposi[1] = 105.0f*ANGLEPAI;
osciconn2_circleposi[0] = 150.0f*ANGLEPAI;
osciconn2_circleposi[1] = 125.0f*ANGLEPAI;
osciconn3_circleposi[0] = 148.0f*ANGLEPAI;
osciconn3_circleposi[1] = 123.0f*ANGLEPAI;
osciconn[0] = false;
osciconn[1] = false;
osciconn[2] = false;
for (int i=0;i<2;i++)
{
     oscibuttonaction[i] = false;
}
sgconn1_circleposi[0] = 160.0f*ANGLEPAI;
sgconn1_circleposi[1] = 120.0f*ANGLEPAI;
sgconn2_circleposi[0] = 88.0f*ANGLEPAI;
sgconn2_circleposi[1] = 61.0f*ANGLEPAI;
sgconn[0] = true;
sgconn[1] = false;
for (int i=0;i<6;i++)
```

```
        {
            sgbuttonaction[i] = false;
        }
        sgbuttonaction[4] = true;
        ccconn1_circleposi[0] = 132.0f*ANGLEPAI;
        ccconn1_circleposi[1] =  95.0f*ANGLEPAI;
        ccconn2_circleposi[0] = 130.0f*ANGLEPAI;
        ccconn2_circleposi[1] =  90.0f*ANGLEPAI;
        ccconn[0] = false;
        ccconn[1] = false;
        for (int i=0;i<6;i++)
        {
            passbuttonaction[i]=false;
        }
    }
```

H.15 MAIN INITIALIZATION FUNCTION FOR EVENT DETECTIONS

```
    public void initialize()
    {
        allEvents = new WakeupCriterion[17];
        allEvents[0] = new WakeupOnAWTEvent(MouseEvent.MOUSE_DRAGGED);
        allEvents[1] = new WakeupOnAWTEvent(MouseEvent.MOUSE_PRESSED);
        allEvents[2] = new WakeupOnAWTEvent(MouseEvent.MOUSE_RELEASED);
        allEvents[3] = new WakeupOnAWTEvent(MouseEvent.MOUSE_MOVED);
        allEvents[4] = new WakeupOnBehaviorPost(null, OSCION);
        allEvents[5] = new WakeupOnBehaviorPost(null, OSCIOFF);
        allEvents[6] = new WakeupOnBehaviorPost(null, SGON);
        allEvents[7] = new WakeupOnBehaviorPost(null, SGOFF);
        allEvents[8] = new WakeupOnBehaviorPost(null, SGINC);
        allEvents[9] = new WakeupOnBehaviorPost(null, SGDEC);
        allEvents[10] = new WakeupOnBehaviorPost(null, PASSON);
        allEvents[11] = new WakeupOnBehaviorPost(null, DOOROPEN);
        allEvents[12] = new WakeupOnBehaviorPost(null, DOORCLOSE);
        allEvents[13] = new WakeupOnBehaviorPost(null, ANIMATION);
        allEvents[14] = new WakeupOnBehaviorPost(null, INTERACTION);
        allEvents[15] = new WakeupOnBehaviorPost(null, DISCONN);
        allEvents[16] = new WakeupOnElapsedFrames(0);
        alleventsCriterion = new WakeupOr(allEvents);
        mouseandpostidEvents = new WakeupCriterion[16];
        mouseandpostidEvents[0] = new WakeupOnAWTEvent(MouseEvent.MOUSE_DRAGGED);
        mouseandpostidEvents[1] = new WakeupOnAWTEvent(MouseEvent.MOUSE_PRESSED);
        mouseandpostidEvents[2] = new WakeupOnAWTEvent(MouseEvent.MOUSE_RELEASED);
        mouseandpostidEvents[3] = new WakeupOnAWTEvent(MouseEvent.MOUSE_MOVED);
        mouseandpostidEvents[4] = new WakeupOnBehaviorPost(null, OSCION);
        mouseandpostidEvents[5] = new WakeupOnBehaviorPost(null, OSCIOFF);
        mouseandpostidEvents[6] = new WakeupOnBehaviorPost(null, SGON);
        mouseandpostidEvents[7] = new WakeupOnBehaviorPost(null, SGOFF);
```

```
mouseandpostidEvents[8] = new WakeupOnBehaviorPost(null, SGINC);
mouseandpostidEvents[9] = new WakeupOnBehaviorPost(null, SGDEC);
mouseandpostidEvents[10] = new WakeupOnBehaviorPost(null, PASSON);
mouseandpostidEvents[11] = new WakeupOnBehaviorPost(null, DOOROPEN);
mouseandpostidEvents[12] = new WakeupOnBehaviorPost(null, DOORCLOSE);
mouseandpostidEvents[13] = new WakeupOnBehaviorPost(null, ANIMATION);
mouseandpostidEvents[14] = new WakeupOnBehaviorPost(null, INTERACTION);
mouseandpostidEvents[15] = new WakeupOnBehaviorPost(null, DISCONN);
mouseandpostidCriterion = new WakeupOr(mouseandpostidEvents);
wakeupOn(mouseandpostidCriterion);
}
```

H.16 FUNCTION FOR DETECTING EXISTENCE OF PICKABLE CONTROL WHEN MOUSE IS MOVED

```
private boolean isObject(Point3f object, float x, float y)
{
    float d;
    d = (object.x-x)*(object.x-x)+(object.y-y)*(object.y-y);
    if (d < DIFFERENCE)
    {
        return true;
    }
    else
    {
        return false;
    }
}
```

H.17 FUNCTION FOR DETERMINING ID OF CONTROL OBJECT BEING PICKED

```
private int whichObject(float x, float y)
{
    //Detect the control components on the oscilloscope panel
    if (isObject(osci_knobposi[0],   x-osciposi.x, y-osciposi.y)) return 1101;
    if (isObject(osci_knobposi[1],   x-osciposi.x, y-osciposi.y)) return 1102;
    if (isObject(osci_knobposi[2],   x-osciposi.x, y-osciposi.y)) return 1103;
    if (isObject(osci_knobposi[3],   x-osciposi.x, y-osciposi.y)) return 1104;
    if (isObject(osci_knobposi[4],   x-osciposi.x, y-osciposi.y)) return 1105;
    if (isObject(osci_knobposi[5],   x-osciposi.x, y-osciposi.y)) return 1106;
    if (isObject(osci_knobposi[6],   x-osciposi.x, y-osciposi.y)) return 1107;
    if (isObject(osci_knobposi[7],   x-osciposi.x, y-osciposi.y)) return 1108;
    if (isObject(osci_knobposi[8],   x-osciposi.x, y-osciposi.y)) return 1109;
    if (isObject(osci_knobposi[9],   x-osciposi.x, y-osciposi.y)) return 1110;
    if (isObject(osci_buttonposi[0], x-osciposi.x, y-osciposi.y)) return 1201;
    if (isObject(osci_slideposi[0],  x-osciposi.x, y-osciposi.y)) return 1301;
```

```
        if (isObject(osci_slideposi[1],  x-osciposi.x, y-osciposi.y)) return 1302;
        if (isObject(osci_slideposi[2],  x-osciposi.x, y-osciposi.y)) return 1303;
        if (isObject(osci_slideposi[3],  x-osciposi.x, y-osciposi.y)) return 1304;
        if (isObject(osci_slideposi[4],  x-osciposi.x, y-osciposi.y)) return 1305;
        if (isObject(osci_connposi[0],   x-osciposi.x, y-osciposi.y)) return 1401;
        if (isObject(osci_connposi[1],   x-osciposi.x, y-osciposi.y)) return 1402;
        if (isObject(osci_connposi[2],   x-osciposi.x, y-osciposi.y)) return 1403;

        //Detect the control components on the signal generator panel
        if (isObject(sg_knobposi[0],   x-sgposi.x, y-sgposi.y)) return 2101;
        if (isObject(sg_buttonposi[0], x-sgposi.x, y-sgposi.y)) return 2201;
        if (isObject(sg_buttonposi[1], x-sgposi.x, y-sgposi.y)) return 2202;
        if (isObject(sg_buttonposi[2], x-sgposi.x, y-sgposi.y)) return 2203;
        if (isObject(sg_buttonposi[3], x-sgposi.x, y-sgposi.y)) return 2204;
        if (isObject(sg_buttonposi[4], x-sgposi.x, y-sgposi.y)) return 2205;
        if (isObject(sg_buttonposi[5], x-sgposi.x, y-sgposi.y)) return 2206;
        if (isObject(sg_connposi[0],   x-sgposi.x, y-sgposi.y)) return 2401;
        if (isObject(sg_connposi[1],   x-sgposi.x, y-sgposi.y)) return 2402;

        //Detect the control components on the circuit board
        if (isObject(cc_connposi[0],   x-sgposi.x, y-sgposi.y)) return 0;//4401;
        if (isObject(cc_connposi[1],   x-sgposi.x, y-sgposi.y)) return 0;//4402;

        //Detect the control components on the card reader panel
        if (isObject(passbuttonposi[ 0], x-passposi.x-frontleftwallposi.x, y-passposi.y-frontleftwallposi.y))
                return 3201;
        if (isObject(passbuttonposi[ 1], x-passposi.x-frontleftwallposi.x, y-passposi.y-frontleftwallposi.y))
                return 3202;
        if (isObject(passbuttonposi[ 2], x-passposi.x-frontleftwallposi.x, y-passposi.y-frontleftwallposi.y))
                return 3203;
        if (isObject(passbuttonposi[ 3], x-passposi.x-frontleftwallposi.x, y-passposi.y-frontleftwallposi.y))
                return 3204;
        if (isObject(passbuttonposi[ 4], x-passposi.x-frontleftwallposi.x, y-passposi.y-frontleftwallposi.y))
                return 3205;
        if (isObject(passbuttonposi[ 5], x-passposi.x-frontleftwallposi.x, y-passposi.y-frontleftwallposi.y))
                return 3206;
        if (isObject(passbuttonposi[ 6], x-passposi.x-frontleftwallposi.x, y-passposi.y-frontleftwallposi.y))
                return 3207;
        if (isObject(passbuttonposi[ 7], x-passposi.x-frontleftwallposi.x, y-passposi.y-frontleftwallposi.y))
                return 3208;
        if (isObject(passbuttonposi[ 8], x-passposi.x-frontleftwallposi.x, y-passposi.y-frontleftwallposi.y))
                return 3209;
        if (isObject(passbuttonposi[ 9], x-passposi.x-frontleftwallposi.x, y-passposi.y-frontleftwallposi.y))
                return 3210;
        if (isObject(passbuttonposi[10], x-passposi.x-frontleftwallposi.x,
                y-passposi.y-frontleftwallposi.y)) return 3211;
        if (isObject(passbuttonposi[11], x-passposi.x-frontleftwallposi.x,
                y-passposi.y-frontleftwallposi.y)) return 3212;
        //add other components
        return 0;
    }
```

H.18 FUNCTION FOR DETERMINING NEXT KNOB POSITION AFTER MOUSE DRAG AND RELEASE

```
private float RotationPosition(float returnangle, int num, float angleposi[])
{
    for (int i=0; i<num-1; i++)
    {
        if (angleposi[i]>angleposi[i+1])
        {
            if (returnangle<=angleposi[i]&&returnangle>angleposi[i+1])
            {
                if (returnangle>(angleposi[i]+angleposi[i+1])/2.0f)
                {
                    returnangle = angleposi[i];
                    return returnangle;
                }
                else
                {
                    returnangle = angleposi[i+1];
                    return returnangle;
                }
            }
        }
        else
        {
            if (returnangle<angleposi[i])
            {
                returnangle = angleposi[i];
                return returnangle;
            }
            else if (returnangle>angleposi[i+1])
            {
                returnangle = angleposi[i+1];
                return returnangle;
            }
        }
    }
    return returnangle;
}
```

H.19 FUNCTION FOR DETERMINING NEXT SLIDER POSITION AFTER MOUSE DRAG AND RELEASE

```
private float SlidePosition(float returnposi, int num, float slideposi[])
{
    for (int i=0; i<num-1; i++)
    {
        if (returnposi<=slideposi[i]&&returnposi>slideposi[i+1])
        {
```

```
            if (returnposi>(slideposi[i]+slideposi[i+1])/2.0f)
            {
                    returnposi = slideposi[i];
            }
            else
            {
                    returnposi = slideposi[i+1];
            }
        }
    }
    return returnposi;
}
```

H.20 CALCULATING MOUSE ANGLE RELATIVE TO KNOB

```
//Returning the value of the current angle
private float CalAngle(Point3f part, Point3f component, Point3f CurrentPt)
{
    float angle;
    angle = (float)(Math.atan2(CurrentPt.x-component.x-part.x,
            CurrentPt.y-component.y-part.y)/Math.PI);
    angle = (-angle+1.0f)*PAI - PAI/2.0f;
    if (angle<0.0f) angle = angle+2.0f*PAI; //The angle value is negative
    return angle;      //Returning the angle value of 0 to 2*PAI
}
```

H.21 CALCULATING CHANGE IN MOUSE ANGLE

```
//Returning the angle difference between the current angle and last one
private float DeltaAngle(float currentangle, float lastangle)
{
    float delta;
    if (currentangle-lastangle>2.0f)
    {
        // currentangle is in the 4th phase and lastangle is in the 1st phase
        delta = currentangle - lastangle - 2.0f*PAI;
    }
    else if (currentangle-lastangle<-2.0f)
    {
        // currentangle is in the 1st phase and lastangle is in the 4th phase
        delta = currentangle -lastangle + 2.0f*PAI;
    }
    else
    {
        delta = currentangle -lastangle;
    }
    return delta;
}
```

H.22 NORMALIZATING MOUSE ANGLE TO RANGE FROM 0 TO 2PI

```
//Being used to regulate the angle and make it range from 0 to 2*PAI
private float RegulateAngle(float componentangle, float delta)
{
        componentangle = componentangle+delta;
        if (componentangle<0.0f) componentangle=componentangle + 2.0f*PAI;
        if (componentangle>=2.0f*PAI) componentangle=componentangle - 2.0f*PAI;
        return componentangle; //[0, 2*PAI)
}
```

H.23 LIMITING KNOB ANGLE TO WITHIN A SPECIFIC RANGE

```
//Limiting the angle in the rangle between the minimum and maximum
private float LimitAngle(float delta, float componentangle, float circleposi[])
{
        if ((componentangle+delta)<=circleposi[0]||(componentangle+delta)>=circleposi[circleposi.length-1])
        {
                //Not allowed to exceed the scope
                componentangle = RegulateAngle(componentangle, delta);
        }
        return componentangle;
}
```

H.24 LIMITING CLIP ANGLE TO WITHIN A SPECIFIC RANGE

```
//Limiting the angle in the rangle between the minimum and maximum
private float LimitConnAngle(float delta, float componentangle, float circleposi[])
{
        if ((componentangle+delta)<=circleposi[0]&&(componentangle+delta)
                >=circleposi[circleposi.length-1])
        {
                //Not allowed to exceed the scope
                componentangle = RegulateAngle(componentangle, delta);
        }
        return componentangle;
}
```

H.25 FUNCTION FOR BUTTON PRESS OR RELEASE EVENTS

```
//Button action, press or release
private void ButtonAct(Point3f object, TransformGroup trans, boolean tag, float span)
{
    if (tag)
    {
        setPosition(trans, new Point3f(object.x, object.y, object.z-span));
    }
    else
    {
        setPosition(trans, new Point3f(object.x, object.y, object.z));
    }
}
```

H.26 MAIN MOUSE RELEASE EVENT FUNCTIONS FOR KNOBS, CLIPS, SLIDERS AND BUTTONS

```
private void MouseRelease(int obj)
{
    switch (obj)
    {
    //--------------------------------------- for the oscilloscope
    case 1101:
        osci_knobangle[0] = RotationPosition(osci_knobangle[0], osciknob1_circleposi.length,
                osciknob1_circleposi);
        setRotationZ(osciknobTrans[0], osci_knobangle[0]);
        if (tcp_osciservice!=null)
        {
            if (osci_knobangle[0]==osciknob1_circleposi[0])
            {
                tcp_osciservice.SendCmd("ch1position 5");
                positionch1 = 0;
            }
            else if (osci_knobangle[0]==osciknob1_circleposi[1])
            {
                tcp_osciservice.SendCmd("ch1position 4");
                positionch1 = 1;
            }
            else if (osci_knobangle[0]==osciknob1_circleposi[2])
            {
                tcp_osciservice.SendCmd("ch1position 3");
                positionch1 = 2;
            }
            else if (osci_knobangle[0]==osciknob1_circleposi[3])
            {
                tcp_osciservice.SendCmd("ch1position 2");
                positionch1 = 3;
```

```
                    }
                    else if (osci_knobangle[0]==osciknob1_circleposi[4])
                    {
                            tcp_osciservice.SendCmd("ch1position 1");
                            positionch1 = 4;
                    }
                    else if (osci_knobangle[0]==osciknob1_circleposi[5])
                    {
                            tcp_osciservice.SendCmd("ch1position 0");
                            positionch1 = 5;
                    }
                    else if (osci_knobangle[0]==osciknob1_circleposi[6])
                    {
                            tcp_osciservice.SendCmd("ch1position 10");
                            positionch1 = 6;
                    }
                    else if (osci_knobangle[0]==osciknob1_circleposi[7])
                    {
                            tcp_osciservice.SendCmd("ch1position 9");
                            positionch1 = 7;
                    }
                    else if (osci_knobangle[0]==osciknob1_circleposi[8])
                    {
                            tcp_osciservice.SendCmd("ch1position 8");
                            positionch1 = 8;
                    }
                    else if (osci_knobangle[0]==osciknob1_circleposi[9])
                    {
                            tcp_osciservice.SendCmd("ch1position 7");
                            positionch1 = 9;
                    }
                    else if (osci_knobangle[0]==osciknob1_circleposi[10])
                    {
                            tcp_osciservice.SendCmd("ch1position 6");
                            positionch1 = 10;
                    }
                    counterch1 = 0;
                    if (ch1on) counter=0;
            }
            break;
        case 1102:
            osci_knobangle[1] = RotationPosition(osci_knobangle[1], osciknob2_circleposi.length,
                osciknob2_circleposi);
            setRotationZ(osciknobTrans[1], osci_knobangle[1]);
        if (tcp_osciservice!=null)
        {
            if (osci_knobangle[1]==osciknob2_circleposi[0])
                tcp_osciservice.SendCmd("ch1verticalscale 0");
                else if     (osci_knobangle[1]==osciknob2_circleposi[1])
                    tcp_osciservice.SendCmd("ch1verticalscale 1");
                else if     (osci_knobangle[1]==osciknob2_circleposi[2])
                    tcp_osciservice.SendCmd("ch1verticalscale 2");
```

```
                    else if      (osci_knobangle[1]==osciknob2_circleposi[3])
                         tcp_osciservice.SendCmd("ch1verticalscale 3");
                    else if      (osci_knobangle[1]==osciknob2_circleposi[4])
                         tcp_osciservice.SendCmd("ch1verticalscale 4");
                    else if      (osci_knobangle[1]==osciknob2_circleposi[5])
                         tcp_osciservice.SendCmd("ch1verticalscale 5");
                    else if      (osci_knobangle[1]==osciknob2_circleposi[6])
                         tcp_osciservice.SendCmd("ch1verticalscale 6");
                    else if      (osci_knobangle[1]==osciknob2_circleposi[7])
                         tcp_osciservice.SendCmd("ch1verticalscale 7");
                    else if      (osci_knobangle[1]==osciknob2_circleposi[8])
                         tcp_osciservice.SendCmd("ch1verticalscale 8");
                    else if      (osci_knobangle[1]==osciknob2_circleposi[9])
                         tcp_osciservice.SendCmd("ch1verticalscale 9");
                    else if      (osci_knobangle[1]==osciknob2_circleposi[10])
                         tcp_osciservice.SendCmd("ch1verticalscale 10");
          }
        counterch1 = 0;
        if (ch1on) counter=0;
        break;
    case 1103:
        osci_knobangle[2] = RotationPosition(osci_knobangle[2], osciknob3_circleposi.length,
            osciknob3_circleposi);
        setRotationZ(osciknobTrans[2], osci_knobangle[2]);
  if (tcp_osciservice!=null)
        {
                    if (osci_knobangle[2]==osciknob2_circleposi[0])
                         tcp_osciservice.SendCmd("ch2verticalscale 0");
                    else if      (osci_knobangle[2]==osciknob3_circleposi[1])
                         tcp_osciservice.SendCmd("ch2verticalscale 1");
                    else if      (osci_knobangle[2]==osciknob3_circleposi[2])
                         tcp_osciservice.SendCmd("ch2verticalscale 2");
                    else if      (osci_knobangle[2]==osciknob3_circleposi[3])
                         tcp_osciservice.SendCmd("ch2verticalscale 3");
                    else if      (osci_knobangle[2]==osciknob3_circleposi[4])
                         tcp_osciservice.SendCmd("ch2verticalscale 4");
                    else if      (osci_knobangle[2]==osciknob3_circleposi[5])
                         tcp_osciservice.SendCmd("ch2verticalscale 5");
                    else if      (osci_knobangle[2]==osciknob3_circleposi[6])
                         tcp_osciservice.SendCmd("ch2verticalscale 6");
                    else if      (osci_knobangle[2]==osciknob3_circleposi[7])
                         tcp_osciservice.SendCmd("ch2verticalscale 7");
                    else if      (osci_knobangle[2]==osciknob3_circleposi[8])
                         tcp_osciservice.SendCmd("ch2verticalscale 8");
                    else if      (osci_knobangle[2]==osciknob3_circleposi[9])
                         tcp_osciservice.SendCmd("ch2verticalscale 9");
                    else if      (osci_knobangle[2]==osciknob3_circleposi[10])
                         tcp_osciservice.SendCmd("ch2verticalscale 10");
          }
        counterch2 = 0;
        if (ch2on) counter=0;
        break;
```

```
case 1104:
    osci_knobangle[3] = RotationPosition(osci_knobangle[3], osciknob4_circleposi.length,
        osciknob4_circleposi);
    setRotationZ(osciknobTrans[3], osci_knobangle[3]);
    if (tcp_osciservice!=null)
    {
        if (osci_knobangle[3]==osciknob4_circleposi[0])
        {
            tcp_osciservice.SendCmd("ch2position 5");
            positionch2 = 0;
        }
        else if (osci_knobangle[3]==osciknob4_circleposi[1])
        {
            tcp_osciservice.SendCmd("ch2position 4");
            positionch2 = 1;
        }
        else if (osci_knobangle[3]==osciknob4_circleposi[2])
        {
            tcp_osciservice.SendCmd("ch2position 3");
            positionch2 = 2;
        }
        else if (osci_knobangle[3]==osciknob4_circleposi[3])
        {
            tcp_osciservice.SendCmd("ch2position 2");
            positionch2 = 3;
        }
        else if (osci_knobangle[3]==osciknob4_circleposi[4])
        {
            tcp_osciservice.SendCmd("ch2position 1");
            positionch2 = 4;
        }
        else if (osci_knobangle[3]==osciknob4_circleposi[5])
        {
            tcp_osciservice.SendCmd("ch2position 0");
            positionch2 = 5;
        }
        else if (osci_knobangle[3]==osciknob4_circleposi[6])
        {
            tcp_osciservice.SendCmd("ch2position 10");
            positionch2 = 6;
        }
        else if (osci_knobangle[3]==osciknob4_circleposi[7])
        {
            tcp_osciservice.SendCmd("ch2position 9");
            positionch2 = 7;
        }
        else if (osci_knobangle[3]==osciknob4_circleposi[8])
        {
            tcp_osciservice.SendCmd("ch2position 8");
            positionch2 = 8;
        }
        else if (osci_knobangle[3]==osciknob4_circleposi[9])
```

```
                    {
                          tcp_osciservice.SendCmd("ch2position 7");
                          positionch2 = 9;
                    }
                    else if (osci_knobangle[3]==osciknob4_circleposi[10])
                    {
                          tcp_osciservice.SendCmd("ch2position 6");
                          positionch2 = 10;
                    }
              }
              counterch2 = 0;
              if (ch2on) counter=0;
              break;
        case 1105:
              break;
        case 1106:
              break;
        case 1107:
              break;
        case 1108:
              osci_knobangle[7] = RotationPosition(osci_knobangle[7], osciknob8_circleposi.length,
                    osciknob8_circleposi);
              setRotationZ(osciknobTrans[7], osci_knobangle[7]);
              if (tcp_osciservice!=null)
              {
                    if (osci_knobangle[7]==osciknob8_circleposi[0])
                    {
                          tcp_osciservice.SendCmd("horizontalscale 0.5 0");
                          sweeptime = 0.5f;
                          cycle=sgfrq*sweeptime;
                    } else if (osci_knobangle[7]==osciknob8_circleposi[1])
                    {
                          tcp_osciservice.SendCmd("horizontalscale 0.25 0");
                          sweeptime = 0.25f;
                          cycle=sgfrq*sweeptime;
                    } else if (osci_knobangle[7]==osciknob8_circleposi[2])
                    {
                          tcp_osciservice.SendCmd("horizontalscale 0.1 0");
                          sweeptime = 0.1f;
                          cycle=sgfrq*sweeptime;
                    } else if (osci_knobangle[7]==osciknob8_circleposi[3])
                    {
                          tcp_osciservice.SendCmd("horizontalscale 0.05 0");
                          sweeptime = 0.05f;
                          cycle=sgfrq*sweeptime;
                    } else if (osci_knobangle[7]==osciknob8_circleposi[4])
                    {
                          tcp_osciservice.SendCmd("horizontalscale 0.025 0");
```

```
                sweeptime = 0.025f;
                cycle=sgfrq*sweeptime;
        }
        else if (osci_knobangle[7]==osciknob8_circleposi[5])
        {
                tcp_osciservice.SendCmd("horizontalscale 0.01 0");
                sweeptime = 0.01f;
                cycle=sgfrq*sweeptime;
        }
        else if (osci_knobangle[7]==osciknob8_circleposi[6])
        {
                tcp_osciservice.SendCmd("horizontalscale 0.005 0");
                sweeptime = 0.005f;
                cycle=sgfrq*sweeptime;
        }
        else if (osci_knobangle[7]==osciknob8_circleposi[7])
        {
                tcp_osciservice.SendCmd("horizontalscale 0.0025 0");
                sweeptime = 0.0025f;
                cycle=sgfrq*sweeptime;
        }
        else if (osci_knobangle[7]==osciknob8_circleposi[8])
        {
                tcp_osciservice.SendCmd("horizontalscale 0.001 0");
                sweeptime = 0.001f;
                cycle=sgfrq*sweeptime;
        }
        else if (osci_knobangle[7]==osciknob8_circleposi[9])
        {
                tcp_osciservice.SendCmd("horizontalscale 0.0005 0");
                sweeptime = 0.0005f;
                cycle=sgfrq*sweeptime;
        }
        else if (osci_knobangle[7]==osciknob8_circleposi[10])
        {
                tcp_osciservice.SendCmd("horizontalscale 0.00025 0");
                sweeptime = 0.00025f;
                cycle=sgfrq*sweeptime;
        }
        else if (osci_knobangle[7]==osciknob8_circleposi[11])
        {
                tcp_osciservice.SendCmd("horizontalscale 0.0001 0");
                sweeptime = 0.0001f;
                cycle=sgfrq*sweeptime;
        }
        else if (osci_knobangle[7]==osciknob8_circleposi[12])
        {
                tcp_osciservice.SendCmd("horizontalscale 0.00005 0");
                sweeptime = 0.00005f;
                cycle=sgfrq*sweeptime;
        }
        else if (osci_knobangle[7]==osciknob8_circleposi[13])
```

```
            {
                tcp_osciservice.SendCmd("horizontalscale 0.000025 0");
                sweeptime = 0.000025f;
                cycle=sgfrq*sweeptime;
            }
            else if (osci_knobangle[7]==osciknob8_circleposi[14])
            {
                tcp_osciservice.SendCmd("horizontalscale 0.00001 0");
                sweeptime = 0.00001f;
                cycle=sgfrq*sweeptime;
            }
            else if (osci_knobangle[7]==osciknob8_circleposi[15])
            {
                tcp_osciservice.SendCmd("horizontalscale 0.000005 0");
                sweeptime = 0.000005f;
                cycle=sgfrq*sweeptime;
            }
        }
        counterch1 = 0;
        counterch2 = 0;
        if (ch1on) counter=0;
        if (ch2on) counter=0;
        break;
    case 1109:
        osci_knobangle[8] = RotationPosition(osci_knobangle[8], osciknob9_circleposi.length,
            osciknob9_circleposi);
        setRotationZ(osciknobTrans[8], osci_knobangle[8]);
        setTriggerPosition();
        break;
    case 1110:
        osci_knobangle[9] = RotationPosition(osci_knobangle[9], osciknob10_circleposi.length,
            osciknob10_circleposi);
        setRotationZ(osciknobTrans[9], osci_knobangle[9]);
        if (osci_knobangle[9]==osciknob10_circleposi[0])
        {
            if (tcp_osciservice!=null)
                tcp_osciservice.SendCmd("horizontalposition 5");
            hposition = -100;
        }
        else if (osci_knobangle[9]==osciknob10_circleposi[1])
        {
            if (tcp_osciservice!=null)
                tcp_osciservice.SendCmd("horizontalposition 4");
            hposition = -80;
        }
        else if (osci_knobangle[9]==osciknob10_circleposi[2])
        {
            if (tcp_osciservice!=null)
                tcp_osciservice.SendCmd("horizontalposition 3");
            hposition = -60;
        }
        else if (osci_knobangle[9]==osciknob10_circleposi[3])
```

```
            {
                 if (tcp_osciservice!=null)
                       tcp_osciservice.SendCmd("horizontalposition 2");
                 hposition = -40;
            }
            else if (osci_knobangle[9]==osciknob10_circleposi[4])
            {
                 if (tcp_osciservice!=null)
                       tcp_osciservice.SendCmd("horizontalposition 1");
                 hposition = -20;
            }
            else if (osci_knobangle[9]==osciknob10_circleposi[5])
            {
                 if (tcp_osciservice!=null)
                       tcp_osciservice.SendCmd("horizontalposition 0");
                 hposition = 0;
            }
            else if (osci_knobangle[9]==osciknob10_circleposi[6])
            {
                 if (tcp_osciservice!=null)
                       tcp_osciservice.SendCmd("horizontalposition 10");
                 hposition = 20;
            }
            else if (osci_knobangle[9]==osciknob10_circleposi[7])
            {
                 if (tcp_osciservice!=null)
                       tcp_osciservice.SendCmd("horizontalposition 9");
                 hposition = 40;
            }
            else if (osci_knobangle[9]==osciknob10_circleposi[8])
            {
                 if (tcp_osciservice!=null)
                       tcp_osciservice.SendCmd("horizontalposition 8");
                 hposition = 60;
            }
            else if (osci_knobangle[9]==osciknob10_circleposi[9])
            {
                 if (tcp_osciservice!=null)
                       tcp_osciservice.SendCmd("horizontalposition 7");
                 hposition = 80;
            }
            else if (osci_knobangle[9]==osciknob10_circleposi[10])
            {
                 if (tcp_osciservice!=null)
                       tcp_osciservice.SendCmd("horizontalposition 6");
                 hposition = 100;
            }
            break;
        case 1301:
osci_slideposi[0].y = SlidePosition(osci_slideposi[0].y, oscislider1_posi.length, oscislider1_posi);
            setPosition(oscislideTrans[0], osci_slideposi[0]);
            if (oscibuttonaction[0]&&osciconn[0]&&osciconn[1])
```

```
            {
                if (tcp_osciservice!=null)
                {
                    if (osci_slideposi[0].y==oscislider1_posi[0])
                        tcp_osciservice.SendCmd("ch1ac");
                    else if (osci_slideposi[0].y==oscislider1_posi[1])
                        tcp_osciservice.SendCmd("ch1gnd");
                    else if (osci_slideposi[0].y==oscislider1_posi[2])
                        tcp_osciservice.SendCmd("ch1dc");
                }
            }
            counterch1 = 0;
            counterch2 = 0;
            if (ch1on) counter=0;
            break;
        case 1302:
            osci_slideposi[1].y = SlidePosition(osci_slideposi[1].y, oscislider2_posi.length,
                oscislider2_posi);
            setPosition(oscislideTrans[1], osci_slideposi[1]);
            if (osci_slideposi[1].y==oscislider2_posi[0])
            {
                stime = System.currentTimeMillis();
                do
                {
                    deltatime = System.currentTimeMillis() - stime;
                } while (deltatime<STEPDELAY);
                if (osci_slideposi[4].x==oscislider5_posi[0])
                {
                    triggerch1 = false;
                    triggerch2 = true;
                    tcp_osciservice.SendCmd("triggerch2");
                }
                else if (osci_slideposi[4].x==oscislider5_posi[1])
                {
                    triggerch2 = false;
                    triggerch1 = true;
                    tcp_osciservice.SendCmd("triggerch1");
                }
                stime = System.currentTimeMillis();
                do
                {
                    deltatime = System.currentTimeMillis() - stime;
                } while (deltatime<STEPDELAY);
                setTriggerPosition();
//              if (tcp_osciservice!=null)
//                  tcp_osciservice.SendCmd("ch1");
                ch1on = true;
                ch2on = false;
                counterch1 = 0;
                if (ch1on) counter=0;
            }
            else if (osci_slideposi[1].y==oscislider2_posi[1])
```

```
{
    stime = System.currentTimeMillis();
    do
    {
        deltatime = System.currentTimeMillis() - stime;
    } while (deltatime<STEPDELAY);
    if (osci_slideposi[4].x==oscislider5_posi[0])
    {
        triggerch1 = false;
        triggerch2 = true;
        tcp_osciservice.SendCmd("triggerch2");
    }
    else if (osci_slideposi[4].x==oscislider5_posi[1])
    {
        triggerch2 = false;
        triggerch1 = true;
        tcp_osciservice.SendCmd("triggerch1");
    }
    stime = System.currentTimeMillis();
    do
    {
        deltatime = System.currentTimeMillis() - stime;
    } while (deltatime<STEPDELAY);
    setTriggerPosition();
//    if (tcp_osciservice!=null)
//        tcp_osciservice.SendCmd("ch2");
    ch2on = true;
    ch1on = false;
    counterch2 = 0;
    if (ch2on) counter=0;
}
else if (osci_slideposi[1].y==oscislider2_posi[2])
{
    stime = System.currentTimeMillis();
    do
    {
        deltatime = System.currentTimeMillis() - stime;
    } while (deltatime<STEPDELAY);
    if (osci_slideposi[4].x==oscislider5_posi[0])
    {
        triggerch1 = false;
        triggerch2 = true;
        tcp_osciservice.SendCmd("triggerch2");
    }
    else if (osci_slideposi[4].x==oscislider5_posi[1])
    {
        triggerch2 = false;
        triggerch1 = true;
        tcp_osciservice.SendCmd("triggerch1");
    }
    stime = System.currentTimeMillis();
    do
```

```
                {
                        deltatime = System.currentTimeMillis() - stime;
                } while (deltatime<STEPDELAY);
                setTriggerPosition();
//      if (tcp_osciservice!=null)
//      tcp_osciservice.SendCmd("alt");
                ch1on = true;
                ch2on = true;
                counterch1 = 0;
                counterch2 = 0;
                if (ch1on) counter=0;
                if (ch2on) counter=0;
        }
        break;
case 1303:
        osci_slideposi[2].y = SlidePosition(osci_slideposi[2].y, oscislider3_posi.length,
                oscislider3_posi);
        setPosition(oscislideTrans[2], osci_slideposi[2]);
        if (tcp_osciservice!=null)
        {
                if (osci_slideposi[2].y==oscislider3_posi[0])
                {
                        tcp_sgservice.SendCmd("d1");

                        stime = System.currentTimeMillis();
                        do
                        {
                                deltatime = System.currentTimeMillis() - stime;
                        } while (deltatime<STEPDELAY);
                        tcp_sgservice.SendCmd("d0");

                        stime = System.currentTimeMillis();
                        do
                        {
                                deltatime = System.currentTimeMillis() - stime;
                        } while (deltatime<STEPDELAY);
                        tcp_osciservice.SendCmd("ch2ac");
                }
                else if     (osci_slideposi[2].y==oscislider3_posi[1])
                        tcp_osciservice.SendCmd("ch2gnd");
                else if (osci_slideposi[2].y==oscislider3_posi[2]) tcp_osciservice.SendCmd("ch2dc");
        }
        counterch1 = 0;
        counterch2 = 0;
        if (ch2on) counter=0;
        break;
case 1304:
        osci_slideposi[3].x = SlidePosition(osci_slideposi[3].x, oscislider4_posi.length,
                oscislider4_posi);
        setPosition(oscislideTrans[3], osci_slideposi[3]);
        if (tcp_osciservice!=null)
        {
```

```
                    if (osci_slideposi[3].x==oscislider4_posi[0])
                        tcp_osciservice.SendCmd("triggernormminus");
                    else if     (osci_slideposi[3].x==oscislider4_posi[1])
                        tcp_osciservice.SendCmd("triggernormplus");
            }
            counterch1 = 0;
            counterch2 = 0;
            if (ch1on) counter=0;
            if (ch2on) counter=0;
            break;
        case 1305:
            osci_slideposi[4].x = SlidePosition(osci_slideposi[4].x, oscislider5_posi.length,
                    oscislider5_posi);
            setPosition(oscislideTrans[4], osci_slideposi[4]);
            if (tcp_osciservice!=null)
            {
                    if (osci_slideposi[4].x==oscislider5_posi[0])
                    {
                        triggerch1 = false;
                        triggerch2 = true;
                        tcp_osciservice.SendCmd("triggerch2");
                    }
                    else if (osci_slideposi[4].x==oscislider5_posi[1])
                    {
                        triggerch2 = false;
                        triggerch1 = true;
                        tcp_osciservice.SendCmd("triggerch1");
                    }
            }
            counterch1 = 0;
            counterch2 = 0;
            if (ch1on) counter=0;
            if (ch2on) counter=0;
            break;
        case 1401:
            osci_connangle[0] = RotationPosition(osci_connangle[0], osciconn1_circleposi.length,
                    osciconn1_circleposi);
            setRotationZ(osciconnTrans[0], osci_connangle[0]);
            if (osci_connangle[0]==osciconn1_circleposi[0])
            {
                    osciconn[0] = true;
                    if (oscibuttonaction[0]&&osciconn[0]&&osciconn[1])
                        OsciSupplement();
            }
            else
            {
                    osciconn[0] = false;
                    if (tcp_osciservice!=null)
                        tcp_osciservice.SendCmd("ch1gnd");
            }
            counterch1 = 0;
            counterch2 = 0;
```

```
            break;
    case 1402:
            osci_connangle[1] = RotationPosition(osci_connangle[1], osciconn2_circleposi.length,
                    osciconn2_circleposi);
            setRotationZ(osciconnTrans[1], osci_connangle[1]);
            if (osci_connangle[1]==osciconn2_circleposi[0])
            {
                    osciconn[1] = true;
                    if (oscibuttonaction[0]&&osciconn[0]&&osciconn[1])
                            OsciSupplement();
            }
            else
            {
                    osciconn[1] = false;
                    if (tcp_osciservice!=null)
                            tcp_osciservice.SendCmd("ch1gnd");
            }
            counterch1 = 0;
            counterch2 = 0;
            break;
    case 1403:
            osci_connangle[2] = RotationPosition(osci_connangle[2], osciconn3_circleposi.length,
                    osciconn3_circleposi);
            setRotationZ(osciconnTrans[2], osci_connangle[2]);
            if (osci_connangle[2]==osciconn3_circleposi[0])
            {
                    osciconn[2] = true;
                    if (sgbuttonaction[5]&&sgconn[1]&&osciconn[2])
                            SgSupplement();
            }
            else
            {
                    osciconn[2] = false;
                    if (tcp_sgservice!=null)
                            tcp_sgservice.SendCmd("d1");
            }
            counterch1 = 0;
            counterch2 = 0;
            break;

    //--------------------------------------- for the signal generator
    case 2101:                  //knob
            stime = System.currentTimeMillis();
            do
            {
                    deltatime = System.currentTimeMillis() - stime;
            } while (deltatime<STEPDELAY);

            if (sgbuttonaction[4]&&sgbuttonaction[5]) //add the unit for the number
            {
                    sgfrq = sgvalue;
                    cycle=sgfrq*sweeptime;
```

```
            if (tcp_sgservice!=null)
                tcp_sgservice.SendCmd("FRQ "+sgdisplayvalue+" HZ abc0");
    }
    else if (sgbuttonaction[3]&&sgbuttonaction[5])
    {
        sgamp = sgvalue;
        if (tcp_sgservice!=null)
        tcp_sgservice.SendCmd("AMP "+String.valueOf(sgvalue/1000.0f)+" V");
    }
    if (sgbuttonaction[5]) postId(SGON);

    counterch2 = 0;
    if (ch2on) counter=0;
    break;

case 2201:      //Power button
    counterch1=0;
    counterch2=0;
    if (ch1on) counter=0;
    if (ch2on) counter=0;

case 2202:
    ButtonAct(sg_buttonposi[1], sgbuttonTrans[0], false, 0.008f);
    if (sgbuttonaction[2])
    {
        sgsquare=!sgsquare;
        if (sgsquare)
        {
            if (tcp_sgservice!=null)
                tcp_sgservice.SendCmd("W3,H0");
        }
        else
        {
            if (tcp_sgservice!=null)
                tcp_sgservice.SendCmd("W1,H0");
        }
    }
    counterch2 = 0;
    if (ch2on) counter=0;
    if (sgbuttonaction[5]) postId(SGON);
    break;

case 2203:
    ButtonAct(sg_buttonposi[2], sgbuttonTrans[1], false, 0.008f);
    if (sgbuttonaction[2])
    {
        sgsquare=!sgsquare;
        if (sgsquare)
        {
            if (tcp_sgservice!=null)
                tcp_sgservice.SendCmd("W3,H0");
        }
```

```
            else
            {
                if (tcp_sgservice!=null)
                    tcp_sgservice.SendCmd("W1,H0");
            }
        }
        counterch2 = 0;
        if (ch2on) counter=0;
        if (sgbuttonaction[5]) postId(SGON);
        break;
    case 2204:       //waveform
        sgsquare=!sgsquare;
        if (sgsquare)
        {
            if (tcp_sgservice!=null)
                tcp_sgservice.SendCmd("W3,H0");
        }
        else
        {
            if (tcp_sgservice!=null)
                tcp_sgservice.SendCmd("W1,H0");
        }
        counterch2 = 0;
        if (ch2on) counter=0;
        if (sgbuttonaction[5]) postId(SGON);
        break;

    case 2205:       //amp
        if (tcp_sgservice!=null)
            tcp_sgservice.SendCmd("AMP "+String.valueOf(sgvalue/1000.0f)+" V");
        counterch2 = 0;
        if (ch2on) counter=0;
        if (sgbuttonaction[5]) postId(SGON);
        break;
    case 2206:       //freq
        if (tcp_sgservice!=null)
            tcp_sgservice.SendCmd("FRQ "+String.valueOf(sgvalue)+" HZ abc0");
        counterch2 = 0;
        if (ch2on) counter=0;
        if (sgbuttonaction[5]) postId(SGON);
        break;
    case 2401:
        sg_connangle[0] = RotationPosition(sg_connangle[0], sgconn1_circleposi.length,
            sgconn1_circleposi);
        setRotationZ(sgconnTrans[0], sg_connangle[0]);
        if (sg_connangle[0]==sgconn1_circleposi[1])
        {
            sgconn[0] = true;
            if (sgbuttonaction[5]&&sgconn[1]&&osciconn[2])
                SgSupplement();
        }
        else
```

```
                {
                    sgconn[0] = false;
                    if (tcp_sgservice!=null)
                        tcp_sgservice.SendCmd("d1");
                }
                break;
        case 2402:
                sg_connangle[1] = RotationPosition(sg_connangle[1], sgconn2_circleposi.length,
                    sgconn2_circleposi);
                setRotationZ(sgconnTrans[1], sg_connangle[1]);
                if (sg_connangle[1]==sgconn2_circleposi[1])
                {
                    sgconn[1] = true;
                    if (sgbuttonaction[5]&&sgconn[1]&&osciconn[2])
                        SgSupplement();
                }
                else
                {
                    sgconn[1] = false;
                    if (tcp_sgservice!=null)
                        tcp_sgservice.SendCmd("d1");
                }
                break;
                //--------------------------------------- for the circuit board
        case 4401:
                cc_connangle[0] = RotationPosition(cc_connangle[0], ccconn1_circleposi.length,
                    ccconn1_circleposi);
                setRotationZ(ccconnTrans[0], cc_connangle[0]);
                if (cc_connangle[0]==ccconn1_circleposi[1])
                {
                    ccconn[0] = true;
                    if (ccconn[0]&&sgconn[1])
                        SgSupplement();
                }
                else
                {
                    ccconn[0] = false;
                    if (tcp_sgservice!=null)
                        tcp_sgservice.SendCmd("d1");
                }
                break;
        case 4402:
                cc_connangle[1] = RotationPosition(cc_connangle[1], ccconn2_circleposi.length,
                    ccconn2_circleposi);
                setRotationZ(ccconnTrans[1], cc_connangle[1]);
                if (cc_connangle[1]==ccconn2_circleposi[0])
                {
                    ccconn[1] = true;
                    SgSupplement();
                }
                else
                {
```

```
                    sgconn[1] = false;
                    if (tcp_sgservice!=null)
                        tcp_sgservice.SendCmd("d1");
            }
        break;
    //--------------------------------------- for the card reader
    case 3201:
        ButtonAct(passbuttonposi[0], passbuttonTrans[0], false, 0.01f);
        break;
    case 3202:
        ButtonAct(passbuttonposi[1], passbuttonTrans[1], false, 0.01f);
        break;
    case 3203:
        ButtonAct(passbuttonposi[2], passbuttonTrans[2], false, 0.01f);
        break;
    case 3204:
        ButtonAct(passbuttonposi[3], passbuttonTrans[3], false, 0.01f);
        break;
    case 3205:
        ButtonAct(passbuttonposi[4], passbuttonTrans[4], false, 0.01f);
        break;
    case 3206:
        ButtonAct(passbuttonposi[5], passbuttonTrans[5], false, 0.01f);
        break;
    case 3207:
        ButtonAct(passbuttonposi[6], passbuttonTrans[6], false, 0.01f);
        break;
    case 3208:
        ButtonAct(passbuttonposi[7], passbuttonTrans[7], false, 0.01f);
        break;
    case 3209:
        ButtonAct(passbuttonposi[8], passbuttonTrans[8], false, 0.01f);
        break;
    case 3210:
        ButtonAct(passbuttonposi[9], passbuttonTrans[9], false, 0.01f);
        break;
    case 3211:
        ButtonAct(passbuttonposi[10], passbuttonTrans[10], false, 0.01f);
        break;
    case 3212:
        ButtonAct(passbuttonposi[11], passbuttonTrans[11], false, 0.01f);
        break;
    //--------------------------------------- for the others
    default:
    }
}
```

H.27 FUNCTION FOR CLIP CONNECTION EVENT FOR OSCILLOSCOPE TERMINALS

```
private void OsciSupplement()
{
    counterch1 = 0;
    if (ch1on) counter=0;
    if (tcp_osciservice!=null)
    {
     if (osci_slideposi[0].y==oscislider1_posi[0]) tcp_osciservice.SendCmd("ch1ac");
     else if      (osci_slideposi[0].y==oscislider1_posi[1]) tcp_osciservice.SendCmd("ch1gnd");
     else if (osci_slideposi[0].y==oscislider1_posi[2]) tcp_osciservice.SendCmd("ch1dc");
    }
}
```

H.28 FUNCTION FOR CLIP CONNECTING EVENT FOR SIGNAL GENERATOR TERMINALS

```
private void SgSupplement()
{
    counterch2 = 0;
    if (ch2on) counter=0;
    if (tcp_sgservice!=null)
        tcp_sgservice.SendCmd("d0");
    stime = System.currentTimeMillis();
    do
    {
        deltatime = System.currentTimeMillis() - stime;
    } while (deltatime<STEPDELAY);

    if (sgbuttonaction[4])  //add the unit for the number
    {
        sgfrq = sgvalue;
        cycle=sgfrq*sweeptime;
        if (tcp_sgservice!=null)
            tcp_sgservice.SendCmd("FRQ "+String.valueOf(sgfrq)+" HZ abc0");
    }
    else if (sgbuttonaction[3])
    {
        sgamp = sgvalue;
        if (tcp_sgservice!=null)
            tcp_sgservice.SendCmd("AMP "+String.valueOf(sgvalue/1000.0f)+" V");
    }
    else if (sgbuttonaction[2])
    {
        if (sgsquare)
        {
            if (tcp_sgservice!=null)
                tcp_sgservice.SendCmd("W3,H0");
```

```
            }
            else
            {
                if (tcp_sgservice!=null)
                    tcp_sgservice.SendCmd("W1,H0");
            }
        }

        stime = System.currentTimeMillis();
        do
        {
            deltatime = System.currentTimeMillis() - stime;
        } while (deltatime<200);

        if (tcp_osciservice!=null)
        {
         if (osci_slideposi[2].y==oscislider3_posi[0]) tcp_osciservice.SendCmd("ch2ac");
         else if      (osci_slideposi[2].y==oscislider3_posi[1]) tcp_osciservice.SendCmd("ch2gnd");
         else if (osci_slideposi[2].y==oscislider3_posi[2]) tcp_osciservice.SendCmd("ch2dc");
        }
    }
```

H.29 FUNCTION FOR TRIGGER SLIDER FOR OSCILLOSCOPE

```
    private void setTriggerPosition()
    {
        if (tcp_osciservice!=null)
        {
            if (osci_knobangle[8]==osciknob9_circleposi[0])
            {
            //     tcp_osciservice.SendCmd("mainlevel 5");
                triggerposition = 0;
                if (osci_slideposi[4].x==oscislider5_posi[0]&&ch2on)
                {
                    if (!triggerch1)
                    {
                        tcp_osciservice.SendCmd("triggerch1");
                        counterch1 = 0;
                        if (ch1on) counter=0;
                        counterch2 = 0;
                        if (ch2on) counter=0;
                    }
                    else
                    {
                        counterch1 = COUNCH1;
                        if (ch1on) counter=COUNTER;
                    }
                    triggerch2 = false;
```

```
                    triggerch1 = true;
            }
            else if (osci_slideposi[4].x==oscislider5_posi[1]&&ch1on)
            {
                if (!triggerch2)
                {
                    tcp_osciservice.SendCmd("triggerch2");
                    counterch2 = 0;
                    if (ch2on) counter=0;
                    counterch1 = 0;
                    if (ch1on) counter=0;
                }
                else
                {
                    counterch2 = COUNCH2;
                    if (ch2on) counter=COUNTER;
                }
                triggerch1 = false;
                triggerch2 = true;
            }
        }
        else if (osci_knobangle[8]==osciknob9_circleposi[1])
        {
//      tcp_osciservice.SendCmd("mainlevel 4");
            triggerposition = 1;
            if (osci_slideposi[4].x==oscislider5_posi[0]&&ch2on)
            {
                if (!triggerch2)
                {
                    tcp_osciservice.SendCmd("triggerch2");
                    counterch2 = 0;
                    if (ch2on) counter=0;
                }
                else
                {
                    counterch2 = COUNCH2;
                    if (ch2on) counter=COUNTER;
                }
                triggerch1 = false;
                triggerch2 = true;
            }
            else if (osci_slideposi[4].x==oscislider5_posi[1]&&ch1on)
            {
                if (!triggerch1)
                {
                    tcp_osciservice.SendCmd("triggerch1");
                    counterch1 = 0;
                    if (ch1on) counter=0;
                }
                else
                {
                    counterch1 = COUNCH1;
```

```
                                if (ch1on) counter=COUNTER;
                        }
                        triggerch2 = false;
                        triggerch1 = true;
                }
        }
        else if (osci_knobangle[8]==osciknob9_circleposi[2])
        {
//      tcp_osciservice.SendCmd("mainlevel 3");
                triggerposition = 2;
                if (osci_slideposi[4].x==oscislider5_posi[0]&&ch2on)
                {
                        if (!triggerch2)
                        {
                                tcp_osciservice.SendCmd("triggerch2");
                                counterch2 = 0;
                                if (ch2on) counter=0;
                        }
                        else
                        {
                                counterch2 = COUNCH2;
                                if (ch2on) counter=COUNTER;
                        }
                        triggerch1 = false;
                        triggerch2 = true;
                }
                else if (osci_slideposi[4].x==oscislider5_posi[1]&&ch1on)
                {
                        if (!triggerch1)
                        {
                                tcp_osciservice.SendCmd("triggerch1");
                                counterch1 = 0;
                                if (ch1on) counter=0;
                        }
                        else
                        {
                                counterch1 = COUNCH1;
                                if (ch1on) counter=COUNTER;
                        }
                        triggerch2 = false;
                        triggerch1 = true;
                }
        }
        else if (osci_knobangle[8]==osciknob9_circleposi[3])
        {
//      tcp_osciservice.SendCmd("mainlevel 2");
                triggerposition = 3;
                if (osci_slideposi[4].x==oscislider5_posi[0]&&ch2on)
                {
                        if (!triggerch2)
                        {
                                tcp_osciservice.SendCmd("triggerch2");
```

```
                    counterch2 = 0;
                    if (ch2on) counter=0;
                }
                else
                {
                    counterch2 = COUNCH2;
                    if (ch2on) counter=COUNTER;
                }
                triggerch1 = false;
                triggerch2 = true;
            }
            else if (osci_slideposi[4].x==oscislider5_posi[1]&&ch1on)
            {
                if (!triggerch1)
                {
                    tcp_osciservice.SendCmd("triggerch1");
                    counterch1 = 0;
                    if (ch1on) counter=0;
                }
                else
                {
                    counterch1 = COUNCH1;
                    if (ch1on) counter=COUNTER;
                }
                triggerch2 = false;
                triggerch1 = true;
            }
        }
        else if (osci_knobangle[8]==osciknob9_circleposi[4])
        {
//      tcp_osciservice.SendCmd("mainlevel 1");
            triggerposition = 4;
            if (osci_slideposi[4].x==oscislider5_posi[0]&&ch2on)
            {
                if (!triggerch2)
                {
                    tcp_osciservice.SendCmd("triggerch2");
                    counterch2 = 0;
                    if (ch2on) counter=0;
                }
                else
                {
                    counterch2 = COUNCH2;
                    if (ch2on) counter=COUNTER;
                }
                triggerch1 = false;
                triggerch2 = true;
            }
            else if (osci_slideposi[4].x==oscislider5_posi[1]&&ch1on)
            {
                if (!triggerch1)
                {
```

```
                    tcp_osciservice.SendCmd("triggerch1");
                    counterch1 = 0;
                    if (ch1on) counter=0;
                }
                else
                {
                    counterch1 = COUNCH1;
                    if (ch1on) counter=COUNTER;
                }
                triggerch2 = false;
                triggerch1 = true;
            }
        }
        else if (osci_knobangle[8]==osciknob9_circleposi[5])
        {
//      tcp_osciservice.SendCmd("mainlevel 0");
            triggerposition = 5;
            if (osci_slideposi[4].x==oscislider5_posi[0]&&ch2on)
            {
                if (!triggerch2)
                {
                    tcp_osciservice.SendCmd("triggerch2");
                    counterch2 = 0;
                    if (ch2on) counter=0;
                }
                else
                {
                    counterch2 = COUNCH2;
                    if (ch2on) counter=COUNTER;
                }
                triggerch1 = false;
                triggerch2 = true;
            }
            else if (osci_slideposi[4].x==oscislider5_posi[1]&&ch1on)
            {
                if (!triggerch1)
                {
                    tcp_osciservice.SendCmd("triggerch1");
                    counterch1 = 0;
                    if (ch1on) counter=0;
                }
                else
                {
                    counterch1 = COUNCH1;
                    if (ch1on) counter=COUNTER;
                }
                triggerch2 = false;
                triggerch1 = true;
            }
        }
        else if (osci_knobangle[8]==osciknob9_circleposi[6])
        {
```

```
//      tcp_osciservice.SendCmd("mainlevel 10");
        triggerposition = 6;
        if (osci_slideposi[4].x==oscislider5_posi[0]&&ch2on)
        {
              if (!triggerch2)
              {
                    tcp_osciservice.SendCmd("triggerch2");
                    counterch2 = 0;
                    if (ch2on) counter=0;
              }
              else
              {
                    counterch2 = COUNCH2;
                    if (ch2on) counter=COUNTER;
              }
              triggerch1 = false;
              triggerch2 = true;
        }
        else if (osci_slideposi[4].x==oscislider5_posi[1]&&ch1on)
        {
              if (!triggerch1)
              {
                    tcp_osciservice.SendCmd("triggerch1");
                    counterch1 = 0;
                    if (ch1on) counter=0;
              }
              else
              {
                    counterch1 = COUNCH1;
                    if (ch1on) counter=COUNTER;
              }
              triggerch2 = false;
              triggerch1 = true;
        }
}
else if (osci_knobangle[8]==osciknob9_circleposi[7])
{
//      tcp_osciservice.SendCmd("mainlevel 9");
        triggerposition = 7;
        if (osci_slideposi[4].x==oscislider5_posi[0]&&ch2on)
        {
              if (!triggerch2)
              {
                    tcp_osciservice.SendCmd("triggerch2");
                    counterch2 = 0;
                    if (ch2on) counter=0;
              }
              else
              {
                    counterch2 = COUNCH2;
                    if (ch2on) counter=COUNTER;
              }
```

```
            triggerch1 = false;
            triggerch2 = true;
        }
        else if (osci_slideposi[4].x==oscislider5_posi[1]&&ch1on)
        {
            if (!triggerch1)
            {
                tcp_osciservice.SendCmd("triggerch1");
                counterch1 = 0;
                if (ch1on) counter=0;
            }
            else
            {
                counterch1 = COUNCH1;
                if (ch1on) counter=COUNTER;
            }
            triggerch2 = false;
            triggerch1 = true;
        }
    }
    else if (osci_knobangle[8]==osciknob9_circleposi[8])
    {
//      tcp_osciservice.SendCmd("mainlevel 8");
        triggerposition = 8;
        if (osci_slideposi[4].x==oscislider5_posi[0]&&ch2on)
        {
            if (!triggerch2)
            {
                tcp_osciservice.SendCmd("triggerch2");
                counterch2 = 0;
                if (ch2on) counter=0;
            }
            else
            {
                counterch2 = COUNCH2;
                if (ch2on) counter=COUNTER;
            }
            triggerch1 = false;
            triggerch2 = true;
        }
        else if (osci_slideposi[4].x==oscislider5_posi[1]&&ch1on)
        {
            if (!triggerch1)
            {
                tcp_osciservice.SendCmd("triggerch1");
                counterch1 = 0;
                if (ch1on) counter=0;
            }
            else
            {
                counterch1 = COUNCH1;
                if (ch1on) counter=COUNTER;
```

```
                }
                triggerch2 = false;
                triggerch1 = true;
            }
        }
        else if (osci_knobangle[8]==osciknob9_circleposi[9])
        {
//      tcp_osciservice.SendCmd("mainlevel 7");
            triggerposition = 9;
            if (osci_slideposi[4].x==oscislider5_posi[0]&&ch2on)
            {
                if (!triggerch2)
                {
                    tcp_osciservice.SendCmd("triggerch2");
                    counterch2 = 0;
                    if (ch2on) counter=0;
                }
                else
                {
                    counterch2 = COUNCH2;
                    if (ch2on) counter=COUNTER;
                }
                triggerch1 = false;
                triggerch2 = true;
            }
            else if (osci_slideposi[4].x==oscislider5_posi[1]&&ch1on)
            {
                if (!triggerch1)
                {
                    tcp_osciservice.SendCmd("triggerch1");
                    counterch1 = 0;
                    if (ch1on) counter=0;
                }
                else
                {
                    counterch1 = COUNCH1;
                    if (ch1on) counter=COUNTER;
                }
                triggerch2 = false;
                triggerch1 = true;
            }
        }
        else if (osci_knobangle[8]==osciknob9_circleposi[10])
        {
//      tcp_osciservice.SendCmd("mainlevel 6");
            triggerposition = 10;
            if (osci_slideposi[4].x==oscislider5_posi[0]&&ch2on)
            {
                if (!triggerch1)
                {
                    tcp_osciservice.SendCmd("triggerch1");
                    counterch1 = 0;
```

```
                if (ch1on) counter=0;
                counterch2 = 0;
                if (ch2on) counter=0;
            }
            else
            {
                counterch1 = COUNCH1;
                if (ch1on) counter=COUNTER;
            }
            triggerch2 = false;
            triggerch1 = true;
        }
        else if (osci_slideposi[4].x==oscislider5_posi[1]&&ch1on)
        {
            if (!triggerch2)
            {
                tcp_osciservice.SendCmd("triggerch2");
                counterch2 = 0;
                if (ch2on) counter=0;
                counterch1 = 0;
                if (ch1on) counter=0;
            }
            else
            {
                counterch2 = COUNCH2;
                if (ch2on) counter=COUNTER;
            }
            triggerch1 = false;
            triggerch2 = true;
        }
    }
  }
}
```

H.30 GENERAL FUNCTION FOR SETTING POSITION OF TRANSFORMGROUP

```
private void setPosition(TransformGroup Trans, Point3f point)
{
    Transform3D t3d = new Transform3D();

    if (Trans!=null)
    {
        Trans.getTransform(t3d);
        t3d.setTranslation(new Vector3d(point));
        Trans.setTransform(t3d);
    }
}
```

H.31 GENERAL ROTATION FUNCTION FOR ROTATING TRANSFORMGROUP RELATIVE TO Z-AXIS

```
private void setRotationZ(TransformGroup Trans, float angle)
{
    Matrix3d rotMat = new Matrix3d();
    Transform3D rt3d = new Transform3D();
    if (Trans!=null)
    {
        Trans.getTransform(rt3d);
        rt3d.getRotationScale(rotMat);
        rotMat.m00 = Math.cos(angle);
        rotMat.m11 = rotMat.m00;
        rotMat.m10 = Math.sin(angle);
        rotMat.m01 = -rotMat.m10;
        rt3d.setRotation(rotMat);
        Trans.setTransform(rt3d);
    }
}
```

H.32 MAIN EVENT RESPONSE FUNCTION

```
public void processStimulus (Enumeration criteria)
{
    WakeupCriterion wakeup;
    AWTEvent[] event;
    int eventId;
    while (criteria.hasMoreElements())
    {
    wakeup = (WakeupCriterion) criteria.nextElement();
    // Mouse AWT event                                        //
    if (wakeup instanceof WakeupOnAWTEvent)
    {
        event = ((WakeupOnAWTEvent)wakeup).getAWTEvent();
        for (int i=0; i<event.length; i++)
        {
            eventId = event[i].getID();
            // Mouse move event                                //
            if (eventId == MouseEvent.MOUSE_MOVED)
            {
                int x_m = ((MouseEvent)event[i]).getX();
                int y_m = ((MouseEvent)event[i]).getY();
                pickCanvas.setShapeLocation(x_m, y_m);
                Point3d eyePos = pickCanvas.getStartPosition();
                pickResult = pickCanvas.pickClosest();

                if (pickResult != null)
                {
                    //Get closest intersection results
```

```
                        PickIntersection pi = pickResult.getClosestIntersection(eyePos);
                        trans = (TransformGroup)
                            pickResult.getNode(PickResult.TRANSFORM_GROUP);
                        Point3d []ptw = pi.getPrimitiveCoordinatesVW(); //reflect global coordinates
                        Point3d []pt = pi.getPrimitiveCoordinates();      //reflect local coordinates

                        if (pt.length==3) //Focus on knob
                        {
                            if (pt[0].z>KNOBFACE&&pt[1].z>KNOBFACE&&pt[2].z>KNOBFACE)
                            {
                                Point3d intPt = pi.getPointCoordinatesVW();       // position of cursor
                                CurrentPt = new Point3f(intPt);
                                setPosition(sphTrans, CurrentPt);
                                Point3f CenterPt = new Point3f(ptw[0]);
                                obj = whichObject(CenterPt.x, CenterPt.y);
                            }
                            else  // Focus on the other faces instead of the front face
                            {
                                setPosition(sphTrans, sphposi);
                                trans = null;
                                obj = 0;
                            }
                        }
                    else
                    {
if (pt[0].z>BUTTONFACE&&pt[1].z>BUTTONFACE&&pt[2].z>BUTTONFACE&&pt[3].z>BUTTONFACE)
                    {
                            Point3d intPt = pi.getPointCoordinatesVW();
                            CurrentPt = new Point3f(intPt);
                            setPosition(sphTrans, CurrentPt);
                    if (pt[0].x>=0&&pt[1].x>=0&&pt[2].x>=0&&pt[3].x>=0) // Focus on connector
                            {
Point3f CenterPt = new Point3f((float)((ptw[2].x+ptw[3].x)/2.0f), (float)((ptw[2].y+ptw[3].y)/2.0f), (float)(ptw[0].z));
                            obj = whichObject(CenterPt.x, CenterPt.y);
                            }
                                                        else                    // Focus on button or slider
                            {
Point3f CenterPt = new Point3f((float)((ptw[0].x+ptw[2].x)/2.0f), (float)((ptw[0].y+ptw[2].y)/2.0f), (float)(ptw[0].z));
                            obj = whichObject(CenterPt.x, CenterPt.y);
                            }
                    }
                        else  // Focus on the other faces instead of the front face
                        {
                            setPosition(sphTrans, sphposi);
                            trans = null;
                            obj = 0;
                        }
                    }
                    }
                        else  // On picked object
```

```
            {
                setPosition(sphTrans, sphposi);
                trans = null;
                obj = 0;
            }
            wakeupOn(alleventsCriterion);
        }
        // Mouse press event                                      //
        if (eventId == MouseEvent.MOUSE_PRESSED)
        {
            if (obj!=0)
            {
            switch (obj)
            {
        // Processing the control components of the oscilloscope ---------
            case 1101:
                    osciknobTrans[0]=trans;
        lastangle = CalAngle(osciposi, osci_knobposi[0], CurrentPt);
        break;
        case 1102:
            osciknobTrans[1]=trans;
            lastangle = CalAngle(osciposi, osci_knobposi[1], CurrentPt);
            break;
        case 1103:
            osciknobTrans[2]=trans;
            lastangle = CalAngle(osciposi, osci_knobposi[2], CurrentPt);
            break;
        case 1104: ·
            osciknobTrans[3]=trans;
            lastangle = CalAngle(osciposi, osci_knobposi[3], CurrentPt);
            break;
            case 1105:
            osciknobTrans[4]=trans;
            lastangle = CalAngle(osciposi, osci_knobposi[4], CurrentPt);
            break;
        case 1106:
            osciknobTrans[5]=trans;
            lastangle = CalAngle(osciposi, osci_knobposi[5], CurrentPt);
            break;
        case 1107:
            osciknobTrans[6]=trans;
            lastangle = CalAngle(osciposi, osci_knobposi[6], CurrentPt);
            break;
        case 1108:
            osciknobTrans[7]=trans;
            lastangle = CalAngle(osciposi, osci_knobposi[7], CurrentPt);
            break;
        case 1109:
            osciknobTrans[8]=trans;
            lastangle = CalAngle(osciposi, osci_knobposi[8], CurrentPt);
            break;
        case 1110:
```

```
                osciknobTrans[9]=trans;
                lastangle = CalAngle(osciposi, osci_knobposi[9], CurrentPt);
                break;
        case 1201:
                oscibuttonTrans[0]=trans;
                oscibuttonaction[0]=!oscibuttonaction[0];
ButtonAct(osci_buttonposi[0], oscibuttonTrans[0], oscibuttonaction[0], 0.015f);
        if (oscibuttonaction[0])
        {
                starttime = System.currentTimeMillis();
                postId(OSCION);
                // Adding the initializing program for the oscilloscope
                if (osciconn[0]&&osciconn[1])
                        OsciSupplement();
                        }
                else
                {
                        postId(OSCIOFF);
                                }
                break;
        case 1301:
                oscislideTrans[0]=trans;
                break;
        case 1302:
                oscislideTrans[1]=trans;
                break;
        case 1303:
                oscislideTrans[2]=trans;
                break;
        case 1304:
                oscislideTrans[3]=trans;
                break;
        case 1305:
                oscislideTrans[4]=trans;
                break;
        case 1401:
                osciconnTrans[0]=trans;
                lastangle = CalAngle(osciposi, osci_connposi[0], CurrentPt);
                break;
        case 1402:
                osciconnTrans[1]=trans;
                lastangle = CalAngle(osciposi, osci_connposi[1], CurrentPt);
                break;
        case 1403:
                osciconnTrans[2]=trans;
                lastangle = CalAngle(osciposi, osci_connposi[2], CurrentPt);
                break;
        // Processing the control components of the signal generator -------
        case 2101:
                sgknobTrans[0]=trans;
                lastangle = CalAngle(sgposi, sg_knobposi[0], CurrentPt);
                break;
```

```
case 2201:
sgbuttonTrans[5]=trans;
sgbuttonaction[5]=!sgbuttonaction[5];
if (sgbuttonaction[5])
{
      sgvalue = 1000;
      sgamp = 1000;
      sgfrq = 1000;
      sgdigit = 4;
      sglast_digit=4;
      sgcurrent_digit=4;
      sgunit = „Hz";
      sgsquare = true;
      cycle=sgfrq*sweeptime;
      if (tcp_sgservice!=null)
      {
            tcp_sgservice.SendCmd(„d0");
            stime = System.currentTimeMillis();
            do
            {
            deltatime = System.currentTimeMillis() - stime;
            } while (deltatime<STEPDELAY);
            if (sgsquare)
            {
                  if (tcp_sgservice!=null)
            tcp_sgservice.SendCmd(„W3,H0");
            }
            else
            {
            if (tcp_sgservice!=null)
                  tcp_sgservice.SendCmd(„W1,H0");
            }
            stime = System.currentTimeMillis();
            do
            {
            deltatime = System.currentTimeMillis() - stime;
            } while (deltatime<STEPDELAY);
tcp_sgservice.SendCmd(„AMP „+String.valueOf(sgamp/1000.0f)+" V");
      }
      if (sgbuttonaction[5]&&sgconn[1]&&osciconn[2])
            SgSupplement();
      postId(SGON);
      // Adding the initializing program for the signal generator
      }
      else
      {
            tcp_sgservice.SendCmd(„d1");
            postId(SGOFF);
      }
ButtonAct(sg_buttonposi[0], sgbuttonTrans[5], sgbuttonaction[5], 0.008f);
break;
case 2202:
```

```
                        sgbuttonTrans[0]=trans;
                        ButtonAct(sg_buttonposi[1], sgbuttonTrans[0], true, 0.008f);
                        if (sgbuttonaction[5])
                        {
                            if (sgdigit>1) sgdigit -=1;
                        }
                        break;

                    case 2203:
                        sgbuttonTrans[1]=trans;
                        ButtonAct(sg_buttonposi[2], sgbuttonTrans[1], true, 0.008f);
                        if (sgbuttonaction[5])
                        {
                                if (sgdigit<sgcurrent_digit) sgdigit +=1;
                        }
                        break;
                        case 2204:
                        sgbuttonTrans[2]=trans;
                        sgbuttonaction[2]=true;
                        sgbuttonaction[3]=false;
                        sgbuttonaction[4]=false;
                    ButtonAct(sg_buttonposi[3], sgbuttonTrans[2], sgbuttonaction[2], 0.008f);
        if (sgbuttonTrans[3]!=null) ButtonAct(sg_buttonposi[4], sgbuttonTrans[3], sgbuttonaction[3], 0.008f);
        if (sgbuttonTrans[4]!=null) ButtonAct(sg_buttonposi[5], sgbuttonTrans[4], sgbuttonaction[4], 0.008f);
                        if (sgbuttonaction[5])
                        {
                        }
                        break;
                    case 2205:
                        sgvalue = sgamp;
                        sgbuttonTrans[3]=trans;
                        sgbuttonaction[2]=false;
                        sgbuttonaction[3]=true;
                        sgbuttonaction[4]=false;
        if (sgbuttonTrans[2]!=null) ButtonAct(sg_buttonposi[3], sgbuttonTrans[2], sgbuttonaction[2], 0.008f);
                        ButtonAct(sg_buttonposi[4], sgbuttonTrans[3], sgbuttonaction[3], 0.008f);

        if (sgbuttonTrans[4]!=null) ButtonAct(sg_buttonposi[5], sgbuttonTrans[4], sgbuttonaction[4], 0.008f);
                        break;

                    case 2206:
                        sgvalue = sgfrq;
                        sgbuttonTrans[4]=trans;
                        sgbuttonaction[2]=false;
                        sgbuttonaction[3]=false;
                        sgbuttonaction[4]=true;
        if (sgbuttonTrans[2]!=null) ButtonAct(sg_buttonposi[3], sgbuttonTrans[2], sgbuttonaction[2], 0.008f);
        if (sgbuttonTrans[3]!=null) ButtonAct(sg_buttonposi[4], sgbuttonTrans[3], sgbuttonaction[3], 0.008f);
            ButtonAct(sg_buttonposi[5], sgbuttonTrans[4], sgbuttonaction[4], 0.008f);
        //      if (sgbuttonaction[5]) postId(SGON);
                        break;
                        case 2401:
```

```
sgconnTrans[0]=trans;
lastangle = CalAngle(sgposi, sg_connposi[0], CurrentPt);
break;
case 2402:
sgconnTrans[1]=trans;
lastangle = CalAngle(sgposi, sg_connposi[1], CurrentPt);
break;
// Processing the control components of the circuit board --------
case 4401:
    ccconnTrans[0]=trans;
    lastangle = CalAngle(sgposi, cc_connposi[0], CurrentPt);
    break;
case 4402:
    ccconnTrans[1]=trans;
    lastangle = CalAngle(sgposi, cc_connposi[1], CurrentPt);
    break;
    // Processing the control components of the card reader --------
case 3201:
    passbuttonTrans[0]=trans;
    ButtonAct(passbuttonposi[0], passbuttonTrans[0], true, 0.01f);
    if (passdigit<6)
    {
        passdisplayvalue =  passdisplayvalue + „*“;
        passstorevalue =  passstorevalue + „0“;
        passdigit++;
    }
    else
    {
         passdisplayvalue = passdisplayvalue.substring(1, 6) + „*“;
        passstorevalue = passstorevalue.substring(1, 6) + „0“;
    }
    postId(PASSON);
    break;
case 3202:
    passbuttonTrans[1]=trans;
    ButtonAct(passbuttonposi[1], passbuttonTrans[1], true, 0.01f);
    if (passdigit<6)
    {
        passdisplayvalue = passdisplayvalue + „*“;
        passstorevalue = passstorevalue + „1“;
        passdigit++;
    }
    else
    {
        passdisplayvalue = passdisplayvalue.substring(1, 6) + „*“;
        passstorevalue = passstorevalue.substring(1, 6) + „1“;
    }
    postId(PASSON);
    break;
    case 3203:
        passbuttonTrans[2]=trans;
        ButtonAct(passbuttonposi[2], passbuttonTrans[2], true, 0.01f);
```

```
                    if (passdigit<6)
                    {
            passdisplayvalue = passdisplayvalue +„*";
                    passstorevalue = passstorevalue +„2";
                    passdigit++;
                    }
                    else
                    {
                    passdisplayvalue = passdisplayvalue.substring(1, 6) +„*";
                    passstorevalue = passstorevalue.substring(1, 6) +„2";
                    }
                    postId(PASSON);
                    break;
            case 3204:
                    passbuttonTrans[3]=trans;
                    ButtonAct(passbuttonposi[3], passbuttonTrans[3], true, 0.01f);
                    if (passdigit<6)
                    {
                        passdisplayvalue = passdisplayvalue +„*";
                        passstorevalue = passstorevalue +„3";
                        passdigit++;
                    }
                    else
                    {
                    passdisplayvalue = passdisplayvalue.substring(1, 6) +„*";
                    passstorevalue = passstorevalue.substring(1, 6) +„3";
                    }
                    postId(PASSON);
                    break;
            case 3205:
                    passbuttonTrans[4]=trans;
                    ButtonAct(passbuttonposi[4], passbuttonTrans[4], true, 0.01f);
                    if (passdigit<6)
                    {
                        passdisplayvalue = passdisplayvalue +„*";
                        passstorevalue = passstorevalue +„4";
                        passdigit++;
                    }
                    else
                    {
                    passdisplayvalue = passdisplayvalue.substring(1, 6) +„*";
                    passstorevalue = passstorevalue.substring(1, 6) +„4";
                    }
                    postId(PASSON);
                    break;
                    case 3206:
                            passbuttonTrans[5]=trans;
                    ButtonAct(passbuttonposi[5], passbuttonTrans[5], true, 0.01f);
            if (passdigit<6)
                    {
                            passdisplayvalue = passdisplayvalue +„*";
                            passstorevalue = passstorevalue +„5";
```

```
                    passdigit++;
                }
                else
                {
                    passdisplayvalue = passdisplayvalue.substring(1, 6) + „*";
                    passstorevalue = passstorevalue.substring(1, 6) + „5";
                }
                postId(PASSON);
                break;
            case 3207:
                passbuttonTrans[6]=trans;
                ButtonAct(passbuttonposi[6], passbuttonTrans[6], true, 0.01f);
                if (passdigit<6)
                {
                    passdisplayvalue = passdisplayvalue + „*";
                    passstorevalue = passstorevalue + „6";
                    passdigit++;
                }
                else
                {
                    passdisplayvalue = passdisplayvalue.substring(1, 6) + „*";
                    passstorevalue = passstorevalue.substring(1, 6) + „6";
                }
                postId(PASSON);
                break;
            case 3208:
                passbuttonTrans[7]=trans;
                ButtonAct(passbuttonposi[7], passbuttonTrans[7], true, 0.01f);
                if (passdigit<6)
                {
                    passdisplayvalue = passdisplayvalue + „*";
                    passstorevalue = passstorevalue + „7";
                    passdigit++;
                }
                else
                {
                passdisplayvalue = passdisplayvalue.substring(1, 6) + „*";
                passstorevalue = passstorevalue.substring(1, 6) + „7";
                }
                postId(PASSON);
                break;
            case 3209:
                passbuttonTrans[8]=trans;
                ButtonAct(passbuttonposi[8], passbuttonTrans[8], true, 0.01f);
                if (passdigit<6)
                {
                    passdisplayvalue = passdisplayvalue + „*";
                    passstorevalue = passstorevalue + „8";
                    passdigit++;
                }
                else
                {
```

```
                passdisplayvalue = passdisplayvalue.substring(1, 6) + „*";
                passstorevalue = passstorevalue.substring(1, 6) + „8";
        }
        postId(PASSON);
        break;
case 3210:
        passbuttonTrans[9]=trans;
        ButtonAct(passbuttonposi[9], passbuttonTrans[9], true, 0.01f);
        if (passdigit<6)
        {
                passdisplayvalue = passdisplayvalue + „*";
                passstorevalue = passstorevalue + „9";
                passdigit++;
        }
        else
        {
                passdisplayvalue = passdisplayvalue.substring(1, 6) + „*";
                passstorevalue = passstorevalue.substring(1, 6) + „9";
        }
        postId(PASSON);
        break;
case 3211:
        passbuttonTrans[10]=trans;
        ButtonAct(passbuttonposi[10], passbuttonTrans[10], true, 0.01f);
        if (passdigit>1)
        {
        passdisplayvalue = passdisplayvalue.substring(0, passdigit-1);
        passstorevalue = passstorevalue.substring(0, passdigit-1);
        passdigit--;
        }
        else
        {
                passdisplayvalue = „";
                passstorevalue = „";
                passdigit = 0;
                }
                postId(PASSON);

        if (dooropen&&doorAlpha.finished())
        {
                postId(DOORCLOSE);
        }
        break;
case 3212:
        passbuttonTrans[11]=trans;
        ButtonAct(passbuttonposi[11], passbuttonTrans[11], true, 0.01f);
                if (!dooropen&&doorAlpha.finished())
                {
                        passdisplayvalue = „";
                        passstorevalue = „";
                        passdigit = 0;
                        postId(PASSON);
```

```
                            postId(DOOROPEN);
                            if (udp_osciservice==null)
                    {
            udp_osciservice = new UDP_OSCI_1("vlab.ee.nus.edu.sg", 9000);
                    }
                            if (tcp_osciservice==null)
                            {
                tcp_osciservice = new TCP_OSCI("vlab.ee.nus.edu.sg", 9875);
                            }
                            if (tcp_sgservice==null)
                            {
                tcp_sgservice = new TCP_OSCI("vlab.ee.nus.edu.sg", 9876);
                            }
                            if (udp_osciservice!=null)
                                udp_osciservice.showCurve();
                            if (!initosci)
                            {
                                if (tcp_osciservice!=null)
                                tcp_osciservice.SendCmd("initialize");

                            stime = System.currentTimeMillis();
                            do
                            {
                            deltatime = System.currentTimeMillis() - stime;
                            } while (deltatime<STEPDELAY);
                            if (tcp_osciservice!=null)
                                tcp_osciservice.SendCmd("alt");
                            stime = System.currentTimeMillis();
                            do
                            {
                                deltatime = System.currentTimeMillis() - stime;
                            } while (deltatime<STEPDELAY);
                            if (tcp_sgservice!=null)
                                tcp_sgservice.SendCmd("d1");
                                initosci=true;
                            }
                            }
                            break;

                            /////////////////////////////   other components
                            default:
                            }
                    wakeupOn(alleventsCriterion);
                    }
            }

            // Mouse release event                            //
            if (eventId == MouseEvent.MOUSE_RELEASED)
            {
                MouseRelease(obj);
                wakeupOn(alleventsCriterion);
            }
```

```
                    // Mouse drag event                                    //
                    if ((eventId == MouseEvent.MOUSE_DRAGGED) &&
                            !((MouseEvent)event[i]).isAltDown() &&
                            !((MouseEvent)event[i]).isMetaDown())
                    {
                            float delta;
                            int x_d = ((MouseEvent)event[i]).getX();
                            int y_d = ((MouseEvent)event[i]).getY();
                            pickCanvas.setShapeLocation(x_d, y_d);
                            Point3d eyePos = pickCanvas.getStartPosition ();
                            pickResult = pickCanvas.pickClosest();

                            if (pickResult != null)
                            {
                                    // Get closest intersection results
                    PickIntersection pi = pickResult.getClosestIntersection(eyePos);
                                    Point3d []pt = pi.getPrimitiveCoordinates();
                            if (pt.length==3)
                            {
                    if (pt[0].z>KNOBFACE&&pt[1].z>KNOBFACE&&pt[2].z>KNOBFACE)
                    {
                            Point3d intPt = pi.getPointCoordinatesVW();
                            CurrentPt = new Point3f(intPt);
                            setPosition(sphTrans, CurrentPt);
                    }
                    else
                    {
                            setPosition(sphTrans, sphposi);
                            MouseRelease(obj);
                            trans = null;
                            obj = 0;
                    }
                    }
                    else
                    {
if (pt[0].z>BUTTONFACE&&pt[1].z>BUTTONFACE&&pt[2].z>BUTTONFACE&&pt[3].z>BUTTONFACE)
                    {
                            Point3d intPt = pi.getPointCoordinatesVW();
                            CurrentPt = new Point3f(intPt);
                            setPosition(sphTrans, CurrentPt);
                    }
                    else
                    {
                            setPosition(sphTrans, sphposi);
                            MouseRelease(obj);
                            trans = null;
                            obj = 0;
                            }
                    }
                    }
                    else
```

```
        {
            setPosition(sphTrans, sphposi);
            MouseRelease(obj);
            trans = null;
            obj = 0;
        }
        switch (obj)
        {
        // Processing the control components of the oscilloscope --------
        case 1101:
            currentangle = CalAngle(osciposi, osci_knobposi[0], CurrentPt);
            delta = DeltaAngle(currentangle, lastangle);
            osci_knobangle[0] = LimitAngle(delta, osci_knobangle[0], osciknob1_circleposi);
            setRotationZ(osciknobTrans[0], osci_knobangle[0]);
            lastangle = currentangle;
            break;
        case 1102:
            currentangle = CalAngle(osciposi, osci_knobposi[1], CurrentPt);
            delta = DeltaAngle(currentangle, lastangle);
            osci_knobangle[1] = LimitAngle(delta, osci_knobangle[1], osciknob2_circleposi);
            setRotationZ(osciknobTrans[1], osci_knobangle[1]);
            lastangle = currentangle;
            break;
        case 1103:
            currentangle = CalAngle(osciposi, osci_knobposi[2], CurrentPt);
            delta = DeltaAngle(currentangle, lastangle);
            osci_knobangle[2] = LimitAngle(delta, osci_knobangle[2], osciknob3_circleposi);
            setRotationZ(osciknobTrans[2], osci_knobangle[2]);
            lastangle = currentangle;
            break;
        case 1104:
            currentangle = CalAngle(osciposi, osci_knobposi[3], CurrentPt);
            delta = DeltaAngle(currentangle, lastangle);
            osci_knobangle[3] = LimitAngle(delta, osci_knobangle[3], osciknob4_circleposi);
            setRotationZ(osciknobTrans[3], osci_knobangle[3]);
            lastangle = currentangle;
            break;
        case 1105:
            currentangle = CalAngle(osciposi, osci_knobposi[4], CurrentPt);
            osci_knobangle[4] = osci_knobangle[4] + currentangle - lastangle;
            break;
        case 1106:
            currentangle = CalAngle(osciposi, osci_knobposi[5], CurrentPt);
            osci_knobangle[5] = osci_knobangle[5] + currentangle - lastangle;
            break;
        case 1107:
            currentangle = CalAngle(osciposi, osci_knobposi[6], CurrentPt);
            osci_knobangle[6] = osci_knobangle[6] + currentangle - lastangle;
            break;
        case 1108:
            currentangle = CalAngle(osciposi, osci_knobposi[7], CurrentPt);
            delta = DeltaAngle(currentangle, lastangle);
```

```
                osci_knobangle[7] = LimitAngle(delta, osci_knobangle[7], osciknob8_circleposi);
                setRotationZ(osciknobTrans[7], osci_knobangle[7]);
                lastangle = currentangle;
                break;
        case 1109:
                currentangle = CalAngle(osciposi, osci_knobposi[8], CurrentPt);
                delta = DeltaAngle(currentangle, lastangle);
                osci_knobangle[8] = LimitAngle(delta, osci_knobangle[8], osciknob9_circleposi);
                setRotationZ(osciknobTrans[8], osci_knobangle[8]);
                lastangle = currentangle;
                break;
        case 1110:
                currentangle = CalAngle(osciposi, osci_knobposi[9], CurrentPt);
                delta = DeltaAngle(currentangle, lastangle);
                osci_knobangle[9] = LimitAngle(delta, osci_knobangle[9], osciknob10_circleposi);
                setRotationZ(osciknobTrans[9], osci_knobangle[9]);
                lastangle = currentangle;
                break;
        case 1301:
                osci_slideposi[0].y = CurrentPt.y-osciposi.y;
                if (osci_slideposi[0].y>oscislider1_posi[0])
                {
                        osci_slideposi[0].y=oscislider1_posi[0];
                }
                if (osci_slideposi[0].y<oscislider1_posi[oscislider1_posi.length-1])
                {
osci_slideposi[0].y=oscislider1_posi[oscislider1_posi.length-1];
                }
                setPosition(oscislideTrans[0], osci_slideposi[0]);
                break;
        case 1302:
                osci_slideposi[1].y = CurrentPt.y-osciposi.y;
                if (osci_slideposi[1].y>oscislider2_posi[0])
                {
                        osci_slideposi[1].y=oscislider2_posi[0];
                }
                if (osci_slideposi[1].y<oscislider2_posi[oscislider2_posi.length-1])
                {
                        osci_slideposi[1].y=oscislider2_posi[oscislider2_posi.length-1];
                }
                setPosition(oscislideTrans[1], osci_slideposi[1]);
                break;
        case 1303:
                osci_slideposi[2].y = CurrentPt.y-osciposi.y;
                if (osci_slideposi[2].y>oscislider3_posi[0])
                {
                        osci_slideposi[2].y=oscislider3_posi[0];
                }
                if (osci_slideposi[2].y<oscislider3_posi[oscislider3_posi.length-1])
                {
osci_slideposi[2].y=oscislider3_posi[oscislider3_posi.length-1];
                }
```

```
                    setPosition(oscislideTrans[2], osci_slideposi[2]);
                    break;
              case 1304:
                    osci_slideposi[3].x = CurrentPt.x-osciposi.x;
                    if (osci_slideposi[3].x>oscislider4_posi[0])
                    {
                          osci_slideposi[3].x=oscislider4_posi[0];
                    }
                    if (osci_slideposi[3].x<oscislider4_posi[oscislider4_posi.length-1])
                    {
                    osci_slideposi[3].x=oscislider4_posi[oscislider4_posi.length-1];
                    }
                    setPosition(oscislideTrans[3], osci_slideposi[3]);
                    break;
              case 1305:
                    osci_slideposi[4].x = CurrentPt.x-osciposi.x;
                    if (osci_slideposi[4].x>oscislider5_posi[0])
                    {
                          osci_slideposi[4].x=oscislider5_posi[0];
                    }
                    if (osci_slideposi[4].x<oscislider5_posi[oscislider5_posi.length-1])
                    {
                          osci_slideposi[4].x=oscislider5_posi[oscislider5_posi.length-1];
                    }
                    setPosition(oscislideTrans[4], osci_slideposi[4]);
                    break;
              case 1401:
                    currentangle = CalAngle(osciposi, osci_connposi[0], CurrentPt);
                    delta = DeltaAngle(currentangle, lastangle);
osci_connangle[0] = LimitConnAngle(delta, osci_connangle[0], osciconn1_circleposi);
                    setRotationZ(osciconnTrans[0], osci_connangle[0]);
                    lastangle = currentangle;
                    osciconn[0] = false;
                    break;
              case 1402:
                    currentangle = CalAngle(osciposi, osci_connposi[1], CurrentPt);
                    delta = DeltaAngle(currentangle, lastangle);
                    osci_connangle[1] = LimitConnAngle(delta, osci_connangle[1], osciconn2_circleposi);
                    setRotationZ(osciconnTrans[1], osci_connangle[1]);
                    lastangle = currentangle;
                    osciconn[1] = false;
                    break;
              case 1403:
                    currentangle = CalAngle(osciposi, osci_connposi[2], CurrentPt);
                    delta = DeltaAngle(currentangle, lastangle);
osci_connangle[2] = LimitConnAngle(delta, osci_connangle[2], osciconn3_circleposi);
                    setRotationZ(osciconnTrans[2], osci_connangle[2]);
                    lastangle = currentangle;
                    osciconn[2] = false;
                    break;
                    // Processing the control components of the signal generator --------
                    case 2101:
```

```
                    currentangle = CalAngle(sgposi, sg_knobposi[0], CurrentPt);
                    delta = DeltaAngle(currentangle, lastangle);
                    sg_knobangle[0] = RegulateAngle(sg_knobangle[0], delta);
                    setRotationZ(sgknobTrans[0], sg_knobangle[0]);
                    if (delta>0.1f&&sgbuttonaction[5])
                    {
                        lastangle = currentangle;
                        postId(SGDEC);
                    }
                    else if (delta<-0.1f&&sgbuttonaction[5])
                    {
                        lastangle = currentangle;
                        postId(SGINC);
                    }
                    break;
            case 2401:
                    currentangle = CalAngle(sgposi, sg_connposi[0], CurrentPt);
                    delta = DeltaAngle(currentangle, lastangle);
            sg_connangle[0] = LimitConnAngle(delta, sg_connangle[0], sgconn1_circleposi);
                    setRotationZ(sgconnTrans[0], sg_connangle[0]);
                    lastangle = currentangle;
                    sgconn[0] = false;
                    break;
        case 2402:
                    currentangle = CalAngle(sgposi, sg_connposi[1], CurrentPt);
                    delta = DeltaAngle(currentangle, lastangle);
            sg_connangle[1] = LimitConnAngle(delta, sg_connangle[1], sgconn2_circleposi);
                    setRotationZ(sgconnTrans[1], sg_connangle[1]);
                    lastangle = currentangle;
                    sgconn[1] = false;
                    break;
        // Processing the control components of the circuit board --------
        case 4401:
                    currentangle = CalAngle(sgposi, cc_connposi[0], CurrentPt);
                    delta = DeltaAngle(currentangle, lastangle);
            cc_connangle[0] = LimitConnAngle(delta, cc_connangle[0], ccconn1_circleposi);
                    setRotationZ(ccconnTrans[0], cc_connangle[0]);
                    lastangle = currentangle;
                    ccconn[0] = false;
                    break;
        case 4402:
                    currentangle = CalAngle(sgposi, cc_connposi[1], CurrentPt);
                    delta = DeltaAngle(currentangle, lastangle);
            cc_connangle[1] = LimitConnAngle(delta, cc_connangle[1], ccconn2_circleposi);
                    setRotationZ(ccconnTrans[1], cc_connangle[1]);
                    lastangle = currentangle;
                    ccconn[1] = false;
                    break;
        default:
        }
        }
        wakeupOn(alleventsCriterion);
```

```
                }
        }

            // Post Behavior event                                //
            if (wakeup instanceof WakeupOnBehaviorPost)
            {
                    eventId = ((WakeupOnBehaviorPost)wakeup).getPostId();
                    // Processing the curve display of the oscilloscope --------
                    if (eventId == OSCION)
                    {
                        if (osciCurvebranch!=null)
                        {
                            osciCurvebranch.detach();
                        }
                        osciCurvebranch = new BranchGroup();
                        osciCurvebranch.setCapability(BranchGroup.ALLOW_DETACH);
                        osciCurvebranch.setPickable (false);
                        grid = new Grid3D(0.01f, 0.25f, 0.18f);
                        osciCurvebranch.addChild(grid);
                        Transtri = new TransformGroup();
Transtri.setCapability(TransformGroup.ALLOW_TRANSFORM_WRITE);
Transtri.setCapability(TransformGroup.ALLOW_TRANSFORM_READ);
                        osciCurvebranch.addChild(Transtri);
                        tri = new Triangle3D(0.01f, 0.006f, 0.006f);
                        Transutri = new TransformGroup();
Transutri.setCapability(TransformGroup.ALLOW_TRANSFORM_WRITE);
Transutri.setCapability(TransformGroup.ALLOW_TRANSFORM_READ);
                    osciCurvebranch.addChild(Transutri);
                    utri = new UTriangle3D(0.01f, 0.006f, 0.006f);
                    setPosition(Transutri, new Point3f(hposition*0.25f/200.0f, 0.082f, 0.001f));
                        Transutri.addChild(utri);
                        coord_1 = new Coord3D_1(0.01f, 0.25f, 0.17f);
                        osciCurvebranch.addChild(coord_1);                // Frame
                        coord_2 = new Coord3D_2(0.01f, 0.25f, 0.17f);
                    osciCurvebranch.addChild(coord_2);                    // x, y-coordinate

                        ///////////////////// Channel 1
                        if (ch1on)
                {
                if (udp_osciservice!=null)
                {
                if (counterch1<COUNCH1)
                {
heightch1 = (float)(udp_osciservice.maximumch1 - udp_osciservice.minimumch1)/14000.0f;
                            //      System.out.println("counterch1="+counterch1);
                        for (int i=0; i<200; i++)
                        {
                        coordinate_Y1[i] = (float)(udp_osciservice.actualch1[i]/1400.0f);
                        if (coordinate_Y1[i]>0.1f) coordinate_Y1[i]=0.1f;
                        if (coordinate_Y1[i]<-0.1f) coordinate_Y1[i]=-0.1f;
                        }
```

```
                        if (counterch1<COUNCH1-1)
                        {
                                if (triggerch1) counterch1++;
                        }
                        else
                        {
                                if (cycle<=0.055)
                                        cycle=0.055f;
if (triggerch1&&osci_slideposi[4].x==oscislider5_posi[1]&&osci_slideposi[3].x==oscislider4_posi[1]) //plus
                        {
                if (coordinate_Y1[100-(int)(5.0f*1.0f/cycle)]<=coordinate_Y1[100+(int)(5.0f*1.0f/cycle)])
                                {
                                        counterch1=COUNCH1;
                                }
                        }
else if (triggerch1&&osci_slideposi[4].x==oscislider5_posi[1]&&osci_slideposi[3].x==oscislider4_posi[0])
//minus
                                {
                if (coordinate_Y1[100-(int)(5.0f*1.0f/cycle)]>=coordinate_Y1[100+(int)(5.0f*1.0f/cycle)])
                        {
                                counterch1=COUNCH1;
                        }
                        }
                        }
                        }
                        }
                        else
                        {
                                heightch1 = 0.0f;
                                for (int j=0; j<200; j++)
                                {
                                        coordinate_Y1[j] = 0.0f;
                                }
                        }
ch1curve3D = new Scope3D_1(0.25f, 0.2f, coordinate_Y1, new Vector3f(0.0f, 0.0f, 0.0015f), hposition, 0);
                                osciCurvebranch.addChild(ch1curve3D);
                                Transbox_11 = new TransformGroup();          //position
                                Transbox_11.setCapability(TransformGroup.ALLOW_TRANSFORM_WRITE);
                                Transbox_11.setCapability(TransformGroup.ALLOW_TRANSFORM_READ);
                                osciCurvebranch.addChild(Transbox_11);
                                box_11 = new Box3D(0.01f, 0.004f, 0.004f);
                                Transbox_11.addChild(box_11);
                                setPosition(Transbox_11, new Point3f(-0.125f, (positionch1-5.0f)*0.018f, 0.001f));

                                if (osci_slideposi[4].x==oscislider5_posi[1]) //Trigger ch1
                                {
setPosition(Transtri, new Point3f(0.125f, 1.1f*(triggerposition-5)*heightch1+(positionch1-5.0f)*0.018f, 0.001f));
                                        Transtri.addChild(tri);
                                }
                                Transbox_12 = new TransformGroup();          //triggered point
                        Transbox_12.setCapability(TransformGroup.ALLOW_TRANSFORM_WRITE);
                        Transbox_12.setCapability(TransformGroup.ALLOW_TRANSFORM_READ);
```

```
        osciCurvebranch.addChild(Transbox_12);
        box_12 = new Box3D(0.01f, 0.004f, 0.004f);
        Transbox_12.addChild(box_12);
    setPosition(Transbox_12, new Point3f(0.0f+hposition*0.25f/200.0f, coordinate_Y1[100], 0.001f));
    }


///////////////////////////////// Channel 2
Transbox_21 = new TransformGroup(); //Vertical position
Transbox_21.setCapability(TransformGroup.ALLOW_TRANSFORM_WRITE);
Transbox_21.setCapability(TransformGroup.ALLOW_TRANSFORM_READ);
        osciCurvebranch.addChild(Transbox_21);
        box_21 = new Box3D(0.01f, 0.004f, 0.004f);
        Transbox_21.addChild(box_21);
        setPosition(Transbox_21, new Point3f(-0.125f, (positionch2-5.0f)*0.018f, 0.001f));
        Transbox_22 = new TransformGroup();
Transbox_22.setCapability(TransformGroup.ALLOW_TRANSFORM_WRITE); //The triggered point
Transbox_22.setCapability(TransformGroup.ALLOW_TRANSFORM_READ);
        osciCurvebranch.addChild(Transbox_22);
        box_22 = new Box3D(0.01f, 0.004f, 0.004f);

        if (ch2on)
        {
            if (sgsquare)
            {
                if (udp_osciservice!=null) //Read the values
                {
                    if (counterch2<COUNCH2)
                    {
                    if ((udp_osciservice.ch2length==55&&osci_slideposi[2].y==oscislider3_posi[2])||(udp_
osciservice.ch2length==56&&osci_slideposi[2].y==oscislider3_posi[2]))
                        {
                            for (int j=0; j<200; j++)
                            {
                                coordinate_Y2[j] = -0.10f;
                            }
                        }
                        else
                        {
                            for (int i=0; i<200; i++)
                            {
            coordinate_Y2[i] = (float)(udp_osciservice.actualch2[i]/1400.0f);
                if (coordinate_Y2[i]>0.1f) coordinate_Y2[i]=0.1f;
                if (coordinate_Y2[i]<-0.1f) coordinate_Y2[i]=-0.1f;
                        }
                        }
                        if (counterch2<COUNCH2-1)
                        {
                            if (triggerch2) counterch2++;
                        }
                        else
                        {
                            if (cycle<=0.055f)
```

```
                                cycle=0.055f;
        if (triggerch2&&osci_slideposi[4].x==oscislider5_posi[0]&&osci_slideposi[3].x==oscislider4_posi[1]) //plus
                                {
                if (coordinate_Y2[100-(int)(5.0f*1.0f/cycle)]<=coordinate_Y2[100+(int)(5.0f*1.0f/cycle)])
                    {
                            counterch2=COUNCH2;
                    }
                }
        else if (triggerch2&&osci_slideposi[4].x==oscislider5_posi[0]&&osci_slideposi[3].x==oscislider4_posi[0])
        //minus
                    {
                if (coordinate_Y2[100-(int)(5.0f*1.0f/cycle)]>=coordinate_Y2[100+(int)(5.0f*1.0f/cycle)])
                {
            counterch2=COUNCH2;
                        }
                    }
                    }
                    }
                    }
                else
                {
                        heightch2 = 0.0f;
                        for (int j=0; j<200; j++)
                        {
                                coordinate_Y2[j] = 0.0f;
                        }
                }
                    if (osci_slideposi[4].x==oscislider5_posi[0]) //Trigger ch2
                    {
            heightch2 = (float)(udp_osciservice.maximumch2 - udp_osciservice.minimumch2)/14000.0f;
        setPosition(Transtri, new Point3f(0.125f, 1.1f*(triggerposition-5)*heightch2+(positionch2-5.0f)*0.018f, 0.001f));
                        Transtri.addChild(tri);
                    }
            setPosition(Transbox_22, new Point3f(0.0f+hposition*0.25f/200.0f, coordinate_Y2[100], 0.001f));
                        Transbox_22.addChild(box_22);
        ch21curve3D = new Scope3D_1(0.25f, 0.2f, coordinate_Y2, new Vector3f(0.0f, 0.0f, 0.0015f), hposition, 0);
                        osciCurvebranch.addChild(ch21curve3D);
                    }
                else  //else of square wave
                {
                        if (udp_osciservice!=null) //Read the values
                        {
                            if (counterch2<COUNCH2)
                            {
                                    if ((udp_osciservice.ch2length==55&&osci_slideposi[2].y==
                                    oscislider3_posi[2])||      (udp_osciservice.ch2length==
                                    56&&osci_slideposi[2].y==oscislider3_posi[2]))
                                {
                                    for (int j=0; j<200; j++)
                                    {
                                        coordinate_Y2[j] = -0.10f;
                                    }
                                }
```

```
                    }
                    else
                    {
                        for (int i=0; i<200; i++)
                        {
                            coordinate_Y2[i] = (float)(udp_osciservice.actualch2[i]/1400.0f);
                            if (coordinate_Y2[i]>0.1f) coordinate_Y2[i]=0.1f;
                            if (coordinate_Y2[i]<-0.1f) coordinate_Y2[i]=-0.1f;
                        }
                    }
                    if (counterch2<COUNCH2-1)
                    {
                        if (triggerch2) counterch2++;
                        }
                        else
                        {
                            if (cycle<=0.055f)
                            cycle=0.055f;
                        if (triggerch2&&osci_slideposi[4].x==oscislider5_posi[0]&&
                            osci_slideposi[3].x==oscislider4_posi[1]) //plus
                        {
                        if (coordinate_Y2[100-(int)(5.0f*1.0f/cycle)]<=
                            coordinate_Y2[100+(int)(5.0f*1.0f/cycle)])
                        {
                            counterch2=COUNCH2;
                        }
                        }
                        else if (triggerch2&&osci_slideposi[4].x
                            ==oscislider5_posi[0]&&osci_slideposi[3].x==oscislider4_posi[0])
//minus
                        {
                        if (coordinate_Y2[100-(int)(5.0f*1.0f/cycle)]>=
                            coordinate_Y2[100+(int)(5.0f*1.0f/cycle)])
                        {
                            counterch2=COUNCH2;
                        }
                        }
                        }
                    }
                }
                else
                {
                    heightch2 = 0.0f;
                    for (int j=0; j<200; j++)
                    {
                        coordinate_Y2[j] = 0.0f;
                    }
                }
                if (osci_slideposi[4].x==oscislider5_posi[0]) //Trigger ch2
                {
                    heightch2 = (float)(udp_osciservice.maximumch2 –
                        udp_osciservice.minimumch2)/14000.0f;
```

```
                    triggerch2coun = TriggerPoint(coordinate_Y2,
                        1.1f*(triggerposition-5)*heightch2+(positionch2-5.0f)*0.018f);
                    setPosition(Transtri, new Point3f(0.125f,
                        1.1f*(triggerposition-5)*heightch2+(positionch2-5.0f)*0.018f, 0.001f));
                    Transtri.addChild(tri);
                }
                else
                {
                    triggerch2coun = 100;
                }
                if (osci_slideposi[4].x==oscislider5_posi[0]&&
                    (triggerposition==0||triggerposition==10||triggerposition==5))
                {
                    triggerch2coun = 100;  //Exceed the scope
                }
                setPosition(Transbox_22, new Point3f(0.0f+hposition*0.25f/200.0f,
                    coordinate_Y2[triggerch2coun], 0.001f));
                Transbox_22.addChild(box_22);
                if (osci_slideposi[2].y==oscislider3_posi[1])
                {
                    triggerch2coun = 100;
                }

                if (osci_slideposi[2].y==oscislider3_posi[2])
                {
                    ch22curve3D = new Scope3D(0.25f, 0.2f, coordinate_Y2, new Vector3f(0.0f, 0.0f,
                        0.0015f), hposition, 0, 0.0f, 5);
                }
                else
                {
                    if (cycle<=0.055f) cycle=0.055f;
                    ch22curve3D = new Scope3D(0.25f, 0.2f, coordinate_Y2, new Vector3f(0.0f, 0.0f,
                        0.0015f), hposition, 100-triggerch2coun, 1.0f/(sweeptime*sgfrq), positionch2);
                }
                osciCurvebranch.addChild(ch22curve3D);
            }
        }
        osciCurvebranchParent.addChild(osciCurvebranch);
        wakeupOn(alleventsCriterion);
    }
    else if (eventId == OSCIOFF)
    {
        if (osciCurvebranch!=null)
        {
            osciCurvebranch.detach();
        }
        wakeupOn(mouseandpostidCriterion);
    }

    // Processing the digital display of the signal generator --------
    if (eventId == SGON||eventId == SGINC||eventId == SGDEC)
    {
```

```
if (sgCurvebranch!=null)
{
    sgCurvebranch.detach();
}
sgCurvebranch = new BranchGroup();
sgCurvebranch.setCapability(BranchGroup.ALLOW_DETACH);
sgCurvebranch.setPickable (false);
if (!sgbuttonaction[2]) //the waveform button is not active
{
    sglast_digit = sgcurrent_digit;
    if (eventId == SGINC)
    {
if (sgvalue + Math.pow(10.0, sgdisplayvalue.length() - sgdigit) < 10000)
    {
    sgvalue += Math.pow(10.0, sgdisplayvalue.length() - sgdigit);
    sgdisplayvalue = String.valueOf(sgvalue);
    sgcurrent_digit = sgdisplayvalue.length();
    if (sgcurrent_digit != sglast_digit) sgdigit += 1;
        if (sgdigit>4) sgdigit=4;
    }
    }
    else if (eventId == SGDEC)
    {
if (sgvalue - Math.pow(10.0,sgdisplayvalue.length() - sgdigit) >= 100)
    {
    sgvalue -= Math.pow(10.0, sgdisplayvalue.length() - sgdigit);
    sgdisplayvalue = String.valueOf(sgvalue);
    sgcurrent_digit = sgdisplayvalue.length();
    if (sgcurrent_digit!=sglast_digit) sgdigit -=1;
    if (sgdigit<1) sgdigit=1;
    }
    }
}
sgdisplayvalue = String.valueOf(sgvalue);

if (sgbuttonaction[4]) //add the unit for the number
{
    sgunit = „Hz";
}
else if (sgbuttonaction[3])
{
    sgunit = „mv";
}
else if (sgbuttonaction[2])
{
    if (sgsquare)
    {
        sgunit = „Square";
    }
    else
    {
        sgunit = „Sine";
```

```
            }
            sgdisplayvalue = „“;
        }
    sgtext = new Text2D(sgdisplayvalue + sgunit, new Color3f(0.0f,1.0f,0.0f),
                              „Times Roman“, 10, Font.PLAIN);
    TransformGroup sgvalueTrans = new TransformGroup();
    sgvalueTrans.setCapability(TransformGroup.ALLOW_TRANSFORM_WRITE);
    sgvalueTrans.setCapability(TransformGroup.ALLOW_TRANSFORM_READ);
    sgvalueTrans.setPickable (false);
    setPosition(sgvalueTrans, new Point3f(-0.08f, -0.01f, 0.011f));
    sgvalueTrans.addChild(sgtext);
    sgCurvebranch.addChild(sgvalueTrans);

    if (!sgbuttonaction[2])
    {
    sgtext = new Text2D(„-“, new Color3f(0.0f,1.0f,0.0f), „Arial Narrow“, 8, Font.BOLD);
    TransformGroup sgchangeTrans = new TransformGroup();
    sgchangeTrans.setCapability(TransformGroup.ALLOW_TRANSFORM_WRITE);
    sgchangeTrans.setCapability(TransformGroup.ALLOW_TRANSFORM_READ);
    sgchangeTrans.setPickable (false);
    setPosition(sgchangeTrans, new Point3f(-0.023f*(4-sgdigit), -0.025f, 0.011f));
    sgchangeTrans.addChild(sgtext);
    sgCurvebranch.addChild(sgchangeTrans);
    }
    sgCurvebranchParent.addChild(sgCurvebranch);
    wakeupOn(mouseandpostidCriterion);
    }
    else if (eventId == SGOFF)
    {
        if (sgCurvebranch!=null)
        {
            sgCurvebranch.detach();
        }
        wakeupOn(mouseandpostidCriterion);
    }

    // Processing the digital display of the card reader --------
    if (eventId == PASSON)
    {
        if (passCurvebranch!=null)
        {
                passCurvebranch.detach();
        }
        passCurvebranch = new BranchGroup();
        passCurvebranch.setCapability(BranchGroup.ALLOW_DETACH);
        passCurvebranch.setPickable (false);
        passtext = new Text2D(passdisplayvalue, new Color3f(0.0f,1.0f,0.0f),
                „Times Roman“, 20, Font.BOLD);
        TransformGroup passvalueTrans = new TransformGroup();
        passvalueTrans.setCapability(TransformGroup.ALLOW_TRANSFORM_WRITE);
        passvalueTrans.setCapability(TransformGroup.ALLOW_TRANSFORM_READ);
        passvalueTrans.setPickable (false);
```

```
        setPosition(passvalueTrans, new Point3f(0.09f-0.03f*(passdigit-1), -0.055f, 0.011f));
        passvalueTrans.addChild(passtext);
        passCurvebranch.addChild(passvalueTrans);
        passCurvebranchParent.addChild(passCurvebranch);
        wakeupOn(mouseandpostidCriterion);
}

// Processing the action for opening or closing the door --------
if (eventId == DOOROPEN)
{
        doorcontrol.setQuat(0, quats[0]);
        doorcontrol.setQuat(1, quats[1]);
        startTime = System.currentTimeMillis();
        doorAlpha.setStartTime(startTime);
        dooropen = true;
        wakeupOn(mouseandpostidCriterion);
}
else if (eventId == DOORCLOSE)
{
        doorcontrol.setQuat(0, quats[1]);
        doorcontrol.setQuat(1, quats[0]);
        startTime = System.currentTimeMillis();
        doorAlpha.setStartTime(startTime);
        dooropen = false;
        wakeupOn(mouseandpostidCriterion);
}

// Processing the mark for animating or interacting --------
if (eventId == ANIMATION)
{
        animating = true;
        wakeupOn(mouseandpostidCriterion);
}
else if (eventId == INTERACTION)
{
        animating = false;
        wakeupOn(mouseandpostidCriterion);
}

// Processing the disconnection --------
if (eventId == DISCONN)
{
        closeAll();
        wakeupOn(mouseandpostidCriterion);
}

if (counter==1)
{
        panel.Connection.setForeground(Color.red);
        panel.Connection.setText(„Wait ....");
}
else if (counter==COUNTER)
```

```
                    {
                        panel.Connection.setForeground(Color.blue);
                        panel.Connection.setText(„Ready ....");
                    }
        }

                    // Frames Elapsed event                              //
                    if (wakeup instanceof WakeupOnElapsedFrames)
                    {
                    if (oscibuttonaction[0])
                    {
                    long endtime = System.currentTimeMillis();
                    if (endtime-starttime>400) //prevent the system from keeping freshing curve
                    {
                        if (counter<COUNTER) counter++;
                        postId(OSCION);
                        starttime = endtime;
                    }
                    }
                    wakeupOn(alleventsCriterion);
        }
            } // the end of the loop while
    } // the end of the function processStimulus()
```

H.33 FUNCTION FOR TRIGGER POINT OF OSCILLOSCOPE

```
    private int TriggerPoint(float data[], float compdata)
    {
        int tempint1 = 199;
        int tempint2 = 1;
        for (int i=100; i<199; i++)
        {
            if (compdata>=data[i]&&compdata<=data[i+1])
            {
                tempint1=i;
                break;
            }
            if (compdata<=data[i]&&compdata>=data[i+1])
            {
                tempint1=i;
                break;
            }
        }
        for (int i=100; i<199; i++)
        {
            if (compdata>=data[200-i]&&compdata<=data[199-i])
            {
                tempint2=200-i;
                break;
            }
```

```
                    if (compdata<=data[200-i]&&compdata>=data[199-i])
                    {
                        tempint2=200-i;
                        break;
                    }
            }
            if ((tempint1-100)<=(100-tempint2))
            {
                return tempint1;
            }
            else
            {
                return tempint2;
            }
        }
    }
```

Appendix I
Program Summary and Screen Capture

Location	Description	Screen Shots
Chapter II Page 22 Figure 2	A simple program for creating a rotating color cube.	
Chapter III Page 37 Figure 8	Using PointArray to declare a set of points on a specific curve.	

Chapter III Page 38 Figure 9	Using LineArray to draw a star shape.	
Chapter III Page 42 Figure 13	Using QuadArray to build a house shaped object.	
Chapter III Page 46 Figure 18	Using LineStripArray, TriangleStripArray and TriangleFanArray to generate typical application graphics.	
Chapter III Page 47 Figure 20	Using LineStripArray to create a colored trapezium.	

Chapter III Page 47 Figure 21	Using LineStripArray to create a 3D trapezoidal structure.	
Chapter III Page 48 Figure 22	Using LineStripArray to create a Tetrahedral.	
Chapter III Page 49 Figure 23	Using LineStripArray to build a DNA type of structure with two helixes jointed at various positions.	
Chapter III Page 50 Figure 24	Using LineStripArray to create a simple 3D maze structure using recursive programming techniques.	
Chapter III Page 51 Figure 25	Using TriangleStripArray to create an hour glass shape based on five points or vertices.	

Chapter III Page 52 Figure 26	Setting PolygonAttributes to the geometry created.	
Chapter III Page 53 Figure 28	Using TriangleStripArray to construct a diamond.	
Chapter III Page 54 Figure 29	Using TriangleFanArray to construct simple examples, where the combination of a number of fanning triangles of the same size gives rise to a circle eventually as the number of vertices is increased.	
Chapter III Page 54 Figure 30	Using TranigleFanArray to construct a two-pole speaker and a laser display.	

Chapter III Page 29 Figure 31	Using TranigleFanArray to construct a two-pole speaker and a laser display.	
Chapter III Page 55 Figure 32	Using TriangleStripArray to onstruct a diamond, where the top and bottom parts of the object are implemented by using two strip arrays.	
Chapter III Page 57 Figure 34	Using IndexedPointArray to display a few points in space.	
Chapter III Page 58 Figure 35	The colors of the vertices, which influence the colors of the lines drawn in the manner as shown in the result in Figure 35, is set in the same way as that for the vertex coordinates.	

Chapter III Page 60 Figure 37	Use of IndexedLineArray to construct a sphere by using a series of circles.	
Chapter III Page 61 Figure 38	Use of IndexedTriangleArray to construct a solid tetrahedral.	
Chapter III Page 62 Figure 39	Figure 39 Code segment and result of DiamondIndexed TriangleArray.java.	
Chapter III Page 64 Figure 40	IndexedQuadArray is very similar to that of IndexedTriangleArray, apart from the fact that the basic shape is changed from a 3-sided triangle to a 4-sided quadrilateral.	
Chapter III Page 65 Figure 41	Using IndexedLineStripArray to create a prism.	
Chapter III Page 66 Figure 42	Using IndexedLineStripArray to create a wedge shape object.	

Chapter III Page 67 Figure 43	Usage of of IndexedTriangleStrip Array to build a trapezoidal object with 8 vertices.	
Chapter III Page 68 Figure 44	Presents another example where a diamond shaped object is constructed.	
Chapter III Page 69 Figure 45	Constructing a pyramid using IndexedTriangleFan Array.	
Chapter III Page 70 Figure 46	Figure 46 Code segment and result of DiamondIndexedTriangle FanArray.java.	

Chapter III Page 71 Figure 47	Figure 47 Constructor and result of Museum_ exhibit.java.	
Chapter III Page 74 Figure 50	Code segment and result for Util.java.	
Chapter IV Page 79 Figure 6	Illustrate how 3 points with different widths can be rendered at different locations.	
Chapter IV Page 80 Figure 7	Shows how spherical or circular points can be rendered.	
Chapter IV Page 81 Figure 9	Second segment of LineAttributesExample1. java and result.	

Chapter IV Page 83 Figure 11	Results from PolygonAttributes Example1.java. Note that the CULL_NONE attribute results in both the front and back of the letter E to be seen even after it has been rotated.	
Chapter IV Page 84 Figure 12	Results from PolygonAttributes Example1.java after changing CULL_NONE to CULL_FRONT. This renders only the front of the letter, resulting in a blank screen after rotation.	

Chapter IV Page 85 Figure 13	Results from PolygonAttributes Example1.java after changing CULL_NONE to CULL_BACK. This renders only the back of the letter, resulting in a blank screen after rotation.	
Chapter IV Page 85 Figure 14	Code segment and result of PolygonAttributes Example2.java.	

Chapter IV Page 85 Figure 15	Results from PolygonAttributes Example2.java after changing POLYGON_ POINT to POLYGON_ LINE (left) and POLYGON_FILL (right).	
Chapter IV Page 86 Figure 16	Code segment and result of AppearanceCOLOR.java.	
Chapter IV Page 87 Figure 17	Code segment and result of Sphere_exhibit. java.	

Chapter IV Page 88 Figure 18	Results from Sphere_exhibit.java with tval equal to 0.3f and tmode given by SCREEN_DOOR (left) and BLENDED (right).	
Chapter IV Page 88 Figure 19	Results from Sphere_exhibit.java with tval/tmode given by 0.7f/NICEST (left), 0.85f/SCREEN_DOOR (middle), and 0.7f/BLENDED, CREEN_DOOR (right).	
Chapter IV Page 90 Figure 21	Second segment and result of render.java.	

Chapter IV Page 90 Figure 22	Results from render.java, after changing the first two parameters in RenderingAttributes(true,true to RenderingAttributes(false,false.	
Chapter IV Page 91 Figure 23	Results from render.java, after changing the third and fourth parameters in RenderingAttributes(true,true,0.0f, RenderingAttributes.ALWAYS to RenderingAttributes(true,true,ALPHA_TEST,RenderingAttributes.GREATER. The value of ALPHA_TEST is 0.4f and 0.9f for the left and right diagram, respectively.	
Chapter IV Page 92 Figure 24	Results from render.java, after changing the fifth and sixth parameters in RenderingAttributes(true,true,0.0f, RenderingAttributes.ALWAYS,true,false to RenderingAttributes(true,true,0.0f, RenderingAttributes.ALWAYS,false,false and RenderingAttributes(true,true,0.0f, RenderingAttributes.ALWAYS,true,true.	
Chapter IV Page 94 Figure 25	Code segment and result of Material_Attribute.java.	

Chapter IV Page 94 Figure 26	Results from Material_ Attribute.java, after changing the diffuse color to blue (0.0f,0.0f, 1.0f), and then the specular color to red (1.0f,0.0f,0.0f), followed by the emissive color to dirty green (1.0f,0.4f,0.4f) resulting in the left, center and right hand displays, respectively.	
Chapter IV Page 95 Figure 27	Results from Material_ Attribute.java, after changing the shininess parameter. The display on the left has a shininess of 128, while that on the right has a shininess of 10.	
Chapter V Page 99 Figure 2	Specifying texture coordinates without any distortion for a quad array plane.	
Chapter V Page 100 Figure 3	Specifying texture coordinates with distortion for a triangular geometry object.	

Chapter V Page 103 Figure 6	Texture modes.		
Chapter V Page 103 Figure 7	Texture map transform.		
Chapter V Page 104 Figure 8	Showing that, by using the optional argument Primitive.		
Chapter V Page 105 Figure 9	Code segment and result for TexCoordGenApp.java.		
Chapter V Page 105 Figure 10	Code segment and result for SphereMap. java.		

Chapter V Page 107 Figure 11	Code segment and result for MultiLevel.java.	
Chapter V Page 108 Figure 13	First code segment and result for Multitexture. java.	
Chapter VI Page 120 Figure 7	Results from using weak white and strong blue ambient light.	

Chapter VI Page 120 Figure 8	Result from using directional light.	
Chapter VI Page 121 Figure 9	Point light and result.	
Chapter VI Page 122 Figure 10	Spot light and results.	
Chapter VI Page 123 Figure 11	Code segment and result for LightAttenApp.java.	

Chapter VI Page 126 Figure 14	Results from using fog.	
Chapter VI Page 127 Figure 15	Using fog with influencing bound smaller than the distances to some objects.	
Chapter VI Page 128 Figure 16	Adding a constant color background and result.	
Chapter VI Page 129 Figure 17	A background based on a 2D image.	

Chapter VI Page 130 Figure 18	A background based on a geometrical modeling.	
Chapter VII Page 136 Figure 1	Code segment and result of DemoPositionInterpolator.java.	
Chapter VII Page 137 Figure 2	Code segment and result of DemoPositionPath Interpolator.java.	
Chapter VII Page 139 Figure 3	Code segment and result of DemoRotationInterpolator.java.	

Chapter VII Page 140 Figure 4	Code segment and result of RotPathInter. java.	
Chapter VII Page 141 Figure 5	Code segment and result of DemoRotPosPath Interpolator.java.	
Chapter VII Page 142 Figure 6	Code segment and result of DemoScaleInterpolator. java.	
Chapter VII Page 143 Figure 7	Code segment and result of RotPosScalePathInter. java.	

Chapter VII Page 144 Figure 8	Code segment and result of RotPosScalePathInter. java.	
Chapter VII Page 145 Figure 9	Code segment and result of DemoTransparency Interpolator.java.	
Chapter VII Page 147 Figure 10	Code segment and result of DemoColor Interpolator.java.	
Chapter VII Page 152 Figure 15	Fifth code segment and result of BillboardDemo. java.	
Chapter VII Page 155 Figure 18	Third code segment and result of LOD.java.	

Chapter VII Page 157 Figure 20	Morph behavior and result.	
Chapter VIII Page 180 Figure 21	Code segment and result of WakeupOnElapsed TimeClock.java.	
Chapter VII Page 182 Figure 24	Second code segment and result of TransformChange.java.	
Chapter IX Page 188 Figure 1	Illustration of picking behavior when the user picks and moves the cube.	
Chapter IX Page 192 Figure 4	Third code segment and result snapshoots for PickBehaviour.java.	

Chapter IX Page 196 Figure 8	Code segment and result for PickRayBehaviour.java.	
Chapter IX Page 200 Figure 13	Result from PickSegmentBehavior.java.	
Chapter IX Page 201 Figure 14	Result from PickConeRayBehavior.java.	
Chapter IX Page 207 Figure 20	First code segment and result for PickCylinderRayBehavior.java.	

Chapter IX Page 209 Figure 22	Result from PickBoundsBehavior.java.	
Chapter IX Page 212 Figure 25	Signal generator control panel.	
Chapter X Page 234 Figure 16	Second code segment and result for SensorBehavior.java.	
Chapter XI Page 244 Figure 6	Code segment and result for MultiViewApp.java.	

Chapter XI Page 247 Figure 8	Projection policy.	
Chapter XI Page 249 Figure 10	Window eyepoint policy and field of view.	
Chapter XI Page 251 Figure 12	Code segment and result for ViewProjectionApp.java.	
Chapter XI Page 254 Figure 15	Code segment and result for MonoscopicPolicyApp. java.	
Chapter XI Page 257 Figure 18	Third code segment and results for ManualEyeApp.java.	

Chapter XI Page 258 Figure 19	Views from changing eye positions.	
Chapter XI Page 261 Figure 22	Portal view system.	
Chapter XI Page 262 Figure 23	Video wall viewing system.	
Chapter XII Page 270 Figure 8	Code segment and screen capture for MultiViewApp.java.	

Chapter XII Page 274 Figure 8	Second code segment and result for SoundTest.java.	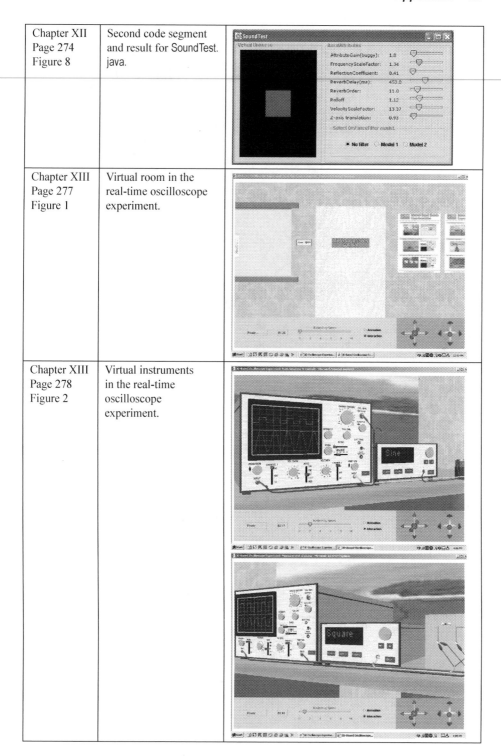
Chapter XIII Page 277 Figure 1	Virtual room in the real-time oscilloscope experiment.	
Chapter XIII Page 278 Figure 2	Virtual instruments in the real-time oscilloscope experiment.	

Chapter XIII Page 282 Figure 5	Texture for realizing the front surface of a button test point, a test point, and a clip.	
Chapter XIII Page 285 Figure 6	Navigating Icons.	
Chapter XIII Page 287 Figure 8	Example picking controls on instruments.	

About the Authors

Chi Chung Ko received the BSc and PhD degrees in electrical engineering from Loughborough University of Technology, UK. He is currently a professor in the department of electrical and computer engineering, National University of Singapore. His current research interests include Internet experimentation, digital signal processing, communications and networks. He is a senior member of IEEE and has written over 250 technical publications in these areas. He has served as an associate editors of the IEEE Transactions on Signal Processing and the IEEE Transactions on Antenna and Propagation. He is also an editor for the EURASIP Journal on Wireless Communications and Networking, as well as the ETRI Journal.

Cheng Chang Dong received the BSEE and MSEE degrees from Harbin Institute of Technology, China, and a PhD degree from Beijing University of Aeronautics and Astronautics, China, in 1990, 1995, and 1999, respectively. From 2000 to 2004, he was a research fellow in the department of electrical and computer engineering at the National University of Singapore (NUS) and the Temasek Laboratories at the Nanyang Technological University (NTU). Currently, he is the managing director of NDI Automation PTE LTD (Singapore).

Index